W9-BWC-750

The Photographic History
of The Civil War

Two Volumes in One.
Forts and Artillery

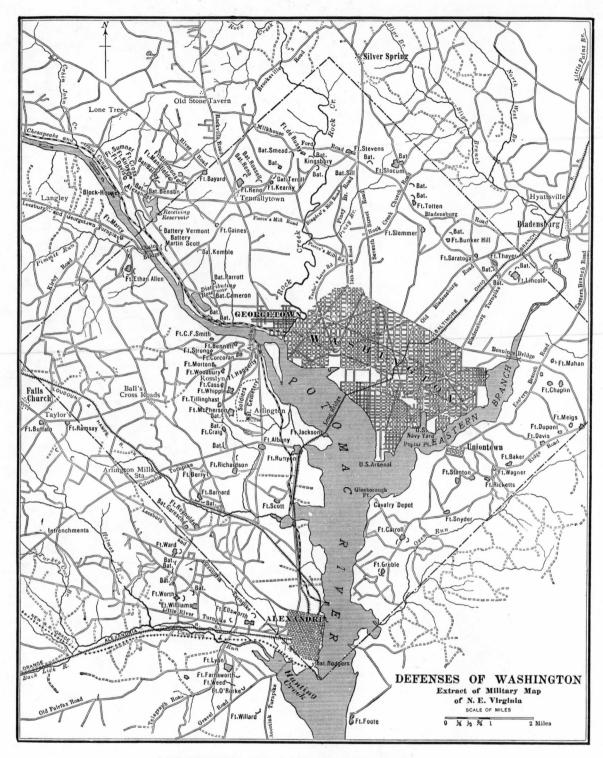

MAP SHOWING THE DEFENSES OF WASHINGTON

SPECIALLY COMPILED FOR THE PHOTOGRAPHIC HISTORY OF THE CIVIL WAR FROM THE OFFICIAL MAP OF THE ENGINEER
BUREAU OF THE U. S. WAR DEPARTMENT, DRAWN 1865

FEDERAL
GUNS
IN
THE GRAND
REVIEW

BEFORE
THE
CAPITOL,
MAY 24,
1865

ARTILLERY BRIGADE IN THE GRAND REVIEW

It was the artillery that defended Washington, as told in Chapter I of this volume. It was "heavy" artillery turned into infantry which sustained the greatest loss in battle—the First Maine and Eighth New York. On every hard-fought open field, it was the artillery that put heart into the infantry, supporting the charge or covering the retreat. No wonder a roar of applause went up on that sunny day in May, while the caissons clanked down Pennsylvania Avenue, and made the cannon rumble again in their bronze and iron throats.

The Photographic History of The Civil War

Complete and Unabridged

TWO VOLUMES IN ONE.

Volume 3
*Forts and Artillery
The Navies

EDITOR

O. E. HUNT

Captain, United States Army ; Instructor in Modern Languages,
United States Military Academy

Contributors

O. E. HUNT
Captain, United States Army

J. W. MALLET
Lieutenant-Colonel, Confederate States Army,
and Superintendent of the Ordnance Laboratories of the Confederate States; Professor of
Chemistry in the University of Virginia

DAVID GREGG McINTOSH
Colonel of Artillery, Confederate States Army

T. M. R. TALCOTT, C.E.
Colonel Commanding Engineering Troops, Army
of Northern Virginia

FREDERICK M. COLSTON
Lieutenant and Ordnance Officer, Alexander's
Battalion of Artillery, Longstreet's Corps,
Army of Northern Virginia

THE BLUE & GREY PRESS

PHOTOGRAPHIC HISTORY OF THE CIVIL WAR

Vol. 3
Forts and Artillery
The Navies

Two Volumes in One.

Copyright © 1987 by The Blue & Grey Press,
a division of Book Sales, Inc.
110 Enterprise Avenue
Secaucus, NJ 07094

Printed in the United Statres of America

ISBN: 1-55521-203-4

CONTENTS

PAGE

Map—THE DEFENSES OF WASHINGTON 2

Frontispiece—"THE ARTILLERY BRIGADE IN THE GRAND REVIEW" 6

Preface 11

THE FEDERAL ARTILLERY AND ARTILLERYMEN 13
    O. E. Hunt

THE CONFEDERATE ARTILLERY—ITS ORGANIZATION AND DEVELOPMENT . . . 55
    David Gregg McIntosh

MEMORIES OF GETTYSBURG 71
    Frederick M. Colston

DEFENDING THE NATIONAL CAPITAL 75
    O. E. Hunt

THE DEFENSES OF CHARLESTON 109

THE ORDNANCE DEPARTMENT OF THE FEDERAL ARMY 123
    O. E. Hunt

THE ORDNANCE OF THE CONFEDERACY 155
    J. W. Mallet and O. E. Hunt

THE AMMUNITION USED IN THE WAR 171
    O. E. Hunt

ENTRENCHMENTS AND FORTIFICATIONS 193
    O. E. Hunt

ENGINEER CORPS OF THE FEDERAL ARMY 219
    O. E. Hunt

REMINISCENCES OF THE CONFEDERATE ENGINEER SERVICE 255
    T. M. R. Talcott

FEDERAL MILITARY RAILROADS 271
    O. E. Hunt

DEFENDING THE CITADEL OF THE CONFEDERACY 303
    O. E. Hunt

Map—THE DEFENSES OF RICHMOND 322

PHOTOGRAPHIC DESCRIPTIONS THROUGHOUT THE VOLUME
    Roy Mason
    Colonel W. R. Hamilton, U. S. A. (Retired)

PREFACE

IT was not a mere sneer that described Napoleon as "only an artillery officer." His method of massing great guns was almost unknown in America when the Civil War opened; the Confederates, to their cost, let two years go by before organizing so as to allow of quick artillery concentration; yet what else could have won Gettysburg for the Federals?

Proper defense against cannon was even less understood until the Civil War.

If Louis XIV's military engineer Vauban had come to life during any battle or siege that followed his death up to 1861, he could easily have directed the operations of the most advanced army engineers—whose fortifications, indeed, he would have found constructed on conventional lines according to his own text-books.

Thus the gunner in Blue or Gray, and his comrade the engineer, were forced not only to fight and dig but to evolve new theories and practices. No single work existed to inform the editors of this History systematically concerning that fighting and digging. No single work described Federals and Confederates alike, and readably told the story of the great events with the guns and behind the ramparts from '61 to '65. That gap it is hoped this volume will fill.

American resourcefulness here became epochal. For siege work great guns were devised and perfected which rendered useless, for all time, most of the immense brick and stone and mortar fortifications existing in the world. The introduction of rifled guns worked as great a revolution in warfare on land as that of the ironclad vessel on the sea.

The photographs in this volume follow the artillery in the field, both Federal and Confederate. They comprehensively illustrate the precaution taken by the Federal engineers to protect the Northern capital from capture. They supplement graphically the technical information in regard to the fabrication of guns and making of ammunition. A dramatic series of views follows the gradual reduction of the Confederate forts and batteries on Morris Island by the Federal besiegers, and the latter's attempts against Sumter.

The photographs in the latter part of the volume reflect the ingenuity of the American soldier in protecting himself on the battlefield; the bridging of broad rivers in the space of an hour by the Engineer Corps; the expert railroading under difficulties of the United States Military Railroad Construction Corps; the Confederate defenses along the James which baffled the Federal army, and preserved Richmond so long free though beleaguered.

I

WITH THE FEDERAL ARTILLERY

LIGHT ARTILLERY—TWO GUNS IN POSITION,
READY TO FIRE

BATTERY A, FOURTH UNITED STATES ARTILLERY, FEBRUARY, 1864

Battery A, Fourth United States Artillery, was one of the celebrated horse batteries of the Army of the Potomac. These photographs, taken by Gardner in February, 1864, represented its four 12-pounder light brass Napoleons "in battery," with limbers and caissons to the rear, and the battery wagon, forge, ambulance, and wagons for transportation, embracing the entire equipage of a light battery in the field. At that time the battery was on the line of the Rappahannock. Three months later it accompanied Sheridan on his

THE BATTERY THAT RODE CLOSEST TO RICHMOND

famous Richmond raid, and on the night of May 12th its members heard men talking within the fortifications of Richmond, dogs barking in the city, and bought copies of the Richmond *Inquirer* from a small but enterprising Virginia newsboy who managed to slip within their lines with the morning papers. Below, beyond "A," another battery is seen in camp. The horses hitched in, and the open limber-chests indicate an approaching inspection. These formed part of Lieutenant-Colonel James Madison Robertson's brigade.

ON THE DAY OF BATTLE—SHELLING EARLY'S TROOPS IN FREDERICKSBURG

Here is no play at war. These guns were actually throwing their iron hail against Marye's Heights across the river on the very day that this photograph was taken by Captain A. J. Russell, the Government photographer. Early that morning the Union guns opened with a roar; at half past ten Sedgwick's gallant Sixth Corps charged up the hill where nearly 13,000 of their comrades had fallen the previous December. Before the assault the field artillery added its clamor to the heavy boom of the big guns, clearing the way for the intrepid Union columns which General Newton led up the once deadly hill to victory.

WORKING THE 32-POUNDERS ON MAY 3, 1863

With a charge of eight pounds of powder these sea-coast guns could throw a shot weighing 32.3 pounds 2,664 yards, or over a mile and a half, with a ten degree muzzle elevation.   The town spread out before the frowning weapons was thus easily within range.   The pieces are mounted on siege carriages.   Two men are handling the heavy swab which must reach a distance nearly twice the length of a man.   The man at the nearest breech is just sighting; the crew are at attention, ready to perform their tasks.   In a companion photograph, taken at the same time (pages 126 and 127 of Volume II), they can be seen waiting to load the piece in the foreground.

THE FEDERAL ARTILLERY AND ARTILLERYMEN

By O. E. Hunt
Captain, United States Army

THE regular troops brought into Washington for its defense at the outbreak of the war included two batteries of field-artillery of exceptional drill and discipline. The presence of these guns and men helped materially to allay the feeling of apprehension, and General Scott, in command of the United States army at the time, was able to assure the inhabitants that he could hold Washington against several times the number that the Confederates could then bring against him, as he knew from experience that the troops which had been hastily enlisted for the Southern cause were still in a very unprepared state.

Most of the organizations participating in the first battle of the war were untried and undisciplined. A few regular companies and batteries made a leaven for the mass, and among those Federal organizations that most distinguished themselves were Ricketts' and Griffin's regular field-batteries.

About half-past two in the afternoon of July 21, 1861, these were ordered forward to the top of the Henry hill, where the battle of Bull Run was raging hottest. They went with a feeling that the regiments ordered to support them were unreliable. For a time there was a lull in the battle. But danger was close at hand. No sooner had Ricketts taken up his position than his men and horses began to fall under the well-directed fire of concealed Confederate sharpshooters. No foe was visible, but death sped from behind fences, bushes, hedges, and knolls. The battery fought with desperate

[18]

THE HENRY HOUSE—AFTER BULL RUN

THE ARTILLERY CENTER OF THE FIRST CIVIL WAR BATTLE

Thus stood the Henry house after the battle of Bull Run, on July 21, 1861. The building is no longer habitable—though the white plaster remaining shows that the destroying cannonade had not brought fire in its train.   At first not in the direct line of fire, the little home suddenly became the center of the flood-tide of the first real conflict of the Civil War when at two-thirty General McDowell sent forward Ricketts' and Griffin's regular batteries.   The former planted their guns within 1,500 yards of Captain (later Brigadier-General) John B. Imboden's Confederate batteries, which were stationed in a slight depression beyond.   A terrific artillery duel at once ensued.   Old Mrs. Henry, bedridden and abandoned by her relatives, lay alone in the house in an agony of terror till one of the first shots put an end to her life of suffering.   The Thirty-third Virginia could restrain themselves no longer, and without orders advanced upon the Federal batteries.   In the dust they were mistaken for a supporting Federal regiment until within point-blank range they fired a volley which annihilated both batteries.   Thenceforth the contending forces surged over the prostrate bodies of cannoneers.   Ricketts, severely wounded, was finally taken prisoner.   At last Johnston's fresh troops arrived, the gray line surged forward, and the much-coveted guns were seized by the Confederates for the last time.

[F—2]

courage. Griffin's battery took its place alongside. There were eleven Union guns pouring shell into—what? Soon were uncovered no less than thirteen Confederate guns at short range. The Confederate batteries were well supported. The Federal guns were not.

The Confederate regiments, seeing the Union batteries exposed, were tempted to come out from their concealment. They pressed cautiously but stubbornly on Ricketts, whose battery, all this time, was wholly occupied with the Confederate artillery. Griffin, absorbed in the fire of his guns against the opposing artillery, was astounded to see a regiment advancing boldly on his right. He believed these troops to be Confederates, but was persuaded by other officers that they were his own supports. Instinctively, he ordered his men to load with canister and trained the guns on the advancing infantry. Persuaded not to fire, he hesitated a moment, and the two batteries were overwhelmed. The supporting regiment fired one volley and fled. The two disabled batteries now became the center of the contest of the two armies. In full view from many parts of the field, the contending forces surged back and forth between the guns, over the prostrate bodies of many of the cannoneers. Ricketts, severely wounded, was finally taken by the Confederates and retained a prisoner. Two more Federal batteries, one a regular organization, crossed the valley to take part in the fight, but were compelled to withdraw.

Finally, with the appearance of Johnston's fresh troops, including more field-artillery, the tide was turned for the last time, and the much coveted guns remained in the hands of the Confederates. Four pieces of Arnold's battery, four of Carlisle's battery, and five of the Rhode Island battery, practically all that were taken off the field, were lost at the clogged bridge over Cub Run. The entire loss to the Federals in artillery was twenty-five guns, a severe blow when ordnance was so precious.

GENERAL GRIFFIN, WHO LED THE FIRST LIGHT BATTERY INTO WASHINGTON

Major-General Charles Griffin stands in the center of his staff officers of the Fifth Army Corps, of which he attained command on April 2, 1865. He was the man who led the first light artillery into Washington, the famous Battery D of the Fifth United States Artillery, known as the "West Point Light Battery." When war was threatening, Colonel Charles Delafield, then Super-intendent of the Military Academy at West Point, directed Lieutenant Charles Griffin, then of the Second Artillery and in-structor in the Tactical Department, to form a light battery of four pieces, with six horses to the piece, and enough men to make the command seventy strong. On February 15, 1861, it left for Washington with its four 12-pounder Napoleons. Re-organized July 4th as Company D of the Fifth United States Artillery, its organizer promoted to its captaincy, its strength increased to 112 men, and equipped with four 10-pounder Parrotts and two 12-pounder gun-howitzers, it proceeded to Arlington and thence to the battlefield of Bull Run. The "West Point Light Battery" was the first to enter the City of Washington in 1861, with Captain Charles Griffin, and Lieutenants Henry C. Symonds and Alexander S. Webb, his subordinates. At Bull Run the battery was wrecked, nearly all its horses killed, and one third of its men either killed or wounded. At West Point there is a memorial tablet to this battery bearing the following names: Bull Run, Mechanicsville, Hanover, Gaines's Mill, Mal-vern Hill, Manassas, Antietam, Fredericksburg, Rappahannock, Wilderness, Spotsylvania, North Anna, Cold Harbor, Weldon, Appomattox. General Griffin commanded the artillery at Malvern Hill, and as leader of the Fifth Corps he received the surren-der of the arms of the Army of Northern Virginia at Appomattox. The Maltese Cross on the flag was the badge of his corps.

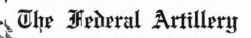 

McClellan was called to Washington and placed in command, and immediately, by his great energy, tact, and professional skill, restored confidence. On his assuming command of the Military Division of the Potomac, the field-artillery of the division consisted of no more than parts of nine batteries, or thirty pieces of various and, in some instances, unusual and unserviceable calibers. Calculations were made for an expansion of this force, based on an estimated strength of the new Army of the Potomac, about to be formed, of one hundred thousand infantry.

Considerations involving the peculiar character and extent of the force to be employed, the probable field and character of the operations, and the limits imposed by the as yet undeveloped resources of the nation, led to the adoption, by General McClellan, of certain recommendations that were made to him by General W. F. Barry, his chief of artillery. The most important of these were: to have, if possible, three guns for each thousand men; one-third of the guns to be rifled and either Parrott or Ordnance Department guns; batteries to be of not less than four nor more than six guns, and then followed a number of important recommendations concerning the tactical organization of the arm.

A variety of unexpected circumstances compelled some slight modifications in these propositions, but in the main they formed the basis of the organization of the artillery of the Army of the Potomac.

The supply of ordnance matériel before the Civil War was in large measure obtained from private arsenals and foundries. This sudden expansion in the artillery arm of the country overtaxed these sources of supply, and the Ordnance Department promptly met the requisitions of the chief of artillery of the Army of the Potomac by enlarging, as far as possible, their own arsenals and armories. The use of contract work was in some instances the cause of the introduction of faulty matériel; and the loss of field-guns on several

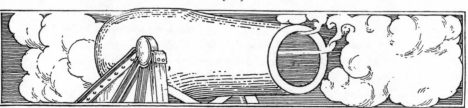

THE ONLY UNION BATTERY THAT FIRED ON YORKTOWN

This photograph of May, 1862, shows Federal Battery No. 1 in front of Yorktown. On May 3, 1862, all of McClellan's encircling guns, with the exception of two batteries, were waiting to open fire, and those two would have been ready in six hours more—when the Confederates evacuated the works defending the city. Fire was actually opened, however, only from this one. It was armed with two 200-pounder and five 100-pounder Parrott rifled guns. The garrison was one company of the famous First Connecticut Artillery, under Captain Burke. It was a great disappointment to the Federal artillerymen, who had worked for a month placing the batteries in position, that there was no chance to test their power and efficiency. McClellan has been criticised for dilatory tactics at Yorktown, but many old soldiers declare that the army under his command inflicted as much damage and suffered far less than the victorious army directed by Grant.

WATCHING THE AP-PROACH OF A SHELL, YORKTOWN, MAY, 1862 This photograph of Battery No. 4, planted for the bombardment of Yorktown, shows a sentinel on the watch, ready to give warning of the approach of a shell and thus enable every man to seek shelter. Beside him is the bomb-proof in which the troops remained under cover when the bombardment was continuous. At Yorktown, the Confederates had an 8-inch mortar with which they did rather indifferent shooting, but the moral effect on the Federal soldiers of the screeching shells was great.

The caliber of these mortars was thirteen inches, and on account of their tremendous weight, 17,000 pounds, it required great labor to place them in position. The projectiles, which were principally used for sea-coast operations, varied in weight, according to character. Their maximum weight was about 770 pounds, and these were fired with a maximum of about seventy-five pounds of powder. The bore of this mortar is 35.1 inches in length. This was a case of war's labor lost, as the Confederates left on May 3d, and McClellan's elaborate siege batteries never had a chance.

battlefields was laid to the breaking of gun-carriages. The Ordnance Department, however, was able to supply the deficiencies as soon as its own plants were running, and artillery officers thereupon expressed their complete satisfaction.

The field-guns were of two kinds—the 3-inch wrought-iron (10-pounder) rifle and the smooth-bore Napoleon 12-pounder. The first was made by wrapping boiler-plate around an iron bar to form a rough cylinder, welding it together, and then boring it out and shaping it up. The second was generally made of bronze, cast solid, then bored and prepared. For short ranges in rough country, the Napoleon gun was preferred to the rifle, as it carried heavier charges and the use of canister in it was more effective.

The siege-guns, in which mobility was less important, were of cast iron. Owing to the length of bore and the relatively small diameter, these guns were also usually cast solid. One of these pieces, the Parrott, was strengthened by a wrought-iron cylinder shrunk over the breech.

Sea-coast guns were generally of cast iron, and the best types were cast hollow and cooled by the Rodman process of playing a stream of water on the interior of the tube while the exterior was kept hot, thus regulating the crystallization of the iron and increasing its durability. To some of the sea-coast guns the Parrott principle of construction was applied.

The imperfectly equipped batteries which were left to the Army of the Potomac after the First Bull Run consisted, as has been noted, of only thirty guns. These had six hundred and fifty men and four hundred horses.

When the army took the field, in March, 1862, the light artillery consisted of ninety-two batteries of five hundred and twenty guns, twelve thousand five hundred men, and eleven thousand horses, all fully equipped and in readiness for field-service. Of this force, thirty batteries were regular and sixty-two volunteer. During the short period of seven months, all the immense amount of necessary matériel had been issued and

[24]

FIFTY-NINE AND A HALF TONS OF ORDNANCE EMPLACED IN VAIN

These mortars of Battery No. 4 were ready to let loose a stream of fire upon Yorktown on the night of May 3d. But that very night the Confederate host secretly withdrew. The great weight of the projectiles these guns could throw was sufficient to crash through the deck of a battleship. For that reason such mortars were generally used for sea-coast fortifications. The projectiles weighed up to 770 pounds. At times, the big mortars were used for siege purposes, although their great weight—17,000 pounds—made them difficult to emplace in temporary works. For thirty days the Union artillerymen had toiled beneath the Virginia sun putting the seven gigantic weapons, seen on the left-hand page, into place. Their aggregate weight was 119,000 pounds, or fifty-nine and a half tons. By garrisoning Yorktown and forcing the Federals to place such huge batteries into position—labor like moles at these elaborate, costly, and tedious siege approaches— General Magruder delayed the Union army for a month, and gained precious time for General Lee to strengthen the defenses of the threatened Confederate capital, while Jackson in the Valley held off three more Federal armies by his brilliant maneuvering, and ultimately turned upon them and defeated two.

the batteries organized, except that about one-fourth of the volunteer batteries had brought a few guns and carriages with them from their respective States. These were of such an odd assortment of calibers that there was no uniformity with the more modern and serviceable ordnance with which most of the batteries were being armed, and they had to be replaced with more suitable matériel. Less than one-tenth of the State batteries came fully equipped for service.

When the Army of the Potomac embarked for Fort Monroe and the Peninsula, early in April, 1862, fifty-two batteries of two hundred and ninety-nine guns went with that force, and the remainder that had been organized were scattered to other places, General McDowell and General Banks taking the greater portion. When Franklin's division of McDowell's corps joined McClellan on the Peninsula, it took with it four batteries of twenty-two guns; and McCall's division of McDowell's corps, joining a few days before the battle of Mechanicsville, also kept its artillery, consisting of the same number of batteries and guns as Franklin's. This made a grand total of sixty field-batteries of three hundred and forty-three guns with the Federal forces.

The instruction of a great many of these batteries was necessarily defective at first, but the volunteers evinced such zeal and intelligence, and availed themselves so industriously of the services of regular officers, that they made rapid progress and attained a high degree of efficiency.

The Confederates having taken a position at Yorktown and erected strong works, a regular siege of the place was ordered. Reconnaissances were made by the artillery and engineer officers to locate the works. A siege-train of one hundred and one pieces was sent down from Washington, and field-batteries of 12-pounders were also used as guns of position. The First Connecticut Heavy and the Fifth New York Heavy Artillery were in charge of the siege-train, and had for its operation a total of twenty-two hundred men.

[26]

MAJOR ASA M. COOK

The three photographs on this page give bits of daily camp-life with the light artillery. In the top photograph Major Asa M. Cook, of the Eighth Massachusetts Light Battery, who also had temporary command of the First, sits his horse before his tent. In the center the artillerymen of the First Massachusetts Light Battery are dining in camp at their ease. Below appear the simple accommodations that sufficed for Lieutenant Josiah Jorker, of the same battery. The First Massachusetts was mustered in August 27, 1861, and saw its full share of service. It fought through the Peninsula campaign, assisted in checking Pope's rout at Bull Run, August 30, 1862, and covered the retreat to Fairfax Court House, September 1st. It served at Antietam,

DINNER TIME
FIRST MASSACHUSETTS LIGHT BATTERY IN CAMP

Fredericksburg, and Gettysburg; at the Wilderness and in the "Bloody Angle" at Spotsylvania the following year. It fought at Cold Harbor, and went to Petersburg, but returned to Washington with the veteran Sixth Army Corps to defend the city from Early's attack. It then accompanied Sheridan on his Shenandoah Valley campaign and fought at the battle of Opequon. It was mustered out, October 19, 1864, at the expiration of its term. The Eighth Battery of Massachusetts Light Artillery was organized for six months' service June 24, 1862. It fought at the second battle of Bull Run, at South Mountain, and Antietam. The regiment was mustered out November 29, 1862.

LIEUTENANT JOSIAH JORKER, WITH THE FIRST MASSACHUSETTS ARTILLERYMEN

The Federal Artillery ❖ ❖

Fourteen batteries of seventy-five guns and forty mortars were established across the Peninsula, the work of constructing emplacements beginning on April 17th and ending on May 3d. During the night of May 3d, the Confederates evacuated Yorktown, and the Federal troops took possession at daylight on the 4th.

The peculiarities of the soil and terrain in the vicinity of the opposing works made the labor of installing the siege-artillery very great. The heavier guns would often sink to the axles in the quicksand, and the rains added to the uncomfortable work. The efforts of the strongest and most willing of the horses with the heavy matériel frequently did not avail to extricate the guns from the mud, and it became necessary to haul them by hand, the cannoneers working knee-deep in mud and water. The First Connecticut Heavy Artillery and the Fifth New York Heavy Artillery excelled in extraordinary perseverance, alacrity, and cheerfulness.

The effect of the delay to the Army of the Potomac was to enable the Confederates to gain strength daily in preparation for the coming campaign. All the batteries of the Union line, with the exception of two, were fully ready to open fire when the Confederates evacuated their positions, and these two batteries would have been ready in six hours more. Circumstances were such, however, that fire was actually opened from only one battery, which was armed with two 200-pounder and five 100-pounder Parrott rifled guns.

The ease with which these heavy guns were worked and the accuracy of their fire on the Confederate works, as afterward ascertained, were such as to lead to the belief that the Confederates would have suffered greatly if they had remained in the works after the bombardment was opened. The desired result, however, had been achieved. The Union army had been delayed a month, and precious time had been gained for General Lee to strengthen the defenses of Richmond while Johnston held off his formidable antagonist.

COWAN AND HIS MEN, MAY, 1862, JUST AFTER THE FIRST FIGHT

These four officers of the First New York Independent Battery seated in front of their tent, in camp on the left bank of the Chickahominy River, look like veterans, yet a year of warfare had not yet elapsed; and their first taste of powder at Lee's Mills had just occurred. First on the left is Andrew Cowan (later brevet-lieutenant-colonel), then lieutenant commanding the battery (he had been promoted to captain at Lee's Mills, but had not yet received his captain's commission). Next is First-Lieutenant William P. Wright (who was disabled for life by wounds received in the battle of Gettysburg), Lieutenant William H. Johnson (wounded at Gettysburg and mortally wounded at Winchester), and Lieutenant Theodore Atkins, sunstruck during the fierce cannonade at Gettysburg, July 3, 1863, and incapacitated for further service in the army. Private Henry Hiser, in charge of the officers' mess at the time, is leaning against the tent-pole. The first Independent Battery of Light Artillery from New York was organized at Auburn and mustered in November 23, 1861. It was on duty in the defenses of Washington until March, 1862, when it moved to the Peninsula by way of Fortress Monroe. Its first action was at Lee's Mills, April 5, 1861; it took part in the siege of Yorktown, and fought at Lee's Mills again on April 16th. It served throughout the Peninsula campaign, and in all the big battles of the Army of the Potomac throughout the war. It helped to repulse Early's attack on Washington, and fought with Sheridan in the Shenandoah. The battery lost during its service two officers and sixteen enlisted men killed and mortally wounded and thirty-eight enlisted men by disease.

To the patient and hard-working Federal artillerymen, it was a source of keen professional disappointment that, after a month's exacting toil in placing siege-ordnance of the heaviest type, the foe did not give them a chance to test its power and efficiency.

It was found by the Federals that the Confederate works about Yorktown were strong. The chief engineer of the Army of the Potomac reported that the outline of the works immediately surrounding the town was almost the same as that of the British fortifications of Cornwallis in the Revolution, but that the works had been thoroughly adapted to modern warfare. Emplacements had been finished for guns of heavy type, of which about ninety-four could have been placed in position. The Federals captured fifty-three guns in good order.

From Yorktown to the front of Richmond, and on the march to the James, the gallant efforts of the artillery seconded the work of the other arms through the battles of Williamsburg, Hanover Court House, Fair Oaks, Mechanicsville, including Gaines' Mill, Savage's Station, Glendale, and Malvern Hill. As General W. F. Barry has stated, "These services were as creditable to the artillery of the United States as they were honorable to the gallant officers and enlisted men who, struggling through difficulties, overcoming obstacles, and bearing themselves nobly on the field of battle, stood faithfully to their guns, performing their various duties with a steadiness, a devotion, and a gallantry worthy of the highest commendation."

At Malvern Hill the artillery saved the army. The position was most favorable for the use of guns. The reserve artillery, under Colonel H. J. Hunt, was posted on the heights in rear of the infantry lines. Sixty pieces, comprising principally batteries of 20-pounders and 32-pounders, had a converging fire from General Porter's line, and all along the crest of the hill batteries appeared in commanding positions. The First Connecticut Heavy Artillery again distinguished itself for the

COWAN'S BATTERY ABOUT TO ADVANCE ON MAY 4, 1862

THE NEXT DAY IT LOST ITS FIRST MEN KILLED IN ACTION, AT THE BATTLE OF WILLIAMSBURG

Lieutenant Andrew Cowan, commanding, and First-Lieutenant William F. Wright, sit their horses on the farther side of the Warwick River, awaiting the order to advance. After the evacuation of Yorktown by the Confederates on the previous night, Lee's Mills became the Federal left and the Confederate right. The Confederate earthworks are visible in front of the battery. This spot had already been the scene of a bloody engagement. The First Vermont Brigade of General W. F. Smith's division, Fourth Corps, had charged along the top of the dam and below it on April 16th and had gained the foremost earthwork, called the "Water Battery." But General Smith received orders not to bring on a general engagement. The Vermonters were withdrawn, suffering heavily from the Confederate fire. Their dead were recovered, under a flag of truce, a few days later. The "slashing" in the foreground of this photograph was in front of earthworks erected by Smith's division after the withdrawal of the Vermonters. The earthworks themselves were about two hundred yards to the rear of this "slashing," and were occupied by the First New York Battery in the center, and strong bodies of infantry to its left and right. The battery is seen halted where a road ran, leading to the Williamsburg road. Loaded shells had been planted inside the Confederate works, so that the feet of the horses or the wheels of the guns passing over them would cause them to explode. The battle of Williamsburg or "Fort Magruder" was fought on May 5th. In that battle the battery lost its first men killed in action.

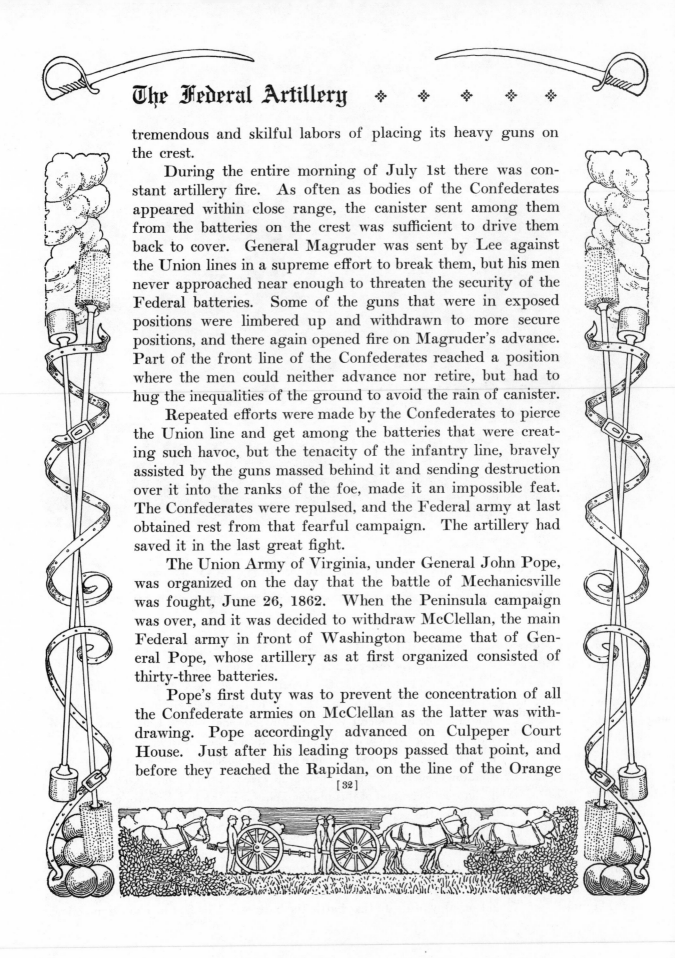

tremendous and skilful labors of placing its heavy guns on the crest.

During the entire morning of July 1st there was constant artillery fire. As often as bodies of the Confederates appeared within close range, the canister sent among them from the batteries on the crest was sufficient to drive them back to cover. General Magruder was sent by Lee against the Union lines in a supreme effort to break them, but his men never approached near enough to threaten the security of the Federal batteries. Some of the guns that were in exposed positions were limbered up and withdrawn to more secure positions, and there again opened fire on Magruder's advance. Part of the front line of the Confederates reached a position where the men could neither advance nor retire, but had to hug the inequalities of the ground to avoid the rain of canister.

Repeated efforts were made by the Confederates to pierce the Union line and get among the batteries that were creating such havoc, but the tenacity of the infantry line, bravely assisted by the guns massed behind it and sending destruction over it into the ranks of the foe, made it an impossible feat. The Confederates were repulsed, and the Federal army at last obtained rest from that fearful campaign. The artillery had saved it in the last great fight.

The Union Army of Virginia, under General John Pope, was organized on the day that the battle of Mechanicsville was fought, June 26, 1862. When the Peninsula campaign was over, and it was decided to withdraw McClellan, the main Federal army in front of Washington became that of General Pope, whose artillery as at first organized consisted of thirty-three batteries.

Pope's first duty was to prevent the concentration of all the Confederate armies on McClellan as the latter was withdrawing. Pope accordingly advanced on Culpeper Court House. Just after his leading troops passed that point, and before they reached the Rapidan, on the line of the Orange

"FLYING ARTILLERY" IN THE ATTEMPT ON RICHMOND

THE CANNONEERS WHO KEPT UP WITH THE CAVALRY—IN THIS SWIFTEST BRANCH OF THE SERVICE EACH MAN RIDES HORSEBACK

Here are drawn up Harry Benson's Battery A, of the Second United States Artillery, and Horatio Gates Gibson's Batteries C and G, combined of the Third United States Artillery, near Fair Oaks, Virginia. They arrived there just too late to take part in the battle of June, 1862. By "horse artillery," or "flying artillery" as it is sometimes called, is meant an organization equipped usually with 10-pounder rifled guns, with all hands mounted. In ordinary light artillery the cannoneers either ride on the gun-carriage or go afoot. In "flying artillery" each cannoneer has a horse. This form is by far the most mobile of all, and is best suited to accompany cavalry on account of its ability to travel rapidly. With the exception of the method of mounting the cannoneers, there was not any difference between the classes of field batteries except as they were divided between "light" and "heavy." In the photograph above no one is riding on the gun-carriages, but all have separate mounts. Battery A of the Second United States Artillery was in Washington in January, 1861, and took part in the expedition for the relief of Fort Pickens, Florida. It went to the Peninsula, fought at Mechanicsville May 23–24, 1862, and took part in the Seven Days' battles before Richmond June 25th to July 1st. Batteries C and G of the Third United States Artillery were at San Francisco, California, till October 1861, when they came East, and also went to the Peninsula and served at Yorktown and in the Seven Days.

and Alexandria Railroad, they encountered the foe. This brought on the battle of Cedar Mountain, the first engagement of the campaign, August 9th. Contact of the advance troops occurred in the morning, and, beginning at noon, the artillery duel lasted until about three o'clock in the afternoon. Then the infantry engagement began, and resulted in the Federal troops being pushed back. The Confederates followed the retiring troops until Federal reenforcements arrived. " Unaware of this," says J. C. Ropes, " Jackson undertook, in his anxiety to reach Culpeper before morning, to shell the Federal troops out of their position, but succeeded in arousing so many sleeping batteries that he shortly discontinued his cannonade, having suffered some loss. The battle of Cedar Mountain was over." The Union troops lost one gun, mired in the mud while withdrawing.

Pope retired across the Rappahannock and Lee concentrated his entire army against him. At the Rappahannock, the commanding positions of the Union artillery on the left bank enabled it to get a superiority of fire over the Confederate guns, which proved very distressing to Lee and baffled his first attempts to cross.

From the Rappahannock to Gainesville, the artillery had little opportunity to go into action. The marching and countermarching by both armies, each under the impression that the other was retreating, finally brought them together on the field of Gainesville, on August 28th. In this sanguinary fight the losses were great, the artillery sustaining its full proportion.

Pope's problem was now to prevent the union of Longstreet and Jackson. At Groveton, near the old Bull Run battle-ground, another bloody encounter took place, and the character of the fighting can best be understood when it is related that the men of General Hatch's division, after fighting for three-quarters of an hour in close range of the foe, retired in good order, leaving one gun in the hands of the Southerners.

A BATTERY THAT FOUGHT IN MANY CAMPAIGNS—"KNAP'S"

The upper photograph is of Independent Battery E of Pennsylvania Light Artillery, known as Knap's Battery, after its captain, Joseph M. Knap. Here the battery is within a strong fortification, guarded by a "slashing" of trees with branches pointing outward, visible beyond the walls. At Antietam, where the battery distinguished itself, there were no entrenchments to protect it from the fire of the Confederates; yet, practically unsupported, it broke up two charges in the thick of the action. Then McClellan's long-range guns materially assisted the Union advance, but later in the day the demand for artillery was so great that when General Hancock asked for more to assist his attenuated line, he could not get them until he finally borrowed one battery from Franklin. After the battle ended (September 17, 1862) and the Confederates withdrew to the south side of the Potomac, General Porter resolved to capture some of the Confederate guns com-

[F–3]

HEADQUARTERS FIRST BRIGADE HORSE ARTILLERY, BRANDY STATION, SEPTEMRER, 1863

Here are some followers of Brigadier-General James Madison Robertson, who won promotion as chief of horse artillery on many fields, from the Peninsula to the Virginia campaigns of 1864. The horse artillery was attached to the cavalry force.

manding the fords. One of the five pieces taken in this exploit on the night of September 19th was a gun which had been captured by the Confederates at the First Bull Run, from Griffin's Battery, D of the Fifth United States Artillery. There is another photograph of Knap's battery in Volume II, page 61. It was organized at Point of Rocks, Maryland, from a company formed for the Sixty-third Pennsylvania and surplus men of the Twenty-eighth Pennsylvania Infantry in September, 1861. Its service included Pope's campaign in Northern Virginia, beside the Maryland campaign which culminated at Antietam. Its next important campaign was that of Chancellorsville, and then came the Gettysburg campaign. The scene of its activities was then transferred to the West, where it fought at Chattanooga, Lookout Mountain and Missionary Ridge. It was with Sherman in the Atlanta campaign, marched with him to the sea, and returned to Washington with the Army of Georgia in time for the Grand Review.

The Confederates afterward said of this incident that the gun continued to fire until they were so close as to have their faces burnt by the discharges. Higher praise than this surely could not have been given the troops of either side.

Then followed the Second Battle of Manassas, a defeat for the Union army, but a hard-fought battle. The artillery continued to fire long after the musketry engagement had ceased, and after darkness had set in. The Federal army retired. General Pope claims not to have lost a gun, but Lee's report states that thirty pieces of artillery were captured during the series of battles. With the battle at Chantilly the campaign closed, and the Federal armies were again concentrated around Washington.

Early in September, Pope was relieved, and the Army of Virginia passed out of existence. Lee crossed into Maryland; McClellan moved up the Potomac with the reorganized Army of the Potomac, and the encounter came at Antietam, but in the mean time Harper's Ferry had again been taken by the Confederates, and seventy-three pieces of artillery and thousands of small arms were added to their store.

On the high ground in the center of his position at Antietam, McClellan placed several batteries of long-range guns. From this position almost the whole of the field of battle could be seen, and, further to the left, where the batteries of the Fifth Corps were placed, a still more complete view could be obtained. The conformation of the ground was such that nearly the entire Confederate line was reached by fire from these central Federal batteries. The Union advance was assisted materially by their fire, but several of them were effectively shelled by the Confederates, who, however, on their counter-attacks, in turn suffered severely from the fire of the Federal guns.

At 10 A.M., September 17th, two of Sumner's batteries were being closely assailed by Confederate sharpshooters, and Hancock formed a line of guns and infantry to relieve them. Cowan's battery of 3-inch guns, Frank's 12-pounders, and

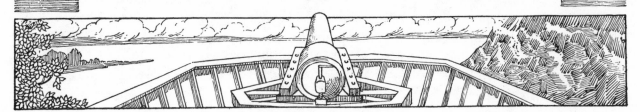

FROM PRIVATE TO BRIGADIER–GENERAL—ROBERTSON, A CHIEF OF ARTILLERY
WHO HELPED THE FEDERALS TO WIN GETTYSBURG

Twenty-three years before the war Brigadier-General James Madison Robertson (first on the left above) was a private in battery F of the Second United States Artillery. Between 1838 and 1848 he became corporal, then artificer, and finally quartermaster-sergeant. On June 28th of that year he was made second-lieutenant, and four years later first-lieutenant. It was not until May 14, 1861, that he attained his captaincy. Then came war, and with it rapid advancement. His quarter of a century of preparation stood him in good stead. In the next four years he was promoted as many times for gallant, brave, and distinguished services on the field, attaining finally the rank of brigadier-general. While Pleasonton's cavalry at Gettysburg was preventing Stuart from joining in Pickett's charge, Robertson led the horse artillery which seconded the efforts of Pleasonton's leaders, Gregg and Buford and Kilpatrick, whose exploits were not second to those of the infantry. For gallant and meritorious service in this campaign Robertson was promoted to lieutenant-colonel. He had been promoted to major for his gallantry at the battle of Gaines' Mill on the Peninsula. He was made colonel May 31, 1864, for gallant and meritorious service in the battle of Cold Harbor, and brigadier-general for distinguished service while chief of horse artillery attached to the Army of the Potomac during the campaign from May to August, 1864, including the battles of the Wilderness, Cold Harbor, Hawes' Shop, and Trevilian Station. He died, a soldier "full of years and honors," January 24, 1891.

Cothran's rifled guns, with their supporting infantry, a brigade, drove away the threatening skirmishers and silenced the Confederate batteries.

The demand for artillery was so great that when General Hancock asked for more guns to assist his attenuated line, the request could not be complied with. However, he borrowed, for a time, from Franklin, one battery, and when its ammunition had been expended, another was loaned him to replace it.

The battle ended September 17th. On the night of the 18th the Confederates withdrew, and by the 19th they had established batteries on the south side of the Potomac to cover their crossing. Porter determined to clear the fords and capture some of the guns. The attempt was made after dark of that day, and resulted in the taking of five guns and some of their equipment. One of these had been taken by the Confederates at the First Bull Run, and belonged to Battery D (Griffin's), Fifth United States Artillery.

We now follow the fortunes of the army to Fredericksburg. Sumner, with fifteen brigades of infantry and thirteen batteries, arrived on the banks of the Rappahannock before a large Confederate force was able to concentrate on the opposite shore, but no attempt was made to cross until just before the battle of December 13, 1862. General Hunt, on the day of the fight, had one hundred and forty-seven guns on the crest above the left bank of the river, in position to command the crossing, and the ground beyond. Besides these, twenty-three batteries, of one hundred and sixteen guns, crossed the river at the lower bridges, and nineteen batteries, of one hundred and four guns, crossed with Sumner's command. The Federal guns were principally 3-inch rifles, 20-pounder Parrotts, and 4½-inch siege-guns. They engaged the Confederates at close range, and the duel was terrific. The reserve line, on the crest of the left bank, aided with all its power, but the result was disastrous to the Federal arms.

We cannot follow the fortunes of the heroes through all

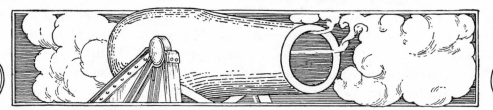

LIGHT ARTILLERY "IN RESERVE"—WAITING ORDERS

It is no parade-ground upon which this splendid battery is drawn up, as the untrodden daisies plainly show. Thus the waving fields of Gettysburg smiled on those July days of 1863—until the hoofs and wheels had trampled all green things to the earth, where they lay crushed beneath the prostrate forms of many a brave soldier of the North and South fighting for what each thought the right. This battery is standing in reserve. At any moment the notes of the bugle may ring out which will send it dashing forward across field and ditch to deal out death and face it from the bullets of the foe. The battery was evidently serving with infantry, as the cannoneers have no mounts. They are standing beside the gun-carriages, upon which they will leap when the battery moves forward. It was no easy matter for them to retain their seats as the heavy wheels cut through the grass and flowers and rebounded from hummocks and tilted sharply over stones. At any moment a horse might fall crippled, and it was their duty to rush forward and cut the traces, and jump aboard again as the gun drove around, or, if necessary, over the wounded animal. The latter was harder for an artilleryman who loved his horses than facing the screaming shells and whistling bullets at the front.

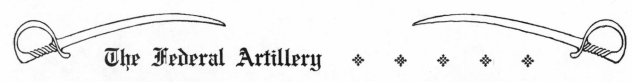

the vicissitudes of the following campaigns. On the Gettysburg field the artillery again contested with the Confederates in probably the most stubborn fighting of the war. General Meade had three hundred guns. The Federal advance was at first gradually forced back to Cemetery Hill, where General Doubleday rallied his troops, and his artillery did excellent service in checking the foe. He relates that the first long line that came on from the west was swept away by the Federal guns, which fired with very destructive effect. On the second day, the angle at the peach orchard furnished opportunities for nearly every phase of an artillery combat. "The power of the arm in concentration was well illustrated, the splendid devotion with which its destructive force was met and struggled against fixed our attention, and the skilful tactics by which its strength was husbanded for the decisive moment are especially to be praised."

Two Pennsylvania batteries on Cemetery Hill which had been captured by the Confederates were recovered in a gallant manner. The cannoneers, so summarily ousted, rallied and retook their guns by a vigorous attack with pistols, handspikes, rammers, stones, and even fence rails—the "Dutchmen" showing that they were in no way inferior to their "Yankee" comrades, who had been taunting them ever since Chancellorsville. After an hour's desperate fighting the Confederates were driven out with heavy loss.

The Federal artillery from Little Round Top to Cemetery Hill blazed "like a volcano" on the third day of the fight. Two hours after the firing opened, the chief of artillery, with the approval of General Meade, caused his guns to cease firing in order to replenish their ammunition supply. This deceived the Confederates, and Pickett's famous charge was made. No sooner was the advance begun than the Federal artillery belched forth all along the line, firing only at the approaching infantry. The brave assailants advanced even to the muzzles of the guns, the mass gradually diminishing as it

A VETERAN BATTERY FROM ILLINOIS, NEAR MARIETTA IN THE ATLANTA

CAMPAIGN

Battery B of the First Illinois Light Artillery followed Sherman in the Atlanta campaign.   It took part in the demonstrations against Resaca, Georgia, May 8 to 15, 1864, and in the battle of Resaca on the 14th and 15th. It was in the battles about Dallas from May 25th to June 5th, and took part in the operations about Marietta and against Kenesaw Mountain in June and July.   During the latter period this photograph was taken. The battery did not go into this campaign without previous experience.   It had already fought as one of the eight batteries at Fort Henry and Fort Donelson, heard the roar of the battle of Shiloh, and participated in the sieges of Corinth and Vicksburg.   The artillery in the West was not a whit less necessary to the armies than that in the East.   Pope's brilliant feat of arms in the capture of Island No. 10 added to the growing respect in which the artillery was held by the other arms of the service.   The effective fire of the massed batteries at Murfreesboro turned the tide of battle.   At Chickamauga the Union artillery inflicted fearful losses upon the Confederates.   At Atlanta again they counted their dead by the hundreds, and at Franklin and Nashville the guns maintained the best traditions of the Western armies.   They played no small part in winning battles.

approached. Their comrades watched them breathlessly until they disappeared in the cloud of smoke. Only a few disorganized stragglers were finally swept back. The deadly canister had broken the spirit of that great Army of Northern Virginia.

In the West, the value of the artillery was no less than in the East. It will be impossible to notice the minor affairs in which field-batteries took an active and a decisive part. In Missouri particularly was this the case. General Lyon, before his untimely death, used this effective weapon to its full capacity, as did Pope, Fremont, Grant, and the other Union leaders who participated in shaping up the campaign against the Confederacy in Missouri and Kentucky.

Early in 1861 the Confederates took possession of a line from Columbus to Bowling Green, Kentucky. Forts Henry and Donelson were in the center, and formed the keystone of the arch. Grant saw their value, and directed himself to their capture. He obtained permission from Halleck and McClellan to reconnoiter up the Tennessee and Cumberland rivers, and sent General C. F. Smith with two brigades from Paducah.

On the strength of Smith's report, Grant made strong representation to Halleck, his immediate superior, that the move was advisable. After some delay, the orders were issued, and Grant moved up the Tennessee with seventeen thousand men. The immediate assault on Fort Henry was threatened by General McClernand, with two brigades, each having two batteries. The work was a solidly constructed bastion fort with twelve guns on the river face, and five bearing inland. It was evacuated without attack from the land forces, as the gunboat bombardment was sufficient to drive out the defenders, but not without considerable damage to the fleet.

Fort Donelson, on the Cumberland, was the next objective. On the 8th of February, 1862, Grant telegraphed to Halleck that he proposed to take Fort Donelson with infantry and cavalry alone, but he moved out from Fort Henry with fifteen thousand men and eight field-batteries. Some of the guns were

A
WISCONSIN
LIGHT BATTERY

AT
BATON
ROUGE, LOUISIANA

The First Wisconsin Independent Battery of Light Artillery saw most of its service in Tennessee, Mississippi, and Louisiana. Its first active work was in the Cumberland Gap campaign, from April to June, 1862. It accompanied Sherman's Yazoo River expedition in December, 1862, and went on the expedition to Arkansas Post in January, 1863. At the siege of Vicksburg it participated in two assaults, May 19th and 22d, and after the fall of Vicksburg, July 4th, it went to the siege of Jackson, Mississippi. The battery was then re-fitted with 30-pounder Parrotts, and ordered to the Department of the Gulf. It left New Orleans April 22, 1864, to go on the Red River campaign. This was taken by the Confederate photographer, A. D. Lytle.

Battery C of the First Illinois Light Artillery served throughout the Western campaigns and accompanied Sherman on his march to the sea. It took part in the siege of Savannah, December 10 to 21, 1864, and served throughout the

campaign of the Carolinas, January to April, 1865. After being present at the surrender of Johnston and his army, it marched to Washington via Richmond, and took part in the grand review. It was mustered out on June 14, 1865.

OFFICERS OF A LIGHT BATTERY THAT MARCHED TO THE SEA

20- and 24-pounders, rifles, and howitzers. Grant's fifteen thousand men found themselves confronted by about twenty thousand entrenched. McClernand pressed to the right, up the river. His artillery was very active. Sometimes acting singly, and then in concert, the batteries temporarily silenced several of those of the Confederates and shelled some of the camps. Outside the main work, about fourteen hundred yards to the west, the Confederates had, after the surrender of Fort Henry, constructed a line of infantry entrenchments, which circled thence to the south and struck the river two and one-quarter miles from the fort. The guns of eight field-batteries were placed on this line.

On the 15th, McClernand's right was assailed and pressed back, and a part of the garrison escaped, but Grant received the unconditional surrender of about fourteen thousand men and sixty-five guns. His own artillery had not increased beyond the eight batteries with which he marched from Fort Henry. These were not fixed in position and protected by earthworks, but were moved from place to place as necessity dictated.

The brilliant feat of arms of Pope and his command in the capture of Island No. 10 added to the growing respect in which the artillery was held by the other combatant arms.

About seven in the morning on April 6, 1862, the Confederate artillery opened fire on the Union camps at Shiloh. Thereupon ensued one of the most sanguinary conflicts of the whole war. Although the Federal artillery was under the direct orders of the division commanders, the fighting was so fragmentary that no concerted attempt was made to use the batteries until, on the retirement of Hurlbut to the vicinity of Pittsburg Landing, some batteries of heavy guns were placed in position to cover the possible retirement of the troops from the front. About forty guns were finally assembled, and their work had an important part in saving the army, for this group of batteries was a large factor in repulsing the attempt of the

HEAVY ARTILLERY THAT MADE MARVELLOUS INFANTRY—DRILLING BEFORE THE WILDERNESS

Save for the drills in the forts about Washington, the big heavy artillery regiments with a complement of 1,800 men had an easy time at first. But in 1864, when General Grant took command of the armies in the field, the heavy artillery regiments in the vicinity of Washington were brigaded, provisionally, for service at the front. On May 19th, at the battle of Spotsylvania, the veterans cracked no end of jokes at the expense of the new troops. "How are you, heavies?" they would cry. "Is this work heavy enough for you? You're doing well, my sons. If you keep on like this a couple of years, you'll learn all the tricks of the trade." They had no more such comments to make after they had seen the "heavies" in action. They bore themselves nobly. Many of the severest casualties during the war were sustained by the heavy artillerists in the Wilderness campaign and at Petersburg.

A LIGHT BATTERY THAT FOUGHT BEFORE PETERSBURG—THE 17TH NEW YORK

The Seventeenth Independent Battery of New York Light Artillery, known as the "Orleans Battery," was organized at Lockport, New York, and mustered in August 26, 1862. It remained in the artillery camp of instruction and in the defenses of Washington until July, 1864, when it was ordered to Petersburg. It took part in the pursuit of Lee, and was present at Appomattox.

Confederates to seize the Landing and cut off Buell's army from crossing to Grant's assistance.

At the battle of Murfreesboro, or Stone's River, the artillery was especially well handled by the Federals, although they lost twenty-eight guns. On the second day, the Confederates made a determined assault to dislodge the Federals from the east bank of the river. The infantry assault was a success, but immediately the massed batteries on the west bank opened fire and drove Breckinridge's men back with great loss. Federal troops were then sent across the river to reenforce the position and the day was saved for the Union cause. The effective fire of the artillery had turned the tide of battle.

In assailing Vicksburg, Grant made four serious attempts to get on the flanks of the Confederate position before he evolved his final audacious plan of moving below the city and attacking from the southeast. In all the early trials his artillery, in isolated cases, was valuable, but the character of the operations in the closed country made it impossible to mass the guns for good effect. The naval assistance afforded most of the heavy gun-practice that was necessary or desirable against the Confederates.

On the last attempt, however, when the troops had left the river and were moving against Pemberton, Grant's guns assumed their full importance. His army consisted of the Thirteenth Army Corps, Major-General McClernand; the Fifteenth Army Corps, Major-General Sherman, and the Seventeenth Army Corps, Major-General McPherson, with an aggregate of sixty-one thousand men and one hundred and fifty-eight guns. The superb assistance rendered to the infantry by the ably handled guns made it possible for Grant to defeat his antagonist in a series of hard-fought battles, gradually move around him, and press him back into Vicksburg. Once there, the result could not be doubtful if the Federal army could hold off the Confederate reenforcements. This it was able to do. The progress of the siege we shall not here consider, except to

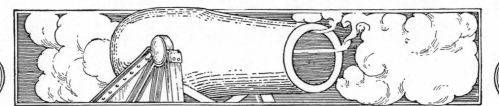

THIS BATTERY STOOD FIFTH IN ITS NUMBER OF CASUALTIES

The First Independent Battery of New York Light Artillery, under command of Captain Andrew Cowan, lost two officers and sixteen enlisted men killed and mortally wounded out of its complement of 150 men. Only four other batteries suffered a greater loss. "Cooper's" Battery B, First Pennsylvania Artillery, lost twenty-one men; "Sands'" Eleventh Ohio Battery lost twenty men (nineteen of them in one engagement in a charge on the battery at Iuka); "Philips'" Fifth Massachusetts Battery lost nineteen men; and "Weeden's" Battery C, First Rhode Island Artillery, lost nineteen men. This photograph shows Cowan's Battery in position within the captured Confederate works on the Petersburg line. The officers and men lived and slept in a work captured from the Confederates, and the horses were picketed back of the emplacements and in the gun-pits as seen underneath.

say that for scientific artillery work on the part of the besiegers it was not surpassed elsewhere in the conduct of the war. Twelve miles of trenches were constructed and armed with two hundred and eight light field-guns and twelve heavy siege-guns. The total loss in guns for the Confederacy during the series of operations was two hundred and sixty, of which one hundred and seventy-two were lost in the city of Vicksburg, and eighty-eight during the preceding campaign. Sixty-seven of these were siege-guns and the rest lighter field-pieces.

From Tullahoma to Chickamauga, Rosecrans skilfully maneuvered his army, to encounter a check that caused a temporary halt in the Union progress. During the first day's fierce fighting at Chickamauga, there were several interchanges of batteries—captures and recaptures. At half-past two in the afternoon of September 19, 1863, the Confederates made a determined assault on the Federal right. Hood's corps met with fearful loss from heavy artillery fire, six batteries opening with canister as the columns approached. On they came relentlessly, but the stubborn courage of the Federal troops, now reenforced, finally drove them back. As darkness was approaching, General Thomas, on the Union left, while re-forming his lines, was fiercely attacked, and the assault was so determined that some confusion resulted, but the artillery again came to the rescue, and, after dark, the Confederates were repulsed, and the first day's conflict ended as a drawn battle.

On the morning of the second day, the attack was made on the Federal left by Polk, but Thomas had entrenched his men and batteries, and the tremendous efforts to dislodge him were repulsed by a storm of musketry and canister, and the attacks failed. After the Federal right was pushed off the field and the conflict raged around Thomas on Horseshoe Ridge, the artillery of Thomas' command created havoc in the ranks of the assaulting columns. As the final attacks were made the ammunition was exhausted, and, in their turn, the infantry saved the artillery by receiving the foe with cold steel. That night

THE "ABOUT-FACED" REDOUBT
THREE DAYS AFTER ITS CAPTURE BY THE FEDERALS

A photograph of June 21, 1864—three days after Cowan's Battery captured this work and turned it against its Confederate builders. When the Eighteenth Army Corps had made its advance on Petersburg, followed by the gallant charges of the Fifteenth, and the fighting of the two following days, all the captured redoubts were occupied and strengthened. Of course, they were made to face the other way. The sand-bag reënforcements were removed and placed on the eastern side, new embrasures and traverses were constructed, and face to face the armies sat down to watch one another, and to begin the huge earthworks and fortifications that became the wonder of the military world. All night long for many months the air was filled with fiery messengers of death. The course of the bomb-shells could be plainly followed by the lighted fuses which described an arc against the sky. The redoubt pictured here is one captured, "about faced," and occupied on June 18th by Cowan's First New York Independent Battery, in the Artillery Brigade of the Sixth Corps. Thus the Union lines advanced, trench by trench, until Lee's army finally withdrew and left them the works so long and valiantly defended. The view looks northwest to the Appomattox.

GENERAL TOMPKINS

Starting as captain of a Rhode Island Battery May 2, 1861, Charles Henry Tompkins became a major August 1, 1861, colonel September 13, 1861, and brevet brigadier-general of volunteers August 1, 1864, for gallant and meritorious service, in the campaign before Richmond, and in the Shenandoah Valley.

BRIGADIER–GENERAL C. H. TOMPKINS

the Federal army retired to Chattanooga. The Confederate victory had been dearly bought.

Sherman started his campaign with fifty-three batteries of two hundred and fifty-four guns. For most of the time the weather was almost as great an antagonist as the Confederates. Crossing swollen streams without bridges, dragging heavy guns through mud and mire, and most of the time stripped of all surplus baggage and equipage, the artillery soldier had few pleasures, no luxuries, and much very hard work.

On the 17th of July, the Confederate Government removed Johnston, and detailed Hood to command his army. The news was received with satisfaction by the Federal troops, for now they were certain of getting a fight to their hearts' content. And so it developed. The battle of Peach Tree Creek, in front of Atlanta, gave a splendid opportunity for the employment of the energies of the batteries that had been dragged so far through the mud by the patient men and animals of Sherman's artillery. "Few battlefields of the war had been so thickly strewn with dead and wounded as they lay that evening around Collier's Mill."

Atlanta captured, Sherman rested his army and then started for the sea, sending Thomas back into Tennessee to cope with Hood. At Franklin and Nashville, the guns maintained the best traditions of the Western forces, and victory was finally achieved against one of the best armies ever assembled by the Confederacy.

The consolidated morning report of the Army of the Potomac for April 30, 1864, showed with that army forty-nine batteries of two hundred and seventy-four field guns, of which one hundred and twenty were 12-pounder Napoleons, one hundred and forty-eight 10-pounder and 3-inch rifles, and six 20-pounder Parrott rifles. In addition to these guns, there were eight 24-pounder Coehorn mortars. Two hundred and seventy rounds of ammunition were carried for each gun. The

"DICTATOR"—THE TRAVELING MORTAR IN FRONT OF PETERSBURG, 1864

This is the 13-inch mortar, a 200-pound exploding shell from which threw a Confederate field-piece and its carriage above its parapet, at a range of nearly two miles. The 17,000 pounds of this mortar made it difficult to move, so it was mounted on an ordinary railroad-car strengthened by additional beams, and plated on top with iron. This engine of destruction was run down on the Petersburg & City Point Railroad to a point near the Union lines, where a curve in the track made it easy to change the direction of the fire. The recoil from a charge of fourteen pounds of powder shifted the mortar less than two feet on the car, which moved a dozen feet on the track. Even the full charge of twenty pounds of powder could be used without damage to the axles of the car. This mortar, whose shell would crush and explode any ordinary field-magazine, terrorized the Confederate gunners, and succeeded in silencing their enfilading batteries on Chesterfield Heights. The activities of this great war machine were directed by Colonel H. L. Abbot, of the First Connecticut Heavy Artillery. Other photographs of it, with officers and men, are shown on pages 186 and 187, Volume III.

[F—4]

CAMP OF HEAVY ARTILLERY ON THE WAY TO PETERSBURG

On May 16, 1864, the date of this sweeping photograph, the movement against Petersburg had begun. The heavy guns which these two regiments were about to serve before Petersburg were sent by steamer and rail, so no ordnance is visible in this peaceful-looking camp on the banks of the beautiful river. The First Massachusetts Heavy Artillery had been ordered from the defenses of Washington to join the Army of the Potomac at Belle Plain, Virginia. It was to form part of the second brigade, third division, Second Army Corps, of the

THE FIRST MASSACHUSETTS AND SECOND NEW YORK AT BELLE PLAIN, 1864

Army of the Potomac, from May, 1864, to May, 1865. A month after landing at Belle Plain it was at the siege of Petersburg. At Belle Plain it was met by the Second New York Heavy Artillery, also from the defenses of Washington, which formed part of the first brigade, first division, Second Army Corps of the Army of the Potomac, from that time till June, 1865. The latter regiment also proceeded to Petersburg but by a more circuitous route. May 18th to 21st it served at Spotsylvania; June 1st to 12th, it was at Cold Harbor.

succession of battles and flank marches through the Wilderness to the James, up to Petersburg, thence to Appomattox, had taxed the energies and showed the devotion of the men with the guns in the hardest campaign of the war, finally causing the surrender of a remnant of the proud Army of Northern Virginia.

While at Petersburg, an interesting experiment was tried which resulted successfully. A large 13-inch Coehorn mortar was mounted on an ordinary railroad platform car, run down to a point within range of the Confederate works, and halted on a curve so that by a slight movement of the car the direction of the piece could be changed. The mortar, fired with fourteen pounds of powder, recoiled less than two feet on the car, which, in turn, was moved only ten or twelve feet on the track. The firing excited much apprehension in the Confederate works, and was effective in preventing their batteries from enfilading the right of the Union lines.

Major E. S. May, of the British army, has this to say of the Federal artillery in the Civil War:

"We have not by any means exhausted that rich repository of brilliant deeds, and many bright examples are reluctantly omitted. Enough, however, has been said to show that this arm can scarcely be with justice reproached for lack of enterprise during the great struggle. . . . As regards the conduct of officers and men in action, efficient service of guns, and judicious handling on the part of its more prominent leaders, the artillery showed itself in no degree unworthy of the great traditions handed down to it from the previous era, and may point with satisfaction to what it accomplished."

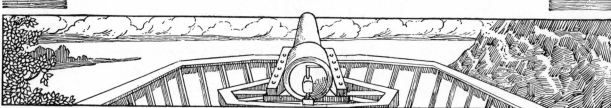

CONFEDERATE
GUNS
AND GUNNERS

THE LARGEST CONFEDERATE GUN AT YORKTOWN——A 64-POUNDER
BURST IN THE EFFORT TO REACH FEDERAL BATTERY NO. 1 IN
McCLELLAN'S WORKS BEFORE THE BELEAGUERED CONFEDERATE CITY

THE CONFEDERATE ARTILLERY—ITS ORGANIZATION AND DEVELOPMENT

By David Gregg McIntosh
Colonel of Artillery, Confederate States Army

THE organization of the Confederate field-artillery during the Civil War was never as symmetrical as that of the cavalry and infantry, and its evolution was slow. This was due in part to the lack of uniformity in the equipment of single batteries, and the inequality in the number of men in a company, running all the way in a 4-gun battery from forty-five to one hundred, and also to the tardiness with which the batteries were organized into battalions with proper staff-officers.

The disposition of the Government was to accept all bodies which volunteered for a particular branch of the service, and this did not tend to due proportions between the different branches. Outside of a limited number of smooth-bore guns in possession of certain volunteer associations, the Government had no equipment of field-artillery to start with. What was found in the arsenals in the Southern States which fell into the hands of the Confederate Government, consisted of old iron guns mounted on Gribeauval carriages, manufactured about 1812, but there was not a single serviceable field-battery in any arsenal.

The few guns belonging to the different States were short of harness, saddles, and other equipment. Not a gun or gun-carriage, and, except during the Mexican War, not a round of ammunition had been prepared in any of the Confederate States for fifty years. When hostilities began, the only foundry for casting cannon was at the Tredegar works in Richmond, and with the exception of a battery of Blakely guns, imported by the State of South Carolina, and a single battery

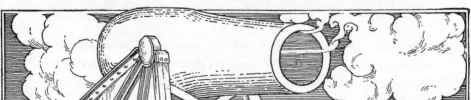

INSIDE A CONFEDERATE "WATER BATTERY," PENSACOLA HARBOR, IN 1861

THIS AND THE FOLLOWING THREE PHOTOGRAPHS WERE TAKEN WITHIN THE CONFEDERATE LINES IN 1861

This vivid view of great events in the making reveals the green Confederate volunteers without uniforms and still inexperienced. They show more enthusiasm than efficiency as they awkwardly handle the guns. It was not long before these quickly recruited gunners had become expert enough to give a good account of themselves. On November 22 and 23, 1861, they sustained and replied to a bombardment by the United States vessels *Niagara* and *Richmond* and by Fort Pickens and the neighboring Union batteries. Although Fort McRee was so badly injured that General Bragg entertained the idea of abandoning it, the plan of the Union commanders to "take and destroy it" was not executed. Time and again when the Federal blockading fleet threatened various points along the Confederate coast, requisitions were sent for these guns, but they were always needed in this fort. At the outset of the Civil War not a gun or gun-carriage, and, excepting during the Mexican War, not a round of ammunition had been prepared in the States of the Confederacy for fifty years. They were forced to improvise all of the vast paraphernalia necessary for war.

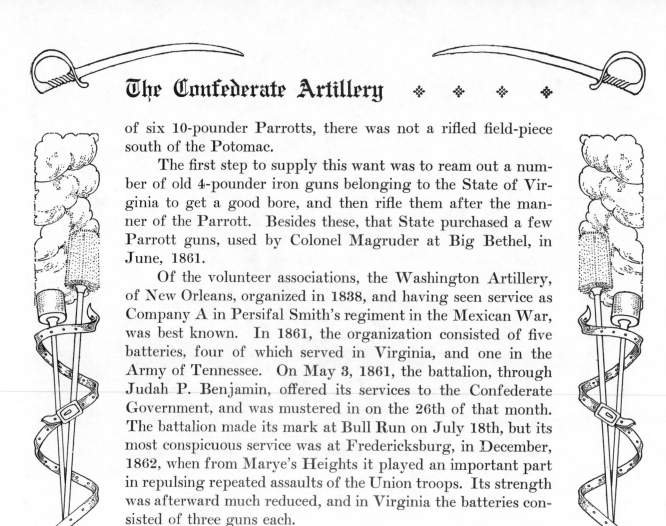

of six 10-pounder Parrotts, there was not a rifled field-piece south of the Potomac.

The first step to supply this want was to ream out a number of old 4-pounder iron guns belonging to the State of Virginia to get a good bore, and then rifle them after the manner of the Parrott. Besides these, that State purchased a few Parrott guns, used by Colonel Magruder at Big Bethel, in June, 1861.

Of the volunteer associations, the Washington Artillery, of New Orleans, organized in 1838, and having seen service as Company A in Persifal Smith's regiment in the Mexican War, was best known. In 1861, the organization consisted of five batteries, four of which served in Virginia, and one in the Army of Tennessee. On May 3, 1861, the battalion, through Judah P. Benjamin, offered its services to the Confederate Government, and was mustered in on the 26th of that month. The battalion made its mark at Bull Run on July 18th, but its most conspicuous service was at Fredericksburg, in December, 1862, when from Marye's Heights it played an important part in repulsing repeated assaults of the Union troops. Its strength was afterward much reduced, and in Virginia the batteries consisted of three guns each.

Next in importance was the Richmond Howitzers, organized at the time of the John Brown raid by George W. Randolph, afterward Confederate Secretary of War. In 1861, it was recruited up to three companies and formed into a battalion, though in the field the first company was never associated with the other two. It has been said that the flower of the educated youth in the South gravitated toward the artillery, and it is claimed that over one hundred men were commissioned from this corps, of every rank from that of second lieutenant to Secretary of War. One of its features was the Howitzer Glee Club, led by Crouch, the author of "Kathleen Mavourneen"; another was the Howitzer Law Club, in which moot-courts were held. Many of its members were from the

[58]

THE CONFEDERATE GUNNERS IN 1861

It is clear that these Confederate gunners at Pensacola are untried and undisciplined, but it is also evident that they are enthusiastic. They are manning the guns which are to open later on Fort Pickens, the first fort on the Confederate coast seized by the Federals, and held by them throughout the war. This was due to the enterprise of Lieutenant Adam J. Slemmer, ably seconded by Lieutenant J. H. Gilman. Lieutenant Slemmer's report says of Lieutenant Gilman: "During the whole affair we have stood side by side, and if any credit is due for the course pursued, he is entitled to it equally with myself." The demand was refused, and Fort Pickens never passed into the hands of the Confederates. The battery seen in this photograph was at Warrington, nearly opposite Fort Pickens. It commanded the entrance to the harbor. General Pendleton, who was a graduate of West Point in the class of 1830, was chief of artillery in Lee's army of Northern Virginia. He entered the war as captain in the artillery corps July 19, 1861, and became colonel and chief of artillery July 21, 1861. The mortar in this photograph is an old style piece dating from before the Mexican war. The new Confederate soldiers had at times to content themselves with very old guns.

BRIGADIER–GENERAL W. N. PENDLETON

University of Virginia, where out of six hundred and four students in 1861 over one-half entered the Confederate service.

Besides these organizations, was the Washington Artillery, of Charleston, South Carolina, organized in 1784; the Marion Artillery, of the same place; Delaware Kemper's Artillery, of Alexandria, and a number of other organizations.

The great bulk of the artillery, however, was composed of companies which volunteered for that branch of the service, and were compelled to accept such equipment as the Government could furnish. This embraced a great variety. There was the small 6-pounder gun, at first largely predominating, and afterward the 12-pounder known as Napoleon, and also the 12-pound and 24-pound howitzer, all of bronze. The rifled guns were somewhat nondescript. Those turned out by the Ordnance Department were generally of 3-inch caliber with five or seven grooves adapted to the same ammunition, though not uniform in length or shape, and varying in weight. Many of these were withdrawn and replaced by guns of the Parrott type, or the 3-inch U. S. pattern.

It was extremely rare at any period of the war to find a battery with uniform equipment. There was at no time in the Army of Northern Virginia more than six or eight batteries of Napoleon guns, and a less number of 3-inch rifles. It seems to have been thought desirable to have a section of rifles and a section of smoothbores. But it was not unusual to find in the same section rifles of different caliber, or a Napoleon with a 6-pounder, or perhaps a howitzer; and in a battery of four guns, there was not infrequently at least three different calibers which required different ammunition. This made the supply of ammunition more difficult and impaired the effectiveness of the battery. Experience taught the value of concentrated fire, and that four Napoleons or four rifles were more effective than the fire of a mixed battery.

The Napoleon and the 3-inch rifle, U. S. pattern, were the favorite guns; the former, because it was equally adapted to the

BRIGADIER–GENERAL E. P. ALEXANDER, WHO COMMANDED LONGSTREET'S
ARTILLERY AT GETTYSBURG

E. P. Alexander was the Confederate officer who commanded Longstreet's eighty guns in the great artillery battle which preceded Pickett's charge at Gettysburg. He entered the Engineer Corps of the Confederate army April 2, 1861, and served on the staff of General G. T. Beauregard as engineer and chief of signal service till August of that year. As chief of ordnance of the Army of Northern Virginia, he distinguished himself on the bloody field of Antietam. He directed the eighty pieces on Longstreet's front at Gettysburg, which prepared the way for Pickett's charge until they had shot away practically all their ammunition. He was acting chief of artillery in Longstreet's corps from September 25, 1863, till February 26, 1864, and was appointed chief of artillery of the corps with which he remained till Appomattox, serving in the Wilderness, at Spotsylvania, and the siege of Petersburg. On February 26, 1864, he had been appointed brigadier-general of Artillery. Within two weeks after Lee's surrender he was at the Brandreth House in New York city attempting to arrange for a commission in the Brazilian army. Later, he became general manager and president of various Southern railroads, Government director of the Union Pacific Railroad Company from 1885 to 1887, and in 1901 engineer arbitrator in charge of the mooted boundary survey between Costa Rica and Nicaragua.

use of shell, spherical case, or canister, and was most effective at close quarters; the latter, because it was light and easily handled, and its range and accuracy remarkable. At the siege of Petersburg, in the summer of 1864, a battery of 20-pound Parrotts from a Confederate work shelled passing trains behind the Union lines, which excited the ire of some 3-inch rifle batteries. The Confederate work was heavily built and well provided with embrasures for the guns, but these were torn away day by day and replaced at night. The range was finally so accurate that if a Confederate cap on a stick was raised over the edge of the parapet, it would immediately be cut down by a shot. The Confederate 30-pound Parrotts did not prove a success. Two of them mounted on Lee's Hill, at the battle of Fredericksburg, burst, one at the thirty-ninth, the other at the fifty-seventh discharge.

Besides the home-made guns, which were all muzzle-loaders, a number of guns of various make, Whitworth, Armstrong, James, Blakely, and Hotchkiss, were brought in through the blockade. Two Whitworths were sent to the Army of Northern Virginia. They had a great reputation for range and accuracy of fire, but beyond the shelling of distant columns and trains, proved a disappointment. The length and weight of the guns were above the average, making them difficult to transport, and the care and length of time consumed in loading and handling impaired their efficiency for quick work.

Transportation, after all, was one of the most difficult problems with the Confederate artillery. Four horses to a piece, and the same to a caisson, was the utmost allowance, excepting, perhaps, the 20-pounder Parrott gun. In consequence, the cannoneers were required to walk, and General Jackson issued more than one order on the subject. When A. P. Hill's artillery was hurrying from Harper's Ferry to Antietam to General Lee's assistance, the first battery to arrive on the field was worked by less than half the complement of men, officers, commissioned and non-commissioned, lending a hand.

COPYRIGHT, 1911, REVIEWS OF REVIEWS CO.

CONFEDERATE ARTILLERISTS

These Confederate artillerists, members of the famous Washington Artillery of New Orleans, had but few field-pieces with which to face their foes when this photograph was taken, early in '62. Some ordnance stores had been secured when the Confederate Government seized coastwise guns and forts.   But a visit to the artillery camps later in the war would have revealed the fact that most of the three-inch rifles, the Napoleons, and the Parrott guns had been originally "Uncle Sam's" property, later captured in battle; and an inspection of the cavalry would have shown, after the first year, that the Southern troopers were armed with United States sabers taken from the same bountiful source.   During the first year, before the blockade became stringent, Whitworth guns were brought in from abroad. But that supply was soon stopped, and the Southerners had to look largely to their opponents for weapons.   The Tredegar Iron Works in Richmond was almost the only factory for cannon, especially for pieces of heavy caliber.   It is estimated by ordnance officers that two-thirds of the artillery in the South was captured from the Federals, especially the 3-inch rifles and the 10-pound Parrotts.

The Confederate Artillery

The forces under General Johnston in May, 1861, while at Harper's Ferry were supplied with the 6-pounder gun and 12-pounder howitzer. When Johnston joined Beauregard at Manassas in July, he brought four brigades with four batteries and two in reserve. Beauregard had eight brigades with thirty-four guns, which, under orders of July 20th, he distributed for the action as follows: Six pieces to Ewell, eight to Jones, eight to Longstreet, and twelve to Cocke. The Washington Artillery at this time had four 12-pound howitzers, four 6-pounders, and three rifles, distributed among the different batteries. Twenty-eight pieces captured in the battle added to the supply.

General Henry A. Wise, in West Virginia, reports about the same time having "ten small pieces, six of iron, three of brass, and one piece, private property," with nine officers and one hundred and seventy-seven men.

In April, 1862, the artillery in Johnston's army had grown to thirty-four batteries, McLaws' Division of four brigades having nine batteries, Toombs' Division of three brigades having two battalions, Longstreet's Division of five brigades having five batteries, with Pendleton's Artillery, thirty-six pieces, and the Washington Artillery in reserve.

In July, 1862, the batteries were distributed as follows:

Longstreet's Division: 6 brigades, 8 batteries
A. P. Hill's " 6 " 9 "
Jones' " 2 " 3 "
D. H. Hill's " 6 " 7 "
Anderson's " 3 " 6 "
McLaws' " 4 " 4 "

This gave thirty-seven batteries to twenty-seven brigades, with Pendleton's First Virginia Artillery of ten companies, Cutt's Georgia Artillery of five companies, and three battalions of eleven companies in reserve.

During the operations around Richmond in August, 1862, the artillery of the army was distributed as follows:

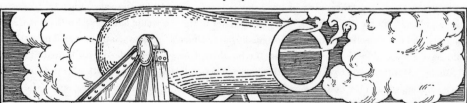

A DISTINGUISHED CONFEDERATE BATTERY FROM TENNESSEE—"RUTLEDGE'S"

This photograph shows the officers of Rutledge's Battery, Company A, First Tennessee Light Artillery. It was taken at Watkin's Park, Nashville, in the latter part of May, 1861, just after the battery was mustered in. The cannon for this battery were cast at Brennon's Foundry, at Nashville, and consisted of four 6-pounder smooth-bore guns, and two 12-pounder howitzers. During the first year of the war the battery took part in several engagements and two notable battles—Mill Springs, or Fishing Creek, and Shiloh. The officers here shown from left to right, starting with the upper row are: Frank Johnson, George W. Trabui, Jack B. Long, James C. Wheeler, E. T. Falconet, A. M. Rutledge, Joe E. Harris, George E. Purvis, J. P. Humphrey, J. Griffith, and M. S. Cockrill. Three of the officers in this picture—Falconet, Rutledge, and Cockrill—were promoted. Captain Rutledge was promoted to be major of artillery and assigned to duty on the staff of General Leonidas Polk. First-Lieutenant Falconet became a captain in the cavalry service, and Second-Lieutenant Cockrill was appointed first-lieutenant and assigned to duty in the ordnance department. rience, and because of heavy losses, the battery was merged, at the expiration of the year for which it had enlisted, with McClurg's Battery, and its history after that time is the history of that battery.

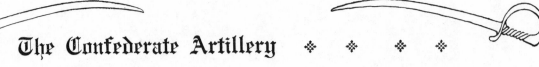

The Confederate Artillery ❖ ❖ ❖ ❖

Jackson's   Corps: 4 divisions, 14 brigades, 17 batteries
Magruder's   "   2   "   6   "   13   "
Longstreet's   "   3   "   15   "   22   "

Pendleton with five battalions, twenty batteries, was held in reserve, and five more unattached, making a total of seventy-seven batteries.

In the Seven Days' Battles around Richmond, General Lee must have found his artillery something of an encumbrance. The artillery numbered about three hundred guns, nearly four guns to every thousand men, of which ninety-eight were in the general reserve. It has been said of the artillery during that time by a critic not unfriendly to the cause, that "it left only the faintest trace of its existence." Its use, generally, was fragmentary and detached, and nowhere did it achieve results comparable to the concentrated fire of the Union batteries at Malvern Hill. It was not until Second Manassas, when S. D. Lee brought eighteen guns to bear on the heavy masses attacking Jackson's right and succeeded in breaking them up in a short half-hour, that the value of concentrated artillery fire was learned. At Fredericksburg, fourteen guns were massed on Jackson's right at Hamilton's Crossing, and were used with brilliant results.

General Lee must have been impressed with the fact that his artillery was unwieldy, for in the expedition into Maryland, in the following fall, many batteries were left behind. In the right wing were one hundred and twelve pieces: forty-five rifles, thirteen Napoleons, and fifty-four short-range. In the left wing one hundred and twenty-three pieces: fifty-two rifles, eighteen Napoleons, fifty-three short-range; and in the reserve fifty-two guns.

On October 14, 1862, fourteen of these batteries were disbanded under general orders, and the men and guns distributed to other commands, and four batteries consolidated into two.

In the winter of 1862–63, the practice of assigning batteries to infantry brigades ceased, and the artillery was organ-

A CONFEDERATE ARTILLERY WRECK AT ANTIETAM

A TRAGEDY OF THE TREMENDOUS CANNONADE—WHY LEE DID NOT RENEW THE BATTLE

The battery-horses lie dead beside the shattered caissons and the litter of corn-cobs where, only a few hours before, they had munched at their last meal. The heavy loss to Lee's artillery in horses, caissons, and guns affected his decision not to renew the battle. From researches of Henderson, the British military historian, it appears that on the morning of September 18, 1862, after the roar of Antietam had died away, General Lee sent for Colonel Stephen D. Lee, and told him to report to General Jackson. They rode together to the top of a hill on which lay wrecked caissons, broken wheels, human corpses, and dead horses. Their view overlooked the Federal right. "Can you take fifty pieces of artillery and crush that force?" asked General Jackson. Colonel Lee gazed earnestly at the serried Union lines, bristling with guns unlimbered and ready for action, but could not bring himself to say no. "Yes, General; where will I get the fifty guns?" "How many have you?" asked General Jackson. "About twelve out of the thirty I carried into the action yesterday." "I can furnish you some, and General Lee says he can furnish you some." "Shall I go for the guns?" "No, not yet," replied General Jackson. "Colonel Lee, can you crush the Federal right with fifty guns?" Although Colonel Lee evaded the question again and again, General Jackson pressed it home. Reluctantly the brave artillery officer admitted: "General, it cannot be done with fifty guns and the troops you have near here." "Let us ride back, Colonel." Colonel Lee reported the conversation to General Lee, and during the night the Army of Northern Virginia, with all its trains and artillery, recrossed the Potomac at Boteler's Ford.

ized into a number of battalions, usually of four batteries, with one or two field-officers with the rank of major or lieutenant-colonel to each. These battalions were supplied with an ordnance officer and a quartermaster. An adjutant was usually detailed from one of the batteries. The battalion commanders reported to the chiefs of artillery of the army corps, and on the march or in battle acted with, and received orders from, the general of the division with which they happened to be.

In the Chancellorsville campaign, Longstreet with two divisions was absent. With the remaining divisions of that corps, there were two battalions of artillery and ten batteries in reserve. With the Second Corps there were four battalions and ten batteries in reserve, with a further general reserve of six batteries, making a total of fifty-one batteries.

On June 4th, prior to the Gettysburg campaign, the army having been divided into three corps, an officer of the rank of colonel was assigned to the command of the artillery of each corps, the battalion organization continuing as before.

Of these, five battalions, with twenty-two batteries, were assigned to the First Corps; five battalions, with twenty batteries, were assigned to the Second Corps; five battalions, with twenty batteries, were assigned to the Third Corps.

The equipment was as follows:

31 rifles,	42 Napoleons,	10 howitzers	= 83 in the 1st Corps
38 "	32 "	12 "	= 82 in the 2d Corps
41 "	26 "	15 "	= 82 in the 3d Corps
	Total		247

The particular equipment in the battalions of the Third Corps was as follows:

Cutts:	10 rifles,	3 Napoleons,	4 howitzers		= 17
Garnett:	11 "	4 "	2 "		= 17
McIntosh:	10 "	6 "			= 16
Pegram:	8 "	9 "	2 "		= 19
Cutshaw:	2 "	5 "	7 "		= 14

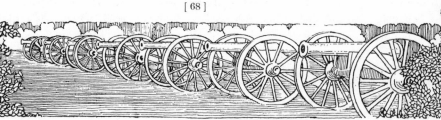

AFTER THE BATTLE OF CHATTANOOGA—CAPTURED CONFEDERATE GUNS

The Confederate artillery was never equal in number or weight to that of the Union armies. In the West these ancient 12-pounder howitzers were mounted on rough wooden carriages, those above, for instance. These guns are aligned in front of General Thomas' headquarters. They were taken late in November, 1863, at the battle of Chattanooga, and the photograph was made early in 1864. Behind the guns can be seen the pole to one of the caissons. When the Confederate armies captured a gun they almost invariably whirled it around, detailed artillerymen to man it, and set it promptly to work, but by this time the Union armies were so well equipped that captured guns might be parked. Many pieces had changed hands several times, and had barked defiance at both armies. The equipment of the Confederate batteries was seldom uniform. Among four guns there might be found three different calibers, requiring different ammunition. The batteries' efficiency was still further impaired during the fight by the inability of the chief of artillery to select positions for his guns, which were often placed so far apart that he was unable to assemble them for concentrated fire. This was due to the custom of apportioning the field-artillery to infantry divisions, and placing them under orders of the brigadier-general, who could not give them proper attention. The plan was not changed until the early part of 1863. In the face of all these difficulties the Confederate artillery made a glorious record.

The Confederate Artillery ❖

There were in Richmond, at this time, three battalions of light artillery and five batteries unattached, besides two divisions with two battalions each of heavy artillery.

The battalion organization continued to the close of the war, the exigencies of the service producing minor changes, and shifting of commands at various times. As many as six or eight batteries were sometimes assigned to a battalion commander.

At the battle of Cold Harbor, the opposite lines at one point approached quite near, and it was discovered that the Union troops were laying a mine, the approach to which was along an open trench. The battalion commander took advantage of a ravine in his rear, and sinking the trail of a smooth-bore gun so that it could be used as a mortar, threw shells with a slight charge of powder and time-fuses aimed to fall and explode in the trench. When the Union forces withdrew and the ground was examined, a number of shells were found in the trench unexploded, showing accuracy of fire, but failure of the fuse.

The organization as described was adopted generally in the Southern and Western armies. In the Department of North Carolina, General Holmes had, in 1861, three brigades to which six batteries were assigned. In the Army of Kentucky, six batteries were assigned to six brigades, with two in reserve.

In 1862, in Bragg's Army of the Mississippi, Polk's Corps contained one division of four brigades, and a battery assigned to each brigade. In Hardee's Corps the batteries were assigned to brigades or divisions, indiscriminately. In Van Dorn's Army of West Tennessee, a battery was assigned to each brigade of infantry. In Kirby Smith's Army of Tennessee, there were two divisions, four brigades to each, and a battery attached to each brigade.

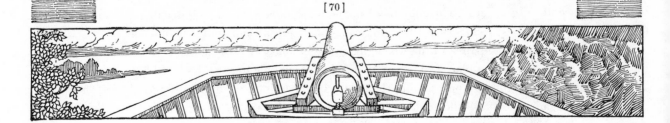

CAPTAIN JOHN DONNELL SMITH

This photograph well reflects the bearing of a representative artillery officer in the Army of Northern Virginia. At the time—May, 1863—he was in Richmond, following the battle of Chancellorsville. He was then First-Lieutenant of Jordan's Battery, Alexander's Battalion of Artillery, First Corps, Army of Northern Virginia. Battery A of Huger's (formerly Alexander's) battalion of Artillery, Longstreet's Corps, Army of Northern Virginia, of which John Donnell Smith later became captain, was then in camp near Bowling Green, Caroline County, Virginia. Captain Smith helped to serve the guns at Gettysburg. On June 4, 1863, prior to the Gettysburg campaign, the army having been divided into three corps, five battalions with twenty-two batteries were assigned to the first, five battalions with twenty batteries were assigned to the second, and five battalions with twenty batteries to the third. The total number of Confederate guns at Gettysburg, including rifles, Napoleons, and howitzers was two hundred and forty-eight. These opposed 320 Union guns, all in action.

MEMORIES OF GETTYSBURG

By F. M. Colston *

ALEXANDER'S battalion of artillery, which I joined in the spring of 1863, had gained renown under Colonel, afterward Lieutenant-General, Stephen D. Lee, especially at Second Manassas and Sharpsburg. This renown was increased under the command of Colonel E. Porter Alexander, afterward brigadier-general and chief of artillery of Longstreet's corps. He had graduated No. 3 at West Point, in 1857, and entered the Engineer Corps of the United States Army. He was more consulted by General Lee than any other artillery officer in the Confederate service. In later life he became president of several railroads, Government director of the Union Pacific Railroad, and engineer arbitrator of the boundary survey between Costa Rica and Nicaragua.

The battalion was composed of six batteries—two more than customary—four Virginia, one South Carolina and one Louisiana. Together with the more noted Washington Artillery of New Orleans, with four batteries, it composed the reserve artillery of Longstreet's corps, Army of Northern Virginia. They were called the " reserve " because they were not specially attached to any division, but kept for use whenever and wherever wanted. Hence the battalion explanation that " we were called 'reserve' because never in reserve."

After taking part in the battle of Chancellorsville, our battalion was moved down to Milford, Caroline County, to refit. On June 3d commenced the forward march that ended at Gettysburg. When we went into action there, July 2d, just south of the peach orchard, the batteries actually charged, action front, with a front of over four hundred yards—the finest sight imaginable on a battlefield. One of the batteries, which was short-handed, had borrowed five men from the adjacent Mississippi regiment. In the fight two were killed and

* Lieutenant and Ordnance Officer in Alexander's Battalion of Artillery, Longstreet's corps.

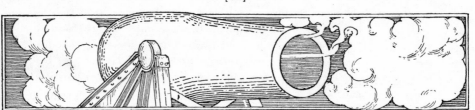

LIEUTENANT–COLONEL FRANK HUGER

After General Alexander became acting chief of artillery, Huger succeeded to the command of his battalion. The fine faces of these officers recall the trying times through which they passed. For the last two years especially, the Confederate field-artillery fought against the odds of lack of horses. Behind them stood no such supply depot as Giesboro outside of Washington, which furnished the Federal armies thousands of fresh horses, and cared for sick ones. A Confederate artillery piece seldom boasted more than four horses after 1862. When some of these were killed, the gun was handled by the horse or horses left and the men of the battery. However, Huger's battalion went through the campaigns of Chancellorsville, Gettysburg, East Tennessee, the Wilderness, Spotsylvania Court House—fought with the Army of Northern Virginia through the siege of Petersburg—and "never had to run." The men boasted they occupied their ground after every fight, and buried their own dead.

PROBLEMS
OF LEE'S
ARTILLERY

W. T. Poague was captain of the Rockbridge Artillery in the Stonewall brigade before he became lieutenant-colonel of artillery, Third Corps. This was in the Army of Northern Virginia. The efficiency of its artillery was crippled until the winter of 1862–63 by the system of attaching the batteries to various brigades and divisions, and not handling it as a separate corps so that its batteries could be massed. The chief of artillery was not even allowed to choose the positions for his guns. But during that winter the artillery was organized into a number of battalions, and the battalion commanders reported to the chiefs of artillery of the army corps, and on the march or in battle acted with and received orders from the general of the division with which they happened to be. After the batteries could be massed they were much more effective as they abundantly proved on the battlefield of Gettysburg and in the later Virginia campaigns.

LIEUTENANT–COLONEL W. T. POAGUE

one wounded, so that we could return only two—which the regiment seemed to think a small return of borrowed property! We then took a position in front of the Emmittsburg road and a little north of the peach orchard. We lay all night there, opposite the center of the Federal line, the cemetery being a little to our left front, and the Round Tops on our right.

At one o'clock the next day the great artillery duel, the heaviest in the history of war to that time and probably not exceeded since, was opened by the previously arranged signal-gun of the Washington Artillery. It was promptly answered by the Federals—and the din of war was on.

The roar of our guns was terrific. The explosion of the Federal shells, with a different sound, added to the tumult. In the midst of it our officers and men engaged were busy with their work, pausing only to give a cheer at the sight of an exploding caisson of the Federals. The work went on mechanically. Few orders were given and those had to be shouted. As soon as Pickett's division passed through our guns on their way to the charge a respite was gained, the dead were removed, the wounded cared for, and the survivors breathed more freely.

The question is often asked, "How does a man feel in such an action?" Comparatively few men are physical and moral cowards. Even when the courage is wanting, the example and opinion of comrades often acts in place of it. Brave men cheerfully acknowledge their appreciation of the danger. The most trying time is "waiting to go in." The silence before the coming battle is oppressive. Many mental and physical exhibitions will be noticed, and if the battle is on, the sight of the wounded men streaming back is disheartening.

But when once engaged, the sense of duty and the absorption of occupation will greatly overcome every other sensation. Every man has his duty to do, and if he does it he will have little time to think of anything else. No place can be considered safe. In this action, a man was standing behind a tree near our battalion, safe from direct fire. But a passing shell exploded just as it passed; the fragments struck him and tossed his dead body out. The sight reassured those who were in the open.

I

DEFENDING THE
NATIONAL CAPITAL

BLOCKHOUSE AT THE CHAIN BRIDGE, ABOVE GEORGETOWN

THIS APPROACH WAS DEFENDED BY FORTS ETHAN ALLEN AND MARCY ON THE
VIRGINIA SIDE, AND BY BATTERIES MARTIN SCOTT, VERMONT, AND
KEMBLE ON THE MARYLAND SIDE OF THE POTOMAC

IN A WASHINGTON FORT

Erect on the parapet is the tall, soldierly figure of Colonel Michael Corcoran of the Sixty-ninth New York, who was subsequently captured and chosen by lot to meet the same fate as Walter W. Smith, prizemaster of the Southern schooner *Enchantress*, taken prisoner, July 22, 1861, and tried for piracy. Neither was executed. The men pictured in their shirt-sleeves, and the heavy shadows cast by the glaring sun, indicate that the time is summer. The soldier with the empty sleeve has evidently suffered a minor injury, and is carrying his arm inside his coat. Several of the officers peer over the parapet, watching for the approach of danger. The first forts located in the defenses south of the Potomac were Fort Runyon, at the land end of the approach of Long Bridge, and Fort Corcoran, covering the approach to the aqueduct. On the night of May 23, 1861, three columns of Federal soldiers crossed the Potomac, one by the aqueduct, one by Long Bridge, and one by water to Alexandria. The smooth-bore guns in the armament of Fort Corcoran were two 8-inch howitzers *en barbette*. The rifled guns consisted of three 3-inch Parrotts *en embrasure*. The term "*en barbette*" refers to the placing of a gun so that the muzzle projected over a wall. "*En embrasure*" indicates a cannon in an opening in the fortification with no protection in front of it. The gun around which the officers above are grouped is an 8-inch sea-coast howitzer. These guns were of iron, and were used principally to flank the ditches of permanent works. They fired especially grape-shot for this purpose. The howitzer is a cannon employed to throw large projectiles with comparatively small charges of powder. It is shorter and lighter than most guns of the same caliber. The chief advantage was in the fact that it could produce at short ranges a greater effect, due to its ability to throw hollow projectiles with bursting charges and case shot. The weight of this gun was about 3,000 pounds, and the usual charge was about four pounds of powder. It is mounted on a wooden carriage. Before it lies a pile of grape-shot.

COLONEL MICHAEL CORCORAN

AND HIS OFFICERS OF THE 69TH NEW YORK, IN FORT CORCORAN, 1861

The First Connecticut Heavy Artillery was organized from the Fourth Connecticut Infantry in January, 1862, and remained on duty in Fort Richardson till April. The regiment acquired a high reputation by serving continuously throughout the four years of warfare actively in the field as heavy artillery. Very few of the other "heavy" regiments in the army saw any service aside from garrison duty, except while acting as infantry. The First Connecticut Heavy Artillery served in the two big sieges of the Army of the Potomac, Yorktown, April and May, 1862, and Petersburg, June, 1864 to April, 1865. Fort Richardson lay on the Virginia line of the Washington defenses about halfway between Fort Corcoran and Fort Ellsworth, in front of Alexandria. Its smooth-bore armament consisted of three 24-pounders on siege carriages *en barbette*, two 24-pounders on barbette carriages *en embrasure*, one 24-pounder field howitzer *en embrasure* and one 24-pounder field howitzer *en barbette*. Its four rifled guns consisted of one 100-pounder Parrott *en barbette*, two 30-pounder Parrott *en embrasure* and one 30-pounder Parrott *en barbette*. It also contained two mortars, one 10-inch siege mortar and one 24-pounder Coehorn.

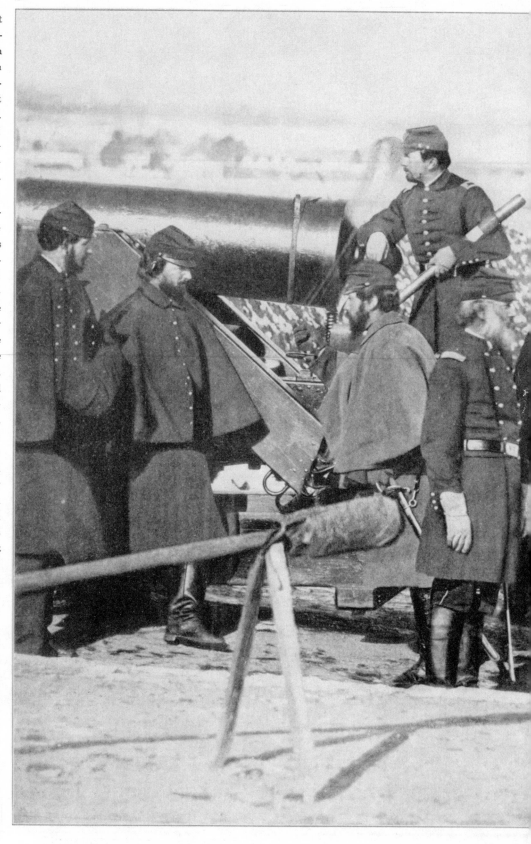

OFFICERS OF THE FIRST CONNECTICUT HEAVY ARTILLERY IN FORT RICHARDSON

A WINTER SCENE IN THE DEFENSES OF WASHINGTON

DEFENDING THE NATIONAL CAPITAL

By O. E. HUNT
Captain, United States Army

THE following conversation took place early in 1861 between General Winfield Scott and Colonel Charles P. Stone, inspector-general of the District of Columbia:

General Scott: " Gosport navy-yard has been burned."

Colonel Stone: " Yes, General."

General Scott: " Harper's Ferry bridge has been burned."

" Yes, General."

General Scott: " The bridge at Point of Rocks was burned some days since."

" Yes, General."

General Scott: " The bridges over Gunpowder Creek, beyond Baltimore, have been burned."

" Yes, General."

General Scott: " They are closing their coils around us, sir."

" Yes, General."

General Scott: " Now, how long can we hold out here? "

" Ten days, General, and within that time the North will come down to us."

General Scott: " How will they come? The route through Baltimore is cut off."

" They will come by all routes. They will come between the capes of Virginia, up through Chesapeake Bay, and by the Potomac. They will come, if necessary, from Pennsylvania, through Maryland, directly to us, and they will come through Baltimore and Annapolis."

[80]

INSIDE
FORT TOTTEN—THREE
SHIFTING SCENES IN A BIG–GUN DRILL

Constant drill at the guns went on in the defenses of Washington throughout the war. At its close in April, 1865, there were 68 enclosed forts and batteries, whose aggregate perimeter was thirteen miles, 807 guns and 98 mortars mounted, and emplacements for 1,120 guns, ninety-three unarmed batteries for field-guns, 35,711 yards of rifle-trenches, and three block-houses encircling the Northern capital. The entire extent of front of the lines was thirty-seven miles; and thirty-two miles of military roads, besides those previously existing in the District of Columbia, formed the means of interior communication. In all these forts constant preparation was made for a possible onslaught of the Confederates, and many of the troops were trained which later went to take part in the siege of Petersburg where the heavy artillery fought bravely as infantry

Defenses of Washington ❖

Later, General Scott asked, " Where are your centers?" and received the reply: " There are three, General. First, the Capitol, where have been stored some two thousand barrels of flour, and where Major McDowell remains every night with from two to three hundred of my volunteers. Second, the City Hall hill, a commanding point, with broad avenues and wide streets connecting it with most important points, having in its vicinity the Patent Office and the General Post Office, in each of which I place a force every night. In the General Post Office we have stored a large quantity of flour. Third, the Executive Square, including the President's house, the War, Navy, State, and Treasury departments, in each of which, and in Winder's building, I place a force every night after dusk.

" The citadel of this center is the Treasury building. The basement has been barricaded very strongly by Captain Franklin of the Engineers, who remains there at night and takes charge of the force. The front of the Treasury building is well flanked by the State Department building, and fifty riflemen are nightly on duty there. The building opposite is also occupied at night. The outposts at Benning's Bridge and the pickets in that direction will, in case of attack in force, retire, fighting, to the Capitol. Those on the northeast and north will, if pressed, retire by Seventh Street to City Hall hill, while those on the northwest and west will, in case of attack, fall back and finally take refuge in the Treasury building, where they will be joined by the detachments guarding the river front when the attack shall have become so marked and serious that only the centers can be held. In the Treasury building are stored two thousand barrels of flour, and perhaps the best water in the city is to be found there. The city is so admirably laid out in broad avenues and wide streets centering on the three points chosen, that concentration for defense on any one of the three is made easy.

" The field-battery can move rapidly toward any outpost where heavy firing shall indicate that the attack there is serious,

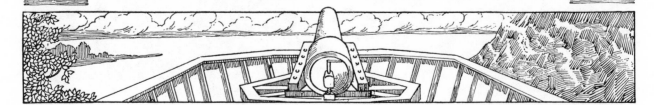

THE SEVENTEENTH NEW YORK ARTILLERY DRILLING BEFORE THE CAPITAL

In the background rises the dome of the Capitol which this regiment remained to defend until it was ordered to Petersburg, in 1864. It appears in parade formation. The battery commander leads it, mounted. The battery consists of six pieces, divided into three platoons of two guns each. In front of each platoon is the platoon commander, mounted. Each piece, with its limber and caisson, forms a section; the chief of section is mounted, to the right and a little to the rear of each piece. The cannoneers are mounted on the limbers and caissons in the rear. To the left waves the notched guidon used by both the cavalry and light artillery.

A LIGHT BATTERY AT FORT WHIPPLE, DEFENSES OF WASHINGTON

This photograph shows the flat nature of the open country about Washington. There were no natural fortifications around the city. Artificial works were necessary throughout. Fort Whipple lay to the south of Fort Corcoran, one of the three earliest forts constructed. It was built later, during one of the recurrent panics at the rumor that the Confederates were about to descend upon Washington. This battery of six guns, the one on the right hand, pointing directly out of the picture, looks quite formidable. One can imagine the burst of fire from the underbrush which surrounds it, should it open upon the foe. At present it is simply drilling.

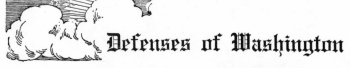

and with the aid of this battery the retreat from that point can be made slowly enough to give time for concentration on that line of the outlying companies in positions not threatened. In case a sharp resistance outside the city may fail to prevent the advance of the enemy, we can occupy the centers until the North shall have had time to come to our relief. All our information tends to show that the force of the enemy which can immediately act against the capital does not exceed five thousand organized men, and before that number can be largely increased our relief will come. These District of Columbia volunteers would be fighting in defense of their homes and would fight well."

After considering the plan outlined General Scott thus replied to Colonel Stone:

"Your plan is good. Your pickets will have to fight well, and must not try to fall back more than fifteen paces at a time and to fire at least once at each halt. This requires good men and good, devoted officers. These soldiers of the District will probably fight as well in defense of their homes as the enemy in attacking them. But you have too many centers. You cannot hold three. You will need all your force concentrated to hold one position against an energetic force equal, or superior in numbers, to all you have. The first center to be abandoned must be the Capitol. It is a fire-proof building. There is little in it that is combustible excepting the libraries of Congress and the Supreme Court, and I do not believe that any Americans will burn public libraries and archives of courts of justice. The second center to be abandoned will be the City Hall hill. Finally, if necessary, all else must be abandoned to occupy, strongly and effectively, the Executive Square, with the idea of firmly holding only the Treasury building, and, perhaps, the State Department building, properly connected. The seals of the several departments of the Government must be deposited in the vaults of the Treasury. They must not be captured and used to deceive

COPYRIGHT, 1911, REVIEW OF REVIEWS CO.

A TRIP AROUND THE DEFENSES OF WASHINGTON—FORT LYON

This photograph is the first of a series illustrating the thirty-seven miles of forts and batteries which surrounded Washington.   After Fort Lyon, in this series, one of the farthest forts to the southwest, comes Battery Rodgers, south of Alexandria; then the entrance to Long Bridge; Forts Corcoran and Woodbury, defending the Aqueduct Bridge; Fort Marcy, the farthest north across the Potomac from Washington; Fort Sumner, the farthest north on the other side of the Potomac; Fort Stevens, farther east; Fort Totten, east of Fort Stevens; Fort Lincoln, still farther south; and finally Fort C. F. Smith, to show the type of construction of the later forts.   Thus the reader completely encircles Washington, and beholds varied types of sixty-eight forts and batteries.   These mounted 807 guns and ninety-eight mortars, with emplacements for 1,120 guns more.   There were also 35,711 yards of rifle-trenches and three blockhouses.   Fort Lyon, above pictured, lay across Hunting Creek from Alexandria.   The Parrott guns were rifled cannon of cast-iron, strengthened at the breech by shrinking a band of wrought-iron over the section which contained the powder charge. The body of the larger Parrott guns was cast hollow and cooled by the Rodman process—a stream of water or air flowing through the interior.   About 1,700 of these guns were purchased by the Federal Ordnance Department during the war and used in the defense of Washington and in the great sieges.

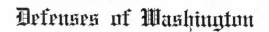

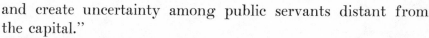

and create uncertainty among public servants distant from the capital."

Then he added: " Should it come to the defense of the Treasury building as a citadel, then the President and all the members of his cabinet must take up their quarters with us in that building. They must not be permitted to desert the capital!"

This conversation, quoted from a Washington historian of the war-time period (Doctor Marcus Benjamin), shows, in brief, the inadequate preparations for the defense of the capital of one of the greatest nations on the face of the globe! On April 19, 1861, troops began to arrive from the North, and the extreme apprehension was for a time quieted, until the battle of Bull Run, on July 21st, threw the country, and especially the population of Washington, into a state of the most intense excitement.

Except for certain river defenses, twelve miles below the city, Washington was entirely undefended at the outbreak of the war. From a hasty glance at the topography, we find that there are no natural fortifications around the city, and that artificial works were necessary throughout. The problem of defense was made greater, also, by the fact that the city was spread out over so much ground. At the time of the Civil War the effective range of the heaviest artillery was between three and four miles, and the engineers recognized the great difficulty of erecting adequate defenses. We find also that public opinion fluctuated and affected the action of Congress in regard to these defenses, to the frequent consternation of the officers charged with their maintenance.

Obviously the first direction from which danger was apprehended was that of the Virginia side. The heights commanding the river were a constant menace to Washington until they could be occupied in force by the Federals. Since no attempts theretofore had been made to fortify the city, it does not appear that sufficient information upon which even

BATTERY
RODGERS

ITS
15-INCH GUN

Battery Rodgers, about half a mile from the southern outskirts of Alexandria, overlooked the Potomac and the mouth of Hunting Creek. Its site was a bluff rising about twenty-eight feet above high water. It was armed with five 200-pounder Parrott guns and a 15-inch Rodman smooth-bore, emplaced in pairs. The parapet was twenty-five feet thick. The 15-inch Rodman gun visible above the bomb-proofs, can be studied below closer at hand. This monster of its time became possible through the discoveries made by Captain Rodman, of the United States Ordnance Department. It is mounted on a center-pintle carriage—that is, the tracks carrying the carriage are completely circular, and the pivot on which it revolves is under the center of the carriage. The timber revetment of the interior slope of the parapet affords greater protection to the garrison; the men can stand close to the wall, and are less apt to be struck by high-angle fire. In the foreground are the entrances to the bomb-proofs, guarded by two sentries who accommodatingly faced the camera.

ALL QUIET ALONG THE POTOMAC,
MAY 18, 1864

AN INTIMATE VIEW OF THE
GREAT RODMAN GUN SHOWN
ON THE PAGE PRECEDING

The 15-inch Rodman gun in Battery Rodgers, near Alexandria, with a gun-detachment around it. The scene was quiet the day this photograph was taken. The gunners little thought that within a few weeks the city would be in a turmoil of excitement from Early's attack on the northern defenses of Washington. This battery was erected to guard the south side of Washington from an attack by the Confederate fleet. The distance to mid-channel was 600 yards, and no vessel of a draft of twenty feet could pass at a greater distance than half a mile. The battery also enfiladed the channel for the full range of its guns. The main face of the work was 135 feet long, and it had flanks of sixty and eighty feet. The wharf at Alexandria is visible to the left, with a steamer loading supplies and a lighter close by. The size of the gun can be judged from the little photograph, on the opposite page, of a soldier who has crawled, feet first, into the muzzle.

a tentative line of works could be planned was at hand, and engineer officers examined the ground as well as they could at the termination of Long Bridge, on the Virginia shore, and also at the Virginia side of the aqueduct. Confederate pickets were observed from the first outbreak of hostilities, and while these parties were apparently unarmed, the officers making reconnaissances to determine the location of works, had necessarily to be prudent in their movements, and accurate observations were impossible.

The first forts located were Fort Runyon, at the land end of the approach to Long Bridge, about a half a mile from the Virginia end of the bridge proper, and Fort Corcoran, covering the approach to the aqueduct. These footholds were secured by a crossing in force on the night of the 23d of May, 1861, of three columns, one by the aqueduct, one by Long Bridge, and one by water to Alexandria. The nearness of Alexandria, and the fact that it commanded the river, made its occupation a matter of prime importance from the outset. Fort Ellsworth, on Shuter's Hill, one half-mile west of the town, was located and fortified by the column crossing by water. During the eight weeks following the crossing, and up to the time of General McDowell's advance on Manassas, officers and troops were hard at work on the entrenchments, thus established at three points, to the total neglect of the protection of the city on the eastern and northern sides. These first three works constructed were larger than most of those which followed---the perimeter of Fort Runyon, indeed, exceeding that of any subsequent work.

Of course, these three points were intended to be only footholds for further development of the works, and were, themselves, badly located for isolated defense. Fort Runyon was overlooked by the heights of Arlington, as was Fort Corcoran, though the latter was better situated than the former. Fort Ellsworth was but a weak field-fortification.

The main efforts of the officers were to strengthen the

COMPLETING THE BARRICADE AT ALEXANDRIA

When Brigadier-General Herman Haupt was put in charge of all the railroads centering in Washington in 1861 his first care was to safeguard them as far as possible from the destructive Confederate raiders. He built a stockade around the machine shops and yard of the Orange & Alexandria Railroad, with blockhouses at the points most vulnerable to raiders. The citizens of Alexandria, terrified by their exposed position across the Potomac close to the battlefield of Bull Run, entrenched themselves as best they could, before the great forts about them were completed. The lower view is looking up Duke Street from Pioneer Mill. The heavy stockade, inside the city, suggests how acute were the apprehensions of its inhabitants. The barrier is solid enough to stop a cavalry charge, with the big gates closed. A couple of field pieces, however, could batter it down in short order. Later in the war, such stockades as this would have been built with twenty-five feet of earth banked up in front of them. After the hurried preparations shown in the photograph, the tide of war rolled away into southern Virginia. The stockade for a while remained as a memento of a passing fear.

A STOCKADE IN THE STREET

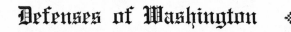

three points at which works had been begun, and no attempts were made looking to the erection of a continuous or a supporting line to stop the advance of the Confederates. The necessity for this was not realized. But the first disaster awoke the military and civil authorities of Washington to the grim fact that the war was not a thing of probably a few weeks' duration, and in the face of a victorious foe there was the great menace of the capture of the Nation's capital with all the dire consequences. It was not the extent of the fortifications that impeded the Confederate army after Manassas, but the fact that there *were* fortifications, and that the Confederates were as badly defeated as the Federals. General Johnston says:

"We were almost as much disorganized by our victory as the Federals by their defeat," and it was conceded by everybody that disorganization and the moral deterrent effect of "fortifications" were mainly responsible for the Confederates not pressing their victory to the logical conclusion of occupying the capital.

The stream of fugitives crowding across Long Bridge and Aqueduct Bridge after the disaster of Bull Run, July 21st, announced to the people of Washington, to the people of the North, and to the people of the world the initiation of a mighty struggle. The echo rang southward, where the cry immediately was taken up, "On to Washington." In the North the echo was, "On to the defense of Washington." Despair in the North was replaced by a dogged determination to prosecute the war to the bitter end, and a few weeks' delay on the part of the Confederates sounded the doom of their chances to take the capital, for every energy of the North was bent, first, to organizing for its defense, and, second, to taking the field in an offensive movement against the Confederates.

General Scott, who had fought in two wars against foreign foes, was bowed down with age, and the tremendous energy necessary to cope with so appalling a situation had left him; so he asked to be relieved by a younger man. All

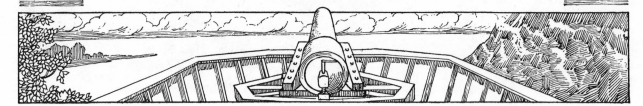

DEFENDERS OF LONG BRIDGE—A BATTERY DRILL

The little boy on the corner is not looking at the cannoneers. Real soldiers and 12-pounder Napoleon field-guns are no novelty to him by now. He is staring at something really new in the summer of '64—the camera. He finds the curious looking box vastly more interesting. The soldiers stationed at the Virginia end of Long Bridge were "caught" by the pioneer photographer at drill. They are in correct position ready for action. The duty of the soldiers with the long swabs on the right of the guns near the muzzle is to sponge them out, and to ram home the new charge. The men on the left near the muzzle place the charge in the gun. The men on the right, back of the wheel, cover the vents until the charge is rammed home. The men on the left, back of the wheel, have duties more complex. They prick the cartridge, insert a friction primer attached to a lanyard, step back, and at the order: "Fire!" explode the primer. Still further to the left of the guns stand the sergeants who are chiefs of pieces. The men behind the limbers cut the fuses for the length of time required and insert them in the shell. It is the duty of the men at their left to carry the charge from the limber and deliver it to the loaders who place it in the gun. Finally, the corporals directly behind the cannon are the gunners who sight the pieces. The remainder are to help prepare and bring up the ammunition from the limber, and to take the places of any disabled. All this is familiar to their companions lounging about the hotel. The time is evidently summer. The boy is barefoot, and the trees are in full bloom.

 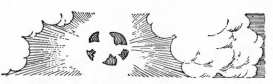

eyes were directed to General McClellan, whose successes had already made him a marked man, and under the direction of that able organizer a more secure feeling immediately appeared. He directed the immediate completion of the fortifications of the city, and also bent his energy to organizing the great Army of the Potomac.

Once the positions on the right bank of the Potomac were reasonably secure through the works just mentioned and such additional defenses as Fort Albany, Fort Scott, and various lines of connecting fortifications, attention was given to the Washington side of the river. In the summer and autumn the Potomac is fordable at points not far above Washington, and as the river became lower apprehension increased that the victorious foe, who still rested at Manassas, would avoid the works on the Virginia side, cross above Georgetown, and attack from the Maryland side of the city. To meet the emergency, works were hurriedly thrown up without that careful preliminary study of the topography which the occasion really demanded.

The securing of the roads was the first consideration. The main road which followed the general line of the crest between Rock Creek and the Potomac, branched at Tennallytown, about a mile south of the District line, and entering and leaving the town were other important roads. As this was on fairly high ground it was selected as a proper point for a work, and Fort Pennsylvania (afterward Fort Reno) was placed there. Thus was established one point of the line of works. Fort Stevens, commanding the Seventh Street Road, running north, and Fort Lincoln, commanding the Baltimore turnpike and the Baltimore and Ohio Railroad, together with Forts Totten and Slocum, between these latter roads and the Seventh Street Road, were all simultaneously started. All these works were on the crest of a somewhat irregular ridge overlooking the valley of Sligo Branch. This carried the general project from Tennallytown, within two miles of the Potomac, around to the north and east of the capital to Anacostia Branch.

The forts on the south side of the Potomac, grouped immediately about the Aqueduct Bridge, were Forts Bennett, C. F. Smith, Strong, Morton, Woodbury, and Corcoran. The latter was a *tete-du-pont*, or defense of a bridge, covering the Virginia end of the Aqueduct Bridge. It was on a slight plateau above the river, but was itself commanded by higher ground around Arlington Heights. In the two center photographs cannoneers are loading big guns in Forts Corcoran and Woodbury. These are both cast-iron muzzle-loading 32-pounder guns, mounted on wooden carriages with front pintles. Technically, the upper part of the mount is the carriage, and the lower part, running on the traverse wheels, is the chassis. The front pintle allowed the gun to rotate through an arc of 180 degrees. An interesting aspect of the loading of

UNION ARCH OF THE WASHINGTON AQUEDUCT

LOADING 32–POUNDERS IN CORCORAN AND WOODBURY

the big gun in Fort Corcoran is the officer holding his thumb over the vent. This was to prevent the influx of oxygen while the charge was being rammed home. After the gun was heated by several discharges, it was possible to fire it merely by removing the thumb from the vent. Woe to the man handling the rammer if the officer inadvertently removed his thumb before the charge was rammed home! The premature discharge following would blow him into atoms, that is, if he should be thoughtless enough to expose his body before the muzzle of the cannon. Many distressing accidents occur in this way, both in peace and war, where amateurs handle the guns. The well-trained artillerist stands aside from the muzzle when ramming home the charge. Fort Corcoran was constructed to defend this important bridge from assault on the Virginia side of the Potomac. Fort Strong was originally Fort De Kalb and with Forts Corcoran, Bennett and Woodbury constituted the defense of the bridge at the time the capital was threatened by the Confederates after Lee's defeat of General Pope's army in August, 1862.

DOWN THE POTOMAC FROM UNION ARCH

The line once established by the location of the larger forts, the process already employed on the Virginia side was used to fill in the gaps. Supporting works of usually less strength, were placed within rifle-range along the crest.

The problem of resting the left of the line on the Potomac, however, was more difficult. There were two matters of paramount importance, the consideration of which indicated a position for the line quite different from that indicated by the topography. It must be remembered that the Chain Bridge crossed the Potomac about three miles above Georgetown, and the receiving reservoir which supplied most of Washington and Georgetown with water was about three and one-half miles from the latter place. The value of the bridge and reservoir rendered their protection necessary. But the high ground, upon which naturally the line of forts should be placed, ran toward the Potomac on a line south of Powder-Mill Run, the stream supplying the reservoir, which approached the river at the point where the bridge crossed. It was obvious that works placed on these heights would not protect the reservoir, and that the bridge would be in the zone of fire of any force attacking the forts. Hence the line of works was broken, and three isolated works, afterward united into one, were placed on high ground to the north of the reservoir, and far enough above the bridge to prevent artillery fire from reaching it.

South of Anacostia Branch the problem at first appeared to be capable of solution by placing bridge-heads, or small forts covering the approaches to the bridges, on the south side. There were two bridges, one at the navy-yard, about two miles up the creek, and Benning's Bridge, some two and one-half miles above the first. In addition, it appeared that there should be at least one large fort overlooking and protecting the navy-yard and the arsenal, which latter was on the point at the confluence of the Anacostia and the Potomac, and which contained large quantities of war-supplies of all kinds. A more critical examination, however, showed the necessity of

A VIEW FROM FORT MARCY—COMPANY A, FOURTH NEW YORK HEAVY ARTILLERY

In front of the tent at the right of the picture sits William Arthur, brother of Chester A. Arthur, the future President. This view was taken from the fort down toward the camp. The Fourth New York Heavy Artillery was organized at New York, November, 1861, to February, 1862. It left for Washington on February 10th. Its first camp was five miles from Chain Bridge, and its second at Fort Marcy. These unusually clear photographs were treasured half a century by T. J. Lockwood, a member of the regiment.

LOOKING FROM THE CAMP TOWARD FORT MARCY

Marcy was the northernmost fort on the west side of the Potomac, lying above Chain Bridge. Its armament consisted of three 24-pounders *en barbette*, two 12-pounder howitzers, six 30-pounder Parrotts, three 20-pounder Parrotts and three 10-pounder Parrotts, all *en embrasure*. It also mounted one 10-inch siege mortar and two 24-pounder Coehorn mortars. It overlooked the Leesburg and Georgetown Turnpike.

fortifying the entire length of the crest between the Anacostia and Oxen Run, a distance of about six miles. This was done, and toward the end of the year 1861 these works were well toward completion. Likewise were the works along the entire perimeter of the defensive line encircling the capital, on both sides of the Potomac.

By the spring of 1862 there were, surrounding Washington, twenty-three forts on the Virginia side of the Potomac, fourteen forts and three batteries from the Potomac around by the north and east of the city to the Anacostia, and eleven forts south of the Anacostia, with the right of the line resting on the Potomac. Of these, Fort Runyon, already noted as covering Long Bridge on the Virginia side, was the largest, with a perimenter of one thousand five hundred yards, but the size of the remainder varied to a minimum of one hundred and fifty-four yards. Most of them were enclosed works, and some were lunettes, or partially closed works, with the unclosed side occupied by stockades. The armament was principally 24- and 32-pounders, some smooth-bore and some rifled, with a few lighter field-guns. Magazines were provided that had a capacity each of about one hundred rounds of ammunition, and some of the most important works had bomb-proof shelters, where about one-third of the garrison could sleep secure from artillery fire.

The curious fluctuation of public feeling toward the fortifications can be seen when we remember that, before the Manassas campaign, they were very lightly regarded; immediately after that campaign and the defeat of Bull Run, there was a fever heat of apprehension and demand for protection. When General McClellan's splendidly organized army took the field against the foe, there was a certainty that the war was about to be ended, and a corresponding decrease of regard for the defenses; and we shall see later how the ebb of the tide again caught the public and sent it scurrying behind the forts. When McClellan left Washington for the front, the act

IN FORMIDABLE FORT SUMNER
APRIL 5, 1864

Fort Sumner, a semi-closed work, lay highest up the river of all the forts defending Washington. It was northwest of the receiving reservoir, overlooking the Potomac, and commanded by the fire of its heavy guns the opposite shore in front of the works of the Virginia side. Its great armament made it a formidable fort. Of smooth-bore guns it had three 8-inch siege-howitzers and two 32-pounder sea-coast guns *en embrasure*, and six 32-pounder and four 24-pounder sea-coast guns *en barbette*. Its rifled guns were two 100-pounder Parrotts *en barbette*, four 4½-inch rifles *en embrasure*, two 4½-inch rifles *en barbette*, and six 6-pounder James rifles *en embrasure*. It also boasted three mortars, one 10-inch siege-mortar, and two 24-pounder Cochorns, and there were thirteen vacant platforms for field and siege-guns. The terrain on which the work was placed was such as to enable it to shelter a large body of troops with natural cover. The first gun on the right in this photograph is a 32-pounder sea-coast gun in an embrasure; the second is a 4½-inch rifle in an embrasure; the third is a 100-pounder Parrott *en barbette;* and the gun on the left is a 4½-inch rifle *en barbette*. The first and fourth guns are on wooden sea-coast carriages; the second on a siege-carriage; and the Parrott rifle on a wrought-iron sea-coast carriage.

ONE OF THE HEAVY ARTILLERY REGIMENTS THAT WASHINGTON LACKED IN '64

The Third Pennsylvania heavy artillerists, as they drill in Fort Monroe, April, 1864, are the type of trained big gun fighters that Washington needed by thousands when Early swept up to Fort Stevens, threatening to take it three months after this picture was taken.

of Congress making appropriations for the defenses of the capital read as follows:

" Be it enacted, etc., etc., that the sum of one hundred and fifty thousand dollars be, and the same is hereby, appropriated, out of any money in the Treasury not otherwise appropriated, for completing the defenses of Washington; *Provided,* That all arrearages of debts incurred for the objects of this act shall be first paid out of this sum: *And Provided Further,* That no part of the sum hereby appropriated shall be expended in any work hereafter to be commenced."

General J. G. Barnard, who, prior to the passage of the act above quoted, had been in engineering charge of the works, was, after the disasters of the first campaign under McClellan, placed also in command. He says that it was evident to all that the line north of the Potomac was not adequately defended at the time of the above act, and that after the disasters in Virginia the work was prosecuted with all vigor, new works being thrown up and the old ones strengthened, notwithstanding the act of Congress. Public opinion demanded these measures as imperative necessities, thus demonstrating the return of affection for forts and bombproofs. Even with the utmost endeavors of General Barnard, assisted by a large force of competent engineers, the defenses, in December, 1862, were far from satisfactory. Congress had not removed its prohibition against the commencement of new works, but here we witness one of the exhibitions of the masterful nature of the great war secretary, Stanton. He authorized General Barnard to continue the work of construction, and to begin such new works as were necessary. It was evident, however, that the expenditures would continue indefinitely, and ultimately would amount to a very large sum. In order to have a sufficient justification in the face of the Congressional prohibition, Secretary Stanton convened a board of officers whose judgment could be relied on for an unbiased decision. This board spent two months in examining

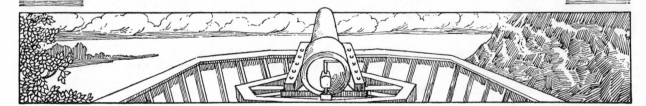

MEN OF THE THIRD MASSACHUSETTS HEAVY ARTILLERY IN FORT STEVENS

Fort Stevens, on the north line of the defenses of Washington, bore the brunt of the Confederate attack in the action of July 12, 1864, when Early threatened Washington. The smooth-bore guns in its armament were two 8-inch siege-howitzers *en embrasure*, six 24-pounder siege-guns *en embrasure*, two 24-pounder sea-coast guns *en barbette*. It was also armed with five 30-pounder Parrott rifled guns, one 10-inch siege-mortar and one 24-pounder Coehorn mortar. Three of the platforms for siege-guns remained vacant.

COMPANY K, THIRD MASSACHUSETTS HEAVY ARTILLERY, IN FORT STEVENS, 1865

Washington was no longer in danger when this photograph was taken, and the company is taking its ease with small arms stacked—three rifles held together by engaging the shanks of the bayonets. This is the usual way of disposing of rifles when the company is temporarily dismissed for any purpose. If the men are to leave the immediate vicinity of the stacks, a sentinel is detailed to guard the arms. The Third Massachusetts Heavy Artillery was organized for one year in August, 1864, and remained in the defenses of Washington throughout their service, except for Company I, which went to the siege of Petersburg and maintained the pontoon bridges.

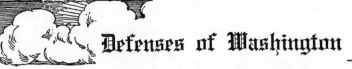 

critically all the works, completed, under construction, and projected. The findings of the board were, in brief, as follows:

That there were (in December, 1862) surrounding Washington, fifty-three forts and twenty-two batteries; that the perimeter of the entire line of fortifications was thirty-seven miles; that the armament consisted of six hundred and forty-three guns and seventy-five mortars; that the total infantry garrison needed for a proper manning of the defenses was about twenty-five thousand; that the total artillery garrison necessary was about nine thousand, and that a force of three thousand cavalry was necessary to make reconnaissances in order to give warning of the approach of the foe. In accordance with the recommendations of the board, Congress raised the embargo on funds for further defense preparation, and, during 1863, several important new works were opened and completed, and the old ones kept in a high state of efficiency. One of the most notable new works was Battery Rodgers at Jones' Point, near Alexandria, for defense against the Confederate vessels. During 1864, one large fort, McPherson, was commenced on the Virginia side between Long Bridge and Aqueduct Bridge but not completed, and some smaller ones built. With these exceptions the time was devoted to keeping in good repair those already constructed. These included some water batteries that had been constructed in 1862 as a supplementary aid to the forts in repelling naval attacks.

The amount of work that was expended on the defenses of Washington during the war was indicated by the fact that, at the close of the war, in April, 1865, the fortifications consisted of sixty-eight enclosed forts and batteries, whose aggregate perimeter was thirteen miles, eight hundred and seven guns, and ninety-eight mounted mortars, and emplacements for one thousand one hundred and twenty guns, ninety-three unarmed batteries for field-guns, thirty-five thousand seven hundred and eleven yards of rifle-trenches, and three blockhouses. The

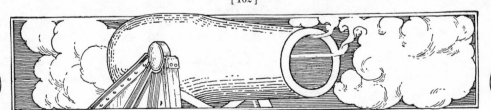

JAMES RIFLES BEHIND THE FORT TOTTEN RAMPARTS

The first gun, in the foreground, is a James rifle on a siege-carriage, the second a James rifle on a sea-coast carriage, the third a James rifle on a siege-carriage, and the fourth a Columbiad on a sea-coast carriage. Fort Totten had many magazines and bomb-proofs.

WITH THE COLUMBIADS AT FORT TOTTEN

The total armament of Fort Totten consisted of two 8-inch howitzers, eight 32-pounder sea-coast Columbiads, one 100-pounder Parrott rifle, three 30-pounder Parrott rifles, four 6-pounder James rifles, one 10-inch siege-mortar, and one 24-pounder coehorn mortar.

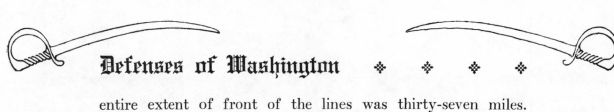

entire extent of front of the lines was thirty-seven miles. Thirty-two miles of military roads, besides those previously existing in the District of Columbia, formed the means of interior communication.

"Sensitiveness for the safety of Washington influenced every combination and every important movement of troops in the Virginia theater." General McClellan proposed, in January, 1862, to transfer the Army of the Potomac to the lower Chesapeake, for an advance on Richmond. A council of division commanders decided that McClellan's plan was good, but that the forts on the right bank of the Potomac for the defense of the capital must be garrisoned by a full quota, and that those on the Washington side be occupied in force—in brief, not less than forty thousand men ought to be left for the defense of Washington. McClellan sought to combine his own necessities with the exigencies which had arisen in connection with the protection of the capital, and included in the number of troops left for the defense those which he sent to the Shenandoah. The field-commanders always insisted that the best way to defend Washington was to attack Richmond. However, the Secretary of War decided that McClellan's inclusion of the Shenandoah troops in the defenders of the capital was not justifiable, and the recall of McDowell from the Army of the Potomac and all the subsequent controversies growing therefrom are matters of record.

Although General Pope's army operated between the Confederates and Washington, there was a great feeling of uneasiness on account of the inadequacy of the works, and the fact that the garrison had been reduced to add to Pope's field-army. But "nevertheless they deterred Lee from pushing further against Washington his offensive movements . . . and thereby saved the Nation from much greater calamities than actually befell us in this most disastrous year." The garrisons were "commanded, generally, by artillery officers of the army, and by them instructed in the service of sea-coast-, siege-, and

Eighteen forts, four batteries of heavy artillery, and twenty-three of light artillery were located between Fort Sumner, on the Potomac above Georgetown, and Fort Lincoln, near Bladensburg, commanding the Baltimore and Ohio Railroad and the upper Anacostia. Fort Lincoln was profusely but not heavily armed. It had two 8-inch siege-howitzers, six 32-pounder sea-coast guns, one 24-pounder siege-gun, three 24-pounder sea-coast guns, four 12-pounder field-guns, and eight 6-pounder field-guns *en barbette*, with two 24-pounder field-howitzers *en embrasure*. This concludes the list of the smooth-bores, but there were also a 100-pounder Parrott and four 20-pounder Parrotts. Fort Lincoln was a bastioned fort of four

THE INTERIOR OF FORT LINCOLN

faces. One of the 20-pounder Parrotts is just visible over the top of the storehouse, and the 100-pounder is in full view in the far corner of the fort. This was one of the first points fortified on the Northern lines about Washington. The spade, seen leaning against the house to the left of the pile of boxes, was the great weapon of warfare. The lower photograph shows Company H of the Third Massachusetts Heavy Artillery manning the guns. Their muskets have been leaned against the parapet, and the pile of shells to the right makes the great guns glaring down the valley seem formidable indeed. The Third Massachusetts was organized from unattached companies of heavy artillery in August, 1864, for the defense of Washington.

COMPANY H, THIRD MASSACHUSETTS HEAVY ARTILLERY, IN FORT LINCOLN

field-guns of the forts," and " they soon became an unrivaled body of artillerymen. Their long connection with particular works inspired them with pride in their perfection and preservation, while the zeal and military knowledge of their commanders prompted and enabled them to render aid to the engineers in modifying and strengthening the forts and in developing the lines."

Such was the confidence felt by everyone in General Grant that when, in 1864, he withdrew practically the entire garrison of Washington for his field-army—a thing that McClellan had wanted to do and was prevented—there was little or no opposition raised. But this very action left Washington a tempting morsel for a daring raider, and the Confederate commander was not long in taking advantage of that fact. Lee was hard pressed, and he sought to create a diversion by sending Early to threaten, and, if possible, to capture Washington. This ruse of threatening the national capital had been successful before, and he hoped that Grant also might be influenced by it. Early left Lee's army under orders to attack and destroy General Hunter's army in the Shenandoah and then to threaten Washington. Several times during the raid, Lee communicated with Early, leaving the decision of returning or moving on to the judgment of Early, according to the circumstances in which he found himself. On the 10th of July he was within sixteen miles of Washington, in Maryland, and defeated a small detachment of Federal cavalry. Hasty preparations were made in the defenses to muster all the troops possible to repel the invader.

General Early attacked the works on the Seventh Street Road but was repulsed, and during the night of the 12–13th of July, 1864, he withdrew and retired toward Conrad's Ferry, on the Potomac. He stated later: " McCausland [one of his brigade commanders] reported the works on the Georgetown pike too strong for him to assault. We could not move to the right or left without its being discovered from a signal

THE GARRISON OF FORT C. F. SMITH—COMPANY F, SECOND NEW YORK HEAVY ARTILLERY

In these photographs of 1865, the defenses of Washington have served their turn; it is more than a year since they were threatened for the last time by General Early and his men. But the panoply of war continues. Everything is polished and groomed. During four long years the guns in Fort C. F. Smith have been swabbed out daily and oiled, to be ready for a thunderous reception to the Confederates. The fort, one of the later constructions, lay to the northwest of Fort Corcoran. Its armament of smooth-bore guns consisted of one 8-inch sea-

COMPANY L, AT DRILL

coast howitzer *en barbette*, four 24-pounders on siege carriages *en embrasure*, and three 12 - pounder howitzers *en embrasure*. Of rifled guns it boasted six 4½-inch Rodmans *en embrasure*, and two 10-pounder Parrotts *en embrasure*. It also mounted three 8-inch siege-mortars. There were six vacant platforms for further guns. The Second New York Heavy Artillery remained in the defenses of Washington till May, 1864, when it joined the Army of the Potomac. It lost 114 officers and men killed and mortally wounded, and 247 by disease.

station on the top of Soldiers' Home, which overlooked the country, and the enemy would have been enabled to move in his works to meet us. Under the circumstances, to have rushed my men blindly against the fortifications without understanding the state of things, would have been worse than folly. If we had any friends in Washington none of them came out with any information, and this satisfied me that the place was not undefended. . . . After interchanging views with my brigade commanders, being very reluctant to abandon the project of capturing Washington, I determined to make an assault on the enemy's works at daylight the next morning, unless some information should be received before that time showing its impracticability, and so informed those officers. During the night a despatch was received from General Bradley T. Johnson, from near Baltimore, informing me that he had received information, from a reliable source, that two corps had arrived from Grant's army, and that his whole army was probably in motion. This caused me to delay the attack until I could examine the works again, and, as soon as it was light enough to see, I rode to the front and found the parapets lined with troops. I had, therefore, reluctantly to give up all hopes of capturing Washington, after I had arrived in sight of the dome of the Capitol and given the Federal authorities a terrible fright."

This was the last time Washington was threatened; and the fortifications saved the city. The garrison unaided could not have done so.

[The defenses of Washington presented many problems in the nature of formal fortification and concentration of troops that did not apply to the capital of the Confederacy. Lee's army was the surest defense of Richmond whose fall necessarily followed the defeat of the Confederate forces. Nevertheless, a scheme of defense was early adopted and this will be found discussed in an interesting chapter, in the preparation of which Captain Hunt has received the valuable assistance of Colonel T. M. R. Talcott, commanding the engineer troops of the Army of Northern Virginia.—THE EDITORS.]

[108]

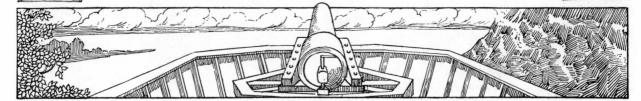

V

ATTACK
AND DEFENSE
AT CHARLESTON

THE MORNING AND EVENING GUN—SUMTER

THIS PIECE THAT TIMED THE GARRISON OF THE BELEAGUERED FORT
LOOKS OUT ACROSS THE MARSHES OF CHARLESTON HARBOR—
IN THESE GILLMORE'S MEN SET UP THEIR BATTERIES, WITH
WHAT RESULTS THE FOLLOWING SERIES OF PICTURES SHOWS

GILLMORE STUDYING THE MAP OF CHARLESTON IN 1863, WHILE HE DREW
HIS "RING OF FIRE" ROUND THE CITY

MAP EXPLAINING THE PHOTOGRAPHS
ON THE PAGES THAT FOLLOW

Brigadier-General Quincy Adams Gillmore
is the man who surrounded Charleston with
a ring of fire. On the map which he is studying the words "East Coast, South Carolina"
are plainly legible. A glance at the map
to the right will reveal that coast, along
which his guns were being pushed when this
photograph was taken, in 1863. It will also
reveal the progress illustrated by the succession of photographs following—the gradual reduction of Battery Wagner, at the
north end of Morris Island before Charleston,
by a series of parallels. On the facing page
are scenes in Battery Reynolds on the first
parallel and Battery Brown on the second.
Then come Batteries Rosecrans and Meade
on the second parallel, shown on successive
pages. The "Swamp Angel" that threw
shells five miles into the city of Charleston
comes next, and then the sap-roller being
pushed forward to the fifth and last parallel,
with Battery Chatfield on Cumming's Point.
On the next page is Battery Wagner. The

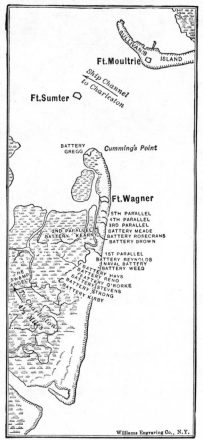

remaining scenes are inside Charleston. The
last page shows the effect of the bombardment
of Fort Sumter. Thus a sequent story is told
in actual photographs of the siege operations about Charleston. Quincy Adams Gillmore was graduated first in his class at West
Point. He served as an assistant engineer
in the building of Fortress Monroe from 1849
to 1852, and later became assistant instructor
of practical military engineering at West
Point. When the war broke out he had
abundant opportunity to put his learning to
the test, and proved one of the ablest military
engineers in the Federal service. He acted
as chief engineer of the Port Royal expedi-
tionary corps in 1861–62; was chief engineer
at the siege of Fort Pulaski, Georgia, from
February to April, 1862, conducted the land
operations against Charleston, fought at
Drewry's Bluff, and in the defense of Washington against Early. On March 13, 1865,
he was brevetted successively brigadier-
general and major-general in the regular
army, and on December 5, 1865, he resigned
from the volunteer service He was the author
of many engineering books and treatises.

THE PARROTT IN BATTERY STRONG

This 300-pounder rifle was directed against Fort Sumter and Battery Wagner. The length of bore of the gun before it burst was 136 inches. It weighed 26,000 pounds. It fired a projectile weighing 250 pounds, with a maximum charge of powder of 25 pounds. The gun was fractured at the twenty-seventh round by a shell bursting in the muzzle, blowing off about 20 inches of the barrel. After the bursting the gun was "chipped" back beyond the termination of the fracture and afterwards fired 371 rounds with as good results as before the injury. At the end of that time the muzzle began to crack again, rendering the gun entirely useless.

TWO PARROTTS IN BATTERY STEVENS

Battery Stevens lay just east of Battery Strong. It was begun July 27, 1863. Most of the work was done at night, for the fire from the adjacent Confederate forts rendered work in daylight dangerous. By August 17th, most of the guns were in position, and two days later the whole series of batteries "on the left," as they were designated, were pounding away at Fort Sumter.

GUNS IN BATTERY RENO TRAINED ON BATTERY WAGNER

Both the batteries on this page were "on the left," that is, across a creek from Morris Island proper. Battery Hays was begun on July 15, 1863, in preparation for an attack on Battery Wagner set for July 18th. Within sixty hours from breaking ground, the platforms were made, the earthworks thrown up and revetted with sand-bags—as shown—magazines constructed and fifteen Parrott guns in place, ready to open fire. At ten o'clock they began the bombardment of Wagner, in conjunction with the fleet, and kept it up until dusk, when a determined but unsuccessful assault was made. Battery Reno was one of the "breaching batteries" against Fort Sumter. The work was begun July 27th, and on August 17th four 100-pounder Parrott rifle guns, one 8-inch and one 10-inch Parrott gun, the largest guns then made, were in place. The ground was flat and marshy. No obstructions interfered with the bombardment.

PARROTTS IN BATTERY HAYS TRAINED ON SUMTER

BATTERY REYNOLDS, ON THE FIRST PARALLEL AGAINST BATTERY WAGNER

The surprised Confederates discovered at dawn of July 24, 1863, the new line thrown forward from Battery Reynolds and the naval battery on the first Union parallel. Two direct assaults on Battery Wagner having been repulsed with great loss of life, the advance upon the work was made by a series of parallels. The batteries were ready in sixty hours from the time of breaking ground, most of the work being done in the night during heavy rains. The second parallel, six hundred yards in ad-

SAILORS IN THE NAVAL BATTERY

vance, was established July 23d, by a flying-sap along the narrow strip of shifting sand. The moon was so bright until midnight that no work could be done, but from twelve till dawn a parapet ten feet thick and one hundred seventy-five feet long was completed, six howitzers were placed, an entanglement was put up a hundred yards in advance, and a large bomb-proof magazine finished in the center of an old graveyard. Slowly but surely the Federal forces were working their way to the northern end of Morris Island.

BATTERY BROWN, ON THE SECOND PARALLEL

BURST GUN IN BATTERY ROSECRANS—LIFE IN THE "PARALLELS"

It was not the bursting of a gun in the works that caused the troops most concern, but the Confederate fire. Major Thomas B. Brooks describes dodging shells in the parallels on Morris Island in August, 1863: "The fire from Wagner, although inflicting much less real injury, up to this time, than the aggregate fire from the other batteries of the enemy, still gives far greater interruption to the working parties, on account of our nearness to the fort. 'Cover—Johnson or Sumter,' gives sufficient warning for those in the trenches to seek partial shelter, if the shell is seen to be coming toward them; but 'Cover, Wagner,' cannot be pronounced before the shell has exploded and done its work. At these cautionary words, I have often observed soldiers, particularly Negroes, fall flat on their faces, under the delusion that they were obtaining cover from mortar-shells exploding over them, when, in truth, their chances of being hit were much increased . . . On one occasion, a soldier was observed to place an empty powder-barrel over his head, to shield him from heavy shells."

THE 100–POUNDER PARROTTS IN BATTERY ROSECRANS

"'WARE SHARPSHOOTERS!'"—SERVING THE PARROTTS IN BATTERY MEADE

At ten o'clock on the night of July 28th, orders were issued to construct Battery Meade and Battery Rosecrans in the second parallel. The positions were laid out and work begun on them before midnight. Work progressed rather slowly, however, because the Confederate sharpshooters picked off every man who stuck his head above the parapet. Several men were wounded at a distance of thirteen hundred yards. Consequently all the work that required any exposure was done at night. Another cause of delay was the lack of earth; when trenches were dug more than three feet deep the spring tides flooded them. Besides, the work was frequently interrupted by finding dead bodies, either in coffins or wrapped in blankets only. On an old map Morris Island was called "Coffin Land"; it had been used as a quarantine burying-ground for Charleston. In spite of such discouragements, the men standing in front of the headquarters at the bottom of the page continued their labors. By August 17th the five immense Parrott guns stood ready to fire against Sumter. Thus the Federal army advanced, parallel by parallel, toward Battery Wagner at the end of Morris Island, until the final "flying-sap" took them up to its very walls, and it was carried by assault. But the defenders had other strings to their bow, as Gillmore's amphibious diggers discovered. Though now occupying the stronghold that commanded the harbor from the south, the Federals got no farther.

HEADQUARTERS OF THE FIELD OFFICER OF THE SECOND PARALLEL

[F—8]

One of the most famous guns in the Civil War was the "Swamp-Angel." The marsh here surely deserved the name. The two engineers who explored it to select a site for the battery carried a fourteen foot plank. When the mud became too soft to sustain their weight, they sat on the plank and pushed it forward between their legs. The mud was twenty feet deep, and men on such a plank could start waves rippling across the oozy surface by jumping up and down. It is said that one of the officers detailed for the construction of the platforms called for "twenty men, eighteen feet long!" In spite of these difficulties piles were driven in the marsh at a point that commanded the city of Charleston and a platform at length laid upon it. On August 17,

THE "SWAMP–ANGEL"—ONE OF THE FAMOUS GUNS OF '63

1863, an 8-inch, 200-pounder Parrott rifle was skidded across the marsh and mounted behind the sandbag parapet. On the night of August 21st, after warning had been sent to the Confederate commander, General Beauregard, the gun was fired so that the missiles should fall in the heart of Charleston. Sixteen shells filled with Greek fire were sent that night. On August 23d, at the thirty-sixth discharge, the breech of the gun was blown out and the barrel thereby thrown upon the sand-bag parapet as the photograph shows. From the outside it looked to be in position for firing, and became the target for Confederate gunners. Two weeks later two 10-inch mortars were mounted in place of the Parrott. It was later mounted in Trenton.

AFTER THE 36TH SHOT—THE "SWAMP–ANGEL" BURST

SAP-ROLLER AT THE HEAD
OF THE FLYING-SAP

This remarkable picture was taken while the flying-sap was being pushed forward to the fifth (and last) parallel. The action of September 6th is thus reported by Major T. B. Brooks: "The general commanding ordered General Terry to take and hold the ridge, and place the resources of the command at his disposal for that purpose. It was accomplished at 6:30 P.M. by a brilliant charge of the Twenty-fourth Massachusetts Volunteers, Colonel Francis A. Osborn commanding, supported by the Third New Hampshire Volunteers, Captain Randlett commanding. Sixty-seven prisoners were captured. They were

afraid to retire on account of their own torpedoes, as they informed us, and had too little time, even if there had been no torpedoes. No works, excepting rude rifle-pits in the excellent natural cover afforded by the ridge, were found. . . . The moment the ridge was gained the work of entrenching was begun under the superintendence of Captain Walker." The balance of the report tells about the fifth parallel and the flying-sap, which took them up to Battery Wagner and the battery renamed Chatfield on Cumming's Point, in order to commemorate Colonel John L. Chatfield, killed July 18th, at Battery Wagner.

FIRING THE BIG GUN
CHATFIELD

ONE OF THE MOST POWERFUL GUNS OF THE CONFEDERACY, IN FORT MOULTRIE

This huge gun in Fort Moultrie was designed to throw 600-pound shells. With such defenders Charleston became the best-fortified city on the Confederate sea-coast, and proved a stumbling-block to both the Federal army and navy. Fort Moultrie was on Sullivan's Island, guarding the right-hand entrance to the harbor. Charleston was finally evacuated February 17, 1865, after Sherman's march to the sea.

WAGNER AND GREGG

These two forts (Wagner shown above; Gregg to the right) were captured successively in the slow approach by parallels along Morris Island, preceding the evacuation of Charleston. Both Wagner and Gregg were evacuated September 6, 1863. General Beauregard, the Confederate commander, states that Wagner was an inconsiderable work. General Gillmore, whose forces occupied the place, insists that it was an exceedingly strong fort. Its bomb-proofs would hold 1,500 or 1,600 men, and eighteen pieces of heavy ordnance were captured when it finally fell.

GUNS THAT WERE NOT NEEDED
THE SOUTH BATTERY IN CHARLESTON ITSELF
THE FEDERAL FLEET NEVER GOT BEYOND THE HARBOR FORTS

The upper photograph shows two 10-inch Columbiads in the White Point or "South" Battery, in Charleston. This was situated on the extreme southeast point between the Ashby and Cooper Rivers. It was established for the purpose of affording a last opportunity to stop vessels that might get past Fort Sumter into the inner harbor. Sumter, however, was so far out, and with Moultrie, Gregg, and the others proved so effectual a barrier to the harbor's mouth, that no use was found for the guns here in the city itself. How close they were to the heart of the city is shown by the gun in the lower photograph, emplaced on the battery directly in front of the public square. Charleston was the birthplace of secession, and was prepared to make a stout defense. Sumter almost single-handed held out until inland communications were cut, and the city was evacuated February 17, 1865.

ONE OF THE "SOUTH BATTERY" GUNS
DIRECTLY ON THE PUBLIC SQUARE

WRECK OF THE GIANT BLAKELY GUN AT CHARLESTON

This was an English gun, all steel, to which the principle of "initial tension" was successfully applied. From the breech to the trunnions of the Blakely gun it was pear-shaped, for the purpose of resisting the tremendous power-pressures. By "initial tension" is meant intentional strain in the metal of the gun, scientifically placed, so as to counteract in a measure the strains set up by the powder discharge. There is an inner tube, on the outside of which bands are shrunk so as to set up a strain of extension in the exterior band. By properly combining these strains the extreme tension due to the powder gases at their moment of greatest expansion does not affect the gun as injuriously as if these initial strains were not present. This was among the earliest form of cannon to be successful with this principle of "initial tension," a fundamental element in the scientific design of the best modern built-up guns.

VIEW FROM THE REAR

THE ONLY GUN IN THE LINE OF FIRE

The city of Charleston was fortified up to its very doorsteps, as is evidenced by these three photographs of the wrecked carriage of the immense Blakely gun on the Battery. The only battery in the path of the Federal fire was that containing this monster piece. Under date of January 6, 1864, Major Henry Bryan, Assistant Inspector-General at Charleston, reported that from August 21, 1863, to January 5, 1864, the observer in the steeple of St. Michael's Church counted 472 shells thrown at the city. Of

LOOKING OUT TO SEA

a total of 225 investigated, 145 struck houses, nineteen struck in yards, and sixty-one struck in the streets and on the edge of the burnt district. Only about one third of these burst. The section of the city most frequently struck was bounded on the north by Market Street from East Bay to Meeting, down Meeting to Horlbeck's Alley, and along Horlbeck's Alley to Tradd Street; on the south by Tradd Street from the corner of King to Church Street, down Church Street to Longitude Lane, along that to East Bay; and on the east by East Bay Street.

LOOKING NORTHEAST

This view shows the street running at right angles to the one in the adjoining photograph.

THE HEART OF THE CITY

This shows how close to the dwelling houses the Federal shells must have fallen during the bombardment.

These views show the result of the bombardment from August 17 to 23, 1863. The object was to force the surrender of the fort and thus effect an entrance into Charleston. The report of Colonel John W. Turner, Federal chief of artillery runs: "The fire from the breaching batteries upon Sumter was incessant, and kept up continuously from daylight till dark, until the evening of the 23d. . . . The fire upon the gorge had, by the morning of the 23d, succeeded in destroying every gun upon the parapet of it. The para-

pet and ramparts of the gorge were completely demolished for nearly the entire length of the face, and in places everything was swept off down to the arches, the *débris* forming an accessible ramp to the top of the ruins. Nothing further being gained by a longer fire upon this face, all the guns were directed this day upon the southeasterly flank, and continued an incessant fire throughout the day. The demolition of the fort at the close of the day's firing was complete, so far as its offensive powers were considered." So fared Sumter.

WHERE SHOT AND SHELL STRUCK SUMTER

SOME OF THE 450 SHOT A DAY

THE LIGHTHOUSE ABOVE THE DÉBRIS

VI

THE ORDNANCE
OF THE
FEDERAL ARMIES

A FEDERAL TRANSPORT IN APRIL, 1865, TAKING ARTILLERY DOWN THE
JAMES RIVER.   THE VIEW IS NEAR FORT DARLING ON DREWRY'S BLUFF

THE ORDNANCE DEPARTMENT OF THE FEDERAL ARMY

By O. E. Hunt
Captain, United States Army

THE provision of muskets and cannon for the vast army of volunteers that flocked to Washington in answer to President Lincoln's call for troops, presented a problem hardly second in importance to the actual organization and training of these citizen soldiers. As the United States had but a small regular army, there were no extensive stores of arms and munitions of war, nor were there large Government manufactories or arsenals adequate to supply great armies. The opening of the Civil War found the Federal War Department confronted, therefore, with an extraordinary situation. From scientific experiment and the routine of a mere bureau, whose chief duties were the fabrication and test of the ordnance required by the small regular army, the Ordnance Department suddenly was called upon to furnish from its all too meager supply, tens of thousands of weapons for the different arms of the service, on a scale quite unprecedented in the military operations theretofore attempted in the United States.

Enjoying a reputation for scientific and painstaking work, especially in the making of large cast-iron cannon, it early became apparent that, in the event of hostilities, there must be a wide extension of the activities of the Ordnance Department. Accordingly, at the outbreak of the war the Ordnance Department was reorganized, and the new organization provided for a chief of ordnance with the rank of brigadier-general, two colonels, two lieutenant-colonels, four majors, twelve captains, twelve first lieutenants, and twelve second lieutenants.

[124]

BAYONETS, HOWITZERS AND REVOLVERS OF THE CIVIL WAR DAYS

The soldiers are part of Company L of the Second New York Heavy Artillery. They were armed with rifles provided with musket bayonets. This bayonet was a very effective weapon. The blade was made of steel, eighteen inches long. To give lightness and stiffness, its three faces were grooved in the direction of the length, or "fluted." The blade was joined to the socket, which fitted over the muzzle, by a "neck" which, due to the change of direction, had to be made very strong. During the Civil War there was more actual use of the bayonet than since, but the presence

of the bayonet still gives a moral effect both to the defender and assailant. The upper photograph shows two 24-pounder smooth-bore guns in Fort C. F. Smith in the deenses of Washington. The carriages are those usually used with siege guns, the heavy scooped-out block on the trail being for the purpose of holding the base of the gun when it was being transported. These 24-pounders were for short range. In the lower photograph "Captain Schwartz, the sharpshooter," is holding a revolver which looks exceedingly clumsy compared to the neat twentieth-century weapons.

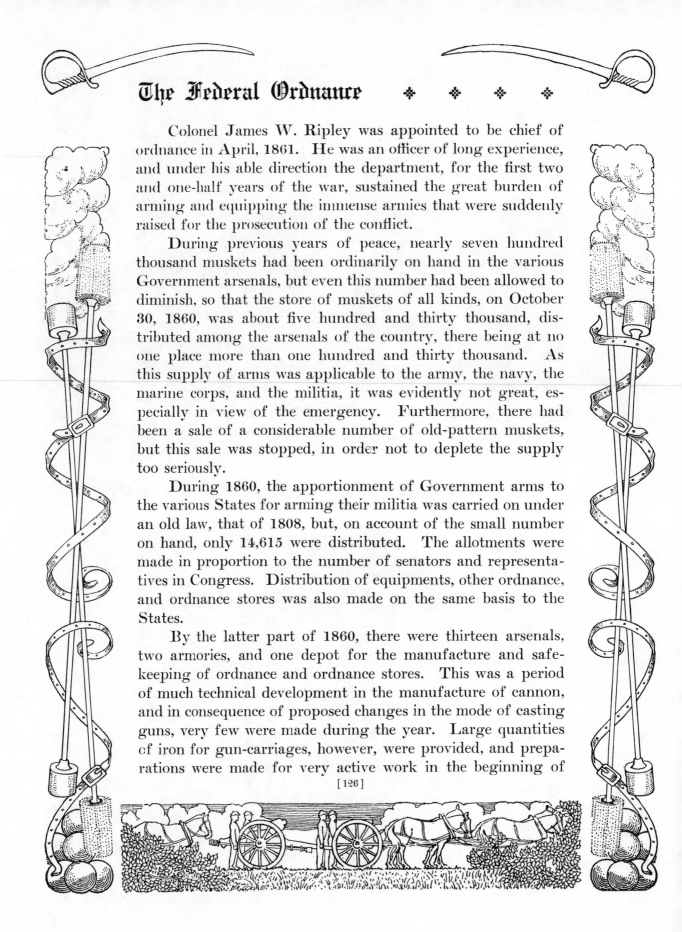

The Federal Ordnance ❖ ❖ ❖ ❖

Colonel James W. Ripley was appointed to be chief of ordnance in April, 1861. He was an officer of long experience, and under his able direction the department, for the first two and one-half years of the war, sustained the great burden of arming and equipping the immense armies that were suddenly raised for the prosecution of the conflict.

During previous years of peace, nearly seven hundred thousand muskets had been ordinarily on hand in the various Government arsenals, but even this number had been allowed to diminish, so that the store of muskets of all kinds, on October 30, 1860, was about five hundred and thirty thousand, distributed among the arsenals of the country, there being at no one place more than one hundred and thirty thousand. As this supply of arms was applicable to the army, the navy, the marine corps, and the militia, it was evidently not great, especially in view of the emergency. Furthermore, there had been a sale of a considerable number of old-pattern muskets, but this sale was stopped, in order not to deplete the supply too seriously.

During 1860, the apportionment of Government arms to the various States for arming their militia was carried on under an old law, that of 1808, but, on account of the small number on hand, only 14,615 were distributed. The allotments were made in proportion to the number of senators and representatives in Congress. Distribution of equipments, other ordnance, and ordnance stores was also made on the same basis to the States.

By the latter part of 1860, there were thirteen arsenals, two armories, and one depot for the manufacture and safe-keeping of ordnance and ordnance stores. This was a period of much technical development in the manufacture of cannon, and in consequence of proposed changes in the mode of casting guns, very few were made during the year. Large quantities of iron for gun-carriages, however, were provided, and preparations were made for very active work in the beginning of

IN THE WASHINGTON ARSENAL YARD—A ROW OF "NAPOLEONS"

This type of piece was used extensively during the war, and was usually made of bronze. Its exterior was characterized by the entire absence of ornament, and was easily distinguished from the older types of field-guns. The weight of the piece was 1,200 pounds. It fired a twelve-pound projectile, also case-shot and canister. The charge for solid projectiles and case was two and a half pounds of powder; for canister, two pounds. This gun had as long range and as accurate as any of the heavier guns of the older models, while the strain of the recoil on the carriage was not nearly so heavy as in the older guns. This yard was always kept in immaculate order.

1861. Likewise, in the manufacture of gunpowder the department had determined there should be an improvement. The sudden strain on the large guns of quick-burning powders had caused some to burst, and the problem confronting the experts was to produce a slow-burning powder that would not cause the great initial strain of the quick-burning kinds, without sacrifice of velocity or range.

As showing the distribution of ordnance supplies at the outbreak of the war, it may be stated there were stored in arsenals in the South about one hundred and thirty-five thousand small arms of all patterns. These fell into the hands of the Confederates, depleting considerably the already small supply for the use of the Union armies.

In verbal reports to the Secretary of War, about the 23d of April, 1861, the chief of ordnance suggested that, in view of the limited capacity of the arsenals, there should be purchased from abroad from fifty thousand to one hundred thousand small arms and eight batteries of rifled cannon. There was no immediate action on this request; on the contrary, efforts were made to encourage the private manufacturers in the Northern States to increase the capacity of their plants. This, it was foreseen, would lead to an endless variety of arms soon being in use in the service, unless special effort was made to provide a uniform pattern. The Springfield model of the United States rifle was then being manufactured at the armories of the Government at a cost of a little less than fourteen dollars, and it was estimated that it could be made in private armories for twelve dollars, so that, with a proper margin of profit, it could be sold to the Government for the cost of manufacture in Government factories. The United States musket then, as nearly always since, had no superior in the world.

The patriotic efforts of the States to assist the general Government were well shown by the action of New York in purchasing, early in 1861, twenty thousand Enfield rifles from England, with an initial purchase of one hundred thousand

LADIES AND OFFICERS IN THE INTERIOR COURT, WASHINGTON ARSENAL

These leisurely ladies and unhurried officers do not betray the feverish activity which existed in the Union Ordnance Department throughout the war. By the latter part of 1860 there were thirteen arsenals, two armories and one depot for the manufacturing and safe-keeping of ordnance and ordnance stores in the United States. There were stored in arsenals in the South about 61,000 small arms of all patterns which fell into the hands of the Confederates. About April 23, 1861, the Chief of Ordnance suggested that, in view of the limited capacity of the arsenals, there should be purchased from abroad from 50,000 to 100,000 small arms and eight batteries of rifled cannon. There was no immediate action on this request. Early in 1861 the State of New York purchased 20,000 Enfield rifles from England, with an initial purchase of 100,000 rounds of ammunition. Efforts were made to encourage the private manufacturers in the Northern States to increase the capacity of their plants, and to provide a uniform pattern. The Springfield model of United States rifle was then the standard. The arsenal was kept in model condition throughout the war. In the yard were stored thousands of heavy and light cannon, with hundreds of thousands of projectiles of every description. Hundreds of extra wheels, besides promiscuous material piled in order, were kept there always ready for issue.

rounds of ammunition. This was followed by an inquiry made of the chief of ordnance to ascertain whether the same ammunition could be manufactured in the Government arsenals, for issue to the troops armed with the Enfield. Necessarily, the answer was " No," and the chief of ordnance, on June 17, 1861, reported to the Secretary of War that the issue of " fancy " arms to troops about to be mustered into the service of the United States was highly undesirable. By the end of December, 1861, however, it was found that the capacity of the various arsenals of the Government was not equal to the great output necessary, and that the practice of buying by contract had to be recognized to a great extent. The States had already sent troops for service armed with numerous patterns of rifles, and it was impracticable to rearm all of them.

On January 25, 1862, the chief of ordnance reported to Secretary Stanton that, under the administration of his predecessor, Secretary Cameron, it had been tentatively decided to have, if possible, but one caliber of rifles, and to cause the necessary changes to be made to accomplish this. It was found that there were in the arsenals but ten thousand rifles of .58-inch caliber, the standard size deemed best for the military service, and it was decided to ream up to that size all arms of less caliber. The Government shops were working to their utmost capacity, and could not make the alterations without serious injury to the necessary business from an interruption of the operations and consequent diminution of the output. Certain private firms took over all the small arms that were to be changed, paid the Government a price almost equal to the original cost price, reamed them to the standard size, put on sword-bayonets, and returned them to the Government at a slight advance, sufficient to cover the cost of the work and give a small margin of profit. Thereby, the service secured a supply of arms that would take the regulation ammunition.

The consensus of expert opinion at the time inclined toward the use of the muzzle-loader in preference to

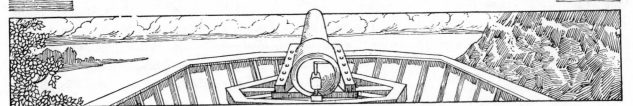

A 17,000-POUND SEA-COAST MORTAR IN THE WASHINGTON ARSENAL

This leviathan of the shore dwarfs by its size the big guns visible in the background. Some idea of its huge proportions can be gained by figuring its diameter by the height of the man leaning against it. The bore of this mortar was 35.1 inches in length, and the maximum charge was about 75 pounds of powder. It was employed principally for sea-coast fortifications, where it was expected to operate against the decks of vessels, the great weight of the projectiles being exceedingly destructive. These mortars were sometimes used for siege purposes, as at Yorktown, but their great weight made them difficult to move and emplace in temporary works.

[F— 9]

the breech-loading rifle, and the repeaters of the day were considered especially undesirable for military purposes. Those in use were complicated in their mechanism, liable to get out of order, and more difficult of repair than the more simple weapon. Besides, with the repeaters, the ammunition was so heavy and the expenditure so rapid, that the supply was soon exhausted, while, owing to the excessive rapidity of fire, the soldier took less care in aiming, with the net result that the value of his ammunition was much less than by the old method of loading.

The question of a repeating rifle was, however, much discussed. Before the war opened there was no weapon of this type considered altogether suitable for military purposes. Inventors immediately began producing models and improving upon them, and the Government armories afforded favorite places for the work of these men. One of the best models was the Spencer, patented in 1860. This was a very ingenious weapon, which was made at the Harper's Ferry Armory. Compared with a revolver, it was quicker in action and held more cartridges, while having the advantage of the better enclosed rifle construction. In this rifle, for the first time, the problem of a closed breech and barrel, as in a single loader, was successfully solved. Theretofore, rapidity of fire had been associated only with the revolver principle. By operating the lever which formed the trigger-guard, the breech-block was given two motions—one rotary, and the other one of depression. The magazine was a tube in the stock, having a spring which fed the cartridges toward the breech mechanism.

All throughout the war this gun and similar types did splendid service, notwithstanding the fact that the prevailing opinion among ordnance experts was in favor of the muzzle-loader. It is stated that, at Ball's Bluff, one regiment of Confederates was armed with the repeater and did great execution. Due to the use of the Spencer rifle by a part of General Geary's troops at Gettysburg, a whole division of Ewell's corps was

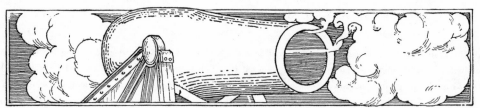

A DAHLGREN 11-INCH SMOOTH-BORE NAVAL GUN, OPPOSITE YORKTOWN

The Dahlgren guns of large caliber were made of cast iron, solid and cooled from the exterior. The powder-chamber was of the "Gomer" form—almost a cone with the base forward and of the size of the bore of the gun, so that when the projectile was rammed home it would not go entirely down to the bottom of the cavity, but would leave a powder-chamber behind it so shaped that the gases had access to a greater surface of the projectile than if the bore had been cylindrical to the base. The 11-inch Dahlgren had a bore of 132 inches in length, a maximum diameter of thirty-two inches, and a weight of 16,000 pounds. The service charge of powder was fifteen pounds, the maximum twenty pounds, and the weight of the solid shot 170 pounds. It sometimes fired a shell weighing 130 pounds.

A 10-INCH COLUMBIAD IN BATTERY SEMMES

With a charge of fifteen pounds of powder this gun, above Farrar's Island on the James River, could throw a shot weighing 123 pounds 3,976 yards, or as far as the Dutch Gap Canal, over two miles away.

AN 8-INCH PARROTT AND A RODMAN GUN

In this battery at Yorktown are a pear-shaped Rodman gun and the long slim lines of an 8-inch Parrott in front. The latter is reënforced by an extra part shrunk over the powder chamber.

repulsed by inferior numbers. Of this an eye-witness said, "The head of the column, as it was pushed on by those behind, appeared to melt away or sink into the earth, for though continually moving it got no nearer." In the West, it was found that a regiment armed with the Spencer was more than a match for a division armed with the old Springfield. In 1863, the Winchester was patented, and was an improvement over the former models of repeaters—and from that time to the end of the war these and kindred types were greatly sought after by new regiments going to the front.

During the first part of the war, so great was the demand for muskets that Secretary Stanton approved a recommendation of the chief of ordnance on August 8, 1862, for a somewhat lenient interpretation of the contracts with private establishments delivering small arms. General Ripley stated that it had been found impossible to hold contractors to the literal, strict compliance with all the terms of their contracts. In view of the fact that contractors had expended large sums for equipping their factories, and having in mind the urgent need for great quantities of small arms, as close an inspection at the private factories as in the United States armories was not carried on. Arms were not rejected for small blemishes not impairing the serviceability of the weapon. The main points insisted on were that they should be of standard caliber to take the Government ammunition, and that the stocks, barrels, locks, and other essential parts should be of the strongest quality. Otherwise, the matter of acceptance or rejection was left in the hands of the inspector.

The greatest difficulty was experienced in securing iron for the manufacture of small arms and cannon. Up to August, 1862, a sufficient quantity of American iron could not be procured, and the department was forced to buy abroad. On August 8th of that year, the Secretary of War was informed by the chief of ordnance that the use of American iron was what the ordnance officers were striving for without success.

THE DIVERSITY OF THE FEDERAL ORDNANCE—WIARD GUN BATTERIES

This view of the Washington Arsenal yard shows three batteries of Wiard steel guns. This was only one of many types which added to the complexity of the armaments of the Federal ordnance. It is recorded that the artillery with Rosecrans's army February 8, 1863, included thirty-two 6-pounder smooth-bores, twenty-four 12-pounder howitzers, eight 12-pounder light Napoleons, twenty-one James rifles, thirty-four 10-pounder Wiard steel guns, two 6-pounder Wiard steel guns, two 16-pounder Parrotts, and four 3-inch rifle ordnance guns. Of the batteries here shown, two were rejected on account of reported defects in the guns.

A 6–POUNDER WIARD—A MODERN–APPEARING TYPE

Every inducement had been offered to manufacturers to prepare iron of a suitable quality; the highest prices had been offered, and a great many samples had been tested. Whenever American iron of acceptable quality was presented, it was always used in preference to foreign iron, other things being equal. The chief of ordnance stated that he had no doubt there was a sufficient quantity of good American material, but up to that time the producer had not furnished it, and a resort to foreign markets was a necessity.

The difficulties experienced with small arms were repeated with the ammunition. When the Army of the Potomac took the field in the middle of March, 1862, for the Peninsula campaign, the Ordnance Department held, at the Washington Arsenal, sixteen million five hundred thousand rounds of small-arms ammunition, for five different kinds of arms, in reserve. This ammunition was for smooth-bore muskets, caliber .58; foreign muskets of various makes, caliber .577, and nondescript, unclassified muskets, caliber .54. For carbines and pistols of various kinds, one million rounds were in reserve. For artillery there were sixty-four thousand two hundred projectiles for three kinds of 6-pounders, three kinds of 12-pounders, and one kind each of 10-, 20-, 24-, and 32-pounders. The mere mention of these various classifications is sufficient to indicate the strain under which the department was laboring. But this task was met and well done, for history seldom records a shortage of ammunition that could be traced to the ordnance officers.

In February, 1863, there were on hand in the ordnance armories and arsenals nearly one hundred and thirty-seven million rounds of small-arms ammunition, and up to that time, since the opening of the war, nearly fifty-five million pounds of lead had been purchased for use in making bullets.

The development of rifled cannon was in an experimental stage when the war opened. There had been a decided movement toward the adoption of these guns in 1859, simultaneously

THE BIGGEST GUN OF ALL—THE 20–INCH MONSTER FOR WHICH NO TARGET WOULD SERVE

A photograph of the only 20-inch gun made during the war. It weighed 117,000 pounds. On March 30, 1861, a 15-inch Columbiad was heralded in *Harper's Weekly* as the biggest gun in the world, but three years later this was exceeded. In 1844 Lieutenant (later Brigadier-General) Thomas Jefferson Rodman of the Ordnance Department commenced a series of tests to find a way to obviate the injurious strains set up in the metal, by cooling a large casting from the exterior. He finally developed his theory of casting a gun with the core hollow and then cooling it by a stream of water or cold air through it. So successful was this method that the War Department, in 1860, authorized a 15-inch smooth-bore gun. It proved a great success. General Rodman then projected his 20-inch smooth-bore gun, which was

THE BIGGEST GUN IN THE WORLD.

We publish on page 205 an accurate drawing of the great Fifteen-inch Gun at Fort Monroe, Virginia; and also a picture, from a recent sketch, showing the experiments which are being made with a view to test it. It is proper that we should say that the small drawing is from the lithograph which is published in MAJOR BARNARD'S "Notes on Sea-Coast Defense," published by Mr. D. Van Nostrand. of this city.

This gun was cast at Pittsburgh, Pennsylvania, by Knapp, Rudd, & Co., under the directions of Captain T. J. Rodman, of the Ordnance Corps. Its dimensions are as follows:

Total length	190	inches.
Length of calibre of bore	156	"
Length of ellipsoidal chamber	9	"
Total length of bore	165	"
Maximum exterior diameter	48	"

NEWS OF MARCH 30, 1861

made in 1864 under his direction at Fort Pitt, Pittsburg, Pennsylvania. It was mounted at Fort Hamilton, New York Harbor, very soon afterwards, but on account of the tremendous size and destructive effect of its projectiles it was fired only four times during the war. It was almost impossible to get a target that would withstand the shots and leave anything to show what had happened. These four shots were fired with 50, 75, 100 and 125 pounds of powder. The projectile weighed 1,080 pounds, and the maximum pressure on the bore was 25,000 pounds. In March, 1867, it was again fired four times with 125, 150, 175 and 200 pounds of powder, each time with an elevation of twenty-five degrees, the projectile attaining a maximum range of 8,001 yards. This is no mean record even compared with twentieth century pieces.

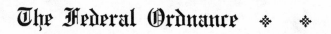

with their introduction into the foreign services. Prior to that time, artillerists and inventors had directed their attention to the production of a projectile on the expanding system. This method of making the projectile take the rifling had been more or less successful with the bullet, and it was hoped that a device could be invented which would permit the use of the same principle with larger projectiles. The board of rifled ordnance, in 1859, expressed an opinion that such would be the case, with the exception of one member, who recommended the continuation of experiments with flanged projectiles and similar types. However, the Charrin projectile, an expanding type, was adopted at first, but proved to be unsatisfactory and was withdrawn. The introduction of rifled cannon did not simplify the question of calibers.

Up to the summer of 1862, there were made, in the arsenals of the Government and in certain private establishments, bronze rifled guns of 3.67 and 3.8 inches, and large numbers of iron rifled cannon of 2.9 and 3.0 inches. There had been already both smooth-bore and rifled guns of 4.62 inches, and guns of 4.5 inches were also made. The great objection to the smaller calibers was that the range was needlessly great, and the shell too small to be of practical value. With the system of expanding projectiles at first adopted, the question of exact calibers was not of such great importance, for by the method used for accommodating the projectile to the rifling, the same shot could be used for both the 3.67-inch and the 3.8-inch gun.

Bronze had been adopted as a standard metal for field-guns in 1841, and served the purpose excellently until the introduction of rifled cannon, when the increased strain due to the imparting of the rotary motion to the projectile proved too great, and the metal was too soft to stand the wear on the rifling. It was then found that wrought iron served the purpose best, and of this material 3-inch muzzle-loading guns were made. On the introduction of breech-loaders, forged steel proved to be more satisfactory. However, many Parrott rifled

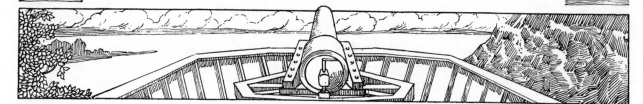

HANDLING HEAVY GUNS—TOWING A PIECE FROM A CONFEDERATE BATTERY ON THE JAMES

It was no slight task to move the heavy ordnance, after the James River was opened and Richmond had fallen. The barge in the upper photograph has sunk deep into the water and lists heavily. A crowd of men are busy handling it. The tripod at Broadway Landing in the lower photograph had legs about as thick as the body of a man, but it looks none too large to handle the big guns lying beneath. Judging from the height of the sentry standing by its left leg, the guns are ten feet long. Both of them are reënforced at the breech.

A TRIPOD SWINGING PARROTT GUNS BY THE APPOMATTOX, AT BROADWAY LANDING

cast-iron field-guns were successfully used. These received a reenforcement of wrought iron shrunk around the base. A considerable number of the bronze Napoleon guns were, however, retained, and did effective service at short ranges.

For heavier ordnance cast iron was early found to be the most suitable material, and proved entirely satisfactory until the adoption of the rifled systems. The American smooth-bore type of ordnance was the best in the world. In 1860, the Ordnance Department adopted Colonel Rodman's method of interior cooling of a hollow cast tube, and in 1863 the extreme effort was made to produce a heavy gun, resulting in a successful 20-inch smooth-bore throwing a shot weighing 1080 pounds. The heavy rifled guns of the Civil War period were somewhat untrustworthy, however, and many accidents resulted. In consequence, their use was limited principally to those built on the Parrott principle, and the great mass of the heavy artillery used by the Union armies was of the smooth-bore type.

The expenditures of the Government on account of the Ordnance Department for the fiscal year ending June 30, 1863, were over $42,300,000. The principal purchases that were made during the year consisted of 1577 field-, siege-, and sea-coast cannon, 1,082,841 muskets, 282,389 carbines and pistols, over 1,250,000 cannon-balls and shells, over 48,700,000 pounds of lead, and over 259,000,000 cartridges for small arms, in addition to nearly 6,000,000 pounds of powder.

These purchases were made necessary by the fact that the arsenals and armories under the direct control of the department were not able to produce all of this immense quantity of war matériel. But the progress toward obtaining greater facilities for the production of these supplies was very great. The Secretary of War, in his report of the operations of the War Department for 1863, made note especially of the tremendous work done by the ordnance officers and the personnel under their direct charge. He stated that the resources of the country for the production of arms and

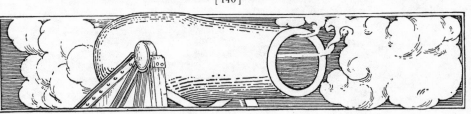

BRINGING UP THE MORTARS AT BUTLER'S CROW'S NEST

So annoying to the Union force at Dutch Gap, digging the canal in 1864, did the fire of the Confederate batteries become, that a battery and lookout were established above the canal. The upper photograph shows the big mortars of the battery being placed in position. They are old style 10-inch mortars and very difficult to handle. A lookout with a crow's-nest on top can be seen in the trees. This is where the signal men did their work. During the imprisonment of the Confederate fleet above Chaffin's Bluff, their crews and officers served ashore. So close were the Confederate batteries that with a spy-glass some naval officers actually recognized some of their former companions in the Federal service. That it was no easy task to install this battery is clear from the gigantic paraphernalia to move big guns, shown in the lower photograph. This was a giant sling-cart used by the Federals in removing captured ordnance from the batteries on the James River below Richmond, after there was no more use for the battery shown above. By means of this apparatus the heaviest siege and sea-coast cannon could be moved. The cart was placed over the piece, ropes run under the trunnions and the cascabel, or knob, on the rear of the gun, and a large pole placed in the muzzle for the accommodation of another rope.

A SLING CART MOVING A HEAVY GUN

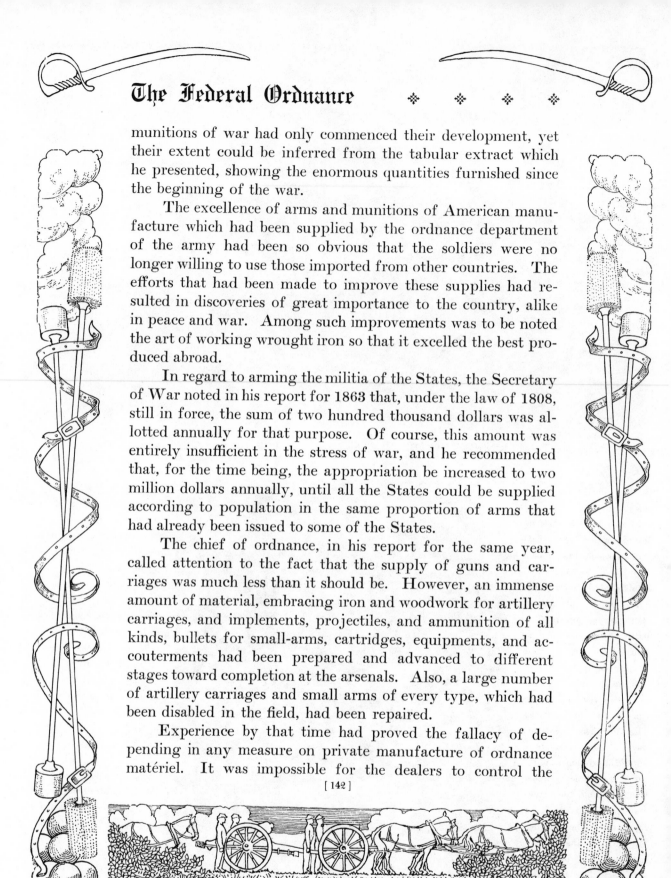

munitions of war had only commenced their development, yet their extent could be inferred from the tabular extract which he presented, showing the enormous quantities furnished since the beginning of the war.

The excellence of arms and munitions of American manufacture which had been supplied by the ordnance department of the army had been so obvious that the soldiers were no longer willing to use those imported from other countries. The efforts that had been made to improve these supplies had resulted in discoveries of great importance to the country, alike in peace and war. Among such improvements was to be noted the art of working wrought iron so that it excelled the best produced abroad.

In regard to arming the militia of the States, the Secretary of War noted in his report for 1863 that, under the law of 1808, still in force, the sum of two hundred thousand dollars was allotted annually for that purpose. Of course, this amount was entirely insufficient in the stress of war, and he recommended that, for the time being, the appropriation be increased to two million dollars annually, until all the States could be supplied according to population in the same proportion of arms that had already been issued to some of the States.

The chief of ordnance, in his report for the same year, called attention to the fact that the supply of guns and carriages was much less than it should be. However, an immense amount of material, embracing iron and woodwork for artillery carriages, and implements, projectiles, and ammunition of all kinds, bullets for small-arms, cartridges, equipments, and accouterments had been prepared and advanced to different stages toward completion at the arsenals. Also, a large number of artillery carriages and small arms of every type, which had been disabled in the field, had been repaired.

Experience by that time had proved the fallacy of depending in any measure on private manufacture of ordnance matériel. It was impossible for the dealers to control the

ROWS OF FEDERAL ORDNANCE AT THE BROADWAY LANDING DEPOT, 1865

In the background are Parrott and Brooke rifles—the former belonging to the Federal army and the latter captured from the Confederates. To the left are lighter field-guns, some rifles, and some smooth-bores. The small, low carriages in front of the field-pieces are for small mortars. Two Rodman smooth-bores are lying dismounted on the ground. There is a marked difference between the heavy Parrott, probably a 100-pounder, in the traveling position on the carriage at the right of the photograph and the howitzer on the small carriage alongside. This photograph gives some idea of the tremendous output of the Union ordnance department during the latter years of the war. In the year ending June 30, 1864, it spent $38,500,000, and the supplies produced included 1,750 caissons and carriages, 802,525 small arms, 8,409,400 pounds of powder, nearly 1,700,000 projectiles for cannon, and nearly 169,500,000 rounds of small-arms ammunition, besides miscellaneous supplies. In the lower left-hand corner are some sling carts to handle the smaller guns.

fluctuation in the market of labor and raw material, even if they so desired, and no private establishment could afford to carry on hand a large stock of ordnance stores such as would meet possible demands from the Government. Warned by repeated failures to procure supplies, the chief of ordnance had taken energetic measures, as far as the funds appropriated would permit, to enlarge the principal arsenals, viz.: Watertown, Massachusetts; Watervliet, West Troy, New York; Allegheny, Pennsylvania; St. Louis, Missouri; Washington, and Benicia, California.

Owing to the development of the resources of the United States, less material had been purchased abroad during the year ending June 30, 1863, than at previous periods of the war, and the Ordnance Department determined that still less should be acquired in Europe in the future. The only articles of which there appeared to be a possible lack were sulphur and saltpeter. During the year the reserve supply of saltpeter had been held intact, and all the powder necessary had been purchased, while the supply of sulphur had been augmented.

In the matter of small arms, the country, by June 30, 1863, was entirely independent. The supply from the Springfield Armory alone was capable of equipping two hundred and fifty thousand troops a year, and the private manufacturers were fully able to supply two hundred and fifty thousand more. Of carbines for cavalry, the capacity of established factories under contract with the Government was at least one hundred thousand annually, and of pistols not less than three hundred thousand.

The duties of officers commanding armories and arsenals and their responsibilities were almost without limitation, involving the control and disbursement of vast quantities of the public money, and the supervision of almost every branch of the mechanic arts. The department, due to the untiring energies of its personnel, both commissioned and enlisted, aided by the large body of civilian employees in service, had been able

A MAMMOTH SEA–COAST CANNON AIMED BY WOODEN WEDGES—1861

This Rodman smooth-bore gun in Port Royal, South Carolina, is mounted on a wooden carriage of a type prevalent during the war. These carriages were sufficiently strong to carry the guns of that time, being made of selected oak, beech, ash, hickory, cypress, or some other durable and resisting wood; but at the close of the war the increased size and power of the guns had surpassed the strength of the old carriages, and the Ordnance Department was confronted with the problem of replacing all the old carriages and making iron carriages for the guns then in process of construction. The elevating device seen on this carriage is primitive, consisting of wooden wedges to be inserted, one on top of another, until the required elevation of the breach was obtained. The recoil on firing sent the piece back, and it was loaded in its recoil position. The piece was returned "in battery" by inserting the bars in the holes in the wheels of the upper carriage. The piece is centered on a pivot, and wheels running on the circular track allow it to be "traversed." This was known as a "center-pintle" carriage. It could be revolved in a complete circle.

to meet successfully all the exigencies of the great war, and to keep supplies going out constantly to a tremendous army operating over a territory as large as Europe. And the quality of the ordnance supplied had surpassed anything theretofore used in the armies of the world.

During the year ending June 30, 1863, over twenty thousand officers had been accountable to the department for ordnance and ordnance stores, and over eighty thousand returns should have been made to the office of the chief of ordnance. All of the accounts rendered for supplies had to be carefully checked, and this involved an immense amount of labor. Many of the returns that were due were not submitted by officers in the field, however, their time being fully occupied with the sterner duties of war.

The activities of the department required an expenditure for the next year of over $38,500,000. The supplies produced included 1760 pieces of ordnance, 2361 artillery caissons and carriages, 802,525 small arms, 8,409,400 pounds of powder, nearly 1,700,000 projectiles for cannon, and nearly 169,500,-000 rounds of small-arms ammunition, besides miscellaneous supplies. In addition to this, large quantities of matériel were repaired after service in the field.

The capacity of the arsenals for the production of munitions was vastly increased, as far as the amount of the Congressional appropriations would permit. By this time, the superiority of the articles fabricated in the Government workshops had received unanimous recognition, and the increased facilities had enabled these factories to reduce the cost below that of private manufacture. The Springfield Armory could, by June 30, 1864, turn out three hundred thousand of the finest muskets in the world, annually, and the arsenal at Rock Island, Illinois, was under construction, and promised a great addition to the capacity of the Ordnance Department. There were, in the hands of troops in the field, one and one-quarter million small arms, and the stock on hand in the armories and

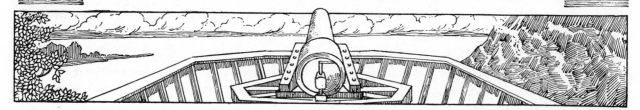

PULASKI'S PARAPETS AFTER THE CAPTURE

One of the first siege exploits of General Quincy A. Gillmore was the reduction of Fort Pulaski, at the mouth of the Savannah River, which fell April 11, 1862. The upper photograph shows the Third Rhode Island Artillery at drill in the fort, and the lower shows battery A, looking toward Tybee. Behind the parapet is part of the remains of the covered way used by the Confederates during the bombardment. The parapets have been repaired, all is in order, and a lady in the costume of the day graces the fort with her presence. Pulaski mounted forty-eight guns in all. Twenty bore upon Tybee Island, from which the bombardment was conducted. They included five 10-inch Columbiads, nine 8-inch Columbiads, three 42-pounders, three 10-inch mortars, one 12-inch mortar, one 24-pounder howitzer, two 12-pounder howitzers, twenty 32-pounders, and two 4½-inch Blakely rifled guns. Against these General Gillmore brought six 10-inch and four 8-inch Columbiads, five 30-pounder Parrotts, twelve 13-inch and four 10-inch siege mortars, and one 48-pounder, two 64-pounder and two 84-pounder James rifles. The most distant of the batteries on Tybee Island was 3,400 yards from the fort, and the nearest 1,650. Modern siege-guns can be effective at a dozen miles. Modern field artillery has a maximum effective range of 6,000 yards. In the Civil War the greatest effective range of field artillery was about 2,500 yards, with rifled pieces.

arsenals available for issue had been increased to three-quarters of a million.

The introduction of breech-loaders for the military service throughout was now very generally recommended. The success of the Spencer, the Sharp, and some other types of repeaters had brought them prominently to notice. The great objections to the breech-loading small arm, in addition to that heretofore mentioned, were that these pieces were heavier than the muzzle-loaders, did not shoot as accurately, were more expensive, and more liable to get out of repair. Besides, dampness penetrated between the barrel and the breech; there was greater risk of bursting; the cartridges were troublesome to make and expensive to buy; the ammunition was heavier, and the projecting pin of the cartridge, then thought a necessity, was liable to cause an explosion by being accidentally struck.

When the war closed, the activities of the Ordnance Department were at their height. Forty-three million one hundred and twelve thousand dollars were spent during the last year, and the main efforts were directed toward providing the same types of matériel that had theretofore been supplied. The manufacture of arms at the national armories was reduced as rapidly as consistent with the economic interests of the Government. With a view to changing the old muzzle-loaders to breech-loaders, extensive experiments were made, but had not, by that time, produced any satisfactory results. The Secretary of War recognized that the importance of the matter demanded that time be taken in reaching a decision, and insisted that no model which had defects of well-known character be accepted. The department had permitted about five thousand of the Springfields to be altered to suit a plan tentatively adopted, and these rifles were issued to troops, but at the time of the cessation of hostilities these were still undergoing tests, and the plan had not been found satisfactory.

There were one million Springfields on hand in the armories, and about one-half million captured muskets of domestic

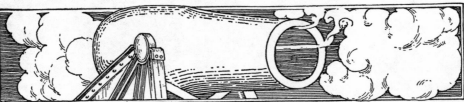

McCLELLAN'S GUNS AND GUNNERS READY TO LEAVE YORKTOWN

This photograph of May, 1862, shows artillery that accompanied McClellan to the Peninsula, parked near the lower wharf at Yorktown after the Confederates evacuated that city. The masts of the transports, upon which the pieces are to be loaded, rise in the background. On the shore stand the serried ranks of the Parrott guns. In the foreground are the little Coehorn mortars, of short range, but accurate. When the Army of the Potomac embarked early in April, 1862, fifty-two batteries of 259 guns went with that force. Later Franklin's division of McDowell's Corps joined McClellan with four batteries of twenty-two guns, and, a few days before the battle of Mechanicsville, McCall's division of McDowell's Corps joined with an equal number of batteries and guns. This made a grand total of sixty field batteries, or 353 guns, with the Federal forces. In the background is part of a wagon train beginning to load the vessels.

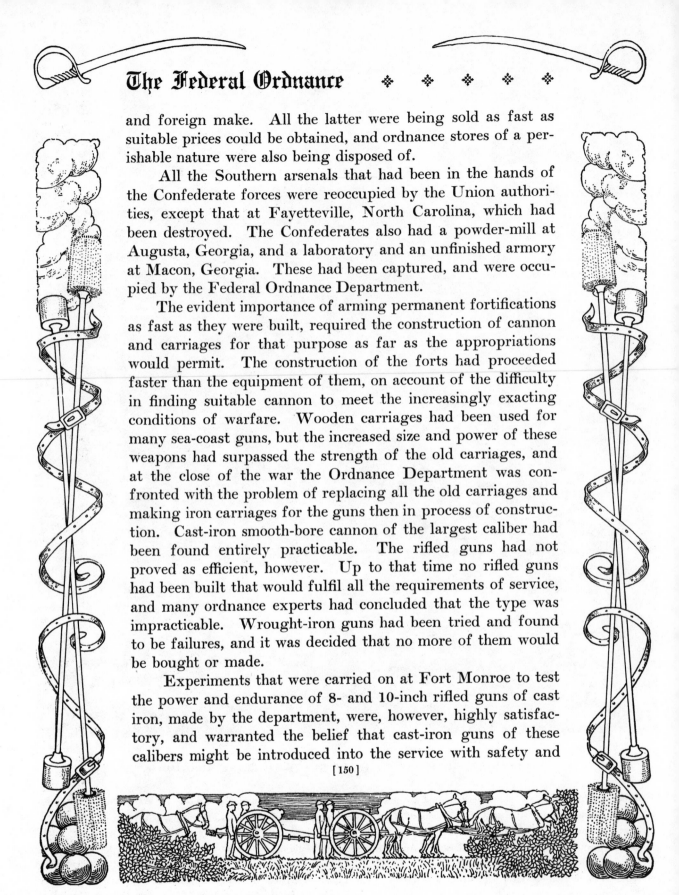

and foreign make. All the latter were being sold as fast as suitable prices could be obtained, and ordnance stores of a perishable nature were also being disposed of.

All the Southern arsenals that had been in the hands of the Confederate forces were reoccupied by the Union authorities, except that at Fayetteville, North Carolina, which had been destroyed. The Confederates also had a powder-mill at Augusta, Georgia, and a laboratory and an unfinished armory at Macon, Georgia. These had been captured, and were occupied by the Federal Ordnance Department.

The evident importance of arming permanent fortifications as fast as they were built, required the construction of cannon and carriages for that purpose as far as the appropriations would permit. The construction of the forts had proceeded faster than the equipment of them, on account of the difficulty in finding suitable cannon to meet the increasingly exacting conditions of warfare. Wooden carriages had been used for many sea-coast guns, but the increased size and power of these weapons had surpassed the strength of the old carriages, and at the close of the war the Ordnance Department was confronted with the problem of replacing all the old carriages and making iron carriages for the guns then in process of construction. Cast-iron smooth-bore cannon of the largest caliber had been found entirely practicable. The rifled guns had not proved as efficient, however. Up to that time no rifled guns had been built that would fulfil all the requirements of service, and many ordnance experts had concluded that the type was impracticable. Wrought-iron guns had been tried and found to be failures, and it was decided that no more of them would be bought or made.

Experiments that were carried on at Fort Monroe to test the power and endurance of 8- and 10-inch rifled guns of cast iron, made by the department, were, however, highly satisfactory, and warranted the belief that cast-iron guns of these calibers might be introduced into the service with safety and

LIGHT FIELD GUNS—A PIECE OF "HENRY'S BATTERY," BEFORE SUMTER IN 1863

Battery B of the First United States Artillery became known as "Henry's Battery" from the name of its young commander, Lieutenant Guy V. Henry (afterward a brigadier-general; later still a conspicuous figure in the Spanish-American War). It took part in the siege operations against Forts Wagner and Gregg on Morris Island, and against Sumter and Charleston, from July to September, 1863. Bronze had been adopted as a standard metal for field guns in 1841, and many of the field batteries were equipped with bronze 12-pounder napoleons. The metal proved too soft to stand the additional wear on rifled guns, however, and it was then found that wrought iron served the purpose best. Later forged steel proved more satisfactory for breech loaders.

AFTER THE ATTEMPT ON SUMTER—THIRD NEW YORK LIGHT ARTILLERY

NAPOLEON GUN IN BATTERY NO. 2, FORT WHIPPLE

The lush, waving grass beautifies this Union fort, one of the finest examples of fortification near Washington. The pieces of ordnance are in splendid condition. The men at the guns are soldierly but easy in their attitudes. They are evidently well-drilled crews. The forked pennant of the artillery flies defiantly above the parapet. But there are no longer any Confederates to defy. The nation is again under one flag, as former Confederate leaders proved by leading Union troops to victory in 1898. Fort Whipple was a mile and a half southwest of the Virginia end of the Aqueduct bridge. It was a "semi-permanent" field work, completely closed, having emplacements for forty-one heavy guns. The gun in the foreground is a 12-pounder smooth-bore, a Napo-

PEACE AT THE DEFENSES OF WASHINGTON

leon. During four years it has been carefully oiled, its yawning muzzle has been swabbed out with care, and a case has been put over it to keep it from rusting in foul weather. In the case of larger guns, the muzzles were stopped up with tampions. Now the rust may come, and cobwebs may form over the muzzle, for nearly fifty years have passed and Americans have fought side by side, but never again against each other. As splendidly as the Confederates fought, as nobly as they bore themselves during the Civil War, still more splendid, still more noble has been their bearing since under the common flag. Nothing could add more luster to their fame than the pride and dignity with which they not only accepted the reunion of the parted nation, but have since rejoiced in it and fought for it.

advantage. A 12-inch rifle was also under test, and had been fired, by the time the war closed, three hundred and ninety times, with a charge of powder weighing fifty-five pounds, and throwing a 600-pound projectile. This was almost conclusive in favor of the gun. Some of the large Parrott rifles used in the siege of Charleston showed remarkable endurance —one of them, a 4.2-inch 30-pounder having fired four thousand six hundred and six rounds before bursting.

After the great pressure of war was over, the department undertook the duties of cleaning, repairing, preserving, and storing the tremendous quantities of war matériel that had accumulated. Fire-proof warehouses were constructed at Watervliet, Frankfort, and Allegheny arsenals, three great magazines were constructed at St. Louis Arsenal, and one each at Washington and Benicia arsenals. The Harper's Ferry Armory had suffered so much in the stress of war that it was in bad repair, and was abandoned. At the Springfield Armory, the work was confined to cleaning, repairing, and storing the small arms used during the conflict, and to making preparations for the conversion of the old Springfield muskets, the best in the world of their kind, into rifled breech-loaders, the new type which the experience of war had brought into being.

France had sent an army into Mexico. The United States declared this a violation of the Monroe Doctrine, and the issue was doubtful. The Ordnance Department expected further trouble, but was fully prepared for it. The able officers of the department and the devoted personnel under their direction had made an institution unsurpassed in history. Be it for peace or war, no concern was felt for the outcome, for arms, equipments, and miscellaneous stores for nearly two million men were ready for issue, or already in the hands of troops. This was the net result of the great labors of the men of the department. But France realized the power of the United States, withdrew her forces from the support of Maximilian, and the crisis was past.

VII

ORDNANCE
OF THE
CONFEDERACY

EARLY CONFEDERATE ORDNANCE — WHAT REMAINED IN 1863 OF THE
FAMOUS "FLOATING BATTERY" THAT AIDED THE SOUTH CARO-
LINIANS TO DRIVE ANDERSON AND HIS MEN OUT OF SUMTER IN 1861

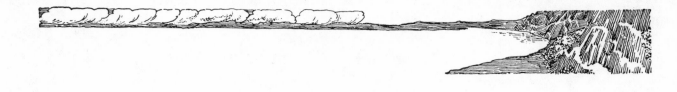

THE ORDNANCE OF THE CONFEDERACY

By J. W. Mallet

Lieutenant-Colonel, Confederate States Army, and Superintendent of the Ordnance Laboratories of the Confederate States

And O. E. Hunt

Captain, United States Army

AT the beginning of the Civil War the Confederate States had very few improved small arms, no powder-mills of any importance, very few modern cannon, and only the small arsenals that had been captured from the Federal Government. These were at Charleston, Augusta, Mount Vernon (Alabama), Baton Rouge, and Apalachicola. The machinery that was taken from Harper's Ferry Armory after its abandonment by the Federals was removed to Richmond, Virginia, and Fayetteville, North Carolina, where it was set up and operated. There were some State armories containing a few small arms and a few old pieces of heavy ordnance. There was scarcely any gunpowder except about sixty thousand pounds of old cannon-powder at Norfolk. There was almost an entire lack of other ordnance stores—no saddles and bridles, no artillery harness, no accouterments, and very few of the minor articles required for the equipment of an army. There was a considerable number of heavy sea-coast guns at the fortified seaports, and others were seized on board men-of-war at Norfolk and among the stores of the Norfolk Navy-Yard. The supply of field-pieces amounted to almost nothing. The States owned a few modern guns, but the most of those on hand were old iron guns, used in the war of 1812–15.

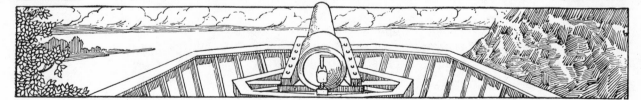

IMPORTED

FROM

FRANCE

"RIFLES"

INVENTED BY

JOHN M. BROOKE,

C. S. N.

AN OLD

COLUMBIAD

IRON BANDS ADDED

The French 12-pounder bronze field-guns in the top photograph were made by Le Place Frères in Paris. They weighed 1,200 pounds and fired a projectile weighing 25¼ pounds with a charge of 2½ pounds of powder. The Southern output was large, of the bronze 12-pounders known as Napoleons. During 1863 and 1864, no less than 110 of these were manufactured at the Augusta arsenal under the direction of General George W. Rains of the Confederate ordnance service. In the lower photograph is an old cast-iron Columbiad, strengthened at the Tredegar Iron Works at Richmond, by the addition of iron bands, after the manner of the Brooke heavy artillery invented by John M. Brooke, formerly of the United States navy, the designer of the ironclad *Virginia*—better known as the *Merrimac*. The gun in the middle of the second photograph is a light Brooke rifle—a 3-inch gun. Its length was about seventy inches, the diameter of the barrel at the muzzle was eleven inches, and the piece weighed nearly 900 pounds. The weight of the projectile was ten pounds with a powder charge of one pound. The maximum effective range of these guns was 3,500 yards, and the time of flight fifteen seconds, with an elevation of fifteen degrees.

The Confederate Ordnance

In the arsenals captured from the Federals, there were about one hundred and twenty thousand muskets of old types, and twelve thousand to fifteen thousand rifles. In addition to these, the States had a few muskets, bringing the total available supply of small arms for infantry up to about one hundred and fifty thousand. With this handicap, the States entered the greatest war in American history. President Jefferson Davis said that "it soon became evident to all that the South had gone to war without counting the cost."

At first, all the ordnance and ordnance supplies of the United States in the Southern arsenals and armories were claimed by the States in which they were found. This caused no little delay in the acquisition of necessary ordnance stores by the Confederate Government, due to the necessity for negotiating for their transfer. The first steps toward provision for ordnance needs were taken while the Government was still at Montgomery, Alabama. An Ordnance Department was organized. Colonel Josiah Gorgas, a graduate of the United States Military Academy in the class of 1841, was appointed chief of ordnance about the end of February, 1861. The department immediately sent out purchasing-officers. Of these, Commander Raphael Semmes (afterward Admiral Semmes) was sent to New York, where, for a few weeks, he was able to buy ordnance stores in considerable quantity and ship them to the South; and Colonel Caleb Huse was soon afterward sent to London to act as general purchasing-agent in England and on the European continent. He remained on this duty throughout the war, and did invaluable service to the Confederate cause.

The seat of the Confederate Government having been moved to Richmond, Colonel Gorgas there proceeded to organize the center of activity of the Ordnance Department. There were four main sources of supply: arms on hand at the beginning of the war, those captured from the United States, those manufactured in the Confederacy, and those imported

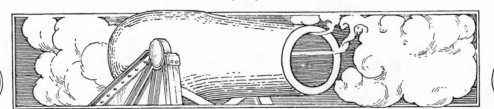

GUNS JUST SEIZED BY CONFEDERATES—1861

The photograph of the cannoneers in their hickory shirts, and the long line of cannon, was taken by J. D. Edwards of New Orleans. This is one of the Confederate sand-bag batteries bearing on Fort Pickens. The Northern administration not only failed to take steps at the outset of the war to protect the great navy-yard at Norfolk, but it also surrendered that at Pensacola. The former could have been retained had the incoming administration acted more promptly. With the loss of these two great establishments to the Union went some thousands of cannon which aided immensely to arm the Southern batteries. This was one more source from which the Confederacy secured her guns. All of the big guns in the coastwise forts were old-time Columbiads placed there in 1856.

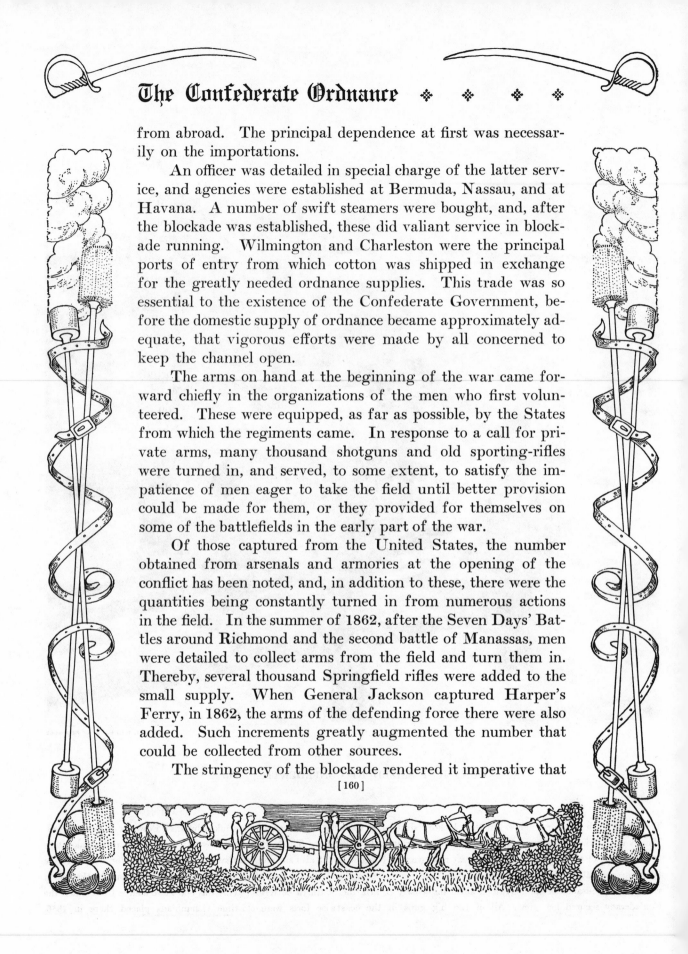

from abroad. The principal dependence at first was necessarily on the importations.

An officer was detailed in special charge of the latter service, and agencies were established at Bermuda, Nassau, and at Havana. A number of swift steamers were bought, and, after the blockade was established, these did valiant service in blockade running. Wilmington and Charleston were the principal ports of entry from which cotton was shipped in exchange for the greatly needed ordnance supplies. This trade was so essential to the existence of the Confederate Government, before the domestic supply of ordnance became approximately adequate, that vigorous efforts were made by all concerned to keep the channel open.

The arms on hand at the beginning of the war came forward chiefly in the organizations of the men who first volunteered. These were equipped, as far as possible, by the States from which the regiments came. In response to a call for private arms, many thousand shotguns and old sporting-rifles were turned in, and served, to some extent, to satisfy the impatience of men eager to take the field until better provision could be made for them, or they provided for themselves on some of the battlefields in the early part of the war.

Of those captured from the United States, the number obtained from arsenals and armories at the opening of the conflict has been noted, and, in addition to these, there were the quantities being constantly turned in from numerous actions in the field. In the summer of 1862, after the Seven Days' Battles around Richmond and the second battle of Manassas, men were detailed to collect arms from the field and turn them in. Thereby, several thousand Springfield rifles were added to the small supply. When General Jackson captured Harper's Ferry, in 1862, the arms of the defending force there were also added. Such increments greatly augmented the number that could be collected from other sources.

The stringency of the blockade rendered it imperative that

CHIEF OF THE

CONFEDERATE

ORDNANCE

DEPARTMENT

Colonel (later Briga-
dier-General) Josiah
Gorgas served as chief
of ordnance of the
Confederate States
Army throughout the
war. He it was who
sent Colonel (later
Brigadier - General)
George W. Rains to
Augusta to build the
great powder-plant.
Facing an apparently
insuperable difficulty,
in the matter of am-
munition, Rains re-
sorted to first princi-
ples by collecting 200,-
000 pounds of lead in
Charleston from win-
dow-weights, and as
much more from lead
pipes in Mobile, thus
furnishing the South
essential means of
prolonging the war.

BRIGADIER–GENERAL JOSIAH GORGAS

Julius A. de Lagnel was
made captain of the Artillery Corps on March 16,
1861, and major of the
Twentieth Battalion of
Virginia Artillery, July 3,
1862. He was appointed
brigadier-general of the
provisional Army of the
Confederate States, April
15, 1862, but declined the
appointment. During most
of his service he was in
the ordnance bureau at
Richmond, Virginia, ably
seconding Colonel Gorgas.

MAJOR JULIUS A. DE LAGNEL

AN ORDNANCE

OFFICER

OF HIGH

RESOURCEFULNESS

every effort be made to increase the domestic manufacture of all kinds of ordnance and ordnance stores. In arranging for the manufacture of arms and munitions at home, establishments of two different kinds were placed in operation: those which were intended to be permanent, built and equipped for their special purpose and intended to concentrate work on a large scale, and those of a more temporary character, capable of yielding results in the shortest time, and intended to meet the immediate demands of the war, with such resources as the country then afforded.

The first of the permanent works undertaken was a first-class powder-mill, the erection and equipment of which were placed in charge of Colonel George W. Rains, of North Carolina, a graduate of the United States Military Academy in the class of 1842. The mill was placed at Augusta, Georgia, and its construction was commenced in September, 1861. The plant was ready to begin making powder in April, 1862, and continued in successful operation until the end of the war, furnishing all the gunpowder needed, and of the finest quality. Competent critics say of this mill, that, notwithstanding the difficulties in the way of its erection and maintenance, it was, for its time, one of the most efficient powder-mills in the world.

Another permanent work erected was a central ordnance laboratory for the production of artillery and small-arms ammunition and miscellaneous articles of ordnance stores. This was decided on in September, 1861, placed in charge of Lieutenant-Colonel J. W. Mallet, and located at Macon, Georgia. It was designed to be an elaborate establishment, especially for the fabrication of percussion-caps, friction-primers, and pressed bullets, in addition to heavier ordnance supplies. Special machinery was made in England and shipped, but did not reach its destination in time for use. A large instalment including a most powerful pair of engines, had reached Bermuda when blockade running practically came to an end, near the close of the war.

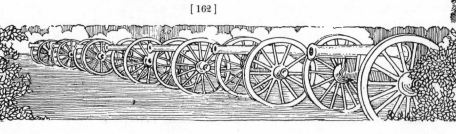

COPYRIGHT, 1911, PATRIOT PUB. CO.

A CONFEDERATE GUN THAT RAN THE BLOCKADE

RICHMOND
1865

Beside the home-made guns, which were all muzzle-loaders, a number of guns of various makes, Whitworth, Armstrong, James, Blakely, and Hotchkiss, were brought in through the blockade. The gun in this photograph is a modified 12-pounder breech-loading Whitworth. The breech was open when the picture was taken. The breech mechanism was adopted from the British Armstrong type and from the French system. In the Armstrong breech-loading gun the breech-block has the full screw that is seen here. The item taken from the French system was the manner of swinging the block back after the screw had become disengaged. The large ring through which the breech-block passes is hinged to the right side of the breech of the gun. Two Whitworths were sent

BRIGADIER–GENERAL
GABRIEL J. RAINS

Gabriel J. Rains of North Carolina was a colonel in the infantry corps March 16, 1861, and was appointed brigadier-general September 23d of that year. He was in charge of the bureau of conscription till December, 1862, and was made chief of the torpedo service June 17, 1864.

to the Army of Northern Virginia. One of them was used in an attempt to knock over General Benjamin F. Butler's famous signal-tower. They had a great reputation for range and accuracy of fire, but beyond the shelling of distant columns and trains proved a disappointment. The length and weight of the gun were above the average, making it difficult to transport, and the care and length of time consumed in loading and handling impaired its efficiency for quick work. The cross-section of this gun was a hexagon with rounded corners. The twist was very rapid, and the projectiles were made long. The diameter of the bore was 2.75 inches, its length 104 inches, its weight 1,092 pounds, and it fired a 12-pound projectile with a usual load of 1.75 pounds of powder.

[F—11]

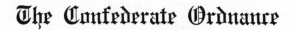

The Confederate Ordnance

The third establishment projected to be permanent was a large central armory, equipped with a complete plant of machinery for the fabrication of small arms, and to which the Harper's Ferry machinery, which had been temporarily installed at Richmond and Fayetteville, was to be removed. This was put in charge of Lieutenant-Colonel J. H. Burton, who had gained experience at the factory in Enfield, England. It was determined to locate this armory at Macon, also. The buildings were begun in 1863, but they were not so far advanced toward completion as the laboratory when the end of the war arrested the work.

As a consequence of the necessity for immediate supply of arms and munitions to enable the armies to keep the field, resort was had to temporary arsenals and armories—at least they were designated as "temporary," although they were actually permanent, as far as the purposes of the war which the Confederacy waged was concerned.

The work was scattered among a number of available places throughout the South. Herein entered the problem of transportation by rail. The railroads were not very amply equipped at the outbreak of the war, and were overburdened in operation to such an extent that it would have been impossible to transport material to any single point from great distances, or to secure similar transportation for finished products over long lines. It was, moreover, uncertain how far any one place could be depended upon as secure from molestation by the foe. And there was not time for the removal of the plants from the localities in which they were when the Confederacy took possession of them, and various temporary ordnance works grew up about existing foundries, machine-shops, and railroad repair-shops, and at the various United States arsenals and ordnance depots. The chief localities that were thus utilized were Richmond, Virginia; Fayetteville, North Carolina; Charleston, South Carolina; Augusta, Savannah, and Macon, Georgia; Nashville and Memphis, Tennessee; Mount Vernon

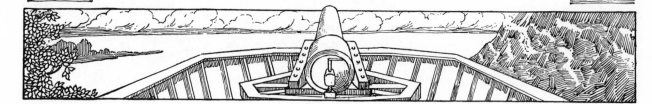

CONFEDERATES AND THEIR SMALL ARMS IN 1861

This remarkable photograph of the encampment of the Perote Guards of New Orleans was found in the Major Chase home in Pensacola, Florida, in 1862, after the city was evacuated by the Confederates. The comparison is striking between the careless garb of the men and the business-like small arms stacked and carried by the sentry. "Bright muskets" and "tattered uniforms" went together. Soldiers could be found all through the camps busily polishing their muskets and their bayonets with wood ashes well moistened.

THE BOWIE KNIFE— CONSIDERED BY THE NORTHERN PRESS OF '61 AN IMPORTANT WEAPON

An article "concerning fire-arms" published in *Harper's Weekly* of August 2, 1861, states that "the bowie knife is usually from ten to fifteen inches in length, with a blade about two inches wide. It is said to owe its invention to an accident which occurred to Colonel Bowie during a battle with the Mexicans; he broke his sword some fifteen inches from the hilt, and afterward used the weapon thus broken as a knife in hand-to-hand fights. This is a most formidable weapon, and is commonly in use in the West and Southwest." As much space is devoted to the description of the bowie knife as is given to siege artillery. An illustration in the same journal for August 31, 1861, shows "Mississippians practising with the bowie knife." The Mississippians are engaged in throwing the knives. The heavy blades are seen hurtling through the air and burying their points in a tree. Grasping his bowie knife in the above photograph stands E. Spottswood Bishop, who started out as a private, was promoted to captain in the Twenty-fifth Virginia Cavalry, wounded five times, and elected colonel of his regiment by its officers. On the right is David J. Candill, who was transferred from the Twenty-fifth to the Tenth Kentucky Cavalry, and was promoted to lieutenant-colonel of his regiment. He was severely wounded in active service in his native State.

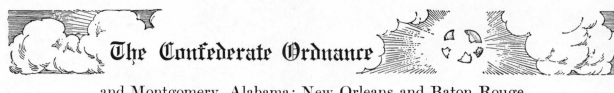

and Montgomery, Alabama; New Orleans and Baton Rouge, Louisiana; Little Rock, Arkansas, and San Antonio, Texas. The events of the war soon compelled the abandonment of some of these, and from time to time others were added to the list, as, for instance, Columbia, South Carolina; Atlanta and Columbus, Georgia; Selma, Alabama, and Jackson, Mississippi. Of these, Atlanta and Selma became most important.

Heavy artillery at the beginning of the war was manufactured only at Richmond at the Tredegar Iron Works. Later in the war, excellent heavy artillery was produced at Selma, first in conjunction with the naval officers, and later by them alone.

Field-artillery was made and repaired chiefly at Richmond and at Augusta, small arms at Richmond and Fayetteville, caps and friction-primers at Richmond and Atlanta, accouterments to a great extent at Macon, while cast bullets and small-arms cartridges were prepared at almost all of the works.

After the Federals took possession of the copper mines of Tennessee, there was great anxiety as to the future supply of copper, both for bronze field-guns and for percussion-caps. The casting of bronze guns was immediately stopped, and all the available copper was utilized in the manufacture of caps. It soon became apparent that the supply would be exhausted and the armies rendered powerless unless other sources of supply were discovered. No reliance could be placed on the supply from abroad, for the blockade was stringent, although large orders had been forwarded. Of course, the knowledge of this scarcity of copper was kept from the public as much as possible. In this emergency, it was concluded to render available, if possible, some of the copper turpentine- and apple-brandy-stills which were in North and South Carolina in large numbers. This work was entrusted to Lieutenant-Colonel Leroy Broun, commanding the Richmond Arsenal.

In spite of the difficulties to be overcome and the constantly increasing pressure for immediate results, the Confederate Ordnance Department was able to boast of some useful

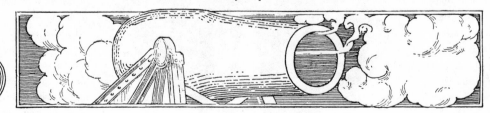

CONFEDERATE GUNS—PRACTICALLY EVERY TYPE USED IN THE CIVILIZED WORLD IN 1865

In the collection of captured Confederate artillery on the wharves of Richmond awaiting shipment North in April, 1865, might be found practically every type of gun made and used by the civilized nations of the world, besides some patterns entirely obsolete. The first sources of Confederate artillery were the captured navy-yards and arsenals. Purchasing agents were sent to Europe and some guns were imported from abroad. This was eventually checked by the Federal blockade. One of the principal places of manufacture was the Trede-gar Iron Works in Richmond. Large quantities of ordnance were also obtained from all battlegrounds of the war where the Confederates held the field for a time following the battle. Due to these various sources of supplies the ordnance material was varied and incongruous. The wagon in the foreground is a tool-wagon, but observe the light wheels. Just over the top of this wagon is visible a caisson, complete, with the fifth, or spare wheel, on the back. In the chests of the caisson are stored projectiles and powder which cannot be carried in the limber of the gun. Below several brass mountain-howitzers appear. Mountain artillery must be light enough to be carried on the backs of pack animals if necessary. The howitzer used for this purpose was a short, light 12-pounder, weighing 220 pounds. When a carriage was used, it was mounted on a low, two-wheeled one. The projectiles were shell and case-shot, and the charge was half a pound of powder.

CONFEDERATE BRASS HOWITZERS

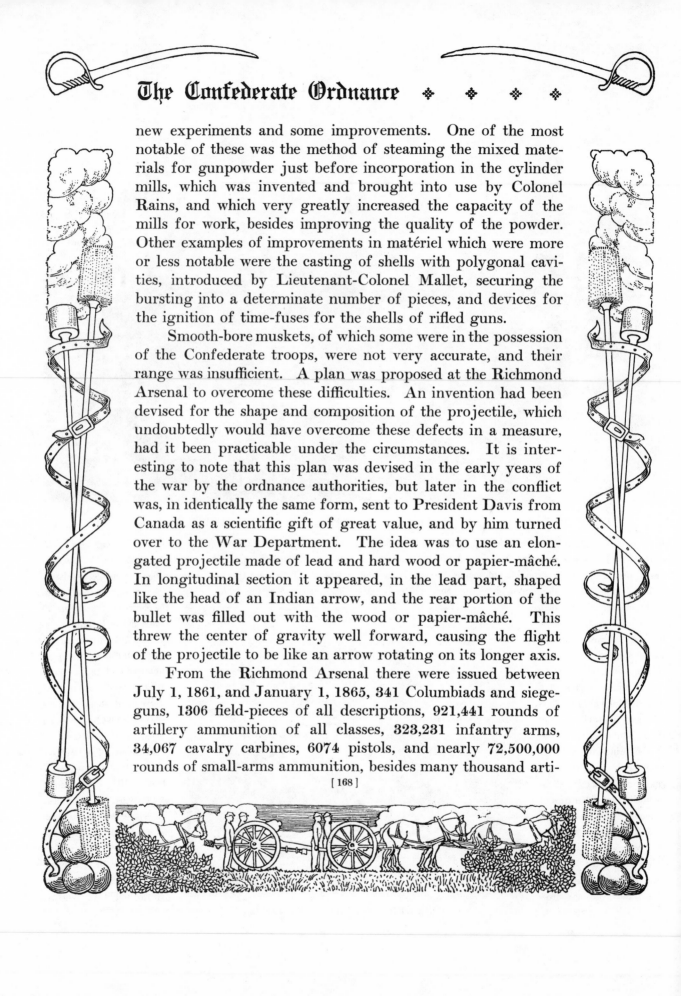

new experiments and some improvements. One of the most notable of these was the method of steaming the mixed materials for gunpowder just before incorporation in the cylinder mills, which was invented and brought into use by Colonel Rains, and which very greatly increased the capacity of the mills for work, besides improving the quality of the powder. Other examples of improvements in matériel which were more or less notable were the casting of shells with polygonal cavities, introduced by Lieutenant-Colonel Mallet, securing the bursting into a determinate number of pieces, and devices for the ignition of time-fuses for the shells of rifled guns.

Smooth-bore muskets, of which some were in the possession of the Confederate troops, were not very accurate, and their range was insufficient. A plan was proposed at the Richmond Arsenal to overcome these difficulties. An invention had been devised for the shape and composition of the projectile, which undoubtedly would have overcome these defects in a measure, had it been practicable under the circumstances. It is interesting to note that this plan was devised in the early years of the war by the ordnance authorities, but later in the conflict was, in identically the same form, sent to President Davis from Canada as a scientific gift of great value, and by him turned over to the War Department. The idea was to use an elongated projectile made of lead and hard wood or papier-mâché. In longitudinal section it appeared, in the lead part, shaped like the head of an Indian arrow, and the rear portion of the bullet was filled out with the wood or papier-mâché. This threw the center of gravity well forward, causing the flight of the projectile to be like an arrow rotating on its longer axis.

From the Richmond Arsenal there were issued between July 1, 1861, and January 1, 1865, 341 Columbiads and siege-guns, 1306 field-pieces of all descriptions, 921,441 rounds of artillery ammunition of all classes, 323,231 infantry arms, 34,067 cavalry carbines, 6074 pistols, and nearly 72,500,000 rounds of small-arms ammunition, besides many thousand arti-

A GIANT CONFEDERATE SLING–CART TO CARRY SIEGE-GUNS

This giant sling-cart was built by the Confederates for the purpose of handling the two 12-inch guns that were cast at the Tredegar Iron Works, in Richmond, just before the evacuation. These guns weighed nearly fifty thousand pounds each. The size of the cart can be estimated by comparing it with the man visible through its spokes in the upper photograph. The wheels are more than eleven feet high. The cart required twelve mules and one hundred and fifty men with drag ropes to move it, when carrying only an 8-inch rifle or a heavy Columbiad over bad roads. The big guns were slung underneath the cart by ropes so as to clear the ground by a few inches. It was captured by the Federals, and used in the removal of the ordnance from Drewry's and Chaffin's bluffs.

cles of other ordnance and ordnance stores. The enormous number of pieces of artillery issued were, of course, not all made at the arsenal, but had been obtained by manufacture, by purchase, or by capture. The Richmond *Enquirer,* on the day after the evacuation of Richmond, said that, assuming the issues from the Richmond Arsenal to have been half of all the issues to Confederate troops, which was approximately true, and that 100,000 of the Federals had been killed, it would appear that about 150 pounds of lead and 350 pounds of iron were fired for every man killed, and, furthermore, assuming that the proportion of killed to wounded was about one to six, it would appear that one man was wounded for every 200 pounds fired. These figures exaggerated the form of the old belief that it took a man's weight in lead to kill him in battle.

Considering the general lack of previous experience in ordnance matters, the personnel of the corps, both at the arsenals and in the field, deserved great praise for intelligence, zeal, and efficiency. Many names of officers deserve to be remembered. Among the most prominent were Lieutenant-Colonels J. H. Burton, superintendent of armories; T. L. Bayne, in charge of the bureau of foreign supplies; I. M. St. John, at the head of the niter and mining bureau; Lieutenant-Colonel J. W. Mallet, in charge of the Central Laboratory at Macon, Georgia; Lieutenant-Colonel G. W. Rains, of the Augusta powder-mills and Arsenal; Lieutenant-Colonel Leroy Broun, commanding the Richmond Arsenal; Major M. H. Wright, of the Atlanta Arsenal; Lieutenant-Colonel R. M. Cuyler, of the Macon Arsenal; Major J. A. De Lagnel, of Fayetteville; Major J. T. Trezevant, of Charleston Arsenal; Lieutenant-Colonel J. L. White, of Selma Arsenal; Lieutenant-Colonel B. G. Baldwin, chief of ordnance, Army of Northern Virginia; Lieutenant-Colonel H. Oladowski, chief of ordnance, Army of Tennessee, and Major W. Allen, chief ordnance officer, Second Corps, Army of Northern Virginia.

VIII

AMMUNITION

13-INCH SHELLS
FOR
THE SEA COAST
MORTARS

These missiles, filled with explosive, and trailing a fiery fuse, shrieked like lost souls in their flight, that covered nearly two and a half miles from the gaping mouths of the tremendous mortars looking like huge bull-frogs with their muzzle elevation of forty-five degrees. The shells seen in this photograph

show the larger hole where the time fuse was inserted, and the indentations which enabled the gunners to handle them with a sort of pincers carried by two men. The mortars were manned by the famous First Connecticut Heavy Artillery, prominent in many important engagements from the Peninsula to the Petersburg Campaign. Companies served on the Bermuda Hundred lines in 1864, also at Fort Fisher.

THE AMMUNITION USED IN THE WAR

By O. E. Hunt
Captain, United States Army

UNTIL the middle of the nineteenth century there was but little improvement in cannon or gunpowder. One reason for this was that bronze and iron were used for making guns, and these metals could not withstand the exceedingly great pressures of heavy charges of powder unless the cannon were cast so large as to be unmanageable. No scientific treatment of the subject of gun-strains had been attempted previous to this time, because it was assumed that all the powder in a charge was converted instantaneously into gas.

Powder and ball for small arms were originally carried loose and separately. Gustavus Adolphus, King of Sweden, first made an improvement by providing separate receptacles for each powder charge; these were called cartridges (Latin *carta*, or *charta*) from their paper envelopes. He subsequently combined the projectile with the powder in the paper wrapper, and this, until about 1865, formed the principal small-arms ammunition.

However, not all of the ammunition used in the Civil War was prepared in this form, and from the fact that powder and ball were carried separately arose the danger of inadvertently loading the piece with more than one charge at a time. Even in the use of the two in one package, inasmuch as there was usually nothing to prevent the reloading of the gun before the previous cartridge had been fired, there still remained this danger. As a consequence, it was reported that nearly half of the muskets abandoned on the field of Gettysburg were found to contain more than one load, and some of

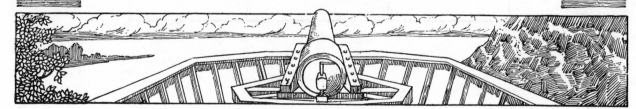

AMMUNITION IN FEDERAL FORT No. 9, ATLANTA

While Sherman rested his soldiers before their march to the sea, this view was taken of Federal Fort No. 9, looking northwest toward Forts Nos. 8 and 7 at Atlanta. Bags of charges for the 12-pounders in the embrasures are ranged along the parapet in exposed positions that they never would have occupied if there had remained any danger of an assault. The bags are marked "12 Pdr. Model. 1857." These were for the brass Napoleons, the most popular guns for field-artillery during the war. In the lower photograph of Confederate works near Petersburg appear boxes in which the cartridges for rifles had been served out. Evidently, they have been hastily ripped open and cast aside. On the further box, lying upside down, are the words "ball cartridges." Beside lie a few shells for field-guns, although the guns themselves have been withdrawn. The photograph was taken after these works passed into the hands of the Federals, and the silent witnesses of a feverish moment under fire tell their own story. The order at drill was, "tear cartridge." The ends of them were usually bitten open, especially in action. At one end of the cartridge came the bullet, then the powder, and the other end was torn open in order to free the powder when it was rammed home.

AFTER THE FIRING

them had three or four. In the excitement, men were observed to load, make a motion mechanically as if to fire the piece, fail to notice that it had not been discharged, and then hasten to put another load on top of the first.

The state of the arts required the first breech-loading ammunition to be in a paper or cloth package. However, as it was impossible to prevent the escape of the gas, the joint required for rapid loading was generally placed in front of the chamber, from which position the soldier suffered least from the discharge. To facilitate loading, the mechanism of the gun was so arranged that, the paper or cloth cartridge having been broken or bitten open, the bullet acted as a stopper to hold the powder in place until the piece was closed.

The next improvement in ammunition was the introduction of the metallic cartridge-case. This was invented in France, and was first used by troops in our Civil War. It contained all the components of the ammunition in a case that protected them from the weather, and thus prevented the deterioration of the powder. The principal purpose of the case, however, has been to act as a gas-check, to prevent the escape of the gases to the rear and to permit the use of an easily operated breech-mechanism.

Being rigid and of fixed dimensions, the metallic cartridge was first used extensively in magazine rifles. There was, at first, a great objection, however, limiting the use of these rifles for military purposes, and that was the rapid consumption of ammunition, which soon exhausted the supply on the person of the soldier. The caliber of the guns was large and the ammunition heavy; hence only a small amount could be carried.

A fulminate, or firing-composition, has always been required for the ignition of the powder, in whatever form it has been used. For loose powder and for paper or cloth cartridges, a percussion-cap, fitted over a vent communicating with the powder in the breech of the gun, served the

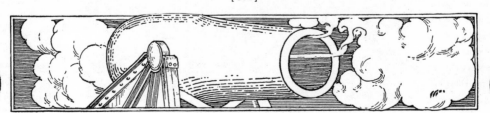

AMMUNITION STORED IN THE WASHINGTON ARSENAL—1864

An essential factor in the winning of pitched, open battles was a plentiful supply of ammunition. At Gaines' Mill, in June, 1862, the Union soldiers found it difficult to cheer convincingly when they had shot away all their cartridges, and found themselves separated from their ammunition wagons by the fast-swelling Chickahominy. The ammunition train always took precedence on the march.

SCHOONERS PILED WITH CARTRIDGE-BOXES—HAMPTON ROADS, DECEMBER, 1864

By 1864, the problem of getting ammunition expeditiously to the front had been solved, and there were no more such shortages as at Gaines' Mill. In this photograph, the harbor of Hampton Roads swarms with ammunition schooners, transports, coal barges, and craft of every sort. The decks of the schooners in the foreground are piled high with cartridge-boxes.

purpose. In the first practicable form of metallic cartridge, the composition was placed in the rim which formed the base of the cartridge, and which enabled it to be withdrawn after discharge—the rim thus serving two purposes. These rim-fire cartridges answered very well until the powder charges became heavier, when it was discovered that the weakening of the metal by folding to make the rim caused it to sheer off at the edge of the chamber of the gun, and the copper, of which they were made, would expand and render it almost impossible to extract the shell. And since the fulminate had to be placed entirely around the rim, a greater quantity was used than necessary for firing, and the distribution was imperfect, thus causing misfires. A pin-fire cartridge was invented, but proved unsatisfactory. A pin projected from the rim and was intended to be struck by the hammer of the gun; but, of course, any object striking it would cause an explosion, and it was dangerous. Neither the pin-fire nor the rim-fire cartridges could be reloaded.

On June 25, 1864, the chief of ordnance of the United States army reported that among the most important changes in firearms evolved from the experience of the war was the metallic cartridge-case. Linen had been in use, but copper was much superior. The case formed a perfect gas-check; it gave the benefit of allowing a fulminate to be used in the case itself, which was an advantage over the former method of using a cap; there was a gain of time in that the piece did not have to be recapped with each new load; there was greater ease of loading, and the ammunition was waterproof.

For the field-artillery of both services there were supplied solid shot, case, and shell with time-fuses and with percussion-fuses. Solid shot were designed for destroying the heavy walls of fortifications, or for some similar purpose, but were used also in the field. The other forms of ammunition were used against troops. Case was of two kinds—canister, which separated at the muzzle of the piece in consequence of the shock

CONFEDERATE AMMUNITION—SOLID SHOT AND A CHARGE OF GRAPE

This view of the Confederate works at Yorktown, in 1862, shows an 11-incl. Dahlgren smooth-bore naval gun. Several of these were taken from the Norfolk Navy-Yard. On the ground is a solid shot and a charge of grape. Grape-shot consisted of a number of small projectiles secured together by a series of iron plates containing holes in which the shot is held. In addition to the common cast-iron shells not intended to pierce iron, forged steel shells were used. In the days of smooth-bore guns, bar shot, chain shot, grape-shot, hot shot, shrapnel and canister were in use. Shrapnel are shaped like shell, but have thinner walls and are filled with lead or iron balls. A small bursting-charge breaks up the case in the air and the balls scatter like shot from a shotgun. In canister the balls, larger than those in shrapnel, are sunk in soft wood disks piled up to form a cylinder and the whole covered with a tin case; or, in small calibers, the balls are simply pushed in sawdust and enclosed in a cylindrical tin case. Grape, shrapnel and canister were all three known as case-shot.

of discharge, and shrapnel, which separated at a distance, due to the presence of a bursting charge which scattered the contents of the receptacle.

The shell was a hollow projectile, containing also a bursting charge, intended for destructive effect at a distance. One of its principal purposes was in the destruction of walls of masonry and other solid construction. By using percussion-fuses the shell would penetrate, and then burst, opening out a breach; and by the addition of further shots in the same place, an opening could be made through which assaulting troops could pass.

The ammunition used by the Federal siege-artillery was of prime importance in the conduct of the war. The siege-guns consisted of mortars, smooth-bore guns, and rifles. All the ammunition received preliminary tests at the factories, and a great portion of it also by target practice in the defenses of Washington. The records of this practice were the most complete ever compiled regarding artillery ammunition, and covered all features of the firing; therefore, when it was issued to the troops in the field, they were informed of the proper results to be expected, as far as the target practice could be simulated to field firing. Experiments were also made at Washington with the Confederate ammunition that had been captured, and certain of the features of that ammunition received very favorable notice from the Federal ordnance officers.

The mortars were designed to throw a shell containing a bursting charge, and carrying either a time-fuse or a percussion-fuse. The time-fuse was ignited by the propelling charge, before leaving the gun. At times this fuse was uncertain in its action, as it would become extinguished during flight or on striking, and the bursting charge, which was intended to cause the damage, would not explode. The percussion-fuse was not ignited by the propelling charge in the mortar, but contained a fulminate that was ignited by a plunger of some description which moved when the shell was fired or when it

PROJECTILES IN THE SEA–COAST FORTS

The guns of the parapet of Fort Putnam were siege guns of heavy caliber. Shells with metal rims made soft to take the grooves of the rifling are stacked up in the foreground. The projectiles by the chassis in Battery Magruder were 8.5-inch Armstrong rifle-shot, which could be used as shell or solid shot at pleasure. They had a cavity for the insertion of a bursting charge, which, with its percussion-fuse, was not inserted unless it was desired to fire the projectile against advancing

SHELLS IN FORT PUTNAM, SOUTH CAROLINA

PROJECTILES IN MAGRUDER BATTERY, YORKTOWN

INTERIOR OF FORT JOHNSON, MORRIS ISLAND

troops as shell. These had a terrific effect, bursting at times into more than 200 pieces. The view of Fort Johnson reveals both spherical solid shot and oblong shell. The latter are slightly hollowed out at the base, in order to secure a better distribution of the gases generated when the pieces were discharged. The stack of projectiles around the two 100-pounder Parrott guns in the lower view of Fort Putnam are for these rifles. Their weight was eighty-six pounds—although the guns were known as 100-pounders—and the powder charge was ten pounds. The projectile for the 3-inch field-gun on the top of the parapet weighed ten pounds, and the powder charge was one pound.

INTERIOR OF FORT PUTNAM, MORRIS ISLAND

struck, thereby communicating the flame to the bursting charge. Of course, these were not always sure.

Whether the one or the other form of fuse was used, depended on the purpose of the firing. If against troops, it was desirable to cause the shell to burst in their midst, and not to allow it to penetrate the ground. If desired for the destruction of earthworks or magazines, it had to be exploded after the penetration. In the former case the time-fuse, and in the latter the percussion-fuse was used.

At Fort Scott, near Washington, in October, 1863, an experiment was tried to test the value of spherical case-shot when fired from mortars. The 10-inch shell was filled with 12-pound canister-shot, and the bursting charge was loose. The capacity of the shell was thirty-eight of that size balls, but twenty-seven only were used. They were inserted through the fuse-hole, and two and a half pounds of bursting powder placed on top of them. The shell weighed ninety pounds and each of the balls forty-three hundredths of a pound, making a total weight of about one hundred and four pounds. A charge of one pound six ounces of mortar-powder gave a range of eight hundred yards with a time of flight of thirteen seconds.

The experiments showed that the fragments scattered a great deal and the balls had ample power to kill. They penetrated the ground from three to seven inches in a turf where, when thrown by a man with his whole strength, they entered less than one inch. A little calculation showed that the velocity must have been over two hundred feet per second, and as the projectiles weighed nearly half a pound each, there was easily sufficient force to disable a man or a beast. The practicability of the shot having been fully determined, a field-trial was given which proved conclusive.

The projectile was used in the battle of the Petersburg mine, where General Hunt's orders for the artillery were to use every exertion to quiet the batteries of the foe bearing on

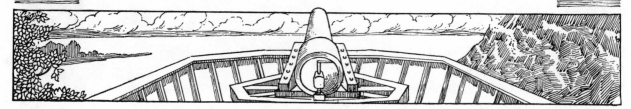

IN CASTLE PINCKNEY—428-POUND PROJECTILES

A BIG GUN IN CAS–TLE PINCKNEY

The gun overlooking the parapet of Castle Pinckney is a 15-inch Columbiad which used a powder charge of 40 pounds. The projectile weighed 428 pounds. A large number of these projectiles are stacked in the foreground. With an elevation of twenty degrees, the maximum range of this gun was 3,787 yards, or a little over two miles. This fort

POWDER MAGAZINE IN BATTERY RODGERS

was used as a prison for Union captives in 1861. In Battery Rodgers, within the corporate limits but nearly half a mile below the wharves and populous portion of the city of Alexandria, there were two magazines, one twelve by thirty feet and the other twelve by eighteen feet interior dimensions. These were sunk entirely below the *terre plein*, and protected by a cover of earth seventeen and a half feet thick, armed with five 200-pounders.

the point of assault. A battery of 10-inch mortars was placed near the subsequent location of Fort Rice, and directed its fire, at a range of eight hundred yards, upon a salient battery of the Confederates, from which much trouble was anticipated. Not a shot was fired from the Confederate battery after its range was obtained, and from information received afterward from a Southern officer, it was found that the men could not remain at their guns after the showers of balls began falling, every thirty seconds, around them.

The ordinary mortar-shell was the one used largely in all the operations. At Yorktown, the Confederates had an 8-inch mortar with which they did rather indifferent shooting, but the moral effect on the Federal soldiers of the screeching shells was great. Accordingly, the Federals thereafter paid close attention to the training of men for the use of a similar type of mortar, and at Petersburg there was a good opportunity to reply in kind. The Confederate gunners, now feeling the effect of the fire from the other side, and having for a time no bombproofs in which to take shelter, were appalled by the sudden opening of the Federal mortars. The lines were so near together that the soldiers were under the necessity of keeping their works closely guarded to prevent their being taken by assault, and the moral effect was very depressing. One case is related of a Confederate soldier having been blown entirely over the parapet of the work by the explosion of one of the Federal 8-inch mortar-shells, and his body lay out of reach of his friends, who were compelled to keep under cover by the Federal sharpshooters.

As soon as the Confederates could place mortars in position at Petersburg, they opened on the besiegers, and thereafter the fire was severe. The Federal expenditure of mortar ammunition was over forty thousand rounds, and that of the Confederates was estimated to have been not much less.

The incident of the so-called "Petersburg Express," when the Federals mounted a 13-inch sea-coast mortar on a railroad

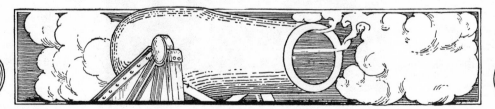

THE LABORATORY FOR SMALL AMMUNITION AT RICHMOND

This photograph was taken the day the new flag of the Confederate States of America was thrown to the breeze on top of Libby prison. The entire supply of gunpowder in the Confederacy at the beginning of the conflict was scarcely sufficient for one month of active operations. Not a pound was being made throughout its limits. The comparatively small amount captured at the Norfolk navy-yard, with that on hand from other sources, was promptly distributed to the army gathering on the Potomac, to Richmond, Yorktown, Pensacola, Mobile, and New Orleans. Scarcely any remained for the force assembling under the command of General Albert Sidney Johnston in Kentucky. In the face of these difficulties, Colonel (later General) George W. Rains was given *carte blanche* to take charge of the manufacture of gunpowder. He established immense works in Augusta, Georgia. So extensive were they that at no time after their completion were they worked to their full capacity. They were never run at night. They satisfied in little more than two days the urgent call of General Ripley at Charleston for cannon-powder, to replace the twenty-two thousand pounds consumed during the action with the iron-clad fleet. The Richmond laboratory made 72,000,000 cartridges in three and a half years, nearly as much as the others in the Confederate States combined.

platform car, was very impressive for the Confederates. The car was moved within easy range of the Confederate works, and halted at a curve in the track, so that, by moving it a few feet either way, the direction of fire could be changed. Much apprehension was excited in the defenders' works by the huge missiles, and observers reported that one of the shells, on explosion, threw a Confederate field-gun and carriage above the parapet of the works. The range was about thirty-six hundred yards.

Although the first really successful application of rifled cannon to warfare occurred in the Italian campaign of Napoleon III, in 1859, the problem of a projectile that would satisfactorily take the rifling of the gun had not been solved, and up to the outbreak of the Civil War in America the employment of such guns was, on this account, an uncertain undertaking. During the years from 1861 to 1865, there was continual trouble in finding a projectile that would take the rifling successfully without injury to the gun, but developments were such during the war that, at its close, the problem consisted principally in deciding between the various types of projectiles. Both belligerents devoted much time to the solution of these difficulties. Many inventions had temporary vogue, and then gradually were laid aside, so that even experienced ordnance officers could not, at the close of the conflict, tell exactly what the prevailing opinion as to types was at any particular date.

In the Federal service, experience caused the rejection of a number of varieties of rifled projectiles. For the siege of Petersburg there were used those of Parrott, Schenkl, and Hotchkiss. The first was fired by the Parrott guns, and the others by the ordnance guns. Case-shot and shell were used with all the systems, and solid shot in the Parrott and Hotchkiss. The guns were also supplied with canister not designed to take the rifled motion.

Observations made throughout the war by the Federal

REMOVING POWDER FROM CONFEDERATE TORPEDOES

1864

In this photograph is one of the stations established for extracting powder from the torpedoes dredged up by the Federal gunboats in the James. When the activities of the Army of the Potomac centered about the James and the Appomattox in 1864 and 1865, it became the paramount duty of the coöperating navy to render the torpedo-infested streams safe for the passage of transports and supply vessels. The powder in these channels helped to guard Richmond from the Union gunboats. In the foreground sit two old salts discussing ways and means of rendering one of the deadly infernal machines harmless, while all about in this quiet nook lie remains of the dreaded submarine menaces that were constantly being placed in the channel by the Confederates.

artillery officers, supplemented by data collected elsewhere, showed that the penetrations of the elongated rifled projectiles were variable, depending largely on the direction maintained by the axis of the projectile. When the axis remained coincident with the trajectory or nearly so, the penetration exceeded that of the round shot of the same weight by about one-fourth, even at the shortest ranges, though greater charges were used for the guns firing the latter shot. Whenever the axis of the projectile was turned, as the slightest obstruction would cause it to do, the penetration was greatly reduced. There was a noticeable tendency to curve upward after entering an earth embankment. The percussion shells, which were designed to explode on impact, attained usually about three-fourths of their entire penetration before bursting, and time-fuses, prepared to burn a certain number of seconds after leaving the gun, frequently became extinguished on entering the dirt.

With ordinary clay-loam, parapets and magazines required at least a thickness of sixteen feet to resist the 6.4-inch projectile (100-pounder) and twelve feet to resist smaller calibers. In new earth not well settled, those thicknesses had to be increased. Earthen parapets of the proper dimensions could not be injured greatly by rifled shells of any caliber less than 6.4 inches, and not permanently by those if the garrison were active in repairing the damage.

The moral effect of the shells as they went shrieking over the heads of the troops was frequently great. In describing an engagement, a Confederate private soldier said that the reports of cannon were incessant and deafening; that at times it seemed as if a hundred guns would explode simultaneously, and then run off at intervals into splendid file-firing. No language could describe its awful grandeur. Ten thousand muskets fired in volleys mingled in a great roar of a mighty cataract, and it seemed almost as if the earth were being destroyed by violence. The shells howled like demons as they sailed over the heads of the troops lying close to their impro-

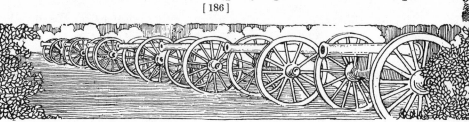

THE DAY AFTER   DANGER EVER
THE EXPLOSION THAT   PRESENT WITH MILL—
REACHED GRANT'S QUARTERS   IONS OF POUNDS OF POWDER

On the 9th of August, 1864, the quiet of noon at City Point was shattered by a deafening roar. Shot and shell were hurled high in the air. Fragments fell around the headquarters of General Grant. Only one member of his staff was wounded, however—Colonel Babcock. "The lieutenant-general himself," wrote Major-General Rufus Ingalls in his official report, "seems proof against the accidents of flood and field." A barge laden with ordnance stores had blown up, killing and wounding some 250 employees and soldiers, throwing down over 600 feet of warehouses, and tearing up 180 feet of wharf. Seventy men were killed and 130 wounded, according to contemporary report. This view was taken the next day.

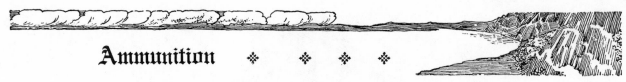

vised shelter, and caused the men to crouch into the smallest possible space and wish for the little red cap of the fairy story, which would make the wearer invisible.

But it was the Hotchkiss shell that made the infernal noise which caused the bravest to duck his head. Though no more destructive than the others, its mere sound worked on the men's nerves, and the moral effect was powerful. The tremendous scream of the missile was caused by a ragged edge of lead which remained on the shell as it left the gun. When the light was favorable, and with the observer standing behind the gun, a peculiar phenomenon was often observed. The projectile seemed to gather the atmosphere as it sped along, just as our globe carries its atmosphere through space, and this apparently accounted for the statement that sometimes men were killed by the wind of a cannon-ball.

Hand-grenades were sometimes used with great effect when the troops were close. The grenade was ignited by the act of throwing, and had the peculiar value that, due to the arrangement of the fuse, the enemy could not utilize the same missile to throw back. It could be thrown about one hundred feet, but as the fragments scattered nearly two hundred yards, the assailant had to seek cover himself to prevent injury from his own grenade.

The variety of rifled projectiles used by the Confederates was very great. This was due to the fact that their ordnance had to be procured from whatever source possible, and the differences in ammunition were, of course, greater than those of the guns. About seventy different kinds of projectiles were in use at one time.

One of these devices was a cupped copper plate, fastened to the shell by a screw, and held firm by radial grooves. It was used principally for the larger calibers, and took the rifling very well. However, one objection to it was that the copper plates often became detached and were liable to cause damage to troops in front of the guns.

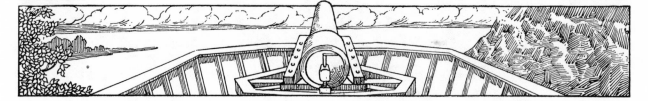

CONFEDERATE TORPEDOES, SHOT AND SHELL COLLECTED IN THE CHARLESTON ARSENAL

Conical-ended torpedoes, as well as several different kinds of shot and shell, make up the heterogeneous collection in the yard of the Charleston Arsenal. The breech and several pieces of the huge Blakely gun used in the defense of the city also appear. In two years, the powder and ordnance works at Augusta turned out among other things 110 field-guns, mostly bronze 12-pounder Napoleons, 174 gun-carriages, 115 caissons, 343 limbers to field artillery, 21 battery wagons, 31 traveling forges, 10,535 powder-boxes, 11,811 boxes for small-arm ammunition, 73,521 horseshoes, 12,630 pounds of nitric acid, 2,227 ounces of fulminate of mercury, 2,455 complete saddles, 2,535 single sets of artillery harness, 2,477 signal rockets, 85,800 rounds of fixed ammunition, 136,642 artillery cartridge-bags, 200,113 time-fuses, 476,207 pounds of artillery projectiles, 4,580,000 buckshot, 4,626,000 lead balls, 1,000,000 percussion caps, and 10,760,000 cartridges for small-arms. General Rains, who was in charge of these works, was able to supply these records for 1863 and 1864 only.

Another device consisted of making the projectiles of wrought iron, with the base cup-shaped like the lead bullet for the small arms. There were also systems resembling the Federal Parrott projectiles, and a type that had a sabot like the Schenkl of the Federal service, except that most of the sabots were made of lead. The Whitworth, Hotchkiss, Armstrong, and Blakely types were very effective.

Lieutenant-Colonel J. W. Mallet, who was in charge of the Confederate States Central Laboratory at Macon, Georgia, devised a shell having a polyhedral cavity, instead of a conical or spherical one, in order to provide for a definite number of pieces when it burst. In explanation of his improvement, Colonel Mallet said that it obviously was not a matter of indifference into what number of pieces the shell might separate on bursting; that if the pieces were very small the destructive effect of each would be insignificant, while, on the other hand, if the pieces were large and few in number, the chance of objects in the neighborhood being hit would be slight. With the size of the fragments known, in order to produce a certain effect, it was clearly desirable that the shell should burst into as many pieces of that size as possible, and the fragments should be projected as equally as possible in all directions about the center of explosion. As ordinary shells then made were either spherical or elongated, it was almost impossible to tell along which lines the case would break, since the interior surface was symmetrical and parallel to the exterior. To effect the desired object, Colonel Mallet proposed to cast shells with the polyhedral cavity, so that there would be certain lines of least resistance, along which the shell would be certain to separate.

Prior to the invention of this device, the efforts to cause the shell to burst into equal parts had been confined to the "shrapnel shell" and the "segment shell." In both of these types the walls of the case were thin, and enclosed a definite number of pieces of metal which would scatter as the shell

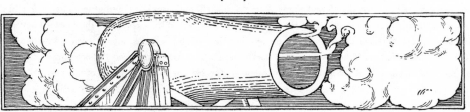

SOLID SHOT, MORTAR SHELLS AND GRAPE IN RICHMOND RUINS

In this photograph piles of solid shot, mortar-shells, and boxes of ammunition are seen lying amidst the ruins of the Tredegar Iron Works.   The foreground is covered with a miscellaneous collection of grape and débris. The shot held together by two, three, four, and in some cases five plates, are grape.   All these missiles, made to be hurled in the faces of the advancing Union armies, now lie on the ground, helter-skelter, at their mercy. They will never cleave the Virginia air, shrieking their messages of death.   The war is over, and every true American, South and North, is proud that it was fought so well, glad to be a citizen of the reunited nation, and more than happy that no more lives are to be sacrificed to the preservation of those principles of brotherhood and unity which make it the greatest Republic in the world and that such a scene as this will never be repeated.

burst. It was a matter of indifference as to how large or how small the pieces of the case became.

In the use of this new form of shell for the 6-, 12-, 24-, and 32-pounders, the cavities were completely filled with powder. Musket or rifle powder always gave the best results with the 6-pounder, and fine-grained cannon powder was suitable for the others.

The Federal artillery paid the Confederate service the compliment of appreciating the improvements in shells, and in 1867, General Henry L. Abbot, of the Corps of Engineers, in a report on siege-ordnance used during the war, stated that there were two improvements in mortar-shells introduced by the Confederates which, in his judgment, should be adopted into the United States service. He did not state who was responsible for the innovations in the Confederate service, but the reference was to the shells perfected by Colonel Mallet and to the providing of certain mortar-shells with ears, to permit greater ease of handling.

Many failures of the Confederate artillery were attributed by their officers to defective ammunition, yet they unanimously pronounced the service of their Ordnance Department, which supplied it, to be the best possible under the circumstances. To illustrate the difficulties under which the department labored, it may be remembered that all the operations had to be organized from the foundation. Waste had to be prevented, and a system of accounting established. The raw troops had no conception of the value of ammunition, and frequently it was lost or damaged through neglect. Although the Confederate armies were never in condition to use ammunition as lavishly as the Federals, the supply never failed in great emergencies, and no disaster has been attributed to its scarcity; and, in fact, whatever scarcity there was must be attributed principally to the inability of the army to carry it, and not to the inability of the Ordnance Department to supply it in sufficient quantities.

[192]

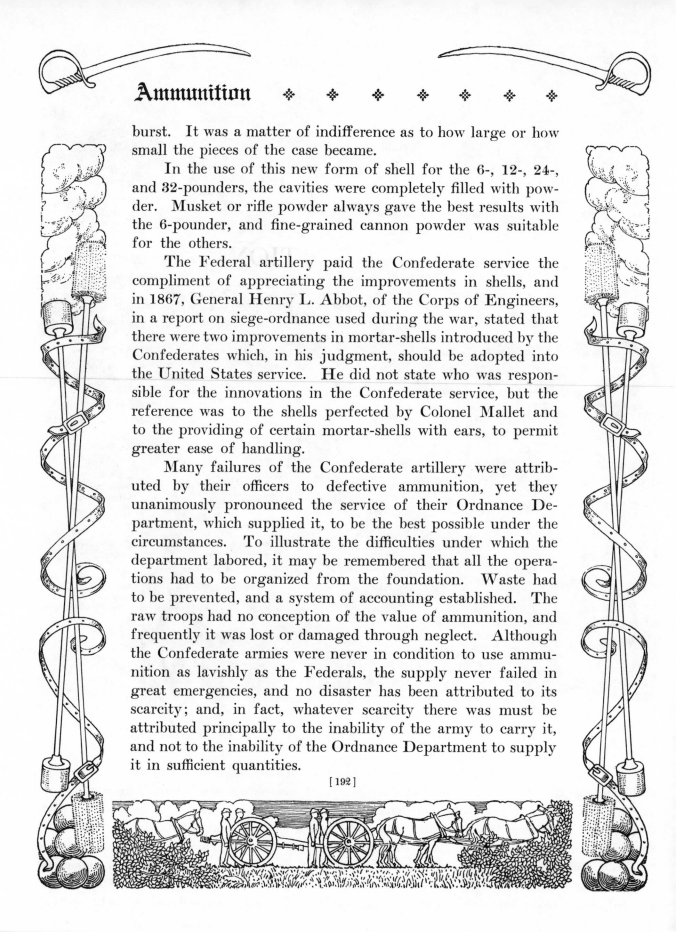

IX

ENTRENCHING
AND
FORTIFICATION

CONFEDERATE ABATIS—COLLECTED AT PETERSBURG, TO BE PLACED IN
POSITION AGAINST GRANT'S ATTACK

ENTRENCHMENTS
AND FORTIFICATIONS

By O. E. Hunt
Captain, United States Army

THE development of the use of earthworks in war between civilized nations has been due to the adoption and increase of power of long-range firearms. The introduction of the breech-loading rifle, of comparatively recent date, has served to give a still greater impetus to the subject of field-works for the protection of the forces engaged, and to-day the spade is second in importance only to the rifle. " Hasty entrenchments," as they are known by soldiers, were first used largely in the American Civil War.

Even at that time, General Sherman expressed his belief that earthworks, and especially field-works, were destined to play a conspicuous part in all future wars, since they enabled a force to hold in check a superior one for a time, and time is a valuable element in all military operations.

At the beginning of the Civil War, the opinion in the North and South was adverse to the use of field-works, for the manual labor required to throw them up was thought to detract from the dignity of a soldier. The opinion prevailed in some quarters that masked batteries were not devices of civilized warfare; and the epithet of " dirt-diggers " was applied to the advocates of entrenchments. Expressions were heard to the effect that the difference ought to be settled by " a fair, stand-up fight, in the open."

" Self-preservation " as a law of nature, and " necessity," as the mother of invention, soon impressed themselves, however, on the officers and men confronting one another in the field—

HOW THE PIONEER PHOTOGRAPHER HELPED TO FORTIFY

The lettering on the wagon curtain, "Photographic Wagon, Engineer Department," explains how the problem of preserving the visual teachings of war was solved for the Union Government. Vast strides in photography were being made by the pioneers Brady, Gardner, and Captain Poe. Diagrams and sketches gave place to actual reflections of the engineering problems which were overcome. Here is the first instance of field-photography for a war department. This photograph reveals the interior of Union Fort Steadman, in front of Petersburg, and its bomb-proof quarters in traverses. On the right is a photographic wagon of the Engineer Corps. The attendant is taking his ease in its shade. This photographic outfit was maintained for the purpose of keeping an official record of matters of professional engineering interest, and good use was made of it. In the West, Captain O. M. Poe was performing a similar service as chief of photography of the United States Engineer Corps. General John Gross Barnard was General Grant's chief of engineers in the East. The accompanying set of photographs of fortifications is largely from these sources.

the first maxim dictating that it was better to dig dirt than to stand up and be shot at, and the second quickly pointed the way to make dirt digging effective. Great necessity and the stern experience of war drove erroneous notions from the heads of the combatants, and before the conflict had progressed far, we find both armies digging trenches without orders, whether in the presence of the enemy or not.

One of the historians of the war has stated that they waited neither for orders, deployment of skirmishers, nor even for formation of lines. The standing rule, adopted by common consent without a dissenting voice, was that they should proceed with this work without waiting for instructions. It mattered not that their lines might soon be moved. A little labor and effort on the soldiers' part at the opportune time often saved a life later.

It was the good common sense of the troops that led them to understand the value of even slight protection. The high intelligence of the individual American soldier made it a simple matter for him to grasp this fundamental truth of his own accord. He did not need to be educated to it by his officers; he knew it by instinct as soon as the enemy began firing at him. Nor was the initiative in the matter of seeking both natural and artificial protection caused by his knowledge of the art of war. Certain features of the art came to him instinctively, and this was one of them.

The Confederates made great use of earthworks, and by their aid were able to hold the Federals, in superior numbers, at half-rifle-shot distance on many hard-fought fields. On many occasions they extemporized protection and dug themselves into rifle-pits, hid their artillery in gun-pits and behind epaulments on the flanks of their infantry lines, and thus made their positions impregnable.

The rapidity with which adequate protection from rifle fire could be obtained by the use of bayonets, tin cups, knives, and other parts of the equipment which the soldier always had

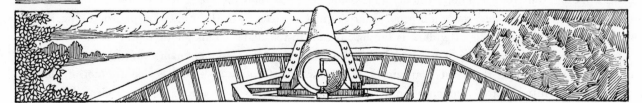

THE ENGINEER PHOTOGRAPHER BEFORE ATLANTA, 1864—A CAPTURED CONFEDERATE FORT

A CLOSER VIEW OF THE ENTANGLEMENTS ON MARIETTA STREET—CHEVAUX-DE-FRISE

with him, early became a surprise to everyone; and it did not take long to discover that a short additional time and a little more work rendered that same pit safe from ordinary direct artillery fire. In loose soil, a few minutes sufficed to throw up a mound of earth a foot high and fifteen inches in thickness, by about two feet in length, for cover against bullets, and this was often topped by a knapsack. It was not believed when the war broke out that a man could save his life by lying behind such a slight cover, but before the campaign on the Peninsula was over, every man of both armies knew it.

The Confederates threw up works on the field of Manassas immediately after their victory. The position was well chosen and the entrenchments were very well constructed. To increase the appearance of strength a number of embrasures were filled with "quaker guns," so-called by the Federals—being simply logs shaped to resemble cannon and placed in position to deceive the foe. These lines were located and the works thrown up, not with the object of assuming the offensive, but to hold the advantage they had gained until it should be decided what further operations should be undertaken. Consequently, their entrenchments were for defensive purposes only, as the quaker guns indicated.

The Federal plan of campaign having been decided on, the information reached the Confederates before the Union army was started for the Peninsula, and Manassas was evacuated immediately. The quaker guns were still in position when the Federals took possession of the Manassas works. When McClellan arrived on the Peninsula, he found that the Confederates were there ahead of him in sufficient force to place works across from Yorktown, utilizing, in a large measure, the trace of the old Revolutionary works of Lord Cornwallis, and strengthening the parapets to fulfil the more modern conditions of warfare. The Yorktown works were built for the same general purposes as the Manassas lines— for defense. And they served the purpose admirably, for

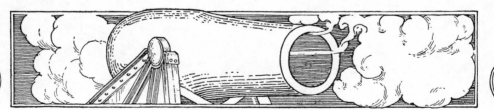

CLOSER STILL TO THE ATLANTA FORT

PICKET FENCES TO STOP SHERMAN'S ATTACK

Picket fences with shaped and molded points, dangerous to the small boy's breeches in times of peace, have been utilized by the Confederates to delay Sherman's men for that fatal instant which loses many lives to a charging line. These seem proportionately as effective as the *chevaux-de-frise*, in the rear—logs pierced by sharpened spokes and the elaborate ditches and embankments, and palisades constructed in the works all about Atlanta. Historians have declared that no clear conception of Sherman's remarkable campaign to Atlanta can be had unless the difficult character of the country and the formidable nature of these artificial defenses are remembered. Practically every foot of the way from Ringgold to Atlanta was entrenched.

Earthworks and Forts ❖ ❖ ❖ ❖ ❖

McClellan's army was delayed a month before the Confederates evacuated.

The preliminary reconnaissances by the Federal engineers persuaded McClellan that a regular siege of Yorktown was necessary, and accordingly strong works were erected opposite those of the Confederates. Emplacements for heavy guns and parapets to protect them were pushed to completion. Regular siege-works, consisting of "parallels" and "approaches," were projected. The Confederates held the position until the last moment, and just as fire was about to be opened on them they abandoned the lines. By that time the works of defense had assumed almost the proportions of a fortress. Enormous labor was required to effect this, and, correspondingly, the labors of the besiegers were great. The low-lying ground of the Peninsula was under water part of the time from the tremendous rains, and the heavy guns of both armies sank into the mud, and it required tremendous exertions to extricate them. Yet, without fighting, the purpose of the Confederates was attained—that of delay; and, while many guns had to be abandoned, the expense was compensated for by the increased preparations of the main Confederate army.

But, notwithstanding the lessons in fortification given both combatants by these operations, the individual soldier did not appreciate, to any great extent, his own responsibility in the matter of entrenchments, since these Yorktown works were on a large scale and used by the entire masses of men of the hostile armies. It was in the campaign to follow that the important instruction in the art was to come.

The progress of the Federals was energetically disputed by inferior numbers in field-works at Williamsburg, which was not so solidly fortified as Yorktown. A large fort with six redoubts barred the road into the town, but, with the flanks not well protected, the position could be turned, and the Union troops did not wait to undertake a siege. At Mechanicsville, Gaines' Mill, Seven Pines, Malvern Hill, and Harrison's

FEDERAL FORTIFICATIONS AT ALLATOONA PASS, GEORGIA

When Sherman's army passed this point—early in June, 1864—entrenching was becoming a fine art with the American armies. From the battle of New Hope Church, on May 25th, almost every advanced line on either side entrenched itself as soon as its position was taken up. Not to be outdone by their Western comrades, the great armies operating in Virginia also got down and "dug dirt." In timber, huge logs were placed in position and covered with earth. Without timber, the parapets were often made as much as fifteen feet thick, to stop artillery fire. Even on the march the Western armies found time to make gabions of wattles with marvelous celerity.

THE TYPICAL HEAD–LOG WITH SKIDS—SHERMAN'S DEFENSE BEFORE ATLANTA

If a shell drove back one of the head-logs in this photograph, it might crush and maim the soldiers in the trenches but for the skids across the trenches. The head-log was placed on top of the earth parapet, with a space left under the log to permit the men to fire.

Landing, the works thrown up by the Federals were increasingly strong, and the private soldier gradually learned his own individual responsibility in preparing the earth-and-log protection.

In the Seven Days' Battles, while they were on the defensive, the Union troops took advantage of all sorts of protection —woods, rail fences, trees, irregularities of the ground, and houses, but made little use of earthworks. There were so many of the other forms of protection and time was so precious that earthworks did not figure much in their calculations.

The last scene of the Peninsula campaign was placed at Malvern Hill, and Harrison's Landing, which was strongly fortified. There was thrown up an improvised fortress where, after several days of victorious pursuit of the Federals, the Confederates were checked.

The system of fortifications in this first campaign paralyzed the offensive movements on both sides, saving first the Confederates and then the Federals probably from total defeat, and proving beyond doubt that entrenchments of even the slightest character gave excellent results in defensive operations, but also that they must be constructed " with a celerity that defied the rapid march of the opposing army and with an ability and aptitude that enabled a defender to transform an entire field of battle into an improvised fortress."

Yet, despite the experiences of this campaign, the lesson was not fixed in the minds of the combatants. The former schools of military teaching still showed their effects. In the campaign between Lee and Pope, in 1862, but little use was made of field-works, and at Antietam Lee fortified only a part of his line, though strictly on the defensive. But Antietam evidently taught the lesson anew, for we find that same Confederate army at Fredericksburg with lines that defied the efforts of the assailants as effectually as permanent fortifications could have done.

The manner of construction of these works of hasty entrenchment usually was this: The men, deployed in a line of

"GUNS"

THE CONFEDERATES

ABANDONED

AT MANASSAS

These are some of the earliest Confederate fortifications. The works were thrown up on the field of Manassas immediately after their victory. The position was well chosen and the entrenchments very well constructed. As seen in the upper photograph, the time was before the soldiers had learned to "dig dirt"; the works are rather thrown up than dug down. A happy combination of the two was later adopted by both the Confederate and Union armies. To increase the appearance of strength in 1861, a number of embrasures were filled with "quaker guns," so called by the Federals on account of the unwarlike nature of the followers of that faith. These were simply logs shaped to resemble cannon and placed in position to deceive the foe. The end projecting from the fortifications was painted black to make the deception more complete. This was a particularly amusing subterfuge on the part of the Confederates, so destitute of cannon. They had captured a few pieces at the first battle of Manassas, but their supply was still woefully inadequate.

A

"QUAKER GUN"

AT CENTREVILLE

skirmishers, would dig, individually, shallow trenches about four or five feet by two, with their longest dimension toward the foe, and throw up the earth in a little mound of a foot or fifteen inches in height, on the side toward the opponent. This would result in a line of such excavations and mounds, each individually constructed and without any communication with its neighbors. Then the neighbors would dig out the ground between them and throw it to the front, thus forming a continuous line of earthern parapet; but, if their antagonists were firing, or danger was near, it was preferable to deepen the trenches and throw up a larger earth protection before joining the individual trenches. In the rear of such hasty works, heavier lines often were constructed by large forces working with spades.

Semi-permanent works were used both in the East and in the West. Island No. 10, Forts Henry and Donelson, and other small works were all of a permanent or semi-permanent character, having more or less of the scientific touch that followed the old school of fortification. But little was known in the West of the art of hasty entrenchments for some time. At Shiloh, the Federal camps were not entrenched, although the foe was known to be somewhere in the vicinity. General Sherman said that the reason for the lack of field-works was that their construction would have made the new men timid. As a matter of fact, the value of them was not realized by anyone, except that it was known, of course, that heavy works were capable of withstanding an attacking body several times the strength of the defending force.

But, after Shiloh, Halleck took command and erected earthworks nearly every foot of the way from Pittsburg Landing to Corinth, Mississippi, a distance of at least twenty miles, and then prepared for a regular siege of the latter place, where his army outnumbered that of Beauregard about two to one. His approach took a month, at the end of which time Beauregard evacuated Corinth without loss.

This cautious advance marked the first use of

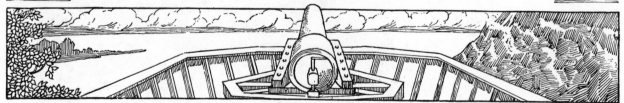

A CONFEDERATE WATER BATTERY THAT DEFENDED VICKSBURG

The natural fortifications around Vicksburg rendered it well-nigh impregnable, and it was made completely so by S. H. Lockett, chief engineer of the defenses under General Pemberton. Only starvation finally reduced the beleaguered force. In two unsuccessful assaults thousands of Federal soldiers were shot down. An instance of the spirit in which Americans fight is related by Lieutenant Roswell Henry

CONFEDERATE WORKS BEHIND VICKSBURG

WHERE GRANT'S ARMY WAS HELD FOR OVER SIX WEEKS

Mason, who led his company of the Seventy-second Illinois Infantry into the city. The soldiers started in with three full days' rations in their haversacks. The gaunt and hungry Confederates lined the road on either side. "Hey, Yank, throw us a hard-tack," they called; or "Hey, Yank, chuck us a piece of bacon." When Mason's company halted in the city not a haversack contained a morsel of food.

entrenchments at every halt. In at least two of the great battles during the preceding period of the war—Bull Run and Shiloh—no entrenchments to speak of had been used. Now, Halleck, going to the extreme in the other direction, lost valuable time constructing trenches for which a little effort at reconnaissance would have told him there was no use. With such good preliminary preparation we should be prepared to see field-fortifications used everywhere more lavishly. And we are not disappointed in finding that both parties to the controversy had now learned their lesson.

At Stone's River, or Murfreesboro, the Federals entrenched a part of their extreme left and the Confederates their right and center before the battle. On the first day, the Federal right was driven back, and during the following night the Confederates entrenched practically all of the remainder of their line. The net result of the battle was a drawn fight, the opponents not daring to attack each other's works seriously. A wholesome respect had grown for hasty entrenchments. The " dirt-diggers " were coming to the front.

The defensive warfare carried on to the end by the Confederates in the West placed them most of the time behind their temporary or semi-permanent works. All the forts along the Mississippi were, necessarily, of the strongest character, assuming the importance of permanent fortifications, armed with heavy guns and manned by small permanent garrisons and, during Grant's and Banks' campaigns, by larger garrisons, pushed in from the field. All of these stronger places had to be taken by the process of regular siege.

When Bragg retired from Murfreesboro, he entrenched several lines between that place and Chattanooga, but Rosecrans, by consummate strategic skill, turned him out of all of them without fighting serious battles. On the battlefield of Chickamauga, the infantry and artillery of Thomas' wing of the Federal army stood " like a rock " behind entrenchments and barricades of earth, fence rails, and logs. Bragg, attacking

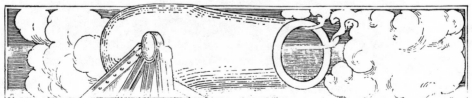

CONSTRUCTING GABIONS FOR GRANT'S ATTACK ON PETERSBURG

The basket-like objects in this photograph are gabions. On the top of one row lie sand-bags. The soldier is seated on three short fascines, and in the background are some long fascines on another row of gabions. A gabion is a cylindrical basket with no bottom, which may be placed in a fortification and filled with earth. Gabions make an exceedingly strong defense, since the dirt remains even if the baskets are smashed. Thousands of gabions were used in the entrenchments of both attacking and defending forces at Petersburg. Fascines consist of small branches or twigs tied by wire or rope or thongs of some tough vine. They vary in length according to whether they are to be used in the construction of works or filling in a ditch. They hold the earth at a steeper slope than the natural slope when the earth is loose. Gabions are also useful for revetments from their perpendicularity; through sand-bags, a foot or two might be added to their height.

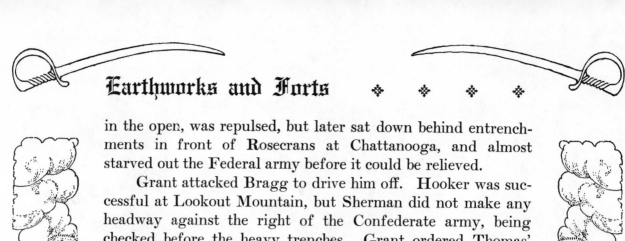

in the open, was repulsed, but later sat down behind entrenchments in front of Rosecrans at Chattanooga, and almost starved out the Federal army before it could be relieved.

Grant attacked Bragg to drive him off. Hooker was successful at Lookout Mountain, but Sherman did not make any headway against the right of the Confederate army, being checked before the heavy trenches. Grant ordered Thomas' men to take the works at the foot of Missionary Ridge and halt. Because of the Federal defeat at Chickamauga, it is reported that Grant feared that the men of Thomas' army could not be trusted to stand under heavy pressure, and he did not want them to go farther than the foot of the ridge. He ordered that they stop there, after driving the Confederates from the trenches. But the lines kept on, higher, higher, and the clouds of battle became larger as they ascended. Seeing the line disobeying orders, Grant turned to Thomas, who was near, and inquired by whose orders the men had gone beyond the foot of the mountain, to which Thomas is said to have replied, "By their own, I think." Grant's rejoinder was: "If they succeed, all right. But if they don't, some one will suffer for this." The works at the top were heavy; but Thomas' troops succeeded, and no one suffered except the gallant men of both sides who fell.

Grant went East, turning over the command of the Western Federal armies to Sherman, who prepared to attack Johnston, entrenched around Dalton, in northern Georgia. Buzzard's Roost formed the strongest portion of Johnston's line, which consisted of heavy fortifications on the heights, in front of which lighter lines had been placed. Sherman felt this position, found it almost impregnable, made a flank movement, and turned Johnston out of his stronghold. In the retaining attack on the works, the Federal troops took a portion of the lower lines of entrenchments, but found the upper works too strong. The turning movement having succeeded, the Union troops withdrew from the front, and Johnston retired to

[208]

THE "SAP" AND THE "COONSKIN" TOWER AT VICKSBURG, 1863

In the center rises "Coonskin" Tower, a lookout and station for sharpshooters.   It was built under the direction of Lieutenant Henry C. Foster of the Twenty-third Indiana Infantry.   In honor of his raccoon-fur cap, the soldiers nicknamed him "Coonskin."   The sap-roller, shown in the illustration below, was used for construction of a sap or trench extending toward the defenders' works in a siege.   A famous sap appears in the upper photograph—that built by Logan's busy men, winding its way toward the strong redan of the veteran Third Louisiana Regiment on the Jackson Road.   First a parallel is opened—that is, a trench is constructed parallel to the besieged entrenchments.   From this are constructed several approaches, or saps, to enable an approach to be made under cover to a position where a second parallel may be.   These are built in a zigzag direction, so that the defender cannot enfilade the trench, except when very close to the opposing works, when it is frequently necessary to approach directly.   Here is where the sap-roller comes into play.   It is rolled at the head of the trench in such a manner as to protect the workmen from their opponents' fire.   It must therefore be thick enough to stop bullets.   To construct a sap-roller in the form shown, two cylindrical baskets of the same length are made, a small one to form the interior wall, and a larger one for the outer wall.

A SAP-ROLLER READY FOR SERVICE

Resaca, and thence to succeeding positions until Atlanta was reached. Direct assaults on entrenchments nearly always failed with heavy loss.

By this time it was thoroughly understood that the function of breastworks, whether of earth, logs, rails, or other material, was to give the advantage to the defense, and consequently everyone recognized that good troops behind such protection could hold off three or four times their number of equally good troops making the assault. This was the proportion depended on, and the calculations of the commanding generals were made accordingly. It was usually considered that troops in the works were inferior to the assailants if they did not succeed in withstanding the attack of several times their own strength.

Naturally, also, the character of the works changed somewhat with increasing experience. With rifles, an entrenched line was almost certain to be able to dispose effectually of an approaching force which had eight hundred yards over which to advance in the open, or over ground partially open. In woods, an abatis, or entanglement, was an effectual aid in stopping the advance before it reached the works, since it delayed the line, and enabled the defenders to get a close-range fire on the assailants.

Beginning with the battle at New Hope Church, on the 25th of May, 1864, almost every advanced line, of either side, entrenched itself as soon as the position was taken up. Whenever an organization was moved, its commander sent out a skirmish line ahead of the new position, for the protection of the men engaged in entrenching; caused an inspection of the ground to be made by competent officers to determine the location of the trenches, and then ordered his men to work. The workers stacked their arms, took tools from the wagons or availed themselves of those carried by the troops, and each small organization—company or battalion—entrenched its own part of the line. In timber, huge logs were placed in position and

"SOFT" WALLS BETTER DEFENSES THAN "HARD"—FORT SUMTER

In 1863, the stone walls of Sumter were soon breached by the guns of the Federal fleet, but behind the breaches rose many feet of gabions filled with earth. These were replaced as fast as the guns of the fleet dislodged the soft earth. General G. T. Beauregard wrote in his official report of February 8, 1863: "The introduction of heavy rifled guns and iron-clad steamers in the attack of masonry forts has greatly changed the condition of the problem applicable to Fort Sumter when it was built, and we must now use the few and imperfect means at our command to increase its defensive features as far as practicable." This beautiful view of Fort Sumter in 1865, clear in every detail, one of Barnard's photographic masterpieces, shows the battered parapets of the fort strengthened again and again by gabions. The humble baskets not only served this purpose, but kept flying pieces of the more solid construction which they reënforced from maiming the garrison. One would hardly imagine that the declivity in the center of the mass of gabions had once been a well-chiseled flight of steps. This kind of fortification deteriorated very rapidly unless constantly repaired. In Sumter the work of repairing was particularly heavy, following one bombardment after another throughout the four years of the war. It was not until February 17, 1865, after Sherman's great march, that the fort was evacuated.

[F—14]

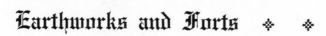

covered with earth. Without timber, the parapets were often made as much as fifteen feet thick, to stop artillery fire. A head log, under which the men could fire, was frequently utilized. When struck by a large projectile, of course a log in that position was liable to be thrown backward and injure a number of men. Various methods were used to prevent its coming back, and one device, to prevent injury to the men in case it did come back, was to place skids under it, perpendicular to the line of the parapet, and extending back across the trench so that it would slide over the heads of the men.

Except for special works, all these lines were constructed by the enlisted men with very little direction from the officers, and foreign officers visiting the troops are quoted as being astonished very often at seeing troops of the line performing what, to them, seemed technical engineering duties which, in their services, would be done by trained officers and men.

The Confederates, on their part, occasionally were able to erect their works beforehand, for, when it was decided to retire, the decision was always arrived at deliberately, and time taken to survey the ground more thoroughly than was possible on the side of the assailants. These works having been erected with more thoroughness than those in the immediate vicinity of the foe, more elaborate preparations frequently were made to defend the works. Devices such as *chevaux-de-frise,* consisting of logs pierced by sharpened spokes, were sometimes resorted to, and palisades were constructed in the ditches of strong works. One historian has remarked that no clear conception of the remarkable campaign to Atlanta can be had unless the difficult character of the country and the formidable nature of these artificial defenses are remembered.

Returning to the armies of the Potomac and of Northern Virginia, we find that, at Chancellorsville, Hooker lost precious time by stopping, after attaining Lee's flank, and entrenching, instead of making an immediate attack; and another entrenched line—this time of value—was taken up after Howard

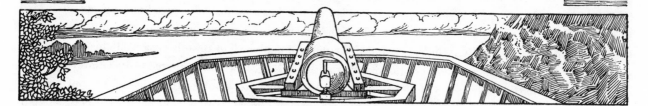

FIGHTING WITH SHARPENED STICKS—PRIMITIVE BUT EFFECTIVE PROTECTION

For its murderous artillery fire every dawn and dusk during the nine months' siege of Petersburg, Union Fort Sedgwick was named by the Confederates "Fort Hell." It was located some three miles south of Fort McGilvery on the southern end of the inner line of Federal entrenchments, east of Petersburg. "Hell" feared invasion in this instance, as the bristling row of slender sharpened sticks planted in the salient witnesses. They were simply light palisades, held by putting poles through holes in a sill, and then fixing the whole in a horizontal position. They look absurdly ineffectual, these sharpened sticks designed to stop the onslaught of an assaulting column, but when another row of them and another and yet another awaited the assailants, their movements were retarded so that they became exposed to fire.

MAJOR–GENERAL D. P. WOODBURY

THE ENGINEER WHO BUILT THE PONTOON BRIDGES AT FREDERICKSBURG

Under the command of regular officers the volunteer engineers soon reached a high point of efficiency. On the Peninsula a brigade, consisting of the Fifteenth and Fiftieth New York Volunteer Engineers, was commanded by Brigadier-General Daniel Phineas Woodbury, a West Point graduate of the class of 1836, and a captain of engineers at the outbreak of the war. In the Peninsula campaign the engineers were active in constructing fortification and building bridges. "Woodbury's Bridge" across the Chickahominy did notable service. Gallant and meritorious conduct in this campaign secured General Woodbury the rank of colonel in the United States Army. At Fredericksburg similar service connected with the work of the pontoon trains brought for him the rank of brigadier-general. He was brevetted major-general August 15, 1864.

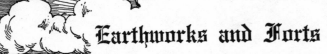

had been driven in by Jackson's flank march and attack. At Gettysburg, the Army of the Potomac made no concerted effort to entrench, but relied largely on natural obstacles.

But a decided change in the record of events commenced when the final campaign started from the Rapidan under Grant, in 1864. We already have noted how, in the Western armies, the art of entrenching had been highly developed. Not to be outdone by their Western comrades, the great armies operating in Virginia now got down and systematically " dug dirt." Each force hugged the ground with bulldog tenacity. The end was coming. Everyone saw that the war must stop, and neither army felt that it was the one that was going to meet defeat.

The great battles of the Wilderness, Spotsylvania, and Cold Harbor, on the way to Petersburg, were but a succession of attacks upon improvised fortresses, defeats for the assaulting troops, flank movements to a new position, new entrenchments, new assaults, new flank movements, and so on continuously. The stronger Northern army never overcame the weaker Southern legions so long as the latter remained in the trenches. The preponderance of numbers enabled the Federal armies to extend ever to the left, reaching out the long left arm to get around the flank of the Confederate positions. This was the final operation in front of Petersburg. To meet the continuously extending left of the Federals, Lee's lines became dangerously thin, and he had to evacuate his works. He was not driven out by the foes assaulting the works themselves until his lines became so thin that they were broken by weight of numbers. Here the principle that already had been demonstrated was again shown to be true—one American in the trench was worth several Americans outside—for all Americans are intrinsically equal.

While these stirring events of the East were occurring, Schofield at Franklin, Tennessee, attacked by Hood, proved again that the increasing faith in hasty field-works was not ill

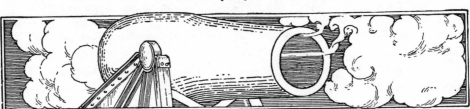

FORT SEDGWICK, WHERE THE GARRISON HELD ITS GROUND

Although the Union Fort Sedgwick before Petersburg was not as elaborate a piece of engineering as the bastioned Forts Wadsworth and Dushane, which commanded the Weldon Railroad, it was nevertheless an exceedingly well-constructed example of field-works. It had to be so in order to stand up against the vindictive fire of Fort Mahone. From this fastness the determined Confederates incessantly tried to render Sedgwick susceptible to assault, thus enabling them to break through and relieve the Army of Northern Virginia from its predicament. The Petersburg campaign was not exactly a formal siege, but the operations of two armies strongly entrenched, either of which at any moment was likely to strike a powerful blow at the other. An abatis, or entanglement, lies to the right in front of the thick earthworks with their revetments of gabions. The Confederates never dared to attempt to carry this huge field fort. They finally selected the far weaker Fort Stedman as the point for their last dash for liberty. Below is another section of the gabion entrenchments of Fort Sedgwick, heightened by sandbags. These fortifications, very effective when occupied and kept in repair, began to fade away under the weather, and the depredations of the residents of the locality in search of fire wood. A few years after the war hardly a vestige of them remained. Rainstorms had done more damage than the tons of Federal shells.

SEDGWICK—GABIONS HEIGHTENED BY SAND–BAGS

placed. With only a light line of works, he was able to withstand the onslaughts of one of the best armies of the Confederacy and withdraw with all his trains and supplies, after inflicting a very large loss on the Southerners and sustaining a comparatively light one himself. Had the conditions been reversed, Hood's army would probably have done as well as Schofield's. They were all Americans of the same intrinsic quality. One force was behind breastworks, slight as they were, and the other was the assaulting party. Again, at Nashville, Thomas and Hood contended on equal terms behind their respective lines, but when Thomas became sufficiently strong he was able to drive Hood out of his works and then defeat him, as he did, on December 16, 1864.

The cost of assaults on entrenchments during all these late campaigns of the war was tremendous. The losses in Grant's army from the time he crossed the Rapidan until he reached the James—a little over a month—were nearly equal to the strength of the entire Confederate army opposing him at the outset. Again, at Petersburg, the attack cost the Union army, in killed and wounded, a number almost equal to the entire force of the foe actually opposed.

As for the profile, showing the strength of parapet of the works employed, there was no fixed rule, and the troops used arbitrary measures. Ten to fifteen feet of fairly solid earth generally sufficed to withstand the heaviest cannon, while a thickness of two feet and a low parapet would protect against rifle fire. If logs or other heavy timber were at hand, the thickness of the parapet could be correspondingly reduced. It was found that even a slight work, if held by strong rifle fire, always prevailed against the advancing force, unless the latter attacked in overwhelming numbers.

Of the stronger fortifications on each side, those exemplifying the best types were the defenses of Washington, of Richmond and Petersburg, of Vicksburg, Port Hudson, and New Orleans, and the works at Mobile, Fort Fisher, Fort Pulaski,

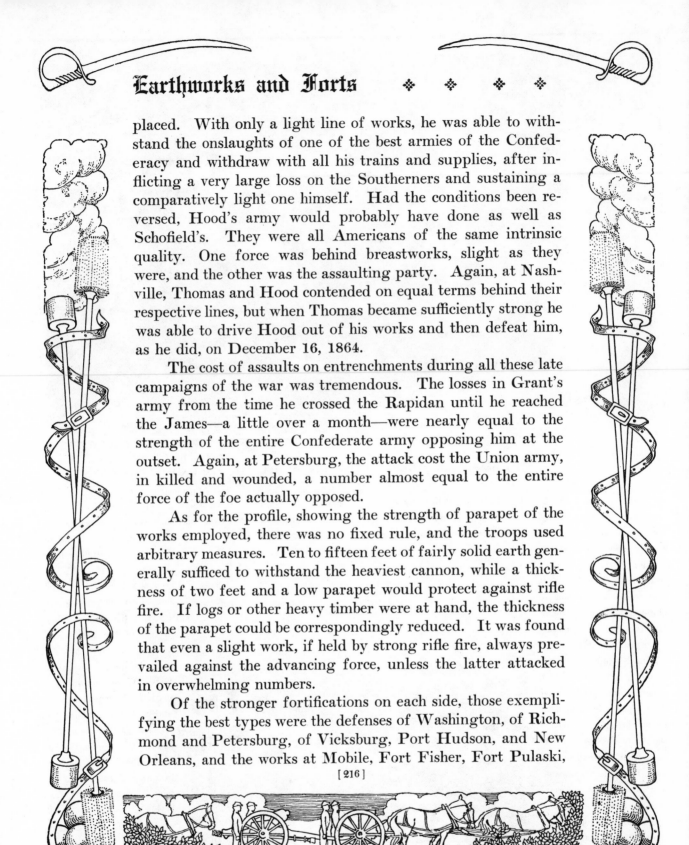

BURROWS OF GRANT'S SOLDIERS BESIEGING PETERSBURG

In these bomb-proof quarters of Fort Sedgwick, and many others, the Federals sought protection. When the artillery fire was not making it "Fort Hell" in fact as well as in name, the bullets of the Confederate sharpshooters were singing over the salient and the breastworks. A cap on a stick thrust above the breastworks was invariably carried away. Many a man taking a hasty glance over the parapet to note the effect of his own fire was killed. Barrels and gabions were used to lengthen the chimneys needed for heating the underground huts. The distance between the main lines, at Fort Sedgwick, was about fifteen hundred feet, and between the pickets only two hundred.

CONFEDERATE ENTRENCHMENTS AS FAR AS THE EYE COULD REACH

The Confederate fortifications in defense of Petersburg were among the most substantial and strongest erected during the war. These tremendous works were built with a degree of skill that has since made them a wonder to military men. They were undermined and blown up by Union troops at the famous "Crater," but were never carried in a front attack till the final assault after which Lee withdrew.

and Charleston. These were all elaborate and designed to sustain sieges and assaults of the heaviest character.

There were also other strong fortifications that fulfilled the requirements of modern warfare absolutely. The improvements in weapons necessitated changing and, in some instances, entirely abandoning the older conceptions of fortresses, and American ingenuity devised works far better adapted to the powerful weapons of destruction that had been secured and developed by both parties to the conflict.

The habit of making themselves secure at all times became so much second nature that it was not confined to the field of battle. This fact excited the very great interest of foreign observers. In the latter part of the war, whenever the troops halted for whatever purpose, if for nothing more than a short rest on the march, they instinctively entrenched themselves. Even before a fire was built, food prepared, or camp necessities provided for, they frequently set to work to provide a shelter from the foe, and the rapidity with which a serviceable cover could be erected was always a cause for remark. These improvised works were abandoned with the same unconcern with which they were erected. It was entirely a matter of course.

Even by casual inspection and comparison of results, the trade-mark of the American soldier will be found on many of the devices used by the other armies of the world to-day for hasty protection in the field, from the inclemencies of the weather, the disagreeable features of camp-life, and from the enemy. In common with the mark left by the individuality of his civilian comrade, the soldier's initiative has so impressed foreign observers that the effect on other nations is evident. In no profession has the American type stood out more preeminent than in that of soldiering, and in no feature of the military art has that same individuality impressed itself more than in the construction of devices for protection against the winged messengers of death loosed so lavishly by the enemy.

X

THE
FEDERAL
ENGINEERS

PONTONIERS ON THE DAY OF BATTLE

ROWING THE PONTOONS INTO PLACE, FOR SEDGWICK TO CROSS TO THE REAR
OF LEE'S ARMY—RAPPAHANNOCK RIVER, MAY 3, 1863

THE
ENGINEERS DIG
A ROAD FOR THE ARMY

The rapid movement of an army and its supplies wins victories and makes possible the execution of effective strategy. Road-making is no less essential to the success of a soldier than the handling of a musket. The upper photograph shows Major Beers of the Fiftieth New York Engineers, on horseback, directing his battalion at road-making on the south bank of the North Anna River May 24, 1864. A wagon-train of the Fifth Corps is crossing the bridge by Jericho Mills, constructed on the previous day by Captain Van Brocklin's company of the Fiftieth New York Engineers. In the lower photograph Major Beers has apparently ridden away, but the soldiers are still hard at work. The wagon-train continues to stream steadily over the bridge.

50TH N. Y.
HARD AT WORK IN
GRANT'S ADVANCE, MAY, 1864

A
CLOSER VIEW
MAKING THE DIRT FLY

Here the reader comes closer to the line of sturdy engineers exerting their muscles in behalf of the Union. The train is over the bridge by this time; only a single wagon is seen, probably attached to the engineer corps. Farther up the river a number of the men not on this detail have gone in swimming. A couple of tents are visible on the bank near the end of the bridge. The busy diggers do not even glance at the men floating on the river below. They are making a road where an army has to pass. Many new ways had to be constructed to enable the supply trains to reach their various commands. South of the river Sheridan's cavalry was operating. There were continuous engagements on the line of the North Anna River from May 22d to 26th, and at any moment the Confederates might appear from the woods and open fire on the engineers.

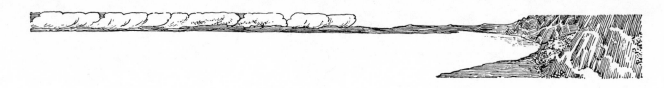

ENGINEER CORPS OF THE FEDERAL ARMY

By O. E. Hunt
Captain, United States Army

IN modern military operations, no more striking examples of the importance of engineer troops and their work can be found than in the American Civil War. For much of the country over which this great struggle was waged, proper maps were wanting, and frequently roads and bridges had to be built before military movements could be executed. Rivers had to be bridged by pontoons and semi-permanent structures; entrenchments and fortifications had to be constructed when camp was made or a definite position taken for defense or siege, and finally, the men doing this had always to consider the laying-aside of axe and spade, and, shouldering the musket, take their place on the firing-line, where they gave an account of themselves second to none of the combatant organizations. Such conditions of warfare were in striking contrast to those under which the great wars of Europe had been fought, for in the campaigns of Frederick, of Napoleon, and of Moltke, practically every inch of the territory was known and mapped. Military operations took place where well-built roads made travel easy; where permanent forts and walled cities were found, and fighting in swamps or on mountaintops was unknown. In short, with the formal military science of the day, the American engineers so combined characteristic ingenuity and the lessons of civil life that the progress and success of the battling ranks were made possible under conditions never before encountered in a great war.

The inception of the present Corps of Engineers in the

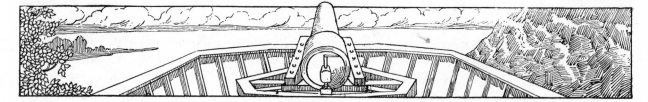

WHEN THE BRIDGE WAS FINISHED AT FRANKLIN'S CROSSING
APRIL 29, 1863

Hopeful and proud these pontoniers of Hooker's engineer battalion stand upon their just-completed bridge —rushed across in one hour and ten minutes. The bridge "train," wagons and boats, had been masked about a mile from the river in dense woods. Then the boats were carried to the river at night and were actually launched before the Confederates were aware of the enterprise. Troops were ferried across in the face of musketry fire from the opposite bank, and the Confederates were driven off. Captain A. J. Russell, who took this photograph, followed close upon this action. In photographs of Franklin's Crossing taken subsequently, the trees have been chopped down, but here the earth, freshly upturned to make an approach to the bridge, and the little pup-tents just going up across the river, both indicate that the soldiers have just arrived. They were not aware that Jackson was to circle Hooker's right in the woods, take him in reverse and cut him off from United States Ford—and that he was to be huddled into a corner in the Wilderness, hurrying messages to Sedgwick's corps to come to his relief. This bridge, three hundred and ninety feet long, was moved bodily to Fredericksburg and there placed in position on the following Sunday during the battle of Fredericksburg Heights, where Sedgwick finally stormed the position that four months before had cost Burnside nearly 13,000 men. This was one of the most successful exploits of the engineer corps during the entire war.

United States army was in 1802. By the act of Congress, of the 16th of March of that year, it was established to consist of one engineer, with the rank of major; two assistant engineers, with the rank of captain; two assistant engineers, with the rank of first lieutenant; two assistant engineers, with the rank of second lieutenant, and ten cadets. The same act authorized the President to make promotions on account of merit whenever he deemed fit, so that the corps, as finally constituted, should not exceed one colonel, one lieutenant-colonel, two majors, four captains, four first lieutenants, and four second lieutenants. The act also provided that the corps, thus constituted, should form a military academy at West Point.

The charge and superintendency of the Military Academy remained in the hands of the Corps of Engineers until July 13, 1866, when, by act of Congress of that date, control passed to the War Department at Washington, and the direct management of the academy to such officers as might be detailed by the President from any of the branches of the service. The Corps of Engineers was thus responsible for the instruction of the officers whose services were invaluable to both the Federal and Confederate armies during the memorable four years of the Civil War.

When the war between the North and South began, there were two organizations of engineers, the Corps of Engineers and the Corps of Topographical Engineers. They were merged in 1863, and thenceforth existed as one organization.

By the act of Congress of August 3, 1861, the Corps of Engineers was reorganized to consist of one colonel, two lieutenant-colonels, four majors, twelve captains, fifteen first lieutenants, fifteen second lieutenants, forty sergeants, forty corporals, eight musicians, two hundred and fifty-six artificers, and two hundred and fifty-six privates—a total of forty-nine commissioned officers and six hundred enlisted men. At the same time the Topographical Engineers were constituted with a total of forty-two commissioned officers. At the end of the

AMATEURS OF '61—UNITED STATES ENGINEERS

This photograph exhibits some unformed engineers the first year of war, with all their experience before them. They had built no bridges at that time, and were not inured to turning from their work to grasp a musket or tranquilly to continue their labor while the dead and wounded from the Confederate sharpshooters' bullets fell thick about them. The uniforms and accouterments are new.

PROFESSIONALS OF '64—GROUP OF COMPANY B, UNITED STATES ENGINEERS

These veterans of Company B as they sit in their camp outside of Petersburg are no longer amateurs, but professionals. Their close-set mouths and steady eyes tell the story of Yorktown, Fredericksburg, along the Potomac and the James; of mighty siege works around Petersburg. They are no longer spick and span as in 1861, but they look much more efficient in their army shirts and loose blouses.

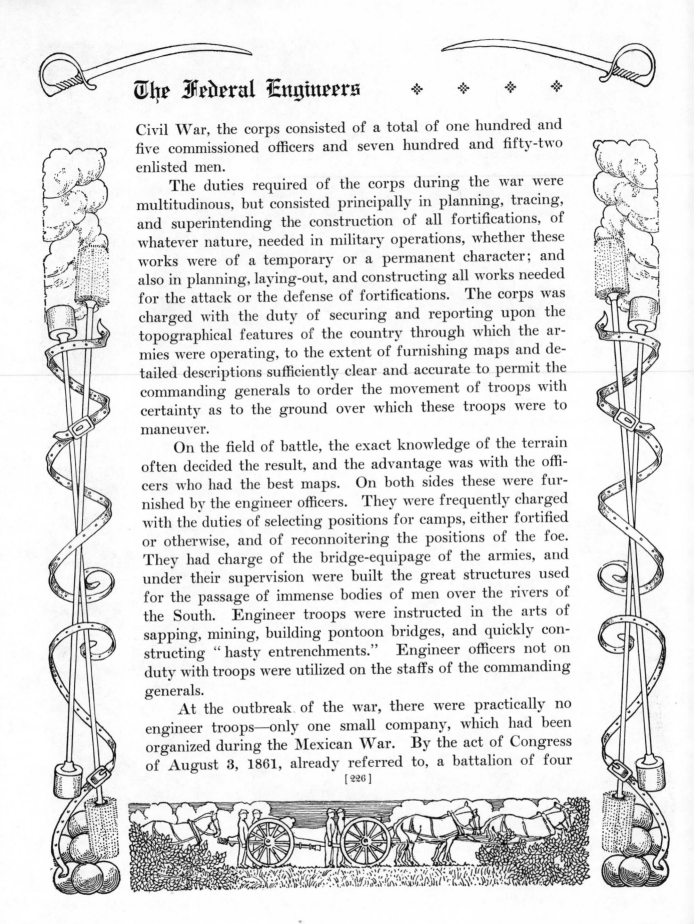

The Federal Engineers

Civil War, the corps consisted of a total of one hundred and five commissioned officers and seven hundred and fifty-two enlisted men.

The duties required of the corps during the war were multitudinous, but consisted principally in planning, tracing, and superintending the construction of all fortifications, of whatever nature, needed in military operations, whether these works were of a temporary or a permanent character; and also in planning, laying-out, and constructing all works needed for the attack or the defense of fortifications. The corps was charged with the duty of securing and reporting upon the topographical features of the country through which the armies were operating, to the extent of furnishing maps and detailed descriptions sufficiently clear and accurate to permit the commanding generals to order the movement of troops with certainty as to the ground over which these troops were to maneuver.

On the field of battle, the exact knowledge of the terrain often decided the result, and the advantage was with the officers who had the best maps. On both sides these were furnished by the engineer officers. They were frequently charged with the duties of selecting positions for camps, either fortified or otherwise, and of reconnoitering the positions of the foe. They had charge of the bridge-equipage of the armies, and under their supervision were built the great structures used for the passage of immense bodies of men over the rivers of the South. Engineer troops were instructed in the arts of sapping, mining, building pontoon bridges, and quickly constructing "hasty entrenchments." Engineer officers not on duty with troops were utilized on the staffs of the commanding generals.

At the outbreak of the war, there were practically no engineer troops—only one small company, which had been organized during the Mexican War. By the act of Congress of August 3, 1861, already referred to, a battalion of four

BLOCKHOUSE BUILT FOR THE DEFENSE OF THE ORANGE & ALEXANDRIA RAILROAD

This blockhouse was near Hunting Creek, close to the Orange & Alexandria Railroad, and covering the bridge over the creek on the Telegraph Road. The walls were built of large logs from sixteen to eighteen inches in diameter. Loop-holes for musketry were cut through the walls, just above the earthern bank, and were "splayed," or widened, toward the inside to permit a greater field of fire. Embrasures for 12-pound howitzers were cut on every face. Two such guns were placed in each blockhouse of this type. Each was provided with a magazine below the floors, arranged for a garrison of sixty men. The lower cut shows a square blockhouse near the Virginia end of Aqueduct Bridge. This structure had two stories, with the upper projecting over the lower, and loop-holes in the floor of the upper story to permit the defenders to fire down on the heads of assailants near the walls. The entrance was through the door in the upper story, to which access was gained over the drawbridge from the top of the trestle. These blockhouses had not much strength, and were useful chiefly for moral effect, although, in case of necessity, a stubborn resistance could have been put up by defenders.

BLOCKHOUSE NEAR AQUEDUCT BRIDGE, ARLINGTON HEIGHTS, VIRGINIA

companies was provided for, and was assigned to the Army of the Potomac. It was utilized in constructing the defenses of the city of Washington in the winter of 1861–62, and during that time received instruction in the duties which it afterward performed so well in the field.

On February 24, 1862, the battalion was sent to Harper's Ferry, Virginia. There, under the greatest of difficulties, it constructed a pontoon bridge across the Potomac. The river was a raging torrent, the water being fifteen feet above the normal level, and filled with huge cakes of drifting ice and quantities of débris. It was with the utmost exertions that the pontoons could be pulled into position, and, once placed, they had to be secured with ships' anchors and chain-cables. But the structure was completed in about eight hours, and General Banks' corps, with all its trains and artillery, crossed safely and without delay. For a time the battalion was engaged in keeping the bridge in position and in good repair. General McClellan, himself an engineer of renown, stated in a letter to Secretary of War Stanton that it was one of the most difficult operations of the kind ever performed.

Immediately after returning to Washington from Harper's Ferry, the engineer troops, with their bridge-equipage, were sent to Fort Monroe, in Virginia, and were moved thence, on April 4th, to a camp near Yorktown, in preparation for the Peninsula campaign. In front of Yorktown the battalion was engaged in constructing trenches and lines of communication, and in superintending and instructing details of soldiers who were unfamiliar with methods of modern warfare. At this period of the war (1862), the troops of the infantry and the cavalry had received no training in the construction of field-fortifications. Consequently, the duty fell heavily on this battalion of men who had received such instruction.

Orders to construct a bridge across the Chickahominy River were received late on the afternoon of the 31st of May. The river was rising rapidly, and the night was extremely dark.

THE MEN WHO MADE MÁPS—TOPOGRAPHICAL ENGINEERS BEFORE YORKTOWN

This photograph of May, 1862, affords the last chance to see the Topographical Engineers at work as a distinct organization. At the time this view was taken they still existed as a separate branch, their duties were the compilation of maps and other topographical data for the use of the army; but by act of March 3, 1863, the Corps of Topographical Engineers was abolished and merged into the Corps of Engineers. Time and again on the field of battle the exact knowledge of locality decided the result. Great advantage lay with the officers who had the most reliable and detailed maps. None such existed of the theater of war in Virginia, and on this corps fell the duty of providing all topographical data necessary for the Army of the Potomac. The officers were all highly trained in engineering work, especially in the surveys necessary for their maps, and in their preparation. In this photograph is a surveyor's level, and on the table a map in process of preparation. The enlisted men in this corps were of very high caliber and their work was of inestimable value.

Consequently, the work had to be postponed until daylight, but communication was opened with the opposite bank by 8:15 A.M. Soon another span was built, and the troops were engaged in road-making in the vicinity of the two river-crossings, to keep open the passages across the low, swampy lands through which the river runs. A third structure, of combined cribwork and trestle, was then constructed, some distance below the two pontoon bridges. Of this last passageway, General Barnard, chief engineer of the Army of the Potomac, remarked that it was an excellent structure, capable of bearing all arms and affording direct communication, in place of that by the inconvenient roads across the pontoon bridges.

At Mechanicsville and Gaines' Mill, the engineer troops did valiant service in the construction of trenches and other field-works. By this time the other troops were gaining the necessary experience, and toward the end of the Peninsula campaign the hastily constructed entrenchments of the entire army were models of completeness and speed in building. Road-work, in this desolate region, was of the most fatiguing kind, but was well and thoroughly done. The few men available from the engineer battalion aided as the instructors of the other troops engaged, and, by the time the movement began toward Malvern Hill, nearly all the troops of the Army of the Potomac had become accomplished in the arts of road-making, bridge-building, and entrenching. At Malvern Hill, the engineer battalion was posted as infantry, after preparing the front of the line by "slashing" or felling trees, to impede the advance of the Confederates and to afford an open field of fire to the defending troops.

After leaving Harrison's Landing on the withdrawal from the Peninsula, the battalion was sent to Fort Monroe to replenish its matériel, and thence to the mouth of the Chicka-hominy, where, in a short time, a fine pontoon bridge was constructed for the passage of McClellan's entire army.

This bridge was 1980 feet long, and for the most part was

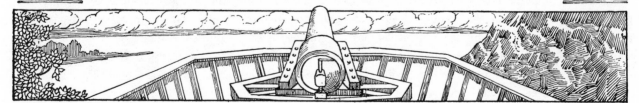

THE CHIEF
ENGINEER OF
GENERAL
GRANT

THE
FORTIFIER
OF
NEW YORK

MAJOR–GENERAL JOHN GROSS BARNARD

ENGINEERS, EAST AND WEST

When the war broke out, General John Gross Barnard had just published "Dangers and Defences of New York" (1859) and "Notes on Sea-Coast Defence" (1861). He was immediately summoned to Washington as chief engineer in charge of constructing the defenses. Later he became chief engineer of the Army of the Potomac with the rank of brigadier-general and chief engineer of General Grant. General Barnard had graduated from the Military Academy at West Point in the class of 1833, fought

BRIGADIER-GENERAL O. M. POE

through the Mexican War, where he fortified Tampico, and was for four years in charge of the defenses of New York. At the close of the war he was brevetted major-general. General O. M. Poe did for Sherman in the West what General Barnard did for Grant in the East. He labored constantly in the construction of defenses for the numerous bridges along the line of railroad, fortified many strategic points, made surveys and issued maps, and secured an invaluable photographic record of the engineering in Sherman's campaigns. Many examples are reproduced in this History.

 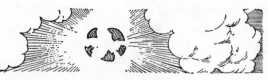

built by successive pontoons—placing the boats in the bridge, one at a time. A portion was built by rafts—i. e., by building a long section separately and placing it in position when complete. The floor was covered with straw to prevent wear. Competent authorities characterized this structure as one of the most extensive known to military history.

On August 18th, after the army had crossed the river, dismantling was begun, the parts being placed in the pontoons, and, within five hours after the work was commenced, rafts of pontoons had been made up, and the whole was on the way to Hampton, near Aquia Creek, on the Potomac.

These troops rendered invaluable service at the battle of Antietam. The night before the conflict they made three of the fords of Antietam Creek possible for artillery, by cutting down the banks and paving the bottom, where it was soft, with large stones. After the battle, by request of its officers, the battalion was assigned to duty as infantry, and it supported one of the batteries in the advance, when the Federals moved away from the Antietam, several weeks later.

On December 11th, a bridge was thrown across the Rappahannock, under fire, at a point known as Franklin's Crossing. Troops embarked in pontoons and were ferried across. Then they stormed the Confederate rifle-pits on the river bank and held them until the passageway was completed. After the battle of Fredericksburg the pontoons were removed.

The following winter, in 1863, a reorganization took place, and the Corps of Topographical Engineers was merged into the Corps of Engineers.

During the Chancellorsville campaign, April and May, 1863, the battalion again constructed a bridge across the Rappahannock at Franklin's Crossing. The bridge train was massed about a mile from the river, in dense woods. At night the boats were carried by infantrymen to the river, without the Confederates being aware of the movement until the boats were actually in the water. Troops were ferried across in the

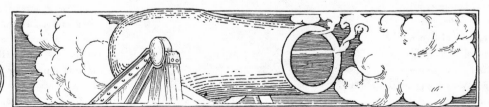

A FEW WEEKS BEFORE THE WILDERNESS—THE FIFTIETH NEW YORK ENGINEERS IN CAMP

The tents in this winter camp at Rappahannock Station, March, 1864, are substantial and roomy wooden huts roofed with tent canvas. To the left is the park of the train. The pontoon-boats are ready on their wagons. All the bridge material awaits transportation.

TWO MONTHS LATER IN 1864

THE ENGINEER CORPS AT WORK

Lee's army, in retiring across the North Anna River before Grant's army in May, 1864, destroyed the permanent bridge at this point. By the summer of 1864 half an hour sufficed for the experienced engineers to lay a bridge like this, after the arrival of the bridge train.

face of musketry fire from the opposite bank. After the Southerners had been driven away, the bridge, three hundred and ninety feet long, was built in one hour and ten minutes. Another was immediately laid, and during the battle of Fredericksburg Heights these two were moved bodily to Fredericksburg and there placed in position. On May 4th, the matériel was hastily removed to the north bank, and the last plank was scarcely up when a force of Confederates appeared on the opposite shore.

Between Chancellorsville and Gettysburg, the engineers were engaged in building roads and bridges in the lines of the Federal army, and the individual officers, not on duty with the troops, were employed in reconnaissances, map-making, and on duty as staff-officers.

Through Gettysburg, back to Virginia soil, and on toward Richmond, the weary army again took its way, and throughout all the attendant hardships the faithful engineers worked for the welfare and efficiency of the other troops. There were numerous occasions during which they had to submit to fire from the opposing army without any opportunity to reply. Their duties were too important to permit them to suspend operations for so trivial an annoyance as being shot at.

The appointment of General Grant to the command of all the armies of the United States in the field, marked a turning-point for the troops of the Army of the Potomac, especially affecting the Engineer Corps. On March 10, 1864, he visited that army, the headquarters of which were near Brandy Station, in Virginia, and announced his intention of remaining with it in future campaigns, leaving General Meade in direct command, and transmitting all orders through him. The army was then lying on the north bank of the Rapidan.

Accurate maps and topographical information of the country between the Rapidan and Richmond were much needed. Reconnaissances had been made as far as the fords of the Rapidan, and that part of the country was well known,

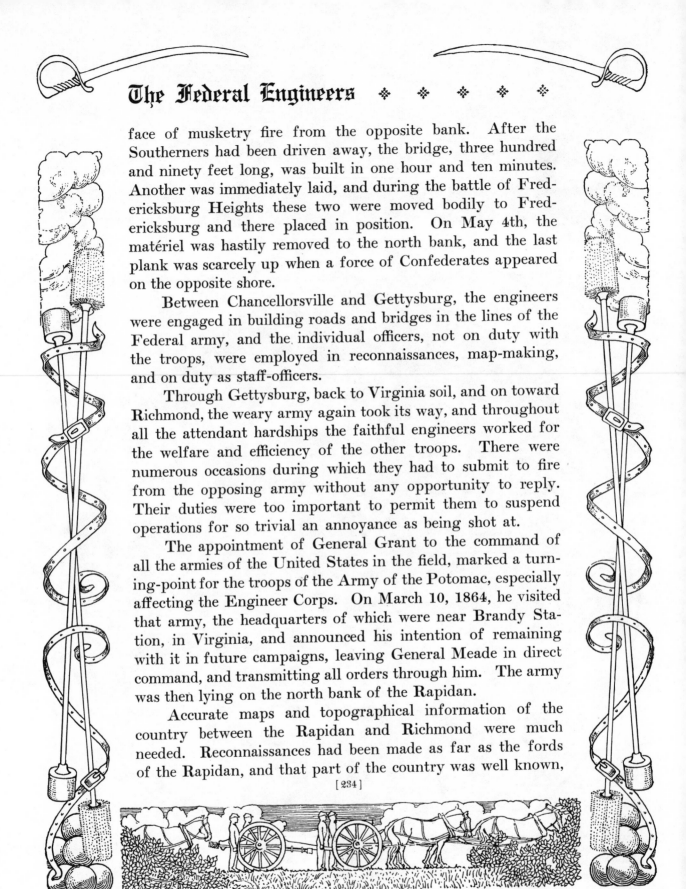

A CANVAS PONTOON BOAT ASSEMBLED READY FOR BUSINESS—MARCH, 1864

When dismantled, the canvas pontoon boats occupied a surprisingly small space. Thus the capacity of a train for bridge material of this kind was very much greater than for that of the wooden pontoons. The latter, however, gave better and more lasting service. The canvas became water-tight if well soaked. These pontoon boats were "knocked down" to be transported; the canvas was folded into a compact bundle and stowed in one of the wagons of the train. The parts of each boat were always kept together, so that they could be assembled at any time. The canvas, all in one piece, was laid out smooth on

CANVAS PONTOON BRIDGE, NORTH ANNA RIVER

the ground, the bottom pieces of the frame put in place, the tenons of the uprights and the braces inserted in their corresponding mortises, the gunwales together with the end-pieces placed on the top, and the canvas then brought up over the sides and lashed tightly over the gunwales, by ropes eye-spliced into the eyes of the sides. The inside end-pieces were then carried around the bow and stern and lashed, and the outer pieces brought up over the ends and lashed in the same manner as the sides. The boat was then allowed to soak in the water for a time. Each boat was twenty-one feet long, five feet wide, and two and a half feet deep.

THE BRIDGE FROM UPSTREAM, JERICHO MILLS

BENHAM'S WHARF AT BELLE PLAIN

ONE MONTH BEFORE HIS FAMOUS BRIDGE ACROSS THE JAMES

"Belle Plain, Upper Wharf, erected by Engineer Corps, General Benham, Chief, May 15, 1864." So reads the inscription made by the photographer on his negative. The few words recall important events. At this time Grant was in the midst of his unsuccessful attempt to circumvent Lee and the Army of Northern Virginia at Spotsylvania. The work shown in this photograph was but child's play compared with the undertaking just one month later, when Grant finally decided to cross the James. One hour before noon on June 15th, General Benham received orders to prepare a pontoon-bridge across the James River for the passage of the entire army. In anticipation of this order, pontoons had been sent from Fort Monroe, and the work was started under Major Duane. General Benham reported to General Meade at the position selected, and was directed to proceed at once with the construction. General Meade smiled at the enthusiasm of Benham when he remarked that he would not sleep till the bridge was finished. About five and a half hours after Benham's arrival, a telegram was received from General Meade inquiring about the progress of the work. The indefatigable engineer was able to reply that the last bolt was in position, and that the troops could begin to move when they wished.

and the movements of the army between that river and Mine Run in Virginia, in November and December, 1863, had furnished considerable information concerning that region. The latter experience had proved that the existing maps of the country to be traversed were valueless for the purposes of marching and fighting an army. The country was of the worst topographical nature possible, and, although in one of the oldest States of the Union, there were but few reliable maps. Consequently, this information had to be obtained in advance of the army.

A party composed of regular and volunteer officers and soldiers, under Colonel N. Michler, of the Engineer Corps, was directed to undertake this work. Their labors commenced after crossing the Rapidan. Every road within the lines of the army had to be surveyed and mapped, and the work extended as far as possible to the front and the flanks. The maps were immediately reproduced on the field and distributed as far as time would permit. Revised editions of the maps were published as often as new information was collected. In this way, several editions of eleven maps were arranged and issued, comprising surveys covering an area of seven hundred and thirty square miles. These were also corrected by instruments carried by the supply train and by maps captured from the Confederates.

Before the army started from its winter quarters on the north of the Rapidan, in the spring of 1864, for the last great campaign, there had been twelve hundred maps made and issued. After the start, and before the end of the siege of Petersburg, about sixteen hundred were issued from new surveys.

In addition to the duties of surveying the country and making and distributing maps, the officers of the corps were charged with the work of selecting positions and directing their fortification. On the morning of the 3d of June, a gallant assault by the whole Union army was directed against

PONTOON-BRIDGE WHERE GRANT CROSSED THE JAMES IN JUNE, 1864

Strips of water a few hundred feet wide often nullify the plans for entire armies. This page of pontoon-bridges gives some idea of the inestimable services of the Engineer Corps. In the upper photograph is one of the pontoon-bridges across the James, at Powhatan Point, near Harrison's Landing, which was used by part of General Grant's army in the march from Cold Harbor to Petersburg. Below to the left is shown a pontoon-bridge over the James with a movable draw, to let vessels pass through. On the right is the pontoon-bridge at Broadway Landing on the Appomattox, over which General Smith's corps moved to make the first attack on Petersburg.

PONTOON-BRIDGE WITH AN OPEN DRAW   PONTOON-BRIDGE ACROSS THE APPOMATTOX

the Confederate entrenchments at Cold Harbor. But the Federals were baffled in their attempts to drive the Confederates across the Chickahominy. Colonel Michler, with his officers, was directed to assist Major Duane, chief engineer of the Army of the Potomac, in making a reconnaissance of the Confederate positions to ascertain their strength. Never were two lines of battle more closely arrayed. At places they were separated by no more than forty to one hundred yards, the men hugging the ground closely, and each army silently awaiting the determined attack of the other. The mettle of each had been felt and keenly appreciated by its opponent.

Colonel Michler and Major Duane made a careful examination of the location of the two lines, and reported to General Grant and General Meade the impracticability of storming the Confederate position, especially in front of the Second and Eighteenth corps, there being no suitable place in the rear for the massing of troops for an attack. The army was then directed to entrench on lines to be selected by the engineer officers, and until the 9th of June it lay confronting the Confederates.

On that date, Michler and Duane were ordered to select a line in rear of that occupied by the army, to be held temporarily by two divisions, which would enable the army to retire and move again by the flank, under cover. The lines were chosen by the engineers. Entrenchments were planned, and the troops began fortifying. At the same time, several of the engineer officers continued the reconnaissance to determine the best route for the contemplated movement.

On the 13th of June, by direction of the commanding general, engineer detachments proceeded in advance of the army to the James River, to reconnoiter the ground along its banks for two purposes—first, to enable the army to cross to the south side, and second, to fight a battle, if necessary, to protect the crossing. Lines covering the point of crossing were selected, entrenched, and held. Colonel Michler was

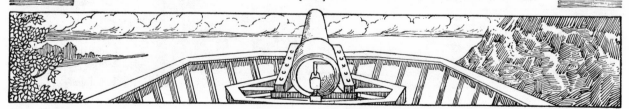

SOLDIERS BY THE UPPER PONTOON BRIDGE AT DEEP BOTTOM—JAMES RIVER, 1864

To construct a pontoon bridge the first boat launched was rowed up-stream a short distance. The anchor was let go. Its rope was then paid out sufficiently to drop the boat down into position. A second anchor was dropped a short distance down-stream, if the current proved irregular. The second boat was placed in position by the same process. Then the sills of the bridge, called "balk," could be placed across by floating the second boat alongside the first, placing the ends of the balk, usually five in number, across the gunwale, and then shoving the boat into position by pushing on the inner ends of the balk. These ends had heavy cleats so that they could be engaged over the further gunwale of each boat. The

THE GROUP SHIFTS—THE SENTRY RETURNS

third boat was then placed in position by repeating the process. Then the "chess" layers commenced. The "chess" were the boards forming the flooring of the bridge. After the floor was laid the side rails, visible on the top of the flooring, were laid, and lashed to the balk through slits which were left between the boards for that purpose. This stiffened the whole structure and held the floor in place. Usually an up-stream anchor was necessary on every boat, and a down-stream anchor on every second or third. The floor of the bridge was usually covered with earth or straw to deaden the sound and preserve the chess. In these two photographs the engineers are just completing a bridge across the James.

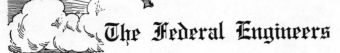 

then directed to locate a line on the south side where the Second Corps, after crossing, could entrench and protect the remainder of the army during the dangerous movement.

One hour before noon, on June 15th, General H. W. Benham, of the Engineer Corps, was ordered by General Grant to prepare a pontoon bridge across the James River for the passage of the army. In anticipation of this order, pontoons had been sent from Fort Monroe, and work was started under direction of Major Duane. General Benham was at Fort Monroe when he received the order, but arrived at the site of the bridge, just above Fort Powhatan, about five o'clock in the afternoon. The work was accomplished by four hundred and fifty men under the immediate command of Captain G. H. Mendell, of the regular service, who had for this purpose a body of regulars and volunteers under his charge.

General Benham reported to General Meade at the position selected, and was directed to proceed at once with the construction. General Meade smiled at the enthusiasm of Benham when he remarked that he would not sleep until the bridge was finished. The regulars were placed at the east end and the volunteers at the west end, and work was commenced on several parts of the bridge simultaneously—by the method known to the engineers as that of " simultaneous bays." About five and a half hours after Benham's arrival, a telegram was received from General Meade asking the progress on the bridge, and the engineer was able to reply that the last bolt was in position, that a gap had been left, according to orders, but the bay necessary to connect the span was ready, and that in fifteen minutes from the time the order was given the communication would be complete from shore to shore, a distance of twenty-two hundred feet.

The gap was closed, but the bridge was not required until six o'clock in the morning of the next day. At that time the regulars were relieved, and the bridge continued under the charge of the volunteers until it was dismantled, three days

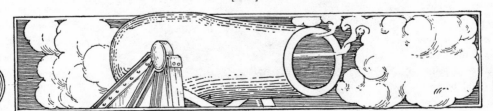

THE DUTCH GAP CANAL

NOVEMBER, '64—DIGGING

APRIL, '65—COMPLETION

After General Beauregard had repulsed the attempt of General Butler to move along the south bank of the James on Richmond, and had "bottled up" Butler at Bermuda Hundred, the Federal commander cast about for other means to accomplish his object. The opposing lines of entrenchments touched the river at Trent's Reach, a broad and shallow portion of the James completely commanded by Confederate batteries. Moreover, General Butler himself had built a line of obstructions across it after his retreat from Drewry's Bluff, much against the advice of the naval men in the river. The army seemed more afraid of the Confederate flotilla than were the men who would have to fight it on water. Butler had been fearful, however, that he would be cut off from his base of supplies at City Point, so he ordered the vessels to be sunk in the channel and made the formidable

obstructions a mile south of the Bluff, where the Confederates soon built Battery Dantzler. The river, however, was so crooked that two miles below Trent's Reach at Dutch Gap, only 174 yards separated the lower river from the upper. If the Federals could cut through this neck, they could avoid the Confederate works and move on up the river by boat as far as the works at Chaffin's Bluff and Drewry's Bluff. Captain Peter S. Michie, of the United States Engineers, later a brigadier-general, was detailed to dig a canal through at Dutch Gap. This would cut off four and a half miles of river. The excavation was forty-three yards wide at the top, twenty-seven at the water level, and thirteen and five tenths yards wide at a depth of fifteen feet below water-level. It was ninety-three feet deep at the northwest end and thirty-six feet deep at the southeast end. The total excavation was nearly 67,000 cubic yards. The greater portion of the digging was done by colored troops who showed the utmost bravery under the constant fire of the Confederate batteries on the river.

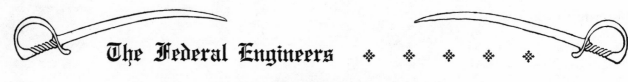

later. The repairs and the adjustments required during the continuous use of the bridge were attended to by the volunteers.

Beginning at six o'clock in the morning of June 16th, a continuous column of wagons (nearly six thousand), nearly all the artillery, cavalry, and infantry present, together with more than three thousand head of beef-cattle for the Subsistence Department continued to cross the bridge for forty hours, without a single accident to man or beast.

The officers and men in charge of the bridge were allowed very little sleep during this time, and General Benham relates that he had only about four hours' sleep in the eighty that the bridge was in operation. He said it was in anxiety, not to say in trembling, that he saw the destinies of that whole army committed to the frail structure, with steamers and other vessels drifting against it, and with so much of its planking previously worn through by careless use on the Rappahannock; while he did not dare stop that stream of men and supplies for a moment, in order to make repairs.

At length, the last animal was over by 7 P.M., on June 18th, and the guardians of the frail path commenced to breathe freely again, when, to their consternation, the Confederate artillery, about a mile away, began shelling. The pontoniers almost gave up hope of withdrawing the bridge in safety; but it was ordered up, and General Benham directed its removal in three rafts. This was successfully accomplished before three o'clock in the morning of the 19th, and the great bridge reached City Point, the Federal headquarters, about sunrise of that day, a souvenir of the most successful bridge of boats in the military history of the world.

Compared with the bridge built by the same troops over the Chickahominy two years before, this James River bridge was the greater feat. In the latter case, the water was deep for the greater portion of the distance, in some places nearly eighty-five feet, with a strong current running. In the former, the stream was comparatively shallow for most of the

SUNK BY A CONFEDERATE SHELL—BUTLER'S DREDGE-BOAT

Here is the dredge-boat that had deepened the southern approaches to the Dutch Gap canal, as it lay after being sunk by a Confederate shell on Thanksgiving Day, 1864.   It was later raised and bomb-proofed to insure its finishing the work.   This view is to the east, showing a Union lookout-tower on the north bank of the James River, and some monitors in the right distance.   The digging of the canal was begun on August 10, 1864, and was intended to enable Union monitors and gunboats to pass up the James to Richmond.   The bend of the river which it cut off was filled with obstructions placed there by General Butler himself, and was commanded by the Confederate Battery Dantzler.   After September 29th, when the Confederate Fort Harrison, north of the James, was captured by the Union troops, the canal was not needed, but work was continued until some four months afterwards it was ready.   After the war it was a welcome channel for vessels on the James.   January 1, 1865, when the bulkhead at the northern end of the excavation was blown up with twelve thousand pounds of powder, the fallen earth and débris obstructed the entrance.   It could be entered by small boats, but it was never used for the passage of armed vessels.   The size of the dredge-boat can be judged by the figures of the two men beside it.

distance, and a great portion of the bridge could be built on trestles, whereas, in the James River construction, only about two hundred feet could be built of trestling.

On July 9, 1864, an order was issued directing operations against Petersburg by regular siege-works. This required a survey of the topography of the country and the positions of the lines of both armies. A map was made by the engineers which was constantly used as a reference by all the officers concerned in laying out and constructing these works. The engineers planned the regular entrenchments and approaches as far as possible, but, because of the multiplicity of duties devolving upon them, much of this work was delegated to other officers, who closely followed the plans indicated on the maps furnished.

At noon, on June 25th, a mine was begun by the troops in front of Petersburg. This was not undertaken by engineer troops, but was under the direction of Lieutenant-Colonel Henry Pleasants, Forty-eighth Pennsylvania Volunteers, and was executed by his own men. General Meade and General Grant sanctioned the project, and plans were adopted for an assault on the entire Confederate line when the mine should explode. The majority of the men employed in the work were miners from the coal regions of Pennsylvania, and the necessary expedients were familiar to them, without special instructions from the engineers. The excavation was commenced without special tools, lumber, or any of the materials usually required for such work. By late afternoon, on July 23d, the excavations were deemed complete. Eighteen thousand cubic feet of earth had been removed.

The mine was charged on the afternoon and evening of the 27th, with three hundred and twenty kegs of powder, each containing about twenty-five pounds. Altogether, there were eight magazines connected by wooden tubes which were half filled with powder. These tubes met at the inner end of the main gallery, and fuses were laid along this gallery to the exit. As

CELEBRATING

AN

ANNIVERSARY

ENGINEERS

ON

JULY 4, 1864

Thus the officers of the Fiftieth New York Engineers celebrated the victories of Gettysburg and Vicksburg in front of Petersburg July 4, 1864. At the head of the table sits Lieutenant-Colonel Ira Spaulding. On his right is Charles Francis Adams, later a leading American historian. Often in front of Petersburg just a few more shovelfuls of earth meant the saving of lives. The veterans in the lower photograph are bearded and bronzed; the muscles beneath their shabby blue tunics were developed by heavy, constant manual labor. The operations in this campaign marked a development in field-fortifications, opened virtually a new era in warfare. The siege was not a bombardment of impregnable fortifications. It was a constant series of assaults and picket-firing on lines of entrenchments in the open. By July, 1864, the earthworks to the east had been almost finished, although much of this exacting labor had been performed at night and under a galling fire. During August, the engineer corps extended the lines south and southeast of the beleaguered city. But meanwhile the Confederates had been hard at work also. They had fewer men to hold their lines and to carry on the work, but it was accomplished with great devotion, and under able management and direction. The soldiers in the trenches lived in bomb-proofs.

GROUP OF COMPANY D, UNITED STATES ENGINEERS, IN FRONT OF PETERSBURG, AUGUST, 1864

there was not a sufficient length of fuse at hand to lay it in one piece, several pieces spliced together had to be used. An inspection of the work indicated that it was perfect.

Orders were given to fire the mine at three o'clock in the morning of July 30th. The fuse was lighted at 3.15 A.M., but the charge failed to explode. The defect was repaired, the fuse again lit, and at twenty minutes to five the mine exploded.

The shock was terrific. For nearly an hour the defenders of the adjacent works appeared paralyzed. Through a misunderstanding, the Federal assault was a failure, and many lives were sacrificed. From an engineering point of view, the enterprise was a success. Tactically, it was a failure.

From the moment the Federal troops appeared before Petersburg until the evacuation of the town, the duties of the Engineer Corps were very exacting. Every man was engaged in superintending and assisting in the construction of the technical part of the siege-works. Whenever the battalion was assembled, it was held ready for duty as infantry, and in several cases of emergency was used to strengthen weak points.

A final attempt was made by General Lee, while shut up in Petersburg and Richmond, to divert attention from himself and the Confederate capital by sending General Early up through the Shenandoah valley into Maryland and against Washington. Practically all the garrison at the Federal capital had been withdrawn from the defenses of the city to reenforce the Army of the Potomac. The troops left behind fit for duty did not suffice to man the armaments of the forts, of which the Engineer Corps and artillery had constructed a line of about thirty-seven miles in length.

Colonel Alexander, of the Corps of Engineers, was the only officer of the corps whose personal attention could be given to these defenses. Two of the officers in the office of the chief engineer were ordered to his assistance, and the officers of the corps on fortification duty on the sea-coast, north and east

WHEN IT WAS JUST A QUESTION OF TIME BEFORE PETERSBURG

It was an unexpected "war-time scene" before the cottage of Colonel Nathaniel Michler of the Engineer Corps at Brant House, near Petersburg. It recalls the prelude to Tennyson's "Princess," and the boy telling of the Christmas vacation in his deserted college halls, who "swore he long'd at college, only long'd, all else was well, for she society." How much more must the boys around Petersburg, some of whom had not seen their womenkind for three years or more, have longed for their presence and all the sweetness and daintiness and gentleness that it implied. It was only a question of time now when stoutly defended Petersburg would succumb before the vigor of the Northern assault. Now and again an officer was fortunate enough to receive a visit from his wife, or, as this picture proves, even from his little boy. The neat cottage shows with what success the Engineer Corps could turn from entrenching to the more gentle art of domestic architecture.

 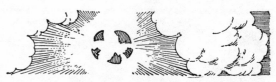

of the city, who could be sent to Washington, were detached from their duties and ordered to report at the capital at once.

But the improvised organization within the city, and the expected arrival of large reenforcements, of which Early had information, impelled him to withdraw after making a light attack, and the city was saved. The engineer officers that had been withdrawn from their work on the seaboard were immediately returned to their respective stations.

In the West, the operations of the Federal engineers shed luster on their corps. Fort Henry, Fort Donelson, and Vicksburg are names that are held in memory as demonstrating the high achievements of the scientific soldiers whose skill overcame great odds. Seventeen field- and subaltern-officers of the corps served constantly in the Western Federal armies, and though they had no regular engineer troops under them, the volunteers who received training from these officers proved their worth. Their labors at Chattanooga, Tennessee, under Captain (afterward Colonel) Merrill, rendered that important position impregnable. Knoxville, Tennessee, likewise withstood terrific onslaughts, having been fortified with great skill.

The army under Sherman had with it nine able engineers, under Captain O. M. Poe, who labored constantly in the construction of defenses for the numerous bridges along the line of railroad, fortified many strategic points, made surveys and issued maps, reconnoitered the positions of the Confederates, and managed the pontoon-bridge service.

Sherman started from Atlanta for the sea-coast, November 16, 1864. Hood had moved north into Tennessee. The Union army under Thomas had been sent to Nashville. The engineers fortified Franklin, but Schofield, with two corps of Thomas' army, was not strong enough to hold it. At Nashville the skill of the engineers, under Captain (afterward General) Morton and Captain Merrill, had enabled General Thomas to take his stand and hold on until he was ready to move against Hood.

[250]

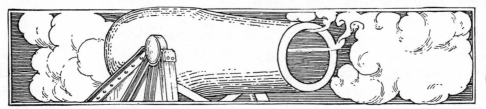

MAP–MAKING FROM PULPIT ROCK, LOOKOUT MOUNTAIN

The tripod signal in the background was erected by Captains Dorr and Donn, of the United States Coast Survey, in the triangular survey of the triple battlefield for making the official maps. In the West, the operations of the Federal engineers shed luster on their corps. Seventeen field and subaltern officers served constantly in the Western Federal armies; and though they had no regular engineer troops under them, the volunteers who received training from

A TRIPOD FOR SURVEYING THE BATTLEFIELD

these officers proved their worth. The army under Sherman had with it nine able engineers under Captain O. M. Poe, under whose supervision a number of the photographs which are reproduced in this work were taken. He fortified many strategic points, made surveys and issued maps, reconnoitered the positions of the enemy, and managed the pontoon-bridge service. Captain Poe was a trained engineer officer, a graduate of West Point. He was commissioned as brigadier-general of volunteers and brevetted brigadier-general of the regular army.

THE ENGINEERS IN KENTUCKY—HEADQUARTERS AT CAMP NELSON

In the West, Forts Henry and Donelson and Vicksburg are names that are held in memory as demonstrating the high achievements of the Engineer Corps. Its labors at Chattanooga, under Colonel Merrill, rendered that important position impregnable. The work at Knoxville likewise withstood terrific onslaught. At Nashville the skill of the engineers enabled General Thomas to take his stand until he was ready to move against Hood. Throughout the Atlanta campaign Sherman showed implicit confidence in his engineers.

ALL DONE BUT
THE DRAW

SPANNING THE
TENNESSEE
RIVER

WORK OF
THE WESTERN
ENGINEER CORPS

AFTER
THE BATTLES
AT CHATTANOOGA

The Federal Engineers ❖ ❖ ❖ ❖

The importance of these defenses was mainly in enabling Thomas to concentrate his army at a depot well stored with munitions of war, and to hold his opponent, who was flushed with his successful march from Atlanta, in check, until the Union army was fully prepared. It is conceded by all critics that the labors of the engineer troops on these works were abundantly well spent. During the same eventful period, the fortifications constructed by them at Murfreesboro were successfully held and defended by a portion of Thomas' army.

No mention has been made of the immensely valuable services of all the engineer officers in the conduct of sieges throughout the war. No small portion of the conflict consisted in the besieging of important fortified places, and the manner in which these duties were discharged elicited high praise from all the commanding generals who had to do with such operations. Henry, Donelson, Vicksburg, Fort Fisher, the defenses of Charleston, Mobile, Savannah, and other places were all notable for the work of the besiegers, whose engineers directed and superintended the construction of the works of approach.

Justice to posterity demands that an accurate record of all the important military events of the war be preserved. No small part of that record had to be shown by maps. The chief engineer of the army directed the engraving, lithographing, photographing, and issuing of these maps, of which about twenty-four thousand five hundred sheets were sent out during the Civil War. The carefulness of the compilation often has been demonstrated. The hostile operations came to an end with the surrender of the last Confederate armed forces, but, for the construction of a basis on which accurate history might later be built, the Engineer Corps of the army continued its invaluable labors in making record of these events, which could be best depicted in map-form and in official reports. We have not even yet fully realized the immense worth of these documents of the great struggles during the Civil War.

X

THE
CONFEDERATE
ENGINEERS

A " COVERED WAY " IN FORT PULASKI, APRIL, 1862—THE GARRISON
HERE MADE A CONTINUOUS BOMB-PROOF BY LEANING TIMBERS
AGAINST THE INNER WALL OF THE FORT AND
THEN COVERING THEM WITH EARTH

REMINISCENCES OF THE CONFEDERATE ENGINEER SERVICE

By T. M. R. TALCOTT

*Colonel Commanding Engineer Troops, Army of Northern Virginia,
Confederate States Army*

[The text of this article is of especial value since it embraces personal reminiscences in a field where few official records or maps are available; namely, the operation of the engineer troops with the Army of Northern Virginia. The chapter is broadened by illustrations showing engineering works of the Confederate army in the West and South. —The Editors.]

THE account of the services rendered to the Southern Confederacy by its engineers must be largely, if not wholly, from memory, owing to the loss of records pertaining to this branch of the Confederate military service. The following, therefore, must be considered merely a reminiscence of the Civil War preserved in the memory of an individual participant in the events of the four years, from April, 1861, to April, 1865.

Prior to April, 1861, the State of Virginia maintained the hope that wise counsels would prevail, and urged forbearance; but mindful of the old adage, " In time of peace prepare for war," an appropriation was made for river, coast, and harbor defenses, and the services of a competent military engineer were secured to plan and superintend the work. Thus it happened that, when the Ordinance of Secession was passed by the Constitutional convention of the State of Virginia, on the 16th of April, 1861, in answer to Lincoln's call for her quota of the seventy-five thousand troops, no time was lost in organizing a State corps of engineers to prepare defenses against the then inevitable invasion of the State.

BRIGADIER-GENERAL DANVILLE LEADBETTER   MAJOR-GENERAL J. F. GILMER

CONFEDERATE ENGINEERS WHO MADE THEIR MARK

When it is realized that few of the officers in the Confederate Engineers Corps had any previous practice as military engineers, although some of them had been educated at military academies, and that no engineer troops were provided for by the Confederate Congress until 1863, the work accomplished by the Confederate engineers seems all the more marvelous. The Confederate coastwise defenses were strengthened in a way that baffled the blockading fleet, and no two armies have ever been entrenched in the field as were the armies of the South and North before Petersburg. Walter H. Stevens became major in the Confederate Corps of Engineers March 16, 1861. He was made colonel the following year, and brigadier-general August 28, 1864. He was chief engineer of the Army of Northern Virginia before Petersburg, and surrendered at Appomattox. Danville Leadbetter also became a major in the Engineer Corps March 16, 1861. He was a brigadier-general of the Provisional Army of the Confederate States February 27, 1861. J. F. Gilmer was lieutenant-colonel of the Engineer Corps in 1861. He became brigadier-general in the Confederate army in 1862, and major-general in 1863. During most of his service he was chief of the engineer bureau.

BRIGADIER-GENERAL WALTER H. STEVENS

The Confederate Engineers ❖

The moment that the Norfolk Navy-Yard was evacuated, the erection and armament of batteries along the Elizabeth River was begun to prevent its recapture; and thus Virginia came into possession of a thoroughly equipped navy-yard, at which the *Merrimac*, some time later, was converted into the ironclad *Virginia*, and the guns needed for the speedy armament of batteries for the defense not only of the Elizabeth, James, and York rivers, but also against attacks on Norfolk and Richmond by other lines of approach, were obtained.

Subsequently, the Virginia Corps of Engineers was merged into that of the Confederate States; and the cost of completing the defenses begun by the State of Virginia was borne by the Confederate Government.

Very few of the officers in the Confederate corps had any previous practice as military engineers, although some of them had been educated at military academies. In this respect the North had a decided advantage over its opponents. No engineer troops were provided for by the Confederate Congress until 1863, when two regiments were authorized and organized, in time to take part in the campaigns of 1864. Prior to that time, such duties as pertain to engineer troops were performed by details from divisions, generally known as Pioneer Corps, under the direction of officers of the Engineer Corps attached to such divisions.

Of the two regiments of engineer troops, the First Regiment and two companies of the Second Regiment were organized for service with the Army of Northern Virginia. The other eight companies of the Second served elsewhere than in Virginia, several of them in the Trans-Mississippi Department.

During the first three years of the war when pontoon bridges were needed, they were handled by the Pioneer Corps, or other details from the ranks, under the direction of officers of the Engineer Corps. The bridge on which General Lee's army recrossed the Potomac near Williamsport after the battle of

AN INGENIOUS DEVICE OF THE CONFEDERATES IN PULASKI

The Confederates had swung upwards the muzzle of this 8-inch smooth-bore sea-coast gun within Fort Pulaski, so that it could be used as a mortar for high-angle fire against the Federal batteries. General Hunter and General Gillmore's troops, supported by the gunboats, had erected these on Jones Island and Tybee Island. Fort Pulaski, commanding the entrance to the Savannah River and covering the passage of blockade runners to and from Savannah, early became an important objective of the Federal forces at Hilton Head. It was of the greatest importance that shells should be dropped into the Federal trenches, and this accounts for the position of the gun in the picture. There was no freedom of recoil for the piece, and therefore it could not be fired with the "service" charge or full charge of powder. Reduced charges, however, were sufficient, as the ranges to the opposing batteries were short. With this and other ingenious devices the little garrison kept up its resistance against heavy odds. It finally surrendered on April 11, 1862.

[F—17]

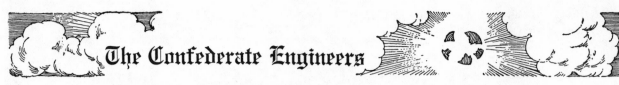

Gettysburg was an illustration of the corps' resourcefulness; for in this instance pontoon boats were lacking. The expedition with which material was collected, boats built, and the bridge constructed was most creditable.

The pontoon bridges for the engineer troops in Virginia were built at Richmond under the direction of the engineering bureau, and were in accordance with the plans and specifications prescribed by Captain (afterward General) George B. McClellan, United States Corps of Engineers, in one of the engineering papers published some years prior to the War between the States.

The pontoon bridge consisted of flat-bottomed boats, with longitudinal timbers to connect them, and planks for the flooring, all of which were lashed together with cords, so that they could be quickly assembled and as readily taken apart. The transportation of them required wagons specially constructed for the purpose. Provision had, of course, to be made to hold the boats in position against strong currents in streams to be crossed, by anchors or guy-lines to the shore.

When the campaign opened in 1864, the engineer troops attached to the Army of Northern Virginia, which was then at Orange Court House, were used first as infantry to guard the depot of supplies at Guiney's Station, and afterward to support a cavalry brigade which held the Telegraph road, on the extreme right of General Lee's position in Spotsylvania County, where it crossed the Ny, one of the four streams which form the Mattapony River. At this point earthworks were constructed, and the position was held until after the battle of Spotsylvania Court House, when it was turned by the flank movement of General Grant; and General Lee retired to the line of the North Anna River.

During General Grant's demonstration against Richmond, the engineer troops were used to strengthen the works which withstood his attacks at Cold Harbor; but anticipating the necessity at any time for a prompt movement across the

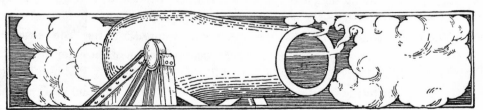

PULASKI—THE ANGLE WHERE THE FEDERALS CONCENTRATED THEIR FIRE

RIFLED CANNON VS. BRICKS

These two photographs of Fort Pulaski at Savannah, taken in April, 1862, after the bombardment by the Federal batteries, show very clearly how the Confederate Engineers learned that the old-fashioned brick wall was of no use against modern guns. The time had passed for brick and stone fortresses. Granite was found to be weaker than sand. Any yielding substance which would slow down and finally stop the great projectiles, and which could be shoveled back into position, no matter how much of it was displaced by a shell, proved far superior to any rigid substance. The ruins of Fort Pulaski taught the Confederates how to defend Fort Sumter—which was evacuated but never fell. In General Gillmore's Re-

port on Charleston he says: "One hundred and ten thousand six hundred and forty-three pounds of metal produced a breach in Fort Pulaski which caused the surrender of that permanent and well constructed brick fortification, while one hundred and twenty-two thousand and thirty pounds of metal failed to open the bomb-proof of Fort Wagner, a sand work extemporized for the war. . . . It must not be forgotten, in this connection, that in the former case the brick wall stood nearly vertical, and all the débris formed by the shots immediately fell into the ditch, and no longer afforded any protection to the wall left standing; while in the latter the mass was so formed that a large proportion of the sand displaced fell back and again within an area attempted to be breached."

INSIDE THE BREACHED CASEMATE (SEE ABOVE)

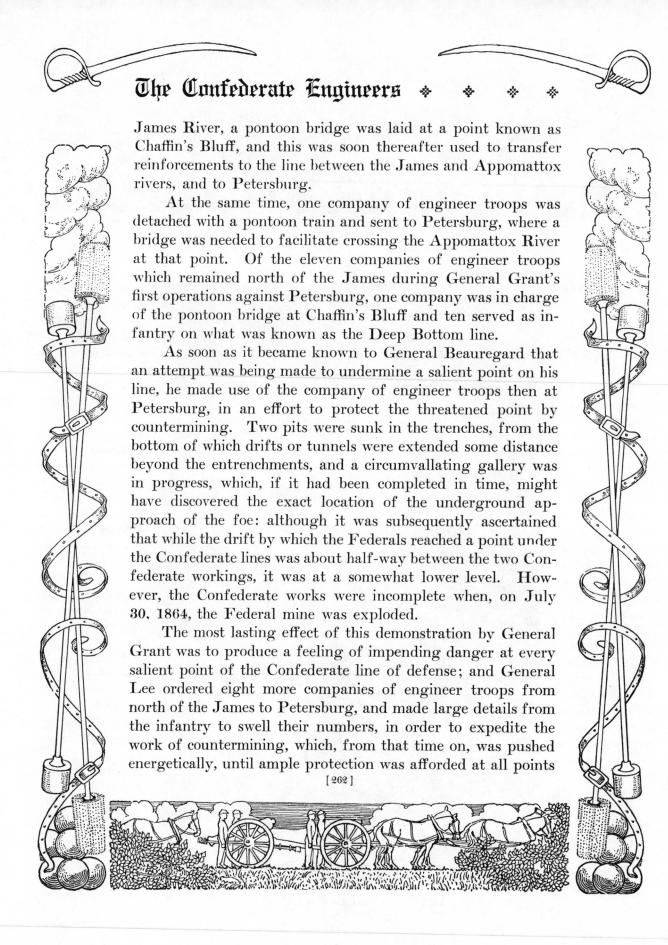

The Confederate Engineers ❖ ❖ ❖ ❖

James River, a pontoon bridge was laid at a point known as Chaffin's Bluff, and this was soon thereafter used to transfer reinforcements to the line between the James and Appomattox rivers, and to Petersburg.

At the same time, one company of engineer troops was detached with a pontoon train and sent to Petersburg, where a bridge was needed to facilitate crossing the Appomattox River at that point. Of the eleven companies of engineer troops which remained north of the James during General Grant's first operations against Petersburg, one company was in charge of the pontoon bridge at Chaffin's Bluff and ten served as infantry on what was known as the Deep Bottom line.

As soon as it became known to General Beauregard that an attempt was being made to undermine a salient point on his line, he made use of the company of engineer troops then at Petersburg, in an effort to protect the threatened point by countermining. Two pits were sunk in the trenches, from the bottom of which drifts or tunnels were extended some distance beyond the entrenchments, and a circumvallating gallery was in progress, which, if it had been completed in time, might have discovered the exact location of the underground approach of the foe: although it was subsequently ascertained that while the drift by which the Federals reached a point under the Confederate lines was about half-way between the two Confederate workings, it was at a somewhat lower level. However, the Confederate works were incomplete when, on July 30, 1864, the Federal mine was exploded.

The most lasting effect of this demonstration by General Grant was to produce a feeling of impending danger at every salient point of the Confederate line of defense; and General Lee ordered eight more companies of engineer troops from north of the James to Petersburg, and made large details from the infantry to swell their numbers, in order to expedite the work of countermining, which, from that time on, was pushed energetically, until ample protection was afforded at all points

ONE OF THE GUNS THAT HAD TO BE DUG OUT—FORT McALLISTER

Digging out the guns was an every-morning duty of the garrison in Fort McAllister, defending Savannah, during the three bombardments of the Federal monitors and gunboats—January 27, February 1, and March 3, 1863. Every night the cannon in the fort became buried with dirt thrown up by the Federal shells, yet every morning they were roaring defiance again at the attacking fleet. No Federals set foot here until the little garrison of 230 men were confronted by Sherman's army of 100,000 and stormed on December 13, 1864.

FORT MORGAN, MOBILE BAY, ALABAMA

Fort Morgan, on the right of the entrance to Mobile Bay, was one of the strongest of the old brick forts. By August, 1864, it had been greatly strengthened by immense piles of sandbags, covering every portion of the exposed front toward the neck of the bay. The fort was well equipped with three tiers of heavy guns, one of the guns at least, of the best English make, imported by the Confederates.

exposed to attack by mining. These underground defenses included, besides the necessary pits, over two and one-half miles of drifts or tunnels.

In addition to the countermining at Petersburg, the engineer troops were used to strengthen the fortifications and to build a branch railroad to facilitate the delivery of supplies. During the investment of Richmond and Petersburg, two pontoon bridges were maintained across the Appomattox River, and one across the James at Chaffin's Bluff; and additional pontoon trains were provided in case they should be needed.

Anticipating the necessity for the abandonment of Richmond and Petersburg, General Lee, during the winter of 1864–65, required the engineer troops to rebuild Bevill's Bridge over the Appomattox River west of Petersburg, and to send a pontoon bridge to the Staunton River in Charlotte County.

The engineer troops also prepared a map showing the routes to the different crossings of the Appomattox River, to be used whenever the army should be withdrawn from Richmond and Petersburg. This map has since been lithographed by the United States Government.

In March, 1865, when the right of General Lee's position was seriously threatened, engineer troops strengthened the defenses at Hatcher's Run; but the main body of them served in the trenches in place of the infantry withdrawn to extend still further westward a line which was already more than thirty miles in length.

The Confederate reverse at Five Forks, which cut off a part of Lee's army from Petersburg and forced it to retire to the north side of the Appomattox River, was closely followed by the loss of a part of the entrenchments before that city, and this necessitated an interior line of defense, pending the withdrawal of the main body of General Lee's army to the north side of the Appomattox River. This new line of breastworks was thrown up hurriedly, in part by the engineer troops, but chiefly by negro laborers. This was probably the only time

SEA FACE OF FORT FISHER—MIGHTIEST FORTRESS OF THE SOUTHERN CONFEDERACY

Along the North Carolina coast, near Wilmington, guarding the port longest open to blockade-runners, lay these far-flung earthworks. Heavy timbers were heaped fifteen to twenty-five feet thick with sand, sodded with luxuriant marsh-grass. Below appears some of the destruction wrought by the fire of the Federal war-ships. Here are the emplacements next to the angle of the work on the left of the sea face, and a bomb-proof under the traverse. The first gun on the right is a 10-inch Columbiad dismounted by the assailants' fire. Only the old-style two-wheeled wooden carriage, without chassis, can be seen, at the top of the bank—ready to tumble over. The next gun is also a 10-inch Columbiad which has been knocked off its wooden barbette carriage; the third, a 6⅜-inch rifle, on a two-wheeled wooden carriage. The carriage has been knocked entirely off the bank, and is lying in the pool of water. The only gun left mounted is the 10-inch Columbiad to the left. The fort finally succumbed to the terrific fire of the Federal fleet on January 15, 1865.

BEHIND THE RAMPARTS—HAVOC FROM FEDERAL SHELLS

that the Confederates required negro laborers to work under fire, and to their credit be it said that they performed their task with apparent willingness.

The engineer troops were the last to leave the city of Petersburg, for the destruction of the bridges devolved upon them. They retired from the north bank of the river early in the morning of April 3, 1865, under a scattering fire from the advance guard of the Federals.

Then followed a day's march to Goode's Bridge, and the crossing of the Appomattox River at that point, not only of the army and its wagon trains, but also of a large number of other wagons, carriages, buggies, and riders on horseback, Government and State officials, bank-officers with their specie, and many private individuals seeking safety for themselves and their belongings.

It had been planned to use the newly built Bevill's Bridge, which was the nearest to Petersburg, for the troops and trains from that point, Goode's Bridge for troops from Richmond, and a pontoon bridge at Genito for all not connected with the army; but by reason of high water, which covered the approaches, Bevill's Bridge was useless. The pontoons for Genito, which were ordered from Richmond two days before, failed to arrive, and thus everything converged at Goode's Bridge and the railroad bridge at Mattoax.

This awkward situation was relieved to some extent by hurriedly laying a rough plank flooring over the rails on the railroad bridge, which made it practicable for vehicles to cross at Mattoax.

The crossing to the south side of the Appomattox River having been effected in some confusion, but, owing to the light of the moon, without accident, both the railroad and pontoon bridges were destroyed before daylight; and the engineer troops moved on to Amelia Court House, where some rest but very inadequate rations awaited them.

Soon orders came from General Lee to push on to Flat

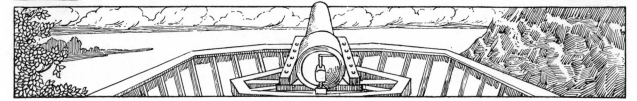

FORT FISHER

EFFECT OF THE NAVAL BOMBARDMENT OF DECEMBER, 1864

In 1864, a larger force than ever had assembled under one command in the history of the American navy was concentrated before Fort Fisher, North Carolina, under Admiral David D. Porter. Sixty vessels, of which five were ironclads, arrived in sight of the ramparts on the morning of December 20th. After a futile effort to damage the fort by the explosion of the powder-boat *Louisiana* on the night of December 23d, the fleet sailed in to begin the bombardment. The *New Ironsides*, followed by the monitors, took position as close in as their drafts would permit. The *Minnesota, Colorado,* and *Wabash* followed near. With a deafening roar and a sheet of flame, these frigates discharged their broadsides of twenty-five 9-inch guns, driving the garrison into their bomb-proofs. On Christmas Day, the bombardment was resumed by the larger vessels and the ironclads, while the smaller vessels covered the landing of General Butler's troops from the transports which had just arrived. The fort proved too strong to take by assault, and the troops were withdrawn. The fort did not fall until January 15, 1865. This photograph shows the effect of the terrific bombardment of the Federal fleet.

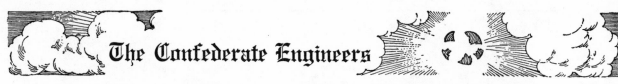

Creek, where the failure of an old country bridge and the absence of practicable fords delayed the crossing of that stream. The outlook at that point on the line of march was evidently disturbing to General Lee, for on arrival of the engineer troops late in the afternoon, for which he had waited, he impressed upon the colonel in command of them the necessity for strenuous efforts to effect as rapid a crossing of Flat Creek as possible, emphasizing his instruction by saying that a captured order from General Grant to General Ord, who was at Jetersville, indicated an attack early next morning.

Timber was felled; a new bridge was built; the last vehicle had passed over it, and the engineer troops were already in motion toward Amelia Springs, when a Federal battery unlimbered on a near-by hill and fired a few shells to expedite the movement of as tired and hungry a body of Confederate troops as could have been found that morning in General Lee's army, where fatigue and hunger were familiar conditions.

When the engineer troops, which had been rejoined by the companies detached for service north of the James River and had made a respectable showing in strength, reached Sailor's Creek, where the rear guard of the army was in line of battle, expecting an immediate attack, the general in command looked pleased and said they were just what he was looking for to reenforce a weak spot in his line. To decline such an honor was not within the range of military possibilities, but an order from General Lee, which a courier had been seeking to deliver, made it imperative to move on to the assistance of the wagon trains. A heavy ordnance train, which was stalled in an effort to surmount a steep hill over a bad road and to cross a creek through swampy ground, was causing serious delay, and a number of wagon trains were parked in the fields, waiting for their turn to move on.

While this congestion was being partially relieved, the battle of Sailor's Creek was fought, which resulted in defeat to the Confederates, who were falling back in disorder toward

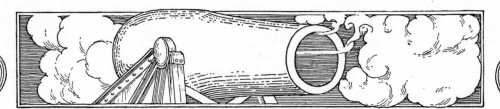

WHERE THE SAILORS ATTACKED—THE MOUND BATTERY AT FORT FISHER

In this photograph unexploded 12-inch shells can be plainly seen upon the beach, as they fell on January 13, 1865, in the terrific fire from the Federal fleet under Rear-Admiral Porter. This was the land face; the portion to the left was the angle of the work. The land assault by the sailors on January 15th, was repulsed with a loss of some three hundred killed and wounded. At the western end of the works, however, the army under General Alfred H. Terry succeeded in effecting an entrance and captured the fort that evening.

ONE OF THE HUGE TRAVERSES, AFTER THE BOMBARDMENT

A traverse in an earthwork built perpendicular to the main work in order to limit the destructive area of shells. The traverses at Fort Fisher rose twelve feet above the twenty-foot parapet, ran back thirty feet, and exceeded in size any previously known to engineers.

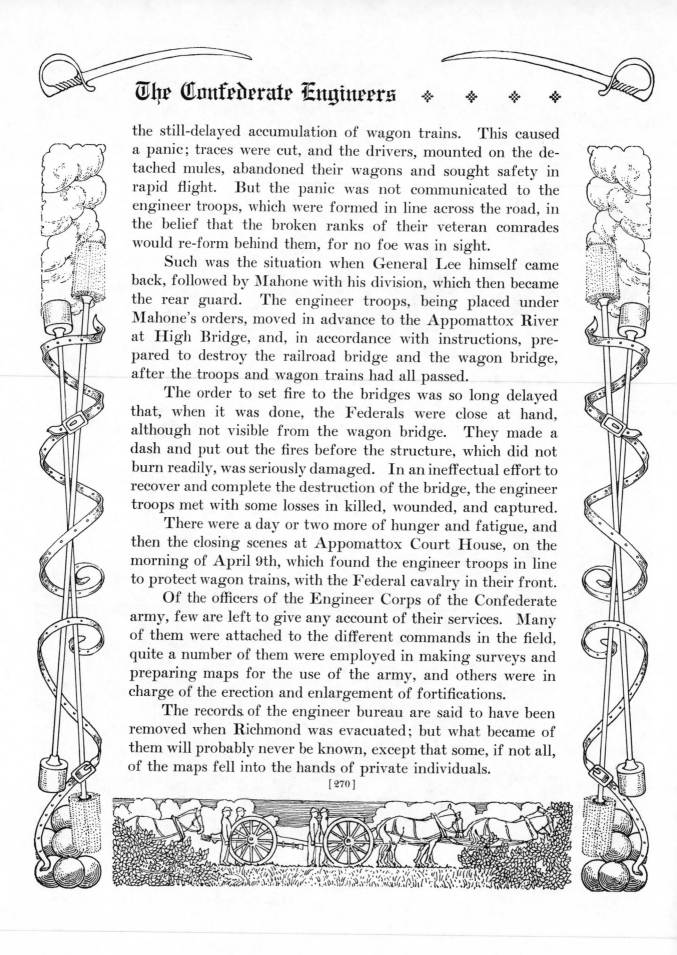

the still-delayed accumulation of wagon trains. This caused a panic; traces were cut, and the drivers, mounted on the detached mules, abandoned their wagons and sought safety in rapid flight. But the panic was not communicated to the engineer troops, which were formed in line across the road, in the belief that the broken ranks of their veteran comrades would re-form behind them, for no foe was in sight.

Such was the situation when General Lee himself came back, followed by Mahone with his division, which then became the rear guard. The engineer troops, being placed under Mahone's orders, moved in advance to the Appomattox River at High Bridge, and, in accordance with instructions, prepared to destroy the railroad bridge and the wagon bridge, after the troops and wagon trains had all passed.

The order to set fire to the bridges was so long delayed that, when it was done, the Federals were close at hand, although not visible from the wagon bridge. They made a dash and put out the fires before the structure, which did not burn readily, was seriously damaged. In an ineffectual effort to recover and complete the destruction of the bridge, the engineer troops met with some losses in killed, wounded, and captured.

There were a day or two more of hunger and fatigue, and then the closing scenes at Appomattox Court House, on the morning of April 9th, which found the engineer troops in line to protect wagon trains, with the Federal cavalry in their front.

Of the officers of the Engineer Corps of the Confederate army, few are left to give any account of their services. Many of them were attached to the different commands in the field, quite a number of them were employed in making surveys and preparing maps for the use of the army, and others were in charge of the erection and enlargement of fortifications.

The records of the engineer bureau are said to have been removed when Richmond was evacuated; but what became of them will probably never be known, except that some, if not all, of the maps fell into the hands of private individuals.

XII

THE RAILROADS
AND
THE ARMIES

THE LOCOMOTIVE "FRED LEACH," AFTER ESCAPING FROM THE CONFEDERATES — THE HOLES IN THE SMOKESTACK SHOW WHERE THE SHOTS STRUCK, AUGUST 1, 1863, WHILE IT WAS RUNNING ON THE ORANGE AND ALEXANDRIA RAILROAD NEAR UNION MILLS

WHAT LINCOLN CALLED THE "BEANPOLE AND CORNSTALK" BRIDGE, BUILT OVER POTOMAC CREEK

This famous "beanpole and cornstalk" bridge, so named by President Lincoln, amazed at its slim structure, was rushed up by totally inexpert labor; yet in spite of this incompetent assistance, an insufficient supply of tools, wet weather and a scarcity of food, the bridge was ready to carry trains in less than two weeks. First on this site had been the original railroad crossing—a solidly constructed affair, destroyed early in the war. After the destruction of the "beanpole and cornstalk" bridge by the Union troops when Burnside evacuated Fredericksburg, came a third of more solid construction, shown in the upper photograph on the right-hand page. The bridge below

THE THIRD BRIDGE, PHOTOGRAPHED APRIL 12, 1863—BELOW, THE FOURTH

is the fourth to be built for the Richmond, Fredericksburg and Potomac Railroad at this point. The United States Military Railroad Construction Corps by this time possessed both trained men and necessary tools. Work on this last bridge was begun Friday, May 20, 1864, at five A.M.; the first train passed over Sunday, May 22d, at four P.M. Its total length was 414 feet, and its height was eighty-two feet. It contained 204,000 feet of timber, board measure, but the actual time of construction was just forty hours. The photograph was taken by Captain A. J. Russell, chief of photographic corps, United States Military Railroads, for the Federal Government.

FEDERAL MILITARY RAILROADS

By O. E. Hunt
Captain, United States Army

WITH miles of black and yellow mud between them and the base of supplies, and a short day's ration of bacon and hardtack in their haversacks, the hearts of the weary soldiers were gladdened many times by the musical screech of a locomotive, announcing that the railroad was at last up to the front, and that in a short time they would have full rations and mail from home. The armies that operated in Virginia and in Georgia greeted, very often, the whistle of the engine with shouts of joy. They knew the construction corps was doing its duty, and here was the evidence.

In the strict sense of the term, there were but few military railroads in the United States during the Civil War, and these few existed only in portions of the theater of war in Virginia, in Tennessee, and in Georgia. Roads owned by private corporations were seized, from time to time, and operated by the Governments of both sides as military necessities dictated, but, technically, these were not military roads, although for the intents and purposes to which they were all devoted, there should be no distinction drawn. The operation of a railroad under Government military supervision, while retaining its working personnel, made of it a military road in every sense.

Great railroad development in this country began during the second quarter of the nineteenth century. The United States Government, about 1837, adopted the policy of loaning to railroad companies officers of the army who had made a scientific study of this new means of communication, and the result was a benefit to the roads and the Government.

[274]

"THEY KNEW THE CONSTRUCTION CORPS WAS DOING ITS DUTY"

CAMP OF THE CORPS AT CITY POINT IN JULY, 1864

The construction corps of the United States Military Railroads had a comparatively easy time at City Point under General McCallum. There was plenty of hard work, but it was not under fire, and so expert had they become that the laying of track and repairing of bridges was figured merely as a sort of game against time. The highest excitement was the striving to make new records. It had been otherwise the year before. General Herman Haupt, then General Superintendent of all the military railroads, had applied for and received authority to arm, drill and make the military railroad organization to some extent self-protective. This was on account of the numerous depredations committed along the Orange and Alexandria Railroad. Bridges were destroyed and reconstructed (that over Bull Run for the seventh time), trains troubled by marauders, and miles of track destroyed by the armies. These men in their camp at City Point look alert and self-sufficient. The investment of Petersburg had begun, and their troubles were practically over.

Constructing companies were assisted in carrying out their ambitious projects, and the Government profited greatly by the experience gained by the officers so detailed. " In this manner army officers became the educators of an able body of civil engineers, who, to this day, have continued the inherited traditions, methods, discipline, *esprit de corps,* and the high bearing of their distinguished predecessors."

General Grant spoke very enthusiastically of the work of the railroads and wagon roads operated for him during the Virginia campaign of 1864, when his army had to be supplied by wagons over the extremely difficult roads, from the termini of railroad lines that were pushed into the Wilderness as far as possible, and from ever-shifting bases on the rivers, where the lack of dockage facilities made the work of handling freight very arduous. He particularly complimented the officers in charge of the trains on the fact that very little special protection had to be given them.

General Sherman, in his memoirs, notes that his base of supplies during the campaign of 1864 was Nashville, supplied by railroads and the Cumberland River, thence by rail to Chattanooga, a secondary base, and by a single-track railroad to his army. The stores came forward daily, but an endeavor was made to have a constant twenty days' supply on hand. These stores were habitually in the wagon trains, distributed to the corps, divisions, and regiments, and under the orders of the generals commanding brigades and divisions. Sherman calculated that, for this supply, he needed three hundred wagons for the provision train of a corps and three hundred for the forage, ammunition, clothing, and other necessary stores—a total of six hundred wagons per corps. It was recognized as impossible for the wagons to go a great distance from the terminus of the railroad and still maintain their maximum efficiency of operation, and hence the efforts made to keep his railroad construction up to the rear of his army.

The construction, operation, and repair of the railroads

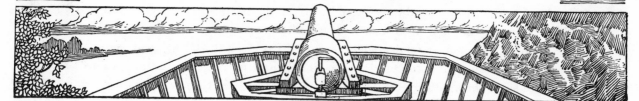

GENERAL HAUPT INSPECTING THE MILITARY RAILROAD—1863

THE SCENE IS NEAR BULL RUN—GENERAL HAUPT STANDS AT THE RIGHT—THE ENGINE HAS BEEN NAMED AFTER HIM

On the embankment stands General Haupt overseeing the actual work on the railroad. This photograph gives an indication of the secret of his success—no detail was too small for him to inspect. He was a graduate of the United States Military Academy in the class of 1835. He resigned his commission soon after graduation, and entered the railroad service in the State of Pennsylvania. His especial forte was bridge-building. In 1846 he became identified with the Pennsylvania Railroad, and in 1865 he became interested in the Hoosac Tunnel project in Massachusetts, which he carried to successful completion. In April, 1862, Secretary of War Edwin M. Stanton summoned him to Washington and put him in charge of rescuing the railways and transportation service from the chaos into which they had fallen. At first employed as a civilian, he was given later the rank of colonel, and at the second battle of Bull Run was commissioned brigadier-general of volunteers. His work was magnificent, and he soon had the railroads running smoothly. On account of differences with General Pope, he retired to his home in Massachusetts in July, 1862. A few days later he received from the War Department the following telegram: "Come back immediately; cannot get along without you; not a wheel moving on any of the roads." General Haupt returned, and the wheels began to move. On September 14, 1863, D. C. McCallum succeeded Haupt.

of the Federal Army of Virginia and the Army of the Potomac were, until September 9, 1863, largely in the hands of Herman Haupt, who, for a time, also held general superintendence over all the military roads of the United States.

In April, 1862, the great war secretary, Edwin M. Stanton, sent an urgent telegram to Mr. Haupt, requesting him to come to Washington. Knowing that Congress would probably exercise a certain amount of supervision over his work if he entered the Government service, and having had a discouraging experience already with legislative bodies, he hesitated to undertake the work which Secretary Stanton pressed upon him. However, having been assured by the joint committee of Congress having such matters in charge that his interests would not be sacrificed, he immediately began the task of rescuing the railway and transportation service of the Federal armies from the apparently irreparable chaos into which it had fallen. Secretary Stanton knew his ground when he confided this work to Haupt. He also knew his man, and the absolute integrity and fearless energy that he was capable of putting into any enterprise he undertook.

At first, Haupt was employed as a civilian. On April 27, 1862, however, he was appointed aide-de-camp on the staff of General McDowell, whom he had known at West Point, and with whom he was soon on the closest terms, both personally and officially. On May 28th, he was given the rank of colonel, which he held until the second battle of Bull Run, when he was commissioned a brigadier-general.

The first important work under Haupt's direction was the reconstruction of the railroad from Aquia Creek to Fredericksburg. This became, on reopening, the first strictly military road in the United States during the war. At Aquia Creek, the large wharf had been completely destroyed and the railroad track torn up for a distance of about three miles, the rails having been carried away and the ties burned. All the bridges in the vicinity had been destroyed by burning and their

A PROBLEM SOLVED BY THE ENGINEERS

It was a long step from Cæsar's wooden bridges to the difficulties which confronted the United States Construction Corps in the Civil War. Here is an example of its work. Time and again, during 1862–63, the bridges on the line of the Orange & Alexandria Railroad were destroyed by both sides in advance and in retreat. It remained for the army engineers to reconstruct them. It was a work requiring patience and unceasing activity, for speed was of prime importance. These structures, capable of supporting the passage of heavy railroad trains, and built in a few hours, were conspicuous triumphs which the American engineers added to the annals of war.

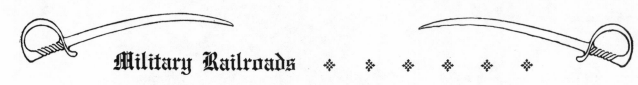

Military Railroads ❖ ❖ ❖ ❖ ❖ ❖ ❖ ❖

abutments blown up. The road-bed had been used by wagons and cavalry and was badly cut up.

The first bridge to be constructed on the line was at Accakeek Creek. This was built complete, with a span of about one hundred and fifty feet and an elevation of thirty feet, in a little more than fifteen hours on May 3 and 4, 1862. The next and most serious obstruction was the deep crossing of Potomac Creek. Here was built what is known as a deck bridge, of crib and trestle-work, four hundred feet long and eighty feet high. As before, totally inexpert labor was employed, and only a very few officers who had any knowledge of that kind of work were available. With this incompetent assistance, with an insufficient supply of tools, with occasional scarcity of food, and several days of wet weather, the work was nevertheless advanced so rapidly that in nine days the bridge was crossed by foot passengers, and in less than two weeks an engine was passed over, to the intense delight of the soldiers, by whose labor the structure had been erected. It was completed on May 13th. After President Lincoln first saw this bridge he remarked: "I have seen the most remarkable structure that human eyes ever rested upon. That man, Haupt, has built a bridge across Potomac Creek, about four hundred feet long and nearly a hundred feet high, over which loaded trains are running every hour, and, upon my word, . . . there is nothing in it but bean-poles and corn-stalks."

The railroad bridge across the Rappahannock at Fredericksburg was constructed next in about the same time as that across Potomac Creek, and was six hundred feet long and forty-three feet above the water, with a depth of water of ten feet. This structure was built under the immediate supervision of Daniel Stone.

The excitement created by General Jackson's invasion of the Shenandoah, in 1862, caused orders to be issued to McDowell to intercept him. The railroads were unserviceable, and it became Haupt's duty to make such repairs as would

BUILDING PORTABLE BRIDGE-TRUSSES

AT WORK IN THE CARPENTER-SHOP

EXPERIMENTS WITH BOARD TRUSSES

LOADING A BRIDGE TO TEST IT

TESTING A "SHAD-BELLY" BRIDGE

TRIAL OF A "SHAD-BELLY" BRIDGE

BRIDGES WHILE YOU WAIT, BY THE CONSTRUCTION CORPS

Early in 1863, after Burnside was relieved and while the Army of the Potomac was lying at Fredericksburg under Hooker, the construction corps experimented busily with portable trusses and torpedoes. Records of the experiments were made by photographs, and these views served for the education of other Federal armies. Above are some of the very photographs that instructed the Federal armies in "bridge-building while you wait." Hooker's first plan of operations, given in confidence to General Haupt, required large preparations of railroad-bridge material. Although the plans were subsequently changed, use was found for all of this material.

enable McDowell's forces to reach the Valley, at Front Royal, in time, if possible, to get in rear of the Confederates. McDowell was then in command of the Department of the Rappahannock, and Haupt was his chief of construction and transportation.

The road to be repaired was the Manassas Gap Railroad. It was promptly put in order from Rectortown to Piedmont, but the equipment was insufficient to enable it to sustain the amount of work suddenly thrown upon it. Besides, the operation of military railroads was not understood, and the difficulties were constantly increased by military interference with the running of trains and by the neglect and, at times, absolute refusal of subordinates in the supply departments to unload and return cars. The telegraph was, at this period, so uncertain an instrument that it was considered impracticable to rely on it for the operation of trains. Consequently, a schedule was arranged. But here again there was trouble. Even the War Department consented to having this schedule broken up by unwarranted interference, and the operators were compelled to return to the uncertain telegraph for train despatching.

Colonel Haupt stated, in a report of these difficulties to the War Department on June 6th, that the road had theretofore been operated exclusively by the use of the telegraph, without the aid of any schedule or time-table for running the trains; that such a system might answer if the telegraph were always in order, operators always at their posts, and the line exclusively operated by the railroad employees; but when in operation it was frequently appropriated to military purposes. In consequence, he had, on one occasion, been compelled to go eighteen miles to get in telegraphic communication with the superintendent to learn the cause of the detention of trains, and had been compelled, after waiting for hours, to leave without an answer, the telegraph line being in use for military messages.

As a further evidence of the unreliability of the telegraph

GUARDING THE "O. & A." NEAR UNION MILLS

Jackson's raid around Pope's army on Bristoe and Manassas stations in August, 1862, taught the Federal generals that both railroad and base of supplies must be guarded. Pope's army was out of subsistence and forage, and the single-track railroad was inadequate.

DÉBRIS FROM JACKSON'S RAID ON THE ORANGE AND ALEXANDRIA RAILROAD

This scrap-heap at Alexandria was composed of the remains of cars and engines destroyed by Jackson at Bristoe and Manassas stations. The Confederate leader marched fifty miles in thirty-six hours through Thoroughfare Gap, which Pope had neglected to guard.

for railroad use, Colonel Haupt stated that, even if a wire and operators were provided for the exclusive use of the road, the line would be so liable to derangement from storms and other causes that it could be considered only as a convenience or an auxiliary. As a principal or sole means of operation it was highly unreliable, and was not a necessity.

In order, then, to get some kind of service, the use of the telegraph had again to be abandoned, and even a schedule was dispensed with. Trains received orders to proceed to Front Royal with all speed consistent with safety, returning trains to give the right of way, and all trains to send flagmen in advance. These flagmen were relieved as soon as exhausted. The trains were run in sections, and after considerable experience in this method of operation, a certain measure of success was obtained.

McDowell's orders had been to intercept Jackson; he had personally hurried through Manassas Gap with the troops in advance, and was at Front Royal when, on May 31st, an engineer officer reported to him that there was a bad break in the railroad just west of the summit of the gap, with the track torn up and rails and ties thrown down the mountainside. McDowell sent a hurried note to Haupt, who was east of the gap, and he replied by the same messenger that the general need feel no uneasiness, for, if the rails were within reach, the break could be repaired in a few hours. On June 1st, soon after daylight, the men of the construction corps reached the scene of the wreck and found it in bad shape, but set to work immediately. The broken cars were tumbled over the bank in short order. The track gang was divided into two parties, working toward each other from the ends of the break. The rails and ties were hauled up from the side of the mountain below, and by ten o'clock an engine passed over and was sent to report to General McDowell. Notwithstanding the quick work done throughout, Jackson escaped up the Valley, and the pursuit was fruitless.

BEFORE THE FRESHET OF APRIL, '63

THE BRIDGE OVER BULL RUN THAT KEPT THE CONSTRUCTION CORPS BUSY

The United States Military Railroad Construction Corps got much of its training at this point. The bridge over Bull Run near Union Mills was one of the most frequently reconstructed of the war. This photograph, taken from upstream, shows its appearance before it was carried away by the freshet of April, 1863. On the pages following it appears in several stages of destruction and reconstruction after that event. This neighborhood was the scene of numerous guerrilla raids after the battle of Chancellorsville, May 2, 1863. It was visited with fire and sword again and again by both the Federals and Confederates, as the fortunes of war gave temporary possession of this debatable bit of ground, first to one side and then to the other.

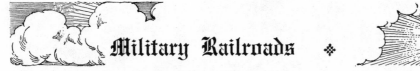

Military Railroads ✦

After the withdrawal of McDowell from the Valley, there was a lull in the active operations, and the construction corps was reorganized. Up to this time it had been composed of details of soldiers. It was now made up of a permanent personnel, assisted by details when necessary. Under date of June 11, 1862, a set of regulations was promulgated by Colonel Haupt for the guidance of the corps, and on June 20th, Haupt, believing that he had accomplished the purpose for which he was brought to Washington by the Secretary of War, sent in a letter of resignation, stating that the communications were then all open, the roads in good condition, the trains running according to schedule, abundant supplies of stores for a week or more in advance already transported, and no probability of any new work for the construction corps for several weeks. As characteristic of Secretary Stanton, it may be noted that this letter was never answered.

On June 26th, General Pope assumed command and persistently declined to notice Haupt or the duties he had been performing. McDowell tried to persuade him to do so, but Pope declared that all such matters should be run by the Quartermaster's Department. Consequently, Colonel Haupt went to Washington, reported the state of affairs to an assistant secretary of war, and proceeded to his home in Massachusetts. The understanding was that he was to return if needed. Soon after his arrival home he received from the War Department the following telegram, "Come back immediately; cannot get along without you; not a wheel moving on any of the roads." He reported to General Pope at Cedar Mountain, and received orders to dictate such directions as he deemed necessary to the chief of staff. Orders were thereupon issued, placing Haupt in entire charge of all transportation by railroad within the lines of operation of Pope's army. This was August 18th. On August 19th, the Secretary of War confirmed the order issued by General Pope on the previous day.

During the retreat of General Pope, the railroads under

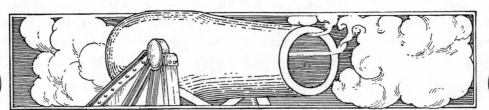

LIFTING THE 59,000–POUND ENGINE "VIBBARD" FROM THE DRAW OF LONG BRIDGE

This scene of March, 1864, suggests some of the difficulties which confronted the superintendent of military railroads during the war. Long Bridge, from the railroad-man's viewpoint, was not a very substantial structure. J. J. Moore, chief engineer and general superintendent of military railroads of Virginia, reported to Brigadier-General D. C. McCallum, under the date of July 1, 1865, that he experienced great difficulty in keeping it secure for the passage of trains. On August 22, 1864, the draw at the south end of the bridge was nearly destroyed by a tug, with a schooner in tow, running into it, and February 18, 1865, an engine broke through the south span of the bridge, the entire span being wrecked. The rescue of the "Vibbard," which weighed 59,000 pounds and cost $11,845, was apparently effectual; the same report states that it ran 5,709 miles at a total cost of $4,318.78 in the fiscal year ending June, 1865.

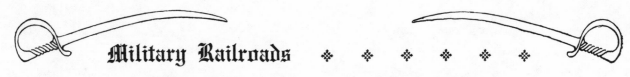

the direction of the chief of construction and transportation
rendered great aid in the transportation of troops and in the
removal of the wounded from the front. The supply of the
army was kept up at the same time. This would have been
entirely impossible in the early days of the war, yet the necessity of having one head for this service had not yet impressed
itself on all the general officers of Pope's army, for we find
interference with the operation of trains from officers who
would not have done so if they had realized the importance of
non-interference. There has been some controversy regarding
the non-arrival of troops at the front during this campaign, and
the point has been made that it was impossible to secure rail
transportation. It appears that the railroad was a single-track
one, with a limited equipment of cars and engines, and necessarily it was impossible to forward troops with the rapidity
that could have been desired, but under the circumstances the
operation of the trains was as successful as could have been
hoped for.

In consequence of the interference by subordinates with
the running of trains, a positive order was issued by General
Halleck to all concerned, directing that no military officer
should give any orders, except through the chief of the construction corps, that would affect the operation of the road,
and that all orders must come from either General Pope or
General Halleck, except in case of attack on the road, in which
case the officials of the road were to consult the commander
of the nearest body of troops.

By August 26th, it was evident that the railroad could be
relied on for nothing more than the necessary supplies for
Pope's army, except in cases where the trains should happen
to be unemployed, in which case troops could be forwarded.
A schedule for use in such event was provided. Transportation was to be furnished in the following order: First, subsistence for men in the field; second, forage; third, ammunition;
fourth, hospital stores; fifth, infantry regiments that had seen

On September 14, 1863, General Haupt was relieved from further duty in the War Department, and turned over his duties to Colonel (later Major-General) D. C. McCallum, who was appointed Superintendent of Military Railroads. The efficient operation of the roads with the Army of the Potomac continued, and received the enthusiastic praise of General Grant. Engines for the military railroad at City Point had to be transported by water. In the lower photograph the "General Dix" is seen being landed at City Point.

MAJOR–GENERAL D. C. McCALLUM
AN OFFICER PRAISED BY GENERAL GRANT

This engine weighed 59,000 pounds and cost $9,500. It was credited with a record of 16,776 miles at the comparatively low cost of $6,136.62 during the fiscal year ending June, 1865. Behind it is the tender piled up with the wood which was used for fuel in those days. This is what necessitated the gigantic stacks of the wood-burning engines. The "General Dix" has evidently been put into perfect condition for its trips over the uneven track of the railway from City Point to the army lines at Petersburg.

LANDING THE MILITARY ENGINE "GENERAL DIX" AT CITY POINT, 1864–5

service, and staff horses; sixth, infantry regiments that had not seen service; and the following were ordinarily refused transportation, although the positive rule was laid down that nothing necessary for military service was to be refused transportation if such was available—batteries, except in cases of emergency, were to march; cavalry was to march; mules and wagon-horses were to be driven; wagons, ambulances, and other vehicles were to be hauled over the common roads.

In addition to the regular duties of construction, repair, and operation of the railroads, the construction corps did valiant service in securing information of the Confederates and also of Pope's army, which for a time was cut off from communication with the Federal capital. Their telegraph operators would go as far forward as possible, climb trees, reconnoiter the country, and send back by wire all the information they could gather. As soon as the Confederates had withdrawn from the vicinity of Manassas, the corps promptly began repairing road-beds, tracks, and bridges. Pope's army was soon resupplied and the intense feeling of apprehension allayed.

In the latter part of 1862, W. W. Wright, an assistant in the work of the corps, was placed in charge of the Cumberland Valley Railroad, which was wholly under military supervision. Later in the war, Wright was in charge of Sherman's railroads during the great Atlanta campaign in 1864. For his guidance with the Cumberland road the instructions were: First, not to allow supplies to be forwarded to the advanced terminus until they were actually required; second, only such quantities were to be forwarded as could be promptly removed; third, cars must be promptly unloaded and returned; fourth, to permit no delay of trains beyond the time of starting, but to furnish extras when necessary.

When Burnside's corps evacuated Fredericksburg upon the withdrawal of the Federal forces from the Rappahannock line before the second Bull Run campaign, all the reconstructed work at Aquia Creek and some of the bridges on the

THE CONSTRUCTION CORPS TURNS TO WHARF-BUILDING

The construction corps of the United States Military Railroads was as versatile in its attainments as the British marines according to Kipling—"Soldier and Sailor, too." This busy scene shows construction men at work on the wharves which formed the City Point terminal to Grant's military railroad, connecting it with the army in front of Petersburg. This hastily constructed road was about thirteen miles long, measured in a straight line and not counting the undulations, which, if added together, would have made it several miles in height.

TROOPS AT CITY POINT READY TO BE TAKEN TO THE FRONT BY RAIL

THE SUPPLY ROUTE WHEN THE RAILROADS WERE WRECKED

When the Army of the Cumberland under Rosecrans retreated from the field of Chickamauga, with 16,000 of its 62,000 effectives killed and wounded, it concentrated at Chattanooga. The Confederates under Bragg held the south bank of the Tennessee, and from the end of the railroad at Bridgeport there was a haul of sixty miles to Chattanooga. Twenty-six miles of railroad, including the long truss bridge across the Tennessee River and the trestle at Whiteside, a quarter of a mile long and one hundred and thirteen feet high, had been destroyed. Rosecrans' only route to supply his army was the river. It was Lieutenant-Colonel (later Brigadier-General) William G. Le Duc who saved from a freshet the first flat-bottomed boat, the *Chattanooga*, which carried 45,000 rations up to Kelley's Ferry, whence the haul was only eight miles to the Army of the Cumberland—instead of sixty. Later more boats were built, and the railroad repaired, but it was Le Duc's ingenuity in rescuing the nondescript craft, built by Captain Edwards, from the oaks along the river and an old boiler as raw material, that saved the army many pangs of hunger, if not general starvation. The sixty-mile haul over the rough mountain-roads from Bridgeport to Chattanooga was no longer whitened with the bones of the suffering draft animals who were being killed by thousands in the desperate effort to bring food to the army. In the photograph opposite the other end of the line—Bridgeport, Alabama— is shown as it appeared April 2, 1863. Prince Felix Salm-Salm, a German soldier of fortune, was the Commander of this post. He served on the staff of General Louis Blenker and later was commissioned Colonel of the Eighth New York Volunteers, a German regiment. His final rank was Brigadier-General.

ARMY BOATS ON THE TENNESSEE—1864

railroad, including the "bean-pole and corn-stalk" bridge, had been again destroyed, this time by Federal troops. General Haupt had protested against it, but without avail. On October 26th, after the memorable battle of Antietam, McClellan requested that the Aquia Creek and Fredericksburg railroad wharves and road be reconstructed. Haupt reported that the task was now much more formidable than before; that he had protested against the destruction of the wharves and the tearing up of the road, and especially against the burning of the "bean-pole and corn-stalk" bridge over Potomac Creek; that this work was a piece of vandalism on the part of Federal troops that could have been prevented, and that it was entirely unnecessary. Nothing was done immediately toward this reconstruction, but strict orders were issued to prevent further depredations of similar character.

On the replacing of McClellan by Burnside, in 1862, the rebuilding of these structures was carried to completion, and again they were in serviceable condition for the campaign which ended so disastrously to the Federals at Fredericksburg.

W. W. Wright was instructed, on December 11, 1862, to prepare for the construction of a bridge over the Rappahannock for the passage of Burnside's army. The rebuilding of the railroad bridge was again commenced, but the battle began and forced suspension of the work, and it was not finished. The battle resulted in a check to the Federal forces, and the forward movement of the Army of the Potomac was stopped. Nothing more of importance occurred in connection with military railroad operations while Burnside was in command. After he was removed, and while the army was lying near Fredericksburg under Hooker, the construction corps was experimenting with trusses and torpedoes; and the U-shaped iron for the destruction of rails was perfected.

The battle of Chancellorsville was fought; Hooker was repulsed, and the same annoyances of guerrilla raids were experienced on the Orange and Alexandria road as had been

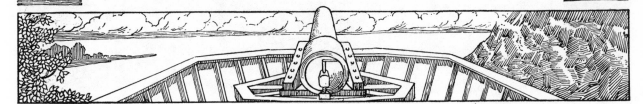

THE STRUCTURE THAT STAYED—THREE TIMES HAD THE CONFEDERATES DESTROYED THE BRIDGE AT THIS POINT—BRIDGEPORT, ALABAMA

This bridge of 1864 over the Tennessee, on the Nashville and Chattanooga Railroad at Bridgeport, Alabama, was the fourth in succession. Three previous bridges had been destroyed by the Confederates. But the United States Military Railroad Construction Corps, then under the command of Colonel D. C. McCallum, seemed like the mythical giant Antæus to rise twice as strong after each upset. So it was only for a short time that supplies were kept out of Chattanooga. So confident did Sherman become during his great Atlanta campaign of their ability to accomplish wonders, that he frequently based his plans upon the rapidity of their railroad work. They never failed him. Colonel W. W. Wright directed the transportation, and General Adna Anderson directed repairs to the road, including the reconstruction of the bridges, but this latter work was under the immediate direction of Colonel E. C. Smeed. How well it was done is evidenced by these two photographs. In the lower one the broad wagon-way below the railroad trestles can be examined.

previously felt elsewhere. On June 28, 1863, Hooker was relieved by General Meade. The crucial period of the war came at Gettysburg. The construction corps, under the personal direction of General Haupt, rendered invaluable service. Haupt had made Gettysburg his home for part of the time he was a resident of the State of Pennsylvania, and knew every road in the vicinity. He gave great assistance in divining Lee's direction of march, and by the great exertions of the corps the railroad communications were kept open, the wounded handled with celerity, and after the battle there was a sufficient supply on hand of nearly all kinds of provisions.

On September 14, 1863, General Haupt was relieved from further duty in the War Department, and turned over his work to Colonel D. C. McCallum, who was appointed superintendent of military railroads. The efficient operation of the roads with the Army of the Potomac continued, and received the enthusiastic praise from General Grant which already has been noted.

Extensions aggregating nearly twenty-two miles in length were built to the railroad from City Point, in order to supply Grant's forces in the lines before Petersburg. After the repulse of General Rosecrans at Chickamauga, in September, 1863, it was deemed necessary to send reenforcements from the Eastern armies, and the military-railroad officials were called upon to know if the movement of the number of troops designated was practicable. Colonel McCallum soon gave an affirmative answer, and the result was the transfer of Hooker, with two corps, about twenty-two thousand men, over twelve hundred miles in eleven and one-half days. For this service Colonel McCallum was appointed brevet brigadier-general.

The Knoxville-Chattanooga road was the next to be opened, and then the Nashville-Johnsonville line. In all of this work the corps introduced new methods to replace the older ones. All of this was preparatory to the advance on Atlanta, in 1864.

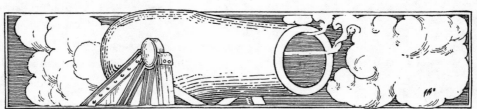

A MILL WRECKED TO BUILD A BRIDGE

CUMBERLAND RAVINE TRESTLE

This trestle across the Cumberland Ravine was rushed up from trees and other materials ready to hand. One source of supply was the mill by the mountain torrent. Few boards remain on the structure as the soldiers lounge about it. While Sherman's army advanced on Atlanta, again and again a long high bridge would be destroyed, and miles of track totally obliterated, by the retiring Confederates. But close upon their heels would come the construction corps: the bridge and track would be restored as if by magic, and the screech of an approaching locomotive would bring delight to the Federals and disappointment to the Confederates. With any materials they found ready to hand the construction corps worked at marvellous speed.

Military Railroads ❖ ❖ ❖ ❖ ❖

In the great Atlanta campaign, the railroad work of every kind was probably the best of the war. The hard schools of Virginia and around Chattanooga had prepared the railroad corps to initiate greater exhibitions of skill and efficiency. General Sherman had such confidence in the abilities of the construction corps to keep pace with him that he frequently risked advances which depended entirely on rapid railroad work behind the corps of his army, feeling assured that the rail communications would keep up with his movements. They did, and the moral effect of a screaming locomotive constantly close in the rear of his army, notwithstanding the tremendous destructive efforts of the Confederates in their retreat, was very great on both armies. A long, high bridge would be destroyed, miles of track totally obliterated, and the Confederates would retire; the Federals would advance, cross the stream in the face of opposition, and no sooner across than, to the consternation of the Confederates and the delight of the Federals, an " iron devil " would immediately set up its heartrending (delightful) screech, announcing that, march as hard and as fast as they might, neither army could get away from the end of the railroad.

The marvelous celerity with which bridges were repaired or rebuilt, new mileage of track opened, and the operation of the road carried on, notwithstanding the numerous breaks by raiding parties, will always remain a bright page in the history of the Civil War. Colonel W. W. Wright directed the transportation and remained most of the time with Sherman; General Adna Anderson directed repairs to the road, including the reconstruction of the bridges, but this latter work was under the immediate direction of Colonel E. C. Smeed. All of these officers had had previous experience in military and civil railroading that fitted them admirably for the work. General Sherman says the operation of his railroads was brilliant; that the campaign could not have been prosecuted without the efficient service which he received; that altogether there were

MILITARY TRAIN ON THE CUMBERLAND RAVINE TRESTLE—BELOW, THE CHAT-
TAHOOCHIE BRIDGE

Underneath this picture of the army trestle (seen from down-stream on the second page preceding) is reproduced a panoramic view of the Chattahoochie Bridge—the most marvelous feat of military engineering to
date (July, 1864). It was 800 feet long, nearly 100 feet high, and contained about twice as much timber as
was required for the "beanpole and cornstalk bridge," shown on page 272. It was completed in four and
a half days, from the material in the tree to the finished product. This would be record time even now.

AN 800-FOOT RAILROAD BRIDGE BUILT IN FOUR AND ONE-HALF DAYS

SWIFT REPAIR WORK BY THE MILITARY RAILROAD CORPS

DISMANTLED BY
A FRESHET
CONSTRUCTION
CORPS TO THE
RESCUE

It was not only the daring Confederates with which the United States military construction corps had to contend, but the elements as well. In April, 1864, a freshet swept away this much abused structure. The standard size parts, ready prepared, were stacked in the railroad yards awaiting calls from the front. Cars were held always ready, and the parts ordered by wire were hurried away to the broken bridge as soon as a competent engineer had inspected the break and decided what was needed. The remainder of the work of the corps after this material reached the spot was a matter of minutes, or at the most of a few hours. The lower photograph shows the Bull Run bridge being repaired.

THE TRACK OVER BULL RUN CLEAR AGAIN—CONSTRUCTION CORPS AT WORK

The parts of this railroad crossing over Bull Run near Union Mills, were of the standard size found most suitable for emergencies. This was fortunate, because the bridge was destroyed seven times. A work of this character could be put up in a very few hours. Repairing the masonry abutments, of course, consumed the greatest length of time, but even these grew like

THE BRIDGE THAT WAS DESTROYED SEVEN TIMES

magic under the efforts of the construction corps. The lower photograph shows the same bridge reënforced with trusses. These standard size trusses and other parts of bridges were carefully made by the skilled engineers of the construction corps, and tested under weights greater than any they would conceivably be called upon to bear. These parts were kept constantly on hand so that repairs could be rushed at short notice.

REËNFORCED WITH TRUSSES—TRANSFORMED INTO A STANDARD BRIDGE

473 miles of road from Louisville, through Nashville and Chattanooga, to Atlanta, 288 miles of which were constantly subject to raids from the foe—the portion from Nashville to Atlanta; that this single-stem road supplied one hundred thousand men and thirty-five thousand animals for one hundred and ninety-six days; and that to have delivered as much food by wagon would have been entirely impossible, since even to have hauled as much a short distance would have taken thirty-six thousand eight hundred six-mule wagons, and, when the state of the roads was considered, an attempt to supply by these means would have been an absurdity. Whereupon he reiterated that the Atlanta campaign would have been an impossibility without the railroads.

When Sherman evacuated Atlanta, preparatory to his march to the sea, he destroyed the railroad in his rear, blew up the railroad buildings in the city, sent back his surplus stores and all the railroad machinery that had been accumulated by his army, and, as far as possible, left the country barren to the Confederates. The stores and railroad stock were safely withdrawn to Nashville, and after the dispersion of Hood's army the construction corps again took the field, reconstructed the road to Chattanooga, then to Atlanta, and later extended it to Decatur, Macon, and Augusta.

At one time, just prior to the close of the war, there were 1,769 miles of military railroads under the direction of General McCallum, general manager of the military railroads of the United States. These roads required about three hundred and sixty-five engines and forty-two hundred cars. In April, 1865, over twenty-three thousand five hundred men were employed. The results of the work of the corps were recognized throughout the world as remarkable triumphs of military and engineering skill, highly creditable to the officers and men.

XIII

THE DEFENSE
OF
RICHMOND

THE CAPITOL AT RICHMOND UNDEFENDED, WHILE LEE AND HIS
REMNANT WERE SWEPT ASIDE—APRIL, 1865

DEFENDING THE CITADEL OF THE CONFEDERACY

By O. E. Hunt
Captain, United States Army

The Editors desire to express their grateful acknowledgment to Colonel T. M. R. Talcott, C. E., C. S. A., for a critical examination of this chapter and many helpful suggestions. Colonel Talcott was major and aide-de-camp on the staff of General Robert E. Lee, and later Colonel First Regiment Engineer Troops, Army of Northern Virginia, with an intimate knowledge of the Richmond defenses and is able to corroborate the statements and descriptions contained in the following pages from his personal knowledge.

AFTER the admission of Virginia to the Confederacy, General Lee was detailed as military adviser to the President, and several armies were put in the field—those of the Potomac, the Valley, the Rappahannock, the Peninsula, and Norfolk. It was not until the spring of 1862, when Richmond was threatened by a large Federal army under McClellan, that these forces were united under Johnston's command—Lee continuing as military adviser to the President until Johnston was wounded at Seven Pines, when the command fell to the leader whose brilliant defense of the citadel of the Confederacy from that time until the close of the great struggle excited the admiration of friend, foe, and neutral, alike.

Owing to the importance of Richmond, General Lee found himself always compelled to keep the one object in view —the defense of the capital of his State and Government.

For the safety of the city it was necessary that the approaches should be rendered defensible by small bodies of

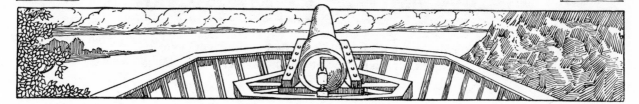

UP THE JAMES AT LAST—1865

These Federal gunboats would not be lying so far up the river—above the Dutch Gap Canal, near Fort Brady—unless the breaking of Lee's lines at Petersburg had forced the evacuation of Richmond, and of the batteries which lined the shores of the river-approach to the city. The Confederate batteries are silent now; and the dreaded Confederate fleet has been destroyed by orders of its own commander. The ironclad, *Virginia*, which never fired a shot, lies in the mud near Chaffin's Bluff opposite Fort Darling, sunk in a last desperate attempt to obstruct the approach of the Federal fleet. Now follows a scene of peace. It is wash-day, as can be seen from the lines of clothing hanging in the rigging of the gunboats and of the converted ferryboat down the river. The latter will soon return to its former peaceful use.

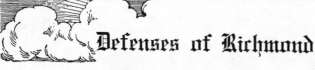 

troops, so that the main body of the Army of Northern Virginia could be utilized in strategic operations, without danger of the fall of the capital into the hands of small raiding parties from the Federal forces.

The energies of the Richmond Government were exerted in so many directions in preparing for the struggle that the immediate preparations for the defense of the capital had to proceed very uncertainly. On June 14th, General Lee reported to Governor Letcher that the work on the redoubts which had been projected was going on so slowly that he deemed it his duty to call the governor's attention to the matter.

Lee had, during the previous month, taken the precaution to fortify the James River below the mouth of the Appomattox, by having works erected on the site of old Fort Powhatan, about twelve miles below the confluence of the two rivers, and at Jamestown Island, Hardin's Bluff, Mulberry Island, and Day's Point.

In July, 1861, the citizens of Richmond were aroused to their patriotic duty of helping in the fortification of the city, and, by formal resolution of a committee on defenses, proposed that the city bear its proportionate share of the expense, and that their officers consult with those of the general Government as to the strength and location of the works. It was decided to employ the services of such free negroes as would be available in the city, under the superintendence of competent officers. To these resolutions the Secretary of War replied on July 12th, concurring in the views expressed, and saying that the question of the division of expense should be adjusted easily, inasmuch as there was a duty on the part of the Government to provide its share toward the protection of its capital; that the militia would be armed, equipped, and drilled immediately, and that the construction of the fortifications would be pushed.

The works erected during the spring and summer of 1861 in and around Norfolk and on the James River and the Peninsula, were provided for by an appropriation by the State of

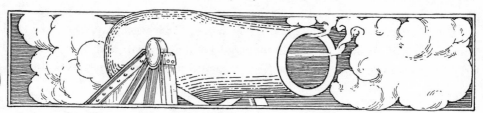

THE ARSENAL AT RICHMOND (AFTER THE FIRE)

After Richmond was selected as the Capital of the Confederate States it was deemed absolutely vital to hold the city at all costs. Aside from the impression which its fall would have made on European nations that might side with the Confederacy, its great iron-works were capable of supplying a large part of the *matériel* for the artillery of the armies and for the navy. It provided railroad supplies in considerable quantities. Its skilled artisans furnished labor essential in the technical branches of both the military and naval services during the first year or more of the war. Now, as the political center of the new Government, its importance was enhanced a hundredfold. The actual fortifications of the city were never completed. The Army of Northern Virginia, under its brilliant and daring tactician, Lee, proved the strongest defense. Field-artillery was made in Augusta, Georgia. But here, in the Tredegar Iron Works, was the only source of heavy caliber guns, of which the Confederacy stood in such woeful need.

THE TREDEGAR WORKS FOR HEAVY GUNS

Defenses of Richmond ✦ ✦ ✦ ✦

Virginia for " river, coast, and harbor defenses " made previous to the secession of the State.

On October 9th, Major Leadbetter, acting chief of the engineer bureau, reported to the Secretary of War that the pressure of work of all kinds on the city, State, and general governments had been such that but little progress had been made on the Richmond defenses. Only six guns, 32-pounders, had been mounted, while some thirty others were on hand without carriages. A few of the carriages were being built, but the work was moving slowly for the want of skilled labor to devote to that particular project. When the Norfolk Navy-Yard fell into the hands of the Confederates, there had been obtained a considerable supply of 32-pounder Dahlgrens, and army gun-carriages were being made for these at Norfolk, but this supply was limited, and the demand was so great that none could be spared for Richmond itself.

By this time, the State authorities were anxious that the whole responsibility for the fortifications should be assumed by the Confederate Government, and Major Leadbetter recommended that these wishes be observed. The greatest difficulty which he apprehended for the general Government was the lack of competent engineer officers. A number of officers of the line had been detailed as acting engineers, and with these it was hoped to carry the work to a successful conclusion.

But it was not until the end of February, 1862, that the chain of works was fairly well started. It consisted of eighteen closed or semi-closed forts, and seven outworks. The entire circuit was about twelve miles, and the designs of all the forts were good, and the proposed distances of the works from the city varied from less than a mile to more than a mile and a half from the outskirts. The complete armament would require two hundred and eighteen heavy guns.

The armament, however, was never fully furnished, for it was decided by the Virginia State authorities that the line was too near the city, and that, if closely assailed, there was

With the possible exception of Charleston at the seaside, Richmond was the best-defended city in the Confederacy. Vicksburg proved long and difficult of capture on account of the natural formation of the land, and Petersburg lay behind an army entrenched; but the series of Confederate batteries along the James River, up which the Union army and navy were trying to advance, rendered the stream impassable to the navy and the city above impregnable against the army. These guns look solitary and deserted with no one but the photographer's assistant in the picture. But each was attended by an eager crew, so long as the Confederacy held the reaches of the James. The serving of

TWO HEAVY
CONFEDERATE
SIEGE GUNS
NORTH OF
DUTCH GAP
CANAL

NAVY
BROADSIDE
42–POUNDER
WITH
REËNFORCED
BREECH

these guns marked the last great stand of the Confederacy. Union assailants will testify to how bravely and desperately they were fought. The Confederacy was calling on every man capable of bearing arms. The Federals could easily have duplicated their own armies in the field. All of these guns are mounted on old-fashioned wooden carriages. The elevating device of the gun in the upper picture differs materially from the screws for that purpose in the lower. The breech was elevated by means of handspikes, using the sides of the carriage as fulcra, and retained in the desired position by the series of checks visible on its breech. Even with these clumsy devices the guns proved too formidable for the Federal fleet.

danger that it might be destroyed even before the forts were taken. It was apparent that the lines should be extended further toward the Chickahominy, and also above and below the city they should be placed much further out. But the inner line of forts was so well built and otherwise judiciously located, that these works could be used as a support for the more advanced positions.

The principal objection to the armament was that the guns were all *en barbette,* thus exposing them and the men too much. But, by the end of February, only eleven guns had been mounted on the north side of the river, with twelve more ready to mount, while, on the south side, there were but two mounted and no others on hand. It was estimated that, even with the entire possible armament in sight, it would take at least three months to complete the instalment of the guns; but not one single piece more was then to be had.

So far as the heavy artillery of its defenses was concerned, Richmond was in almost a helpless condition. Every engineer who expressed himself felt that the danger, however, was not from the north, as that quarter was well protected by the field-army, but from the south by the approach of a land force, and along the James by the approach of a hostile fleet.

A certain amount of unsatisfactory progress was made on the works and armament; but to strengthen the river approaches, five batteries, mounting over forty guns, with provision for more, had been erected by the middle of March along the river at points below Drewry's Bluff.

By that time the control of the defenses had been transferred from the State of Virginia to the Confederate Government, and an officer of the Government placed in charge. The opinion that the works were too near the city was confirmed by the Government engineers, but, as much work had already been done on them, it was directed that they be completed as they had been originally planned, and that, in case of emergency, the secondary works to fill the gaps and those

THE RIVER APPROACH

To hold at bay the Federal navy, waxing strong on the rivers as it was practically supreme on the sea-coast, taxed the Confederates in 1864 especially. The James River emptying into Chesapeake Bay offered the invaders a tempting means of approach. So at every point of advantage in its sinuous course through the bottom lands of Virginia, a Confederate battery was placed to sweep a reach of the river. The big guns, cast and bored in Richmond, were mounted along the river in her defense. So skilfully was this work conducted that the Federal gunboats never reached Richmond until after Lee

UNION

MONITORS

HELD

AT BAY

DECEMBER,

1864

CONFEDERATE

GUNS

ALONG THE

JAMES RIVER

DEFENDING

RICHMOND

retreated from Petersburg. The banks of the James often reëchoed to the thunder of the naval guns during the last year of the war. Battery after battery was silenced, yet Drewry's and Chaffin's Bluffs held firm, while the torpedoes and obstructions in the river made it impossible to navigate. On this page appear two of the Confederate guns that frowned above Dutch Gap. The lower one is in Battery Brooke, whence the deadly fire interfered with Butler's Canal, and is a homemade naval gun. The upper one was a Columbiad with reënforced breech. Both of them are mounted on old style wooden carriages.

to cover the city at a greater distance could be constructed by the troops assigned to the defense, aided by such other labor as could be obtained. It was decided to be an injudicious waste of labor to build the outer works before the stronger inner line was completed, even though the latter was too near the city. Very few more guns were procured, however, and it seemed of doubtful propriety to place so many heavy guns in such a contracted space.

McClellan's Peninsula campaign was bringing his army dangerously near the Confederate capital. Hurried preparation of the unfinished works placed them in as strong a condition as possible, and the outer line was started. When the Federal army began its advance from Yorktown, there were only three guns in position on Drewry's Bluff, but, owing to the fear that the Union gunboats would ascend the river past the batteries further down, several ship's guns were also mounted to cover the obstructions in the channel.

On May 15th, a fleet of Union gunboats under Commander John Rodgers ascended the James and engaged the batteries at Drewry's Bluff. The seven heavy guns now on the works proved most effective against the fleet. After an engagement of four hours the vessels withdrew, considerably damaged.

From information then in the possession of the Confederates, it was supposed that McClellan would change his base to the James in order to have the cooperation of the navy, and it was hoped that he could be successfully assailed while making the change if he crossed above the mouth of the Chickahominy. The repulse of the Union fleet at Drewry's Bluff created a greater feeling of security in Richmond, and there arose a determination that the honored capital city of the Old Dominion and of the Confederacy should not fall into the hands of foes.

The battle of Seven Pines, on May 31st, initiated by Johnston while McClellan's army was divided, stopped the progress of the Federals, but the serious wounding of Johnston caused

WHAT LINCOLN SAW

THE LAST OF THE UNDAUNTED CONFEDERATE FLOTILLA—"VIRGINIA," "PATRICK HENRY" AND "JAMESTOWN" SUNK

Here are some of the sights presented to the view of President Lincoln and Admiral Porter aboard the flagship *Malvern*, as they proceeded up the James on the morning of April 3, 1865, to enter the fallen city of Richmond. To the right of the top photograph rise the stacks of the Confederate ram *Virginia*. Near the middle lie the ruined wheels of the *Jamestown*. And in the bottom picture, before Fort Darling appears the wreck of the *Patrick Henry*. All these were vessels of Commodore Mitchell's command that had so long made

COAL SCHOONERS WRECKED TO BLOCK THE JAMES—(BELOW) DREWRY'S BLUFFS

every effort to break the bonds forged about them by a more powerful force, afloat and ashore. The previous night Lincoln, as Admiral Porter's guest on the deck of the *Malvern*, had listened to the sound of the great engagement on shore and had asked if the navy could not do something to make history at the same time. When told that the navy's part was one merely of watchfulness, the President responded, "But can't we make a noise?" Porter at once telegraphed to his fleet-captain to open upon the forts; then the air was rent with the sound of great guns up the river. Soon, rising even louder, came the sound of four great explosions one after another—the blowing up of Commodore Mitchell's vessels.

Defenses of Richmond

the command to devolve upon General G. W. Smith until June 2d, when President Davis assigned General Lee to the command of the Army of Northern Virginia.

Lee felt that if McClellan could not be driven out of his entrenchments, there was danger that he would move by successive positions, under cover of his heavy guns, to within shelling distance of Richmond; and to prevent this contingency, Jackson was to fall on the Federal right flank to help drive McClellan from his position. The movement was so skilfully made that the Federal commanders in the Valley and the authorities in Washington were completely deceived, and the Union army now found itself on the defensive, and the history of the Peninsula campaign records the retreat of McClellan instead of a close investment of Richmond.

During these operations, the field-works thrown up by the Confederate army constituted the principal auxiliary defenses, but as these were not in positions proper for the immediate defense of the city, they were of no particular value after the removal of the forces to other positions. As soon as the army could recover from the strain of the ordeal through which it had passed, Lee turned his attention to the fortifications immediately surrounding the capital.

On July 13th, he directed the Engineer Corps to prepare a system of defenses from Drewry's Bluff encircling the approaches to Manchester from the south, and, on the 31st, he directed that the construction of the outside lines north of the James be resumed. At the same time, more guns were ordered to be placed on the Drewry's Bluff defenses, as well as on the other works along the south side of the James. The works of Petersburg were strengthened also.

When Lee started for the Rapidan to enter on the campaign against Pope, all the troops of the Army of Northern Virginia were withdrawn from the fortifications of Richmond, and relieved from garrison duty and from the work of construction by the troops of General D. H. Hill's command.

[314]

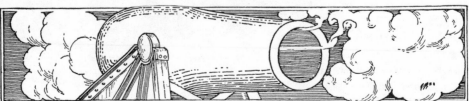

BATTERY BROOKE—GUNS THAT BOTHERED BUTLER

Halfway between the Confederate Fort Darling at Drewry's Bluff and the Dutch Gap Canal, which General Butler was busily constructing, the Confederates had dug this powerful work. Its establishment r e n - dered the construction of the Dutch Gap Canal a futile military operation. After 140 days spent in excavating it, Butler, on New Year's Day, 1865, exploded 12,000 pounds of powder under the bulkhead; but it fell back into the opening. Under the fire from the guns of Battery Brooke the obstruction could not be removed nor could the canal be dredged sufficiently to admit of the passage of vessels. The picture looks south along the main ramparts, fronting east on the river. While the Army of the Potomac was fully occupied at Petersburg, this battery bellowed out hearty defiance to the fleet by night and day. The strong Confederate fortifications cn the James between the Appomattox and Richmond were effective in keeping General Butler bottled up in Bermuda Hundred.

BOMB-PROOF IN BATTERY BROOKE

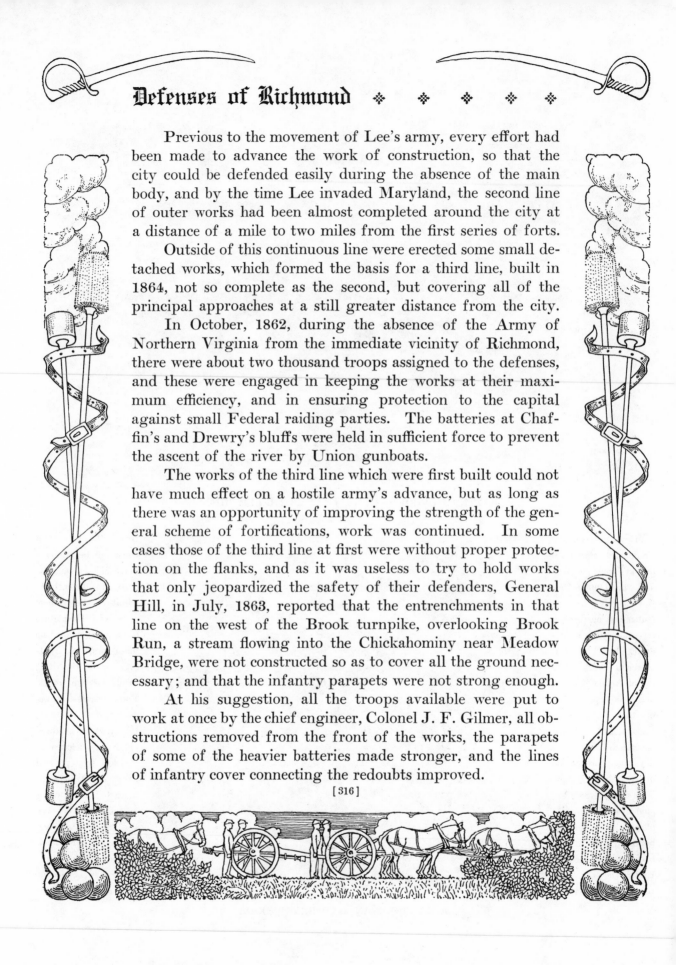

Defenses of Richmond ❖ ❖ ❖ ❖ ❖

Previous to the movement of Lee's army, every effort had been made to advance the work of construction, so that the city could be defended easily during the absence of the main body, and by the time Lee invaded Maryland, the second line of outer works had been almost completed around the city at a distance of a mile to two miles from the first series of forts.

Outside of this continuous line were erected some small detached works, which formed the basis for a third line, built in 1864, not so complete as the second, but covering all of the principal approaches at a still greater distance from the city.

In October, 1862, during the absence of the Army of Northern Virginia from the immediate vicinity of Richmond, there were about two thousand troops assigned to the defenses, and these were engaged in keeping the works at their maximum efficiency, and in ensuring protection to the capital against small Federal raiding parties. The batteries at Chaffin's and Drewry's bluffs were held in sufficient force to prevent the ascent of the river by Union gunboats.

The works of the third line which were first built could not have much effect on a hostile army's advance, but as long as there was an opportunity of improving the strength of the general scheme of fortifications, work was continued. In some cases those of the third line at first were without proper protection on the flanks, and as it was useless to try to hold works that only jeopardized the safety of their defenders, General Hill, in July, 1863, reported that the entrenchments in that line on the west of the Brook turnpike, overlooking Brook Run, a stream flowing into the Chickahominy near Meadow Bridge, were not constructed so as to cover all the ground necessary; and that the infantry parapets were not strong enough.

At his suggestion, all the troops available were put to work at once by the chief engineer, Colonel J. F. Gilmer, all obstructions removed from the front of the works, the parapets of some of the heavier batteries made stronger, and the lines of infantry cover connecting the redoubts improved.

BIG
GUNS
NEAR
RICHMOND

FORT
DARLING
JAMES
RIVER

The narrow reach of the James is swept in both directions by the gun in the upper picture—a large Brooke rifle, made at the Tredegar Iron Works in the Confederate Capital. The gun below is a Columbiad with Brooke reënforcement. It is mounted within Fort Darling, and points down the James toward Chaffin's Bluff, visible beyond the bend to the left. Drewry's Bluff commanded this portion of the river so completely that it was chosen as the site of the first hastily constructed defenses of Richmond in 1862, and was subsequently so strengthened as to be almost impregnable. The guns there mounted remained the guardians closest to the Capital on the James until the withdrawal of Lee with his remnant of the Army of Northern Virginia from Petersburg rendered them useless in 1865.

THE FALL OF RICHMOND

When the news reached Richmond, April 2, 1865, that Lee's slender lines had been broken below Petersburg and that the city was forthwith to be abandoned, pandemonium ruled for a brief space of time. All that day by train and wagon, by horse and on foot, the people fled from the city. Early in the evening bands of ruffians appeared, and pillaged and caroused until the arrest of their ringleaders. The magazines were exploded, and Richmond flamed up to the sky, turning the darkness into daylight. There was little sleep

NEGRO REFUGEES WITH THEIR HOUSEHOLD GOODS ON THE CANAL

that night. Next morning an immense pall seemed to hover over the city that was a capital no more. That day the Union columns of blue marched into Richmond, and the sky was rent with their cheers as they swept into Capitol Square. Forty-eight hours after that memorable still Sunday morning when the news of the break in Lee's lines reached Richmond, the city again lay quiet, her buildings charred, her people sorrow laden. The Sunday following Lee surrendered at Appomattox. The armies in the West shortly yielded.

By the time of the arrival of the Confederate army at Cold Harbor, the third line of defenses had been run northeast from Chaffin's Bluff to the Charles City road, which was crossed four and one-half miles outside of the city, thence directly north to the ground overlooking the swampy lowlands of the Chickahominy, where it terminated abruptly, its flank commanding New Bridge, five miles outside of Richmond. From here, detached works held the ground upstream overlooking the river, and connected with the lines that had been started on ground overlooking the Chickahominy bottoms directly north of the city the year before. These were now completed, and the lines of detached works followed the right bank of Brook Run to its source and then bent toward the James, across the Deep Run turnpike and the plank road, four miles up the James from the outskirts of the city. The completion of this line resulted in there being three strong lines of defense.

The weary ten months which followed tested the strength of the gradually weakening defense. All realized that the fall of Petersburg meant the fall of Richmond, and that the patient toil on the miles of entrenchments around the capital finally had had the effect of causing the blow to fall elsewhere. Two expeditions were sent by Grant against the lines to the north of Richmond, but not in sufficient strength to test the works. The principal object was to weaken the forces defending Petersburg so as to permit a successful assault to be delivered.

The Federal army, under able leaders tested in the furnace of war, exhausted every device to break through the Petersburg lines. They tried them by assault, by mining, by flanking, and by bombardment. Lee's genius, seconded by that of his officers, and maintained by the gallant devotion of his troops, held on till the army was worn out and the stretching of the lines by constant extension to meet the Federal movements to the left, finally caused them to be so weak as to break under a Federal assault. Petersburg was abandoned, and Richmond fell.

THE CAPTURED MAP OF THE DEFENSES OF RICHMOND

This map of the defenses of Richmond was found on the body of the Confederate Brigadier-General John R. Chambliss, by Federal cavalrymen under Gregg. Chambliss had been killed in an engagement with these troopers near White Oak Branch, seven miles from Richmond, on August 16, 1864. Early that month Grant heard that reënforcements were being sent to General Early in the Shenandoah for the purpose of threatening Washington. In order to compel the recall of these troops, and to cause the weakening of the Confederate lines before Petersburg, Hancock took the Second and part of the Ninth Corps and Gregg's cavalry to the north side of the James, threatening the works of Richmond. On the morning of August 16th, Gregg advanced on the right of the Federal line toward White's Tavern, near White Oak Branch. It was here that the action, the death of Chambliss, and the capture of the map took place. Even with the plans of the Southerners thus unexpectedly in their possession, the Federals were unable to pass these defenses until Lee's little army had been forced aside.

The Photographic History
of The Civil War

TWO VOLUMES IN ONE.
The Navies

A VISION OF THE BY-GONE
THE SLOOP–OF–WAR "PORTSMOUTH" OF THE OLD NAVY

Here is a sight the like of which never will be seen again—the U. S. sloop-of-war "Portsmouth" at anchor and drying out her sails. An honorable record did this old corvette leave behind her. Of the type of vessel that had fought in the War of 1812, she had gone through the Mexican War, and had chased and captured many a slaver. But a year or so ago, she was still afloat as the training-ship of the New Jersey state militia. She has every sail up except her head-sails and studding sails. As can be seen at a glance, she was a very lofty craft, and though clewed up, she has her sky-sails, her royals, her topgallant-sails, her topsails, set on every mast. "Excellent, whether sailing, steering, working, scudding, lying to, or riding at anchor in a seaway, she sometimes got her sternboard in stays." With this single exception, reported Commander Armstrong, "she possesses the finest qualities of any ship I ever sailed in; rolls as easy as a cradle, and stands up under her canvas like a church." Lying under her stern is the captain's gig; her other boats seem to have been called away; probably one of the watches has gone ashore.

The Photographic History of The Civil War

Complete and Unabridged

TWO VOLUMES IN ONE.

Volume 3
Forts and Artillery
*The Navies

EDITOR

O. E. HUNT

Captain, United States Army ; Instructor in Modern Languages,
United States Military Academy

Contributors

O. E. HUNT

Captain, United States Army

J. W. MALLET

Lieutenant-Colonel, Confederate States Army,
and Superintendent of the Ordnance Laboratories of the Confederate States; Professor of
Chemistry in the University of Virginia

DAVID GREGG McINTOSH

Colonel of Artillery, Confederate States Army

T. M. R. TALCOTT, C.E.

Colonel Commanding Engineering Troops, Army
of Northern Virginia

FREDERICK M. COLSTON

Lieutenant and Ordnance Officer, Alexander's
Battalion of Artillery, Longstreet's Corps,
Army of Northern Virginia

THE BLUE & GREY PRESS

CONTENTS

PAGE

Frontispiece—THE SLOOP-OF-WAR "PORTSMOUTH" OF THE OLD NAVY . . . 4

Preface 11

Introduction—THE FEDERAL NAVY AND THE BLOCKADE 13
    French E. Chadwick

THE ORGANIZATION OF THE FEDERAL NAVY 41

THE ORGANIZATION OF THE CONFEDERATE NAVY 71

FIRST EXPEDITIONS OF THE FEDERAL NAVY 91

THE BLOCKADE 105

THE BIRTH OF THE IRONCLADS 129

THE MOST FAMOUS AMERICAN NAVAL BATTLE 153

THE MOST DARING FEAT 183

FIGHTING ON THE MISSISSIPPI 205

THE ACTIONS WITH THE FORTS 235

NAVAL ACTIONS ALONG THE SHORES 261

THE SEA LIFE OF '61 277

THE CONFEDERATE CRUISERS AND THE "ALABAMA" 287

NAVAL CHRONOLOGY, 1861–1865 307

PHOTOGRAPH DESCRIPTIONS THROUGHOUT THE VOLUME
    James Barnes
    Robert Sloss

PREFACE

FEW annals in the history of the United States are of greater and more compelling interest than those connected with the achievement of its sailors. The descendants of Drake and Frobisher, led by John Paul Jones, Perry, Bainbridge, Porter, and other illustrious naval heroes in the days of lofty spars and topsails, made a name for themselves both on the sea and on the lasting scrolls of history. Their records, penned by historians and novelists, form brilliant pages in American literature. Therefore, it was not strange that a conflict in which officers and seamen of the same race and speech, graduates of the same historic Naval Academy and sailing the same seas and along the same shores, met in heroic struggle, should form a story second to none in its fascination and interest.

The Civil War ships and the men who fought them are distinctive in naval history, not for immensity of single battles or extent of total destruction, but for diversity of action, the complete realization of the ironclad as a fighting vessel, and the development of the torpedo as a weapon of destruction. Readers are fortunate in finding, at the outset of this volume, the scholarly appreciation by Admiral Chadwick of the essential part played by the navies in the war, while the battles at sea and on inland waters are described by Mr. Barnes with a vividness possible only to a naval historian to whom the sea and its sailors long have been objects of sympathetic study.

The photographic record of the great American conflict

Preface

is particularly striking in this volume. Never before has there been assembled such a pictorial and actual record of fleets and sailors, Union and Confederate. The stately frigate with walls of live-oak, the newly born ironclad, the swift blockade-runner, the commerce-destroying cruiser, which left its indelible mark on the American merchant marine no less than on international law, and last, but not least, the actors in scenes of the great naval drama appear on the pages that follow, in an illustrated " catalogue of the ships " that even Homer in his stately Iliad could have envied.

INTRODUCTION

BY

FRENCH E. CHADWICK

THE VALUE OF DISCIPLINE—PRACTICE ON THE "MENDOTA"

THOUGH LAMENTABLY UNPREPARED FOR WAR IN '61, THE FEDERAL NAVY BY 1864 SET AN
EXAMPLE OF CONSTANT ARDUOUS TRAINING AND DRILL, EVEN DURING LULLS IN THE ACTUAL
FIGHTING SUCH AS WHEN THIS PHOTOGRAPH WAS TAKEN, ON THE JAMES RIVER IN 1864

CUSTODIANS OF THE COAST

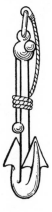

Looking out from the mouth of every important harbor along the Southern seacoast, the Confederates were confronted by just such a grim menace as this. Riding at anchor or moving swiftly from point to point, the Federal fighting-ships, with sleepless vigilance, night and day sought every opportunity to destroy the vessels which attempted to keep up the commercial intercourse of the Confederacy with the outside world. At first it was chiefly a "paper blockade," and the fact that its mere announcement accorded to the Confederacy the status of belligerents was hailed at the South as a fortunate diplomatic mistake. Swift merchantmen abroad were easily induced to enter the bold enter-prise which meant such profitable trade; laughing at the inadequate Federal patrol, they began to dump huge cargoes of the munitions of war at every Southern port, taking in return cotton, so necessary to keep the looms of Europe going. With the rapid growth of the Federal navy the blockade, whose early impotence had been winked at by European powers, became more and more a fact. The cordon was drawn tighter and tighter from the Potomac to the Rio Grande. One venturesome vessel after another was overhauled or driven ashore and both they and their cargoes became the rich prizes of the Federal navy. While this served vastly to increase the difficulty and danger of dealing

A FLEET OF FEDERAL BLOCKADERS IN 1864

with the South, it did not deter greatly the bold spirits to whom this war-time commerce was so profitable and necessary, and down to the fall of the last Southern seaport swift blockade-runners were found that could continue to show the beleaguering fleet a clean pair of heels. From the war's very beginning the Confederates were hopeful of being able to oppose the Federal navy with fighting-vessels that would raise the blockade, but they could not build boats fast enough, and almost as soon as they were finished they were captured or destroyed in one bold attempt after another to contend with the superior numbers that opposed them. Once at Mobile and again at Charleston, after a naval victory the Confederates proclaimed the blockade raised, only to find that in a few days the investing fleet had been doubled in strength. Meanwhile the blockade-runners continued to ply between Nassau, Bermuda, and other convenient depots and the ports of the Confederacy. Charleston, S. C., and Wilmington, N. C., the two most closely guarded ports, continued to be made by these greyhounds of the sea until the Federal land forces at last compassed the evacuation of the towns. Enormous as was the quantity of the merchandise and munitions of war that got by the blockade, it was the work of the Federal navy that first began to curtail the traffic, and finally ended it,

CONFEDERATES IN THE NEWLY–CAPTURED PENSACOLA FORT—1861

Full of enthusiasm and military spirit, but suspecting little what trials lay before them, the Confederate volunteers pictured here are drilling at one of the forts that had been abandoned by the Federal Government, even before the momentous shot was fired at Sumter. Fort Pickens, through the forethought of Commander Henry Walke, who disobeyed his orders most brilliantly and successfully, had been saved to the Federal Government. The other batteries and forts at Pensacola, however, had been handed over to the Confederacy, and here we see the men in gray, early in '61, taking advantage of the gift. Note the new uniforms, the soldierly and well-fed appearance of the men, the stores of ammunition for the great guns.

WHERE THE BLOCKADERS CAME TOO LATE

Many of these soldiers pictured here were soon fighting miles away from where we see them now; a great many were drafted from New Orleans, from Mobile, Savannah, and Charleston; Florida and Georgia furnished their full quota to the Confederate army. This photograph was taken by Edwards, of New Orleans, who, like his confrère Lytle, succeeded in picturing many of the stirring scenes and opening tableaux of the war; they afterward took advantage of their art and used their cameras as batteries at the command of the Confederate secret service, photographing ships and troops and guns of the Federal forces, and sending them to the commanding generals of their departments. Over the chase of the gun is Pensacola harbor.

INTRODUCTION—THE FEDERAL NAVY
AND THE BLOCKADE

By F. E. Chadwick
Rear-Admiral, United States Navy

THE American Civil War marks one of the great social reconstructions which are ever taking place as we advance from plane to plane of mentality. The American and the French revolutions; the overthrow of European feudalism by Napoleon, who was but the special instrument of a great movement, are among the special reconstructions more immediately preceding that of 1861, but all had, in a way, a common impulse—the impulse which comes from having arrived at a new mental outlook.

Such revolutions may be bloodless if mental development is equal to meeting the emergency, as it was in the formation of the American Constitution, in 1787. They are, however, far more apt to be in blood, as was that of 1861, which was brought about by the immense and rapid development, in the last century, of mechanism, the press, and the mobility of populations. We had to step to a new mental, moral, and psychic plane, and war was made certain by the want of a wisdom and foresight which, in the circumstances, it was, perhaps, too much to expect.

The present volume deals with the part taken by the navy in the great contest—a part of vastly greater importance than has generally been recognized. Historians are, however, beginning to see that the rôle of the navy was a vital one, absolutely necessary to success; that the blockade was a constrictive force which devitalized Southern effort. Whatever doubt may have existed at the outset as to the strategy of the

[18]

THE "SABINE," THE FIRST BLOCKADER IN THE SOUTH ATLANTIC

The towering masts of this fine sailing frigate arrived in Pensacola Harbor on April 12, 1861, the day Fort Sumter was fired upon. With the "Brooklyn," she landed reënforcements at Fort Pickens. On May 13th, Captain H. A. Adams of the "Sabine" issued notice of the blockade at Pensacola, the first Atlantic port to be thus closed. The "Sabine," like her prototypes, the "United States" and the "Constitution," mounted 44 guns. She sailed on the expedition to Paraguay in 1858–9, and became one of the first ships of the old navy to see active service in the Civil War. She served in Admiral Du Pont's squadron on the expedition to Port Royal in November, 1861. Her commander on that expedition was Captain Cadwalader Ringgold. It was largely due to the heroic efforts of his officers and crew that 650 marines were saved from drowning when the transport "Governor" foundered on the 3d. In February, 1862, when the "new-fangled" "Monitor," the latest "Yankee notion" in war vessels, was going begging for officers and men, a crew was at last formed largely of volunteers from the "Sabine." Of such stuff were made the tars of the old American sailing-ships of war

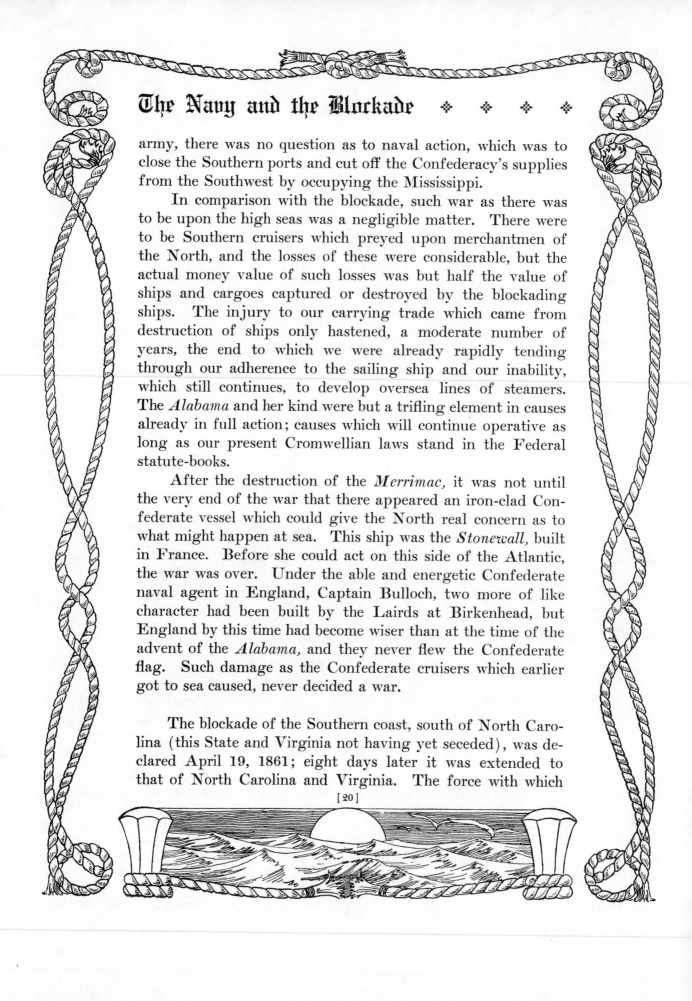

The Navy and the Blockade ❖ ❖ ❖ ◈

army, there was no question as to naval action, which was to close the Southern ports and cut off the Confederacy's supplies from the Southwest by occupying the Mississippi.

In comparison with the blockade, such war as there was to be upon the high seas was a negligible matter. There were to be Southern cruisers which preyed upon merchantmen of the North, and the losses of these were considerable, but the actual money value of such losses was but half the value of ships and cargoes captured or destroyed by the blockading ships. The injury to our carrying trade which came from destruction of ships only hastened, a moderate number of years, the end to which we were already rapidly tending through our adherence to the sailing ship and our inability, which still continues, to develop oversea lines of steamers. The *Alabama* and her kind were but a trifling element in causes already in full action; causes which will continue operative as long as our present Cromwellian laws stand in the Federal statute-books.

After the destruction of the *Merrimac,* it was not until the very end of the war that there appeared an iron-clad Confederate vessel which could give the North real concern as to what might happen at sea. This ship was the *Stonewall,* built in France. Before she could act on this side of the Atlantic, the war was over. Under the able and energetic Confederate naval agent in England, Captain Bulloch, two more of like character had been built by the Lairds at Birkenhead, but England by this time had become wiser than at the time of the advent of the *Alabama,* and they never flew the Confederate flag. Such damage as the Confederate cruisers which earlier got to sea caused, never decided a war.

The blockade of the Southern coast, south of North Carolina (this State and Virginia not having yet seceded), was declared April 19, 1861; eight days later it was extended to that of North Carolina and Virginia. The force with which

CAUGHT BY HER OWN KIND

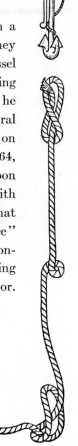

The blockade-runner "A. D. Vance." It frequently took a blockade-runner to catch a blockade-runner, and as the Federal navy captured ship after ship of this character they began to acquire a numerous fleet of swift steamers from which it was difficult for any vessel to get away. The "Vance" brought many a cargo to the hungry Southern ports, slipping safely by the blockading fleet and back again till her shrewd Captain Willie felt that he could give the slip to anything afloat. On her last trip she had safely gotten by the Federal vessels lying off the harbor of Wilmington, North Carolina, and was dancing gleefully on her way with a bountiful cargo of cotton and turpentine when, on September 10, 1864, in latitude 34° N., longitude 76° W., a vessel was sighted which rapidly bore down upon her. It proved to be the "Santiago de Cuba," Captain O. S. Glisson. The rapidity with which the approaching vessel overhauled him was enough to convince Captain Willie that she was in his own class. The "Santiago de Cuba" carried eleven guns, and the "Vance" humbly hove to, to receive the prize-crew which took her to Boston, where she was condemned. In the picture we see her lying high out of the water, her valuable cargo having been removed and sold to enrich by prize-money the officers and men of her fleet captor.

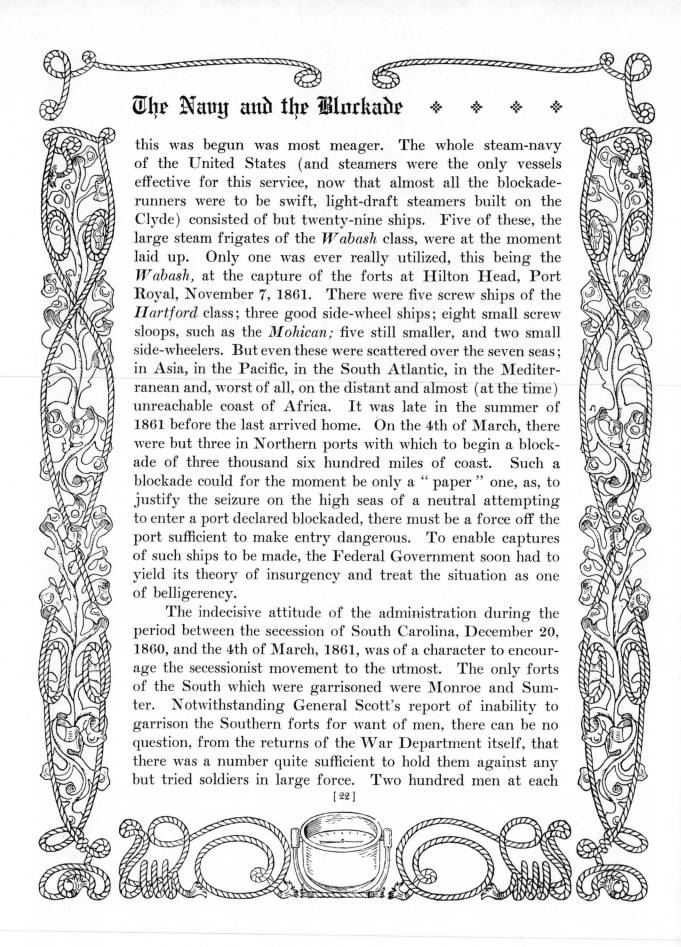

this was begun was most meager. The whole steam-navy of the United States (and steamers were the only vessels effective for this service, now that almost all the blockade-runners were to be swift, light-draft steamers built on the Clyde) consisted of but twenty-nine ships. Five of these, the large steam frigates of the *Wabash* class, were at the moment laid up. Only one was ever really utilized, this being the *Wabash,* at the capture of the forts at Hilton Head, Port Royal, November 7, 1861. There were five screw ships of the *Hartford* class; three good side-wheel ships; eight small screw sloops, such as the *Mohican;* five still smaller, and two small side-wheelers. But even these were scattered over the seven seas; in Asia, in the Pacific, in the South Atlantic, in the Mediterranean and, worst of all, on the distant and almost (at the time) unreachable coast of Africa. It was late in the summer of 1861 before the last arrived home. On the 4th of March, there were but three in Northern ports with which to begin a blockade of three thousand six hundred miles of coast. Such a blockade could for the moment be only a " paper " one, as, to justify the seizure on the high seas of a neutral attempting to enter a port declared blockaded, there must be a force off the port sufficient to make entry dangerous. To enable captures of such ships to be made, the Federal Government soon had to yield its theory of insurgency and treat the situation as one of belligerency.

The indecisive attitude of the administration during the period between the secession of South Carolina, December 20, 1860, and the 4th of March, 1861, was of a character to encourage the secessionist movement to the utmost. The only forts of the South which were garrisoned were Monroe and Sumter. Notwithstanding General Scott's report of inability to garrison the Southern forts for want of men, there can be no question, from the returns of the War Department itself, that there was a number quite sufficient to hold them against any but tried soldiers in large force. Two hundred men at each

A FIGHTING INVENTOR
REAR–ADMIRAL JOHN A. DAHLGREN ON BOARD THE U. S. S. "PAWNEE" IN CHARLESTON HARBOR

Over the admiral's right shoulder can be seen the ruins of the still unsurrendered Fort Sumter. It was for his services on land that Dahlgren was made rear-admiral, Feb. 7, 1863. He had been employed on ordnance duty between 1847–57. With the exception of a short cruise, he had spent the ten years in perfecting the Dahlgren gun, his own invention. In 1862 he was chief of the Bureau of Ordnance. From this he stepped into command of the South Atlantic blockading squadron, July 6, 1863. From that time on he showed the qualities of a great commander in active service. Not only did he bravely and wisely direct the naval activities in Charleston Harbor, but in February, 1864, he led the naval expedition up the St. John's River that was to coöperate with the troops in gaining a hold in Florida. In December, 1864, he coöperated with General Sherman in the capture of Savannah, and on Feb. 18, 1865, he had the satisfaction of moving his vessels up to Charleston, the evacuated city that he had striven so long to capture.

would have been ample to hold the important forts below New Orleans, at Mobile, Pensacola, Savannah, and Wilmington. There were at the Northern posts, which might, of course, have been completely denuded of men with safety, over one thousand men. Fort Monroe was sufficiently garrisoned for protection; the total garrison of Sumter was but eighty-four. As it was, the other forts had simply to be entered and occupied by the raw secessionist volunteers. Such occupancy, which gradually took place, naturally gave an immense impetus to the Southern movement. Had these forts been occupied by Federal troops and had Sumter been properly reenforced, there can be little question that secession would have ended with the act of South Carolina. For with her ports in Federal hands, the South was powerless. Communication with the exterior world was to her a necessity in the strongest meaning of the word, because she was lacking in many things of vital importance. She could not have gone to war; she would not have gone to war, in so helpless a situation.

Even the one effort to hold any of these forts, the retention of which was so vital, was made abortive by the action of Scott in causing to be embarked in New York, in the merchant steamer *Star of the West,* a raw company of artillery under a lieutenant for the reenforcement of Fort Sumter, instead of a force of the older soldiers from Fort Monroe, in the *Brooklyn.* The *Star of the West* made a feeble effort to enter Charleston Harbor. She was fired upon, and seeing no colors hoisted at Sumter or sign of assistance from the fort, turned and went to sea. Had the *Brooklyn* been sent, as President Buchanan, to his credit be it said, intended, and as had been first arranged, the secessionist battery would not have dared to fire upon the powerful man-of-war, or, had it dared, the few guns of the battery or of all of the improvised defenses, none of which had before fired a shot, would have been quickly silenced by the *Brooklyn's* guns; the ship would have occupied the harbor; Sumter would have been manned and provisioned, and

[24]

LEADERS OF DIPLOMACY IN 1863

SECRETARY SEWARD AND NINE FOREIGN DIPLOMATS AT THE TIME WHEN CONFEDERATE CRUISERS ABROAD WERE AN INTERNATIONAL PROBLEM

No military picture of moving troops, no group of distinguished generals, could possibly hold the interest for students of the history of the Civil War that this photograph possesses. It is the summer of 1863. Gathered at the foot of this beautiful waterfall, as if at the end of a day's outing for pleasure, are ten men of mark and great importance. Here are William H. Seward, American Secretary of State, standing bareheaded, to the right. With him, numbered so that the reader can easily identify them, are (2) Baron De Stoeckel, Russian Minister; (3) M. Molena, Nicaraguan Minister; (4) Lord Lyons, British Minister; (5) M. Mercier, French Minister; (6) M. Schleiden, Hanseatic Minister; (7) M. Bertenatti, Italian Minister; (8) Count Piper, Swedish Minister; (9) M. Bodisco, Secretary Russian Legation; (10) Mr. Sheffield, Attaché British Legation; (11) Mr. Donaldson, a messenger in the State Department. These were ticklish times in diplomatic circles. Outwardly polite to one another, and on an occasion such as this probably lowering the bars of prescribed convention, many of these men would have liked to know what was going on in the brains of their associates, for diplomacy is but a game of mental hide-and-seek. More than any one else would Mr. Seward have desired at this moment to be gifted in the art of mind-reading. He would have liked to hear from Lord Lyons exactly what stand the British Government was going to take in relation to the Confederate cruisers that had been outfitted in Great Britain. He would have liked to hear also from Minister Mercier more on the subject of the vessels building in France that he had been in correspondence with John Bigelow about, and he would have liked to know exactly what Napoleon III was trying to do in Mexico, in the ambitious game of which Maximilian was a pawn. The Nicaraguan Minister would have appreciated a word himself on the latter subject; and Lord Lyons, in view of the presence of the Russian fleet, would have liked to pick the brain of Baron De Stoeckel, whose royal master, the Czar, had made such firm offers of friendship to the United States at just this hour. Mr. Schleiden, in view of what was to happen in the next few years, would have welcomed an outburst of confidence from M. Mercier, and for that matter, so would M. Bertenatti. But here they are, sinking all questions of statecraft and posing for the photographer as if the game of diplomacy was far from their minds and they were ordinary "trippers" seeing the sights

Charleston Harbor would have been permanently in the hands of the Federal authorities.

Equal folly, inefficiency, and, in cases, disloyalty were shown in the failure to take steps to protect the great navy-yard at Norfolk and in the surrender of that at Pensacola. The former could have been saved had the incoming administration acted more promptly; the latter could, at any moment in the two months succeeding its surrender in January, have been reoccupied, had there been a show of wisdom in government affairs. With the loss of these two great establishments went the loss of some thousands of cannon, which went to arm the Southern batteries. Had these untoward events not happened, affairs would have assumed a very different phase; for a time, at least, war would have been deferred, and soberer thought might have had its weight.

Whether it were better that the war should be fought, and the pick of the manhood of the South and much of that of the North perish, need not be discussed; but the patent fact remains that the failure to employ the *Brooklyn* instead of the *Star of the West,* the failure to garrison the other forts of the South, the failure to save Norfolk and Pensacola were governmental failures of surpassing ineptitude and folly, only to be made good by four years of a war which brought three millions of men into the field, six hundred ships to close the Southern ports, engulfed the treasure of the North, and laid waste the South. The change to our new mental and psychical plane, a change which had to be made, was dearly bought for want of wisdom and foresight beyond our powers at the moment.

Leaving aside the what-might-have-beens and coming to things as they happened, the blockade, by the end of 1861, had become so effective that in the governmental year of 1861–62, the total cotton exported from the South was but thirteen thousand bales as against the two million of the previous season. During the quarter beginning September 1, 1861, less

FOREIGN ALLIES

Here in the harbor of Alexandria, Va., the crew of the Russian frigate " Osliaba" have climbed into the rigging to view with the officers on the bridge the strange land to which they had been sent on a friendly mission. England was almost openly hostile to the North at the beginning of the war, while France better concealed its sympathies. Its diplomats were highly in favor of joining with Germany and Italy to aid Maximilian in setting up his monarchy in Mexico. The Federal navy was confronted from the start, not only with the problem of the blockade, but with that of providing sufficient fighting-ships to enable it to contend successfully with the navies of foreign powers in case complications arose. When Emperor Alexander ordered his warships to proceed to American waters, there was an end to rumors of foreign hostilities; and when one division of the Russian fleet entered New York Harbor and the other the Golden Gate, feasts of welcome awaited both officers and men who had come to augment the Federal navy at its most critical period.

than one thousand bales of cotton left Charleston Harbor, as against one hundred and ten thousand for a like period in 1860; but four thousand four hundred bushels of rice as against twenty-three thousand; one thousand five hundred barrels of naval stores as against thirty-three thousand. Only thirty-two thousand and fifty bales of cotton left Charleston from July 1, 1861, to April 1, 1863.*

How much this means may be seen by the remarks of Alexander H. Stephens, Vice President of the Confederate States, in a speech on November 1, 1862. He said:

I was in favor of the Government's taking all the cotton that would be subscribed for eight-per-cent. bonds at ten cents a pound. Two million bales of last-year's crop might have been counted on. This would have cost the Government a hundred million bonds. With this cotton in hand and pledged, any number short of fifty of the best iron-clad steamers could have been contracted for and built in Europe —steamers at two millions each could have been procured. Thirty millions would have got fifteen. Five might have been ready by the 1st of January last to open one of our blockaded ports. Three could have been left to keep the port open, while two could have conveyed the cotton across, if necessary. Thus, the debt could have been paid with cotton at a much higher price than it cost, and a channel of trade kept open until others could have been built and paid for in the same way. At less than one month's present expenditure on our army, our coast might have been cleared. Besides this, at least two million more bales of the old crop might have been counted on; this, with the other, making a debt in round numbers to the planters of two hundred million dollars. But this cotton, held in Europe until the price shall be fifty cents a pound [it went much higher], would constitute a fund of at least one billion dollars, which not only would have kept our finances in sound condition, but the clear profit of eight hundred million dollars would have met the entire expenses of the war for years to come.†

* Schwab.

† M. L. Avary. *Recollections of Alexander H. Stephens. His Diary, etc.*, 1910.

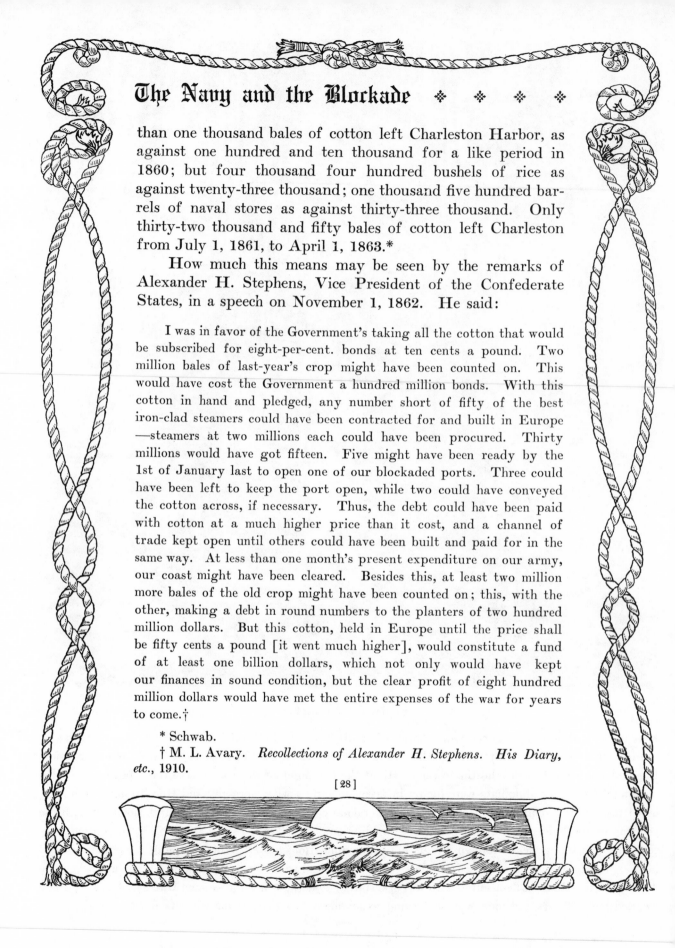

A FRIENDLY VISITOR

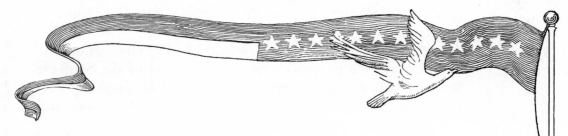

The Russians, although in some degree a maritime nation, did not devote much attention to their navy, as can be seen from a glance at this picture of one of the visiting Russian vessels during the Civil War, the "Osliaba." In another photograph has been shown a group of their sailors. They are as different in appearance from the trim American and English men-of-warsmen as their vessel is different from an American or English man-of-war. The Russian sailors were all conscripts, mostly taken from inland villages and forced to take up a sea-faring life in the service of the Czar. There had to be a sprinkling of real seamen among the crew, but they, like the poor serfs from the country, were conscripts also. The Russian harbors are practically cut off from the world by ice for at least five months of the year. This fact has prevented Russia from taking a place among maritime nations. It has been Russia's purpose to reach warm-water harbors that has brought on two of its greatest wars.

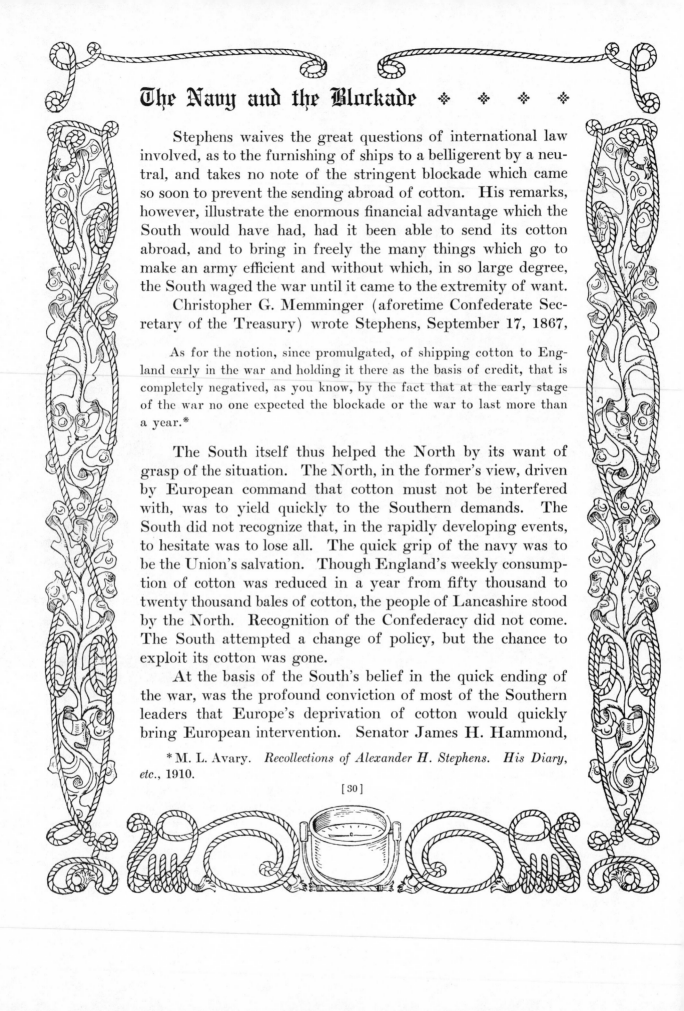

The Navy and the Blockade ❖ ❖ ❖ ❖

Stephens waives the great questions of international law involved, as to the furnishing of ships to a belligerent by a neutral, and takes no note of the stringent blockade which came so soon to prevent the sending abroad of cotton. His remarks, however, illustrate the enormous financial advantage which the South would have had, had it been able to send its cotton abroad, and to bring in freely the many things which go to make an army efficient and without which, in so large degree, the South waged the war until it came to the extremity of want.

Christopher G. Memminger (aforetime Confederate Secretary of the Treasury) wrote Stephens, September 17, 1867,

As for the notion, since promulgated, of shipping cotton to England early in the war and holding it there as the basis of credit, that is completely negatived, as you know, by the fact that at the early stage of the war no one expected the blockade or the war to last more than a year.*

The South itself thus helped the North by its want of grasp of the situation. The North, in the former's view, driven by European command that cotton must not be interfered with, was to yield quickly to the Southern demands. The South did not recognize that, in the rapidly developing events, to hesitate was to lose all. The quick grip of the navy was to be the Union's salvation. Though England's weekly consumption of cotton was reduced in a year from fifty thousand to twenty thousand bales of cotton, the people of Lancashire stood by the North. Recognition of the Confederacy did not come. The South attempted a change of policy, but the chance to exploit its cotton was gone.

At the basis of the South's belief in the quick ending of the war, was the profound conviction of most of the Southern leaders that Europe's deprivation of cotton would quickly bring European intervention. Senator James H. Hammond,

*M. L. Avary. *Recollections of Alexander H. Stephens. His Diary, etc.*, 1910.

MESSENGERS FROM THE CZAR OF RUSSIA

Here again the reader is introduced to some guests of the North—the officers of one of the little fleet that put into the Hudson and paid visits along the coast. It was not the Russian people at large who showed any friendliness to the United States during the Civil War; they knew little, cared less, and were not affected by the results of the conflict more than if it had been waged between two savage tribes in the heart of Africa. It was the Czar, for reasons of state or for his own purposes—which are much the same thing— who made the friendly overtures. Still smarting from the crushing disaster of the Crimea, where England, France, and Sardinia had combined to aid the hated Turk in keeping the Russians from the Bosphorus and the Mediterranean, the Czar would have given a great deal to have seen the "Trent" affair open hostilities between America and the mother country. Great Britain then would have its hands full in guarding its own shores and saving its Canadian possessions. The eyes of Napoleon III. were directed westward also at this time. King Victor Emmanuel, of Sardinia, who in '61 had had placed on his head the crown of United Italy, was trying to juggle the disjointed states of his new kingdom into harmony. Besides this, the Czar had unproductive land to sell—Alaska. It was Russia's chance. This friendship was in the game of diplomacy. But different from what Russia expected was the attitude of England.

of South Carolina, in a speech in the Senate on March 4, 1858, had said:

> But if there were no other reason why we should never have war, would any sane nation make war on cotton? Without firing a gun, without drawing a sword, should they make war on us we could bring the whole world to our feet. . . . What would happen if no cotton was furnished for three years? I will not stop to depict what everyone can imagine, but this is certain: England would topple headlong and carry the whole civilized world with her, save the South. No, you dare not make war on cotton. No power on earth dares to make war upon it.

And again:

> I firmly believe that the slaveholding South is now the controlling *power* of the world—that no other power would face us in hostility. This will be demonstrated if we come to the ultimate . . . cotton, rice, tobacco, and naval stores command the world, and we have sense enough to know it.

With such views, and they were practically the views of the whole South, it is not surprising that, with the belief that to withhold cotton would bring the world to terms, the South was slow to adopt such ideas as those put forth by Stephens. It was soon to be reduced largely to its own resources. " Buttons were made of persimmon seeds; tea of berry leaves; coffee of a variety of parched seeds; envelopes and writing-paper of scraps of wall-paper; shoes of wood and canvas." *

The South, however, aided by adventurous British merchants and her own able secret service abroad, of which Captain Bulloch, formerly of the United States navy, was the head, displayed a wondrous energy. Notwithstanding the blockade, the advent of very fast shallow-draft steamers, built principally on the Clyde and specially for the purpose of running the blockade, did much to alleviate the situation for the Confederacy until the Federal navy's hold on the coast gradually tightened. The

*Schwab.

MANNING THE YARDS—A VISITOR FROM BRAZIL

The lack of skill at manning yards that is pictured here shows that in Civil War times the Brazilians, never a maritime nation, had much to learn. Occasionally during the war, along the South Atlantic coast, while the blockade was still in existence and rigidly enforced, strange vessels would be seen by the cordon of outlying scouts, and more than once mistakes were narrowly averted. It was hard to tell under what guise a blockade-runner might approach the starting-line for the final dash for shore. In July, 1864, late one evening, a vessel was seen approaching and her actions were so peculiar that a little gunboat started at once for the guard-ships and made report. Two vessels were despatched to intercept the stranger. There was a slight fog and the moon was bright, a combination that made it impossible to see more than a few yards ahead. All at once the mist lifted, and there—lying within half pistol-shot between the two Federal cruisers—lay the suspected one. Immediately she was hailed and told to surrender. A voice replied through the speaking trumpet in broken English, stating that she was the French sloop-of-war "Alerte," and wished to make the nearest port, as she was suffering from "occasional discomposure of her engines." This having been ascertained to be the truth, the Frenchman was allowed to drop anchor for repairs. Now and then visitors from South American ports would also drop in, and in this picture of the barkentine-rigged side-wheeler is shown a Brazilian warship.

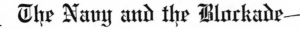

United States was backward then, as in fact it always has been, if the truth be spoken, in marine engineering. Changes came in machinery and material of construction abroad which we were slow to follow, so that the high-powered and lean model of the Clyde iron-built blockade-runner had a distinct advantage in speed over her chasers. Thus, even during the last two months of 1864, the imports of Charleston and Wilmington comprised over eight million five hundred thousand pounds of meat, one million five hundred thousand pounds of lead, nearly two million pounds of saltpeter, five hundred thousand pairs of shoes, three hundred and sixteen thousand pairs of blankets, over five hundred thousand pounds of coffee, sixty-nine thousand rifles, forty-three cannon, ninety-seven packages of revolvers, and two thousand six hundred and thirty-nine packages of medicine. The traffic across the Mexican border was of the same character, but there was still the gantlet to be run of the Mississippi River, now in Federal possession through the dauntless spirit of Farragut, greatest of naval commanders, not excepting Nelson himself.

But the grip of the navy was closing upon the Confederate ports. Charleston was, with the aid of the army, at last closed. Savannah was sealed; Mobile and New Orleans had, of course, long before been lost, as also Pensacola. Wilmington, so long closely watched, finally fell after the capture of Fort Fisher, and then happened that which, as already explained, might have occurred in the beginning had the Buchanan administration but acted with vigor, that is, the complete segregation of the South from the rest of the world. She still had men in plenty, but men to be effective must be fed and clothed. With open ports the war could have been indefinitely continued. With ports closed, the Southern armies were reduced to a pitiful misery, the long endurance of which makes a noble chapter in heroism.

The whole naval warfare of the secession period was thus one of closure. It was a strife to control the waters of the

[34]

THE FLEET THAT CLEARED THE RIVER

"A spear-thrust in the back" was delivered to the Confederacy by the inland-river fleet that cut it in two. The squadron of Flag-Officer Davis is here lying near Memphis. Thus appeared the Federal gunboats on June 5, 1862, two miles above the city. Fort Pillow had been abandoned the previous day, but the Confederate river-defense flotilla still remained below and the Federals, still smarting from the disaster inflicted on the "Cincinnati," were determined to bring on a decisive engagement and, if possible, clear the river of their antagonists. Meanwhile four new vessels had joined the Federal squadron. These were river steamers which Charles Ellet, Jr., had converted into rams in the short space of six weeks. Their principle was as old as history, but it was now to be tried for the first time in aid of the

MEMPHIS, TENNESSEE ON THE HEIGHTS

Federal cause. On these heights above the river the inhabitants of Memphis were crowded on the morning of June 6, 1862, as the Federal squadron moved down-stream against the Confederate gunboats that were drawn up in double line of battle opposite the city. Everyone wanted to see the outcome of the great fight that was impending, for if its result proved adverse to the Confederates, Memphis would fall into Federal hands and another stretch of the Mississippi would be lost to the South. In the engagement at Memphis two of the Ellet rams accompanied the squadron—the "Queen of the West" commanded by Charles Ellet, and the "Monarch" commanded by his younger brother, Major Alfred Ellet. The Confederate flotilla was destroyed, but with the loss of Charles Ellet, from a mortal wound.

LIEUTENANT–COLONEL
ALFRED W. ELLET

ONE OF THE THREE
ELLETS AT MEMPHIS

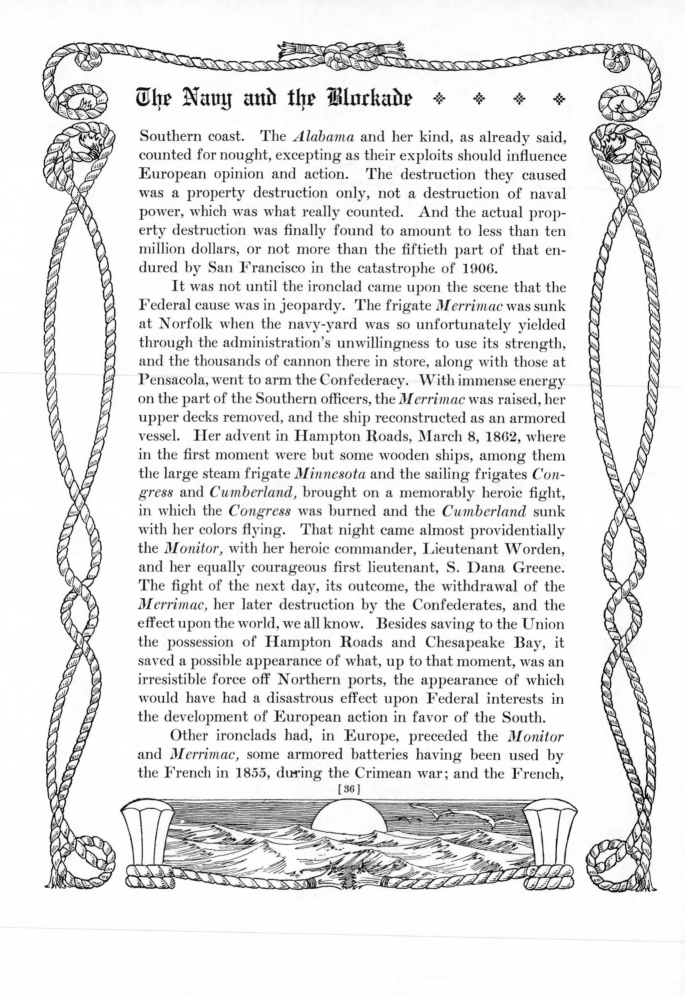

Southern coast. The *Alabama* and her kind, as already said, counted for nought, excepting as their exploits should influence European opinion and action. The destruction they caused was a property destruction only, not a destruction of naval power, which was what really counted. And the actual property destruction was finally found to amount to less than ten million dollars, or not more than the fiftieth part of that endured by San Francisco in the catastrophe of 1906.

It was not until the ironclad came upon the scene that the Federal cause was in jeopardy. The frigate *Merrimac* was sunk at Norfolk when the navy-yard was so unfortunately yielded through the administration's unwillingness to use its strength, and the thousands of cannon there in store, along with those at Pensacola, went to arm the Confederacy. With immense energy on the part of the Southern officers, the *Merrimac* was raised, her upper decks removed, and the ship reconstructed as an armored vessel. Her advent in Hampton Roads, March 8, 1862, where in the first moment were but some wooden ships, among them the large steam frigate *Minnesota* and the sailing frigates *Congress* and *Cumberland,* brought on a memorably heroic fight, in which the *Congress* was burned and the *Cumberland* sunk with her colors flying. That night came almost providentially the *Monitor,* with her heroic commander, Lieutenant Worden, and her equally courageous first lieutenant, S. Dana Greene. The fight of the next day, its outcome, the withdrawal of the *Merrimac,* her later destruction by the Confederates, and the effect upon the world, we all know. Besides saving to the Union the possession of Hampton Roads and Chesapeake Bay, it saved a possible appearance of what, up to that moment, was an irresistible force off Northern ports, the appearance of which would have had a disastrous effect upon Federal interests in the development of European action in favor of the South.

Other ironclads had, in Europe, preceded the *Monitor* and *Merrimac,* some armored batteries having been used by the French in 1855, during the Crimean war; and the French,

THE "BLACKHAWK," PORTER'S FAMOUS MISSISSIPPI FLAGSHIP
PHOTOGRAPHED OFF MEMPHIS, JUNE, '64

This wooden vessel, formerly a powerful river steamer, was armed and added to the Mississippi squadron soon after Porter took command. She was the admiral's flagship on the first expedition up the Yazoo. As the Stars and Stripes were run up on the courthouse at Vicksburg, July 4, 1863, the "Blackhawk," bearing Admiral Porter and his staff, swept proudly up to the levee and received on board General Grant, with many of his officers. They "were received with that warmth of feeling and hospitality that delights the heart of a sailor." Outwardly unmoved, Grant received the congratulations of the officers of the navy upon the greatest victory of the war so far—a victory which the river squadron had helped so materially to win. Again the "Blackhawk" steamed away on active service as Porter's flagship to lead the futile Red River expedition.

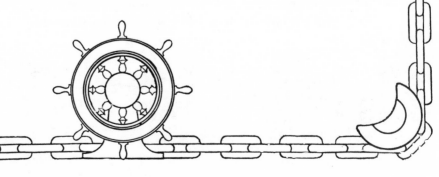

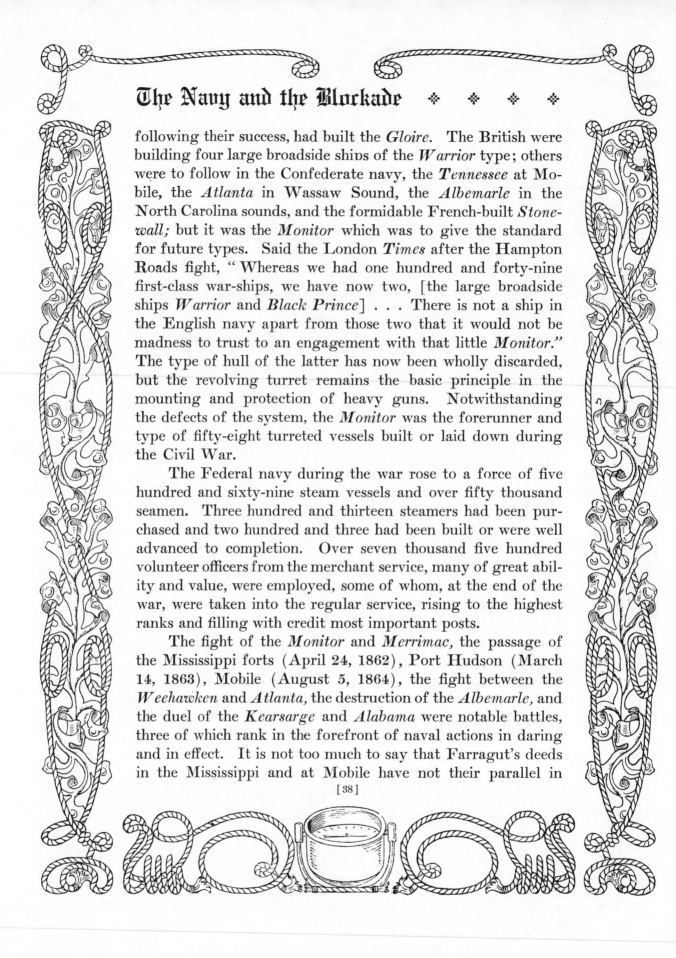

following their success, had built the *Gloire*. The British were building four large broadside ships of the *Warrior* type; others were to follow in the Confederate navy, the *Tennessee* at Mobile, the *Atlanta* in Wassaw Sound, the *Albemarle* in the North Carolina sounds, and the formidable French-built *Stonewall;* but it was the *Monitor* which was to give the standard for future types. Said the London *Times* after the Hampton Roads fight, "Whereas we had one hundred and forty-nine first-class war-ships, we have now two, [the large broadside ships *Warrior* and *Black Prince*] . . . There is not a ship in the English navy apart from those two that it would not be madness to trust to an engagement with that little *Monitor*." The type of hull of the latter has now been wholly discarded, but the revolving turret remains the basic principle in the mounting and protection of heavy guns. Notwithstanding the defects of the system, the *Monitor* was the forerunner and type of fifty-eight turreted vessels built or laid down during the Civil War.

The Federal navy during the war rose to a force of five hundred and sixty-nine steam vessels and over fifty thousand seamen. Three hundred and thirteen steamers had been purchased and two hundred and three had been built or were well advanced to completion. Over seven thousand five hundred volunteer officers from the merchant service, many of great ability and value, were employed, some of whom, at the end of the war, were taken into the regular service, rising to the highest ranks and filling with credit most important posts.

The fight of the *Monitor* and *Merrimac,* the passage of the Mississippi forts (April 24, 1862), Port Hudson (March 14, 1863), Mobile (August 5, 1864), the fight between the *Weehawken* and *Atlanta,* the destruction of the *Albemarle,* and the duel of the *Kearsarge* and *Alabama* were notable battles, three of which rank in the forefront of naval actions in daring and in effect. It is not too much to say that Farragut's deeds in the Mississippi and at Mobile have not their parallel in

COPYRIGHT, 1911, PATRIOT PUB. CO.

THE SILENCED GUNS AT FORT FISHER—THE FINAL LINK IN THE BLOCKADING CHAIN, 1865

The wreckage in this picture of the dilapidated defenses of Fort Fisher marks the approaching doom of the Confederate cause. The gun dismounted by the accurate fire of Porter's fleet and the palisade broken through by the attackers from the sea-front are mute witnesses to the fact that the last port of the South has been effectually closed and that all possibility of securing further supplies and munitions of war from the outside world is at an end. Since the beginning of hostilities Fort Fisher had kept open the approach to Wilmington, North Carolina, and even at the beginning of 1865 the blockade-runners were able in many cases to set at naught the efforts of the Federal squadron to keep them out of Wilmington. The fall of Fort Fisher, making the blockade at last a complete accomplished fact from the Potomac to the Rio Grande, marked the last act in the long drama of achievements by the navy in a war that could never have been won so soon without its help. Nor could the navy alone have closed the port. In the second attack the army had to help.

naval history. Says Charles Francis Adams, " It may safely be claimed that the running of the forts at the mouth of the Mississippi and the consequent fall of New Orleans was as brilliant an operation, and one as triumphantly conducted, as Sherman's march through Georgia," which, as he mentions later, was itself made possible by the undisputed maritime supremacy of the North. " Throttling the Confederacy by the blockade throughout," he says, " the navy was also a spear-thrust in its back."

Great, however, as was the effect of cutting in twain the Confederacy by the occupancy of the Mississippi, much greater was the effect of the monotonous and unheroic work of the blockade in Atlantic waters. By the end of the war there were captured and destroyed, in all, one thousand five hundred and four vessels, of a value of over thirty million dollars, much of which was British property. Large as was the money value, it was as nothing in comparison with the effect in deciding the great question at issue, through the loss of that without which the South could not live.

The failure of historians, with few exceptions, through nearly fifty years to recognize this great service done by the navy, shows a want of philosophic perception without which history is but a diary of events. Blockade is from a dramatic standpoint but a poor offset to great battles with thousands killed and wounded, the losses in which come keenly to tens of thousands of men and women. The fortunes of a million men in an army thus overshadow in the mind of the great public those of a comparatively meager fifty thousand in ships, and a blockade may go unnoticed by the public in war, much as the constant diplomacy of the navy goes unnoticed in peace.

To place New Orleans, Mobile, and Hampton Roads in the category of commonplace events is not to know war. As acts, they are among the lime-lights of history; in results, two, at least, were among the most momentous; for whatever went far to save this Union must be in such a category.

I

THE ORGANIZATION
OF THE
FEDERAL NAVY

GEORGE BANCROFT—FOUNDER
OF THE NAVAL ACADEMY

ALREADY NOTABLE AS A HISTORIAN IN 1845, BANCROFT SIGNALIZED HIS ENTRANCE INTO PRESIDENT POLK'S CABINET, AS SECRETARY OF THE NAVY, BY FOUNDING THE NAVAL SCHOOL, LATER THE ACADEMY AT ANNAPOLIS

JACK–TARS OF THE OLD NAVY

A glance at these seasoned men ranged alongside the 9-inch pivot-gun of the sloop-of-war "Wissahickon" gives us an idea of the appearance of the men of the old navy. The face of the gun-captain standing near the breach of his gun shows that he is a sailor through and through. There are very few landsmen pictured here. The old Jack-tar, standing fourth in the right row, who has turned his cap into a ditty bag, harks back to the fighting days when steam had hardly been thought of. He is a survivor of the War of 1812, and remembers the days of Bainbridge, of Decatur, Stewart, and Biddle. Even the younger men have no look of the volunteer about them; they are deep-sea sailors, every one. The "Wissahickon" was one of the Federal cruisers that had put out in search of the

THE PIVOT-GUN OF THE "WISSAHICKON" AND ITS CREW

Confederate commerce-destroyers. She was in the fleet of Admiral Farragut at New Orleans and ran the batteries at Vicksburg. Late in 1862 she was in Carolina waters and in January, 1863, participated in the first attacks on Fort McAllister. She was in Admiral Dahlgren's fleet during the stirring operations in Charleston harbor and returned to South Carolina waters toward the close of 1864, where she captured numerous prizes, enriching her officers and crew. The sailors on few of the Federal vessels had a more varied and adventurous experience of the war than did those of the "Wissahickon," and the faces in the picture, both old and young, are those of men ready at any and all times for a fight or a frolic on their beloved ship.

THE OLD NAVY—THREE VETERANS OF THE LINE

In the center of this war-time photograph rides the famous frigate "Constitution." She was one of the four fighting-ships the construction of which, under Act of Congress of March 27, 1794, marked the birth of an adequate navy to protect the commerce of the young republic. She was the third to be launched, October 21, 1797, at Boston. Her exploits in the harbor of Tripoli in 1804 and her great fight with the "Guerrière" soon made her name a household word to all Americans. Full of years and honors in 1861, she was lying at Annapolis as a training-ship at the outbreak of the War of the Rebellion, and was in great danger of falling into the hands of the Confederates. General Benjamin F. Butler, who was in the vicinity with the Eighth Massachusetts Regiment, sent a detachment that guarded the old ship till she was towed to Newport, where she arrived May 9th under Lieutenant-Commander G. W. Rodgers, with officers and midshipmen from the Military Academy aboard. At the extreme right of the picture is the "Macedonian," originally a British sloop-of-war captured by the U. S. frigate "United States" in 1812. She was a spick-and-span new

"SANTEE," "CONSTITUTION," AND "MACEDONIAN"

vessel then. In 1852–4 she sailed in Commodore Perry's fleet that opened Japan to American commerce. The outbreak of the war found her lying at Vera Cruz. The frigate on the left, the "Santee," was a later addition to the navy, also mounting fifty guns. She served on blockade duty, chiefly in the Gulf, during the war. There, while lying off Galveston, November 7, 1861, in command of Captain Henry Eagle, some of her crew performed one of the most brilliant naval exploits that marked the beginning of hostilities. Lieutenant James E. Jouett volunteered to run into the harbor and destroy the Confederate steamer "General Rusk" and the schooner "Royal Yacht." Near midnight the little party in two launches pulled boldly into the harbor. When almost upon the "General Rusk," Lieutenant Jouett's launch grounded and was run into by the second launch. With the Confederates thus aroused and several steamers speeding to find him in the darkness, Lieutenant Jouett nevertheless determined to board. After a thrilling encounter, he made prisoners of the crew and destroyed the schooner, returning with a loss of one killed and six wounded.

ORGANIZATION OF THE FEDERAL NAVY

WHEN President Lincoln and his administration found themselves confronted with the most stupendous problem that any nation had had as yet to face, there was one element in their favor that counted more heavily than any other, an element whose value has been overlooked by the early historians of the war. It was the possession not only of a navy but of shipyards and a vast merchant marine from which to draw both vessels and men, and thus to increase the Northern fighting efficiency at sea.

Though both North and South were wholly unprepared for the gigantic struggle, at the command of the Federal Government were inexhaustible resources. Manufactories and establishments of all kinds were at hand, together with ship-building yards that had turned out a merchant marine which, previous to the outbreak of hostilities, had gained the commerce-carrying supremacy of the world. These factors and advantages were of tremendous importance in contributing to the final success of the Federal cause. Not only was the part of the trained sailor significant, but the mechanic and inventor found a peculiar scope and wide field for development in the application of their genius and talents to the navy's needs. In five years, the whole science of naval warfare was to be changed; the wooden fleets of Europe were to become antiquated and practically useless, and the ironclad whose appearance had been adumbrated was now to become a reality for all sea fighting.

Ninety ships of war made up the United States navy at the opening of the year 1861, but of these only forty-two were in any measure ready for active service; the remainder were

THE FLAGSHIP "WABASH"—THE PRIDE OF THE NAVY IN '61

Sights such as this photograph conveys have passed forever. The type of vessel pictured here is now as obsolete as the great "Harry" of King Henry VIII or a Spanish galleon of King Philip. But what a beautiful sight she presents; the long clean sweep of her spar-deck, her standing rigging as taut as fiddle-strings, and all her running gear coiled and flemished down—no wonder that the "Wabash" was the pride of the navy, and that her crew pointed to the name on their caps with pride when they were ashore. The "Wabash" was a steam frigate of the first rating. No finer vessel could have been found in any foreign navy. She displaced 3,274 tons, carried two 10-inch pivot guns on her spar-deck and a broadside of fourteen 8-inch guns; on her gun-deck she carried twenty-eight 9-inch guns and two 12-pounders. On the deck stands a little group of three—Admiral Du Pont, who was in command of the South Atlantic blockading squadron, her Captain, C. R. P. Rodgers, and Commander Corbin. Until the ironclad appeared, such ships as the "Wabash", though small in number, gave to the United States navy a prestige wherever the flag was flown.

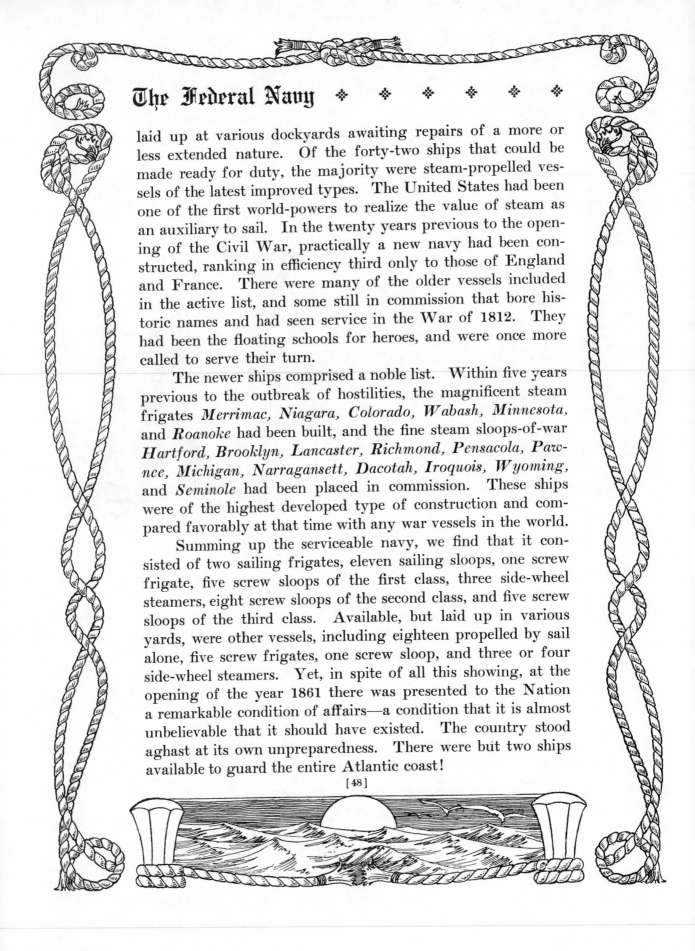

laid up at various dockyards awaiting repairs of a more or less extended nature. Of the forty-two ships that could be made ready for duty, the majority were steam-propelled vessels of the latest improved types. The United States had been one of the first world-powers to realize the value of steam as an auxiliary to sail. In the twenty years previous to the opening of the Civil War, practically a new navy had been constructed, ranking in efficiency third only to those of England and France. There were many of the older vessels included in the active list, and some still in commission that bore historic names and had seen service in the War of 1812. They had been the floating schools for heroes, and were once more called to serve their turn.

The newer ships comprised a noble list. Within five years previous to the outbreak of hostilities, the magnificent steam frigates *Merrimac, Niagara, Colorado, Wabash, Minnesota,* and *Roanoke* had been built, and the fine steam sloops-of-war *Hartford, Brooklyn, Lancaster, Richmond, Pensacola, Pawnee, Michigan, Narragansett, Dacotah, Iroquois, Wyoming,* and *Seminole* had been placed in commission. These ships were of the highest developed type of construction and compared favorably at that time with any war vessels in the world.

Summing up the serviceable navy, we find that it consisted of two sailing frigates, eleven sailing sloops, one screw frigate, five screw sloops of the first class, three side-wheel steamers, eight screw sloops of the second class, and five screw sloops of the third class. Available, but laid up in various yards, were other vessels, including eighteen propelled by sail alone, five screw frigates, one screw sloop, and three or four side-wheel steamers. Yet, in spite of all this showing, at the opening of the year 1861 there was presented to the Nation a remarkable condition of affairs—a condition that it is almost unbelievable that it should have existed. The country stood aghast at its own unpreparedness. There were but two ships available to guard the entire Atlantic coast!

[48]

WITH ALL SAILS SET

Despite the presence of magnificent force and might in the great modern vessel of war that rates from twelve to twenty thousand tons, there is little that suggests the romance of the sea about the huge mass of steel, magnificent and formidable though it may appear. The modern ship is sexless, or rather masculine. But no one would apply to such a fine old war-vessel as is pictured here, the training-ship "Saratoga," anything less than the sailor's half-endearing term of femininity. Ships, just as we see this one, fought in the War of the Revolution, and, with hardly a change, the "Saratoga" appears here as in the Mediterranean she forged ahead in chase of one of the Barbary pirates, or maneuvered to escape from a British seventy-four in the War of 1812. In the older days, she would not have had the handy double topsails which give her one more yard to each mast. Perhaps with single topsails she looked still handsomer. It required seamanship in those days to make a landfall. Dead reckoning was "dead reckoning" with a vengeance. Nowadays, after the departure has been taken and the ship laid on her course, the revolutions of the engines, the knowledge of ocean currents, and the spinning taffrail log give a navigating officer a technical knowledge of his whereabouts. It was different when they depended on the wind alone. It was in the school of the sailing-ship that most of the officers who fought in the Civil War had been trained. The "Saratoga" was one of Commodore Perry's fleet when he sailed to Japan, in 1852. Just previous to the outbreak of the war she had been engaged in putting down piracy in the West Indies, and long after the war was started she was hovering off the western coast of Africa, capturing the "Nightingale," a slaver with over 960 slaves herded between decks. During the war she was used mainly as a school-ship.

The Federal Navy ❖ ❖ ❖ ❖ ❖

At Hampton Roads lay the steam sloop *Brooklyn*, and at New York lay the store-ship *Relief,* that mounted but two guns. The remainder of the serviceable ships actually in commission were scattered in all parts of the earth. The *Niagara,* a screw frigate and the first built by Steers, the famous clipper-ship constructor, was the farthest away from the Atlantic ports. She was on special duty in Japanese waters, and in the best of circumstances could not report where her services were most needed for several months.

The rest of the ships on foreign stations would require from a week to a month to gain home waters. Of the forty-eight ships that were in dock or in the navy-yards, there was none that could be prepared for service within a fortnight, and there were many that would require a month or more before they would be ready.

From the time of the secession of South Carolina, in December, 1860, to the time of the declaration of war, valued officers of the navy whose homes were in the South had been constantly resigning from the service. The Navy Department was seriously hampered through their loss. Shortly after the opening of the war, it became necessary to curtail the course at the Naval Academy at Annapolis, and the last-year class was ordered on active duty to fill the places made vacant by the many resignations. At the opening of the war, the Federal navy had fourteen hundred and fifty-seven officers and seventy-six hundred seamen. This number was constantly increased throughout the war, and at the close there were no less than seventy-five hundred officers and fifty-one thousand five hundred seamen.

When the Lincoln administration came into power in 1861, the Secretary of the Navy under the Buchanan administration, Isaac Toucey, of Hartford, Connecticut, was succeeded by his fellow townsman, Gideon Welles, whose experience as chief of the bureau of provisions and clothing in the Navy Department from 1846 to 1849 had familiarized

THE "COLORADO"—A FRIGATE OF THE OLD NAVY

The "Colorado" was one of six 40-gun screw frigates, the pride and strength of the Federal navy in '61. Like most of her sister-ships of the old navy, the "Colorado" (built for sea fighting) was prevented by her size from getting up the narrow channels, and her gallant commander, Theodorus Bailey, had to lead the fleet at New Orleans past the forts in another vessel. On September 14, 1861, at Pensacola, volunteers from the "Colorado's" crew in four boats, led by Lieutenant J. H. Russell, carried off a "cutting out" expedition. They drove the stubbornly resisting crew from the Confederate privateer "Judah" and destroyed the vessel.

him with the details of department work. Under Welles, as assistant secretary, was appointed Gustavus V. Fox, a brilliant naval officer, whose eighteen years in the service had well fitted him for the work he was to take up, and whose talents and foresight later provided valuable aid to the secretary. At the head of the bureau of yards and docks was Joseph Smith, whose continuous service in the navy for nearly a half-century and whose occupancy of the position at the head of the bureau from 1845 had qualified him also to meet the unlooked-for emergency of war.

Under the direction of the secretary, there were at this time a bureau of ordnance and hydrography, a bureau of construction, equipment, and repair, a bureau of provisions and clothing, and a bureau of medicine and surgery. It was soon found that these bureaus could not adequately dispose of all the business and details to come before the department, and by act of Congress of July 5, 1862, there was added a bureau of navigation and a bureau of steam engineering. The bureau of construction, equipment, and repair was subdivided into a bureau of equipment and recruiting and a bureau of construction and repair.

In William Faxon, the chief clerk of the Navy Department, Secretary Welles found the ablest of assistants, whose business ability and mastery of detail were rewarded in the last months of the war by his being appointed assistant secretary while Mr. Fox was abroad.

With the organization of the new Navy Department, steps were taken at once to gather the greater number of the ships of the Federal fleets where they could be used to the utmost advantage. Work on the repairing and refitting of the ships then laid up in the various navy-yards was begun, and orders were given for the construction of a number of new vessels. But in the very first months of the actual opening of the war, the Navy Department dealt itself the severest blow that it received during the whole course of hostilities.

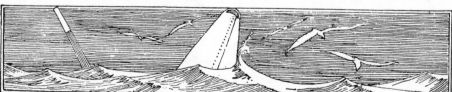

GIDEON WELLES, WAR SECRETARY OF THE FEDERAL NAVY

Rarely has so stupendous a task confronted a man as that which fell to the lot of Lincoln's Secretary of the Navy. In ordinary times the man fit for that office must be a statesman, a constitutional lawyer, a judge of international law and national obligations, as well as a man of sound judgment and executive ability of the highest order. These qualities Gideon Welles possessed in a marked degree. At the time he took his seat in the Cabinet the Navy Department was entirely unprepared for the work that was immediately required of it, work perhaps more arduous than had ever before been demanded of the maritime power of any government. The whole-management of the navy during the war indicated the most remarkable administrative ability on the part of the Secretary. The herculean tasks required were performed without ostentation, with a firm and sagacious hand that never wavered before ungenerous and ignorant criticism. Not only was the physical side attended to with marvelous promptness and efficiency, but the policies of the Administration were frequently shaped by his wise influence.

The Federal Navy ❖

Lying at the Gosport Navy-Yard at Norfolk, Virginia, were some of the navy's strongest, most formidable, and most historic ships—the steam frigate *Merrimac*, of forty guns, that was soon to make the world ring with her name; the sloop-of-war *Germantown*, of twenty-two guns; the *Plymouth*, of the same number, and the brig *Dolphin*.

There were, besides, the old sailing vessels whose names were dear to the country: to wit, the *Pennsylvania*, a line-of-battle ship; the *United States, Columbus, Delaware, Raritan,* and *Columbia*. There was also on the stocks, and unfinished, a ship of the line, the *New York*.

There is not time or space in this short preamble to enter into the reasons for what happened, but through blunders and a feeling of panic, the fiat went forth that the navy-yard and all it contained should be destroyed. On the night of April 20th, this order was carried into effect, and over two million of dollars' worth of Federal property was destroyed, besides vast stores and ammunition. Thousands of cannon fell into the hands of the new-born Secessia. It was a bitter chapter for the cooler heads to read. All along the coast of the Southern States, other vessels which could not be removed from docks or naval stations were seized by the Confederate Government or destroyed by orders from Washington.

As if suddenly recovered from the fever of apprehension that had caused so much destruction, the Federal Government soon recognized its necessities, and the Navy Department awoke to the knowledge of what would be required of it. Immediately, the floating force was increased by the purchase of great numbers of vessels of all kinds. Of these, thirty-six were side-wheel steamers, forty-two were screw steamers, one an auxiliary steam bark, and fifty-eight were sailing craft of various classes. These vessels mounted a total of five hundred and nineteen guns, of which the steam craft carried three hundred and thirty-five. In addition to these, the navy-yards were put to work at the building of new vessels, twenty-three being

FROM THE OLD NAVY TO THE NEW

THE SLOOP–OF–WAR "PENSACOLA," FIRST IN LINE WITH FARRAGUT

The "Pensacola" was the type of United States fighting-ship that marks the transition from the old navy to the new, consummated by the Civil War. Steam had superseded sail, armor plate was still to come. Farragut could never get used to it, contending that in old wooden ships like the "Hartford" a shot would pass clean through both sides, doing less damage than when penetrating an ironclad. The "Pensacola" formed a splendid type of the steam sloop-of-war, of which the "Hartford," Farragut's famous flagship, was the latest addition to the navy at the outbreak of the war. When Farragut fought his way past the forts below New Orleans, the "Pensacola" (after the grounding of the "Cayuga") was first in line. Her captain, Henry W. Morris, deliberately slowed up and stopped frequently opposite the forts, as did the "Mississippi," so that their powerful batteries might take effect while the smaller vessels got by.

in process of construction at the close of the year in the Government shipyards, and one at the New York Navy-Yard being built by a private contractor.

Every place where serviceable ships could be laid down was soon put to use, and in private yards, at the close of 1861, twenty-eight sailing vessels were being constructed, fourteen screw sloops, twenty-three screw gunboats, and twelve side-wheelers. Besides these, there were early on the ways three experimental iron-clad vessels, the value and practicability of which in battle was at this time a mooted question.

One of these three soon-to-be-launched ironclads was an innovation in naval construction; one hundred and seventy-two feet in length, she was over forty-one feet in beam, and presented a free-board of only eighteen inches above the water. Almost amidships she carried a revolving turret, twenty-one feet in diameter and nine feet high. The inventor of this curious craft, which was building at the Continental Iron Works in New York, had absolute faith in her future, a faith that was shared by very few naval men of the day. On the 9th of March, 1862, this "freak," this "monstrosity," this "waste of money" fought her first battle, and marked the closing of one era of naval history and the opening of another. Ericsson and the *Monitor* are names linked in fame for all time to come.

The other two ironclads that were contracted for in 1861 were on the lines of the battle-ship of the day. Heavily armored with iron and wood, they were adapted to the mounting of heavier guns than were then generally in use. No wooden vessel could live for a moment in conflict with them, broadside to broadside.

From the very first, the Lincoln administration had fully understood and comprehended the naval weakness of the South. But not only this, it knew well her dependence on other countries for supplies and necessities, and how this dependence would increase. Almost the first aggressive act was

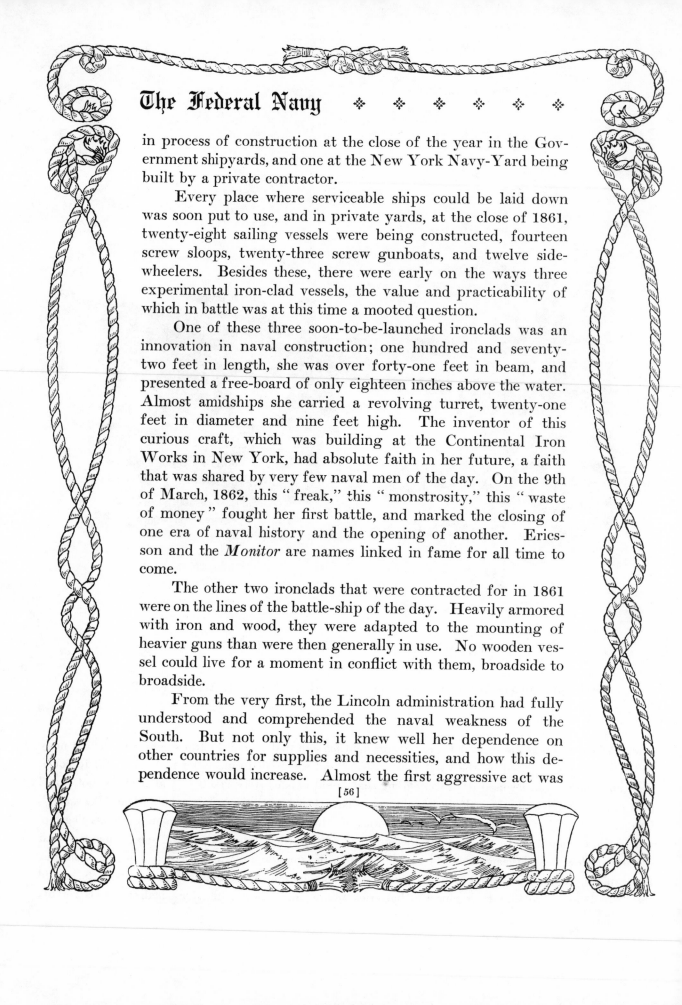

FORERUNNERS OF THE LIGHT–DRAUGHT GUNBOAT—FERRYBOATS CONVERTED INTO WAR–VESSELS

In these pictures are seen two of the navy's converted ferryboat fleet. The "McDonough" (above) was taken while on duty near Hilton Head by a lieutenant of volunteers who possessed one of those rare new instruments, a camera. She was quite thoroughly armored. Under command of Lieutenant-Commander Bacon she was lying in Stono River, February 1, 1863, when the "Isaac Smith," going up the river to make a reconnaissance, was entrapped by three concealed Confederate batteries. The "McDonough" got under way to the assistance of the "Isaac Smith," but was unable to stand the fire of the heavy rifled guns that finally caused the surrender of the "Isaac Smith." Thus these improvised gunboats went bravely to their tasks, sometimes winning single-handed against superior force, sometimes paying the penalty of their boldness in cruising up rivers and about sounds and bayous where hostile batteries and gunboats lay concealed or where troops were ambushed ready to pick off the pilot and anyone else who showed himself. The necessities of this sort of inland warfare taught the navy the value of the light-draught.

THE GUNBOAT "PARKS"

to declare a blockade of the Atlantic coast south of the Chesapeake, and this was quickly followed by proclamations extending it from the Gulf to the Rio Grande. Long before there
were enough vessels to make the blockade effective, this far-
reaching action was taken. But now, as the navy grew, most of
the purchased ships were made ready for use, and before the
close of 1861, were sent southward to establish and strengthen
this blockade, and by the end of the year the ports of the Confederacy were fairly well guarded by Federal vessels cruising
at their harbors' mouths. The expedition to Hilton Head and
the taking of Forts Walker and Beauregard had given the
navy a much coveted base on the Southern shore. Still, every
month new vessels were added, and there was growing on the
Mississippi a fleet destined for a warfare new in naval annals.
Seven ironclads were built and two remodeled under the supervision of Captain James B. Eads. There were also three
wooden gunboats, and later on, in the summer of 1862, at the
suggestion of Flag-Officer Davis, the fleet of light-draft vessels, known as " tin-clads," was organized.

For some time the gunboats and " tin-clads " operating
in conjunction with the Western armies had been under the
supervision of the War Department, and separate from the
navy entirely. But very soon this was to be changed, and the
entire Mississippi forces and those engaged in the Western
and Southern waters came under the jurisdiction of the Navy
Department. Officers were detached to command of these
nondescripts and " tin-clads " that rendered such gallant service; experienced gunners and bodies of marines were sent out
to lend discipline and cohesion to the land sailors who, up to
this time, had been carrying on the river warfare. The blockade called for more and more energy along the Atlantic coast;
very early the " runners " began to try the dangerous game of
eluding the watching cordon.

Providing these vessels with officers and crews taxed the
Navy Department to a great extent. There were not enough

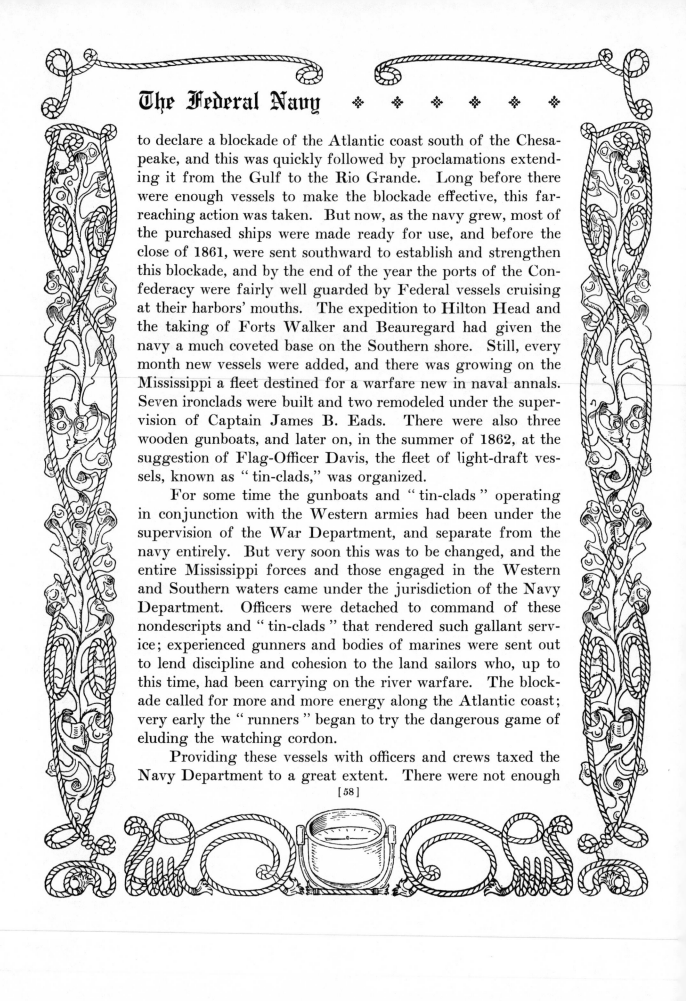

A FORGOTTEN FIGHTER ON THE PAMUNKEY

Here on the Pamunkey River, her ports dropped and exposing her gaping gun-muzzles, lies one of the vessels hastily converted into gunboats to serve the early needs of the navy along the shores and rivers of the Atlantic coast. Manned by brave men who rendered yeoman service for the Federal cause, many of these small craft sank into oblivion, over-shadowed by the achievements of the great monitors and ironclads which were eventually provided by the Navy Department for service along the shore. Some of the converted ferryboats, when their term of charter was up, returned to their wonted peaceful occupation before hostilities ceased; others served till the end, and then, doffing their armor, returned to commercial life. Such vessels were early useful in the York and Pamunkey Rivers in aid-ing the military efforts to advance upon Richmond by way of the Peninsula. White House on the Pamunkey was twice the base of the Federal army, and the Peninsula was a contested field till near the close of the war. Flotillas of these small vessels were constantly rendering aid to the army in keeping communications open and safe.

experienced men then in the navy to officer more than a small portion of the ships brought into service, and it was necessary to call for recruits. The merchant marine was drawn on for many valuable men, who filled the stations to which they were assigned with credit to themselves and the navy. It may be said to the credit of both the merchant marine and the " service," however, that the consequent jealousy of rank that at times was shown resulted in nothing more serious than temporary dissatisfaction, and was seldom openly expressed. The men of both callings had been too well trained to the discipline of the sea to question the orders of their superiors, and after the distribution of commissions usually settled down to a faithful and efficient discharge of the duties to which they had been assigned.

From the outset of the war, it appeared more difficult to secure enlistments for the navy than for the army, and with the constant addition of ships it finally became necessary to offer large bounties to all the naval recruits in order to keep the quota up to the required numbers. During the war the United States navy built two hundred and eight vessels and purchased four hundred and eighteen. Of these, nearly sixty were ironclads, mostly monitors.

With the introduction of the ironclad and the continual increase of the thickness and efficiency of the armor as the war progressed, the guns of the navy also changed in weight and pattern. The advent of the ironclad made necessary the introduction of heavier ordnance. The manufacturers of these guns throughout the North were called upon to provide for the emergency. At the beginning of the war, the 32-pounder and the 8-inch were almost the highest-power guns in use, though some of the steam vessels were provided with 11-inch Dahlgren guns. Before the war had closed, the 11-inch Dahlgren, which had been regarded as a " monster " at the start, had been far overshadowed, and the caliber had increased to 15-inch, then 18-inch, and finally by a 20-inch that came so

FROM THE MERCHANT MARINE—THE "FORT JACKSON"

Here the U. S. S. "Fort Jackson" lies in Hampton Roads, December, 1864. This powerful side-wheel steamer of 1,770 tons burden was a regular river passenger-steamer before she was purchased by the Federal Government and converted into a gunboat of the second class. Her armament consisted of one 100-pounder rifle, two 30-pound rifles, and eight 9-inch smooth-bores. The navy had come to know the need of her type during the latter half of the war. By the end of 1862, 180 purchased vessels had been added to its force. But many of these, unlike the "Fort Jackson," were frail barks in which officers and men "had to fight the heaviest kind of earthworks, often perched at a great height above the water, where their plunging fire could perforate the vessels' decks and boilers or even pass down through their bottoms." But so splendid was the organization and discipline of the navy from the first that inadequacies of equipment were compensated for in a most remarkable degree. The personnel of the navy, both regular and volunteer, was of such a quality that men never questioned the peril which the mere embarking in some of the earlier gunboats entailed. The "Fort Jackson," under Captain B. F. Sands, was in the third line of the fleet that on December 24 and 25, 1864, hurled more than a million and a quarter pounds of shot and shell at Fort Fisher on the Cape Fear River, North Carolina. After the fall of that fort the "Fort Jackson" continued on blockade duty off the North Carolina coast, and during 1865 captured three blockade-runners with valuable cargoes.

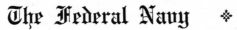

late in the war as never to be used. Rifled cannon were also substituted for the smooth-bore guns.

The navy with which the Federals ended the war belonged to a different era from that with which it started, the men to a different class. Very early in 1862, the number of artisans and laborers employed in the Government navy-yards was increased from less than four thousand to nearly seventeen thousand, and these were constantly employed in the construction and equipment of new ships, embracing all the improvements that could be effectively used, as soon as they were shown to be practical. In addition to these seventeen thousand men, there were fully as many more engaged by private contractors, building and equipping other vessels for the service.

One of the features of the navy in the Civil War, and before referred to, was the " tin-clad " fleet, especially constructed to guard the rivers and shallow waters of the West and South. The principal requirement of these " tin-clads " was that they be of very light draft, to enable them to navigate across the shoals in the Mississippi and other rivers on which they did duty. The lighter class of these vessels drew less than two feet of water, and it was a common saying that they could " go anywhere where the ground was a little damp." They were small side- or stern-wheel boats, and were armored with iron plating less than an inch in thickness, from which they derived the name of " tin-clads." Though insufficient protection to resist a heavy shell, this light plating was a good bullet-proof, and would withstand the fire of a light field-piece, unless the shell chanced to find a vulnerable spot, such as an open port-hole.

These boats were armed with howitzers, and their work against field-batteries or sharpshooters on shore was particularly effective. The heavier class of boats that were used in the river offensive and defensive work was armed with more guns of larger caliber, and their armor-plating was somewhat heavier than that of the little vessels designed to get close to

[62]

FIGHTERS AFLOAT—GUNBOAT MEN ON THE "MENDOTA"

Here on the deck of the "Mendota" on the James River, late in '64, has gathered a typical group of gunboat men. While there are some foreign faces among them, many (particularly the younger ones) betoken the native American that responded to the call to arms by enlisting in the navy. At the outbreak of the war there were but seven thousand six hundred sailors in the Federal navy. It was a matter of no small difficulty to procure crews promptly for the new vessels that were being converted and constructed so rapidly, especially when the military service was making such frequent and sweeping requisitions upon the able-bodied men of the country. Nevertheless, at the close of the war the number of sailors in the navy had been increased to fifty-one thousand five hundred. It was an even more difficult problem to secure competent officers. Volunteers were called for by the Navy Department at the very outset of the struggle. As many of these enrolled as there had been sailors in the navy at the war's outbreak. Many vessels were officered entirely by volunteers, and these men acquitted themselves in a manner no less distinguished than the officers of the regular service. The gun in the picture is one of the "Mendota's" 200-pounder rifles, of which she carried two. In the war the American navy broke away from the old tradition that the effectiveness of a fighting-vessel is in proportion to the number of guns she carries. The distinct tendency became not to divide the weight she could safely bear among numerous guns of small caliber, but rather to have fewer guns of higher efficiency. Many of the small Federal gunboats carried 100-pounder rifles.

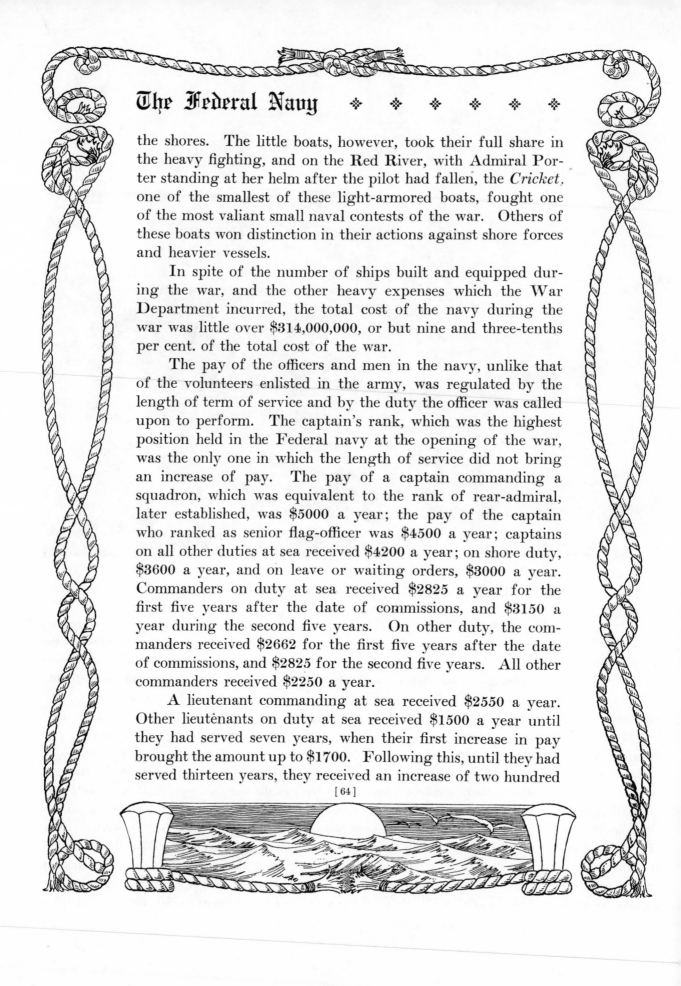

the shores. The little boats, however, took their full share in the heavy fighting, and on the Red River, with Admiral Porter standing at her helm after the pilot had fallen, the *Cricket*, one of the smallest of these light-armored boats, fought one of the most valiant small naval contests of the war. Others of these boats won distinction in their actions against shore forces and heavier vessels.

In spite of the number of ships built and equipped during the war, and the other heavy expenses which the War Department incurred, the total cost of the navy during the war was little over $314,000,000, or but nine and three-tenths per cent. of the total cost of the war.

The pay of the officers and men in the navy, unlike that of the volunteers enlisted in the army, was regulated by the length of term of service and by the duty the officer was called upon to perform. The captain's rank, which was the highest position held in the Federal navy at the opening of the war, was the only one in which the length of service did not bring an increase of pay. The pay of a captain commanding a squadron, which was equivalent to the rank of rear-admiral, later established, was $5000 a year; the pay of the captain who ranked as senior flag-officer was $4500 a year; captains on all other duties at sea received $4200 a year; on shore duty, $3600 a year, and on leave or waiting orders, $3000 a year. Commanders on duty at sea received $2825 a year for the first five years after the date of commissions, and $3150 a year during the second five years. On other duty, the commanders received $2662 for the first five years after the date of commissions, and $2825 for the second five years. All other commanders received $2250 a year.

A lieutenant commanding at sea received $2550 a year. Other lieutenants on duty at sea received $1500 a year until they had served seven years, when their first increase in pay brought the amount up to $1700. Following this, until they had served thirteen years, they received an increase of two hundred

LEARNING NEW LESSONS—THE NAVAL ACADEMY CLASS OF '66

The faces of the graduates of '66, and the view below of part of the Naval Academy grounds at Annapolis, taken in 1866, are the evidence of the peace-footing to which the institution has been restored within a year. The cadets and instructors have returned from Newport in 1865 and resumed their old quarters, from which they had been precipitately driven by the first Confederate move on Washington. The grand veteran "Constitution," the "Old Ironsides" of the navy, had given her pet name to her more powerful descendant, and lying near the center of the picture is now relegated to the position of receiving-ship. At the end of the wharf is tied up the "Santee," on whose deck many a midshipman has paced out the sentry duty with which he was punished for the infringement of regulations. Between the two lies the "Saratoga," now a supply-ship. New students had come to take the places of those who learned the theories and practice of naval warfare with the current exploits of the navy ringing in their ears day by day. Some of the officers who had fought through the great struggle were adding their practical experience, so lately gained, to the curriculum. However, the traditions of the old navy were still predominant; the training of the seaman was still considered essential for the cadets and was enforced as in the old sailing days as the foundation of their education. It was nevertheless the Naval Academy which kept alive for a future generation the valuable experience that had been gained at such a cost in the four years of Civil War.

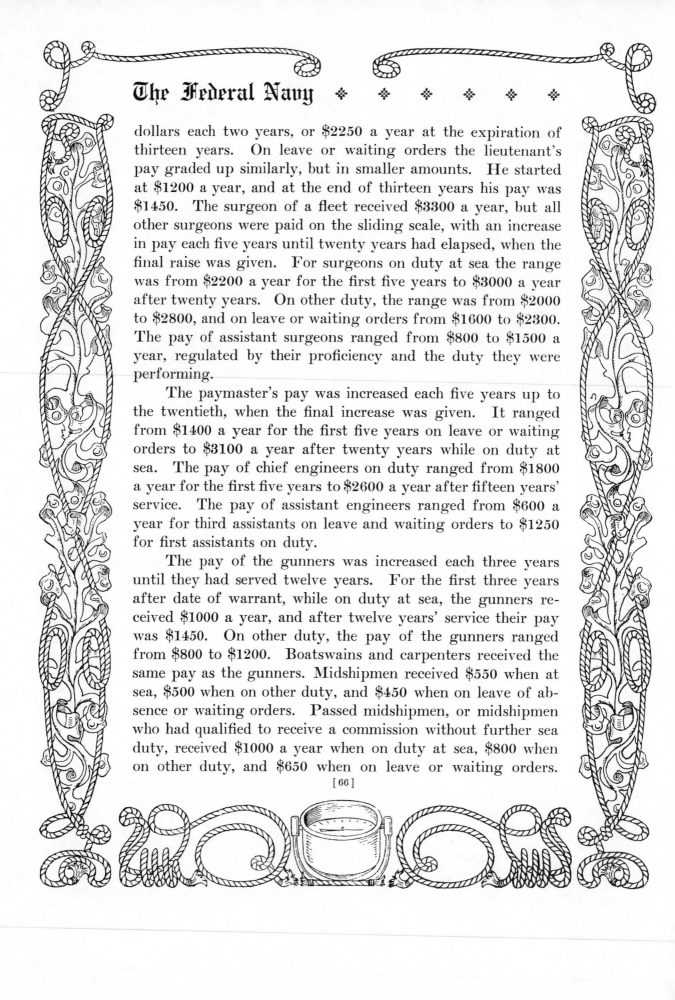

dollars each two years, or $2250 a year at the expiration of thirteen years. On leave or waiting orders the lieutenant's pay graded up similarly, but in smaller amounts. He started at $1200 a year, and at the end of thirteen years his pay was $1450. The surgeon of a fleet received $3300 a year, but all other surgeons were paid on the sliding scale, with an increase in pay each five years until twenty years had elapsed, when the final raise was given. For surgeons on duty at sea the range was from $2200 a year for the first five years to $3000 a year after twenty years. On other duty, the range was from $2000 to $2800, and on leave or waiting orders from $1600 to $2300. The pay of assistant surgeons ranged from $800 to $1500 a year, regulated by their proficiency and the duty they were performing.

The paymaster's pay was increased each five years up to the twentieth, when the final increase was given. It ranged from $1400 a year for the first five years on leave or waiting orders to $3100 a year after twenty years while on duty at sea. The pay of chief engineers on duty ranged from $1800 a year for the first five years to $2600 a year after fifteen years' service. The pay of assistant engineers ranged from $600 a year for third assistants on leave and waiting orders to $1250 for first assistants on duty.

The pay of the gunners was increased each three years until they had served twelve years. For the first three years after date of warrant, while on duty at sea, the gunners received $1000 a year, and after twelve years' service their pay was $1450. On other duty, the pay of the gunners ranged from $800 to $1200. Boatswains and carpenters received the same pay as the gunners. Midshipmen received $550 when at sea, $500 when on other duty, and $450 when on leave of absence or waiting orders. Passed midshipmen, or midshipmen who had qualified to receive a commission without further sea duty, received $1000 a year when on duty at sea, $800 when on other duty, and $650 when on leave or waiting orders.

THE NAVY'S SEAT OF LEARNING

Among the multifarious distinguished services of the scholarly and versatile Bancroft was his founding of the Naval School while Secretary of the Navy in 1845. It was reorganized and renamed the Naval Academy in 1850. In the picture above we see part of the water-front and the landing as it appeared after the war when the peaceful study of naval science had again been resumed here, the Academy having been moved to Newport, Rhode Island, during the war. While George Bancroft, approaching three-score years and ten, was writing history in New York during the great civil struggle, the graduates of the school he founded were making history as officers on the fighting-ships of both North and South. As West Point furnished the military brains for both armies, so Annapolis produced the men whose famous deeds afloat were the glory of both navies. No less than 322 officers resigned from the United States navy and entered the Confederate navy, and 243 of these were officers of the line. Thus nearly a fourth of the officers of the navy at the beginning of 1861 espoused the cause of the South. It was classmate against classmate afloat as well as ashore.

MARINES AT THE WASHINGTON NAVY YARD

AMPHIBIOUS SOLDIERS—1865

This striking picture of an officer and five privates in the United States Marine Corps shows the quality of the men who made up that highly important branch of the service. The United States Marine Corps was established by Act of Congress on July 11, 1798, "as an addition to the present military establishment." On June 30, 1834, another Act for its better organization was passed. The marines were early in the war, not only in minor engagements along the coast incidental to the blockade, but in the first battle of Bull Run, July 21, 1861, where they coöperated with the regular military forces. The marines proved especially useful in the fighting along the Western rivers. When Admiral D. D. Porter took command of the Mississippi squadron, he applied for a force of marines to be carried in suitable vessels accompanying the fleet of gunboats so that the forces could be landed at various points. It was necessary to have trained soldiers at hand to pursue and annihilate these irresponsible raiders, who pillaged on the property of non-combatants

COPYRIGHT, 1911, PATRIOT PUB. CO.

OFFICER AND MEN OF THE U. S. MARINE CORPS

on both sides.   The Navy Department at the time could not furnish the marines that Porter wanted, but the War Department undertook to organize a marine brigade and also to furnish the necessary transports to carry them about.   The command of this was given
to Brigadier-General Alfred Ellet.   Ellet's marine brigade, numbering about 2,000 strong, first sailed up the Tennessee River in April,
1863, to join the flotilla of Lieutenant-Commander Fitch, which was trying to suppress marauding bands in that territory.   On
April 25th, the marine brigade was attacked at Duck River by 700 Confederates under Colonel Woodward, who had mistaken the
Federal vessels for transports.   They were disagreeably surprised when the marines, landing promptly, discomfited them in a sharp
engagement and pursued them for twelve miles inland.   On May 7th, since the waters of the Tennessee had become too low,
the marine brigade joined Admiral Porter's squadron and rendered important service along the Mississippi and the Yazoo.

The Federal Navy ❖ ❖ ❖ ❖ ❖ ❖

Naval chaplains received the same pay as lieutenants. The pay-scale tapered down through the various grades of seamen, until the "boys," which included all the youngsters engaged in the positions of "powder-monkeys," "water-boys," and various other duties, received ten dollars a month and their rations.

Early in the war, the Navy Department was confronted by a serious problem that manifested itself in the numbers of "contrabands," or runaway slaves that made their way into the navy-yards and aboard the Federal ships, seeking protection. These contrabands could not be driven away, and there was no provision existing by which they could be put to work and made useful either on board the ships or in the navy-yards. The situation was finally brought to the attention of the Secretary of the Navy, and he was asked to find some remedy. Under date of the 25th of September, 1861, he issued an order that from that date the contrabands might be given employment on the Federal vessels or in the navy-yards at any necessary work that they were competent to do. They were advanced to the ratings of seamen, firemen, and coal-heavers, and received corresponding pay.

The principal yards where the construction work of the Federal navy was carried on were those at New York, Philadelphia, Portsmouth, and Boston.

Early in the war, the Naval Academy was removed to Newport, Rhode Island, "for safe-keeping," but in 1865, when invasion was an impossibility and the dwindling forces of the South were mostly confined to the armies of Johnston and Lee, south of the James, the academy once more returned to its old home. There were many young men of the classes of 1861 and 1862 who found themselves shoulders high above the rank generally accredited to officers of their years. For deeds of prowess and valor they had been advanced many numbers in the line of promotion. The classes of 1865 and 1866 were very large, and for a long time after the reduction of the naval establishment, promotion in the service became exceedingly slow.

II

ORGANIZATION
OF THE
CONFEDERATE NAVY

1863—BUILDING THE "INDIANOLA," SOON TO BE CAPTURED BY CONFEDERATES

THE "INDIANOLA," ONE OF THE MOST FORMIDABLE IRONCLADS ON THE MISSISSIPPI RIVER, WAS CAP-
TURED BY CONFEDERATE TROOPS ON FEBRUARY 24, 1863. SUCH WAS THE PAUCITY OF SHIPYARDS
AT THE SOUTH, AND THE SCARCITY OF MATERIALS AND SKILLED MECHANICS, THAT THE CAPTURE OF
A FEDERAL VESSEL OF ANY KIND WAS AN EVENT FOR GREAT REJOICING IN THE CONFEDERATE NAVY

THE ORGANIZATION OF THE CONFEDERATE NAVY

ON looking over the history of the rise of the Confederacy, viewed even from the writings of the earlier and more or less partisan historians, a reader will not fail to be impressed with the wonderful resourcefulness that was displayed in meeting the unexpected exigencies of war. Viewed from an absolutely impartial standpoint, the South apparently accomplished the impossible. The young Confederacy succeeded against heavy odds in making something out of almost nothing. There was no naval warfare in the proper sense of the word during the four years' conflict; there were no fleets that met in battle at sea, and only two or three actions that could be touched upon in strictly naval annals. But at the outset, in the making up of the Government of the new republic, there was formed a Navy Department whose accomplishments, struggling against the difficulties that confronted it, were little short of marvelous, considering the limited time, available for preparation, in a country almost barren of ship-yards and other means of providing and equipping sea-going vessels, not to mention warships.

In the closing days of 1860, the secession of South Carolina made the fact apparent to the people of the North and South that the breach was constantly widening between the two sections of the country. Very soon it was perceived that the ever-growing chasm could not be bridged by diplomatic means, and that to sustain the stand they had taken the seceding States would be forced by the urging voices of their leaders to make an appeal to arms.

The South was immeasurably handicapped in more ways than one, but principally by its utter lack of any war-ships,

The Confederacy was able to enter upon the seas early, with a naval force that had to be reckoned with, as a result of its enterprise in seizing the undefended Norfolk Navy-yard only nine days after Sumter was fired upon. As early as February 21, 1861, Jefferson Davis appointed Stephen Mallory as Secretary of the Confederate Navy. He resigned from the United States Senate, where he had represented his State, Florida, and before he joined the Confederate Cabinet the navy-yard in his home town, Pensacola, had been seized, January 10, 1861, by Florida and Alabama State troops. The Federal navy-yards in the South were neither so active nor so well equipped as those at the North. But Norfolk Navy-yard, one of the oldest and most extensive, was provided with everything for the building and finishing of vessels of the largest size. At the time

STEPHEN RUSSELL MALLORY
SECRETARY OF THE CONFEDERATE STATES NAVY

of the secession of Virginia it contained at least 2,000 pieces of heavy cannon, including 300 new Dahlgren guns. The aggregate value of the property there was close to $10,000,000. Most of this fell into the hands of the Confederates. Owing to the possession of the yard equipment, it was here that the Southern naval constructors were first able to exemplify their ideas in ironclad construction by raising the hull of the sunken "Merrimac" and converting her into the armored "Virginia," to strike terror at the heart of the North by her performances in Hampton Roads in 1862. Although the Federals regained possession of Norfolk soon afterward and compelled the destruction of the "Virginia," her record stirred the Confederates to almost superhuman efforts. Secretary Mallory was most active in founding enterprises both at home and abroad for the construction of vessels.

THE BEGINNING OF THE CONFEDERATE NAVY—RUINS OF THE NORFOLK NAVY-YARD, 1862

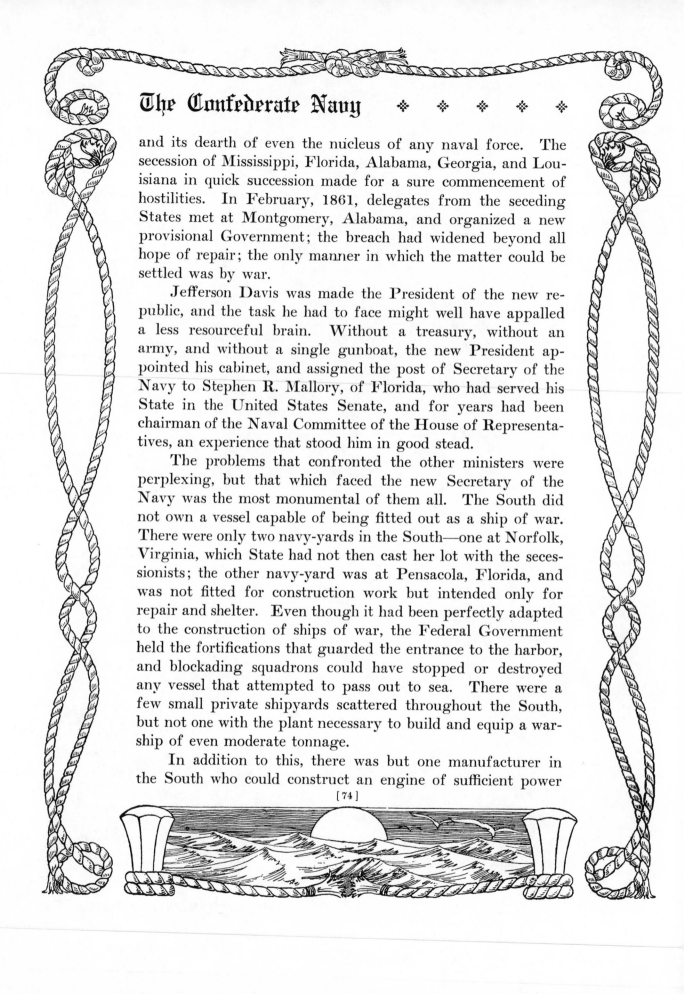

and its dearth of even the nucleus of any naval force. The secession of Mississippi, Florida, Alabama, Georgia, and Louisiana in quick succession made for a sure commencement of hostilities. In February, 1861, delegates from the seceding States met at Montgomery, Alabama, and organized a new provisional Government; the breach had widened beyond all hope of repair; the only manner in which the matter could be settled was by war.

Jefferson Davis was made the President of the new republic, and the task he had to face might well have appalled a less resourceful brain. Without a treasury, without an army, and without a single gunboat, the new President appointed his cabinet, and assigned the post of Secretary of the Navy to Stephen R. Mallory, of Florida, who had served his State in the United States Senate, and for years had been chairman of the Naval Committee of the House of Representatives, an experience that stood him in good stead.

The problems that confronted the other ministers were perplexing, but that which faced the new Secretary of the Navy was the most monumental of them all. The South did not own a vessel capable of being fitted out as a ship of war. There were only two navy-yards in the South—one at Norfolk, Virginia, which State had not then cast her lot with the secessionists; the other navy-yard was at Pensacola, Florida, and was not fitted for construction work but intended only for repair and shelter. Even though it had been perfectly adapted to the construction of ships of war, the Federal Government held the fortifications that guarded the entrance to the harbor, and blockading squadrons could have stopped or destroyed any vessel that attempted to pass out to sea. There were a few small private shipyards scattered throughout the South, but not one with the plant necessary to build and equip a warship of even moderate tonnage.

In addition to this, there was but one manufacturer in the South who could construct an engine of sufficient power

THE "ATLANTA"—FIRST TO RUN THE BLOCKADE FOR THE CONFEDERACY

The "Atlanta" was bought in September, 1861, by Captain James D. Bulloch, secret-service agent of the Confederate States in Europe. She was a new Clyde-built ship, and had made but one or two trips to the north of Scotland, attaining a speed of thirteen knots. She was the first to run the blockade inward for the account of the Confederate Government. She reached Savannah safely on November 12th with a cargo of Enfield rifles, ball cartridges, percussion caps, and various sorts of arms and ammunition. "No single ship," says Captain Bulloch, "ever took into the Confederacy a cargo so entirely composed of military and naval supplies." The "Fingal," as she was originally named, was bottled up by the blockade in Savannah. In January 1862, the Confederates began converting her into an ironclad of the "Merrimac" type. She was cut down to the main deck and widened amidships. A casemate was built upon her deck. Then she was heavily armored and fitted with a formidable ram and a spar torpedo. On July 3d she steamed down the Savannah River on her trial trip, causing great apprehension among the Federals for the safety of the fleet about Port Royal. After her capture by the Federals on June 17, 1863, the Confederates attempted to build other ironclads at Savannah. The "Savannah" was completed, fully armed, and manned, and the "Milledgeville," the same armored type, was nearly so when the city was evacuated in 1865.

RUINS OF THE MACHINE-SHOP AT THE NORFOLK NAVY-YARD

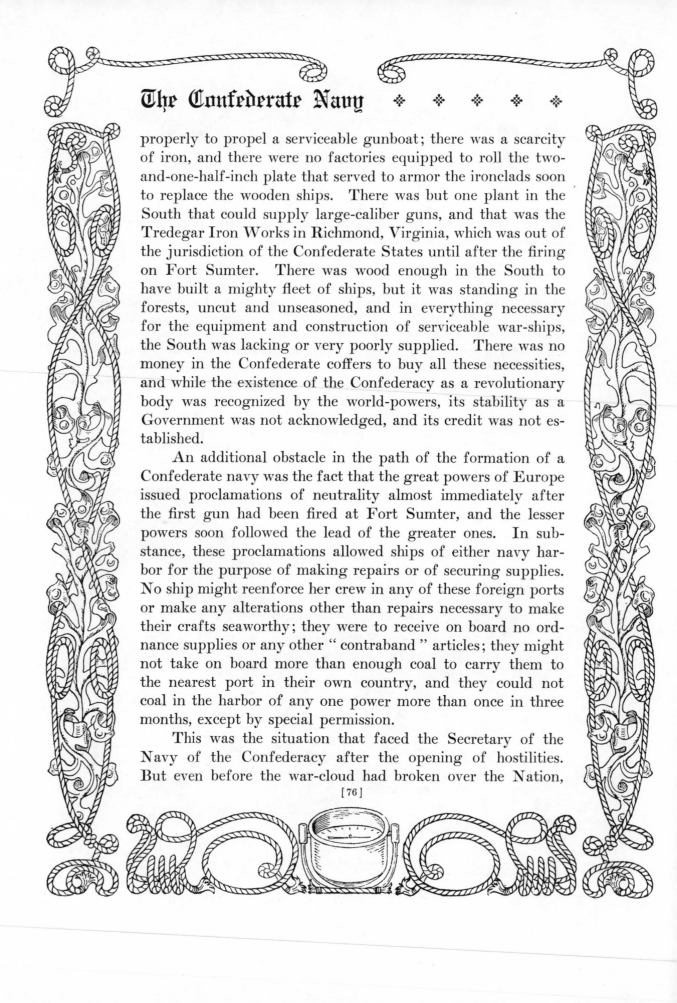

properly to propel a serviceable gunboat; there was a scarcity of iron, and there were no factories equipped to roll the two-and-one-half-inch plate that served to armor the ironclads soon to replace the wooden ships. There was but one plant in the South that could supply large-caliber guns, and that was the Tredegar Iron Works in Richmond, Virginia, which was out of the jurisdiction of the Confederate States until after the firing on Fort Sumter. There was wood enough in the South to have built a mighty fleet of ships, but it was standing in the forests, uncut and unseasoned, and in everything necessary for the equipment and construction of serviceable war-ships, the South was lacking or very poorly supplied. There was no money in the Confederate coffers to buy all these necessities, and while the existence of the Confederacy as a revolutionary body was recognized by the world-powers, its stability as a Government was not acknowledged, and its credit was not established.

An additional obstacle in the path of the formation of a Confederate navy was the fact that the great powers of Europe issued proclamations of neutrality almost immediately after the first gun had been fired at Fort Sumter, and the lesser powers soon followed the lead of the greater ones. In substance, these proclamations allowed ships of either navy harbor for the purpose of making repairs or of securing supplies. No ship might reenforce her crew in any of these foreign ports or make any alterations other than repairs necessary to make their crafts seaworthy; they were to receive on board no ordnance supplies or any other "contraband" articles; they might not take on board more than enough coal to carry them to the nearest port in their own country, and they could not coal in the harbor of any one power more than once in three months, except by special permission.

This was the situation that faced the Secretary of the Navy of the Confederacy after the opening of hostilities. But even before the war-cloud had broken over the Nation,

THE GUNS

OF

THE SAUCY

"TEASER."

ONE OF

THE FIRST

CONFEDERATE

GUNBOATS

THE "TEASER'S"
32-POUNDER

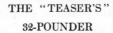

Before the completion of the ironclad "Virginia,"("Merrimac,") the Confederate navy had but five small steamers in the James River to oppose eight of the largest Federal vessels at Hampton Roads. The "Teaser" was a river-tug mounting but one gun at the time, yet in the engagement in which the "Virginia" first appeared the "Teaser," under command of Lieutenant W. A. Webb, C. S. N., boldly used her one gun against the Federal shore battery of sixty. In the upper picture this gun appears, a 12-pounder rifle. Its exposed position is evidence of the courage that was necessary to man it. In the lower picture is seen the 32-pounder that was added to the "Teaser's" armament later. With only these two guns she encountered both the "Maratanza" and the "Monitor," near Haxall's, on the James River, July 4, 1862, and replied valiantly to their fire. The third of the Federal shots, however, pierced her boiler, and her crew were forced to desert her. Many of the vessels procured by the Confederates to piece out its navy were no better built and some not so heavily armed as the "Teaser," yet in river and harbor, in sound and at sea, with few guns they were fought as valiantly as vessels were ever fought against heavy odds.

The Confederate Navy ❖ ❖ ❖ ❖ ❖

Secretary Mallory had started to build up his organization, undismayed by the conditions that he was forced to contend against. There were many Southerners in the Federal navy whose sympathies were with the new Government, and their resignations were daily being handed to the authorities at Washington, and their services tendered to the Confederate States.

Many of the men who left the Federal service were commanders of ships, and there were instances where they might easily have turned their vessels over to the Confederacy, but, without an exception, they returned the ships entrusted to them to the Federal Government before leaving the service, thus " retiring with clean hands." There were also several officers on coast-line vessels that were in Southern ports after the firing of the first gun, who sailed back to the North with their ships before going south to join the Confederates.

Sixteen captains, thirty-four commanders, and seventy-six lieutenants, together with one hundred and eleven regular and acting midshipmen, resigned from the United States Navy. To make provision for these officers, the Confederate service was increased by the Amendatory Act of April 21, 1862, and made to consist of:

Four admirals, 10 captains, 31 commanders, 100 first lieutenants, 25 second lieutenants, 20 masters, in line of promotion; 12 paymasters, 40 assistant paymasters, 22 surgeons, 15 passed assistant surgeons, 30 assistant surgeons, 1 engineer-in-chief, and 12 engineers.

That all the admirals, 4 of the captains, 5 of the commanders, 22 of the first lieutenants and 5 of the second lieutenants shall be appointed solely for gallant or meritorious conduct during the war. The appointments shall be made from the grade immediately below the one to be filled and without reference to the rank of the officer in such grade, and the service for which the appointment shall be conferred shall be specified in the commission. Provided, that all officers below the grade of second lieutenant may be promoted more than one grade for the same service. . . .

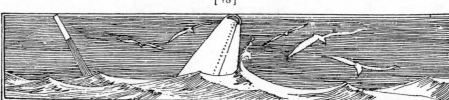

DECK OF C. S. S. "TEASER" AFTER HER CAPTURE BY THE "MARATANZA"

As a consort of the "Virginia" ("Merrimac"), this little converted tug-boat was not afraid in the famous battle in Hampton Roads. Later, no longer under the protecting wing of her huge ironclad leader, she met the "Monitor" and the "Maratanza" near Haxall's, on the James River, July 4, 1862. The little vessel had run aground and was forced to engage her superior antagonists. She opened fire and put a shot into the wheel-house of the "Maratanza," whose answering fire at the third shot exploded a shell in the boiler of the "Teaser." Lieutenant Hunter Davidson and her crew escaped to shore. In the captured vessel were found despatches from which the Federals gleaned valuable information.

THE
"MARATANZA"

AFTER
HER EXPLOIT

The Confederate Navy

One of the first Southern naval men to resign from the Federal Naval Department was Commander Raphael Semmes, who at once went South to enter the service of the new Government. He was sent to the North to secure what arms and ammunition he could, to contract for the delivery of more, and, if possible, to find ships that might serve as a nucleus for the navy of the Confederacy. A large amount of ordnance supplies was delivered or contracted for, but no vessels could be found that would be in the least adapted to service on the high seas, and with this portion of his mission unfulfilled, Semmes returned to Montgomery, twelve days before the firing on Fort Sumter.

Meanwhile, other agents of the Government had been attempting to find suitable ships in the Southern harbors that might be bought. All of these were reported as unsuitable for service as naval vessels, but Commander Semmes, after learning the qualifications of one of them, asked the Secretary of the Navy to secure her, have her altered, give him command, and then allow him to go to sea. The secretary acceded to this request, and the little boat was taken into New Orleans and operations were started to transform her into a gunboat which might fly the Confederate colors and, by harassing the commerce of the North, do her share in the work of warfare. The plans for the reconstruction of the vessel had scarcely been completed when the word was flashed around the world that Fort Sumter had been fired on and had fallen, and the ship, the first of a navy that was to contend against the third largest navy in the world, was christened after the first fort to fall into the hands of the Confederacy, the *Sumter*.

The Navy Department of the South now redoubled its efforts to provide the ships necessary for the defense of its coast and inland rivers. Almost any craft that could be fitted to mount a gun was pressed into service, and as quickly as the means would allow, these boats were prepared for their work, and officers and crews assigned to them.

WORKING ON THE STERN OF THE "INDIANOLA"

After capturing the great ironclad, the Confederates towed their prize over to the east bank of the Mississippi, where she sank, near Jefferson Davis' plantation. Two days later, as they were trying to raise her, they were frightened off by Porter's famous dummy monitor, made of pork-barrels and an old coal-barge, and the next day, although the "harmless monitor" was hard and fast aground, they destroyed the "Indianola" and abandoned her. The "Indianola" had two propellers in addition to her side wheels, and she was worked by seven engines in all. She was heavily armored with 3-inch iron plates. Her clever capture by the Confederates in the darkness was one of the achievements of the Confederate navy; and had it been followed up by the raising of the vessel, the Federals would have had a most formidable antagonist on the Mississippi in the vicinity of Vicksburg, where on the water side they were having things their own way.

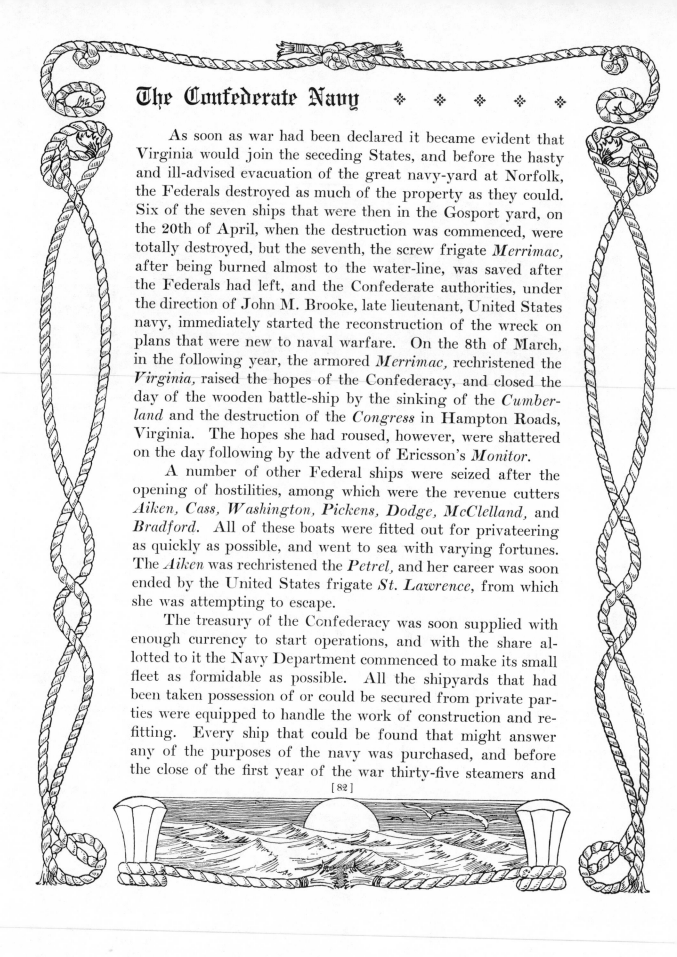

The Confederate Navy ✦ ✦ ✦ ✦

As soon as war had been declared it became evident that Virginia would join the seceding States, and before the hasty and ill-advised evacuation of the great navy-yard at Norfolk, the Federals destroyed as much of the property as they could. Six of the seven ships that were then in the Gosport yard, on the 20th of April, when the destruction was commenced, were totally destroyed, but the seventh, the screw frigate *Merrimac,* after being burned almost to the water-line, was saved after the Federals had left, and the Confederate authorities, under the direction of John M. Brooke, late lieutenant, United States navy, immediately started the reconstruction of the wreck on plans that were new to naval warfare. On the 8th of March, in the following year, the armored *Merrimac,* rechristened the *Virginia,* raised the hopes of the Confederacy, and closed the day of the wooden battle-ship by the sinking of the *Cumberland* and the destruction of the *Congress* in Hampton Roads, Virginia. The hopes she had roused, however, were shattered on the day following by the advent of Ericsson's *Monitor.*

A number of other Federal ships were seized after the opening of hostilities, among which were the revenue cutters *Aiken, Cass, Washington, Pickens, Dodge, McClelland,* and *Bradford.* All of these boats were fitted out for privateering as quickly as possible, and went to sea with varying fortunes. The *Aiken* was rechristened the *Petrel,* and her career was soon ended by the United States frigate *St. Lawrence,* from which she was attempting to escape.

The treasury of the Confederacy was soon supplied with enough currency to start operations, and with the share allotted to it the Navy Department commenced to make its small fleet as formidable as possible. All the shipyards that had been taken possession of or could be secured from private parties were equipped to handle the work of construction and refitting. Every ship that could be found that might answer any of the purposes of the navy was purchased, and before the close of the first year of the war thirty-five steamers and

AN EARLY DEFENDER OF THE MISSISSIPPI
THE CONFEDERATE GUNBOAT
"GENERAL BRAGG"

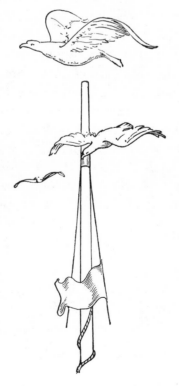

Early in the war, at the suggestion of two Mississippi River steamboat captains, J. E. Montgomery and J. H. Townsend, fourteen river-steamers were seized by the Confederate Government. Their bows were plated with one-inch iron, and pine bulwarks and cotton-bales were used to protect their machinery. They were organized into the river-defense fleet. The "General Bragg," side-wheel steamer, with seven others of these vessels, was stationed below Fort Pillow, under command of J. E. Montgomery, while Flag-Officer Foote was annoying Fort Pillow with his mortar boats. Seizing their opportunity on the hazy morning of May 10, 1862, the Confederate vessels moved up the river, bent on breaking up Foote's mortar-boat parties. The "General Bragg," under command of William H. H. Leonard, steaming far in advance of her con-

sorts, surprised the "Cincinnati" before the rest of the Federal fleet could come to her assistance. In the attack the "General Bragg" received a full broadside from the "Cincinnati," which disabled her and put her out of the action, but not until she had rammed the Federal gunboat, tearing a great hole in her side and flooding her shell-room. She was towed to the shore and sank in eleven feet of water. The career of this Confederate river-defense flotilla was brief, however, for on the 6th of June, when Charles Ellet's rams had been added to the fleet of the Federals in the engagement off Memphis, the Confederate fleet was put out of commission. This picture of the "General Bragg" was taken after she had been raised and refitted by the Federals and added to Porter's fleet on the Mississippi, where she served creditably till the war's close.

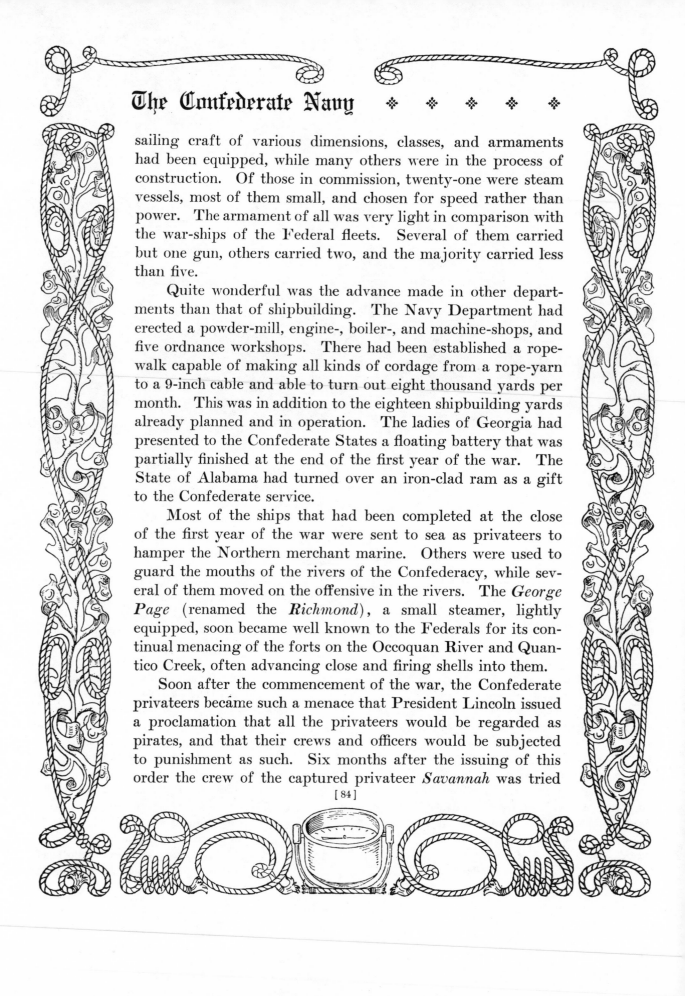

sailing craft of various dimensions, classes, and armaments had been equipped, while many others were in the process of construction. Of those in commission, twenty-one were steam vessels, most of them small, and chosen for speed rather than power. The armament of all was very light in comparison with the war-ships of the Federal fleets. Several of them carried but one gun, others carried two, and the majority carried less than five.

Quite wonderful was the advance made in other departments than that of shipbuilding. The Navy Department had erected a powder-mill, engine-, boiler-, and machine-shops, and five ordnance workshops. There had been established a rope-walk capable of making all kinds of cordage from a rope-yarn to a 9-inch cable and able to turn out eight thousand yards per month. This was in addition to the eighteen shipbuilding yards already planned and in operation. The ladies of Georgia had presented to the Confederate States a floating battery that was partially finished at the end of the first year of the war. The State of Alabama had turned over an iron-clad ram as a gift to the Confederate service.

Most of the ships that had been completed at the close of the first year of the war were sent to sea as privateers to hamper the Northern merchant marine. Others were used to guard the mouths of the rivers of the Confederacy, while several of them moved on the offensive in the rivers. The *George Page* (renamed the *Richmond*), a small steamer, lightly equipped, soon became well known to the Federals for its continual menacing of the forts on the Occoquan River and Quantico Creek, often advancing close and firing shells into them.

Soon after the commencement of the war, the Confederate privateers became such a menace that President Lincoln issued a proclamation that all the privateers would be regarded as pirates, and that their crews and officers would be subjected to punishment as such. Six months after the issuing of this order the crew of the captured privateer *Savannah* was tried

THE "GENERAL PRICE"—A CONFEDERATE WAR–BOAT THAT CHANGED HANDS

This was one of the fourteen river-steamers condemned and seized for the Confederate Government by General Lovell at New Orleans, January 15, 1862. Converted into a war-boat, she took a bold part in the engagement near Fort Pillow, which resulted in the sinking of the "Cincinnati." She arrived on the scene just as the "General Bragg" was disabled and boldly rammed the Federal gunboat for the second time, when a shot from the "Carondelet" disabled her. In the engagement with the Ellet rams off Memphis, she met the same fate as the "General Bragg" and the other vessels. She and the "General Beauregard," while making a dash from opposite sides upon the "Monarch," both missed that speedy vessel and collided with each other. The "General Price" was so badly injured that her captain ran her upon the Arkansas shore, to be added to the prizes won by the Ellet rams. The action put an end to the river-defense flotilla of the Confederates. Like the Federal river fleet at first, this organization was not under control of the Confederate navy, which, on the Mississippi, was commanded by Flag-Officer George N. Hollins, C. S. N. General Polk and the whole Mississippi delegation had urged upon the Confederate Congress the fitting out of this independent flotilla, which cost more than the million and a half dollars appropriated for it. The Confederate General Lovell at New Orleans had no faith in its efficiency because of his belief that the fleet was not properly officered. He stated emphatically that "fourteen Mississippi captains and pilots would never agree about anything after they once got under way."

for piracy, but the jury disagreed. While awaiting a new trial, the Confederacy imprisoned an equal number of officers of the Federal army, who were held as prisoners of war, and notified the Federals that whatever punishment was inflicted upon the privateersmen would be imposed upon the officers who were held as hostages. The great nations of the world refused to accept the ultimatum of the Union that the privateers were practising piracy, and from that time to the close of the war the men captured on privateers were treated as prisoners of war.

Now took place, on the part of the Confederate Navy Department, a most important move which opened a new chapter in naval history. On the 9th of May, 1861, Secretary Mallory, convinced that the resources of the Confederacy were not sufficient to complete a navy that would be adequate to maintain the defenses of the waterways of the South, commissioned James D. Bulloch to go to England and attempt to have some suitable ships constructed there, informing him at the same time that the necessary funds would be secured and placed at his disposal by the representatives of the Confederacy in England. The matter of building war-vessels in England presented many difficulties, for, under the British policy of neutrality, any ship of either of the warring powers that took on any armament or other equipment that was classed as contraband, was guilty of a breach of the neutrality agreement, and might be taken possession of by the British Government.

Captain Bulloch, a graduate of Annapolis, was well suited to the task, and he at once entered into negotiations for the building of two ships, which were to be delivered to him personally as his property. While built on the general lines of ships that would be suitable for privateering, they were not to be armed or in any way equipped as battle-ships by their makers. In spite, however, of all the precautions taken, the ships were not more than half completed before the suspicions of the Federal agents were aroused. But, though they were

REMARKABLE PHOTOGRAPHS OF CONFEDERATE RAMS—THE "ALBEMARLE"

THE CAPTURED RAMS

These pictures are remarkable as being among the scant remaining photographic evidence of the efforts made by the Confederacy to put a navy into actual existence. The "Albemarle" was built at the suggestion of two men whose experience had been limited to the construction of flat-boats. Under the supervision of Commander James W. Cooke, C. S. N., the vessel was completed; and on April 18, 1864, she started down the river, with the forges and workmen still aboard of her, completing her armor. Next day she sank the "Southfield." In the picture she is in Federal hands, having been raised after

THE CONFEDERATE RAM "LADY DAVIS"

Cushing's famous exploit had put her *hors du combat.* The "Lady Davis," formerly a tug, was purchased in Baltimore and was the first war-vessel to be put afloat by the State of South Carolina, March 13, 1861. She made several captures of Federal vessels around Charleston and was in Tattnall's little fleet on the sounds. In the picture she is in sharp and significant contrast with the huge sailing frigate whose wooden sides and many guns already belong to a past era. The efforts that brought such vessels as the "Albemarle" and the "Lady Davis" into the war marked the beginning of a new American navy. In these pictures both of these formidable vessels have been stripped.

morally certain that the ships were to serve in the Confederate navy, there was no tangible evidence upon which they could be detained, and both boats were completed and sailed out of English waters without any contraband stores aboard them. They were later equipped at other ports from ships that had carried out their arms and ammunition. Bulloch remained in Europe during the greater part of the war, and was a valuable assistant to the Secretary of the Navy of the Confederacy.

During the time in which he was superintending the gathering of this foreign-built force, Secretary Mallory was also organizing his department for efficient work in providing for the needs of all naval forces. He organized a bureau of orders and details, a bureau of ordnance and hydrography, a bureau of provisions and clothing, which also had charge of the paying of the naval forces, and a bureau of medicine and surgery. These bureaus were headed by competent men, and the detailed work of the department was soon being carried on in a thorough, business-like manner.

The matter of securing recruits was easily handled; there was no time when the number of men enlisted was not more than was necessary to man all the ships in the service. The men enlisted in the navy who could not be sent to sea were usually assigned to garrison the forts on the coast and along the rivers, while at times they were called upon to serve in the field with the regular army.

Most of the ships that were built for the Confederacy abroad were manned largely by recruits gathered on foreign shores, some of them being natives of the Confederate States, and others men who sympathized with the cause sufficiently to fight under its colors. The danger in running these boats through the blockading squadrons that lined the Confederate shores and the impossibility of getting men out of the ports on other ships, made it necessary to take what men could be secured. These vessels, however, were always officered by Confederates bearing Government commissions.

APRIL, 1865—ALL THAT WAS LEFT OF THE IRONCLAD RAM "VIRGINIA NO. 2"

The Confederates had built the "Virginia No. 2" for the defense of the James River. She was commanded by Commodore R. B. Pegram, C. S. N., and was the flagship of Commodore John K. Mitchell, C. S. N., who with two other gunboats opposed the Federal fleet that was attempting to work its way up to Richmond. The pierced and battered smokestack of the "Virginia" shows how bravely she stood up to the fire of the Federal monitors and the Howlett's house batteries. The "Virginia" and her consorts were active in shelling General Butler's Dutch Gap canal. On October 22, 1864, the "Virginia" discovered a new Federal masked battery nearly two miles below Chaffin's Bluff. With her consorts she stood up for two hours against the fire of the 100-pounder Parrott rifles on the shore, at a range of 500 yards. On the night of January 23, 1865, Commodore Mitchell of the "Virginia" and

his fleet attempted to pass below the Federal obstructions in the river, but both the "Virginia" and the "Richmond" grounded and were exposed all the next day to a ruinous fire from the Federal batteries and gunboats. One 15-inch solid shot tore a terrific hole in the "Virginia," killing six and wounding fourteen of her crew. The tide at last floated her and the "Richmond." Nothing daunted, she again led the fleet down the river in a night expedition. The squadron reached Point of Rocks and was discovered by the Federals who, training a calcium light upon the channel, poured a terrific fire from their batteries. The "Virginia's" pilot was driven from the wheel-house. The Confederate gunboats retired. As the Federal lines were drawn more closely around Petersburg and Richmond, the "Virginia" at last was sunk with other vessels in the channel of the James as an obstruction to navigation.

The Confederate Navy ❖ ❖ ❖ ❖ ❖

The pay of the officers of the Confederate navy was based on a sliding scale, regulated by the length of service and the occupation of the officer, as was the law in the Federal service. The pay, however, was larger. An admiral received $6000 a year; a captain's pay, when commanding a squadron, $5000; on any other duty at sea, $4200; on other duty, $3600, and on leave or awaiting orders, $3000. The pay of other officers was to be regulated by length of service, but as the first increase in pay was to come after five years' service, none of the officers benefitted by it. The pay of a commander on duty at sea was $2825 a year for the first five years after the date of commission, and on other duty, $2662. Commanders on leave or awaiting orders received $2250. Lieutenants commanding at sea received $2550; first lieutenants on duty at sea received $1500 a year, and the same when on other duty. When on leave or awaiting orders they received $1200 a year. Second lieutenants when on duty at sea received $1200 a year, and when on leave or on other duty received $1000. Surgeons on duty at sea received $2200 and when on other duty $2000 a year.

At Richmond, very early in the struggle, a naval school was established by Secretary Mallory and placed under the command of Lieutenant William H. Parker, a former officer of the United States navy, who, at the outbreak of the war, had already seen twenty years of service.

In July, 1863, the steamship *Patrick Henry,* then at Richmond, was converted into a school-ship. She was ordered to remain at anchor off Drewry's Bluff in the James River to lend assistance, if necessary, to the defense of the capital. In the fall of the year the Confederate States Naval Academy was formally opened with an efficient corps of professors.

Throughout the exciting times of 1864–65 the exercises of the school were regularly continued, and many of the students gave a good account of themselves before the war was over.

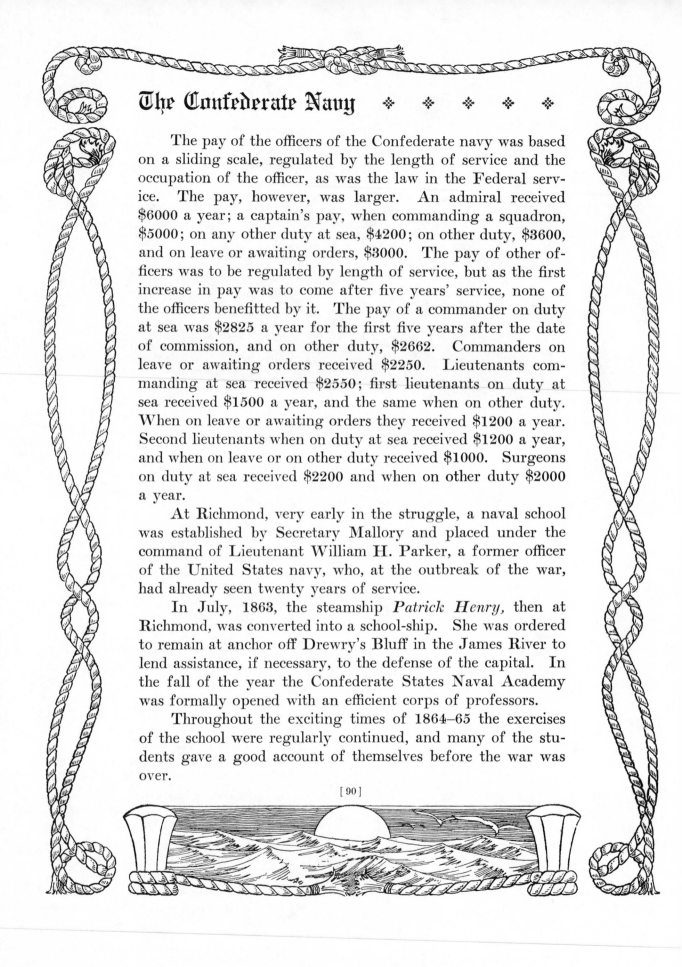

III

FIRST EXPEDITIONS
OF THE
FEDERAL NAVY

THE "PAWNEE"—ONLY 1,289 TONS, BUT THE HEAVIEST FEDERAL VESSEL IN THE POTOMAC
WHEN THE WAR BEGAN—SHE RECEIVED THE SURRENDER OF ALEXANDRIA, VA., IN MAY,
1861, AND FOUGHT GALLANTLY IN THE FIRST EXPEDITION AGAINST HATTERAS, AUGUST, 1861

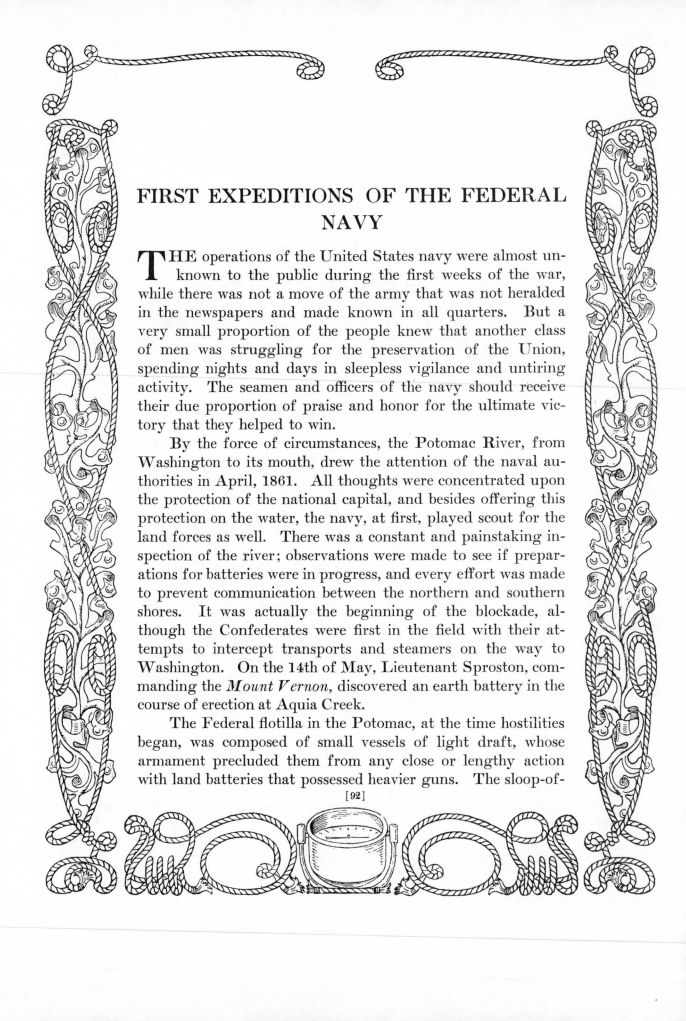

FIRST EXPEDITIONS OF THE FEDERAL NAVY

THE operations of the United States navy were almost unknown to the public during the first weeks of the war, while there was not a move of the army that was not heralded in the newspapers and made known in all quarters. But a very small proportion of the people knew that another class of men was struggling for the preservation of the Union, spending nights and days in sleepless vigilance and untiring activity. The seamen and officers of the navy should receive their due proportion of praise and honor for the ultimate victory that they helped to win.

By the force of circumstances, the Potomac River, from Washington to its mouth, drew the attention of the naval authorities in April, 1861. All thoughts were concentrated upon the protection of the national capital, and besides offering this protection on the water, the navy, at first, played scout for the land forces as well. There was a constant and painstaking inspection of the river; observations were made to see if preparations for batteries were in progress, and every effort was made to prevent communication between the northern and southern shores. It was actually the beginning of the blockade, although the Confederates were first in the field with their attempts to intercept transports and steamers on the way to Washington. On the 14th of May, Lieutenant Sproston, commanding the *Mount Vernon*, discovered an earth battery in the course of erection at Aquia Creek.

The Federal flotilla in the Potomac, at the time hostilities began, was composed of small vessels of light draft, whose armament precluded them from any close or lengthy action with land batteries that possessed heavier guns. The sloop-of-

ON THE "PAWNEE"—THE SHIP THAT SAW SUMTER CAPTURED

The quarterdeck and starboard battery of U. S. S. "Pawnee" appear here from photographs taken in Charleston Harbor. Here on the morning of April 12, 1861, officers and crew watched in an agony of suspense the pitiless iron rain that fell upon Sumter in the bombardment that began the Civil War. The "Pawnee," the "Pocohontas," the "Harriet Lane," and the "Baltic," together with two tugs, had sailed from New York with provisions and reënforcements for Major Anderson's little garrison. As the vessels approached Charleston Harbor, before daylight of April 12th, they heard the boom of shotted guns; and in the gray dawn, smoke rose sullenly in the direction of Sumter. When daylight disclosed the Stars and Stripes still waving over the fort, amid the roar of heavy artillery, Com-

GUNS OF THE "PAWNEE"

mander Stephen Clegg Rowan, of the "Pawnee," immediately volunteered to run his vessel in to the relief of the garrison. Lieutenant Gustavus V. Fox, later Assistant Secretary of the Federal Navy, in command of this expedition, would not consent to such a perilous undertaking, and the fleet lay helplessly by until the surrender of the heroic defenders at four o'clock in the afternoon of the 13th. The next day the garrison was taken off in the "Baltic." The "Pawnee" was next assigned to patrol duty in the Potomac, and on May 24th, in coöperation with the zouaves of the lamented Ellsworth, compelled the Confederates to evacuate Alexandria. Lieutenant Reigart B. Lowry landed and took formal possession of the town, with a detachment of seamen. This was the first Federal foothold in Virginia.

war *Pawnee* was the largest vessel in the river, and she was only of about thirteen hundred tons and carried a battery of fifteen guns. The commander of this vessel, Stephen C. Rowan, co-operating with the ill-fated Colonel Ellsworth and his regiment of Zouaves, took possession of the town of Alexandria, Virginia, May 24, 1861, and it was the navy that hoisted the Stars and Stripes once more over the custom-house.

There was an apparent fruitlessness in a naval force continually contending with shore batteries. If one was silenced and its gunners driven off, the odds were that it would be re-erected the next night, and the work would have to be done all over again. Constantly did the Navy Department request from the Secretary of War that a land force should act with it in the destruction of the Potomac batteries. But General McClellan declared that he could not spare the troops. As a naval writer of that day has pictured the situation, it can be well understood:

"Under such circumstances, the service of the Potomac flotilla was probably among the most fatiguing and discouraging of the war. The crews of the vessels spent a great portion of their nights in rowing up and down the river on picket duty, watching for mail-carriers, smugglers, and spies of all kinds; and in the daytime the ships were often aground on the bars and shoals, in spite of all precaution. They were in hourly danger of being opened upon by masked batteries, which could be constructed unseen in the thick undergrowth of the shores; their quarters in the little steamers were exceedingly uncomfortable; their prizes were rowboats, and small, worthless river craft. . . . For their reward, these hard-working, much-enduring men received too often only the complaints of the country that nothing was done, and sneers at the inefficiency of the Navy Department, and especially of the Potomac flotilla."

As we look back upon these times, when North and South were on tiptoe with excitement, it was remarkable that the Government had not made, before the end of May, any really

[94]

COPYRIGHT, 1911 REVIEW OF REVIEWS CO.

ON DANGEROUS DUTY—OFFICERS ON THE "PHILADELPHIA"

This river vessel was early pressed into service for one of the most important and danger-ous performances of the navy in the war. After Virginia seceded, the Confederates promptly removed all lightships and buoys from the Potomac, completely cutting off Wash-ington from the North. Selected by ballot of a board made up of the chiefs of departments at Washington, Lieutenant Thomas Stowell Phelps was entrusted as an officer "skilled in surveying" with the perilous task of resurveying the channel and replacing guiding marks. He was given the armed tender "Anacostia" and the "Philadelphia" for this work. Four 12-pound army field-pieces were mounted at either end of the latter vessel and covered with old canvas to conceal them. The crew and a company of the Seventy-first New York were kept carefully concealed below, while on the deck Phelps stood fearlessly at work. Near Aquia Creek it was particularly important that the river should be surveyed. Phelps ran boldly up under the guns of the Confederate batteries and worked for two hours, with the Confederate gunners, lock-strings in hand, plainly visible. Years afterward Colonel Wm. F. Lynch, C. S. A., who commanded the battery, explained that he had not given the order to fire because the "Philadelphia" seemed to him to be "the property of some poor devil who had lost his way and from her appearance was not worth the powder." The "Philadelphia" was also flagship in the expedition, March 13–14, 1862, to Albemarle Sound, North Carolina, where Commodore S. C. Rowan invaded the Southern inlets.

hostile move except that of occupying Alexandria. But, at the time of this occupation, the Confederates had already erected three strong earthworks at the railway terminus at Aquia Creek, Virginia, and other batteries were protecting the landing, three being mounted in positions on the higher ground, back of the river.

On the 29th of May, the *Thomas Freeborn,* a paddle-wheel steamer of about two hundred and fifty tons, mounting three guns, with the *Anacostia,* a small screw steamer of about two hundred tons, and the *Resolute,* less than half the latter's size, came down the river. Commander James H. Ward was at the head of the little squadron, whose largest guns were but 32-pounders. Upon reaching Aquia Creek, Ward engaged these batteries. Little damage was done, but these were the first shots fired by the navy in the Civil War. On the 1st of June, the action was renewed with great vigor. The *Pawnee* had joined the squadron, every vessel of which had been hit more than once, but although Commander Ward relates that more than a thousand shot had been discharged within range, he had no damage to report, which was, as he wrote, " truly remarkable," and later in the war, when gunnery practice had improved, it would have been impossible. Again, on the 2d of June, the *Pawnee* attacked the batteries, and though struck a number of times, had no casualties to report.

On the 5th, the steamer *Harriet Lane,* of historic memory, attacked the Confederate batteries at Pig Point, near Hampton Roads, and Captain John Faunce, while bearing testimony to the gallant conduct of the officers and men under his command, regretfully announced that he had five casualties on board his little vessel.

On the 27th of June, the navy lost its first officer and it was no other than the gallant Commander Ward, of the *Freeborn,* who was shot and mortally wounded while in the act of sighting the bow gun. A party had been landed in order to clear the ground at Mathias Point, and this had been surprised

ON THE "FREEBORN"

SHOWING HOW WARD, THE FIRST FEDERAL COMMANDER, WAS LOST

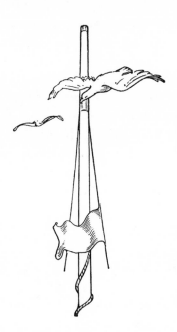

This photograph of 1861, long in the possession of the family of Commander James Harman Ward, and here reproduced for the first time, is the only vestige of a visual record of his brave deed on June 27th, the same year. In the picture, taken on the deck of the little improvised gunboat "Freeborn," the man sighting the gun has reverently donned the blouse and straw hat of Commander Ward to show how that brave officer stood when he received his mortal wound. After the firing on Sumter, the lull in the excitement had brought no respite for the navy, and the duty of patrolling the Potomac night and day devolved first upon Commander Ward. In addition to the "Freeborn," a side-wheel steamer carrying but three guns, his squadron consisted of the "Anacostia" and the "Resolute," carrying two guns each. With these vessels, on May 31st, he boldly attacked the Confederate batteries at Aquia Creek and next day, with the assistance of the "Pawnee," the Confederates were driven from their works. Again supported by the "Pawnee," on June 27th, Commander Ward attacked the Confederates at Mathias Point. While a body of sailors from his consort, under command of Lieutenant James C. Chapman, effected a landing, the gunboats kept up a rapid fire. Commander Ward, in his anxiety that this should prove effective, was in the act of sighting a gun himself when he was suddenly wounded in the abdomen and soon expired.

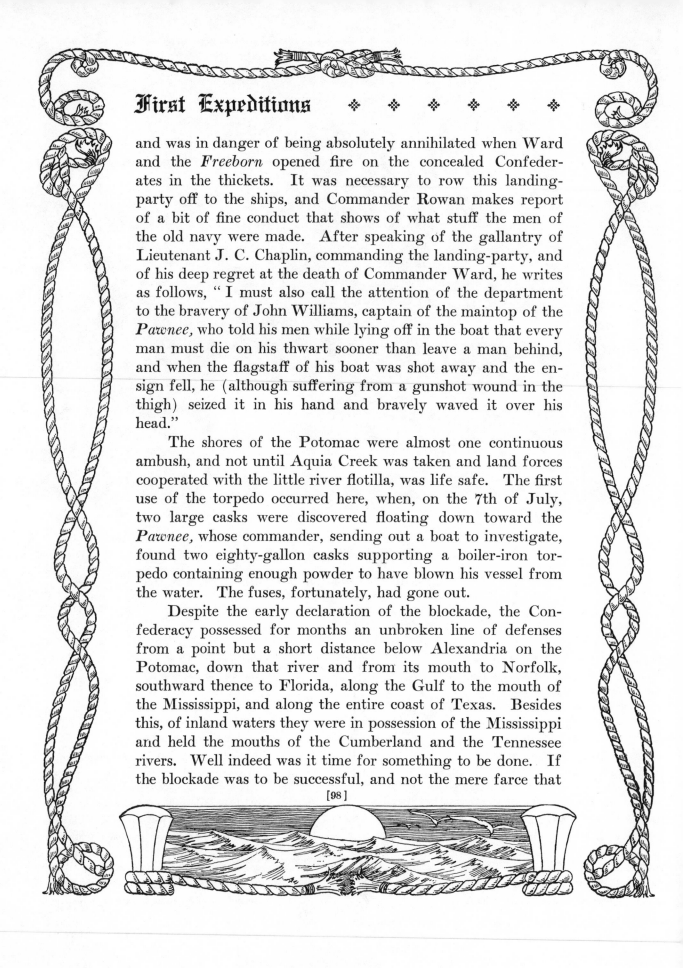

and was in danger of being absolutely annihilated when Ward and the *Freeborn* opened fire on the concealed Confederates in the thickets. It was necessary to row this landing-party off to the ships, and Commander Rowan makes report of a bit of fine conduct that shows of what stuff the men of the old navy were made. After speaking of the gallantry of Lieutenant J. C. Chaplin, commanding the landing-party, and of his deep regret at the death of Commander Ward, he writes as follows, "I must also call the attention of the department to the bravery of John Williams, captain of the maintop of the *Pawnee,* who told his men while lying off in the boat that every man must die on his thwart sooner than leave a man behind, and when the flagstaff of his boat was shot away and the ensign fell, he (although suffering from a gunshot wound in the thigh) seized it in his hand and bravely waved it over his head."

The shores of the Potomac were almost one continuous ambush, and not until Aquia Creek was taken and land forces cooperated with the little river flotilla, was life safe. The first use of the torpedo occurred here, when, on the 7th of July, two large casks were discovered floating down toward the *Pawnee,* whose commander, sending out a boat to investigate, found two eighty-gallon casks supporting a boiler-iron torpedo containing enough powder to have blown his vessel from the water. The fuses, fortunately, had gone out.

Despite the early declaration of the blockade, the Confederacy possessed for months an unbroken line of defenses from a point but a short distance below Alexandria on the Potomac, down that river and from its mouth to Norfolk, southward thence to Florida, along the Gulf to the mouth of the Mississippi, and along the entire coast of Texas. Besides this, of inland waters they were in possession of the Mississippi and held the mouths of the Cumberland and the Tennessee rivers. Well indeed was it time for something to be done. If the blockade was to be successful, and not the mere farce that

AQUIA CREEK LANDING, ON THE POTOMAC—ONE OF THE FIRST FEDERAL NAVY OBJECTIVES

This little landing on the river became at the very outbreak of the war one of the chief objectives of the Federal navy. After the firing upon Sumter, the Confederates seized commanding points from Alexandria southward and mounted batteries of heavy guns as rapidly as possible. Aquia Creek, which was the terminus of the Aquia Creek & Fredericksburg Railroad, was fortified with twenty guns from the captured Norfolk Navy-yard, and was the chief menace to navigation of the Potomac by the Federal vessels. It was the first important duty of the navy to open and maintain the water communications of Washington with the North. If the Confederates could succeed in closing up the Potomac, their boast that the Confederate flag would fly over the National Capitol would not be an idle one, and thus the very first operations of the gunboats in the Potomac were of vital importance to the success of the Federal cause. Under the guns of the two batteries at Aquia Creek, Lieutenant Phelps performed the difficult and dangerous though unsung task of surveying the channel and replacing the buoys in the Potomac. The little flotilla of small vessels in the river carried only a light armament, and until joined by the "Pawnee," a sloop of less than 1,300 tons, was almost powerless against such heavy ordnance as had been mounted by the Confederates. Yet when the "Freeborn" and the "Anacostia" and the "Resolute" boldly advanced to attack Captain W. F. Lynch's batteries at Aquia Creek on May 29, 1861, the guns of the navy spoke out the brave determination which ever characterized that arm of the service throughout the four years of war.

JAMES HARMAN WARD

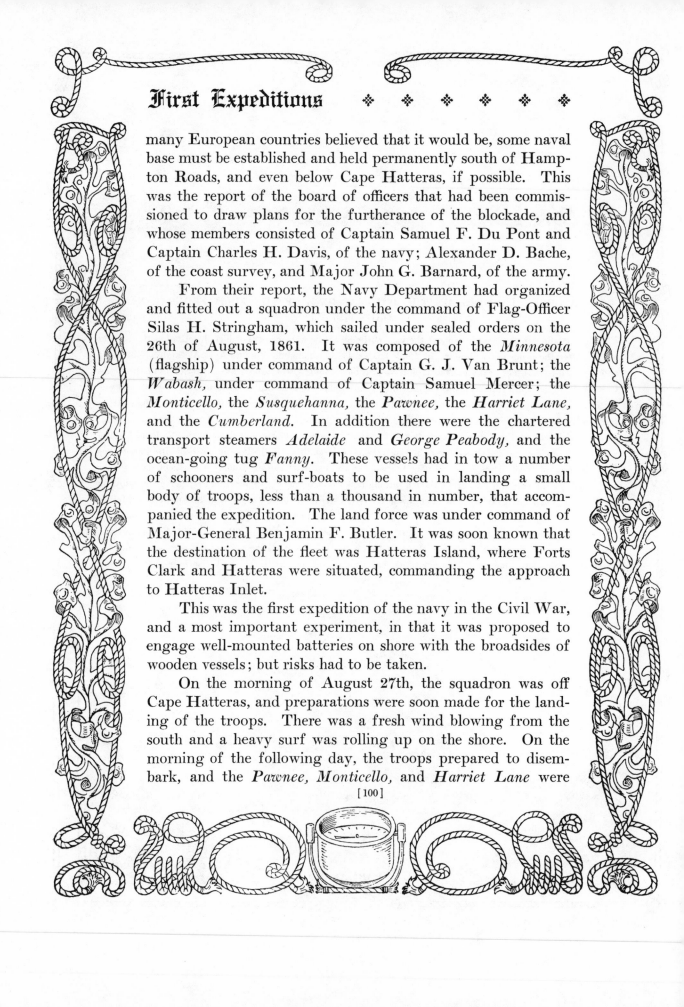

many European countries believed that it would be, some naval base must be established and held permanently south of Hampton Roads, and even below Cape Hatteras, if possible. This was the report of the board of officers that had been commissioned to draw plans for the furtherance of the blockade, and whose members consisted of Captain Samuel F. Du Pont and Captain Charles H. Davis, of the navy; Alexander D. Bache, of the coast survey, and Major John G. Barnard, of the army.

From their report, the Navy Department had organized and fitted out a squadron under the command of Flag-Officer Silas H. Stringham, which sailed under sealed orders on the 26th of August, 1861. It was composed of the *Minnesota* (flagship) under command of Captain G. J. Van Brunt; the *Wabash,* under command of Captain Samuel Mercer; the *Monticello,* the *Susquehanna,* the *Pawnee,* the *Harriet Lane,* and the *Cumberland.* In addition there were the chartered transport steamers *Adelaide* and *George Peabody,* and the ocean-going tug *Fanny.* These vessels had in tow a number of schooners and surf-boats to be used in landing a small body of troops, less than a thousand in number, that accompanied the expedition. The land force was under command of Major-General Benjamin F. Butler. It was soon known that the destination of the fleet was Hatteras Island, where Forts Clark and Hatteras were situated, commanding the approach to Hatteras Inlet.

This was the first expedition of the navy in the Civil War, and a most important experiment, in that it was proposed to engage well-mounted batteries on shore with the broadsides of wooden vessels; but risks had to be taken.

On the morning of August 27th, the squadron was off Cape Hatteras, and preparations were soon made for the landing of the troops. There was a fresh wind blowing from the south and a heavy surf was rolling up on the shore. On the morning of the following day, the troops prepared to disembark, and the *Pawnee, Monticello,* and *Harriet Lane* were

AQUIA CREEK

WHERE THE FIRST SHOTS WERE FIRED BY THE NAVY

The importance of Aquia Creek Landing, on the Potomac, to the navy grew steadily as the advance offensive line which the Confederates had seized upon at the outbreak of the war began to be pushed back into Virginia. As a strategic position the little landing was the scene of many stirring events during the ebb and flow of the military operations. The navy, in coöperating, came to know it as a point of supply. Long before February, 1863, when these pictures were taken, the Potomac flotilla had had its full of the abundance of toil by night and day in the arduous and perilous task of patrolling the great river. Both banks in 1861 were lined with hostile non-combatants; goods were smuggled across constantly by Maryland sympathizers to their fighting friends in Virginia. Federal merchant-vessels were captured in attempting to get up the river to Washington. The suppression of all this fell to the lot of the little flotilla on the Potomac; and the task, which was the real beginning of the blockade, though devoid of glory and fame, was well and thoroughly accomplished and was one of the most praiseworthy achievements of the navy in the war.

ordered to cover their landing. Now the difficulties increased; the iron surf-boats were rolled broadside on the beach, and what men got ashore had to wade through the heavy surf. But three hundred or so succeeded in reaching dry land, a rather forlorn end to the land expedition, as it had no supplies and the ammunition was soaked through. But in the mean time, the *Wabash* got under way, and towing the old *Cumberland* with the *Minnesota* following, led in toward Fort Clark. Soon the battle was on between the land and sea. Flag-Officer Stringham deserves great praise for the way he handled his small squadron; ships were kept in constant movement, and, though well within range, suffered little or no damage from the shots of the fort. The concentrated fire of the vessels upon the little battery, which mounted but five guns, soon bore results. Shortly after noon Fort Clark was abandoned, and the shivering troops that had reached the beach took possession and hoisted the Federal flag.

It was at first thought that Fort Hatteras had surrendered after the short bombardment, but on approaching closer the Confederate batteries once more reopened. The next morning, however, the bombardment being resumed, the fort was seriously damaged, and the powder magazine, having been set on fire, the Confederates hoisted the white flag shortly after eleven o'clock. There was an amusing little note added to the morning's work by the fact that Flag-Officer Barron, who lately had been an officer of the United States navy, refused to surrender the fort to the land forces that now came up from the direction of Fort Clark, the Confederate commander claiming that they had taken no part in the action. Therefore he was rowed off to the flagship, where he gave up his sword to his former friend, Flag-Officer Stringham.

Six hundred and fifteen men and officers were captured at Fort Hatteras, and twenty-five guns, all of which had come from the navy-yard at Norfolk. The moral effect of this easily earned victory was great throughout the North. The real

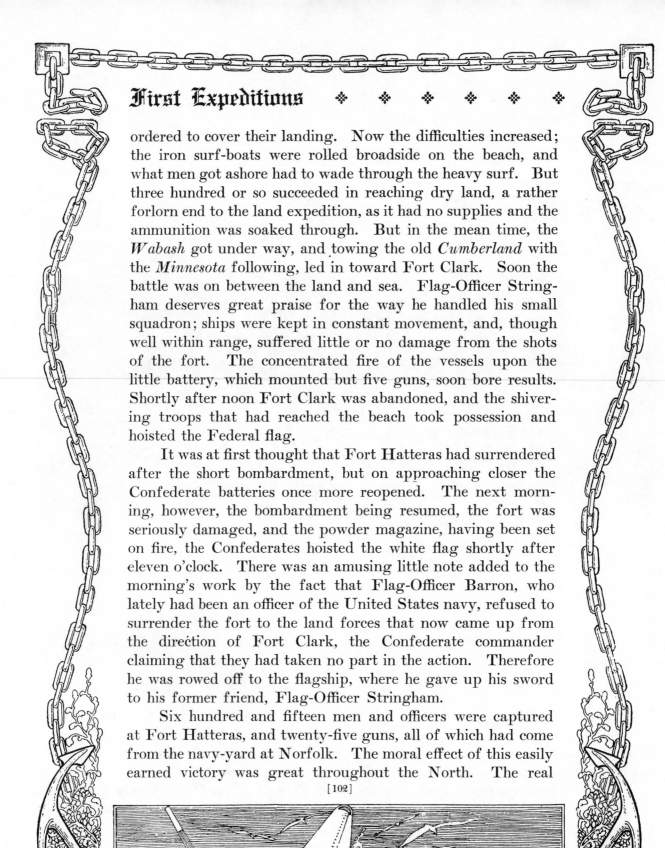

DU PONT AND OFFICERS ON THE "WABASH"

Here are two groups taken on board the "Wabash," which took part in the first real expedition of the navy —to Hatteras. In the lower picture appears the pivot-gun, one of the largest that at that time was fired from the deck of any vessel—a 200-pounder Parrott rifle. The crew are not at quarters, but the condition of the gun shows it was the pet of the forward watch. This gun was on the

THE FORWARD PIVOT-GUN

topgallant forecastle, and had a sweep in every direction except directly aft. At Fort Fisher this gun's crew showed magnificent practice, as they had at Fort Walker, the first engagement at which the big gun had been fired. In the upper picture the little vine growing out of the flower-pot is an evidence of the sailor's desire to make a cabin as much of a home as is possible.

importance of the conflict had not yet been fully realized, but the spirits of all the Northern people were still drooping after the disastrous defeat at Bull Run. They required some salve for their wounded pride, and the successful conclusion of the first naval expedition gave them this and restored confidence, as well. But the most important features were the realization of the plans of the naval committee, and the fact that the victory had gained a base upon the Southern coast for the support of the blockading squadrons, while, at the same time, a foothold was afforded for military invasion.

Stringham's fleet had now almost complete command of the most important passage to the North Carolina sounds. More than one port of entry of the blockade-runners was closed. The important capture of the Hatteras forts was quickly followed by operations along the coast that extended into the various sounds, and a little fort on Beacon Island, Ocracoke Inlet, some twenty miles further south, was captured. It was in an unfinished condition, and was practically abandoned upon receipt of the news of the fall of Forts Clark and Hatteras. Lieutenant Maxwell landed with a small force on Beacon Island and destroyed the guns found there—four 8-inch navy shell-guns and fourteen 32-pounders; then setting fire to a store-ship that he found a few miles beyond, near the little town of Portsmouth, he regained the fleet.

Thus was secured, from Hatteras Inlet southward to Cape Lookout, virtually the entire possession of the coast to the Cape Fear River; northward the occupation of Hatteras controlled the coast as far as Hampton Roads.

IV

_____

THE

BLOCKADE

_____

THE SPEEDY "RHODE ISLAND"—ONE OF THE FEW FEDERAL
CRUISERS SWIFT ENOUGH TO CATCH THE GREYHOUND BLOCK-
ADE-RUNNERS THAT COULD OUTDISTANCE MOST OF THE FLEET

A GREYHOUND CAUGHT—WRECK OF THE BLOCKADE–RUNNER "COLT"

The wreck of this blockade-runner, the "Colt," lies off Sullivan's Island, Charleston Harbor, in 1865. The coast of the Carolinas, before the war was over, was strewn with just such sights as this. The bones of former "greyhounds" became landmarks by which the still uncaptured blockade-runners could get their bearings and lay a course to safety. If one of these vessels were cut off from making port and surrounded by Federal pursuers, the next best thing was to run her ashore in shallow water, where the gunboats could not follow and where her valuable cargo could be secured by the Confederates. A single cargo at war-time prices was enough to pay more than the cost of the vessel. Regular auctions were held in Charleston or Wilmington, where prices for goods not needed by the Confederate Government were run up to fabulous figures. The business of blockade-running was well organized abroad, especially in England. One successful trip was enough to start the enterprise with a handsome profit. A blockade-runner like the "Kate," which made forty trips or more, would enrich her owners almost beyond the dreams of avarice.

THE REMAINS OF THE "RUBY"
SOON AFTER HER CAPTURE BY U. S. S. "PROTEUS," FEBRUARY, 1865

Here on the beach of Morris Island lies all that was left of the swift and doughty blockade-runner " Ruby." She was one of the most successful of her kind. She was busy early in 1862, plying between Nassau and Charleston. Not until February 27, 1865, while trying to get in with an assorted cargo of the type usually denominated "hardware," was she at last entrapped. The Federal screw-steamer " Proteus," Commander R. W. Shufeldt, picked up her scent and gave chase, with the result seen in the picture. It was for taking such risks as these that the captains of the blockade-runners received $5,000 a month instead of the $150 which was the prevailing rate in the merchant service before the war. Officers and crews were paid in like proportion. Coal was worth $20 a ton instead of $4, as formerly. The whole expense of the trip was from three to four times what it would have been in time of peace, and yet a single cargo of cotton was worth from a quarter of a million to a million dollars, and the freight rates in and out ranged from $300 to $1,000 a ton. It was too alluring a business to be deterred by difficulty and danger. As Disraeli remarked, the exploits of the blockade-runners "increase our respect for the energy of human nature."

A LATE CAPTURE—DECEMBER, 1864—FLYING THE BRITISH FLAG

In this blockade-runner is seen the type of vessel in which foreign capital was lavishly invested. She is still flying the British flag, under which she plied her trade, and appears to have been the property of a syndicate of British merchants. In the early stages of the war the Confederacy purchased a number of vessels abroad for use as privateers and blockade-runners. In the beginning the latter were officered by members of the Confederate navy, but later in the war blockade-running became so profitable that the Confederacy could afford to leave it almost entirely to private initiative, rendering such assistance as was needed to enable the vessels to make port or to discharge their cargo in case they were driven on the beach. With the exception of a lighthouse which the Confederates established on the "Mound" near Fort Fisher, there were no guides for blockade-runners at night, except the glow of fires of the ever-busy salt-works and the range lights which were put out in the various channels only after the vessel had exchanged signals with the shore and which were removed immediately after she had made port. It is a remarkable fact that no blockade-runner commanded by an officer of the Confederate navy was ever captured. The famous veteran, the "Robert E. Lee," the best blockade-runner of the Confederacy and long commanded by Lieut.-Commander John Wilkinson, C. S. N., did not meet her fate until October, 1863, on the very first trip she made after Commander Wilkinson had been superseded at Halifax, N. S., by an officer from the merchant marine.

[108]

A FLEET-FOOTED BLOCKADE-RUNNER, WITH TELESCOPING STACKS

This rakish side-wheel steamer was photographed off Norfolk, Va., December, 1864, some time after the boat had been compelled by force of arms to change her occupation from Confederate blockade-running to very useful work with the Federal blockading fleet, under the name of "Fort Donelson." She was of 900 tons burden. Burning anthracite coal, with telescoping smokestacks which could be lowered till almost level with the deck, these vessels left Bermuda and Nassau "on moons"—that is to say, when their arrival off the Southern coast would be attended by as much darkness as possible. Mostly Clyde-built vessels, their first trip would be from some British port with a crew shipped to Bermuda or Nassau "and a market." Little difficulty was experienced in securing recruits willing to take the places of those who did not wish to go the whole cruise. The run-

ners would leave Bermuda and Nassau half a dozen at a time at favorable opportunities, with a regularity and despatcl that the Northern newspapers of the day were fond of commend-ing to the blockading squadron. Old veterans like the "R. E. Lee" and the "Kate" plied with the precision of regular packets. At Havana the blockade-runners were more fre-quent callers than the regular merchantmen between that city and New York. The "Fort Donelson," while in the Federal navy, on August 15, 1864, under command of Acting Vol. Lieut. T. Pickering, captured a suspicious-looking vessel, the "Dacotah," but she was subsequently released. In January, 1865, the "Fort Donelson," under command of Acting Master G. W. Frost, took part in the expedition against Fort Fisher, which dealt such a heavy blow at blockade-running, the business in which she was formerly engaged.

THE BLOCKADE

THERE are two kinds of blockades—military and commercial. A military blockade is merely the equivalent, on the part of a naval force, of that of a siege upon land, and has been practised from the very earliest times. Commercial blockades are instituted with the principal object of stopping an enemy's imports, crippling his trade, and isolating him from commerce with the outside world. In the old monarchies and the republics of antiquity, trade, even when affecting national interest, was held in contempt; there is no record in the histories of early nations of this commercial form of warfare. When Columbus and Vasco da Gama opened the great ocean routes and provided markets that turned royal minds to the value of commerce, international customs and trade relations were entirely changed—the new weapon of the blockade grew suddenly to be an element in warfare. The Dutch provinces of Spain, in their great fight for independence, were the first to make use of it, when they established the commercial blockade of the Scheldt.

The blockade which the United States proclaimed, and at last succeeded in enforcing, against the ports of the Southern Confederacy was of a twofold character; it was both military and commercial, and was recognized by the Supreme Court of the United States as being valid, and sanctioned by both municipal and international law. By the amended proclamation of President Lincoln on the 27th of April, 1861, the whole seacoast of the South Atlantic and the Gulf of Mexico, from Virginia to the Rio Grande, a stretch of over three thousand miles, was interdicted from commercial relations with any foreign shore. But had the President or his advisers perceived the magnitude of the task or apprehended its difficulties and

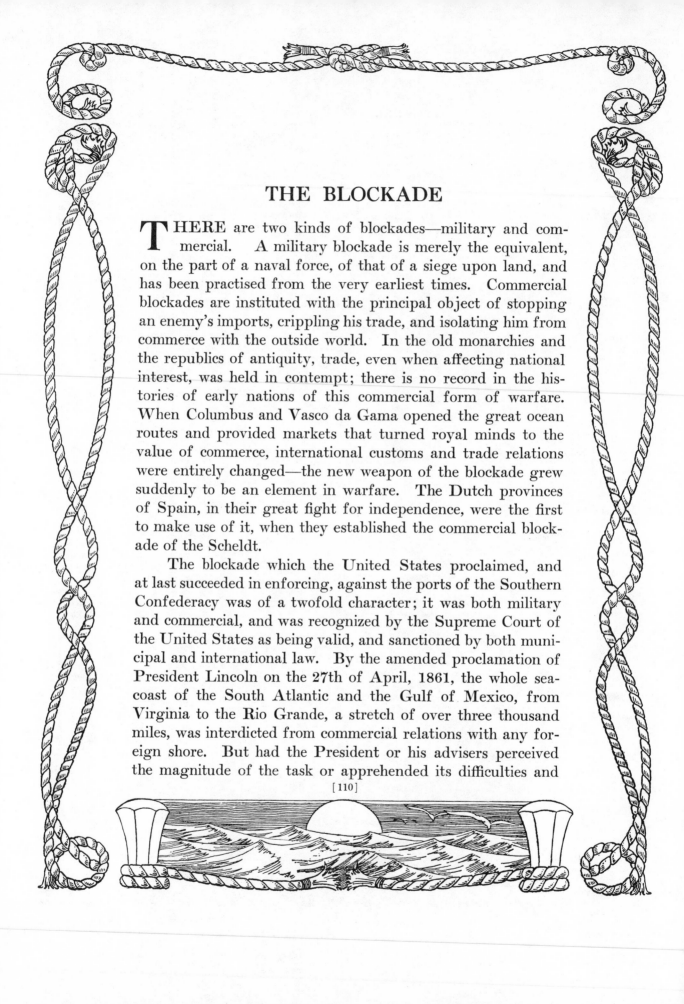

THE FIRST FEDERAL BLOCKADING SQUADRON
PHOTOGRAPHED BY A CONFEDERATE IN '61

This dimmed Confederate photograph of early in 1861 ranks as a unique historical document—for it shows, beyond Fort Pickens on the point of Santa Rosa Island, the Federal squadron that began the blockade on the Atlantic coast. Two tiny figures at the lower right gaze across the waters—Confederates who little dream how mighty a part those ships and their sisters will play in the coming struggle. The view was taken from the lighthouse by Edwards of New Orleans. The relief of Fort Pickens was the first dramatic incident of the war in which the navy played a part. In January, 1861, the "Brooklyn," Captain W. S. Walker, was sent with some United States troops on board to reënforce the little garrison at Fort Pickens. But, owing to the conciliatory policy of the Buchanan Administration, a joint-order from the Secretary of War and the Secretary of the Navy was sent to the naval and military commanders on January 29th, instructing them not to land the troops unless Fort Pickens should be attacked. On April 12th Lieutenant John L. Worden, later of "Monitor" fame, arrived with a special message from Secretary Welles, and that night the fort was saved by soldiers landed from the "Brooklyn."

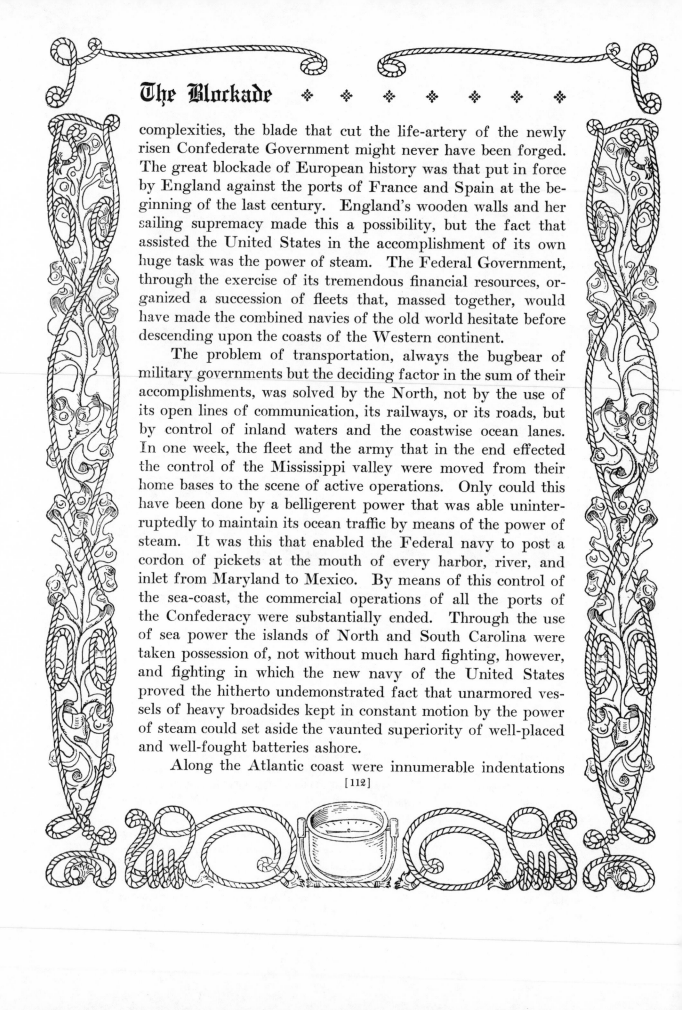

complexities, the blade that cut the life-artery of the newly risen Confederate Government might never have been forged. The great blockade of European history was that put in force by England against the ports of France and Spain at the beginning of the last century. England's wooden walls and her sailing supremacy made this a possibility, but the fact that assisted the United States in the accomplishment of its own huge task was the power of steam. The Federal Government, through the exercise of its tremendous financial resources, organized a succession of fleets that, massed together, would have made the combined navies of the old world hesitate before descending upon the coasts of the Western continent.

The problem of transportation, always the bugbear of military governments but the deciding factor in the sum of their accomplishments, was solved by the North, not by the use of its open lines of communication, its railways, or its roads, but by control of inland waters and the coastwise ocean lanes. In one week, the fleet and the army that in the end effected the control of the Mississippi valley were moved from their home bases to the scene of active operations. Only could this have been done by a belligerent power that was able uninterruptedly to maintain its ocean traffic by means of the power of steam. It was this that enabled the Federal navy to post a cordon of pickets at the mouth of every harbor, river, and inlet from Maryland to Mexico. By means of this control of the sea-coast, the commercial operations of all the ports of the Confederacy were substantially ended. Through the use of sea power the islands of North and South Carolina were taken possession of, not without much hard fighting, however, and fighting in which the new navy of the United States proved the hitherto undemonstrated fact that unarmored vessels of heavy broadsides kept in constant motion by the power of steam could set aside the vaunted superiority of well-placed and well-fought batteries ashore.

Along the Atlantic coast were innumerable indentations

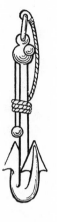
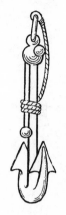

OFFICERS ON DECK OF THE U. S. S. "RHODE ISLAND"

This proved to be one of the most useful of the vessels purchased by the Navy Department during the war. Commissioned in May, 1861, she was one of the last of the Federal warships to go out of service, June, 1865. During the entire war she was commanded by Commander (later Rear-Admiral) Stephen Decatur Trenchard. At the time this picture was taken at Cape Haytien, her executive officers were Lieutenant Pennell, Lieutenant Farquhar, and Master Rodney Brown. Other officers were Chief-Engineer McCutcheon, Captain's Clerk F. C. T. Beck, Paymaster R. Hall Douglas, Paymaster's Clerk, Langdon Rodgers. She had first been employed as a special despatch-boat for the rapid transmission of Government orders to all squadron commanders. Her speed proved so great that she was soon converted into a heavily armed cruiser (twelve guns) and sent to West Indian waters to search for Confederate privateers and blockade-runners. She made numerous prizes and was subsequently transferred to Wilkes' flying squadron. She was finally attached to Admiral Porter's South Atlantic squadron and took part in both attacks on Fort Fisher. For his conduct there Commander Trenchard was specially mentioned in orders by his chief.

that multiplied a thousand times the difficulties of maintaining a strict blockade. From Cape Henry to Matamoras, every bay, sound, harbor, and inlet offered tempting shelter to any craft inward bound and laden with the contraband of war, and from these hidden nooks vessels loaded with cotton for the idle factories of Europe essayed the hazardous voyage that brought the reward of French and British gold.

Remarkable as it may seem, it was the Confederacy that made the first move in the game of blockade. The State of Virginia attempted to close the Potomac and to prevent egress and ingress to the national capital. A total lack of naval force prevented such accomplishment. But the Federal navy's blockade of the Southern ports became ultimately the determining factor in the downfall of the Confederacy. Vicksburg and Port Hudson surrendered as much to Farragut and to Porter as to Grant. Sherman's march to the sea would never have been undertaken had not the Federal fleets already held possession of Port Royal and so strongly invested the harbors of Savannah, Charleston, and Wilmington. In his campaign against Richmond, McClellan sought shelter under the guns of the navy, and Grant was enabled, through the navy's control of the coast, to maintain his base at City Point.

Had Jefferson Davis a navy at his command, the result of the internecine struggle might have been far different. It was the blockade as much as the battles that brought to every Southern home the horrible reality of want that follows in the track of war. The people of the North knew no deprivations, but the women and children of the South, before the conflict ended, were suffering from the lack of the very things that ships, and ships only, could bring them. The watching cordons spread along the coast ultimately precluded the import of articles, not only of trade but of necessity. It was natural that the ports of Virginia and North Carolina received the first attention of the Federal navy.

Agreeable to the requirements of international law, notice

FEDERALS ON THE WHARF AT PORT ROYAL—1862

In these photographs of March, 1862, Federals are busily at work making the newly captured Port Royal the strong and handy Southern base it remained throughout the war. It had become apparent early in the war that, if the blockade were to be made effective, the Federal Government must repossess itself as quickly as possible of the forts guarding the entrances to the important harbors of the South. From the Rio Grande to the Chesapeake the coast defenses were in the hands of the Confederacy. It was impossible for the navy to prevent the ingress and egress of blockade-runners under friendly guns. President Lincoln, in June, 1861, convened a board including Captain Samuel Francis Du Pont and Captain Charles H. Davis, of the navy, Major John G. Barnard, of the army, and Professor Alexander D. Bache, of the coast survey. After careful study they presented a plan to the President. Its first object was to obtain possession of Hatteras Inlet and thus close the main entrance to Albemarle and Pamlico Sounds, which were veritable havens of

refuge to the blockade-runner. This was to be followed up by the capture of Port Royal for a naval base, where vessels could be coaled and repaired without the necessity of being withdrawn from the blockading squadron for the long period required to reach a Northern port. On August 29th a fleet under Flag-Officer Silas H. Stringham, together with a military force commanded by General Benjamin F. Butler, carried out successfully the first of these plans. This was the first expedition in which the army coöperated with the navy. On November 7th another joint expedition, under Flag-Officer Samuel Francis Du Pont, silenced and captured the forts at Port Royal. Then into the sounds had to be sent light-draft gunboats to drive the Confederates from position after position back toward Charleston and Savannah—the first effective step by the Federal navy toward narrowing the field of the blockade-runners, compelling them to seek harbors where the larger vessels of the old navy could be effectively used against them.

STORES AT THE NEWLY CAPTURED BASE

of the blockade was given formally, first at Hampton Roads by Flag-Officer G. J. Pendergast three days after President Lincoln had signed the proclamation declaring it. This was on the 30th of April, 1861. On the 11th of May, Captain W. W. McKean, commanding the frigate *Niagara* which had hastened home from Japanese waters, appeared off Charleston and gave notice to the foreign ships then in that port that the blockading laws would be rigidly enforced. On the 25th of May, he appeared off Pensacola, Florida, and the same day gave notice. Neutral vessels were boarded and warned off the coasts. The steam frigate *Brooklyn,* under Commander C. H. Poor, at the same time proclaimed the blockade at the mouth of the Mississippi, and Lieutenant D. D. Porter, in the *Powhatan,* did the same thing at the entrance to Mobile Bay. The menace had begun. By July, every port had been informed.

Europe, especially England, was at first inclined to laugh at the attempt to close these profitable markets. It was indeed at the outset, in view of the bigness of the task, apparently ludicrous. Here was a coast three thousand five hundred and forty-nine miles long, containing almost two hundred places where anchors could be dropped and cargoes landed. But very soon the shoe began to pinch. As a foreign writer of renown, in reviewing this phase of the war, puts it, "the rapid rise in the prices of all imported commodities in the insurgent States presented the exact measure of the efficiency of the blockade." In December of 1861, when Congress met, the Secretary of the Navy reported that in addition to the regular forces then afloat there had been purchased one hundred and thirty-six vessels; that thirty-four ships had been repaired and put in commission, and that fifty-two vessels were in process of construction, making in all two hundred and sixty-four ships manned, armed, and equipped, and flying the flag of the United States. In the eight months of the war the available navy had been more than trebled.

Engaged in the blockade duty were two separate squad-

THE OUTLYING NAVY-YARD—HILTON HEAD, 1862

These scenes show the activities that sprang up around Hilton Head after the success of the Port Royal expedition. The picture above is of the foundry shop erected by the Federals. Here hundreds of mechanics were kept constantly employed, repairing the iron work needed aboard the gunboats and doing work for which the ships otherwise would have had to go North. The central picture shows the anchor rack, where were kept all sizes of anchors from the small ones used for mooring buoys to those of the largest ships. In the early part of the war hundreds of anchors were

THE ANCHOR RACK

lost to the navy by ships slipping their moorings to stand off-shore in bad weather. Later the employment of long heavy deep-sea cables obviated this necessity, enabling ships to ride out gales. Not a single vessel of the regular navy foundered or was wrecked during the whole war. One of the first things done by the Federal authorities after gaining a foothold at Hilton Head was to replace all buoys and lights. In the lower picture one of the monitors is convoying the new lightship that was sent down from the North to replace the one removed, at the outbreak of hostilities, by the Confederates.

MONITOR AT PORT ROYAL CONVOYING LIGHTSHIP

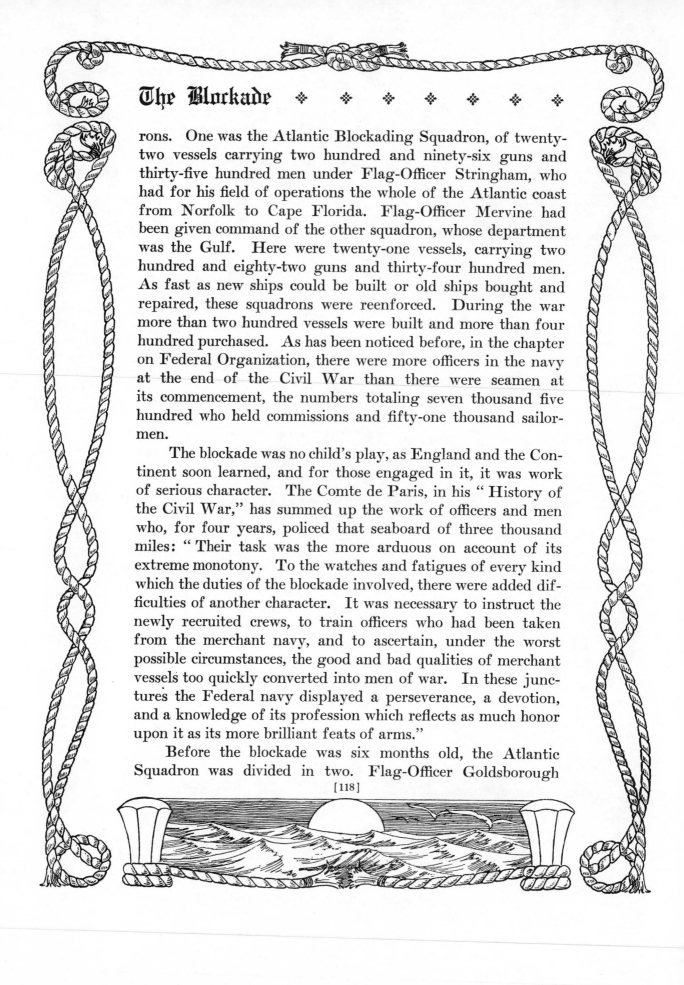

rons. One was the Atlantic Blockading Squadron, of twenty-two vessels carrying two hundred and ninety-six guns and thirty-five hundred men under Flag-Officer Stringham, who had for his field of operations the whole of the Atlantic coast from Norfolk to Cape Florida. Flag-Officer Mervine had been given command of the other squadron, whose department was the Gulf. Here were twenty-one vessels, carrying two hundred and eighty-two guns and thirty-four hundred men. As fast as new ships could be built or old ships bought and repaired, these squadrons were reenforced. During the war more than two hundred vessels were built and more than four hundred purchased. As has been noticed before, in the chapter on Federal Organization, there were more officers in the navy at the end of the Civil War than there were seamen at its commencement, the numbers totaling seven thousand five hundred who held commissions and fifty-one thousand sailor-men.

The blockade was no child's play, as England and the Continent soon learned, and for those engaged in it, it was work of serious character. The Comte de Paris, in his " History of the Civil War," has summed up the work of officers and men who, for four years, policed that seaboard of three thousand miles: " Their task was the more arduous on account of its extreme monotony. To the watches and fatigues of every kind which the duties of the blockade involved, there were added difficulties of another character. It was necessary to instruct the newly recruited crews, to train officers who had been taken from the merchant navy, and to ascertain, under the worst possible circumstances, the good and bad qualities of merchant vessels too quickly converted into men of war. In these junctures the Federal navy displayed a perseverance, a devotion, and a knowledge of its profession which reflects as much honor upon it as its more brilliant feats of arms."

Before the blockade was six months old, the Atlantic Squadron was divided in two. Flag-Officer Goldsborough

When the war broke out, Samuel Phillips Lee, who was born in Virginia in 1811, had already seen twenty-six years of almost continuous service. During the Civil War he was frequently shifted, but everywhere set an example to the service. At the passage of Forts Jackson and St. Phillip he commanded the sloop-of-war "Oneida." He fought conspicuously in the battles of the Mississippi, from New Orleans to Vicksburg. In July of 1862 he was placed in command of the North Atlantic blockading squadron, making the blockade more effective than ever. Late in the war, in the summer of '64, he was transferred to the Mississippi squadron, keeping the Cumberland River open for the army.

The sloop below, attached to the blockading squadron during the war, won quite a name for herself, although not engaged in any of the larger actions, by capturing a number of prizes. In 1861, under Captain C. Green, she caught the blockade-runner "Alvarado" and took the British vessel "Aigburth" at sea laden with contraband intended for the Confederacy. On December 15th, of the following year, she captured the ship "Havelock" and a large brig that was trying to make the coast, laden with cloth and percussion-caps. The "Jamestown" was ordered to the East Indies September 11, 1862, where she remained till after the war's close. She had a roving commission full of adventure.

ADMIRAL S. P. LEE
NORTH ATLANTIC BLOCKADING
SQUADRON, 1862

A FAST SAILER
THE SLOOP-OF-WAR
"JAMESTOWN"

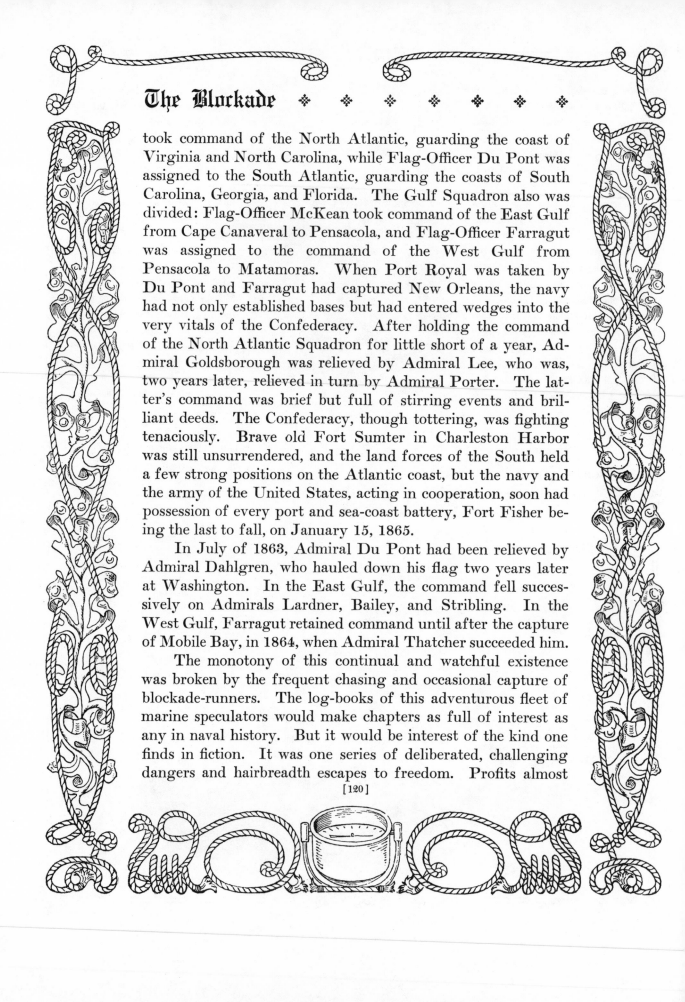

took command of the North Atlantic, guarding the coast of Virginia and North Carolina, while Flag-Officer Du Pont was assigned to the South Atlantic, guarding the coasts of South Carolina, Georgia, and Florida. The Gulf Squadron also was divided: Flag-Officer McKean took command of the East Gulf from Cape Canaveral to Pensacola, and Flag-Officer Farragut was assigned to the command of the West Gulf from Pensacola to Matamoras. When Port Royal was taken by Du Pont and Farragut had captured New Orleans, the navy had not only established bases but had entered wedges into the very vitals of the Confederacy. After holding the command of the North Atlantic Squadron for little short of a year, Admiral Goldsborough was relieved by Admiral Lee, who was, two years later, relieved in turn by Admiral Porter. The latter's command was brief but full of stirring events and brilliant deeds. The Confederacy, though tottering, was fighting tenaciously. Brave old Fort Sumter in Charleston Harbor was still unsurrendered, and the land forces of the South held a few strong positions on the Atlantic coast, but the navy and the army of the United States, acting in cooperation, soon had possession of every port and sea-coast battery, Fort Fisher being the last to fall, on January 15, 1865.

In July of 1863, Admiral Du Pont had been relieved by Admiral Dahlgren, who hauled down his flag two years later at Washington. In the East Gulf, the command fell successively on Admirals Lardner, Bailey, and Stribling. In the West Gulf, Farragut retained command until after the capture of Mobile Bay, in 1864, when Admiral Thatcher succeeded him.

The monotony of this continual and watchful existence was broken by the frequent chasing and occasional capture of blockade-runners. The log-books of this adventurous fleet of marine speculators would make chapters as full of interest as any in naval history. But it would be interest of the kind one finds in fiction. It was one series of deliberated, challenging dangers and hairbreadth escapes to freedom. Profits almost

BOLD BLOCKADERS—THE "PAUL JONES"

This fast side-wheel steamer under Commander C. Steedman saw her first active service in the war in following up the advantages gained by the Federal navy at Port Royal. July 29, 1862, she led three other gunboats up the Ogeechee River to the first attack upon Fort McAllister. The following October she led the expedition to Florida which captured the Confederate batteries on St. John's Bluff. The following year, under Commander A. C. Rhind, she was with the fleet of Rear-Admiral Dahlgren, which captured Fort Wagner on Morris Island in Charleston Harbor, July 18th. Of her seven guns, two were 50-pounder rifles and one a 100-pounder, which made her a very efficient blockader. The trim little gunboat "Marblehead" (shown below), rating something over five hundred tons, was active throughout the war. In April, 1862, under the command of Lieutenant S. Nicholson, she was in the Chesapeake aiding McClellan in his operations before Yorktown. In February, 1863, she joined the blockading squadron, and under Lieutenant-Commanders R. W. Scott and R. W. Meade, Jr., she participated in the operations in the vicinity of Charleston, supporting the movements up the Stono River and the attacks on Morris Island.

THE TRIM GUNBOAT "MARBLEHEAD"

The Blockade ✦ ✦ ✦ ✦ ✦ ✦ ✦

beyond belief were made by the owners of these vessels which were mostly built in Great Britain and were the fastest steaming craft of their day. They were loaded with arms, ammunition, and other supplies needed by the Confederacy, and departed on the return voyage loaded down to their gunwales with cotton. It is a question whether, in the main, the traffic was successful, for so many of these greyhounds were captured by the blockading fleets, and destroyed or wrecked, that in figuring up profit and loss the totals must have almost equaled. During the war the number of blockade-runners destroyed or captured was one thousand five hundred and four. The gross proceeds of the property condemned as lawful captures at sea and prizes to the vessels who took them, before November 1, 1864, amounted to $21,840,000. Subsequently this sum was increased by new decisions of the prize-courts, and actually the total loss to owners who ventured in the business and who principally resided in Great Britain, was in the neighborhood of $30,000,000. The damage paid in the Alabama Claims decision was very little more than half this sum.

The first prize captured off Charleston was the ship *General Parkhill* that was taken by the *Niagara*. The second of Charleston's prizes was the schooner *Savannah* that was taken by the United States brig *Perry* on June 3, 1861. She had been a pilot-boat before the war, and was not in any sense a blockade-runner except for the fact that she had escaped from Charleston and made the open sea. It was intended that she should intercept American merchant vessels, and she was practically a privateer. She had already made one or two prizes when, mistaking the *Perry* for a merchantman, she suffered the consequences. The blockade had more to do with the blockade-runners than with the privateers; the history of these latter vessels, daring as any adventurers in the days of Drake or Frobisher, is of the greatest interest. The careers of the *Sumter* and the brig *Jefferson Davis,* the *Amelia,* the *Dixie,* the *Petrel,* the *Bonita,* the *James Gray,* and many others would

A PURSUER OF MANY PRIZES—THE "SANTIAGO DE CUBA"

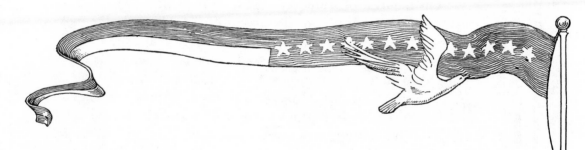

This vigilant blockader was one of the first to see active service. As early as December 3, 1861, Commander D. B. Ridgely brought her ten guns to bear upon the schooner "Victoria" and captured her off Point Isabel on her way to the West Indies with a cargo of cotton. In February of the next year, the "Santiago" caught the sloop "O. K." off Cedar Keys, Florida. The next month she drove a blockade-runner ashore. On April 23, 1862, she captured two schooners and (two days later) a steamer, all on their way from Charleston loaded with cotton. On April 30th she added to her prizes the schooner "Maria," and on May 27th the schooner "Lucy C. Holmes," both with more cotton; on August 3, 1862, at sea, the steamer "Columbia," loaded with munitions of war, and on August 27th the schooner "Lavinia" with a cargo of turpentine. In 1863 the side-wheel steamer "Britannia" and the blockade-runner "Lizzie" were her captures, the former loaded heavily with cotton. Cotton was so valuable at this stage of the war that if a blockade-runner attempted to lighten herself by throwing over a part of her cargo, volunteers were called for from the crew of the closest vessel pursuing to swim out and climb up on the cotton-bales until they could be recovered for their own particular ship after the prize was made. In 1864, after capturing the famous blockade-runner "A. D. Vance" and the "Lucy," the "Santiago de Cuba" served with distinction at Fort Fisher.

make exciting reading. Their careers, however, were all short; many of the blockade-runners kept at sea much longer. The *Robert E. Lee,* under the command of Captain John Wilkinson, C.S.N., ran the blockade no less than twenty-one times, and carried out from six thousand to seven thousand bales of cotton worth two million dollars in gold, at the same time bringing back return cargoes of equal value.

On November 9, 1863, she attempted to run in once more from the island of Bermuda, but Wilkinson and his luck had deserted her; she was under the command of another captain, and was captured off Cape Lookout shoals by the steamer *James Adger* and taken to Boston as a prize. As many of these captured blockade-runners were added to the squadrons off the coast, the hare became a member of the pack of hounds, and not a few of them, like the *Bat, A. D. Vance* and others, helped chase their sister vessels to their death. Over three hundred piled their bones along the shore—in fact, every harbor-mouth of the South was dotted with them.

On the 31st of January, 1863, there took place a brilliant and famous attempt on the part of the Confederate naval forces in Charleston to break the blockade, when the ironclads *Palmetto State* and *Chicora* actually put out from their harbor and steamed some distance out to sea, these rams having engaged several strong Federal gunboats, capturing one and putting the others to flight. Flag-Officer Ingraham, the senior officer of the attack, was fully persuaded that he had broken the blockade, and upon his return to Charleston so reported to General Beauregard. The latter did everything in his power to force this claim upon the attention of foreign governments, for if the consuls of European nations at Charleston would have acted upon such representation, it would have been necessary for the Federal Government to have established a fresh blockade in accordance with the laws of nations. However, to put it briefly, although this intrepid exploit came as a thunderclap to the North, the great Federal armada had

COMMODORE
GERSHOM J. VAN BRUNT, U. S. N.

The gallant commander of the "Minnesota." He and his ship were early in the thick of things and served under Rear-Admiral Goldsborough at Hatteras Inlet. Made commodore July 16, 1862, Van Brunt was actively engaged in blockade duty during the rest of the war.

REAR–ADMIRAL
JAMES L. LARDNER, U. S. N.

In command of the steam frigate "Susquehanna," he formed an active part of Admiral Du Pont's "circle of fire" at Port Royal, November 7, 1861. In 1862–3 he was in command of the East Gulf blockading squadron and in 1864 of the West Indian squadron.

REAR–ADMIRAL
CHARLES WILKES, U. S. N.

A nephew of the celebrated John Wilkes of London, this officer in 1838-42 led the exploring expedition that discovered the Antarctic continent. In 1861 he obtained fame of another kind by seizing Mason and Slidell aboard the British steamer "Trent" and conveying them to Boston in his ship, the "San Jacinto." He had been cruising in the West Indies, looking for the Confederate cruiser

"Sumter," and seized the opportunity for what appeared to be bigger game. Wilkes was thanked by Congress and applauded by the people of the North, but his act nearly brought on a war with England. On August 28, 1862, in command of a flotilla, he destroyed City Point, which was later to become the army base in the closing operations in Virginia. Wilkes afterward did excellent service with his famous "flying squadron," capturing blockade-runners in the West Indian waters.

THE COMMANDER WHO CLOSED IN ON CHARLESTON—DAHLGREN AND HIS STAFF

The South Atlantic blockading squadron was fortunate in being commanded by the best brains of the navy throughout the war. Admiral Du Pont, whose genius had helped to organize the Naval Academy at Annapolis, guided the fortunes of the squadron until July 6, 1863, when he was succeeded by Admiral Dahlgren (seer in the center of picture, his thumb thrust in his coat), who remained in command until after both Savannah and Charleston had fallen. He was chosen by the Administration to recapture Fort Sumter and secure possession of Charleston. The task proved an impossible one. But Dahlgren in coöperation with the military forces captured Morris Island and drew the cordon of the blockade closer about Charleston. Admiral Dahlgren was the inventor of a new form of cannon. He also introduced the light boat-howitzers which proved so useful in the blockading service.

[126]

ADMIRAL DU PONT AND STAFF, ON BOARD THE "WABASH," OFF SAVANNAH, 1863

From left to right: Capt. C. R. P. Rodgers, fleet captain; Rear-Adm. S. F. Du Pont, commanding fleet; Commander Thomas G. Corbin, commanding "Wabash"; Lieutenant Samuel W. Preston, flag-lieutenant; Admiral's Secretary McKinley; Paymaster John S. Cunningham; Lieut. Alexander Slidell McKenzie; Fleet Surgeon George Clymer; Lieut. James P. Robertson; Ensign Lloyd Phenix; Commander William Reynolds, Store-Ship "Vermont"; Lieut.-Com. John S. Barnes, Executive Officer. Rear-Admiral Samuel Francis Du Pont was the man who first made the blockade a fact. To his naval genius the Federal arms owed their first victory in the war. His plan for the capture of Port Royal on the Southern coast was brilliantly carried out. Forming his fleet in a long line, he, in the "Wabash," boldly led it in an elliptical course past first one fort and then the other, completing this "terrible circle of fire" three times till the Confederate guns were silenced. Du Pont's plan of battle became a much followed precedent for the navy during the war, for by it he had won his victory with a loss of but eight killed and twenty-three wounded. A midshipman at the age of twelve, he had got his training in the old navy.

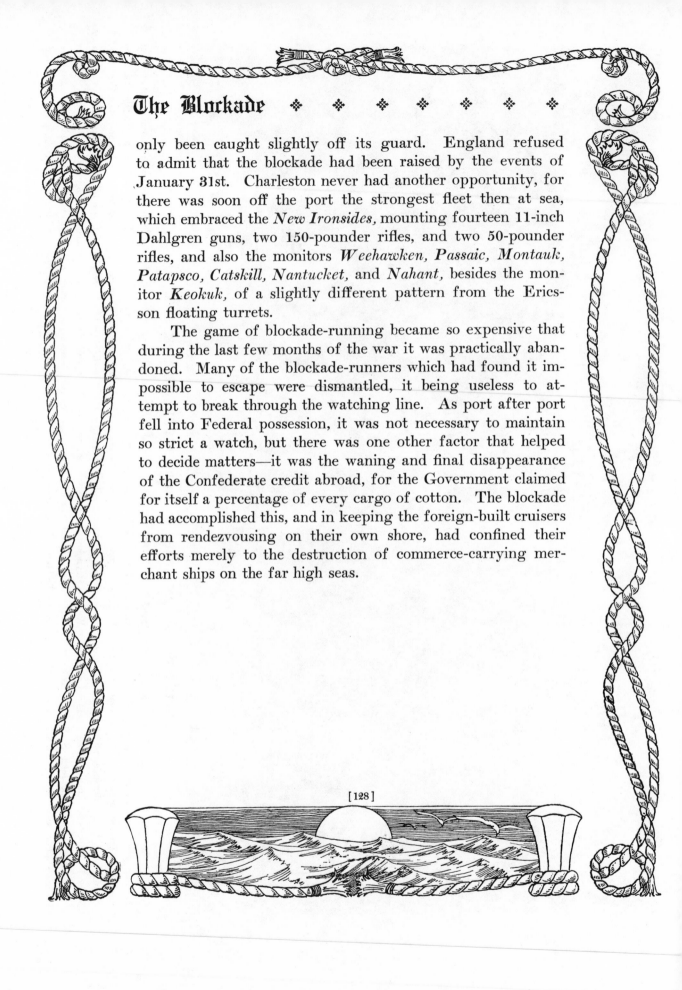

only been caught slightly off its guard. England refused to admit that the blockade had been raised by the events of January 31st. Charleston never had another opportunity, for there was soon off the port the strongest fleet then at sea, which embraced the *New Ironsides,* mounting fourteen 11-inch Dahlgren guns, two 150-pounder rifles, and two 50-pounder rifles, and also the monitors *Weehawken, Passaic, Montauk, Patapsco, Catskill, Nantucket,* and *Nahant,* besides the monitor *Keokuk,* of a slightly different pattern from the Ericsson floating turrets.

The game of blockade-running became so expensive that during the last few months of the war it was practically abandoned. Many of the blockade-runners which had found it impossible to escape were dismantled, it being useless to attempt to break through the watching line. As port after port fell into Federal possession, it was not necessary to maintain so strict a watch, but there was one other factor that helped to decide matters—it was the waning and final disappearance of the Confederate credit abroad, for the Government claimed for itself a percentage of every cargo of cotton. The blockade had accomplished this, and in keeping the foreign-built cruisers from rendezvousing on their own shore, had confined their efforts merely to the destruction of commerce-carrying merchant ships on the far high seas.

V

THE BIRTH OF THE
IRONCLADS

THE RIVER IRONCLAD "ESSEX"

ONE OF JAMES B. EADS' MISSISSIPPI MONSTERS, CONVERTED BY HIM FROM
A SNAG-BOAT, AND COMPLETED IN JANUARY, 1862

THE TYPE FAVORED BY ERICSSON

This splendid picture of the vessel lying at anchor in the James, off Bermuda Hundred, shows clearly the details of the type of perfected monitor most favored by Ericsson. Only a few months after the duel of the "Monitor" and the "Merrimac" in Hampton Roads, no less than thirty-five ironclads of the monitor type were being constructed for the Federal navy. The old Continental Iron Works in New York, that had built the original monitor, were busy turning out six vessels of the "Passaic" class, while others were being rushed up by shipbuilders in the East, and on the Ohio and the Mississippi. Ericsson was already at work upon the huge "Dictator" and "Puritan," each nearly five times as large as the first monitor. These were destined not to be completed till after the close of the war. But the navy-yards at New York, Philadelphia, and Boston were at work upon the four double-turreted monitors of the "Miantonomoh" class. Not satisfied with all this activity, the Navy Department, in September, 1862, let the contracts for nine more monitors similar to the "Passaic" class, but slightly larger. Among these was the "Saugus";

THE SINGLE TURRETED U. S. MONITOR "SAUGUS"

and one of her sister-ships, the "Canonicus," gave her name to the class. The most famous of the nine was the "Tecumseh." Her bold commander, T. A. N.Craven, in an effort to grapple with the Confederate ram "Tennessee" in Mobile Bay, ran through the line of torpedoes and lost his ship, which had fired the first two guns in Farragut's brilliant battle. Ericsson did not approve of the principle of the double-turreted monitor. In the "Saugus" is well exemplified his principle of mounting guns in such a manner that they could be brought to bear in any direction. This object was defeated somewhat in the double-turreted type, since each turret masked a considerable angle of fire of the other. The "Saugus," together with the "Tecumseh" and "Canonicus" and the "Onondaga," served in the six-hour action with Battery Dantzler and the Confederate vessels in the James River, June 21, 1864. Again on August 13th she locked horns with the Confederate fleet at Dutch Gap. She was actively engaged on the James and the Appomattox and took part in the fall of Fort Fisher, the event that marked the beginning of the last year of the war.

THE LATEST TYPE OF "IRON SEA–ELEPHANT" IN 1864

After having steadily planned and built monitors of increasing efficiency during the war, the Navy Department finally turned its attention to the production of a double-turreted ocean cruiser of this type. The "Onondaga" was one of the first to be completed. In the picture she is seen lying in the James River. There, near Howlett's, she had steamed into her first action, June 21, 1864, with other Federal vessels engaging Battery Dantzler, the ram "Virginia," and the other Confederate vessels that were guarding Richmond. The "Onondaga" continued to participate in the closing operations of the navy on the James. Of this class of double-turreted monitors the "Monadnock" and the "Miantonomoh" startled the world after the war was over. Foreign and domestic skeptics maintained that Gustavus Vasa Fox, Assistant Secretary of the Navy, who had earnestly advocated the construction of monitors while the type

THE DOUBLE-TURRETED MONITOR "ONONDAGA"

was still an experiment, had merely succeeded in adding so many "iron coffins" to the navy. It was asserted that no monitor would prove seaworthy in heavy weather, to say nothing of being able to cross the ocean. In the spring of 1866, therefore, the Navy Department determined to despatch the "Miantonomoh" across the Atlantic; and, to show his faith in the "iron coffins" he had advocated, Assistant Secretary Fox embarked on her at St. John, N. B., on June 5th. Meanwhile the "Monadnock" had been despatched around the Horn to San Francisco; her progress was watched with far greater enthusiasm than that of the "Oregon" during the Spanish War. The "Miantonomoh" reached Queenstown in safety, after a passage of ten days and eighteen hours, and about the same time the "Monadnock" arrived at her destination, thus proving beyond cavil both the speed and seaworthiness of the American monitor.

THE BIRTH OF THE IRONCLADS

AN EPOCH IN NAVAL WARFARE

UNDER the date of July 4, 1861, the Secretary of the Navy of the United States, the Honorable Gideon Welles, in his report, explained very clearly the exact position of the iron-clad vessel of war during its period of inception. Caution, and doubt as to the feasibility of such construction are clearly expressed here, and also a certain temerity in the way of expending the departmental allowance:

> Much attention has been given within the last few years to the subject of floating batteries, or iron-clad steamers. Other governments, and particularly France and England, have made it a special object in connection with naval improvements; and the ingenuity and inventive faculties of our own countrymen have also been stimulated by recent occurrences toward the construction of this class of vessel. The period is, perhaps, not one best adapted to heavy expenditures by way of experiment, and the time and attention of some of those who are most competent to investigate and form correct conclusions on this subject are otherwise employed. I would, however, recommend the appointment of a proper and competent board to inquire into and report in regard to a measure so important; and it is for Congress to decide whether, on a favorable report, they will order one or more iron-clad steamers, or floating batteries, to be constructed, with a view to perfect protection from the effects of present ordnance at short range, and make an appropriation for that purpose.

For a long time the armored vessel had been the pet of the inventor, and the building of iron ships of war had been contemplated. To go into the history of such attempts would be to review, in a measure, all the records of the past, for iron-protected ships had been constructed for many years, and as far back as 1583 the Dutch had built a flat-bottomed sailing

JOHN ERICSSON, LL.D.—THE PRECURSOR OF A NEW NAVAL ERA

The battle of Ericsson's "Monitor" with the "Merrimac" settled the question of wooden navies for the world. Born in Sweden in 1803, Ericsson was given a cadetship in the corps of engineers at the age of eleven. In 1839, with several notable inventions already to his credit, he came to America and laid before the Navy Department his new arrangement of the steam machinery in warships. It had been regarded with indifference in England, yet it was destined to revolutionize the navies of the world. In 1841 Ericsson was engaged in constructing the U. S. S. "Princeton." She was the first steamship ever built with the propelling machinery below the water-line, and embodied a number of Ericsson's inventions—among them a new method of managing guns. At the time Ericsson laid his plans for the "Monitor" before the Navy Department, there existed a strong prejudice against him throughout the bureaus because his name had been unjustly associated with the bursting of the "Princeton's" 12-inch gun, February 28, 1844, by which the Secretary of State, the Secretary of the Navy, Cap- tain Kennon, and Colonel Gard- iner were killed. The Naval Board nevertheless had the cour- age to recommend the "Moni- tor," and this last great invention of Ericsson brought him immor- tal fame. He died in New York in 1889. His body was sent back to his native land on board the U. S. S. "Baltimore" as a mark of the navy's high esteem.

vessel that was virtually an ironclad. She accomplished nothing but successfully running ashore, and was captured by the Spaniards, who regarded her as a curiosity.

John Stevens, of Hoboken, New Jersey, submitted plans, during the War of 1812, for an ironclad to the United States Government. They were not acted upon, and America, for a time, watched Europe while she experimented with protecting iron belts, a movement that began soon after 1850, when ordnance had increased in power, penetration, and efficiency.

All that was lacking in the United States up to the year 1861 was a demand, or an excuse, for experiment along the lines of progress in naval construction. It came with the outbreak of the Civil War. As a naval writer, touching upon this subject, has written: " Instead of the mechanical genius of the whole country being devoted to constructions in advance for the discomfiture of a foreign foe, the inventive talents of the two sections were arrayed in hostile competition. The result was the creation of two types of armored steamer, different from each other and from constructions abroad, but each possessing features that have been lasting, and that have been repeated and improved in all subsequent naval shipbuilding."

Being fully aware that there was being built in the old Norfolk Navy-Yard an iron-clad vessel, but quite misinformed as to its power and scope, the Federal Navy Department, on August 7, 1861, advertised for bids for the construction of " one or more iron-clad steam vessels of war . . . of not less than ten or over sixteen feet draft of water, to carry an armament of from eighty to one hundred tons weight."

On September 16th, the board appointed to examine the ideas submitted made a long and exhaustive report. After the preamble occurs the following paragraph that is here quoted verbatim:

J. Ericsson, New York, page 19.—This plan of a floating battery is novel, but seems to be based upon a plan which will render the bat-

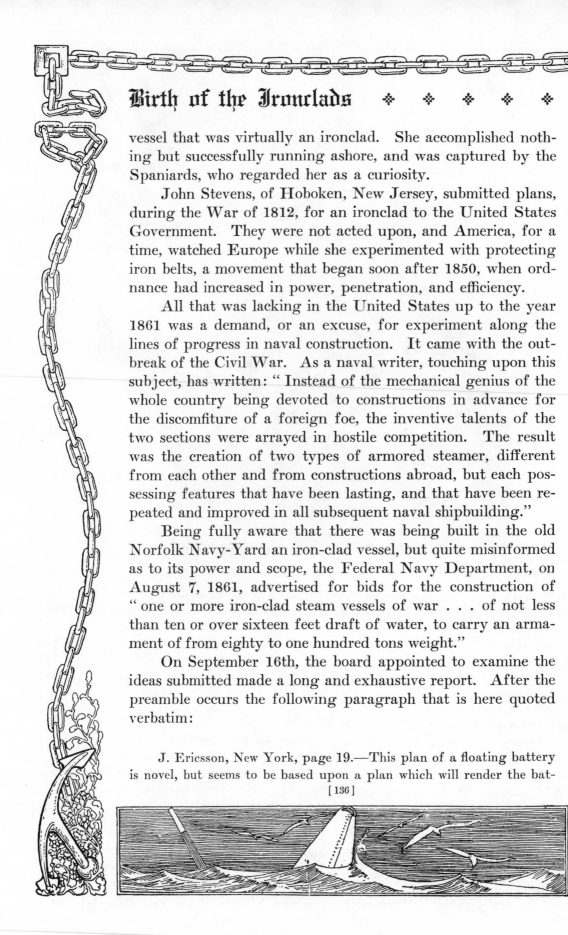

U. S. S. "GALENA"—ONE OF THE THREE FIRST EXPERIMENTS IN FEDERAL IRONCLADS

The Civil War in America solved for the world the question of the utility of armor plate in the construction of war vessels. This problem had been vexing the naval authorities of Europe. France and England were vying with each other at building iron-belted vessels that differed only from the old wooden line-of-battle ships in the addition of this new protection. Following this foreign precedent, Lieutenant John M. Brooke, C. S. N., planned to raise the hull of the "Merrimac" and convert her into an ironclad of original design, which became the standard for all subsequent efforts by the naval constructors of the Confederacy. It was not till October 4, 1861, four months after the Confederacy had raised the "Merrimac," that the first contracts for ironclad vessels were let by the Navy Department. For two months a naval board, appointed by President Lincoln, had been poring over various plans submitted, and finally recommended the adoption of three. A vessel of the foreign type, to be called the "New Ironsides," was to be in effect a floating battery, mounting fourteen 9-inch smooth-bores in her broadsides and two 150-pounder rifles. She proved one of the most formidable vessels of her class. A small corvette, to be called the "Galena," was also ordered, her sides to be plated with three-inch iron. The third was Ericsson's "Monitor."

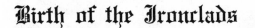

tery shot- and shell-proof. We are somewhat apprehensive that her properties for sea are not such as a sea-going vessel should possess. But she may be moved from one place to another on the coast in smooth water. We recommend that an experiment be made with one battery of this description on the terms proposed, with a guarantee and forfeiture in case of failure in any of the properties and points of the vessel as proposed.

Price, $275,000; length of vessel, 172 feet; breadth of beam, 41 feet; depth of hold, 11½ feet; time, 100 days; draft of water, 10 feet; displacement, 1255 tons; speed per hour, 9 statute miles.

This was the first notice of the famous *Monitor*. The idea of her construction was not exactly new, but no vessel of this class had ever been launched. She resembled, in a measure, the suggested floating battery of Stevens, but still more that proposed in the plans of Theodore R. Timby, of New York, and submitted to the War Department by him in the year 1841. This included specifications and drawings for a revolving iron battery, and practically was the foreshadowing of the *Monitor*. In fact, when the backers of Ericsson came to look into the matter, it was considered advisable to purchase Timby's patents.

There were also built at this time two heavily and almost completely armored ships, both more or less experimental, one, the *Galena,* destined to be a failure, while the other, named the *New Ironsides* and built by contract with Merrick and Sons, of Philadelphia, became, with the addition of the turret principle, the war-ship of future years. She was 232 feet long, 58 feet in beam, and 4120 tons displacement, a large size for that day. Her battery consisted of sixteen 11-inch Dahlgren guns, two 200-pounder Parrott rifles, and four 24-pound howitzers. She was the most formidable ship afloat. Although containing powerful engines, traditions of the older navy still prevailed, and the *New Ironsides* was at first fully rigged as a bark. Soon, however, the cumbersome masts were taken out and replaced with light poles that gave her a still closer appearance

INADEQUATE ARMOR–DECK OF THE "GALENA" AFTER HER GREAT FIGHT

The "Galena" early proved incapable of the work for which she had been planned. It was the belief that her armor would enable her to stand up against the powerful land-batteries of the Confederates. This the "New Ironsides" could do; her sixteen guns could pour in such a hail of missiles that it was difficult for cannoneers on land to stand to their posts. The "Galena," with but six guns, found this condition exactly reversed, and on May 15, 1862, she was found wanting in the attack on Fort Darling, at Drewry's Bluff, the Federal navy's first attempt to reach Richmond. There, under Commander John Rodgers, she came into direct competition with Ericsson's "Monitor." Both vessels were rated in the same class, and their tonnage was nearly equal. The engagement lasted three hours and twenty minutes. The two ironclads, anchored within six hundred yards of the fort, sprung their broadsides upon it, eight guns in all against fourteen. In the action the "Galena" lost thirteen men killed and eleven wounded. A single 10-inch shot broke through her armor and shattered her hull almost beyond repair. The "Monitor" remained entirely uninjured, without the loss of a single man. After the engagement the "Galena" was found to be so cut up that her armor plate was removed and she was converted into a wooden gunboat, thus continuing in service through the war.

to the modern fighting ship. According to reports, the *New Ironsides* was more constantly engaged in action than any other vessel during the Civil War. She was struck by more shot of all weights than any ship that ever floated, yet she suffered little or no damage. Off Charleston, in the engagement with Sullivan's Island, where by constant practice the Confederate gunners had become experts, the great ironclad was hit seventy times within three hours. She survived also the attack of a torpedo that was exploded against her side. During the war she threw in the neighborhood of five thousand 11-inch projectiles. She was later destroyed by fire in the navy-yard at Philadelphia.

As the *Monitor* was being hastened to completion, the *Merrimac,* renamed the *Virginia,* under the direction of the competent and able designers, William P. Williamson, John L. Porter, and John M. Brooke, was being rushed to completion. To these Southern officers, to all the workmen, engineers, and to the men who fought her, belongs a credit that cannot be overestimated. They faced difficulties of which the shipbuilders of the North knew nothing. A wooden frigate burned to the water's edge and sunk, had to be raised, practically rebuilt inside, strengthened in every way, armored with such iron as could be obtained, a slanting deck-house constructed, and an iron bow, or beak, added for purposes of ramming.

The use of the ram was also a revival of an ancient mode of attack. As early as the days of the Greek and Roman triremes and biremes, when hundreds of slaves chained to the oars propelled the vessels through the water at a rapid rate, the ram was in usage. When the days of war vessels propelled by slave-power ended, the ram disappeared. It was not used again until the Civil War and its naval history is not complete without frequent reference to the successful work of this revived but ancient principle. As a Federal naval authority has written about the *Merrimac:* "Indeed, it may not be too much to assert that it was her example, rather than that of the

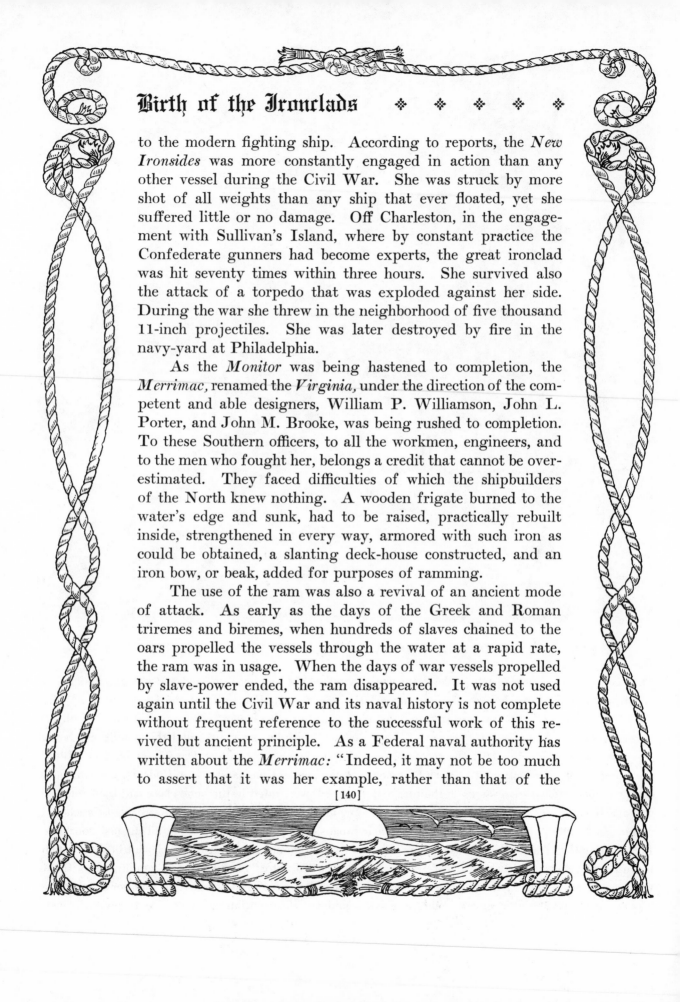

THE FIRST INLAND MONITOR—THE "OZARK"

This hybrid-looking vessel was the first of the Federal attempts to adapt the monitor type of construction to the needs of the navy on the Western rivers. She was a cross between the Ericsson design (which she resembled in her turret and pilot-house) and the early type of river gunboat, apparent in her hull, stacks, and upper works. Her armament consisted of two 11-inch smooth-bores in the turret and a 12-pounder pivot-gun at the stern. Having joined Porter's Mississippi squadron early in 1864, she was the last of the entrapped vessels to get free above the Falls at Alexandria, in the Red River expedition. Porter pronounced her turret all right but considered her hull too high out of water, and declared that she lacked three inches of iron plating on her fifteen inches of oak. Porter had discovered, in running the batteries at Vicksburg, that heavy logs, hung perpendicularly on the sides of his gunboats, prevented shot of heavy size from doing more than slightly indenting the iron plating. He recommended that the three-inch plating of the "Ozark" would be adequate if it were covered on the outside with a facing of wood in addition to the wooden backing within.

THE "OZARK'S" PIVOT-GUN

Monitor, that drew the parting line between the old navies of wood and canvas and the new navies of steel and steam."

There has been rather a controversy as to who first suggested making use of the sunken *Merrimac* as a ram or armored cruiser. It is proved beyond doubt that after the Confederate occupation of the all-but-destroyed and abandoned Norfolk Navy-Yard, many of the vessels that had been sunk were raised, not for use but because they were possible obstructions in the way of navigation. Some of the sailing ships had not been very much injured by submersion—in fact, two, the *Plymouth* and the *Germantown,* could have been refitted and put into commission at no great expenditure of money. But sailing ships, especially of their class, were of no use to the Confederate naval authorities. The *Merrimac,* as soon as she had been raised, floated low, for her topsides had been entirely consumed by fire, and this suggested, apparently to more than one person, the idea of converting her into a floating battery or ram.

There are many claimants to the suggestion. The Confederate Secretary of the Navy, Stephen R. Mallory, in a report made to the Confederate naval committee, wrote as follows:

I regard the possession of an iron-armored ship as a matter of the first necessity. Such a vessel at this time could traverse the entire coast of the United States, prevent all blockade, and encounter, with a fair prospect of success, their entire navy. If, to cope with them upon the sea, we follow their example and build wooden ships, we shall have to construct several at one time, for one or two ships would fall an easy prey to their comparatively numerous steam frigates. But inequality of numbers may be compensated by invulnerability, and thus not only does economy, but naval success, dictate the wisdom and expediency of fighting with iron against wood, without regard to first cost.

The suggestion here quoted was made two months before the above-mentioned paragraph in Secretary Welles' report

THE HEYDAY OF THE MONITOR
A FLEET OF FIVE IN '64

On the Appomattox River, in 1864, lie five of the then latest type of Federal ironclad—all built on the improved Ericsson plan, doing away with the objectionable "overhang" of the deck, dispensed with in order to give greater speed and seaworthiness. By this time the Federal navy had found abundant opportunity to try out the qualities of the monitor type. A monitor presented less than a third as much target area as any one of the old broadside ships that could possibly compete with her armament. Her movable turret enabled her to train her guns almost instantly on an adversary and bring them to bear constantly as fast as they could be loaded, no matter what the position or course of either vessel. If a monitor went aground, she remained a revolving fort irrespective of the position of her hull. A shot to do serious damage must strike the heavy armor of the monitor

squarely. The percentage of shots that could be so placed from the deck of a rolling ship was very small, most of them glancing off from the circular turret and pilot-house or skidding harmlessly along the deck. Only the most powerful land batteries could make any impression on these "iron sea-elephants" which the Federals had learned how to use. Their only vulnerable spot was below the water-line. The boom across the river in the picture, as well as the torpedo-nets, arranged at the bows of the vessels, indicates that the Confederates strove constantly to seize the advantage of this one weakness. The monitors in the James and Appomatox were too vigilant to be thus caught, although hundreds of floating mines were launched in the current or planted in the channel. The fleet, ever on the watch for these, was kept busy raking them up and rendering them harmless for passing ships.

was written, and before the *Merrimac* had been raised. Secretary Mallory had had good training for his position. For several years he had been chairman of the Committee on Naval Affairs of the United States Senate, and had been foremost in his interest in the navy and in the changes that were taking place in naval methods. Although many people of inventive mind and constructive imagination had worked along the lines that were now to be seriously adopted, Secretary Mallory was the first one in a position of authority to take the initiative in a change which abruptly ended the past eras of naval ship building, and inaugurated that of the new.

It was in June, 1861, that a board was appointed to make a survey of the *Merrimac,* draw plans, and estimate the cost of the conversion of that vessel into an iron-clad battery. The board consisted of Lieutenant John M. Brooke, inventor of the Brooke rifled gun, Chief Engineer William P. Williamson, and Lieutenant John L. Porter, chief constructor of the Confederate navy. All of these gentlemen were officers who had seen long service in the navy of the United States. In a letter from Mallory, addressed to Flag-Officer Forrest, Porter and Williamson are mentioned as being the constructor and engineer of the *Merrimac*. John M. Brooke, however, had much to do with her completion. He supervised the placing of the battery inside the armored citadel, which consisted of one 7-inch pivoted Brooke rifle at each end, and eight guns, four in a broadside, six of which were 9-inch Dahlgrens, and two 32-pounder Brooke rifles. In appearance, the *Merrimac,* when completed, resembled very much the Eads ironclads which had appeared on the Mississippi River. An odd coincidence was that the *Monitor* was commissioned as a ship of war on the 25th of February, 1862, and only the day before the *Merrimac,* henceforth known in Confederate annals as the *Virginia,* had received her first commander, Flag-Officer Franklin Buchanan. In the orders issued to him by Secretary Mallory, occur some prophetic paragraphs:

THE "MAHOPAC" ON ACTIVE SERVICE

The monitor "Mahopac," as she floated in the James near Bermuda Hundred in 1864, illustrates one of the newer types completed in 1864. The lower picture gives a good idea of her deck. The gun-ports of her turret are open. The coffin-like hatchway in the foreground was the only means of entrance. In action or rough weather this was tightly closed. Air-holes with their gratings are seen at intervals about the deck, but these too had to be closed during a storm. It was almost a submarine life led by the officers and crew in active service. Every opportunity was seized to get above deck for a breathing space. The "Mahopac" had a crew of 92 men. Her first engagement was with Battery Dantzler in the James River, Nov. 29, 1864. In December, 1864, and January, 1865, the "Mahopac" was in the first line of the ironclads that bombarded Fort Fisher. Her men declared that she silenced every gun on the sea-face of that fort.

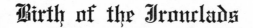

You will hoist your flag on the *Virginia*, or any other vessel of your squadron, which will, for the present, embrace the *Virginia, Patrick Henry, Jamestown, Teaser, Raleigh,* and *Beaufort.*

The *Virginia* is a novelty in naval construction, is untried, and her powers unknown, and the department will not give specific orders as to her attack upon the enemy. Her powers as a ram are regarded as very formidable, and it is hoped that you may be able to test them.

Like the bayonet charge of infantry, this mode of attack, while the most destructive, will commend itself to you in the present scarcity of ammunition. It is one, also, that may be rendered destructive at night against the enemy at anchor.

Even without guns, the ship would be formidable as a ram.

Could you pass Old Point and make a dashing cruise on the Potomac as far as Washington, its effect upon the public mind would be important to the cause.

The reason that the *Merrimac* did not pass Old Point Comfort, or proceed to New York, is told in another place, when she and the little Ericsson *Monitor* met. However, as far as her anticipated work was done, it was successful. With the wooden vessels she had it all her own way. But as of the *Monitor* herself, after the engagement, too high hopes were formed, so, of her antagonist, before she had been tried out, too much was expected.

The monitors failed signally against well-protected shore batteries. As more and more of these turreted vessels were ordered to be constructed during the war, they were divided into classes that differed but slightly from the original type. There were two-turreted, and, even at the last, three-turreted monitors; although the low free-board was maintained, the protecting overhang had disappeared, and this added greatly to their seaworthiness. The tragic loss on the 31st of December, 1862, of the original little vessel, which became a coffin for sixteen of her crew in a gale off Cape Hatteras, had taught ship-designers more than a little. A war-ship must first be seaworthy, and beside having defensive and offensive qualities,

THE "OSAGE" IN 1864

ONE OF THE NEW LEVIATHANS OF THE RIVER

The low, rotating monitor-turret of this ironclad and her great guns saved both herself and the transport "Black Hawk" from capture during the return of the Red River expedition. The "Osage" was a later addition to the squadron; she and her sister ironclad, the "Neosho," were among the most powerful on the rivers. Porter took both with him up the Red River. On the return the "Osage" was making the descent with great difficulty, in tow of the "Black Hawk," when on April 12th she ran aground opposite Blair's plantation. A Confederate force twelve hundred strong, under General Thomas Green, soon appeared on the west bank and, planting four field-pieces, advanced to attack the stranded ironclad. The brisk enfilading fire of the "Lexington" and the "Neosho" did not deter them. Lieutenant-Commander T. O. Selfridge waited till the heads of the Confederates appeared above the river bank. Then he let drive at them with his two big guns, pouring upon them a rain of grape, canister, and shrapnel. General Green, who behaved with the greatest gallantry, had his head blown off. After an hour and a half the Confederates withdrew from the unequal contest, with a loss of over four hundred dead and wounded. The "Osage" was sent to Mobile Bay in the spring of 1865 and was there sunk by a submarine torpedo on March 29th.

A VETERAN OF THE RIVERS—THE "PITTSBURG"

The "Pittsburg" was one of the seven ironclads that Eads completed in a hundred days. She first went into action at Fort Donelson, where she was struck forty times. Two shots from the Confederates pierced her below the guards. She began shipping water so fast that it was feared that she would sink. In turning around to get out of range, she fouled the "Carondelet's" stern, breaking one of her rudders. In going ahead to clear the "Carondelet" from the "Pittsburg," Commander Walke was forced to approach within 350 yards of the fort, which immediately concentrated the fire of the batteries upon that single vessel, whose consorts were all drifting out of action in a disabled condition. It was only by great coolness and courage that the "Carondelet" was extricated after being exposed to a terrific fire for some time. The "Pittsburg" was conspicuous in the fight with the Confederate flotilla at Fort Pillow. She was sent by Admiral Porter on the famous "land cruise" up the Yazoo, which nearly cost him the flotilla. She ran the batteries at Vicksburg and helped to silence the batteries at Grand Gulf, Mississippi. In May, 1863, she was with Admiral Porter on the first Red River expedition and distinguished herself in the action with Fort Beauregard. The next year she was in the second Red River expedition and shared with the other vessels the dangers of the return. She was one of the most serviceable of the first Eads ironclads.

THE "CINCINNATI," A SALVAGED GUNBOAT

The "Cincinnati" was one of the first seven Eads ironclads to be built and was the second to meet disaster. She was Foote's flagship at Fort Henry and in the engagement she was struck thirty-one times. Two of her guns and one of her paddle-wheels were disabled, and her smokestacks, after-cabin, and boats were riddled with shot. She was soon in commission again and joined the flotilla above Island No. 10. In the sudden attack by which the Confederate gunboats surprised the Federal squadron above Fort Pillow, the "Cincinnati" again met disaster and was towed to shallow water, where she sank. Again she was repaired in time to take part in the bombardment of Vicksburg, May 27, 1863, under Lieutenant George D. Bache. Here she gallantly engaged single-handed the batteries on Fort Hill to the north of the town. The terrific hail of grape-shot from the Confederate guns compelled her to close her bow ports. In endeavoring to get away, she was so badly hit that she could barely be gotten into shoal-water before she sank. The Confederates set fire to her a few days later, but even that was not to be the end of the gallant ironclad. After the occupation of Vicksburg, she was raised and found to be not so badly damaged as had been supposed. The next year she was on duty in the Missis- sippi between Fort Adams and Natchez. In 1865 she was sent by Admiral Lee to take part in the final naval operations that led to the fall of Mobile.

MONARCHS OF THE FLOTILLA—THE "LOUISVILLE," ONE OF THE ORIGINAL EADS IRONCLADS

Below appears the Federal ironclad "Benton." As James B. Eads went on constructing gunboats for the Mississippi squadron, he kept improving on his own ideas. The "Benton" was his masterpiece. She was finished soon after the original seven ironclads ordered by the army. Though her engines were slow, she proved to be the most powerful fighting vessel in the Federal Mississippi squadron. She held that distinction till late in 1864, when the river monitors began to appear. The "Benton" was Foote's flagship in the operations around Island No. 10; and when the gallant old officer retired, it was on her deck that he bade good-bye to his officers and men. The "Benton" then became the flagship of Captain Charles Henry Davis, who in her directed the famous battle off Memphis where the Ellet rams proved their prowess. The first commander of the "Benton" was Lieutenant S. Ledyard Phelps. He fought the gunboat in both of the above engagements. The "Benton" was hit twenty-five times while supporting Sherman's unsuccessful assault on Vicksburg from the north, and she was Admiral Porter's flagship when he ran by the batteries at the beginning of the maneuver by which Grant approached and invested Vicksburg from the southward, thus accomplishing the fall of "the key to the Mississippi."

U. S. GUNBOAT "BENTON," TUG "FERN"

THE "GENERAL PRICE," A CAPTIVE BY THE ELLET RAMS

After the "General Price" became a Federal gunboat, the pilot-house was protected and moved forward and other alterations were made. The Ellet rams continued their useful work. Charles Rivers Ellet took the first vessel past the batteries at Vicksburg after Grant had determined upon his venturesome movement upon the city from the south. Admiral Farragut, who had come up from the Red River, requested General Alfred W. Ellet to let him have two of the ram fleet to run the batteries in order to augment the blockade of the Red River. On March 25, 1863, Lieutenant-Colonel J. A. Ellet, in command of the "Lancaster," with his nephew, Charles Rivers Ellet, in command of the "Switzerland," chose a time near daylight for the attempt. "These Ellets were all brave fellows and were full of the spirit of adventure," said Admiral Porter. Scorning the cover of darkness, they got abreast of the batteries, which promptly opened on them in a thundering chorus. A shell exploded the boilers of the "Lancaster" and she went to pieces and sank almost immediately. The "Switzerland" had her boilers perforated by a plunging shot and received other injuries, but she got through; and in her and in other of the Ellet rams, Charles Rivers Ellet performed other distinguished services.

CHARLES RIVERS ELLET

must possess speed. As the class of monitors improved in size and power they rated among the fastest steam vessels afloat. The *Monadnock* and the *Miantonomoh,* the final types, could reach the then wonderful speed of eleven knots, and they proved their seaworthy qualities by riding out gales off the capes, holding to their anchorage when many large vessels and transports had been forced to cut and run.

Toward the end of the war, the various flag-officers who had had, in some cases, ironclads under their command made reports to the United States Navy Department after close observance of these vessels in action. Admiral Goldsborough wrote, in February, 1864, a report in which he says:

Every ironclad, as a matter of course, should be an unexceptionable ram, or, in other words, capable herself of being used as a projectile. She must be turned with every degree of quickness necessary. . . . The turret I regard as decidedly preferable (to broadside) and mainly for these reasons: it renders one gun of a class equivalent to at least two of the same disposed in opposite broadside ports, and this with a great reduction of crew. It admits of the use of much heavier guns. It does not necessarily involve a breadth of beam antagonistic to velocity. It affords a better protection to guns and men, and withal, it secures the fighting of guns longer in a sea-way.

Further on the admiral speaks of the other departure from old types and traditions. He says:

The *New Ironsides,* I regard as a much more efficient type of ironclad than the monitors just discussed, because of her possessing decided advantages over them in the particulars of fitness for general purposes, seaworthiness, relative strength of bottom, or absolute capacity to endure vibration thereat, security against an antagonistic vessel. . . . Had she been planned for turrets, instead of to use guns at broadside ports, she would have been, I think, still more formidable; nor is she unexceptionable in other respects, and among them speed and turning-qualities.

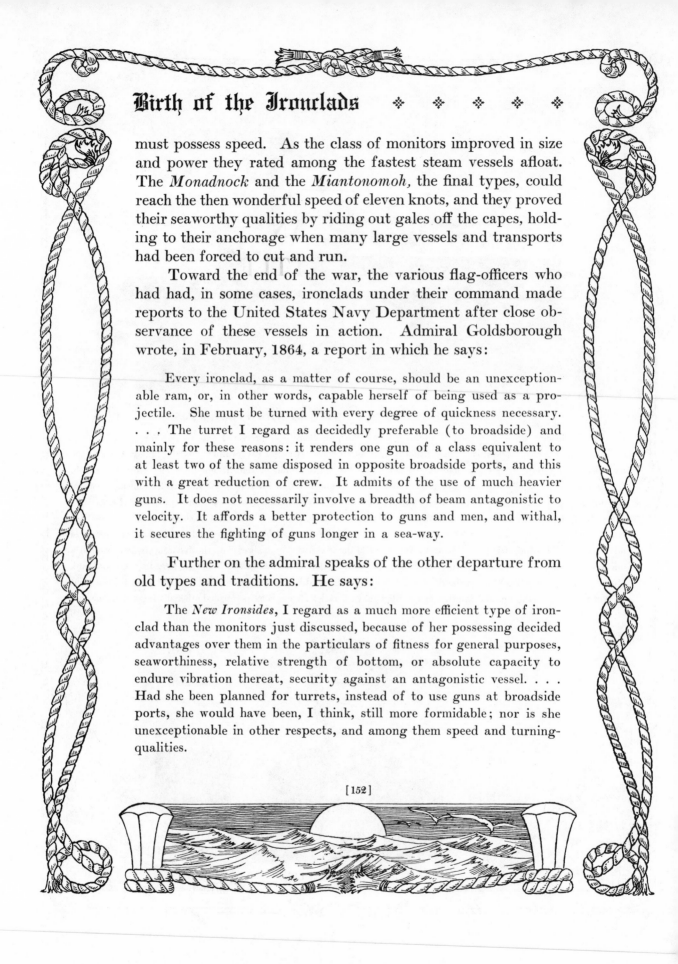

CHAPTER
VI

THE MOST FAMOUS
AMERICAN
NAVAL BATTLE

THE "MONITOR'S" SECOND COMMANDER
A PHOTOGRAPH FOUR MONTHS AFTER "THE MOST FAMOUS FIGHT"

LIEUTENANT W. N. JEFFERS, WHO SUCCEEDED THE GALLANT AND WOUNDED WORDEN
AFTER THE CONTEST, AND COMMANDED THE IRONCLAD "THROUGH MOST OF HER CAREER"

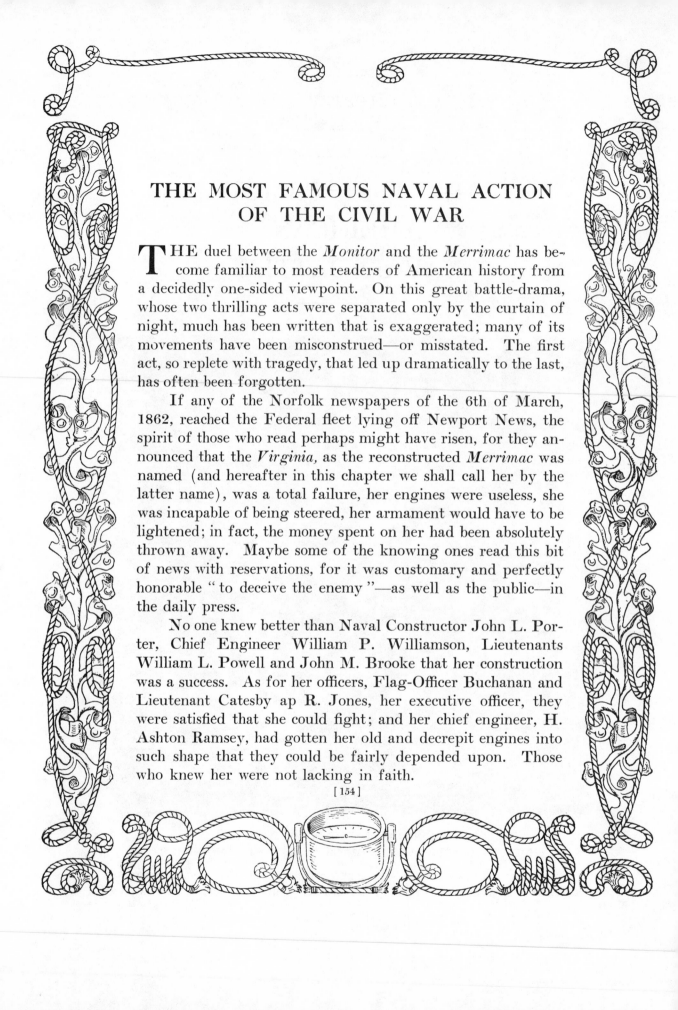

THE MOST FAMOUS NAVAL ACTION
OF THE CIVIL WAR

THE duel between the *Monitor* and the *Merrimac* has become familiar to most readers of American history from a decidedly one-sided viewpoint. On this great battle-drama, whose two thrilling acts were separated only by the curtain of night, much has been written that is exaggerated; many of its movements have been misconstrued—or misstated. The first act, so replete with tragedy, that led up dramatically to the last, has often been forgotten.

If any of the Norfolk newspapers of the 6th of March, 1862, reached the Federal fleet lying off Newport News, the spirit of those who read perhaps might have risen, for they announced that the *Virginia,* as the reconstructed *Merrimac* was named (and hereafter in this chapter we shall call her by the latter name), was a total failure, her engines were useless, she was incapable of being steered, her armament would have to be lightened; in fact, the money spent on her had been absolutely thrown away. Maybe some of the knowing ones read this bit of news with reservations, for it was customary and perfectly honorable " to deceive the enemy "—as well as the public—in the daily press.

No one knew better than Naval Constructor John L. Porter, Chief Engineer William P. Williamson, Lieutenants William L. Powell and John M. Brooke that her construction was a success. As for her officers, Flag-Officer Buchanan and Lieutenant Catesby ap R. Jones, her executive officer, they were satisfied that she could fight; and her chief engineer, H. Ashton Ramsey, had gotten her old and decrepit engines into such shape that they could be fairly depended upon. Those who knew her were not lacking in faith.

THE NORFOLK NAVY-YARD

WHERE THE "VIRGINIA" WAS BUILT

When those two queer-looking craft—the "Monitor" and the "Virginia" ("Merrimac")—approached each other in Hampton Roads on Sunday morning, March 9, 1862, much more hung in the balance to be decided than the mere question of which should win. These were no foreign foes that opposed each other, but men of the same race, and the fighting-machines which they brought into action epitomized the best judgment of men that had been trained in the same navy. The fact that ironclad vessels were to engage for the first time in a momentous conflict was of minor significance. Europe had already taken a long step toward the employment of armor plate; not its place in naval warfare, but the manner in which it was to be given effectiveness by American brains, was at stake. Of these two new armored knights of the sea, the "Virginia"

JOHN M. BROOKE, C. S. N.
DESIGNER OF THE "VIRGINIA'S"
ARMAMENT

(the first to be begun) was the more directly the result of native thought and circumstance. Her hull was all that was left of one of the gallant old fighting frigates built soon after the United States became a nation. The men who planned and superintended her construction were skilled officers of the old navy —John L. Porter and William P. Williamson. Her armament was prepared by another veteran, John M. Brooke, and consisted in part of his own invention, the Brooke rifled gun. She was built at a national navy-yard at Norfolk; and had this not fallen into the hands of the Confederates at the beginning of the war, the remodeled "Merrimac" would never have appeared in Hampton Roads to teach the wooden ships of the old navy the bitter lesson that their usefulness was on the wane and soon to be at an end. The era of the modern warship had come.

With everything on board and steam up, the "total failure" was ready to make her first attack on the 8th of March, 1862. People had crowded down to the water's edge to study her much-heralded "imperfections." What they chiefly noted was that she was very slow, and indeed her speed was not above five knots an hour. Captain William H. Parker, C. S. N., has left so vivid a description of this new departure in naval construction in his "Recollections of a Naval Officer," that the mind's eye can see her perfectly:

The appearance of the *Merrimac* was that of the roof of a house. Saw off the top of a house at the eaves (supposing it to be an ordinary gable-ended, shelving-sided roof), pass a plane parallel to the first through the roof some feet beneath the ridge, incline the gable ends, put it in the water, and you have the *Merrimac* as she appeared. When she was not in action her people stood on top of this roof which was, in fact, her spar-deck.

The Norfolk papers, however, were not so far from wrong. Captain Buchanan commanded her for three days and a little over; Lieutenant Jones, for about the same time, and Flag-Officer Tattnall for forty-five days, yet out of the two months that she was supposed to be in commission and ready to fight, there were actually only about fifteen days that she was not in dock, or laid up in the hands of the navy-yard mechanics.

But to return to the moment of expectation—the morning of the 8th of March. Off Newport News, in Hampton Roads, only six and a half miles from Old Point Comfort and some twelve miles from Norfolk, lay the Federal squadron: the old *Congress* and the *Cumberland* well out in the stream, and farther down toward Fortress Monroe the splendid steam frigates *Minnesota* and *Roanoke,* and the sailing frigate *St. Lawrence.* There were some nondescript vessels and a few decrepit storeships that never counted in the succeeding crowded moments, but certainly six months before it would have been suicide for

CAPTAIN FRANKLIN BUCHANAN, C. S. N., AND CAPTAIN JOSIAH TATTNALL, C. S. N.,
COMMANDING THE "VIRGINIA" ("MERRIMAC")

It was a task of surpassing difficulty and danger that confronted Captain Buchanan when the "Virginia" shipped her anchors on March 8, 1862, and steamed down Elizabeth River to fight a fleet of the most powerful line-of-battle ships in the Federal navy, lying under the guns of formidable land batteries. The "Virginia's" trial trip was this voyage into imminent battle; not one of her guns had been fired; her crew, volunteers from the Confederate army, were strangers to one another and to their officers; they had never even had a practice drill together. The vessel lay too low in the water, and her faulty engines gave her a speed of but five knots, making maneuvering in the narrow channel exceedingly difficult. But Captain Buchanan, who had risen from a sick-bed to take his command, flinched for none of this—nor for the fact that his own brother, McKean, was paymaster on the "Congress." It was one of the most hazardous experiments in all warfare that Captain Buchanan was about to make, and its result revolutionized the American navy. Captain Tattnall, another experienced officer of the old navy, relieved Buchanan on April 11, 1862, and diligently sought a second battle with the "Monitor," but it was not accepted. On May 11th the "Virginia" was destroyed by Tattnall's order.

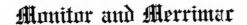

any single vessel of any navy of the world to have challenged this squadron to action. Although the *Congress, St. Lawrence,* and *Cumberland* were sailing vessels, they mounted one hundred and twenty-four guns between them, twenty-two of which were 9-inch; together, their crews amounted to well over a thousand men. The *Minnesota* and *Roanoke* had twelve hundred men between them, and carried over eighty 9-inch and 11-inch guns.

There is no question that the appearance of the *Merrimac,* as she hove in sight accompanied by her consorts, *Beaufort* and *Raleigh,* small river steamers mounting rifled 32-pounders in the bow and carrying crews of about forty men, was a surprise. The *Merrimac,* as she came down the Elizabeth River from Norfolk, had steered very badly. It was necessary for the *Beaufort,* under command of Lieutenant Parker, to pass her a line in order to keep her head straight. Owing to her deep draft, the great ironclad required over twenty-two feet of water to float her clear of the bottom.

About one o'clock in the afternoon the little squadron had swept into the James and turned up-stream. Lying to the last of the flood-tide, the great wooden frigates *Congress* and *Cumberland,* with their washed clothes on the line, were totally unaware of the approach of their nemesis. The *Congress* was just off the point, and the *Cumberland* a short distance above it. It was soon seen that the vessels had at last noticed their untried foe. Down came the lines of washing, signals flashed, and shortly after two o'clock the little *Beaufort,* which was steaming along at the port bow of the *Merrimac,* fired the first shot. Up the flagstaff of the *Merrimac* climbed the signals that spelled the order for close action.

The *Congress* and the *Cumberland,* though taken by surprise, had cast loose, served their guns in marvelous haste, and soon opened a tremendous fire, assisted by the batteries on the shore. The *Merrimac* swept by the *Congress* and made for the latter's consort. The *Cumberland's* broadside was across the

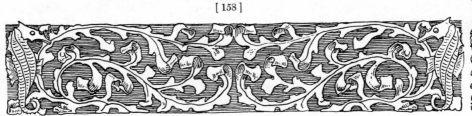

THE "CHEESE BOX" THAT MADE HISTORY
AS IT APPEARED FOUR MONTHS LATER

In this remarkable view of the "Monitor's" turret, taken in July, 1862, is seen as clearly as on the day after the great battle the effect of the Confederate fire upon Ericsson's novel craft. As the two vessels approached each other about half-past eight on that immortal Sunday morning, the men within the turret waited anxiously for the first shot of their antagonist. It soon came from her bow gun and went wide of the mark. The "Virginia" no longer had the broadside of a wooden ship at which to aim. Not until the "Monitor" was alongside the big ironclad at close range came the order "Begin firing" to the men in the "cheese box." Then the gun-ports of the turret were triced back, and it began to revolve for the first time in battle. As soon as the guns were brought to bear, two 11-inch solid shot struck the "Virginia's" armor; almost immediately she replied with her broadside, and Lieutenant Greene and his gunners listened anxiously to the shells bursting against their citadel. They made no more impression than is apparent in the picture. Confident in the protection of their armor, the Federals reloaded with a will and came again and again to close quarters with their adversary, hurling two great projectiles about every eight minutes.

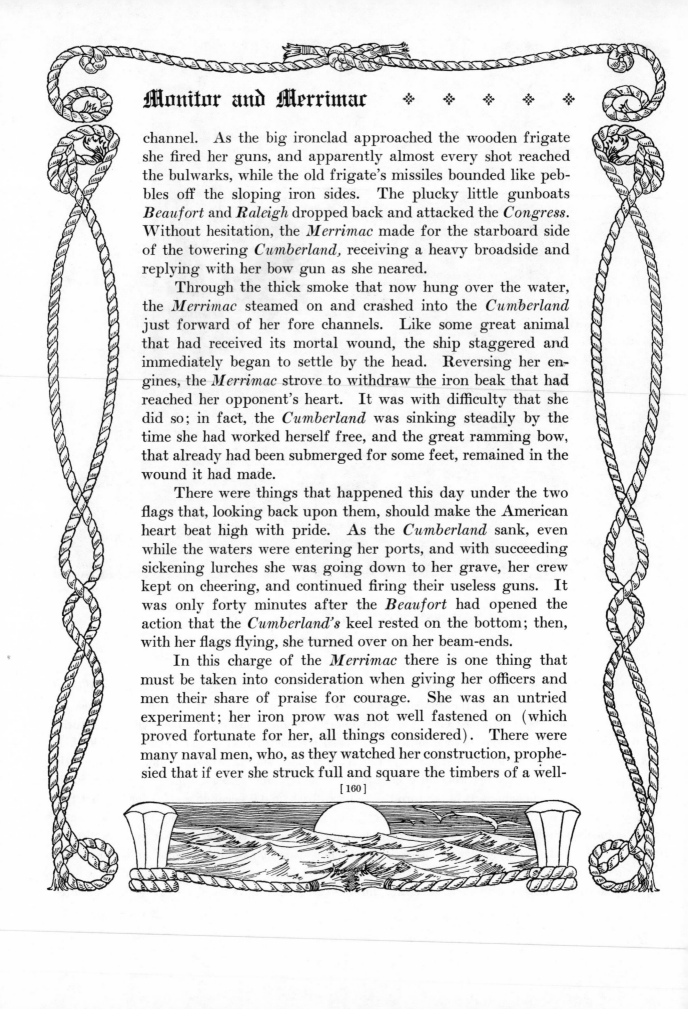

channel. As the big ironclad approached the wooden frigate she fired her guns, and apparently almost every shot reached the bulwarks, while the old frigate's missiles bounded like pebbles off the sloping iron sides. The plucky little gunboats *Beaufort* and *Raleigh* dropped back and attacked the *Congress.* Without hesitation, the *Merrimac* made for the starboard side of the towering *Cumberland,* receiving a heavy broadside and replying with her bow gun as she neared.

Through the thick smoke that now hung over the water, the *Merrimac* steamed on and crashed into the *Cumberland* just forward of her fore channels. Like some great animal that had received its mortal wound, the ship staggered and immediately began to settle by the head. Reversing her engines, the *Merrimac* strove to withdraw the iron beak that had reached her opponent's heart. It was with difficulty that she did so; in fact, the *Cumberland* was sinking steadily by the time she had worked herself free, and the great ramming bow, that already had been submerged for some feet, remained in the wound it had made.

There were things that happened this day under the two flags that, looking back upon them, should make the American heart beat high with pride. As the *Cumberland* sank, even while the waters were entering her ports, and with succeeding sickening lurches she was going down to her grave, her crew kept on cheering, and continued firing their useless guns. It was only forty minutes after the *Beaufort* had opened the action that the *Cumberland's* keel rested on the bottom; then, with her flags flying, she turned over on her beam-ends.

In this charge of the *Merrimac* there is one thing that must be taken into consideration when giving her officers and men their share of praise for courage. She was an untried experiment; her iron prow was not well fastened on (which proved fortunate for her, all things considered). There were many naval men, who, as they watched her construction, prophesied that if ever she struck full and square the timbers of a well-

MEN ON THE "MONITOR" WHO FOUGHT WITH WORDEN

Here on the deck of the "Monitor" sit some of the men who held up the hands of Lieutenant Worden in the great fight with the "Virginia." In the picture, taken in July, 1862, only four months afterward, one of the nine famous dents on the turret are visible. It required courage not only to fight in the "Monitor" for the first time but to embark on her at all, for she was a strange and untried invention at which many high authorities shook their heads. But during the battle, amid all the difficulties of breakdowns by the new untried machinery, Lieutenant S. Dana Greene coolly directed his men, who kept up a fire of remarkable accuracy. Twenty of the forty-one 11-inch shot fired from the "Monitor" took effect, more or less, on the iron plates of the "Virginia." The

ADMIRAL J. L. WORDEN

"Monitor" was struck nine times on her turret, twice on the pilot-house, thrice on the deck, and eight times on the side. While Greene was fighting nobly in the turret, Worden with the helmsman in the pilot-house was bravely maneuvering his vessel and seeking to ram his huge antagonist. Twice he almost succeeded and both times Greene's guns were used on the "Virginia" at point-blank range with telling effect. Toward the close of the action Worden was blinded by a shell striking near one of the peepholes in the pilot-house and the command devolved upon Greene. Worden, even in his agony of pain while the doctor was attending his injuries, asked constantly about the progress of the battle; and when told that the "Minnesota" was safe, he said, "Then I can die happy."

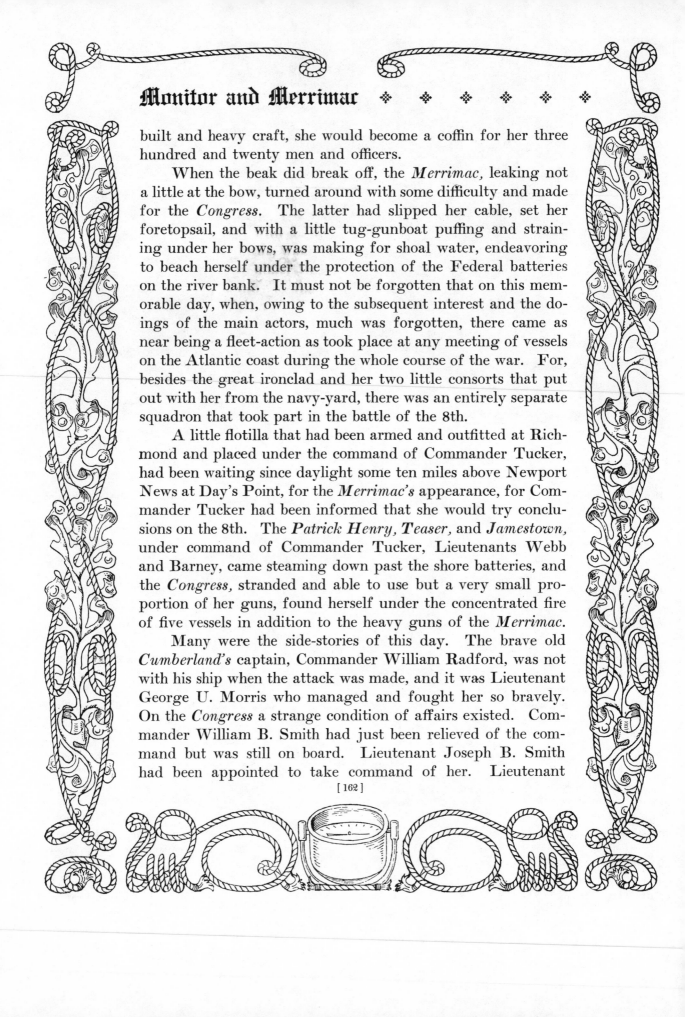

built and heavy craft, she would become a coffin for her three hundred and twenty men and officers.

When the beak did break off, the *Merrimac,* leaking not a little at the bow, turned around with some difficulty and made for the *Congress.* The latter had slipped her cable, set her foretopsail, and with a little tug-gunboat puffing and straining under her bows, was making for shoal water, endeavoring to beach herself under the protection of the Federal batteries on the river bank. It must not be forgotten that on this memorable day, when, owing to the subsequent interest and the doings of the main actors, much was forgotten, there came as near being a fleet-action as took place at any meeting of vessels on the Atlantic coast during the whole course of the war. For, besides the great ironclad and her two little consorts that put out with her from the navy-yard, there was an entirely separate squadron that took part in the battle of the 8th.

A little flotilla that had been armed and outfitted at Richmond and placed under the command of Commander Tucker, had been waiting since daylight some ten miles above Newport News at Day's Point, for the *Merrimac's* appearance, for Commander Tucker had been informed that she would try conclusions on the 8th. The *Patrick Henry, Teaser,* and *Jamestown,* under command of Commander Tucker, Lieutenants Webb and Barney, came steaming down past the shore batteries, and the *Congress,* stranded and able to use but a very small proportion of her guns, found herself under the concentrated fire of five vessels in addition to the heavy guns of the *Merrimac.*

Many were the side-stories of this day. The brave old *Cumberland's* captain, Commander William Radford, was not with his ship when the attack was made, and it was Lieutenant George U. Morris who managed and fought her so bravely. On the *Congress* a strange condition of affairs existed. Commander William B. Smith had just been relieved of the command but was still on board. Lieutenant Joseph B. Smith had been appointed to take command of her. Lieutenant

THE FIRST FIGHTERS OF THE TURRET—THEIR TOUCHING LETTER

In this picture of the " Monitor's" crew taken in July, 1862, are seen the faces of old sailors from the famous old sailing frigate "Sabine," mingled with those of young recruits from the receiving ship "North Carolina." As volunteers these brave fellows had manned the new fighting machine that was to revolutionize the Federal navy. They had weathered the perilous voyage from New York to Hampton Roads in constant danger of foundering. With no rest from the anxiety and exhaustion of that voyage, they had fought the greatest naval battle of modern times under conditions that might well make the stoutest heart quail. Here in a brief respite they have escaped from their murky quarters below deck and are playing checkers and idling about in the sunshine. There were to be but few more glimpses of the sun for some of them, for on December 31st the "Monitor" met the fate which had threatened her on her first voyage, and she became an "iron coffin" in fact as well as in name. Sixteen of her company of sixty-five went down with her off Hatteras. After the famous battle the "Monitor's" crew, still waiting for another opportunity to engage the "Merrimac," had sent the touching letter to Lieutenant Worden of which the following is a portion: " To our Dear and honered Captain:—Dear Sir: These few lines is from your own Crew of the 'Monitor,' Hoping to God that they will have the pleasure of Welcoming you Back to us again Soon, for we are all Ready, able, and willing to meet Death or any thing else, only give us Back our own Captain again. Dear Captain we have got your Pilot-house fixed and all Ready for you when you get well again. . . . But we all join in with our Kindest Love to you hoping that God will Restore you to us again and hoping that your Sufferings is at an end now and we are all so glad to hear that your eye Sight will be Spaired to you again. . . We Remain untill death, your Affectionate Crew, the 'Monitor' Boys." Halting words from brave hearts!

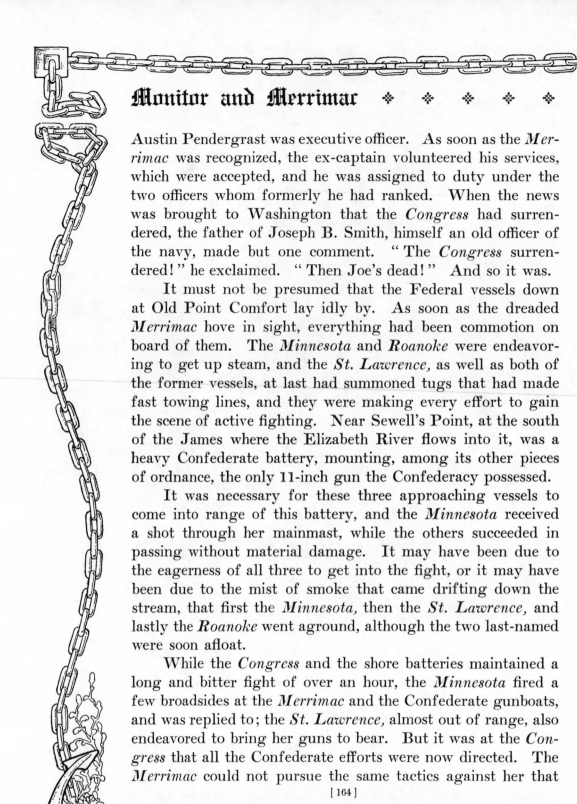

Austin Pendergrast was executive officer. As soon as the *Merrimac* was recognized, the ex-captain volunteered his services, which were accepted, and he was assigned to duty under the two officers whom formerly he had ranked. When the news was brought to Washington that the *Congress* had surrendered, the father of Joseph B. Smith, himself an old officer of the navy, made but one comment. "The *Congress* surrendered!" he exclaimed. "Then Joe's dead!" And so it was.

It must not be presumed that the Federal vessels down at Old Point Comfort lay idly by. As soon as the dreaded *Merrimac* hove in sight, everything had been commotion on board of them. The *Minnesota* and *Roanoke* were endeavoring to get up steam, and the *St. Lawrence,* as well as both of the former vessels, at last had summoned tugs that had made fast towing lines, and they were making every effort to gain the scene of active fighting. Near Sewell's Point, at the south of the James where the Elizabeth River flows into it, was a heavy Confederate battery, mounting, among its other pieces of ordnance, the only 11-inch gun the Confederacy possessed.

It was necessary for these three approaching vessels to come into range of this battery, and the *Minnesota* received a shot through her mainmast, while the others succeeded in passing without material damage. It may have been due to the eagerness of all three to get into the fight, or it may have been due to the mist of smoke that came drifting down the stream, that first the *Minnesota,* then the *St. Lawrence,* and lastly the *Roanoke* went aground, although the two last-named were soon afloat.

While the *Congress* and the shore batteries maintained a long and bitter fight of over an hour, the *Minnesota* fired a few broadsides at the *Merrimac* and the Confederate gunboats, and was replied to; the *St. Lawrence,* almost out of range, also endeavored to bring her guns to bear. But it was at the *Congress* that all the Confederate efforts were now directed. The *Merrimac* could not pursue the same tactics against her that

OFFICERS ON DECK OF THE ORIGINAL "MONITOR"—THE NEWLY FLEDGED
FIGHTER OF THE NAVY

After the brilliant battle in Hampton Roads, high hopes centered in the 'Monitor" for still greater achievements. On May 9, 1862, under Lieutenant-Commander W. N. Jeffers, she led a squadron against the Confederate works at Sewell's Point, and as she engaged them the "Virginia" ("Merrimac") came down the river, but the two antagonists did not give battle to each other. On May 11th the "Virginia" was destroyed by the Confederates and it was determined to send the "Monitor" and several vessels up the James River in an effort to capture Richmond. On May 15th, the Federal vessels were confronted by the hastily constructed Fort Darling at Drewry's Bluff. These works were all that stood between the Federals and the Confederate Capital, but behind them were the former gunners of the "Virginia" ("Merrimac") and the "Monitor" again found them formidable foemen. Although she herself was not seriously injured by their fire, the "Galena" and other of her consorts were so cut up that the attempt to take Richmond by the water route had to be abandoned.

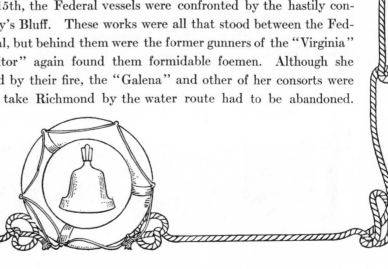

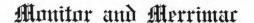

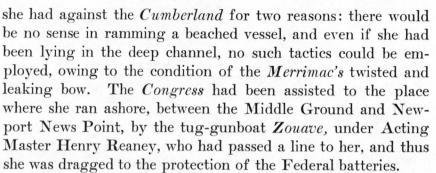

she had against the *Cumberland* for two reasons: there would be no sense in ramming a beached vessel, and even if she had been lying in the deep channel, no such tactics could be employed, owing to the condition of the *Merrimac's* twisted and leaking bow. The *Congress* had been assisted to the place where she ran ashore, between the Middle Ground and Newport News Point, by the tug-gunboat *Zouave,* under Acting Master Henry Reaney, who had passed a line to her, and thus she was dragged to the protection of the Federal batteries.

The decks of the *Congress* were soon littered with the wounded and running with blood; she was afire in the main hold, in the sick-bay, and under the wardroom near the after magazine. No vessel could come to her assistance; the shore batteries under the circumstances offered her little or no protection, and about four o'clock in the afternoon the colors were hauled down. Midshipman Mallory, son of the Confederate Secretary of the Navy, turning to Lieutenant Parker, on the *Beaufort,* pointed to the descending flag, at the same time exclaiming, " I'll swear we fired the last gun." It was true. The little gunboat that had rendered such good account of herself under the same officers in the early actions in North Carolina waters, had fired the first and the last shot of the day.

A strange condition of affairs now followed, and they gave rise to subsequent bitter controversy. Suffice it that when the *Beaufort* and one or two of the other Confederate gunboats, under orders from the flagship to take off the officers and wounded as prisoners and let the crew escape ashore, came alongside the stranded vessel, they were fired upon with both musketry and artillery at close range from the shore. The *Beaufort* was driven off, and the *Merrimac* again opened on the *Congress,* although a white flag had been hoisted to show that she was out of action. Many of the Federal wounded were hit a second time; some were killed; the casualties among the Confederate gunboats, and even on the *Merrimac,* were considerably increased. Lieutenant Pendergrast and Commander

THE LESSON OF THE IRONCLAD—SOME OF THE FIRST TESTS AT THE NAVY–YARD

Here in the Washington Navy-yard, as it appeared on Independence Day, 1866, are the evidences of what the American Civil War had taught not only the United States navy but the world's designers of warships. In four short years of experimentation in the throes of an internecine struggle, the Navy Department had not only evolved the most powerful fighting fleet on the seas of the world, but had stamped it with distinctively American ideas. In the picture, a year after the war, can be seen how the navy had begun to improve the experience it had gained. Already the tests of piercing power of projectiles upon armor plate lie all about, precursors of the steel battleships and big guns that are the marvel of the present day. The wooden hulls of the early monitors rotted away, and as they did so steel construction was gradually evolved. The monitor principle was finally abandoned in its entirety but the turret still remained. Likewise the turtleback construction of the decks of these same vessels remains in the swift and powerful torpedo-boat destroyers.

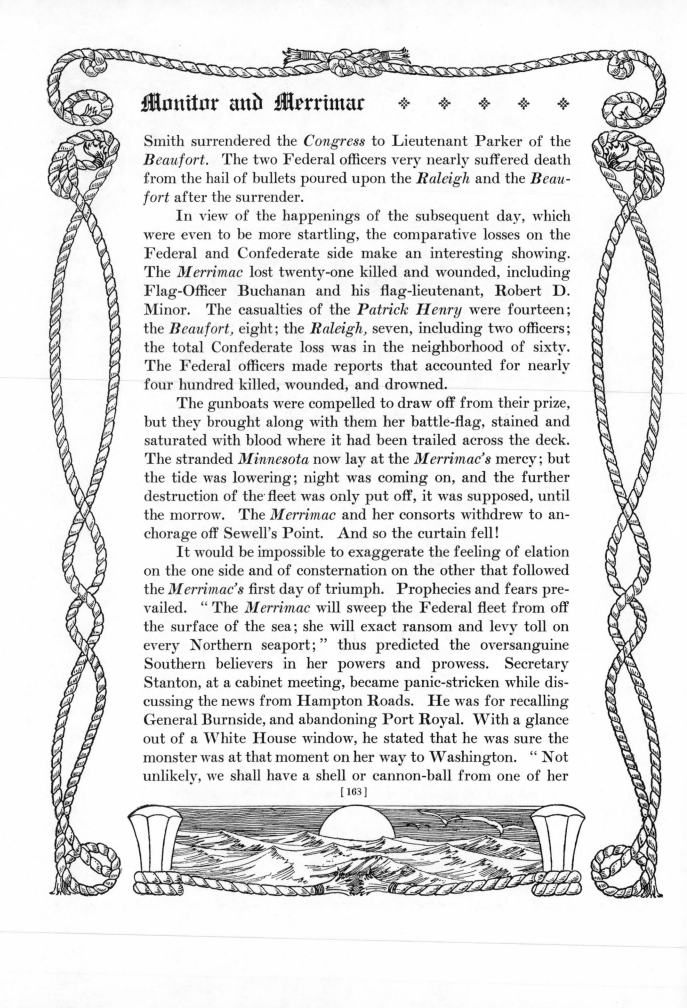

Smith surrendered the *Congress* to Lieutenant Parker of the *Beaufort*. The two Federal officers very nearly suffered death from the hail of bullets poured upon the *Raleigh* and the *Beaufort* after the surrender.

In view of the happenings of the subsequent day, which were even to be more startling, the comparative losses on the Federal and Confederate side make an interesting showing. The *Merrimac* lost twenty-one killed and wounded, including Flag-Officer Buchanan and his flag-lieutenant, Robert D. Minor. The casualties of the *Patrick Henry* were fourteen; the *Beaufort,* eight; the *Raleigh,* seven, including two officers; the total Confederate loss was in the neighborhood of sixty. The Federal officers made reports that accounted for nearly four hundred killed, wounded, and drowned.

The gunboats were compelled to draw off from their prize, but they brought along with them her battle-flag, stained and saturated with blood where it had been trailed across the deck. The stranded *Minnesota* now lay at the *Merrimac's* mercy; but the tide was lowering; night was coming on, and the further destruction of the fleet was only put off, it was supposed, until the morrow. The *Merrimac* and her consorts withdrew to anchorage off Sewell's Point. And so the curtain fell!

It would be impossible to exaggerate the feeling of elation on the one side and of consternation on the other that followed the *Merrimac's* first day of triumph. Prophecies and fears prevailed. "The *Merrimac* will sweep the Federal fleet from off the surface of the sea; she will exact ransom and levy toll on every Northern seaport;" thus predicted the oversanguine Southern believers in her powers and prowess. Secretary Stanton, at a cabinet meeting, became panic-stricken while discussing the news from Hampton Roads. He was for recalling General Burnside, and abandoning Port Royal. With a glance out of a White House window, he stated that he was sure the monster was at that moment on her way to Washington. "Not unlikely, we shall have a shell or cannon-ball from one of her

ONE OF THE "FIGHTING RAFTS"—1864

This fine figure of a monitor lying in the James in 1864 shows clearly the two great principles Ericsson embodied in his plan. Skeptics said that the "Monitor" would never be able to keep an even keel with the waves washing over her low freeboard. Ericsson, who had seen the huge lumber-rafts in his native Sweden riding steadily though almost submerged, knew better. Again it was objected that the discharge of the guns would kill every man in the turret. But as an officer in the Swedish army, Ericsson had learned, by firing heavy guns from little huts, that if the muzzles protruded the concussion within was inconsiderable. Upon these two ideas he built his model that proved so momentous to the American navy. When C. S. Bushnell took the model to Washington, he was referred to Commander C. H. Davis by the other two members of the Naval Board. Davis, upon examining the model closely, told Bushnell that he could "take the little thing home and worship it, as it would not be idolatry, because it was in the image of nothing 'in the heaven above or on the earth beneath or in the waters under the earth.'" It was not long, however, before the completed monitor became the idol of the Federal navy.

guns in the White House before we leave this room." The cabinet, and even Mr. Lincoln himself, were much depressed. For they did not know that the only serious consequence of the great sea-fight, besides the loss of two antiquated wooden ships, would be the revolutionizing of the navies of the world.

Lieutenant (afterward Captain) Parker, commander of the *Beaufort,* who knew the shortcomings as well as the good points of the *Merrimac's* construction, tells of the feeling of the day, and how moral influence in war becomes a factor in times of crises. He writes in the work above cited:

No battle that was ever fought caused as great a sensation through the civilized world. The moral effect at the North was most marvelous; and even now I can scarcely realize it. The people of New York and Washington were in hourly expectation of the *Merrimac's* appearance off those cities, and I suppose were ready to yield at the first summons. At the South, it was expected that she would take Fortress Monroe when she again went out. I recollect trying to explain to a gentleman at the time how absurd it was to expect this of her. I told him that she might bombard Fortress Monroe all day without doing it any considerable damage; that she would get out of ammunition; that she carried but three hundred and fifty men, and could not land a force, even if her boats were not shot away, though they would be; that, in fine, I would be willing to take up my quarters in the casemates there and let the *Merrimac* hammer away for a month—but all to no purpose; the impression had been made on him: a gun mounted on an ironclad must be capable of doing more damage than one on a wooden vessel. An idea once fixed cannot be eradicated; just as we hear people say every day that Jackson at New Orleans defeated the veterans of Waterloo!

As to the *Merrimac* going to New York, she would have foundered as soon as she got outside of Cape Henry. She could not have lived in Hampton Roads in a moderate sea. She was just buoyant enough to float when she had a few days' coal and water on board. A little more would have sent her to the bottom. When she rammed the *Cumberland* she dipped forward until the water nearly entered her bowport; had it done so she would have gone down. Perhaps it was fortunate for her that her prow did break off, otherwise she might not have extricated

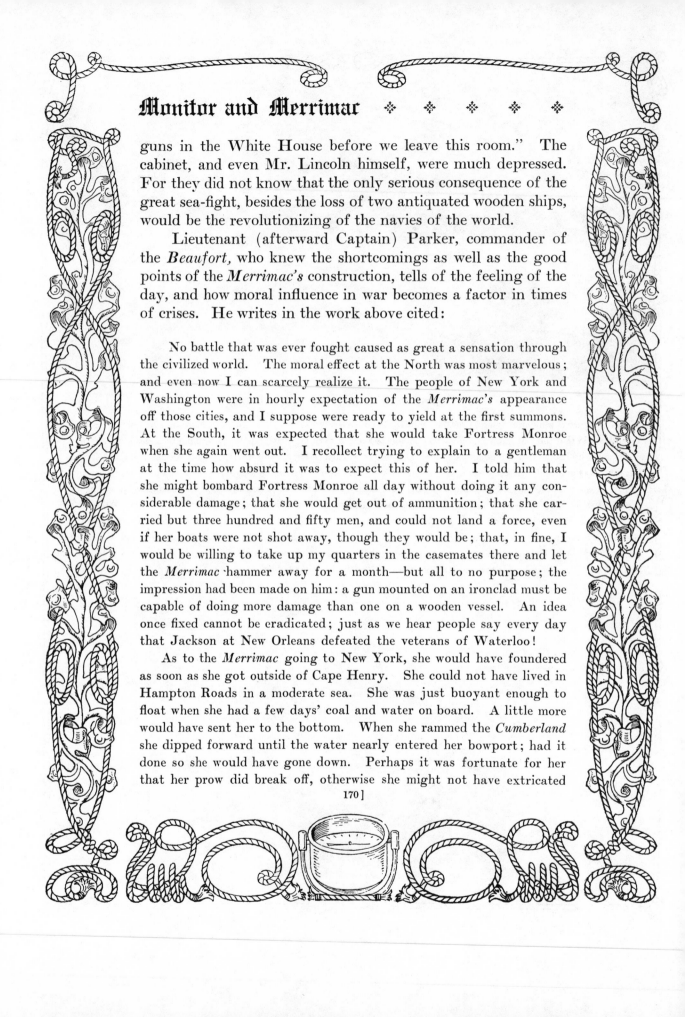

THE FIRST PRIZE OF A MONITOR—FEDERAL OFFICERS ON DECK OF THE CAPTURED CONFEDERATE RAM "ATLANTA"

The honor of the first decisive engagement with one of the formidable ironclads that were constructed by the Confederacy was denied to the original "Monitor." It fell to the monitor "Weehawken," one of seven similar vessels designed by Ericsson for the navy. Under Captain John Rodgers, she, with her sister-vessels, ran first under fire in the attack made upon Fort Sumter and the batteries in Charleston Harbor by Rear-Admiral Du Pont in April, 1863. In June, she and the "Nahant" were blockading the mouth of Wilmington River, Georgia. Early on the morning of the 17th, Captain Rodgers was apprised that the huge Confederate ram, into which the old blockade-runner "Fingal" had been converted, was coming down to raise the blockade. Clearing for action, the "Weehawken" steamed slowly toward the northeastern end of Wassaw Sound, followed by the "Nahant." When about a mile and a half from the "Weehawken," the "Atlanta," which was aground, fired a rifle-

shot at her. The "Weehawken," without replying, approached to within three hundred yards of the ram and opened fire. The first shot broke through the armor and wood backing of the "Atlanta," strewing her deck with splinters and prostrating about forty of her crew by the concussion. The second shot broke only a couple of plates, but the third knocked off the top of the pilot-house, wounding the pilots and stunning the man at the wheel. The fourth shot struck a port-stopper in the center, breaking it in two and driving the fragments through the port. Five shots in all were fired by the "Weehawken" in fifteen minutes. Then the colors of the "Atlanta" were hauled down, a white flag was hoisted, and Commander William A. Webb, C. S. N., put off in a boat to the "Weehawken," where he delivered his sword to Captain Rodgers. The fight was over before the "Nahant" could become engaged. The "Atlanta" was not seriously damaged and was added to the Federal navy, where she did good service.

herself. I served afterward in the *Palmetto State*, a vessel of similar construction to the *Merrimac*, but much more buoyant; yet I have seen the time when we were glad to get under a lee, even in Charleston Harbor. The *Merrimac*, with but a few days' stores on board, drew twenty-two and one-half feet of water. She could not have gone to Baltimore or Washington without lightening her very much. This would have brought her unarmored hull out of the water, and then she would no longer have been an ironclad!

I was not so much surprised at the extravagant expectations of the Southern people, who necessarily knew but little of such matters; but I must say I could not have imagined the extent of the demoralization which existed at Fortress Monroe and in the Federal fleet on the 8th and 9th of March. I have been told by an officer of high rank, who was present in the fort, that if the *Merrimac* had fired a shot at it on the 8th, the general in command would have surrendered it; and, if I am not very much mistaken, I have seen a despatch from that general to the effect that if the *Merrimac* passed Fortress Monroe it must necessarily fall! After this, one can well understand what Napoleon has said in reference to the moral as compared to the physical effect in war.

But John Taylor Wood, C. S. N., a lieutenant on the *Merrimac,* speaks in " Battles and Leaders of the Civil War " of the vessel's condition as she lay at anchor off Sewell's Point:

The armor was hardly damaged, though at one time our ship was the focus on which were directed at least one hundred heavy guns, afloat and ashore. But nothing outside escaped. Two guns were disabled by having their muzzles shot off. The ram was left in the side of the *Cumberland.* One anchor, the smoke-stack, and the steampipes were shot away. Railings, stanchions, boat-davits, everything was swept clean. The flagstaff was repeatedly knocked over, and finally a boarding-pike was used. Commodore Buchanan and the other wounded were sent to the Naval Hospital, and after making preparations for the next day's fight, we slept at our guns, dreaming of other victories in the morning."

Shortly after breakfast-time on the 9th, the *Merrimac,* followed by the Confederate squadron, got under way under a

DECK OF THE "CATSKILL"—THE LEADER OF THE GREAT BOMBARDMENT

On July 10, 1863, under Commander George W. Rodgers, and with Rear-Admiral Dahlgren's flag floating above her, the "Catskill" steamed across the bar into Charleston Harbor and opened fire on Fort Wagner on Morris Island. She was followed by the "Montauk," "Nahant," and "Weehawken," and immediately all the Confederate batteries in Charleston Harbor spoke out their terrific thunder. The "Catskill" was no stranger to that battle-ground; she had seen her first service in Admiral Du Pont's squadron that had failed to silence the defenses of Charleston the preceding April. Now came her supreme test under Admiral Dahlgren. As his flagship she became the especial target. A large percentage of the sixty hits were very severe. Yet the brave men in the turret coolly fired their guns, almost oblivious to the heavy shot that was raining upon their armor. Her pilot-house was broken entirely through by one shot, while her side armor and deck-plates were pierced in many places, making the entrance of the water troublesome. But the "Catskill," after firing 128 rounds, came out of action in good working order. On August 17th Commander Rodgers, while maneuvering for a closer berth in the attack on Fort Wagner, was killed in the pilot-house.

full head of steam, and closely accompanied by the gunboat *Patrick Henry,* headed directly for the *Minnesota* that she counted already as a prize. There is no doubt that despite the *Minnesota's* heavy broadsides she would have become a prey to her reconstructed sister ship, for the original *Merrimac* had been built on the same lines and was practically of the same tonnage and armament.

Only one thing prevented the carrying out of the program, and that was the sudden appearance of the strange little craft that, with her volunteer crew of old sailors, had started from New York on Thursday, the 6th of March, under the command of officers who were not sure whether they would ever reach their destination or not. No power of imagination could invent a more dramatic moment for the arrival of a rescuer than that of the *Monitor's* appearance in Hampton Roads. Late in the afternoon of Saturday, March 8th, as she entered the waters of Chesapeake Bay, there was heard the sound of heavy firing, and Lieutenant John L. Worden, then in command, as he listened intently, estimated the distance to be full twenty miles and correctly guessed that it was the *Merrimac* in conflict with the Federal fleet. While she steamed ahead the *Monitor* was made ready for action, although such preparations were of the simplest character. Before long the flames and smoke from the burning *Congress* could be easily distinguished. At 9 P.M. the *Monitor* was alongside the *Roanoke,* whose commander, Captain Marston, suggested that she should go at once to the assistance of the *Minnesota,* which was still aground.

It was midnight before Lieutenant S. Dana Greene, sent by Worden, reached the *Minnesota* and reported to Captain Van Brunt. While the two officers were talking there came a succession of loud reports, and the *Congress* blew up, as if warning her sisters of the fleet of the fate in store for them. There was little sleep for anyone that night. At seven o'clock in the morning the crew were called to quarters.

THE ARMY'S CHIEF RELIANCE ON THE RIVER—THE DOUBLE-TURRETED MONITOR "ONONDAGA"

While Admiral Porter and his squadron were absent on the Fort Fisher expedition, it was of the greatest importance that an adequate flotilla should be left in the James to preclude the possibility of the Confederate gunboats getting down past the obstructions and making a bold and disastrous attack on City Point, the army base. Having left this huge ironclad fighting-vessel behind, Admiral Porter felt at ease. But the undaunted Confederate Flag-Officer J. K. Mitchell was not to be deterred from making one last attempt to strike a telling blow with the "Virginia" and her consorts. On the night of January 23, 1865, he came down to the Federal obstructions and attempted to get by. When the movement was discovered, contrary to all expectations the great "Onondaga" retreated down the river. The moment might well have been one of the greatest anxiety for the Federals, but in maneuvering, the "Virginia" and the "Richmond" both got aground and the "Onondaga," returning with the "Hunchback" and the "Massasoit," inflicted some telling shots upon them. It was found later by a court-martial that Commander William A. Parker, commanding the division on the James, had made an "error of judgment" in handling the "Onondaga."

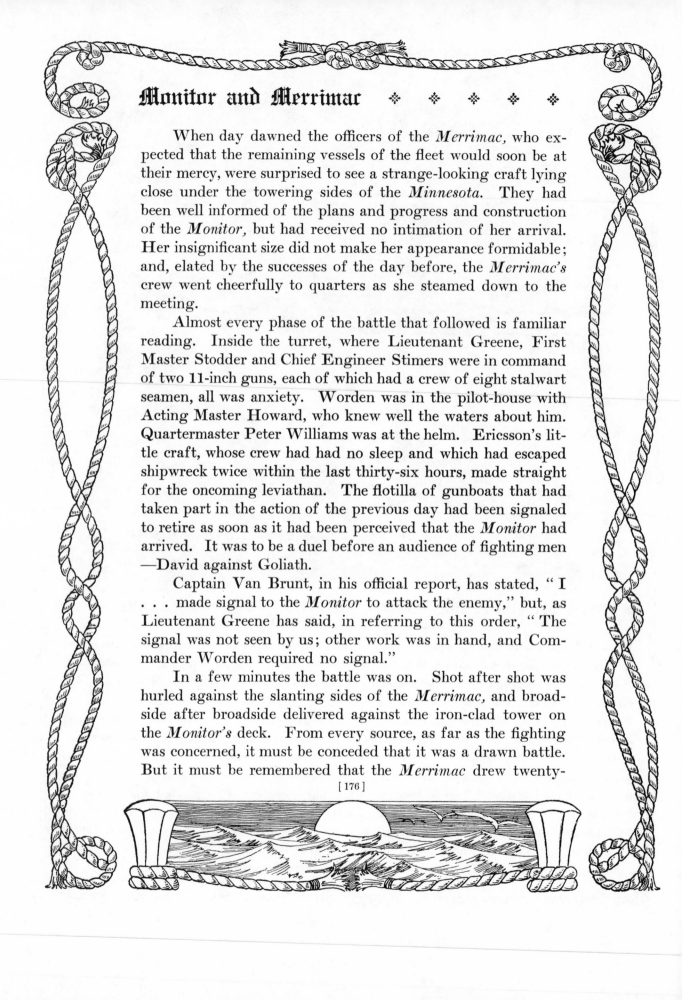

Monitor and Merrimac ✧ ✧ ✧ ✧ ✧ ✧

When day dawned the officers of the *Merrimac,* who expected that the remaining vessels of the fleet would soon be at their mercy, were surprised to see a strange-looking craft lying close under the towering sides of the *Minnesota.* They had been well informed of the plans and progress and construction of the *Monitor,* but had received no intimation of her arrival. Her insignificant size did not make her appearance formidable; and, elated by the successes of the day before, the *Merrimac's* crew went cheerfully to quarters as she steamed down to the meeting.

Almost every phase of the battle that followed is familiar reading. Inside the turret, where Lieutenant Greene, First Master Stodder and Chief Engineer Stimers were in command of two 11-inch guns, each of which had a crew of eight stalwart seamen, all was anxiety. Worden was in the pilot-house with Acting Master Howard, who knew well the waters about him. Quartermaster Peter Williams was at the helm. Ericsson's little craft, whose crew had had no sleep and which had escaped shipwreck twice within the last thirty-six hours, made straight for the oncoming leviathan. The flotilla of gunboats that had taken part in the action of the previous day had been signaled to retire as soon as it had been perceived that the *Monitor* had arrived. It was to be a duel before an audience of fighting men —David against Goliath.

Captain Van Brunt, in his official report, has stated, " I . . . made signal to the *Monitor* to attack the enemy," but, as Lieutenant Greene has said, in referring to this order, " The signal was not seen by us; other work was in hand, and Commander Worden required no signal."

In a few minutes the battle was on. Shot after shot was hurled against the slanting sides of the *Merrimac,* and broadside after broadside delivered against the iron-clad tower on the *Monitor's* deck. From every source, as far as the fighting was concerned, it must be conceded that it was a drawn battle. But it must be remembered that the *Merrimac* drew twenty-

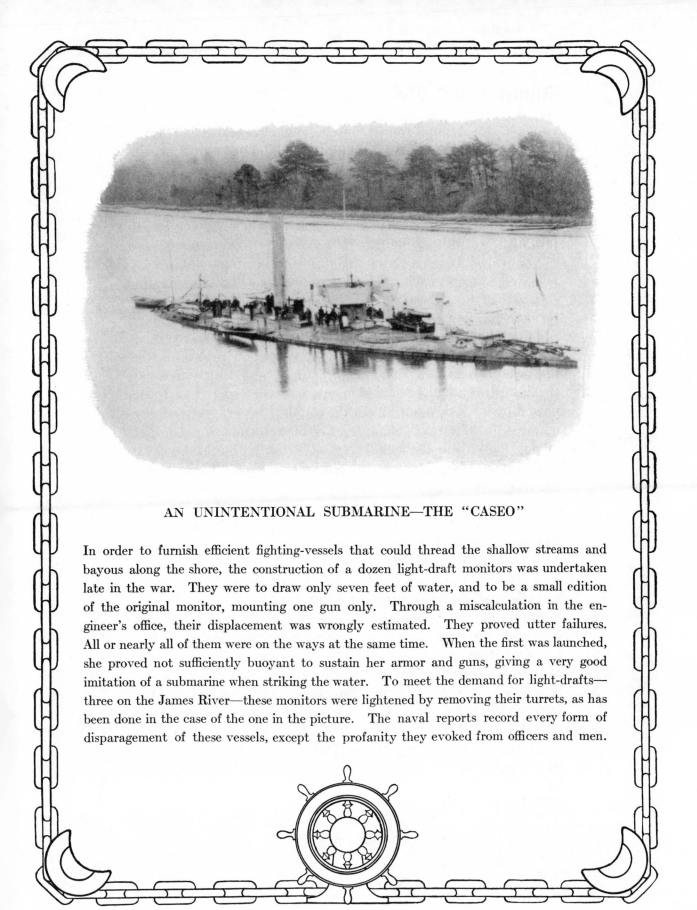

AN UNINTENTIONAL SUBMARINE—THE "CASEO"

In order to furnish efficient fighting-vessels that could thread the shallow streams and bayous along the shore, the construction of a dozen light-draft monitors was undertaken late in the war. They were to draw only seven feet of water, and to be a small edition of the original monitor, mounting one gun only. Through a miscalculation in the engineer's office, their displacement was wrongly estimated. They proved utter failures. All or nearly all of them were on the ways at the same time. When the first was launched, she proved not sufficiently buoyant to sustain her armor and guns, giving a very good imitation of a submarine when striking the water. To meet the demand for light-drafts—three on the James River—these monitors were lightened by removing their turrets, as has been done in the case of the one in the picture. The naval reports record every form of disparagement of these vessels, except the profanity they evoked from officers and men.

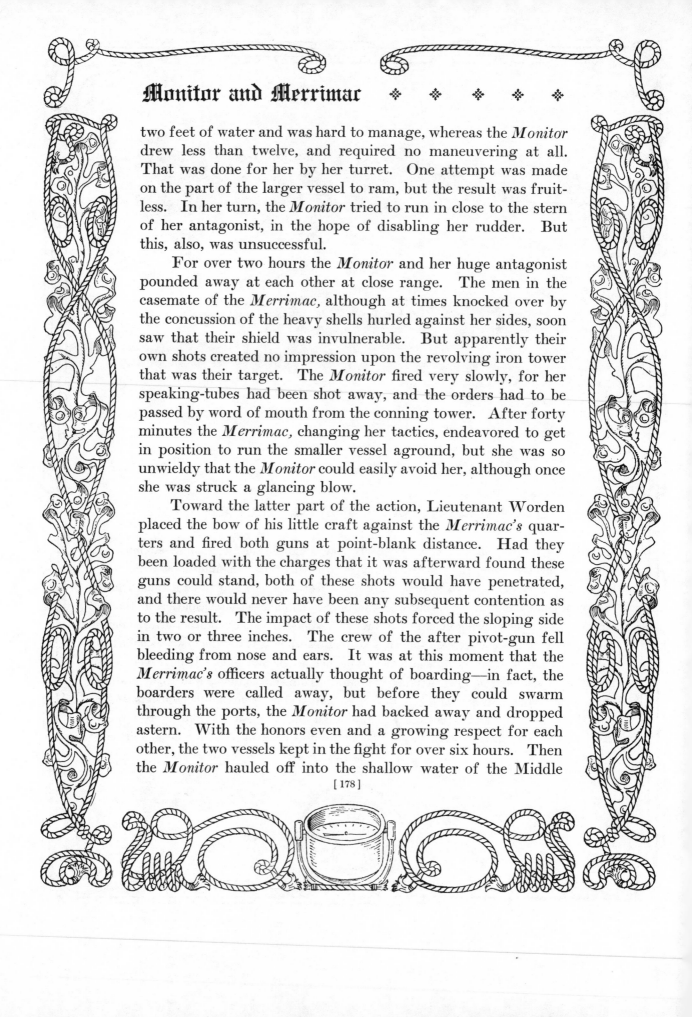

two feet of water and was hard to manage, whereas the *Monitor* drew less than twelve, and required no maneuvering at all. That was done for her by her turret. One attempt was made on the part of the larger vessel to ram, but the result was fruitless. In her turn, the *Monitor* tried to run in close to the stern of her antagonist, in the hope of disabling her rudder. But this, also, was unsuccessful.

For over two hours the *Monitor* and her huge antagonist pounded away at each other at close range. The men in the casemate of the *Merrimac,* although at times knocked over by the concussion of the heavy shells hurled against her sides, soon saw that their shield was invulnerable. But apparently their own shots created no impression upon the revolving iron tower that was their target. The *Monitor* fired very slowly, for her speaking-tubes had been shot away, and the orders had to be passed by word of mouth from the conning tower. After forty minutes the *Merrimac,* changing her tactics, endeavored to get in position to run the smaller vessel aground, but she was so unwieldy that the *Monitor* could easily avoid her, although once she was struck a glancing blow.

Toward the latter part of the action, Lieutenant Worden placed the bow of his little craft against the *Merrimac's* quarters and fired both guns at point-blank distance. Had they been loaded with the charges that it was afterward found these guns could stand, both of these shots would have penetrated, and there would never have been any subsequent contention as to the result. The impact of these shots forced the sloping side in two or three inches. The crew of the after pivot-gun fell bleeding from nose and ears. It was at this moment that the *Merrimac's* officers actually thought of boarding—in fact, the boarders were called away, but before they could swarm through the ports, the *Monitor* had backed away and dropped astern. With the honors even and a growing respect for each other, the two vessels kept in the fight for over six hours. Then the *Monitor* hauled off into the shallow water of the Middle

THE NEW "SEA-ELEPHANT" OF THE NAVY—THE "LEHIGH" IN '64

A naval historian has compared the monitor type of vessel "to the elephant, who swims beneath the surface . . . and communicates through his uplifted trunk with the upper air." In action and in rough weather, the monitor's only means of communication with the upper air are her turret and pilot-house, and from this fact alone it was argued that the monitor type of construction would prove to be an elephant on the hands of the Federal navy. Indeed, on her trial trip Ericsson's "Monitor" came near foundering, and thus she finally met her end in a storm off Cape Hatteras, December 31, 1862. But before this, her faults of construction had been recognized and the Federal Navy Department had undertaken the construction of nine bigger and better monitors. In Charleston Harbor the monitors were hit an aggregate of 738 times, and proved conclusively their superior endurance. The "Lehigh" first made her appearance in the James on an expedition and demonstration made up that river by Acting Rear-Admiral S. P. Lee in July, 1863. In September she was attached to Admiral Dahlgren's fleet. From October 26th to November 4th, under Commander A. Bryson, she and the "Patapsco" were assigned to the special duty of hammering Fort Sumter. On November 16, 1863, she ran aground on Sullivan's Island and was dangerously exposed to the guns of Fort Moultrie for five hours before she could be gotten off.

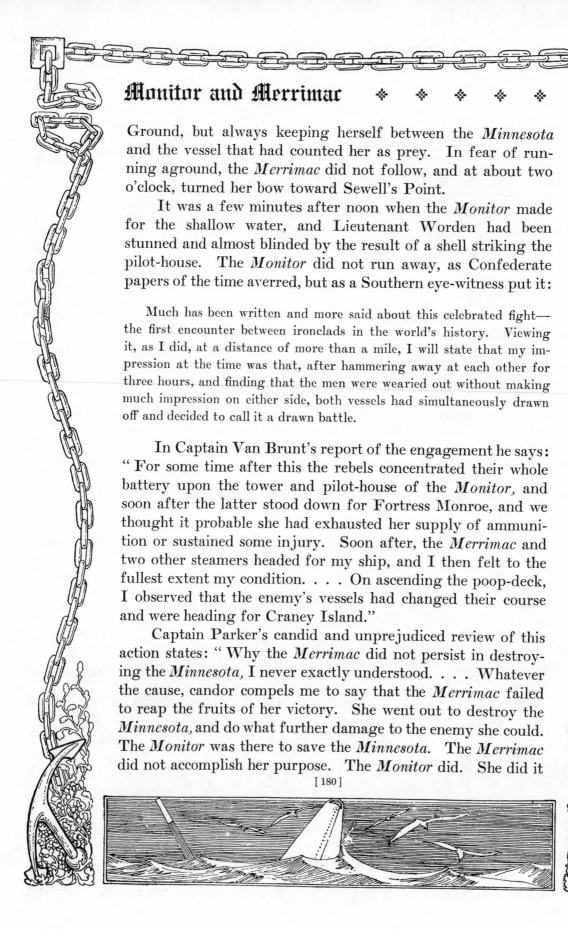

Ground, but always keeping herself between the *Minnesota* and the vessel that had counted her as prey. In fear of running aground, the *Merrimac* did not follow, and at about two o'clock, turned her bow toward Sewell's Point.

It was a few minutes after noon when the *Monitor* made for the shallow water, and Lieutenant Worden had been stunned and almost blinded by the result of a shell striking the pilot-house. The *Monitor* did not run away, as Confederate papers of the time averred, but as a Southern eye-witness put it:

Much has been written and more said about this celebrated fight— the first encounter between ironclads in the world's history. Viewing it, as I did, at a distance of more than a mile, I will state that my impression at the time was that, after hammering away at each other for three hours, and finding that the men were wearied out without making much impression on either side, both vessels had simultaneously drawn off and decided to call it a drawn battle.

In Captain Van Brunt's report of the engagement he says: "For some time after this the rebels concentrated their whole battery upon the tower and pilot-house of the *Monitor,* and soon after the latter stood down for Fortress Monroe, and we thought it probable she had exhausted her supply of ammunition or sustained some injury. Soon after, the *Merrimac* and two other steamers headed for my ship, and I then felt to the fullest extent my condition. . . . On ascending the poop-deck, I observed that the enemy's vessels had changed their course and were heading for Craney Island."

Captain Parker's candid and unprejudiced review of this action states: "Why the *Merrimac* did not persist in destroying the *Minnesota,* I never exactly understood. . . . Whatever the cause, candor compels me to say that the *Merrimac* failed to reap the fruits of her victory. She went out to destroy the *Minnesota,* and do what further damage to the enemy she could. The *Monitor* was there to save the *Minnesota.* The *Merrimac* did not accomplish her purpose. The *Monitor* did. She did it

THE DETACHED BLOCKADERS—JAMES GORDON BENNETT'S YACHT

While Admiral Porter with the fleet was waiting impatiently at Hampton Roads for the start of the much-delayed expedition against Fort Fisher, there was work a-plenty along the coast to keep up the blockade and circumvent the attempts of such Confederate vessels as the "Roanoke" to raise it. The upper picture is of especial popular interest; lying to the right of the despatch-boat and monitor off Port Royal is James Gordon Bennett's yacht "Rebecca," one of the fastest sailing yachts of her time. When she swept into Port Royal flying the Stars and Stripes, she was taken for a blockade-runner until her identity was learned. The officers of the blockading squadron were handsomely entertained aboard her during her stay, and were glad to get the news she brought from the North. On her way back to New York she was frequently mistaken for a blockade-runner and chased. In the lower picture is seen one of the monitors stationed in Ossabaw Sound. Awnings are stretched in the almost tropical sunshine. Yet the vessel is ready for any emergency.

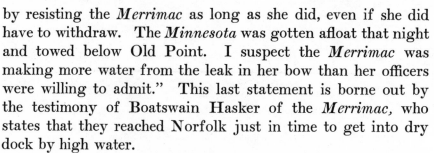

by resisting the *Merrimac* as long as she did, even if she did have to withdraw. The *Minnesota* was gotten afloat that night and towed below Old Point. I suspect the *Merrimac* was making more water from the leak in her bow than her officers were willing to admit." This last statement is borne out by the testimony of Boatswain Hasker of the *Merrimac,* who states that they reached Norfolk just in time to get into dry dock by high water.

But there is no use in fighting all the contested points of this battle over again. It was a drawn fight, bravely fought, and there is honor enough for both. The thrill of the meeting between these two armored ships was in its novelty. The results were in the reconstruction of the navies of the world.

Neither vessel long survived their famous encounter, and the *Merrimac* was the first to finish her days. Owing to Flag-Officer Buchanan's injuries, the command on that memorable 9th of March had fallen on Lieutenant Jones, and he was relieved before the end of the month by Flag-Officer Josiah Tatnall. Though the *Monitor* stayed close at hand, there was no further meeting after her valiant foe was released from the drydock on April 4th.

When Norfolk was evacuated by the Confederates, on the 10th of May, the further disposition of the *Merrimac* became a grave problem. Tatnall had her lightened three feet in order to take her up the James, but the pilots refused to attempt this in the face of a westerly breeze, and now every officer agreed with Tatnall that she must be blown up. This was done on the 11th. The indignation throughout the South was great, but Tatnall was completely exonerated by a court of inquiry.

After the destruction of the *Merrimac,* the *Monitor* went up the James with Commander Rodgers' squadron in the attack on the entrenchments at Drewry's Bluff. Finally on the 31st of December the *Monitor* was sunk in a gale, while on the way to Beaufort, North Carolina, and sixteen of her officers and crew went to the bottom with her.

VII

THE
MOST DARING
FEAT

THE "PORTSMOUTH"

THIS GALLANT OLD SAILING SLOOP PLAYED HER PART IN
FARRAGUT'S PASSAGE OF THE NEW ORLEANS FORTS BY
BROADSIDES ENFILADING THE CONFEDERATE WATER BATTERY,
PROTECTING THE APPROACH OF PORTER'S MORTAR SCHOONERS

THE MOST DARING FEAT—PASSING THE FORTS AT NEW ORLEANS

DAVID GLASGOW FARRAGUT made a sudden leap into fame. Late in the year 1861, he was a member of a retiring-board created by the Navy Department under a new law in order to get rid of superannuated officers. From this position he was suddenly promoted to the command of a fleet, and in a little over three months his name was echoing not only through the country but round the world.

It was Commander David D. Porter, in charge of the steamer *Powhatan* in the Gulf Blockading Squadron, who conceived the idea of running by the powerful forts at the mouth of the Mississippi and capturing the city of New Orleans. His plan was approved by the Secretary of the Navy and the President, and strongly endorsed by Commodore, afterward Rear-Admiral, Joseph Smith. After a consultation in which Commander Porter had a voice, Captain Farragut was selected as the leader of the expedition, and it was Porter who brought to him the first notice of his appointment. This was before the official notification of the Navy Department, for in Farragut's private papers was found an abrupt and mysterious note, dated December 21, 1861, which concludes thus: " I am to have a flag in the Gulf, and the rest depends upon myself. Keep calm and silent. I shall sail in three weeks."

The official notification, addressed to Farragut at Hastings-on-Hudson, New York, where he was stopping with his family, informed him that he was appointed to the West Gulf Blockading Squadron, and that the *Hartford* had been designated as his flagship. Within a fortnight, he received from Secretary of the Navy Gideon Welles the following official orders, dated

U. S. S. "HARTFORD"—FARRAGUT'S PET SHIP

PHOTOGRAPHED IN 1862, AFTER HER PASSAGE OF THE FORTS AT NEW ORLEANS

The flagship "Hartford" lies on the placid bosom of the Mississippi, whose waters reflect her masts and spars as if in a polished mirror. This photograph was taken in 1862 by the Confederate photographer Lytle, who, with his camera set up on the levee, took many of the ships that had survived the fiery ordeal of the forts below. It is evidently but a short time since the "Hartford" had passed through that night of death and terror; her top-gallant masts are housed and everything aloft sent down on deck except her fore, main, and mizzen topsail yards, on which the clewed-up sails are hanging to dry. Her spankers, half-trailed up, are drying out also, as is her flying-jib. Her fore, main, and cross-jack yards are up in place; and not only are the awnings spread above the spar-deck, but the boat awnings are out also, showing that although it is early in the year it must have been a scorching day. Of this beautiful vessel Farragut has written that she "was all that the heart could desire." He trusted himself to her in another memorable engagement when, lashed to her shrouds, he steamed past the forts in Mobile Bay on August 5, 1864, recking not of the Confederate torpedoes liberally planted in the harbor.

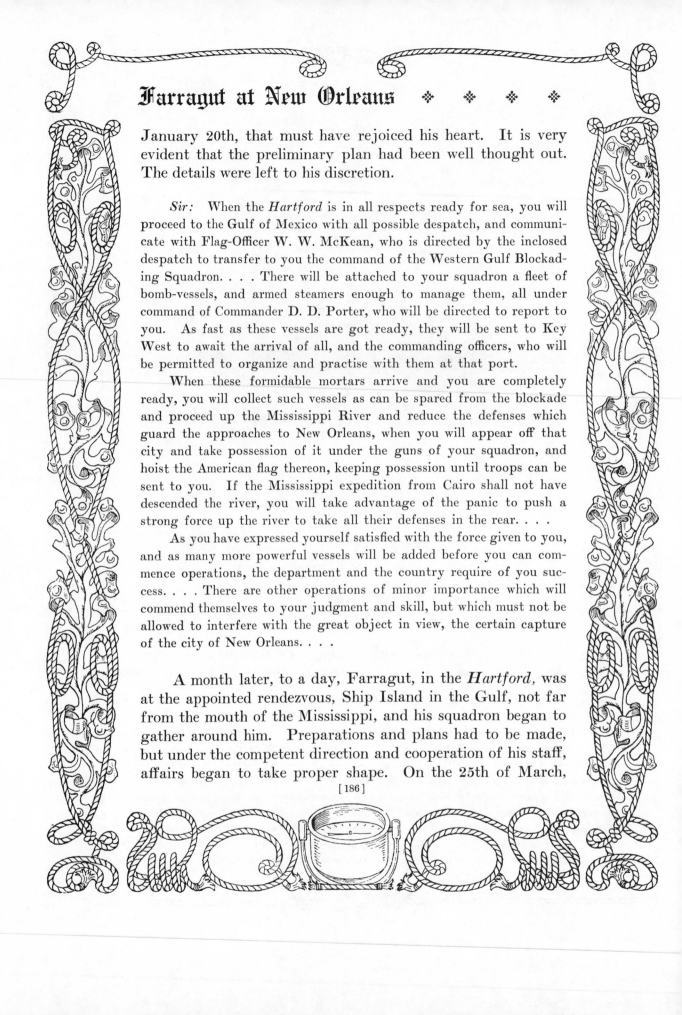

Farragut at New Orleans ❖ ❖ ❖ ❖

January 20th, that must have rejoiced his heart. It is very evident that the preliminary plan had been well thought out. The details were left to his discretion.

Sir: When the *Hartford* is in all respects ready for sea, you will proceed to the Gulf of Mexico with all possible despatch, and communicate with Flag-Officer W. W. McKean, who is directed by the inclosed despatch to transfer to you the command of the Western Gulf Blockading Squadron. . . . There will be attached to your squadron a fleet of bomb-vessels, and armed steamers enough to manage them, all under command of Commander D. D. Porter, who will be directed to report to you. As fast as these vessels are got ready, they will be sent to Key West to await the arrival of all, and the commanding officers, who will be permitted to organize and practise with them at that port.

When these formidable mortars arrive and you are completely ready, you will collect such vessels as can be spared from the blockade and proceed up the Mississippi River and reduce the defenses which guard the approaches to New Orleans, when you will appear off that city and take possession of it under the guns of your squadron, and hoist the American flag thereon, keeping possession until troops can be sent to you. If the Mississippi expedition from Cairo shall not have descended the river, you will take advantage of the panic to push a strong force up the river to take all their defenses in the rear. . . .

As you have expressed yourself satisfied with the force given to you, and as many more powerful vessels will be added before you can commence operations, the department and the country require of you success. . . . There are other operations of minor importance which will commend themselves to your judgment and skill, but which must not be allowed to interfere with the great object in view, the certain capture of the city of New Orleans. . . .

A month later, to a day, Farragut, in the *Hartford,* was at the appointed rendezvous, Ship Island in the Gulf, not far from the mouth of the Mississippi, and his squadron began to gather around him. Preparations and plans had to be made, but under the competent direction and cooperation of his staff, affairs began to take proper shape. On the 25th of March,

[186]

THE MEN WHO DARED—SAILORS ON THE "HARTFORD" AFTER PASSING THE NEW ORLEANS FORTS

On this page of unwritten history McPherson and Oliver, the New Orleans war-time photographers, have caught the crew of the staunch old "Hartford" as they relaxed after their fiery test. In unconscious picturesqueness grouped about the spar-deck, the men are gossiping or telling over again their versions of the great deeds done aboard the flagship. Some have seized the opportunity for a little plain sewing, while all are interested in the new and unfamiliar process of "having their pictures taken." The notable thing about the picture is the number of young faces. Only a few of the old salts whose bearded and weather-beaten faces give evidence of service in the old navy still remain. After the great triumph in Mobile Bay, Farragut said of these men: "I have never seen a crew come up like ours. They are ahead of the old set in small arms, and fully equal to them at the great guns. They arrived here a mere lot of boys and young men, and have now

SPAR–DECK OF THE "HARTFORD"

fattened up and knocked the nine-inch guns about like twenty-four pounders, to the astonishment of everybody. There was but one man who showed fear and he was allowed to resign. This was the most desperate battle I ever fought since the days of the old 'Essex.'" "It was the anxious night of my life," wrote Farragut later. The spar-deck shown below recalls another speech. "Don't flinch from that fire, boys! There is a hotter fire for those who don't do their duty!" So shouted Farragut with his ship fast aground and a huge fire-raft held hard against her wooden side by the little Confederate tug "Mosher." The ship seemed all ablaze and the men, "breathing fire," were driven from their guns. Farragut, calmly pacing the poop-deck, called out his orders, caring nothing for the rain of shot from Fort St. Philip. The men, inspired by such coolness, leaped to their stations again and soon a shot pierced the boiler of the plucky "Mosher" and sank her.

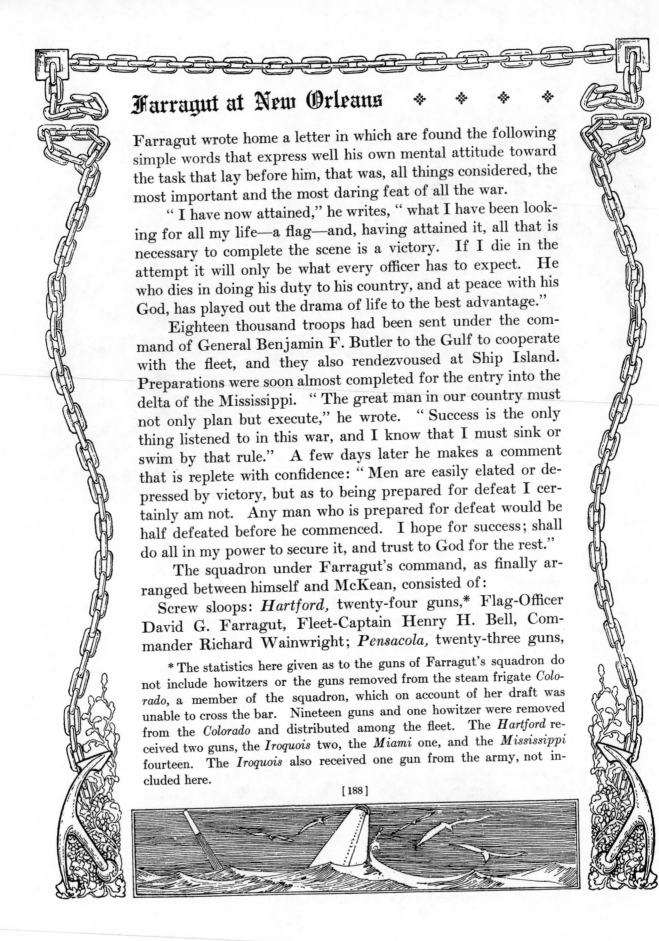

Farragut at New Orleans ❖ ❖ ❖ ❖

Farragut wrote home a letter in which are found the following simple words that express well his own mental attitude toward the task that lay before him, that was, all things considered, the most important and the most daring feat of all the war.

" I have now attained," he writes, " what I have been looking for all my life—a flag—and, having attained it, all that is necessary to complete the scene is a victory. If I die in the attempt it will only be what every officer has to expect. He who dies in doing his duty to his country, and at peace with his God, has played out the drama of life to the best advantage."

Eighteen thousand troops had been sent under the command of General Benjamin F. Butler to the Gulf to cooperate with the fleet, and they also rendezvoused at Ship Island. Preparations were soon almost completed for the entry into the delta of the Mississippi. " The great man in our country must not only plan but execute," he wrote. " Success is the only thing listened to in this war, and I know that I must sink or swim by that rule." A few days later he makes a comment that is replete with confidence: " Men are easily elated or depressed by victory, but as to being prepared for defeat I certainly am not. Any man who is prepared for defeat would be half defeated before he commenced. I hope for success; shall do all in my power to secure it, and trust to God for the rest."

The squadron under Farragut's command, as finally arranged between himself and McKean, consisted of:

Screw sloops: *Hartford,* twenty-four guns,* Flag-Officer David G. Farragut, Fleet-Captain Henry H. Bell, Commander Richard Wainwright; *Pensacola,* twenty-three guns,

* The statistics here given as to the guns of Farragut's squadron do not include howitzers or the guns removed from the steam frigate *Colorado,* a member of the squadron, which on account of her draft was unable to cross the bar. Nineteen guns and one howitzer were removed from the *Colorado* and distributed among the fleet. The *Hartford* received two guns, the *Iroquois* two, the *Miami* one, and the *Mississippi* fourteen. The *Iroquois* also received one gun from the army, not included here.

[188]

DECK OF THE U. S. S. "RICHMOND" AFTER SHE PASSED THE FORTS
THE MEN AT QUARTERS
COMMANDER JAMES ALDEN ON THE BRIDGE

Thus the crew was assembled the morning after that terrible night of fighting past Forts Jackson and St. Philip. The "Richmond" was the third vessel in line in the center division led by Farragut himself. Only two of her crew were killed and four injured, for Commander Alden had carefully prepared a splinter netting which caught the death-dealing pieces of plank and scantling, and prevented them from sweeping the gun-deck. Early in October, 1861, the "Richmond," under Captain John Pope, led the blockading vessels up the delta of the Mississippi to the Head of the Passes, where the stream broadens into a deep bay two miles wide, giving ample room for maneuvers. The Federal vessels were not to remain here long unmolested. In the dim dawn of Oct. 12th, Captain George Nicholas Hollins, C. S. N., stole upon the fleet unobserved. With his ironclad "Ma-

COMMANDER JAMES ALDEN

nassas" he rammed the "Richmond." A coal barge alongside the Federal vessel saved her from serious injury; the "Manassas," whose boilers were damaged by the collision, limped off up-stream. Soon after, three immense fire-rafts were sighted coming down-stream, and Captain Pope gave the signal for retreat. Both the "Richmond" and the "Vincennes" grounded on the bar at the outlet of Southwest Pass and the Confederate vessels again advanced to attack them. But they were driven off by the heavy broadsides and the guns of the plucky little "Water Witch." In command of Lieutenant Francis Winslow, she had not retreated with the other vessels, but had come down to beg Captain Pope to return. After this inglorious affair no further attempt was made to hold the Head of the Passes. A Federal vessel was then stationed off the mouth of each pass.

Captain Henry W. Morris; *Brooklyn,* twenty-four guns, Captain Thomas T. Craven; *Richmond,* twenty-two guns, Commander James Alden.

Side-wheel steamer: *Mississippi,* seven guns, Commander Melancton Smith.

Screw corvettes: *Oneida,* nine guns, Commander Samuel Phillips Lee; *Varuna,* ten guns, Commander Charles S. Boggs; *Iroquois,* seven guns, Commander John De Camp.

Screw gunboats: *Cayuga,* two guns, Lieutenant Napoleon B. Harrison; *Itasca,* four guns, Lieutenant C. H. B. Caldwell; *Katahdin,* two guns, Lieutenant George H. Preble; *Kennebec,* two guns, Lieutenant John H. Russell; *Kineo,* two guns, Lieutenant George M. Ransom; *Pinola,* three guns, Lieutenant Pierce Crosby; *Sciota,* two guns, Lieutenant Edward Donaldson; *Winona,* two guns, Lieutenant Edward T. Nichols; *Wissahickon,* two guns, Lieutenant Albert N. Smith.

In the final plan of action the fleet was divided into three divisions. The first was to be led by Captain Theodorus Bailey, who had transferred his flag from the old *Colorado* to the little gunboat *Cayuga,* and was to be made up of the *Pensacola, Mississippi, Oneida, Varuna, Katahdin, Kineo,* and *Wissahickon;* Farragut led the second, or center, division, composed of the *Hartford, Brooklyn,* and *Richmond,* and Captain Bell, in the *Sciota,* headed the third, having under his command the *Iroquois, Kennebec, Pinola, Itasca,* and *Winona.* Commander Porter, with his little squadron of six armed steamers, the *Harriet Lane, Owasco, Clifton, John P. Jackson, Westfield, Miami,* and *Portsmouth,* was to stay back with the nineteen mortar schooners that continued to pour their great shells into the forts during the passage of the fleet.

General Lovell, in command of the defenses of New Orleans, did not depend entirely upon Colonel Higgins' gunners in Forts St. Philip and Jackson to keep Farragut away from the city. A considerable fleet of war vessels, some belonging to the Government and some to the State, were in the river, and

HUGER, COMMANDER OF THE "McREA" IN THE FEARLESS CONFEDERATE FLOTILLA

Never were braver deeds done by men afloat in ships than were performed by the Southern officers and sailors of the little flotilla of gunboats and river craft that joined with the great forts ashore in disputing the passage of Farragut's fleet up the river. The ram "Manassas," whose thin plating was pierced through and through, charged again and again at the towering wooden walls of the oncoming ships. She struck the "Mississippi," wounding her badly, and all but sank the "Brooklyn." The men on the little tug "Mosher," which pushed the fire-raft against the "Hartford," sank with their vessel. Desperate deeds of courage were performed by every Confederate gunboat engaged in the battle. Commander Kennon, of the "Governor Moore," in his duel with the "Varuna," fired through the bows of his own ship. On board the "McRea," a little sea-going steam barkentine but lightly armed, Commander Thomas B. Huger was killed. It was a remarkable coincidence that, only a few months before, this splendid and gallant officer had been first-lieutenant of the "Iroquois," the very ship from which he received his death-wound. There had been hardly a change in the personnel of the vessel. All of the officers and men on board of her had once obeyed his orders. Not all of the Confederate river-defense fleet took part in the action, but those that were under the command of ex-officers of the navy plunged in almost with mad reck-lessness, disdaining the odds arrayed against them. Had the two power-ful ironclads, the "Mississippi" and the "Louisiana," been finished and in commission, declared the Con-federates, Farragut's fleet would never have reached New Orleans.

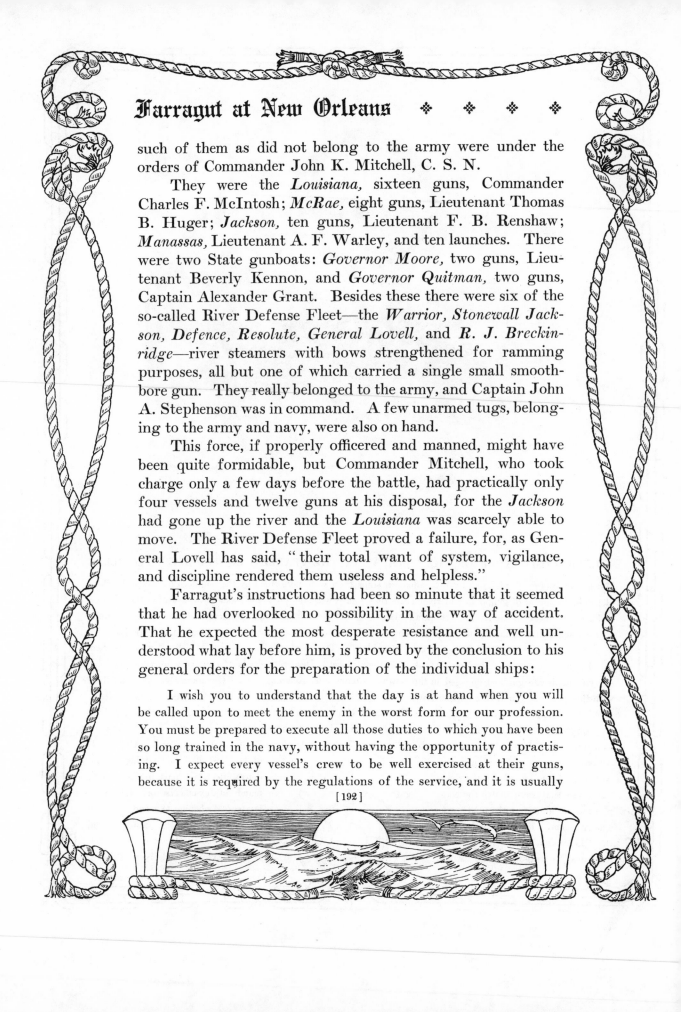

such of them as did not belong to the army were under the orders of Commander John K. Mitchell, C. S. N.

They were the *Louisiana,* sixteen guns, Commander Charles F. McIntosh; *McRae,* eight guns, Lieutenant Thomas B. Huger; *Jackson,* ten guns, Lieutenant F. B. Renshaw; *Manassas,* Lieutenant A. F. Warley, and ten launches. There were two State gunboats: *Governor Moore,* two guns, Lieutenant Beverly Kennon, and *Governor Quitman,* two guns, Captain Alexander Grant. Besides these there were six of the so-called River Defense Fleet—the *Warrior, Stonewall Jackson, Defence, Resolute, General Lovell,* and *R. J. Breckinridge*—river steamers with bows strengthened for ramming purposes, all but one of which carried a single small smoothbore gun. They really belonged to the army, and Captain John A. Stephenson was in command. A few unarmed tugs, belonging to the army and navy, were also on hand.

This force, if properly officered and manned, might have been quite formidable, but Commander Mitchell, who took charge only a few days before the battle, had practically only four vessels and twelve guns at his disposal, for the *Jackson* had gone up the river and the *Louisiana* was scarcely able to move. The River Defense Fleet proved a failure, for, as General Lovell has said, "their total want of system, vigilance, and discipline rendered them useless and helpless."

Farragut's instructions had been so minute that it seemed that he had overlooked no possibility in the way of accident. That he expected the most desperate resistance and well understood what lay before him, is proved by the conclusion to his general orders for the preparation of the individual ships:

I wish you to understand that the day is at hand when you will be called upon to meet the enemy in the worst form for our profession. You must be prepared to execute all those duties to which you have been so long trained in the navy, without having the opportunity of practising. I expect every vessel's crew to be well exercised at their guns, because it is required by the regulations of the service, and it is usually

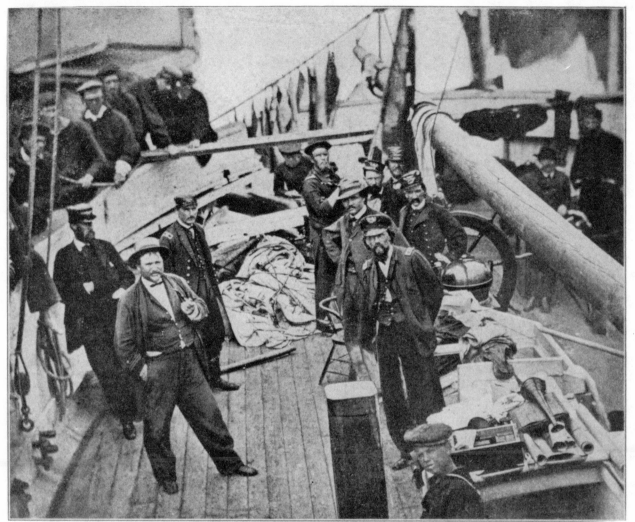

SAVED FROM AN UNTIMELY END—THE "SCIOTA"

This scene on the vessel's deck was photographed shortly after she had been raised after being sunk by a torpedo in Mobile Bay. Two days after the Federal flag was raised over the courthouse in Mobile, the "Sciota," while hurrying across the bay, ran into one of these hidden engines of destruction. A terrific explosion followed and the "Sciota" sank immediately in twelve feet of water. Four of her men were killed and six wounded and the vessel was badly damaged. This was on April 14, 1865. The navy never gives up one of its vessels as a total loss till everything has been done to prove that to be the case; by July 7th the "Sciota" had been raised, repaired, and sent around to Pensacola for her armament, with orders to proceed to New York and go into dry-dock. In the picture the man leaning against the bulwark, with one hand on his coat and the other in his trousers' pocket, is John S. Pearce, one of the engineers of the famous "Kearsarge." In Farragut's squadron below New Orleans the "Sciota," under Lieutenant Edward Donaldson, led the third division of vessels in charge of Commander Henry H. Bell. The "Sciota" did not get under fire of the forts till about 4 A.M. and passed them without much damage. Immediately behind her came the "Iroquois," which was attacked by the "McRae" and another Confederate vessel. The "McRae" was commanded by Lieutenant Thomas Huger, who had been serving on the "Iroquois" at the war's beginning. An 11-inch shell and a stand of cannister aimed from his old ship killed Huger and disabled the "McRae."

the first object of our attentions; but they must be equally well trained for stopping shot-holes and extinguishing fire. Hot and cold shot will, no doubt, be freely dealt to us, and there must be stout hearts and quick hands to extinguish the one and stop the holes of the other.

I shall expect the most prompt attention to signals and verbal orders, either from myself or the captain of the fleet, who, it will be understood, in all cases acts by my authority.

On the 20th of April, Farragut had held a council of his officers in which he expressed the opinion that whatever had to be done would have to be done quickly, as the mortar flotilla that was keeping up a constant bombardment of Fort Jackson and Fort St. Philip was expending shells and ammunitions at a terrific rate. There had been no attempt made to sever the heavy chains that, supported by hulks, crossed almost from one shore to the other opposite Fort Jackson. Farragut had wisely concluded that it and the obstructions were best left alone until immediately before the attempt to run the forts should be made. They really acted as a check on the Confederates themselves, preventing them from making an offensive attack or sending down the numerous fire-rafts that Farragut knew were kept in readiness.

There was one thing that bothered the officers of the fleet more than it did the man upon whose shoulders the whole responsibility rested, and this was the presence in the river of the two powerful iron-clad rams, the *Mississippi* and the *Louisiana*. Had it been known that the former was only about two-thirds completed, and that the *Louisiana,* although her armament had been placed on board of her, was nothing more than a powerful floating battery with such insufficient motive-power that she was unable to leave her moorings, the fears of many would have been allayed. The strength of these vessels, and also of the smaller ram, *Manassas,* had been greatly exaggerated, but the moral effect of their presence had to be taken into account. Farragut had made up his mind that if there was any ramming to be done he intended to do his share of it, even with his

PORTER, WHOSE BOMB–VESSELS BACKED THE FLEET

Admiral David Dixon Porter was born in 1813 and died in 1891. The red blood of the sea-fighter had come down to him unto the third generation. He was the younger son of Commodore David Porter, who won fame in the "Constellation" and "Essex." His grandfather had served with distinction in the nondescript navy of the Colonies in the war for independence. Yet with such a lineage of the free and open sea, Porter, like Farragut, proved that he could adapt himself to the cramped arenas of bay and river. It was for his part in the fall of Vicksburg that he was made rear-admiral in 1863. It was he, too, that was chosen to command the North Atlantic squadron in 1864, when a courageous and steady hand was needed to guide the most important naval operations to a successful outcome. For his services at Fort Fisher he was made vice-admiral in 1866 and was retired with the rank of admiral in 1870.

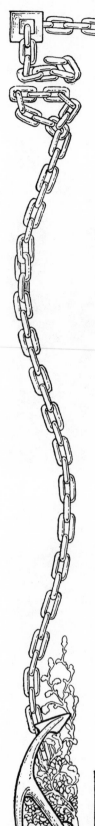

unarmored prows. " These rams are formidable things," he wrote reassuringly, " but when there is room to maneuver, the heavy ships *will run over them.*"

On the night of April 20th, Captain Bell, on board the gunboat *Pinola,* with the *Itasca,* steamed up the river on the daring duty of cutting the chains and making a passageway for the waiting fleet. After adventures and misadventures that included the grounding of the *Itasca,* the chains were removed. Lieutenant Caldwell, in the *Itasca,* dropped part of the chain obstruction to the bottom, and carried away more of it while going down the river. Two of the hulks dragged their anchors and drifted down the stream, and the way was cleared. General M. L. Smith, who had been placed in command of the interior line of works around New Orleans, testified as follows before the board that inquired into the capture of New Orleans:

The forts, in my judgment, were impregnable so long as they were in free and open communication with the city. This communication was not endangered while the obstruction existed. The conclusion, then, is briefly this: While the obstruction existed the city was safe; when it was swept away, as the defenses then existed, it was in the enemy's power.

Farragut, writing home to his family on the 21st of April, refers to this daring performance in the following terms:

Captain Bell went last night to cut the chain across the river. I never felt such anxiety in my life as I did until his return. One of his vessels got on shore, and I was fearful she would be captured. They kept up a tremendous fire on him; but Porter diverted their fire with a heavy cannonade. They let the chain go, but the man sent to explode the petard did not succeed; his wires broke. Bell would have burned the hulks, but the illumination would have given the enemy a chance to destroy his gunboat which got aground. However, the chain was divided, and it gives us space enough to go through. I was as glad to see Bell on his return as if he had been my boy. I was up all night, and could not sleep until he got back to the ship.

CLEARING THE WAY—DECK ON ONE OF PORTER'S MORTAR SCHOONERS

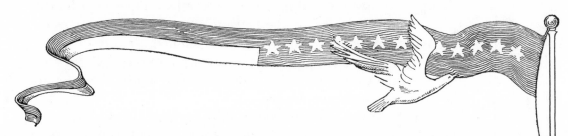

Twenty of these vessels accompanied Farragut's expedition. They were convoyed by six gunboats. Their huge mortars were capable of dropping shells of large caliber within the forts at a distance of 3,680 yards. The mortar schooners were divided into three divisions. Two were stationed behind a natural rampart formed by the west bank of the river, where they were screened from view by a thick growth of wood above which their mastheads rose, affording excellent lookouts. These were further concealed by branches of trees cleverly fastened upon them. Another division was stationed near the east bank, nearer to the forts and in plain view. A terrific bombardment was begun on the morning of April 16th, each mortar schooner firing at intervals of ten minutes throughout the day. Toward five o'clock flames were seen curling up in Fort Jackson. Commander Porter, who pulled up the river in a rowboat, ascertained that the fort itself was burning. It was indeed in a precarious position, as was learned afterward from Colonel Edward Higgins, the Confederate commander of the fort. Had the attempt to pass up the river been made next morning, it would probably have been much easier than on April 24th, when the fleet at last got under way. Throughout the succeeding days of waiting, the mortar flotilla kept up its vigorous bombardment, withdrawing, however, the division on the east bank, which had suffered in its exposed position during the first vigorous attack, and uniting it with the other vessels, which were protected by the screen on woods on the west bank.

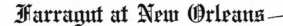

Twice had Farragut been compelled to postpone the advance up the river, but on the night of the 23d everything was in readiness; Lieutenant Caldwell, in a ten-oared boat, made another daring reconnaissance on the evening of the 23d, and reported that the way through the obstructions was clear. Somehow, the Confederates must have known that the time had come, for as early as eleven o'clock they had lighted immense piles of wood along the shores and turned loose their burning rafts. It was five minutes to two on the morning of the 24th when two red lights appeared at the flagship's peak, the signal for getting under way. The first division of eight vessels under command of Captain Bailey passed through the opening in the obstructions and headed for Fort St. Philip. In less than ten minutes Bailey's vessels were replying to the concentrated fire that was poured in upon them. Commander Boggs, on the *Varuna,* accompanied by the *Oneida,* had kept in close to shore, and thus escaped a great deal of the fire of the heavy guns that had been elevated and pointed to cover the midchannel. But now Bailey's division found that there were more than land batteries to contend with—they had to meet the Confederate fleet. The *Varuna,* fired upon and rammed by the Louisiana State gunboat *Governor Moore* and River Defense ram *Stonewall Jackson,* was forced to run into shoal water where she promptly sunk to her topgallant forecastle. The Confederate vessels were so pierced by the *Varuna's* fire that they, too, were run ashore in flames. The *Oneida,* which had already disabled one of the Confederate gunboats, came up and received the surrender of the Confederate Commander Kennon and the crew of the burning *Governor Moore.*

As the *Brooklyn* came through the opening in the barrier, she ran afoul of the little *Kineo* and almost sank her. A few minutes later the ugly shape of the turtle-back ram *Manassas* appeared almost under the *Brooklyn's* bows. Had she not changed her course a little all would have been over, but the blow glanced from the chain armor slung along her sides. In

AFTER A SHOOTING–TRIP ASHORE—OFFICERS ON THE DECK OF THE "MIAMI"

From the time she ran the forts below New Orleans with Farragut, the "Miami" was ever on the go. During 1863–4, under the redoubtable Lieutenant-Commander C. W. Flusser, she was active in Carolina waters. In the Roanoke River, April 1, 1864, she met her most thrilling adventure when she and the "Southfield" were attacked by the powerful Confederate ram "Albemarle." The "Southfield" was sunk, but the "Miami" in a plucky running fight made her escape down the river and gave the alarm.

AN INDEFATIGABLE GUNBOAT—THE "MIAMI"

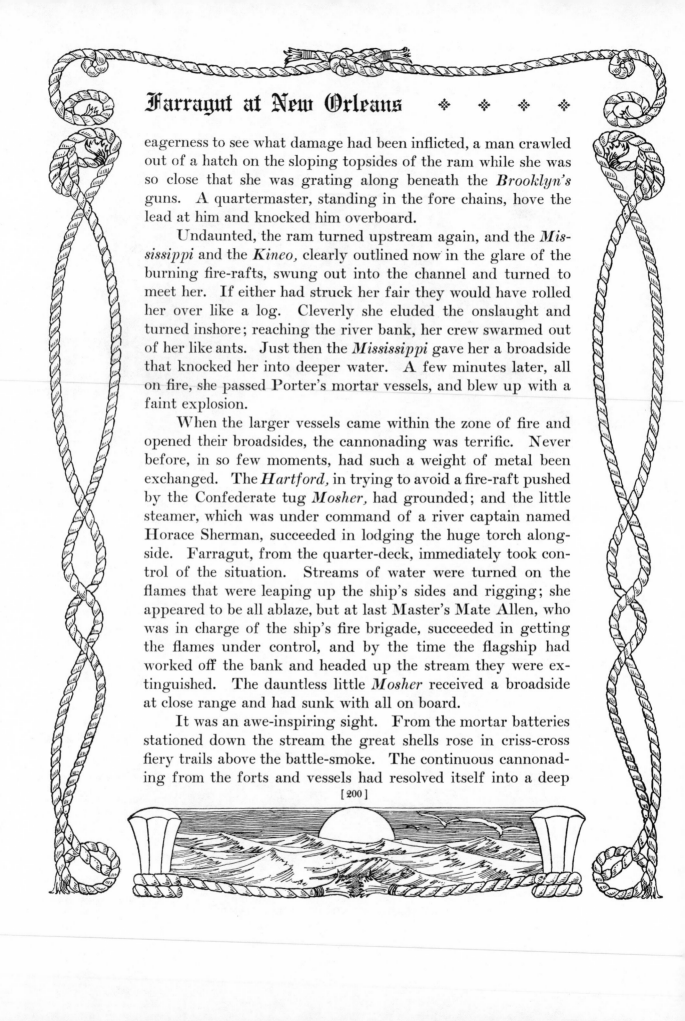

eagerness to see what damage had been inflicted, a man crawled out of a hatch on the sloping topsides of the ram while she was so close that she was grating along beneath the *Brooklyn's* guns. A quartermaster, standing in the fore chains, hove the lead at him and knocked him overboard.

Undaunted, the ram turned upstream again, and the *Mississippi* and the *Kineo,* clearly outlined now in the glare of the burning fire-rafts, swung out into the channel and turned to meet her. If either had struck her fair they would have rolled her over like a log. Cleverly she eluded the onslaught and turned inshore; reaching the river bank, her crew swarmed out of her like ants. Just then the *Mississippi* gave her a broadside that knocked her into deeper water. A few minutes later, all on fire, she passed Porter's mortar vessels, and blew up with a faint explosion.

When the larger vessels came within the zone of fire and opened their broadsides, the cannonading was terrific. Never before, in so few moments, had such a weight of metal been exchanged. The *Hartford,* in trying to avoid a fire-raft pushed by the Confederate tug *Mosher,* had grounded; and the little steamer, which was under command of a river captain named Horace Sherman, succeeded in lodging the huge torch alongside. Farragut, from the quarter-deck, immediately took control of the situation. Streams of water were turned on the flames that were leaping up the ship's sides and rigging; she appeared to be all ablaze, but at last Master's Mate Allen, who was in charge of the ship's fire brigade, succeeded in getting the flames under control, and by the time the flagship had worked off the bank and headed up the stream they were extinguished. The dauntless little *Mosher* received a broadside at close range and had sunk with all on board.

It was an awe-inspiring sight. From the mortar batteries stationed down the stream the great shells rose in criss-cross fiery trails above the battle-smoke. The continuous cannonading from the forts and vessels had resolved itself into a deep

THE "WINONA"—LAST IN THE LINE

This little vessel, mounting but two guns, brought up the rear of the third division in the passage of the New Orleans forts. Following the red stern-light of the "Itasca," she became entangled in the logs and driftwood of the Confederate obstructions on the smoke-clouded river. In backing out she fouled the "Itasca"; both vessels lost nearly half an hour in getting under way again. By this time most of the squadron had passed the forts and daylight was coming fast. Undaunted, Lieutenant Edward Tatnall Nichols of the "Winona" pressed on, a fair mark for the gunners of Fort Jackson. The first shot from the fort killed one man and wounded another; the third and fourth shots killed or wounded the entire gun-crew of her 30-pounder except one man. Still Lieutenant Nichols pressed on to Fort St. Philip. There his vessel and the "Itasca" became the center of such a terrific storm of shot that Commander David D. Porter, of the mortar-boat flotilla, signalled the two little vessels to retire. The "Itasca" had to be run ashore below the mortar-boats. The "Winona" had been "hulled several times, and the decks were wet fore and aft from the spray of the falling shot." She survived to run the batteries at Vicksburg with Farragut. She exchanged a few shells with Fort Morgan in Mobile Bay while on blockade duty there, August 30, 1862.

THE "HARTFORD" AFTER "PASSING THE FORTS" A SECOND TIME

The photographic chronicling of the "most daring deed" would remain incomplete without this presentment of the gallant "Hartford" as she paused at Baton Rouge on a second and peaceful visit in 1882. The rule against the inclusion of any but war-time scenes in this PHOTOGRAPHIC HISTORY has therefore been suspended in favor of this striking photograph—previously unpublished like the others. The people of New Orleans who remembered the "Hartford" in 1862 would hardly have recognized her when, twenty years afterward, she once more steamed up the river and dropped her anchor off the levee. Her appearance, it is seen, was greatly changed; her engines had been altered and she was a much faster vessel than before. When she had passed through the iron hail from the forts,

THE ALTERED APPEARANCE OF THE FAMOUS SHIP ON HER VOYAGE OF PEACE

she was not so trim as she is in this picture. Her top-gallant masts had been sent down and all but her lower yards were on deck; cables were slung along her sides and she was stripped for the fray. Lytle, the Confederate photographer, who had photographed the grand old flagship and her consorts in war-time, also took this photograph of her when she came as a peaceful visitor. The "Hartford" had been for a long time on the European station, and there was hardly a port at which she entered where her name and her fame had not preceded her. Her decks were constantly thronged with visitors, and among her crew were many of the men who had fought with Farragut. These prideful veterans could still point out some of her honorable scars as they told their adventures.

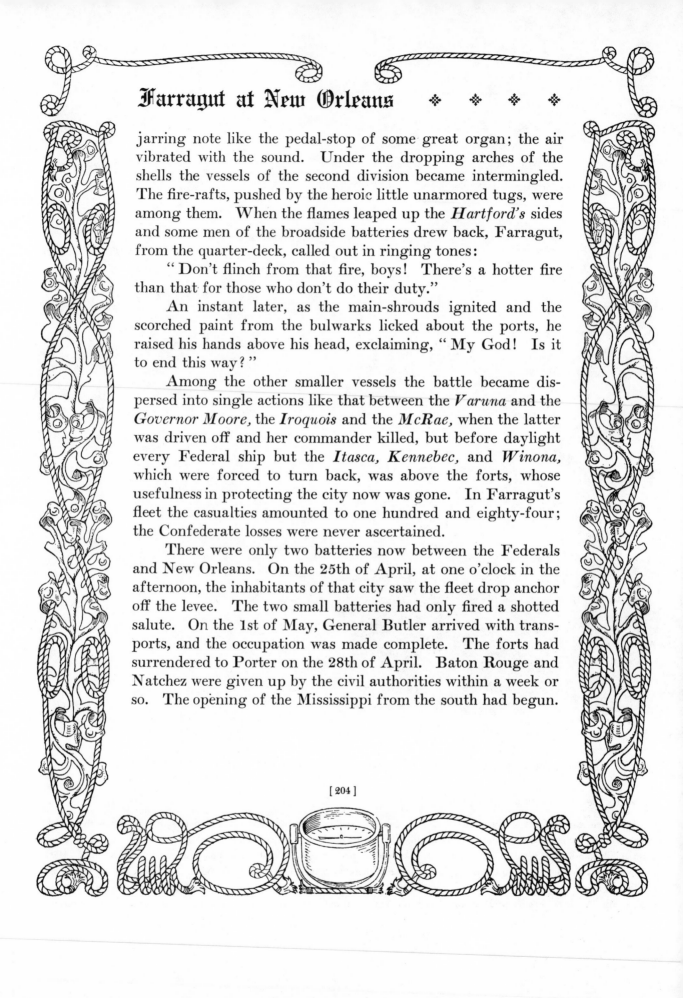

jarring note like the pedal-stop of some great organ; the air vibrated with the sound. Under the dropping arches of the shells the vessels of the second division became intermingled. The fire-rafts, pushed by the heroic little unarmored tugs, were among them. When the flames leaped up the *Hartford's* sides and some men of the broadside batteries drew back, Farragut, from the quarter-deck, called out in ringing tones:

"Don't flinch from that fire, boys! There's a hotter fire than that for those who don't do their duty."

An instant later, as the main-shrouds ignited and the scorched paint from the bulwarks licked about the ports, he raised his hands above his head, exclaiming, "My God! Is it to end this way?"

Among the other smaller vessels the battle became dispersed into single actions like that between the *Varuna* and the *Governor Moore,* the *Iroquois* and the *McRae,* when the latter was driven off and her commander killed, but before daylight every Federal ship but the *Itasca, Kennebec,* and *Winona,* which were forced to turn back, was above the forts, whose usefulness in protecting the city now was gone. In Farragut's fleet the casualties amounted to one hundred and eighty-four; the Confederate losses were never ascertained.

There were only two batteries now between the Federals and New Orleans. On the 25th of April, at one o'clock in the afternoon, the inhabitants of that city saw the fleet drop anchor off the levee. The two small batteries had only fired a shotted salute. On the 1st of May, General Butler arrived with transports, and the occupation was made complete. The forts had surrendered to Porter on the 28th of April. Baton Rouge and Natchez were given up by the civil authorities within a week or so. The opening of the Mississippi from the south had begun.

VIII

FIGHTING
ON
THE MISSISSIPPI

GUNBOAT "NUMBER 53"—AN OFFICER SPYING THE SHORE OPPOSITE BATON ROUGE

A POWERFUL REËNFORCEMENT TO THE RIVER FLEET

This huge vessel was one of the first attempts to develop the Eads type of gunboat. She, with the "Tuscumbia," the "Indianola," the "Lafayette," and the "Chillicothe," was added to the Mississippi squadron after Admiral Porter took command, and all received their baptism in the operations of the Vicksburg campaign, the "Indianola" being captured and destroyed by the Confederates. They were flat-bottomed vessels with side-wheels three-quarters of the way aft, each wheel acting independently of the other so as to give facility in turning in narrow channels, which rendered the broadside guns more effective. They were designed as light-drafts, requiring from five to seven feet of water. The "Choctaw" and her sister-vessel, the "Lafayette," required nine feet. The "Choctaw" mounted three 9-inch smooth-bores and a rifled

THE MONSTER IRONCLAD "CHOCTAW"

100-pounder in her forward casemate. She had a second casemate forward of the wheel where she mounted two 24-pounder howitzers, and a third casemate abaft the wheel containing two 30-pounder Parrott rifled guns. Under Lieutenant-Commander F. M. Ramsay, she was active in the flotilla co-operating with General W. T. Sherman against Haynes' Bluff and Drumgould's Bluff, Mississippi, to distract attention from Grant's famous movement to the south of Vicksburg. She accompanied the expedition that captured Yazoo City on May 21, 1863, and destroyed $2,000,000 worth of Confederate vessels, yards, mills, and other property. On June 7, 1863, she, with the little "Lexington," drove off the Confederate attack on Milliken's Bend, Louisiana. In 1864, she accompanied Admiral Porter on the Red River expedition.

THE "RATTLER"—LEADER OF THE "LAND CRUISE" IN 1863

This little "tinclad" Number 1, the "Rattler," was the flagship of Lieutenant-Commander Watson Smith. Admiral Porter sent him to enter the Yazoo River through Moon Lake, Cold Water, and the Tallahatchie River to attack Vicksburg from that side. This was the most daring and hazardous undertaking attempted by the river navy. The army engineers had cut the levee higher up the Mississippi, but after the water was let in it took some days for it to attain a sufficient level in the vast area flooded. Late in February, Smith and his squadron started out with transports carrying 6,000 troops. Struggling against overhanging trees and masses of driftwood, pausing to remove great trees which the Confederates had felled in their way, the gunboats managed to pick a channel, and approached Fort Pemberton on March 11, 1863. Many of the gunboats had suffered severely from this amphibious warfare. The "Romeo" had her stacks carried away, the "Petrel" had lost her wheel, and the "Chilli-cothe" had started a plank by running upon a submerged stump. The soldiers were grumbling at the constant labor of "digging the gunboats out of the woods." The channel was so obstructed and narrow that only one gunboat at a time could effectually engage Fort Pemberton. After a few days of ineffectual bombardment the expedition was abandoned and the gunboats returned to the Mississippi over the same long, difficult course.

A VIGILANT PATROLLER—THE "SILVER LAKE"

In the picture the "Silver Lake" is lying off Vicksburg after its fall. While Admiral Porter was busy attacking Vicksburg with the Mississippi squadron, Lieutenant-Commander Le Roy Fitch, with a few small gunboats, was actively patrolling the Tennessee and Cumberland Rivers. It was soon seen that the hold upon Tennessee and Kentucky gained by the Federals by the fall of Forts Henry and Donelson would be lost without adequate assistance from the navy, and Admiral Porter was authorized to purchase small light-draft river steamers and add them to Fitch's flotilla as rapidly as they could be converted into gunboats. One of the first to be completed was the "Silver Lake." The little stern-wheel steamer first distinguished herself on February 3, 1863, at Dover, Tennessee, where she (with Fitch's flotilla) assisted in routing 4,500 Confederates, who were attacking the Federals at that place. The little vessel continued to render yeoman's service with the other gunboats, ably assisted by General A. W. Ellet's marine brigade.

THE NAVY'S FRESH-WATER SAILORS

In this group the crew of the "Carondelet" is crowding to get within range of the camera. One of the earliest of the river ironclads, the "Carondelet" was frequently the flagship of Admiral Porter; and her crew, at first recruited from among men who had had little experience afloat, soon learned the art of warfare on inland waters. Great difficulty was experienced at first in manning the river gunboats. Men of the old navy could not be spared, and a large proportion of landsmen had to be enlisted to make up the required complement. Crude as the early crews appeared to the officers of the navy who commanded them, they soon proved their worth; having gotten their sea-legs and sailorlike spirit in the fighting along the rivers, many of them saw service afterward in the blockading squadrons along the coast.

VETERANS IN THE MAKING—CREW OF THE "LAFAYETTE"

In this fine group on the Mississippi ironclad "Lafayette," the photographer has arranged the crew so that a better idea of the faces of the men can be gathered. Many of them are seen to be foreigners, while of the native Americans boys and youths as usual predominate. There is none of the unmistakable look that characterized the crews of the gunboats and ships in Eastern waters. In only a few instances is there any sign of that indescribable sea-faring appearance that marks the old salt. Yet these men could fight as bravely and endure hardship as uncomplainingly as their salt-water comrades. Most of them were recruited from the river towns and communities in the West.

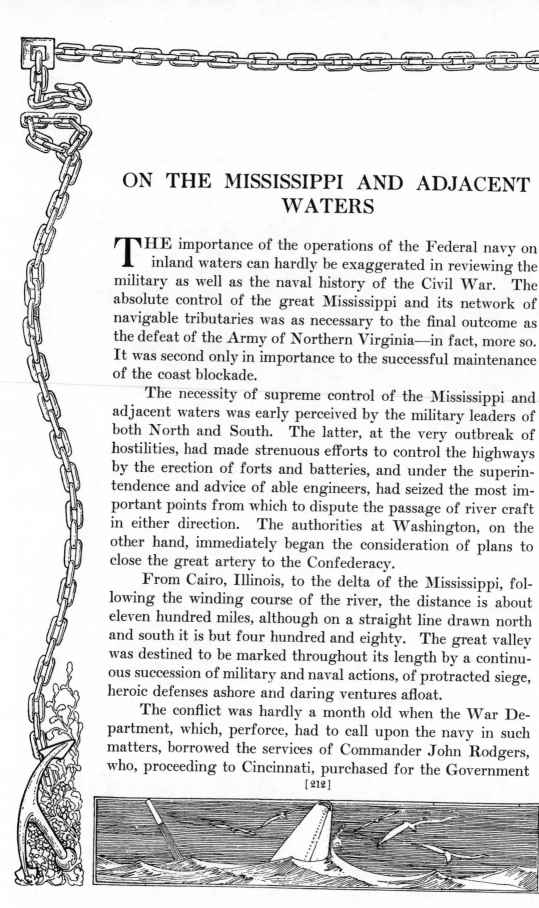

ON THE MISSISSIPPI AND ADJACENT WATERS

THE importance of the operations of the Federal navy on inland waters can hardly be exaggerated in reviewing the military as well as the naval history of the Civil War. The absolute control of the great Mississippi and its network of navigable tributaries was as necessary to the final outcome as the defeat of the Army of Northern Virginia—in fact, more so. It was second only in importance to the successful maintenance of the coast blockade.

The necessity of supreme control of the Mississippi and adjacent waters was early perceived by the military leaders of both North and South. The latter, at the very outbreak of hostilities, had made strenuous efforts to control the highways by the erection of forts and batteries, and under the superintendence and advice of able engineers, had seized the most important points from which to dispute the passage of river craft in either direction. The authorities at Washington, on the other hand, immediately began the consideration of plans to close the great artery to the Confederacy.

From Cairo, Illinois, to the delta of the Mississippi, following the winding course of the river, the distance is about eleven hundred miles, although on a straight line drawn north and south it is but four hundred and eighty. The great valley was destined to be marked throughout its length by a continuous succession of military and naval actions, of protracted siege, heroic defenses ashore and daring ventures afloat.

The conflict was hardly a month old when the War Department, which, perforce, had to call upon the navy in such matters, borrowed the services of Commander John Rodgers, who, proceeding to Cincinnati, purchased for the Government

THE WESTERN NAVAL BASE OF THE UNION—MOUND CITY IN 1862

After Captain Andrew H. Foote took command of the Mississippi flotilla on September 6, 1861, one of his first acts was to establish a depot for the repair of his vessels at Cairo. Since the Government owned no land at this point, the navy-yard was literally afloat in wharf-boats, old steamers, tugs, flat-boats, and rafts. Later, this depot was removed to Mound City, just above Cairo, where ten acres of land were secured. This was frequently under water from freshets, however, and the machine-shops, carpenter-shops, and the like were still maintained in steamers. Captain A. M. Pennock was placed in charge of this depot, and continued to render efficient service in that capacity, looking after the gunboats till the close of the war.

the nucleus of the subsequent river force in the three little wooden steamers, *Conestoga, Lexington,* and *Tyler.* About the time that these small craft had been converted into practicable gunboats, the department made a contract with James B. Eads, of St. Louis, for the construction of seven iron-clad steamers, and so, late in 1861 and early in 1862, there came into being the famous fighters, *Cairo, Carondelet, Cincinnati, Louisville, Mound City, Pittsburgh,* and *St. Louis.* To these were simultaneously added the powerful, converted snag-boats, *Benton* and *Essex,* almost twice the size of any of those built by Eads. The *Benton* proved, despite her slowness, to be the most formidable vessel on the river. She was armored with 3-inch plating, was about one thousand tons burden, and carried two 9-inch guns, seven rifled 42-pounders, and seven 32-pounders, a total of sixteen guns. Thirty-eight mortar-boats completed the Western Flotilla, as first organized.

It was soon evident that friction was bound to exist as long as naval officers were subject to the orders of innumerable military officials who happened to rank them. Nevertheless, it was not until October 1, 1862, that the Western Flotilla was transferred to the control of the Navy Department, and henceforth was called the Mississippi Squadron. During the year 1861 there had been little done by either the army or the navy along the Western border. But the early months of 1862 saw both gunboats and troops in active employment, and so they continued until practically the close of hostilities.

The separate actions that took place have already been covered in detail in previous volumes of this history. The first action of any moment was the capture of Fort Henry, on February 6th, where Flag-Officer Foote's flotilla consisted of the *Cincinnati* (flagship), *Carondelet, St. Louis,* and *Essex,* to which formidable force were added the three small wooden gunboats, *Lexington, Tyler,* and *Conestoga.* This was a joint army and navy movement, a combination of the two able minds of Ulysses S. Grant and Andrew H. Foote. General Lloyd

WORK AFLOAT AND ASHORE—THE NAVAL STATION AT CAIRO

Here the Federal gunboats put in for supplies and minor repairs. The station at Cairo, first established by Captain Foote in September, 1861, soon proved inadequate for the needs of the river squadrons, since all repairs had to be made in the water. The lower picture shows the naval station at Mound City. Here were laid the keels of three of the series of the Eads ironclads, and here the unlucky "Carondelet" was repaired after her injuries at Fort Donelson. The large force of shipwrights, carpenters, mechanics, and engineers was kept constantly at work, often night and day. This was the only naval depot of the river fleet in the West. Said Admiral Porter in 1885: "Those who remember the navy-yard at Mound City, near Cairo, and the large fleet which grew from the small squadron first put afloat, will wonder why we should require so many navy-yards at the present time, when we hardly fit out a dozen vessels in a year."

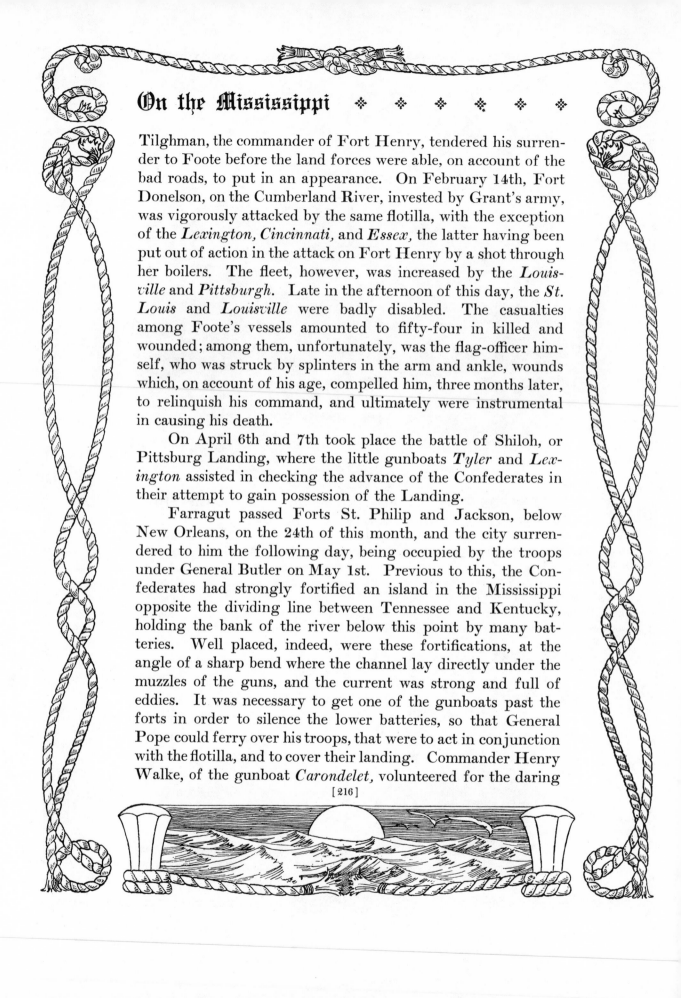

On the Mississippi ❖ ❖ ❖ ❖ ❖ ❖ ❖

Tilghman, the commander of Fort Henry, tendered his surrender to Foote before the land forces were able, on account of the bad roads, to put in an appearance. On February 14th, Fort Donelson, on the Cumberland River, invested by Grant's army, was vigorously attacked by the same flotilla, with the exception of the *Lexington, Cincinnati,* and *Essex,* the latter having been put out of action in the attack on Fort Henry by a shot through her boilers. The fleet, however, was increased by the *Louisville* and *Pittsburgh.* Late in the afternoon of this day, the *St. Louis* and *Louisville* were badly disabled. The casualties among Foote's vessels amounted to fifty-four in killed and wounded; among them, unfortunately, was the flag-officer himself, who was struck by splinters in the arm and ankle, wounds which, on account of his age, compelled him, three months later, to relinquish his command, and ultimately were instrumental in causing his death.

On April 6th and 7th took place the battle of Shiloh, or Pittsburg Landing, where the little gunboats *Tyler* and *Lexington* assisted in checking the advance of the Confederates in their attempt to gain possession of the Landing.

Farragut passed Forts St. Philip and Jackson, below New Orleans, on the 24th of this month, and the city surrendered to him the following day, being occupied by the troops under General Butler on May 1st. Previous to this, the Confederates had strongly fortified an island in the Mississippi opposite the dividing line between Tennessee and Kentucky, holding the bank of the river below this point by many batteries. Well placed, indeed, were these fortifications, at the angle of a sharp bend where the channel lay directly under the muzzles of the guns, and the current was strong and full of eddies. It was necessary to get one of the gunboats past the forts in order to silence the lower batteries, so that General Pope could ferry over his troops, that were to act in conjunction with the flotilla, and to cover their landing. Commander Henry Walke, of the gunboat *Carondelet,* volunteered for the daring

THE "ALBATROSS" WITH THE "HARTFORD," THE ONLY SHIP THAT FOUGHT PAST PORT HUDSON

While Porter had been fighting on the upper Mississippi, Farragut had been busy attending to his large command in the Gulf, but on the 14th of March, 1863, he appeared below Port Hudson. General Banks was to make a simultaneous land-attack upon that post and Farragut was to run the river batteries and join his vessels to those of Porter in an effectual blockade of the Red River, from which the Confederacy drew its trans-Mississippi supplies. The Federal vessels, lashed two and two together, started on their dangerous attempt at eleven o'clock at night, but the Port Hudson garrison discovered them. Lighting bonfires, the Confederates opened with their heavy guns from the bluff a hundred feet above. Lashed to the gallant old flagship "Hartford" was the "Albatross," Lieutenant-Commander John E. Hart. Both vessels in the dense smoke that settled on the river were nearly carried ashore by the five-mile current. The "Hartford" actually did touch ground under the guns of one of the batteries, but with the assistance of the "Albatross" backed off and passed safely above the line of fire. Not so fortunate was the "Genesee," the fastest boat of the squadron. She was lashed to the "Richmond," the slowest boat, and just as they had reached the last battery a plunging shot penetrated to the engine-room of the "Richmond" and so damaged her safety-valves that her engines became useless. Not even with the aid of the "Genesee" could the "Richmond" longer stem the current, and the two had to proceed downstream again past the gauntlet of the Confederate batteries for the second time. Disaster overtook all the other vessels of the squadron, and the "Mississippi" grounded and blew up.

venture, and having prepared his vessel with extra planking and chain cables, and taking alongside a barge loaded with baled hay, started on the night of April 4th to pass the batteries. The feat was accomplished during a terrific rainstorm, and although it was repeated by Lieutenant Thompson in the *Pittsburgh* a night or two later, Walke was the first to tempt what seemed in the minds of the other officers annihilation. The passing of the batteries sealed the fate of Island No. 10, and it was surrendered on April 7, 1862, leaving the Federal fleet free to proceed toward the strongly built Fort Pillow.

A word must be said of the efforts of the Confederate naval forces to resist the downward progress of the Western Flotilla. A number of wooden steamers had been purchased or seized at New Orleans, and six of these, their bows, and in some cases their engines, protected with iron plating and carrying six or seven guns apiece, ascended the river with Commander George N. Hollins as flag-officer. They were the *McRae, Livingston, Maurepas, General Polk, Pontchartrain,* and *Ivy.* The ram *Manassas* was with them, but receiving an injury from a snag, she was sent back to New Orleans. Hollins remained below New Madrid, in the vicinity of Tiptonville, for some time, engaging the shore batteries now occupied by the troops of Generals Pope and Buford. He had resolved to stop the Federal gunboats if they should pass Island No. 10, but he soon began to doubt his ability to do this, and, besides, his powder supply became almost exhausted. So he went down the river in response to an urgent summons from Commander Whittle at New Orleans, incurring thereby the displeasure of the Richmond Government. Most of the fleet was burned at the mouth of the Yazoo, after its guns had been left behind at Fort Pillow, to prevent its falling into the hands of the Federals. The scout-boat *Grampus* and six transports were sunk at Island No. 10 before the surrender. The latter were raised, and one of them became famous as the hospital-ship *Red Rover.*

Hollins' ships were now replaced by a somewhat strange

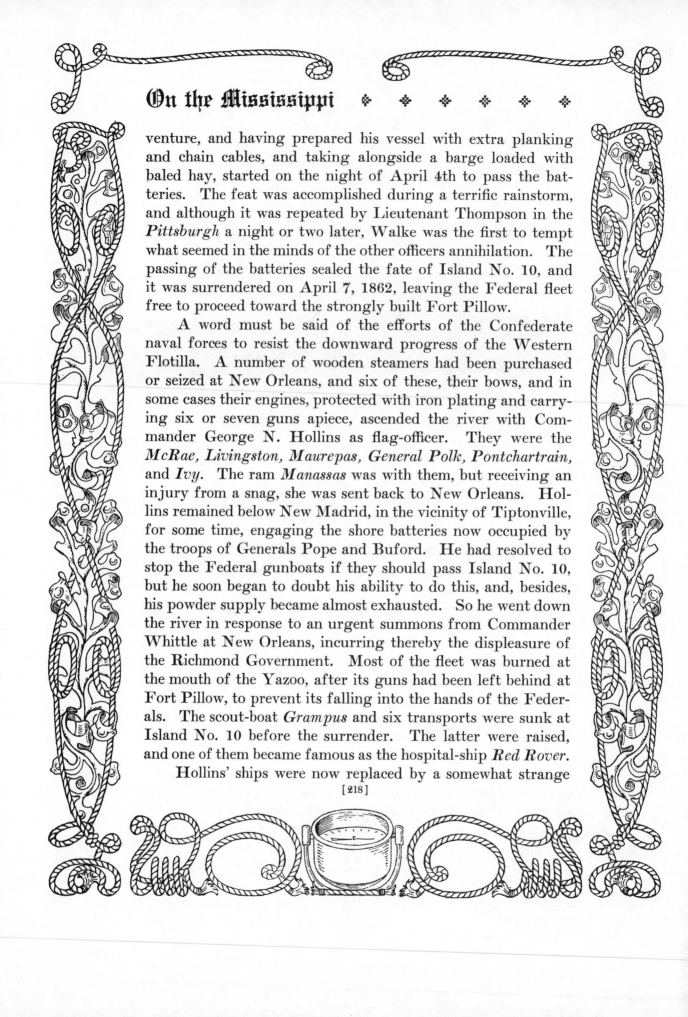

"MY

EXECUTIVE

OFFICER,

MR. DEWEY"

THE

FUTURE ADMIRAL

AS CIVIL WAR

LIEUTENANT

In the fight with the batteries at Port Hudson, March 14, 1863, Farragut, in the "Hartford" lashed to the "Albatross," got by, but the fine old consort of the "Hartford," the "Mississippi," went down—her gunners fighting to the last. Farragut, in anguish, could see her enveloped in flames lighting up the river. She had grounded under the very guns of a battery, and not until actually driven off by the flames did her men leave her. When the "Mississippi" grounded, the shock threw her lieutenant-commander into the river, and in confusion he swam toward the shore; then, turning about, he swam back to his ship. Captain Smith thus writes in his report: "I consider that I should be neglecting a most important duty should I omit to mention the coolness of my executive officer, Mr. Dewey, and the steady, fearless, and gallant manner in which the officers and men of the 'Mississippi' defended her, and the orderly and quiet manner in which she was abandoned after being thirty-five minutes aground under the fire of the enemy's batteries. There was no confusion in embarking the crew, and the only noise was from the enemy's cannon." Lieutenant-Commander George Dewey, here mentioned at the age of 26, was to exemplify in Manila Bay on May 1, 1898, the lessons he was learning from Farragut.

lot of craft, under the control of the army, and known as the River Defense Fleet. They were river steamers, with bows enclosed in iron, and were designed for use as rams. Fourteen vessels in all were thus prepared, and eight were sent up the river in charge of Captain James E. Montgomery to try conclusions with Flag-Officer Foote's powerful ironclads. The opportunity was not long in coming.

Foote, suffering from the wound received at Fort Donelson, was relieved by Captain Charles H. Davis on May 9th. The new commander, who was soon to be promoted to flag-officer, selected the *Benton,* commanded by Lieutenant S. L. Phelps, as his flagship. On May 10th, the bombardment of Fort Pillow by the mortar-boats, which had been going on since the 14th of April, was unexpectedly interrupted by the advance of the River Defense Fleet, which came up bravely from its position under the guns of the fort and actually took the Federal vessels by surprise, the *Cincinnati* being called upon at first to bear the brunt of the onslaught alone. Both she and the *Mound City* had to be beached on account of the injuries they received. There is no doubt that Captain Montgomery, the Confederate commander, showed great bravery in making the attack, but he also proved his discretion by withdrawing upon the advance of the belated *Benton* and *St. Louis,* for with but slight loss and damage he retreated down the river, and had his vessels in good shape four weeks later at Memphis.

A new departure in river fighting began when Colonel Charles Ellet, Jr., came down with his nine rams, which consisted of old stern-wheelers and side-wheelers strengthened by bulkheads, their boilers protected by oak and iron and their bows reenforced with heavy metal sheathing. Colonel Ellet, who had long advocated this style of offensive vessel, had been given independent charge, his orders being simply to cooperate with Flag-Officer Davis and the flotilla. In fact, throughout the whole war, the Ellet rams were under the direction of the War Department. The vessels were unarmed until after the

A BESIEGING "TINCLAD"—THE "MARMORA"

This little "tinclad" Number 2, the "Marmora," under Acting Volunteer Lieutenant Robert Getty, played a lively part in the operations of Admiral Porter's squadron against Vicksburg. She and the "Signal" were the "tinclads" that reconnoitered up the torpedo-infested Yazoo, Dec. 11, 1862, and it was while protecting the "Marmora" from the Confederates along the bank that the luckless "Cairo" met her fate. The "Marmora" was with the fleet in Sherman's futile attack at Chickasaw Bayou. After the fall of Vicksburg, the squadron was divided into detachments to patrol the Mississippi and its tributaries, and the "Marmora" was assigned to the detachment of Lieutenant George M. Bache, the brave commander of the lost "Cincinnati." He, in the little veteran "Lexington," accompanied by the "Cricket" and "Marmora," went up the White River where the Confederates were massing. In the middle of August, 1863, the three little gunboats completely broke up the expedition that was being set afoot by the indefatigable General Price, whom it would have required an army of 20,000 to drive back. The pontoon-bridges in the river were destroyed, completely stopping the advance, and the "Cricket" captured the two vessels in his flotilla.

THE RAM "VINDICATOR" OFF VICKSBURG

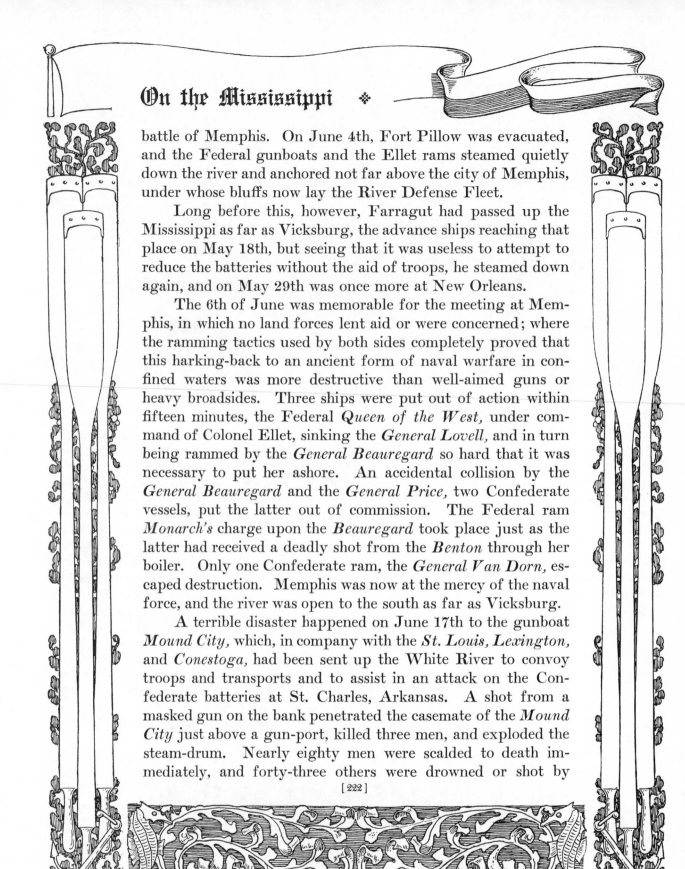

battle of Memphis. On June 4th, Fort Pillow was evacuated, and the Federal gunboats and the Ellet rams steamed quietly down the river and anchored not far above the city of Memphis, under whose bluffs now lay the River Defense Fleet.

Long before this, however, Farragut had passed up the Mississippi as far as Vicksburg, the advance ships reaching that place on May 18th, but seeing that it was useless to attempt to reduce the batteries without the aid of troops, he steamed down again, and on May 29th was once more at New Orleans.

The 6th of June was memorable for the meeting at Memphis, in which no land forces lent aid or were concerned; where the ramming tactics used by both sides completely proved that this harking-back to an ancient form of naval warfare in confined waters was more destructive than well-aimed guns or heavy broadsides. Three ships were put out of action within fifteen minutes, the Federal *Queen of the West,* under command of Colonel Ellet, sinking the *General Lovell,* and in turn being rammed by the *General Beauregard* so hard that it was necessary to put her ashore. An accidental collision by the *General Beauregard* and the *General Price,* two Confederate vessels, put the latter out of commission. The Federal ram *Monarch's* charge upon the *Beauregard* took place just as the latter had received a deadly shot from the *Benton* through her boiler. Only one Confederate ram, the *General Van Dorn,* escaped destruction. Memphis was now at the mercy of the naval force, and the river was open to the south as far as Vicksburg.

A terrible disaster happened on June 17th to the gunboat *Mound City,* which, in company with the *St. Louis, Lexington,* and *Conestoga,* had been sent up the White River to convoy troops and transports and to assist in an attack on the Confederate batteries at St. Charles, Arkansas. A shot from a masked gun on the bank penetrated the casemate of the *Mound City* just above a gun-port, killed three men, and exploded the steam-drum. Nearly eighty men were scalded to death immediately, and forty-three others were drowned or shot by

In the picture above of gunboat "Number 54," the "Nymph," is seen—a typical example of the river steamers that were purchased by the Government and converted into the so-called "tinclads." This kind of vessel was acquired at the suggestion of Flag-Officer Davis, who saw the necessity of light-draft gunboats to operate in shallow waters against the Confederates constantly harassing the flotilla from along shore. These "tinclads" were mostly stern-wheel steamers drawing not more than three feet. They were covered from bow to stern with iron plate a half to three-quarters of an inch thick. When Admiral Porter succeeded Davis in the command of the Mississippi squadron, it had already been reënforced by a number of these extremely useful little vessels. One of Porter's first acts was to use the "tinclads" to prevent the erection of Confederate fortifications up the Yazoo. The "Queen City" ("tinclad" Number 26) was commanded in the Vicksburg campaign by Acting Volunteer Lieutenant J. Goudy, one of those to receive special mention in Admiral Porter's official report on the fall of the besieged town. In June, 1864, the "Queen City" was stationed on the White River, patrolling the stream between Clarendon and Duvall's Bluff, under command of Acting Volunteer Lieutenant G. W. Brown. On the 24th, she was surprised by a Confederate force under General Shelby, who attacked her with artillery about four in the morning. After a sharp struggle of twenty minutes the little "tinclad," with her thin armor riddled with shot, surrendered. After stripping her of the nine guns and her supplies, the Confederates scuttled and burned her. Such were the chances that the "tinclads" constantly took.

TWO WARSHIPS
OF THE
"MOSQUITO FLEET"

"NYMPH" (ABOVE)
AND THE
"QUEEN CITY"

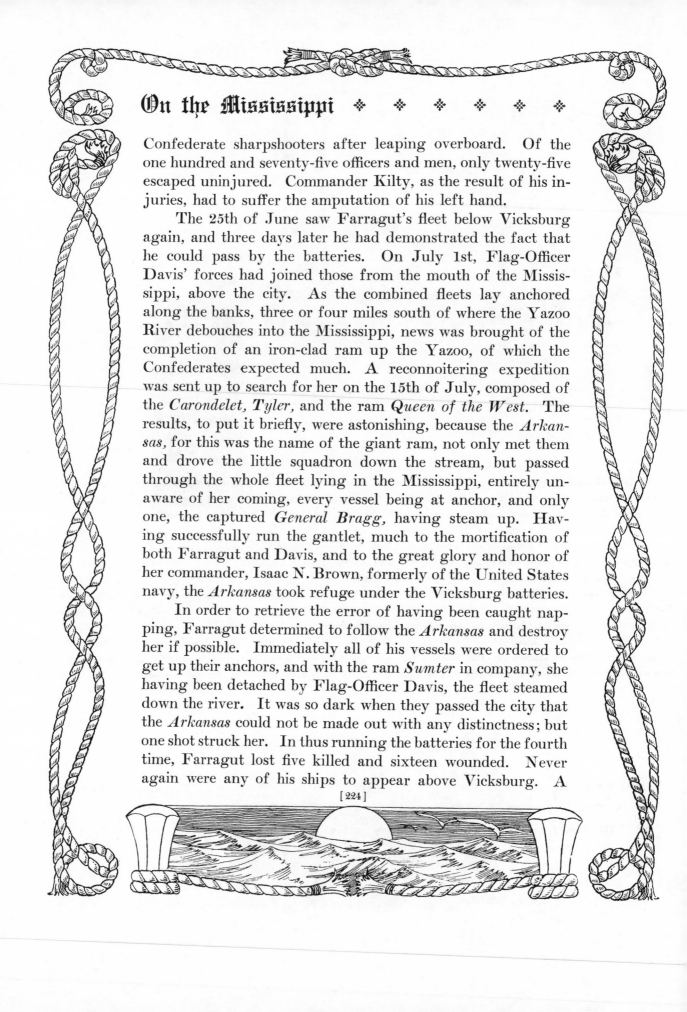

Confederate sharpshooters after leaping overboard. Of the one hundred and seventy-five officers and men, only twenty-five escaped uninjured. Commander Kilty, as the result of his injuries, had to suffer the amputation of his left hand.

The 25th of June saw Farragut's fleet below Vicksburg again, and three days later he had demonstrated the fact that he could pass by the batteries. On July 1st, Flag-Officer Davis' forces had joined those from the mouth of the Mississippi, above the city. As the combined fleets lay anchored along the banks, three or four miles south of where the Yazoo River debouches into the Mississippi, news was brought of the completion of an iron-clad ram up the Yazoo, of which the Confederates expected much. A reconnoitering expedition was sent up to search for her on the 15th of July, composed of the *Carondelet, Tyler,* and the ram *Queen of the West.* The results, to put it briefly, were astonishing, because the *Arkansas,* for this was the name of the giant ram, not only met them and drove the little squadron down the stream, but passed through the whole fleet lying in the Mississippi, entirely unaware of her coming, every vessel being at anchor, and only one, the captured *General Bragg,* having steam up. Having successfully run the gantlet, much to the mortification of both Farragut and Davis, and to the great glory and honor of her commander, Isaac N. Brown, formerly of the United States navy, the *Arkansas* took refuge under the Vicksburg batteries.

In order to retrieve the error of having been caught napping, Farragut determined to follow the *Arkansas* and destroy her if possible. Immediately all of his vessels were ordered to get up their anchors, and with the ram *Sumter* in company, she having been detached by Flag-Officer Davis, the fleet steamed down the river. It was so dark when they passed the city that the *Arkansas* could not be made out with any distinctness; but one shot struck her. In thus running the batteries for the fourth time, Farragut lost five killed and sixteen wounded. Never again were any of his ships to appear above Vicksburg. A

THE TRANSPORT "BLACK HAWK" AFTER HER FIERY TEST—MAY, 1864

The vessel shows the treatment accorded the thirty army transports which, convoyed by Porter's gunboats, went up the Red River in the futile expedition, the object of which was to reach Shreveport. The stacks and pilot-house of the "Black Hawk" have been riddled with Confederate bullets, and she shows the evidences of the continuous struggle through which the fleet passed in the retreat from Grand Ecore. For nearly a month the Federal vessels worked their way slowly down the river. The water was falling rapidly and the vessels, as they nosed their way through the shallow and unfamiliar channel, were constantly running aground. As the military forces had withdrawn to Alexandria, the Confederates, who lined both banks of the river, seized every opportunity to attack the discomfited vessels, and almost daily attempts were made to damage or capture them. The river was full of snags and the vessels had to be lightened; they were "jumped" over sand-bars and logs, fighting every inch of the difficult and laborious journey. Even Admiral Porter himself described the obstacles to be overcome as enough to appall the stoutest heart.

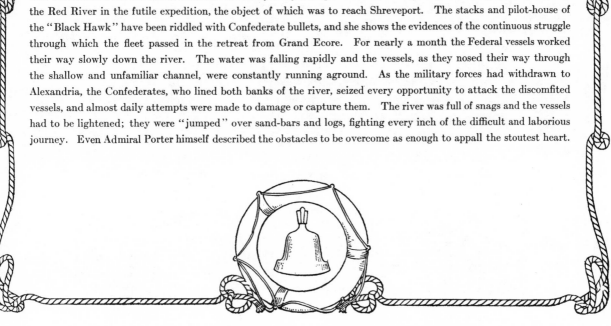

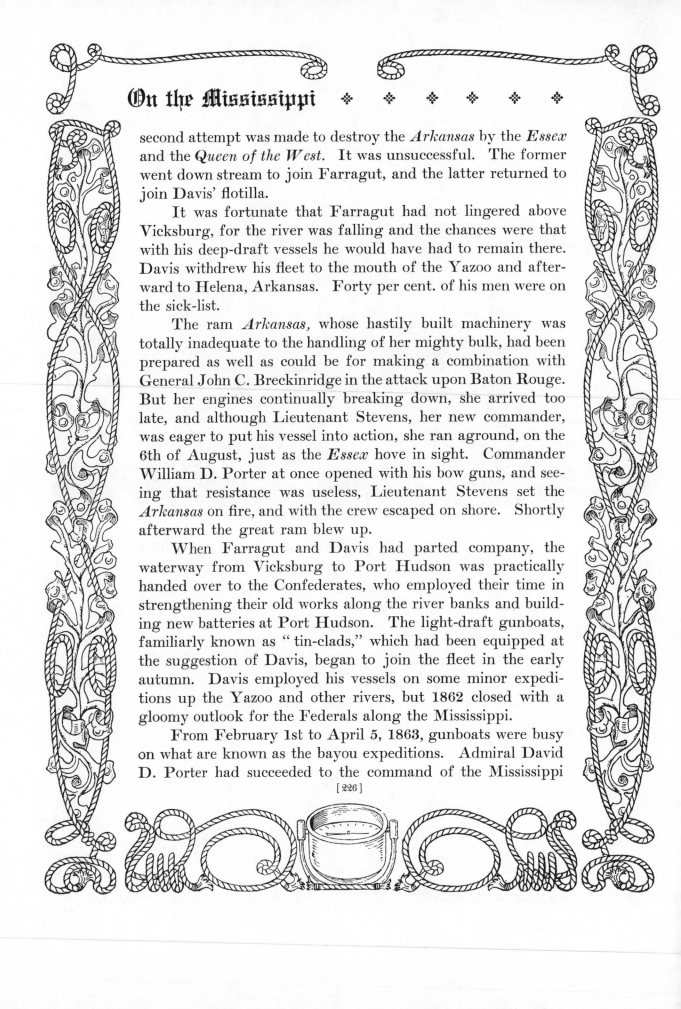

second attempt was made to destroy the *Arkansas* by the *Essex* and the *Queen of the West*. It was unsuccessful. The former went down stream to join Farragut, and the latter returned to join Davis' flotilla.

It was fortunate that Farragut had not lingered above Vicksburg, for the river was falling and the chances were that with his deep-draft vessels he would have had to remain there. Davis withdrew his fleet to the mouth of the Yazoo and afterward to Helena, Arkansas. Forty per cent. of his men were on the sick-list.

The ram *Arkansas,* whose hastily built machinery was totally inadequate to the handling of her mighty bulk, had been prepared as well as could be for making a combination with General John C. Breckinridge in the attack upon Baton Rouge. But her engines continually breaking down, she arrived too late, and although Lieutenant Stevens, her new commander, was eager to put his vessel into action, she ran aground, on the 6th of August, just as the *Essex* hove in sight. Commander William D. Porter at once opened with his bow guns, and seeing that resistance was useless, Lieutenant Stevens set the *Arkansas* on fire, and with the crew escaped on shore. Shortly afterward the great ram blew up.

When Farragut and Davis had parted company, the waterway from Vicksburg to Port Hudson was practically handed over to the Confederates, who employed their time in strengthening their old works along the river banks and building new batteries at Port Hudson. The light-draft gunboats, familiarly known as "tin-clads," which had been equipped at the suggestion of Davis, began to join the fleet in the early autumn. Davis employed his vessels on some minor expeditions up the Yazoo and other rivers, but 1862 closed with a gloomy outlook for the Federals along the Mississippi.

From February 1st to April 5, 1863, gunboats were busy on what are known as the bayou expeditions. Admiral David D. Porter had succeeded to the command of the Mississippi

A CRITICAL MOMENT IN THE RED RIVER EXPEDITION OF APRIL, 1864—FEDERAL TRANSPORTS BELOW THE FALLS

On the second Red River expedition, in 1864, Alexandria was garrisoned and made the effort that base for the army and navy operating both above and below that point, in the effort that had for its ultimate object the recovery of Texas to the Union. The fleet under Admiral Porter started up the Red River from Vicksburg with the transports carrying A. J. Smith's column of 10,000 men. Fort De Russy was captured, and Alexandria and Natchitoches fell into Union hands as they advanced. Banks with his army arrived a week later. At Sabine Cross Roads the vanguard met the Confederates in force. Sufficient care had not been taken to keep the several Union bodies together, and the Confederates under General Taylor defeated Franklin April 8th, and drove him back with a loss of 3,000 out of 11,000 engaged. At Pleasant Hill, A. J. Smith made a stand on April 9th, but was unable to hold his own. An immediate retreat was made, without waiting to bury the dead, and the fleet came near being cut off by low water at Alexandria, but the ingenuity of Colonel Bailey in constructing a dam and water-way enabled it to escape. In the picture the level in front of the hotel is piled with ammunition and supplies—elaborate preparations all wasted.

ENTRAPPED ABOVE THE FALLS—GLOOMY DAYS OF WAITING AND NARROW ESCAPES

Here lies a part of the unlucky fleet that Admiral Porter came near losing in the fruitless expedition up the Red River, which imperilled some of the most valuable gunboats possessed by the Federal navy. First in line is the tow-boat "Brown"; next the steamer "Benefit," whose escape the month before was hair-breadth; then the tug "Dahlia," the tender to Porter's flagship, while the ironclads "Neosho" and "Chillicothe" bring up the rear. The expedition on the part of the navy was undertaken in the assurance that the Red River would, according to its custom, rise at this season of the year. For twenty years it had never failed to rise, but now, in 1864, it did exactly the opposite. Only the light-draft gunboats could be run above the falls by the end of March. Since it was rumored that the Confederates had some formidable ironclads up the Red River, the gunboat "Eastport" was at last hauled over the rocks of the rapids by main strength to lead the expedition. It proved to be her last; she grounded on the return from Grand Ecore, and after

THE FEDERAL FLOTILLA ABOVE ALEXANDRIA, HELD BY THE LOW WATER OF MAY, 1864

heroic efforts to get her off, during which the Confederates kept up constant fighting, she had to be destroyed and abandoned. It looked for a time as if the other vessels of Porter's fleet were to meet the same fate. General Banks had been ordered to give up the expedition and was chafing to get his troops in motion. Meanwhile the officers and men of the navy were working with characteristic courage and determination to save their vessels, now exposed to constant attacks from the Confederates, who grew more and more threatening. The little steamer "Benefit," seen in the picture, had a narrow escape at Grappe's Bluff, where she was attacked on the evening of April 10th, and in less than twenty minutes lost forty-five of her eighty men. Gloomy indeed were the days of waiting above the falls, for both officers and men. One difficulty and disaster followed another. It seemed almost certain that the fated expedition would cost the navy its heaviest and most humiliating loss during the war, but courage and determination won out

HELP AT HAND—THE GUNBOAT "SIGNAL" TOWING MATERIALS FOR THE DAM

On the 1st of May, 1864, thousands of men were set to work upon the famous dam by which Bailey raised the water sufficiently to enable the entrapped vessels to get below the falls. The "Signal" is busily at work towing materials to fill the cribs. Stones were gathered, deserted brick buildings were pulled down, and a large sugar-house a mile below the falls was wrecked and its woodwork, together with its machinery and kettles, were towed up to become a part of the dam. More dangerous work waited the "Signal," however, for on May 4th she and the "Covington," the best two gunboats below the falls, were despatched to convoy the transport "Warner," on which was Lieutenant Simpson of Banks' staff, bearing despatches to Grant, Sherman, and Rosecrans. Near David's Ferry the two gallant little gunboats fought for five hours, on May 5th, against tremendous odds. The Confederates had posted twenty pieces of artillery on the river bank, and against their fire the gunboats stood up bravely. The odds were too heavily against them, however, and the "Covington" was at last abandoned and destroyed, while the "Signal" fell a captive to the Confederates, who sunk her in the channel as an obstruction. Admiral Porter said: "Many of the actions heralded to the world during the late war were much less worthy of notice than this contest between two little gunboats only musket-proof and twenty pieces of artillery."

TRANSPORTS WAITING FOR THE UNION ARMY

THE ARMY SAVING THE NAVY IN MAY, 1864

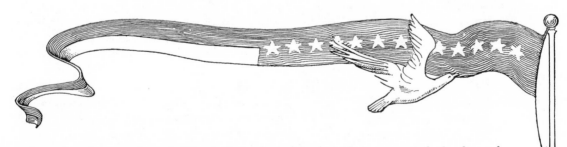

Here the army is saving the navy by a brilliant piece of engineering that prevented the loss of a fleet worth $2,000,000. The Red River expedition was one of the most humiliating ever undertaken by the Federals. Porter's fleet, which had so boldly advanced above the falls at Alexandria, was ordered back, only to find that the river was so low as to imprison twelve vessels. Lieut.-Colonel Joseph Bailey, acting engineer of the Nineteenth Corps, obtained permission to build a dam in order to make possible the passage of the fleet. Begun on April 30, 1864, the work was finished on the 8th of May, almost entirely by the soldiers, working incessantly day and night, often up to their necks in water and under the broiling sun. Bailey succeeded in turning the whole current into one channel and the squadron passed below to safety. Not often have inland lumbermen been the means of saving a navy.

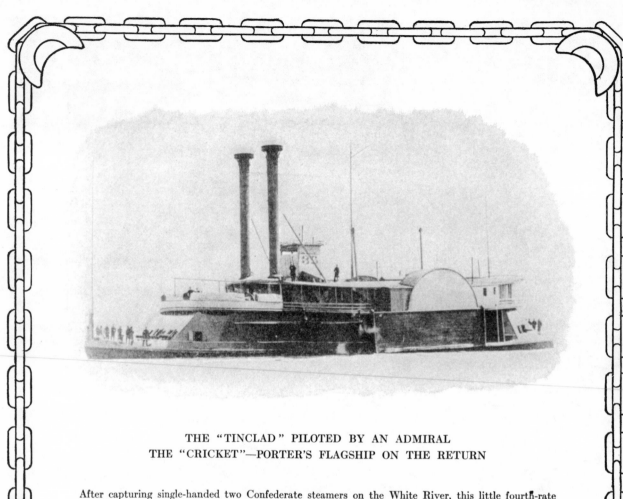

THE "TINCLAD" PILOTED BY AN ADMIRAL
THE "CRICKET"—PORTER'S FLAGSHIP ON THE RETURN

After capturing single-handed two Confederate steamers on the White River, this little fourth-rate vessel took an active part in the bombardment of Vicksburg under command of Acting Master A. R. Langthorne. On the Red River expedition came her great opportunity for distinction. She was chosen by Admiral Porter as his flagship for the return, as the falling water made it necessary to send the heavier vessels ahead with all speed. Porter with the "Cricket," "Fort Hindman," and "Juliet" remained behind to assist Lieutenant-Commander Phelps in his efforts to save the unlucky "Eastport." After getting the injured vessel about fifty miles down the river from Grand Écore, the tinclads were compelled to abandon her, since the river banks were now swarming with hostile forces bent on the capture of the entire squadron. About twenty miles below the wreck of the "Eastport," a Confederate battery had been planted and opened on the "tinclads." The other vessels retreated up-stream, but Porter on the "Cricket" forced his way through. It was all over in five minutes, but in that time the frail vessel was struck 38 times, and 19 shells pierced her. The pilot was wounded and Admiral Porter with great coolness and skill seized the wheel and saved the vessel. So furious was the fight while it lasted that out of the "Cricket's" crew of 50, twelve were killed and nineteen wounded.

FEDERAL GUNBOATS ON THE UPPER TENNESSEE

Federal success at Chattanooga made it important to patrol the upper Tennessee River, and a number of small gunboats were built for that purpose. They were actively engaged above Mussel Shoals in keeping open communications and convoying loaded transports. The "General Grant," under Acting Ensign J. Watson, with the other sturdy little vessels of the land-locked flotilla, aided in restoring order in the thinly settled districts along the river. She and the "General Burnside" engaged a battery which the Confederates had erected above Decatur, Ala., Dec. 12, 1864. On the 22d the "General Thomas" had a brush with some Confederate troops near the same place and they returned her fire with fury. Early in January of 1865 the "Grant," single-handed, silenced Confederate batteries at Guntersville and Beard's Bluff, Ala. Returning a few days later, she destroyed the entire town of Guntersville as punishment for hostile demonstrations against the gunboats. Thus these little vessels were kept busily at work till the close of the war. The "General Sherman" was commanded by Acting Master J. W. Morehead; her executive officer was G. L. McClung, by whose courtesy these fine pictures appear here. The vessels shown above, as they lay in the Tennessee near Bridgeport in March, 1865, are, from left to right, the "General Sherman," No. 60; the "General Thomas," No. 61; the "General Grant," No. 62; and the "General Burnside," No. 63; all named after the military leaders whose strategy had resulted in the recovery of Tennessee to the Union.

GOVERNMENT STEAMBOAT USED ON THE UPPER TENNESSEE IN 1864-65

On the Mississippi ❖ ❖ ❖ ❖ ❖ ❖

Squadron, as the Western Flotilla was now called, and had control of the river between Vicksburg and Port Hudson. Farragut once more entered the river and ran two vessels of his squadron past the works at Port Hudson on the 14th of March, 1863. In doing so, however, the old side-wheeler *Mississippi* grounded under the guns of the fort, where she was set on fire and abandoned. For weeks now the fleet was employed in assisting Grant's army that was slowly closing in upon Vicksburg, which stronghold was to fall on the 4th of July.

The expedition to Shreveport up the Red River, where the fleet under Porter cooperated with the troops under Banks, was a dire failure and came near resulting in a great loss to the squadron. The water in March, 1864, was exceedingly low, and many of the deep-draft vessels could not get above the rapids at Alexandria. However, with some thirty transports, fourteen of the gunboats were dragged up the stream, only to find themselves, when they wished to return at the end of April, helpless above the falls by the receding water. Their rescue, through the aid of the genius, resource, and indefatigable efforts of Lieutenant-Colonel Joseph Bailey, of the Fourth Wisconsin Volunteers, makes a thrilling story. He succeeded in damming the river, thus banking up the water, and by the 13th of May, amid the mighty cheers of the spectators and the lumbermen from Maine and Wisconsin who had built the helpful barrier, the twelve vessels which had been caught had passed down to safety. After Port Hudson fell, except for the Red River expedition, minor skirmishers, and the shelling of guerillas and batteries along the wooded shores, the operations of the navy on the Mississippi and its tributaries were practically over.

When the Federals occupied Chattanooga after the battle of Chickamauga, late in 1863, they needed gunboats on the upper Tennessee River, but none of Admiral Porter's fleet could cross the Mussel Shoals. So several light-draft vessels were built near Bridgeport. They were useful to the army, but saw little active service.

IX

THE ACTIONS WITH THE FORTS

A NAVY GUN ON LAND, 1863

THIS PIECE WAS PLACED ON MORRIS ISLAND IN THE ATTEMPT
TO REDUCE THE CHARLESTON FORTS

THE ACTIONS WITH THE FORTS

By Captain O. E. Hunt, U. S. A., and James Barnes

THE reduction and final capture of the Confederate strongholds that guarded the important ports of entry of the Confederacy on the Atlantic coast and the Gulf were in every case a cooperation between the navy and the army, and to both belong the honor of the successful outcome, which, singly and alone, neither branch of the service could have accomplished.

The old brick and mortar fortress of Pulaski guarded the entrance to the Savannah River. Late in 1861, almost entirely through the use of the navy, the Federals had control of the Atlantic coast, and in the vicinity of Savannah their ships were patrolling the waters of Ossabaw and Wassaw sounds, and their gunboats had penetrated up the Edisto River in the direction of the city. But Pulaski's frowning guns afforded shelter for any blockade-runners that might succeed in eluding the blockading fleet. It was necessary to reduce this strong fortress before a stop could be put to the attempts of the venturesome runners. General Q. A. Gillmore directed the placing of batteries of rifled guns and mortars upon Big Tybee Island, and by the end of February, 1862, other batteries were erected in the rear of the fort, completely enfilading it.

On the 10th of April, 1862, thirty-six heavy rifled cannon and mortars began the bombardment, and after two days of uninterrupted firing, although the fort was gallantly defended, it was so badly battered that it was forced to surrender. But Fort McAllister, at the mouth of the Ogeechee, did not fall until W. T. Sherman had arrived at the end of his march from Atlanta and General Hazen's troops carried the battery by assault.

THE DEMOLISHED BARRIER—FORT PULASKI

These three pictures speak eloquently of the ruin wrought by the combined efforts of the army and navy to gain possession of Fort Pulaski. At the left an 8-inch smooth-bore points upward as the Confederates swung it for use as a mortar against the Federal batteries. Beside it lies one of the mortars, dismounted and rendered useless by the fire from the Federal batteries, while in the lower picture the huge breaches made in the walls of the fort are vividly apparent. It was no easy task to accomplish all this. Without the assistance of the navy it would have been impossible. The "web-footed" gunboats, as Lincoln called them, formed an essential part of the land expedition; floundering through mud, they protected the troops from Tattnall's flotilla while guns were dragged with difficulty over the marshy surface of Jones Island and placed in position. The doomed garrison refused to surrender on April 10, 1862, and for two days withstood a terrible bombardment from the thirty-six heavy-rifled cannon and mortars. Only when the battered fort became utterly untenable was it surrendered on April 12th to the besiegers that surrounded it, ready to open fire again.

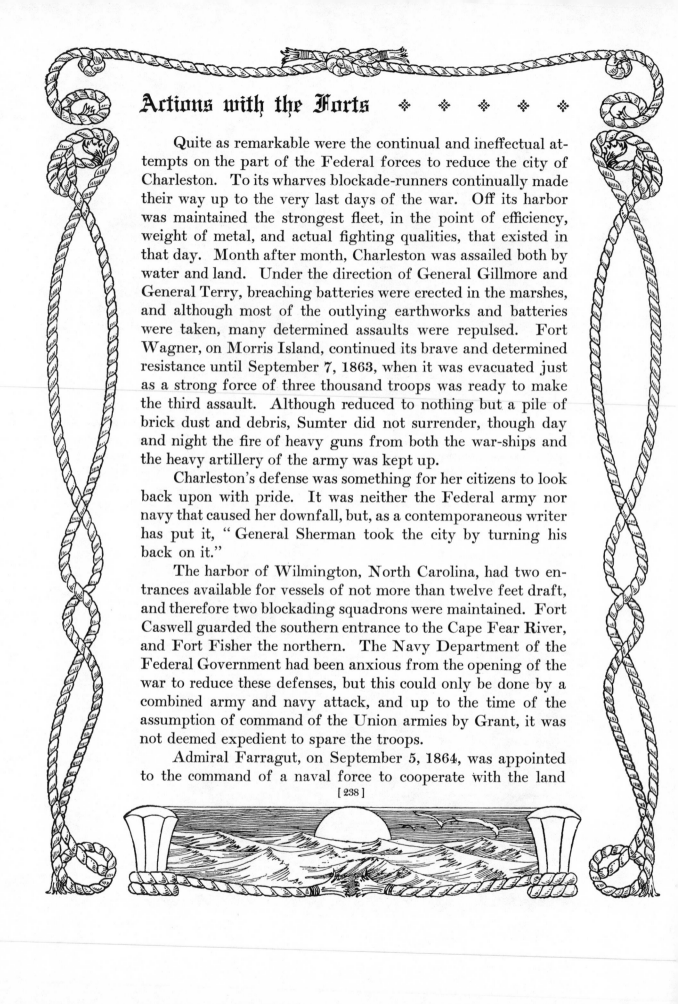

Actions with the Forts   ✦   ✦   ✦   ✦   ✦

Quite as remarkable were the continual and ineffectual attempts on the part of the Federal forces to reduce the city of Charleston. To its wharves blockade-runners continually made their way up to the very last days of the war. Off its harbor was maintained the strongest fleet, in the point of efficiency, weight of metal, and actual fighting qualities, that existed in that day. Month after month, Charleston was assailed both by water and land. Under the direction of General Gillmore and General Terry, breaching batteries were erected in the marshes, and although most of the outlying earthworks and batteries were taken, many determined assaults were repulsed. Fort Wagner, on Morris Island, continued its brave and determined resistance until September 7, 1863, when it was evacuated just as a strong force of three thousand troops was ready to make the third assault. Although reduced to nothing but a pile of brick dust and debris, Sumter did not surrender, though day and night the fire of heavy guns from both the war-ships and the heavy artillery of the army was kept up.

Charleston's defense was something for her citizens to look back upon with pride. It was neither the Federal army nor navy that caused her downfall, but, as a contemporaneous writer has put it, "General Sherman took the city by turning his back on it."

The harbor of Wilmington, North Carolina, had two entrances available for vessels of not more than twelve feet draft, and therefore two blockading squadrons were maintained. Fort Caswell guarded the southern entrance to the Cape Fear River, and Fort Fisher the northern. The Navy Department of the Federal Government had been anxious from the opening of the war to reduce these defenses, but this could only be done by a combined army and navy attack, and up to the time of the assumption of command of the Union armies by Grant, it was not deemed expedient to spare the troops.

Admiral Farragut, on September 5, 1864, was appointed to the command of a naval force to cooperate with the land

HEROIC SACRIFICES AT CHARLESTON—THE FLOATING BATTERY AND THE "CHICORA"

It would have been almost sacrilege to retouch in any way the dim and faded photographs from which these pictures were made. Taken by a Confederate photographer at Charleston in the early part of the war, long lost to view, they preserve sights that inspired the men and women of the South with an intensity of purpose rarely exampled in history. In the upper picture is the famous floating battery built by subscription by the women of Charleston. Its guns were first fired in the attack on Fort Sumter that began the war. From that time forth every nerve was being strained by the Confederacy to put an ironclad flotilla in commission. South Carolina was conspicuous in its efforts to this end. Flag-Officer Duncan N. Ingraham superintended the navy-yard at Charleston and under his direction the "Palmetto State" and the "Chicora" were built. The keel of the latter was laid behind the Charleston post-office in March, 1862, and she was launched the following August. Five hundred tons of iron were required for her armor and the country was scoured by willing searchers for every scrap of metal that could be melted up. On January 31, 1863, the "Chicora" and the "Palmetto State" suddenly came down from Charleston and disabled both the "Mercedita" and the "Keystone State," receiving the former's surrender.

forces for this purpose, General Grant having signified his belief that the army could be ready by the 1st of October of that year. Admiral Farragut's health not permitting his assumption of this duty, it was assigned to Admiral Porter.

For the first attempt at the destruction of Fort Fisher there was used the most gigantic torpedo ever employed in warfare. This consisted of an old gunboat, the *Louisiana,* changed to resemble a blockade-runner and filled with powder. Much doubt as to the value of the experiment was entertained by experienced officers, but it was believed to be worth a trial. On the evening of December 23, 1864, she was towed in almost to the beach, the rest of the fleet keeping well off the coast. Arriving near the beach, she was cast off, and, under her own steam, ran up on the sand three hundred yards from the fort about 11:30 P.M. The slow fuse was lit, the crew deserted her, and at 1:40 A.M. she blew up. The explosion had not the slightest effect on the works. It was a complete failure.

About 12:40 P.M. that day (the 24th) the largest fleet ever assembled under the flag of the United States up to that time, began the naval bombardment. Admiral Porter had under his command fifty-seven vessels, with a total of six hundred and twenty-seven guns.

The garrison had only a limited amount of ammunition, and its commander, Colonel Lamb, gave orders that each gun should be fired only once every half-hour, except by special instructions, and unless the Federals should attempt to run past the works, in which case each gun-commander was to use his piece to its full capacity. This slow fire caused the admiral to believe that the works had been silenced, and he signaled to keep up only a moderate fire to hold down the activities of the garrison and as a notification to General Butler that he could bring in the transports with the troops.

The landing and attack took place on Christmas Day. The fire from the ships was slow and methodical, as at target practice. Great holes were dug in the parapets by the gigantic

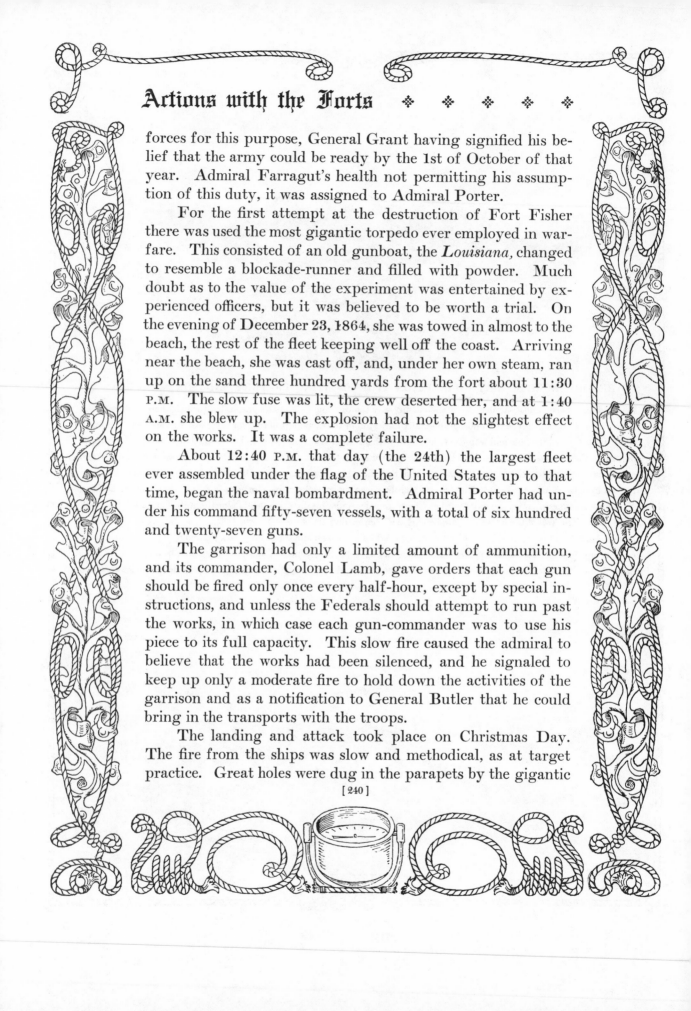

VIEW FROM FORT McALLISTER—UNION VESSELS IN THE ROADSTEAD

In this picture of December, 1864, the Federal vessels lie peaceful before the fort so impregnable to their attacks early the preceding year. The shore appearing below was lined with Georgia sharpshooters by Captain George W. Anderson, Jr., commander of the fort when the monitor "Montauk" and four gunboats advanced to the attack of Feb. 1, 1863. The "Montauk," under Commander John Lorimer Worden, hero of the original "Monitor," was the first Federal ironclad to arrive in Ossabaw Sound. Early on January 27th, it furiously attacked the fort. On this occasion the Federal vessels did not attempt to cross the line of piles and torpedoes. The Confederates were confident that in the second attack attempts would be made to land boat-parties to assault the works, and the sharpshooters were posted to prevent this. Commander Worden and his consorts, however, contented themselves with engaging the fort with their heavy guns and mortars. Although the Federals kept up a terrible fire, it failed to do more damage to the fort than could be repaired at night. The Confederate guns responded vigorously in kind, and the "Montauk" was struck forty-six times.

IN FRONT OF THE PARAPET—FORT McALLISTER

THE "HARTFORD" JUST AFTER THE BATTLE OF MOBILE BAY

This vivid photograph, taken in Mobile Bay by a war-time photographer from New Orleans, was presented by Captain Drayton of the "Hartford" to T. W. Eastman, U. S. N., whose family has courteously allowed its reproduction here. Never was exhibited a more superb morale than on the "Hartford" as she steamed in line to the attack of Fort Morgan at Mobile Bay on the morning of August 5, 1864. Every man was at his station thinking his own thoughts in the suspense of that moment. On the quarterdeck stood Captain Percival Drayton and his staff. Near them was the chief - quartermaster, John H. Knowles, ready to hoist the signals that would convey Farragut's orders to the fleet. The admiral himself was in the port

QUARTERMASTER KNOWLES

main shrouds twenty-five feet above the deck. All was silence aboard till the "Hartford" was in easy range of the fort. Then the great broadsides of the old ship began to take their part in the awful cannonade. During the early part of the action Captain Drayton, fearing that some damage to the rigging might pitch Farragut overboard, sent Knowles on his famous mission. "I went up," said the old sailor, "with a piece of lead line and made it fast to one of the forward shrouds, and then took it around the admiral to the after shroud, making it fast there. The admiral said, 'Never mind, I'm all right,' but I went ahead and obeyed orders." Later Farragut, undoing the lashing with his own hands, climbed higher still.

FARRAGUT AT THE PINNACLE OF HIS FAME

Leaning on the cannon, Commander David Glasgow Farragut and Captain Percival Drayton, chief of staff, stand on the deck of the "Hartford," after the victory in Mobile Bay, of August, 1864. When Gustavus V. Fox, Assistant Secretary of the Navy, proposed the capture of New Orleans from the southward he was regarded as utterly foolhardy. All that was needed, however, to make Fox's plan successful was the man with spirit enough to undertake it and judgment sufficient to carry it out. Here on the deck of the fine new sloop-of-war that had been assigned to him as flagship, stands the man who had just accomplished a greater feat that made him a world figure as famous as Nelson. The Confederacy had found its great general among its own people, but the great admiral of the war, although of Southern birth, had refused to fight against the flag for which, as a boy in the War of 1812, he had seen men die. Full of the fighting spirit of the old navy, he was able to achieve the first great victory that gave new hope to the Federal cause. Percival Drayton was also a Southerner, a South Carolinian, whose brothers and uncles were fighting for the South.

WHERE THE CONFEDERATES FOUGHT FARRAGUT SHOT FOR SHOT

From these walls the gunners of Brigadier-General Richard L. Page, C. S. A., sighted their pieces and gave the Federal vessels shot for shot. It was a fight at close range, since the obstructions in the channel compelled the fleet to pass close under the guns of the fort. During the hour while the vessels were within range, the fort fired 491 shots, about eight a minute. When the fight was thickest the Confederate gunners fired even far more rapidly, enveloping the vessels, and especially the "Hartford" and the "Brooklyn," in a veritable hail of missiles. The fort was an old five-sided brick works mounting its guns in three tiers. It was built on the site of the little redoubt (Fort Bowyer) that had repelled the British fleet in 1814. Within the fort were mounted thirty-two smooth-bores and eight rifles.

INTERIOR OF FORT MORGAN, MOBILE BAY, IN 1864

The entire front wall was reënforced by enormous piles of sand-bags to enable its four feet eight inches of solid brick to withstand the broadsides of the fleet. Although the other fortifications at the entrance to Mobile Bay surrendered the day after the battle, it took more than Farragut's broadsides to reduce Fort Morgan. A siege-train had to be brought from New Orleans and a land attack made by the troops under General Gordon Granger, August, 22, 1864. Not till 3,000 missiles had been hurled into and around the fort by the combined guns of the army and navy did the brave garrison of Fort Morgan surrender after a gallant defense of twelve hours. In the picture some of the damaging effects of the terrific gunnery of the fleet are evident in the sea wall.

shells, until the whole face of the works began to take on the irregularity of the neighboring sand-dunes. The troops, about fifteen hundred men under command of General Weitzel, advanced their skirmish lines to within about seventy-five yards of the fort, capturing a small outwork and over two hundred men. By a personal reconnaissance, Weitzel ascertained that the two days' terrible bombardment by the fleet and the previous explosion of the powder-ship had done no practical injury to the parapets and interior. He therefore reported to Butler and to Admiral Porter that the works could not be taken by assault.

That evening, General Butler notified Admiral Porter that he was convinced that it was impossible to take the fort by assault as the naval fire had not damaged the works, and that he proposed to withdraw all his men and return to Fortress Monroe, which he did on the 27th. This ended the first combined attempt against Fort Fisher.

Admiral Porter was much disappointed at Butler's leaving him, and began to fear that the Confederates would abandon Fort Fisher and entrench themselves further up the river out of reach of his guns. So he attempted to deceive his foe. " I thought it best," he says, " under the circumstances, to let the enemy think we had abandoned the expedition entirely, and sent the fleet to a rendezvous off Beaufort, one or two at a time, to look as if they were crippled."

Evidently the Confederates did not anticipate the early return of the fleet. The supporting army was withdrawn to a point sixteen miles north of Wilmington. No lookout was kept up the coast, and, in consequence, the first tidings of the return were sent from Fort Fisher itself, when, on the evening of the 12th of January, 1865, its few defenders saw from the ramparts the Federal fleet returning.

At that time there were but eight hundred men in the garrison, and about one hundred of them were unfit for duty. The principal, and almost the only, organization represented was the Thirty-sixth North Carolina regiment. Sunrise revealed

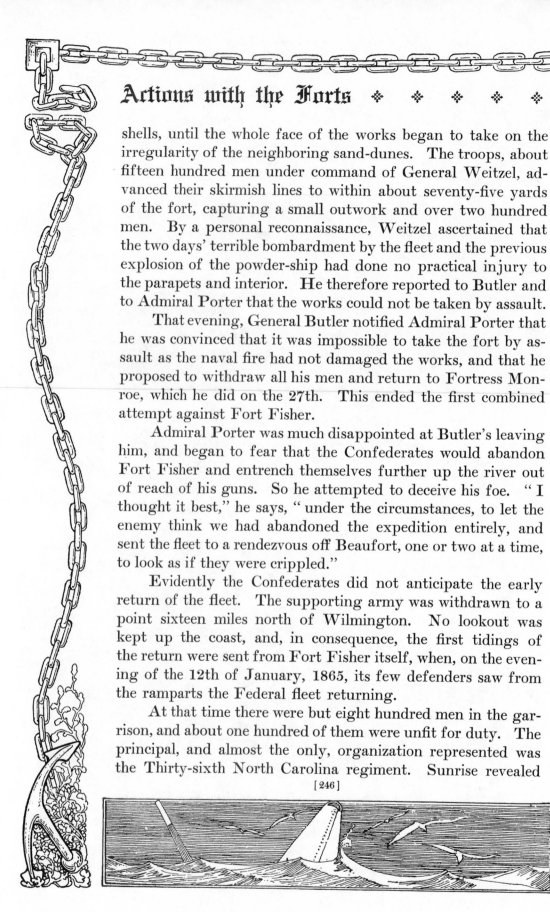

FORT MORGAN—A BOMBARDMENT BRAVELY ANSWERED

The battered walls of Fort Morgan, in 1864, tell of a terrific smashing by the Federal navy. But the gallant Confederates returned the blows with amazing courage and skill; the rapidity and accuracy of their fire was rarely equalled in the war. In the terrible conflict the "Hartford" was struck twenty times, the "Brooklyn" thirty, the "Octorora" seventeen, the "Metacomet" eleven, the "Lackawanna" five, the "Ossipee" four, the "Monongahela" five, the "Kennebec" two, and the "Galena" seven. Of the monitors the "Chickasaw" was struck three times, the "Manhattan" nine, and the "Winnebago" nineteen. The total loss in the Federal fleet was 52 killed and 170 wounded, while on the Confederate gunboats 12 were killed and 20 wounded. The night after the battle the "Metacomet" was turned into a hospital-ship and the wounded of both sides were taken to Pensacola. The pilot of the captured "Tennessee" guided the Federal ship through the torpedoes, and as she was leaving Pensacola on her return trip Midshipman Carter of the "Tennessee," who also was on the "Metacomet," called out from the wharf: "Don't attempt to fire No. 2 gun (of the "Tennessee"), as there is a shell jammed in the bore, and the gun will burst and kill some one." All felt there had been enough bloodshed.

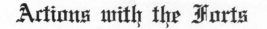

to their astonished gaze a new and what appeared to them a more tremendous aggregation of fighting ships than before, with transports carrying troops. General Alfred H. Terry, with a force of about eight thousand men, had been assigned, this time, to the duty of cooperating with the fleet for the reduction of Fort Fisher. The fleet consisted of forty-nine vessels of the heaviest class, with six hundred and twenty-seven guns.

On the morning of the 13th, the fleet stood close in and engaged the batteries, whose guns replied under the same instructions as during the first bombardment: that is, to husband their ammunition by firing very slowly, except when necessary to concentrate on a special vessel. During the day and night of the 13th, about seven hundred men arrived as reenforcements, making in all about fifteen hundred in the garrison.

The bombardment lasted during the 13th and 14th without abatement. The Federal troops landed on the 13th at a point about four miles north of the fort, and nine days' supplies were sent ashore with them. The advance on the forts was commenced immediately.

When the sun rose on the 15th of December, the streams of shell from the vessels were redoubled, and before noon but one good gun was left on the land face of the fort. By that time the casualties had increased so that the defense had less than twelve hundred men to hold the parapets. Soon after noon a small reenforcement of about three hundred and fifty men, sent by Bragg, succeeded in reaching the works. The defenders could see the assaulting columns getting ready to deliver their attack. A column of sailors and marines was making its way toward the sea face, to cooperate with the infantry on the land side.

In the mean time, the assault on the land face by the infantry was pushed strongly over the works into the interior, taking one section after another against a most obstinate defense. Colonel Lamb was badly wounded, as was General Whiting, the district commander, who was present but had

THE BRAVEST OF THE BRAVE—THE CONFEDERATE IRONCLAD RAM "TENNESSEE"

Mobile Bay, on the morning of August 5, 1864, was the arena of more conspicuous heroism than marked any naval battle-ground of the entire war. Among all the daring deeds of that day stands out superlatively the gallant manner in which Admiral Franklin Buchanan, C. S. N., fought his vessel, the "Tennessee." "You shall not have it to say when you leave this vessel that you were not near enough to the enemy, for I will meet them, and then you can fight them alongside of their own ships; and if I fall, lay me on one side and go on with the fight." Thus Buchanan addressed his men, and then, taking his station in the pilot-house, he took his vessel into action. The Federal fleet carried more power for destruction than the combined English, French, and Spanish fleets at Trafalgar, and yet Buchanan made good his boast that he would fight alongside. No sooner had Farragut crossed the torpedoes than Buchanan matched that deed, running through the entire line of Federal vessels, braving their broadsides, and coming to close quarters with most of them. Then the "Tennessee" ran under the guns of Fort Morgan for a breathing space. In half an hour she was steaming up the bay to fight the entire squadron single-handed. Such boldness was scarce believable, for Buchanan had now not alone wooden ships to contend with, as when in the "Merrimac" he had dismayed the Federals in Hampton Roads. Three powerful monitors were to oppose him at point-blank range. For nearly an hour the gunners in the "Tennessee" fought, breathing powder-smoke amid an atmosphere superheated to 120 degrees. Buchanan was serving a gun himself when he was wounded and carried to the surgeon's table below. Captain Johnston fought on for another twenty minutes, and then the "Tennessee," with her rudder and engines useless and unable to fire a gun, was surrendered, after a reluctant consent had been wrung from Buchanan, as he lay on the operating table.

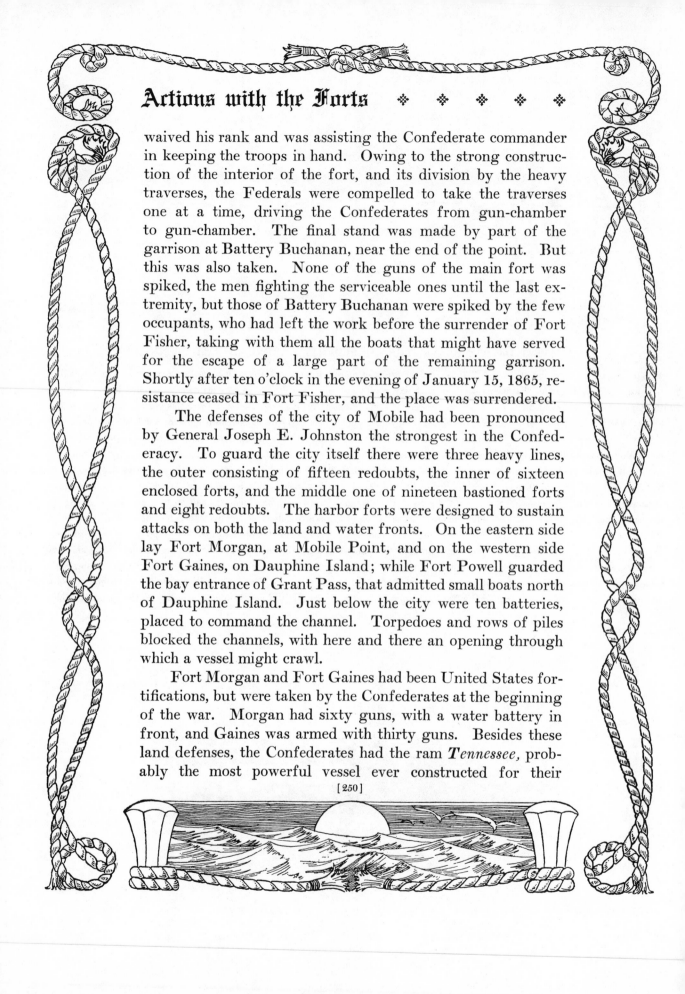

waived his rank and was assisting the Confederate commander in keeping the troops in hand. Owing to the strong construction of the interior of the fort, and its division by the heavy traverses, the Federals were compelled to take the traverses one at a time, driving the Confederates from gun-chamber to gun-chamber. The final stand was made by part of the garrison at Battery Buchanan, near the end of the point. But this was also taken. None of the guns of the main fort was spiked, the men fighting the serviceable ones until the last extremity, but those of Battery Buchanan were spiked by the few occupants, who had left the work before the surrender of Fort Fisher, taking with them all the boats that might have served for the escape of a large part of the remaining garrison. Shortly after ten o'clock in the evening of January 15, 1865, resistance ceased in Fort Fisher, and the place was surrendered.

The defenses of the city of Mobile had been pronounced by General Joseph E. Johnston the strongest in the Confederacy. To guard the city itself there were three heavy lines, the outer consisting of fifteen redoubts, the inner of sixteen enclosed forts, and the middle one of nineteen bastioned forts and eight redoubts. The harbor forts were designed to sustain attacks on both the land and water fronts. On the eastern side lay Fort Morgan, at Mobile Point, and on the western side Fort Gaines, on Dauphine Island; while Fort Powell guarded the bay entrance of Grant Pass, that admitted small boats north of Dauphine Island. Just below the city were ten batteries, placed to command the channel. Torpedoes and rows of piles blocked the channels, with here and there an opening through which a vessel might crawl.

Fort Morgan and Fort Gaines had been United States fortifications, but were taken by the Confederates at the beginning of the war. Morgan had sixty guns, with a water battery in front, and Gaines was armed with thirty guns. Besides these land defenses, the Confederates had the ram *Tennessee,* probably the most powerful vessel ever constructed for their

THE "MONONGAHELA"—A FEARLESS WOODEN SHIP

To this "heart of oak" belongs the distinction of being the first vessel to ram the huge Confederate ironclad "Tennessee." After Farragut, crying, "Damn the torpedoes!" had astounded both the Confederates and his own fleet by running the "Hartford" right through the line of submarine volcanoes, the "Tennessee" moved down with the intention of ramming the wooden ships in turn. She missed the "Hartford" and then the "Richmond," which escaped across the line of torpedoes like the flagship. In attempting to ram the "Lacka-wanna," the Confederate ironclad swung abeam of the channel, exposing her side full and fair to the "Mo-nongahela," which had been fitted with an artificial iron prow. Commander Strong endeavored to seize the opportunity to ram; but, owing to the fact that the "Kennebec" was lashed to her side, the "Mononga-hela" could not attain full speed, and only a glancing blow was struck. Later, when the "Tennessee" came up single-handed to attack the fleet above the forts, Farragut ordered the wooden vessels to try the effect of ramming the ironclad. Again the "Monongahela" was the first to advance to the attack and succeeded in striking the "Tennessee" fair amidships. So violent was the shock that many of the men on both vessels were knocked down. The blow, which would have sunk any vessel in the Federal fleet, did no more harm to the "Tennessee" than it did to the "Monongahela." Her iron prow was wrenched off and the butt-ends of her bow planks were shattered, while only a small leak was started in the "Tennessee."

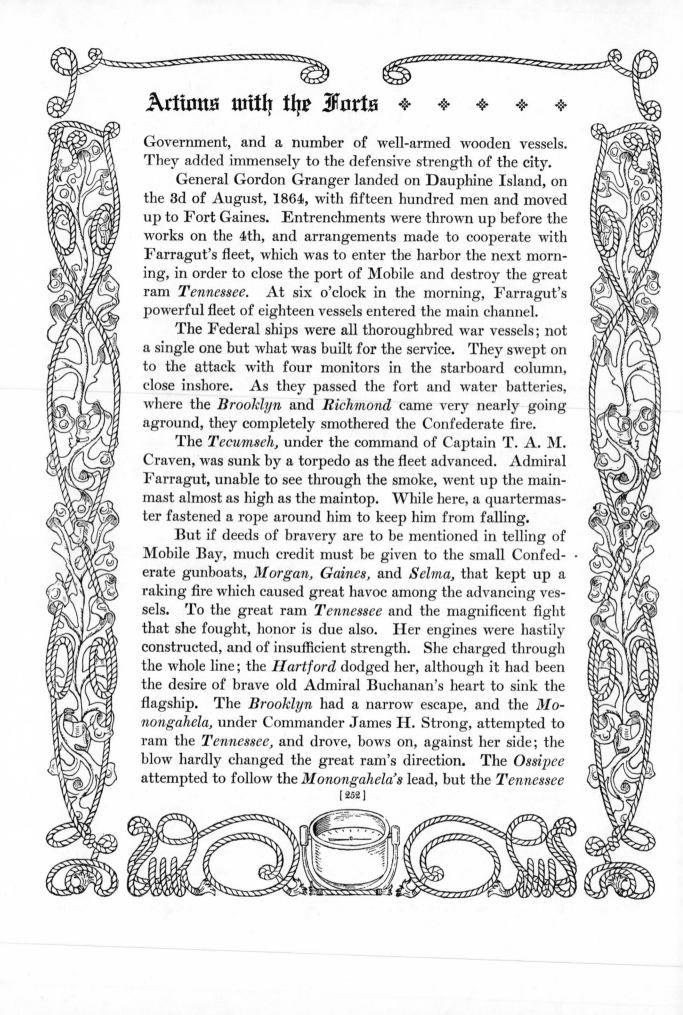

Actions with the Forts ✦ ✦ ✦ ✦ ✦

Government, and a number of well-armed wooden vessels. They added immensely to the defensive strength of the city.

General Gordon Granger landed on Dauphine Island, on the 3d of August, 1864, with fifteen hundred men and moved up to Fort Gaines. Entrenchments were thrown up before the works on the 4th, and arrangements made to cooperate with Farragut's fleet, which was to enter the harbor the next morning, in order to close the port of Mobile and destroy the great ram *Tennessee.* At six o'clock in the morning, Farragut's powerful fleet of eighteen vessels entered the main channel.

The Federal ships were all thoroughbred war vessels; not a single one but what was built for the service. They swept on to the attack with four monitors in the starboard column, close inshore. As they passed the fort and water batteries, where the *Brooklyn* and *Richmond* came very nearly going aground, they completely smothered the Confederate fire.

The *Tecumseh,* under the command of Captain T. A. M. Craven, was sunk by a torpedo as the fleet advanced. Admiral Farragut, unable to see through the smoke, went up the mainmast almost as high as the maintop. While here, a quartermaster fastened a rope around him to keep him from falling.

But if deeds of bravery are to be mentioned in telling of Mobile Bay, much credit must be given to the small Confederate gunboats, *Morgan, Gaines,* and *Selma,* that kept up a raking fire which caused great havoc among the advancing vessels. To the great ram *Tennessee* and the magnificent fight that she fought, honor is due also. Her engines were hastily constructed, and of insufficient strength. She charged through the whole line; the *Hartford* dodged her, although it had been the desire of brave old Admiral Buchanan's heart to sink the flagship. The *Brooklyn* had a narrow escape, and the *Monongahela,* under Commander James H. Strong, attempted to ram the *Tennessee,* and drove, bows on, against her side; the blow hardly changed the great ram's direction. The *Ossipee* attempted to follow the *Monongahela's* lead, but the *Tennessee*

LEADERS ON SEA AND LAND—FARRAGUT AND GRANGER AFTER THE BATTLE OF MOBILE BAY

This splendid picture shows the calm and finely-molded features of the great admiral just after the accomplishment of a feat which save in bravery o'er-topped his great achievement of the passage of the forts below New Orleans. There Farragut had done what was pronounced impossible, but at Mobile he had fought his way through dangers ten times more formidable. Here, with the modesty which ever characterized him, he sits within the captured Fort Gaines on Dauphin Island, discussing with General Gordon Granger plans for the combined attack by which Fort Morgan was taken on August 22, 1864. It was to Granger that Mobile finally surrendered.

passed between them, and made for the *Oneida,* which was not under steerageway.

It was at this exciting moment that the monitors drew up, and the *Winnebago,* forging ahead, took her position between the ram and her seemingly helpless prey. The Federal vessels had been hampered, in a measure, by being lashed side by side in couples, in the way that Farragut had run the batteries at Port Hudson, but now having passed the forts they began to cast off their lashings. Enabled, in the broader water, to maneuver and use their broadsides, they drove the little Confederate fleet before them, the *Selma* surrendering to the *Metacomet,* the *Gaines* being disabled and soon in flames. The *Morgan* sought the protection of Fort Morgan, and during the night steamed ahead to the inner harbor and anchored under the batteries protecting the city of Mobile. The Federal vessels, being now out of range of the forts, dropped anchor and their crews were sent to breakfast.

It was a meal that was never finished. Admiral Buchanan, who had passed through the whole Union line, stopped under the protecting guns of Fort Morgan and looked back up the bay. Turning to Commander Johnston, the brave old admiral, who had taught many of the commanders of the ships opposed to him their lessons in naval tactics, said, " Follow them up, Johnston; we can't let them off that way."

On came the *Tennessee,* one vessel against the entire Federal fleet! Signals flew from the flagship; the monitors were given orders to come into close action, and the *Monongahela, Lackawanna,* and *Ossipee,* which had false iron prows, were ordered to prepare to ram. The *Tennessee* was as unwieldy as a raft of logs; she made no attempt to dodge the blows of her more agile antagonists. The *Monongahela* struck her square amidships, with the only result that she carried away her own bow, and the *Lackawanna,* striking the *Tennessee* on the other side, suffered likewise. The Confederate ram was uninjured. The *Hartford* came bearing down upon her now; the ships met almost bows

[254]

THE FALLEN FORTRESS—TRAVERSES AT FORT FISHER IN 1865

THE "MOUND" AT FORT FISHER

WHERE BLOCKADE–RUNNERS WERE SIGNALED

In the top picture appear six of the gun positions within Fort Fisher, from which the Confederates so long defied the blockading fleet covering the approach and departure of blockade-runners to and from Wilmington, N. C. Only after two powerful expeditions had been sent against it did the Federals finally gain possession of this well-constructed work. In the centre is seen a portion of the "Mound," an artificial eminence used as a lookout. It was on this that the light for the guidance of blockade-runners was established early in the war. The Confederates had destroyed all other aids to navigation along the coast, but it was of the utmost importance that vessels with cargoes for Wilmington should be able to make port and discharge their precious "ballast" in the form of munitions of war. In the view of the bomb-proof at the bottom of the page is evident the pains that have been taken to make the works impregnable. At the point where the brick chimney rises, the cooking for a section of the garrison was done in safety.

THE WELL–SHORED BOMB–PROOF

on, but the *Hartford's* anchor acted as a fender, and with their port sides touching, the two vessels scraped by each other. The solid 9-inch shot from the Federal flagship bounded off the *Tennessee's* sloping sides; she attempted to fire her broadside battery in turn, but her primers failed, and only one shot pierced the *Hartford's* side, exploding on the berth-deck, wounding an officer and killing several men.

In attempting to make a quick turn, with the object of again ramming, the *Hartford* came into collision with the *Lackawanna;* it was a narrow escape, for almost under the spot where Farragut was standing, the flagship was cut down within two feet of the water-line.

But now the monitors came up. From this minute on to the time that the *Tennessee* hauled down her flag, she never fired a shot and was literally hammered into submission. Even after the flag was lowered, the *Ossipee,* that had started another ramming charge and could not stop in time, struck her a slight blow. At the same moment the commanders of the two vessels recognized each other and passed a friendly hail. For over an hour the one-sided fight had been maintained. The *Tennessee* had lost two killed and nine wounded, and the Union fleet, in passing the forts and in the subsequent actions with the gunboats and the ram, had fifty-two killed and one hundred and seventy wounded. There were ninety-three lost by the sinking of the *Tecumseh.*

Fort Powell had been evacuated on the 5th, and Fort Gaines did not long survive the catastrophe to Buchanan's fleet. The siege was pressed, and the Confederates, appreciating that resistance was useless, asked for a truce to arrange terms of surrender. The arrangements were made on the 7th, and the surrender took place on the 8th.

The next day, General Granger moved his command, reenforced by three new regiments, across the bay, landing at Navy Cove, four miles from Fort Morgan, on the bay side of Mobile Point. Each succeeding night slight advances were

PICKED MEN IN THE NAVY—PORTER AND HIS STAFF, DECEMBER, 1864

In this vivid portrait group of Admiral Porter and his staff, taken in December, 1864, appear the men selected by him to aid in accomplishing the fall of Fort Fisher and the conclusion of the navy's most important remaining tasks in the war. At the extreme left stands the young and indomitable Lieutenant W. B. Cushing, fresh from his famous exploit of blowing up the Confederate ram "Albemarle"; fifth from the left, with his arms folded, is Lieutenant-Commander K. R. Breese, another young officer scarcely less daring than Cushing and now Porter's fleet-captain. Lieutenant-Commander Henry A. Adams, Jr., stands on Porter's right. A number of volunteer officers are in the group. Porter was ever quick to recognize the bravery of the volunteers and their value to the service. From the decks of the "Malvern" (shown below) were directed the final operations at sea of the North Atlantic squadron in the war. Fort Fisher by 1864 had become the most formidable line of works in the Confederacy, and it was evident to the navy that this position at the mouth of the Cape Fear River, North Carolina, would have to be reduced if blockade-running into Wilmington was to be broken up. The first attack on Fort Fisher, December 24–25, 1864, was unsuccessful, owing to an unfortunate division in military authority in which General Benjamin F. Butler played an overweening part. After the second attack, January 13–15th, Admiral Porter, from the deck of the "Malvern," witnessed the gallant onslaught of General Terry's troops upon the land side of the fortifications, while 1,600 of his own sailors and 400 marines with pistol and cutlass tried to board the sea face. Amid the cheers of both army and navy, the news of the surrender of the garrison was received very soon afterward.

THE FLAGSHIP "MALVERN" AT NORFOLK

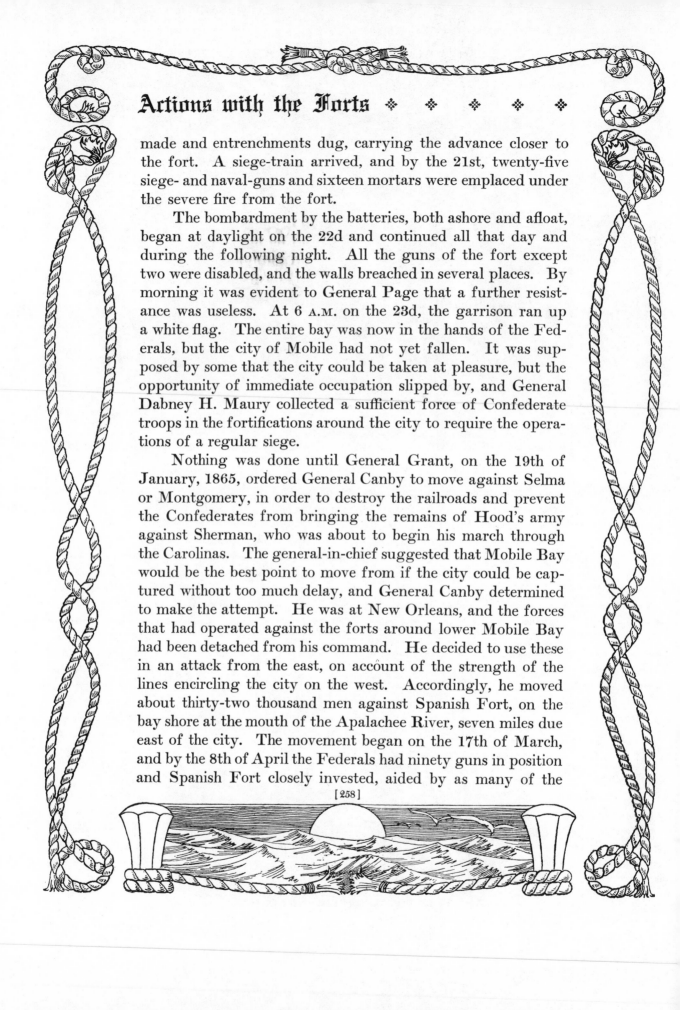

made and entrenchments dug, carrying the advance closer to the fort. A siege-train arrived, and by the 21st, twenty-five siege- and naval-guns and sixteen mortars were emplaced under the severe fire from the fort.

The bombardment by the batteries, both ashore and afloat, began at daylight on the 22d and continued all that day and during the following night. All the guns of the fort except two were disabled, and the walls breached in several places. By morning it was evident to General Page that a further resistance was useless. At 6 A.M. on the 23d, the garrison ran up a white flag. The entire bay was now in the hands of the Federals, but the city of Mobile had not yet fallen. It was supposed by some that the city could be taken at pleasure, but the opportunity of immediate occupation slipped by, and General Dabney H. Maury collected a sufficient force of Confederate troops in the fortifications around the city to require the operations of a regular siege.

Nothing was done until General Grant, on the 19th of January, 1865, ordered General Canby to move against Selma or Montgomery, in order to destroy the railroads and prevent the Confederates from bringing the remains of Hood's army against Sherman, who was about to begin his march through the Carolinas. The general-in-chief suggested that Mobile Bay would be the best point to move from if the city could be captured without too much delay, and General Canby determined to make the attempt. He was at New Orleans, and the forces that had operated against the forts around lower Mobile Bay had been detached from his command. He decided to use these in an attack from the east, on account of the strength of the lines encircling the city on the west. Accordingly, he moved about thirty-two thousand men against Spanish Fort, on the bay shore at the mouth of the Apalachee River, seven miles due east of the city. The movement began on the 17th of March, and by the 8th of April the Federals had ninety guns in position and Spanish Fort closely invested, aided by as many of the

ONE
THE NAVY LOST
LIEUTENANT SAM-
UEL W. PRESTON

This brave and promis-
ing young officer was an
ardent advocate of the
effectiveness of land de-
tachments of sailors and
marines against forts.
At Fort Fisher came the
coveted opportunity and
Preston paid for his be-
lief in it with his life.
The heavy loss on the
beach cast a gloom over
the navy despite the
success of the assaulting
column of soldiers under
General Terry. Ensign
(now Rear-Admiral) Rob-
ley D. Evans was one of
those severely wounded.
The 200-pounder Parrott
gun above was the for-
ward pivot-gun of the
"Wabash" and did as
much damage in the bom-
bardments of Fort Fisher
as any other single gun in
the fleet. The gun-crew
that served it was com-
posed of picked men
and every effective shot
aroused hearty cheers.

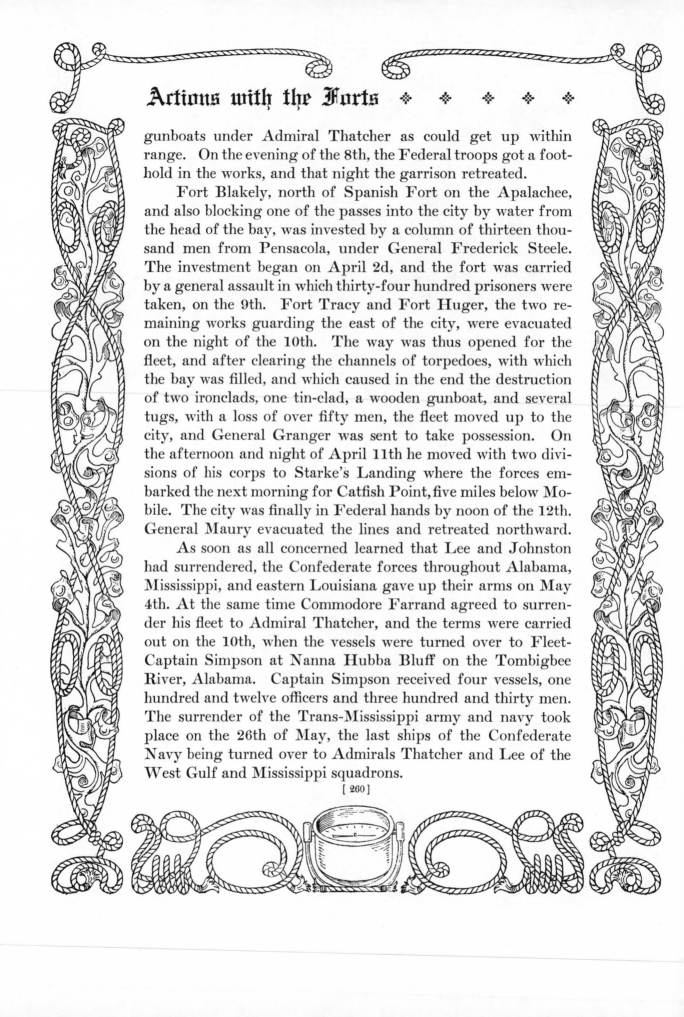

gunboats under Admiral Thatcher as could get up within range. On the evening of the 8th, the Federal troops got a foothold in the works, and that night the garrison retreated.

Fort Blakely, north of Spanish Fort on the Apalachee, and also blocking one of the passes into the city by water from the head of the bay, was invested by a column of thirteen thousand men from Pensacola, under General Frederick Steele. The investment began on April 2d, and the fort was carried by a general assault in which thirty-four hundred prisoners were taken, on the 9th. Fort Tracy and Fort Huger, the two remaining works guarding the east of the city, were evacuated on the night of the 10th. The way was thus opened for the fleet, and after clearing the channels of torpedoes, with which the bay was filled, and which caused in the end the destruction of two ironclads, one tin-clad, a wooden gunboat, and several tugs, with a loss of over fifty men, the fleet moved up to the city, and General Granger was sent to take possession. On the afternoon and night of April 11th he moved with two divisions of his corps to Starke's Landing where the forces embarked the next morning for Catfish Point, five miles below Mobile. The city was finally in Federal hands by noon of the 12th. General Maury evacuated the lines and retreated northward.

As soon as all concerned learned that Lee and Johnston had surrendered, the Confederate forces throughout Alabama, Mississippi, and eastern Louisiana gave up their arms on May 4th. At the same time Commodore Farrand agreed to surrender his fleet to Admiral Thatcher, and the terms were carried out on the 10th, when the vessels were turned over to Fleet-Captain Simpson at Nanna Hubba Bluff on the Tombigbee River, Alabama. Captain Simpson received four vessels, one hundred and twelve officers and three hundred and thirty men. The surrender of the Trans-Mississippi army and navy took place on the 26th of May, the last ships of the Confederate Navy being turned over to Admirals Thatcher and Lee of the West Gulf and Mississippi squadrons.

X

NAVAL ACTIONS
ALONG
THE SHORE

A BUSY SCENE ON THE JAMES, 1864

ARMY TUGS 4 AND 5 IN THE FOREGROUND; THE MONITOR "ONONDAGA" IN THE
OFFING—WITH GRANT AT CITY POINT, THE RIVER BECAME THE
ARTERY FOR ARMY AND NAVY COMMUNICATION

A FERRYBOAT READY FOR BATTLE

Take away the background of this picture of the "Commodore Perry," substitute for it the lonely shore of the Carolina sounds or the Virginia rivers lined with men in gray uniforms, and you have an exact reproduction of how this old converted ferryboat looked when going into action. Here the men have been called to quarters for gun-drill. The gun-captains are at their places and the crews with training lines in hand await the order from the officers above to aim and fire. Many times was this scene repeated aboard the "Commodore Perry" after she sailed with the motley fleet that Admiral Goldsborough led against Albemarle and Pamlico Sounds in January, 1862. In addition to her four 9-inch smooth-bores, the "Perry" carried a 12-pounder rifle and a 100-pounder rifle, it being the policy to equip the light-draft gunboats with the heaviest armament that they could possibly carry. Under command of the brave Lieutenant Charles W. Flusser, the guns of the "Perry" were kept hot as she skurried about the sounds and up the rivers, gaining a foothold for the Federal forces. Flusser, after a record of brilliant service in recovering inch by inch the waters of the Carolinas, lost his life in the "Miami" in the engagement with the "Albemarle."

[262]

AN EMERGENCY GUNBOAT FROM THE NEW YORK FERRY SERVICE

This craft, the "Commodore Perry," was an old New York ferryboat purchased and hastily pressed into service by the Federal navy to help solve the problem of patrolling the three thousand miles of coast, along which the blockade must be made effective. In order to penetrate the intricate inlets and rivers, light-draft fighting-vessels were required, and the most immediate means of securing these was to purchase every sort of merchant craft that could possibly be adapted to the purposes of war, either as a fighting-vessel or as a transport. The ferryboat in the picture has been provided with guns and her pilot-houses armored. A casemate of iron plates has been provided for the gunners. The Navy Department purchased and equipped in all one hundred and thirty-six vessels in 1861, and by the end of the year had increased the number of seamen in the service from 7,600 to over 22,000. Many of these new recruits saw their first active service aboard the converted ferryboats, tugboats, and other frail and unfamiliar vessels making up the nondescript fleet that undertook to cut off the commerce of the South. The experience thus gained under very unusual circumstances placed them of necessity among the bravest sailors of the navy.

The "Commodore Perry," under Lieutenant-Commander C. W. Flusser, was in the division of Commander Rowan, which distinguished itself at Roanoke Island. An old converted ferryboat, she was on the advance line of the action of February 10, 1862, when the signal for a dash at the Confederate gunboats was given. She pursued and captured the "Sea Bird," the flagship of Captain Lynch, C.S.N., upon that occasion, making prisoners of nearly all her officers and crew.

On July 9, 1862, she led two other frail gunboats up the Roanoke River on a reconnaissance. Commander Flusser's orders were to go to Hamilton; and despite the fact that the river banks were lined with sharpshooters, he braved their fire for ten hours, reached his destination, took possession of the Confederate steamer "Nelson," and returned with his prize. Flusser in the old "Perry" achieved a brilliant record on the shallow Carolina waters, where he finally lost his life.

A

PLUCKY

LIGHT-DRAFT

THE

"COMMODORE

PERRY"

THE NAVY ASHORE—CREW OF THE "FOSTER" WITH HOWITZERS

While the Federals with both army and navy closed in upon Richmond, heroic efforts were made by the Confederates to drive them back. Batteries were built along the river banks for the purpose of harassing the gunboats, and it was frequently necessary to land the crews of vessels—such as this detachment from the army gunboat "Foster," near Point of Rocks—in order effectually to drive off hostile detachments. In the lower picture the "Canonicus," one of the newer monitors, is seen coaling on the James. Under Commander E. G. Parrott, the "Canonicus" participated in the six-hour engagement with Battery Dantzler and the Confederate gunboats on June 21, 1864, and on August 16th and 18th, she, with other vessels, engaged the "Virginia" and the "Richmond" and Confederate troops under General R. E. Lee, to cover the

THE GUNBOAT "MASSASOIT"

advance of Federals under General Butler. The "Canonicus" participated in the Fort Fisher expedition, and to her belongs the honor of capturing the British blockade-runner "Deer" off Charleston, February 18, 1865. In the center appears the gunboat "Massasoit." In the last action that took place with the Confederate flotilla on the James, at Trent's Reach, January 24, 1865, it was the "Massasoit" that received the only damage from the guns of the hostile vessels and the battery at Howlett's house. In the two-hour action after the return of the "Onondaga" up-stream, five men on the "Massasoit" were wounded. She was one of the third-class double-ender armored vessels and mounted ten guns. During this action she was commanded by Lieutenant G. W. Sumner, who displayed the utmost coolness and bravery in handling his vessel.

THE MONITOR "CANONICUS"

ALONG THE SHORES

THE movements of the naval forces on the Atlantic coast south of Cape Charles and Cape Henry, and along the borders of the Gulf States, were primarily to forward the maintenance of a strict blockade, and secondly, to act in cooperation with the various land expeditions in the establishment of naval bases and the convoying of troops intended for inland service. The armed ships of the navy lent their mighty aid in the reduction of the formidable forts that commanded the chief ports of entry.

Besides the universal adoption of armor and the recurrence to the ram of ancient days, there were introduced three important principles. They were not new—the minds of our forefathers had roughly imagined them—but they were for the first time put successfully into practice. The first was the revolving turret; the second, the torpedo, in both its forms, offensive and defensive, and the third was the " submergible " and actually the submarine, the diving ship of to-day. The purposes and methods of their employment have not been changed; only in the details of construction and in the perfection of machinery and mechanism can the difference be seen.

The first notice of the torpedo in Civil War annals is when two were found floating down the Potomac on July 7, 1861. They were made of boiler-iron and were intended for Commander Craven's little flotilla that was protecting Washington. Out in the West, when Foote and his gunboats made their way up the Tennessee they actually steamed past, without touching, some mines that had drifted out of the channel. The gunboat *Cairo* was the first victim of this new style of warfare, in the Yazoo River, December 12, 1862.

With the exception of the actions along the Potomac and in

THE BEGINNINGS OF SUBMARINE WARFARE

A CONFEDERATE PHOTOGRAPH OF '64—THE FIRST "DAVID," FIGURING IN AN HEROIC EXPLOIT

This peaceful scene, photographed by Cook, the Confederate photographer at Charleston, in 1864, preserves one of the most momentous inventions of the Confederate navy. Back of the group of happy children lies one of the "Davids" or torpedo-boats with which the Confederates made repeated attempts to destroy the Federal vessels in Charleston Harbor, and thus raise the blockade. The Confederates were the first to employ torpedoes in the war, at Aquia Creek, July 7, 1861. Captain F. D. Lee, C. S. N., was working on designs for a torpedo ram early in the war, and Captain M. M. Gray, C. S. N., in charge of the submarine defenses of Charleston, with a force of sixty officers and men under him, was particularly active in developing this mode of warfare. The "David" in the picture appears to be the first one built in the Confederacy; she was constructed at private expense by Theodore Stoney, of Charleston. She was driven by steam, and on the night of October 5, 1863, in command of Lieut. W. T. Glassell, with a crew of three volunteers from the Confederate gunboats, she succeeded in exploding a torpedo under the new "Ironsides," putting her out of commission for a time. The little "David" was almost swamped. Her crew took to the water to save themselves by swimming. Lieutenant Glassell and James Sullivan, fireman, were captured after being in the water nearly an hour. Engineer C. S. Tombs, seeing that the "David" was still afloat, swam back to her, where he found Pilot J. W. Cannon, who could not swim, clinging to her side. Tombs clambered aboard and pulled Cannon after him, and together they managed to build a fire under the boiler and bring the little vessel safely back to Charleston.

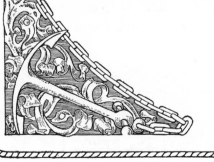

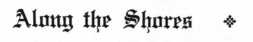

Along the Shores ✦

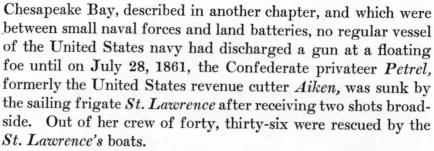

Chesapeake Bay, described in another chapter, and which were between small naval forces and land batteries, no regular vessel of the United States navy had discharged a gun at a floating foe until on July 28, 1861, the Confederate privateer *Petrel,* formerly the United States revenue cutter *Aiken,* was sunk by the sailing frigate *St. Lawrence* after receiving two shots broadside. Out of her crew of forty, thirty-six were rescued by the *St. Lawrence's* boats.

To the Federal navy belongs the honor of achieving the first signal success along the coast, in the bombardment and capture of Forts Hatteras and Clark at Hatteras Inlet, on the 28th and 29th of August, 1861. From Hatteras Inlet offensive operations could be carried on by means of light-draft vessels along the entire coast of North Carolina. The inlet was the key to Albemarle Sound, and was, besides, a good depot for outfitting and coaling, and a refuge, owing to its sheltered position, from the fierce winter storms that raged along the shore.

In the Gulf, there had been some skirmishing. The squadron under Captain John Pope that had been sent, after the escape of the *Sumter* to sea, to the mouth of the Mississippi, had a chance to bring on an action, in October, 1861, with several of the Confederate naval vessels. But Pope's ships got aground in the passes of the delta, and he and his captains exercising undue caution, refused offer of battle and made out into the Gulf. There were two brilliant bits of boat-work at Pensacola and Galveston. Lieutenant John H. Russell cut out and destroyed the unfinished Confederate privateer *Judah,* at the Pensacola Navy-Yard, on September 13, 1861, and Lieutenant James E. Jouett, of the frigate *Santee,* took and destroyed the privateer *Royal Yacht* in Galveston Harbor, in November.

Many were the gallant acts of the enlisted men and petty officers in the fighting along the shore. In the expedition under Flag-Officer Goldsborough against Roanoke Island, in February, 1862, there were two brave little fights between the

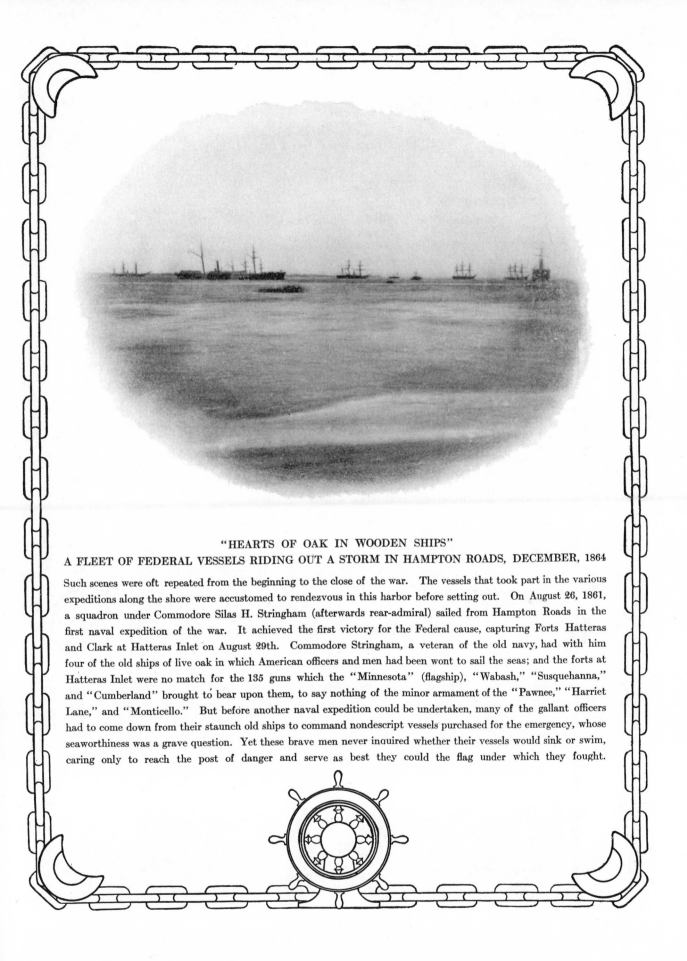

"HEARTS OF OAK IN WOODEN SHIPS"
A FLEET OF FEDERAL VESSELS RIDING OUT A STORM IN HAMPTON ROADS, DECEMBER, 1864

Such scenes were oft repeated from the beginning to the close of the war. The vessels that took part in the various expeditions along the shore were accustomed to rendezvous in this harbor before setting out. On August 26, 1861, a squadron under Commodore Silas H. Stringham (afterwards rear-admiral) sailed from Hampton Roads in the first naval expedition of the war. It achieved the first victory for the Federal cause, capturing Forts Hatteras and Clark at Hatteras Inlet on August 29th. Commodore Stringham, a veteran of the old navy, had with him four of the old ships of live oak in which American officers and men had been wont to sail the seas; and the forts at Hatteras Inlet were no match for the 135 guns which the "Minnesota" (flagship), "Wabash," "Susquehanna," and "Cumberland" brought to bear upon them, to say nothing of the minor armament of the "Pawnee," "Harriet Lane," and "Monticello." But before another naval expedition could be undertaken, many of the gallant officers had to come down from their staunch old ships to command nondescript vessels purchased for the emergency, whose seaworthiness was a grave question. Yet these brave men never inquired whether their vessels would sink or swim, caring only to reach the post of danger and serve as best they could the flag under which they fought.

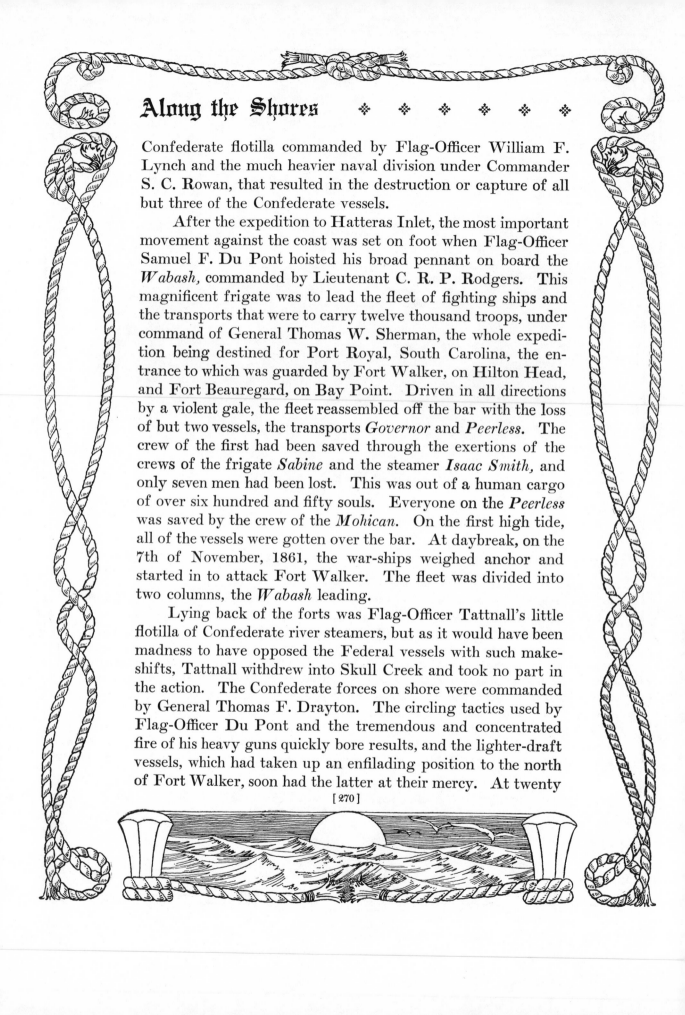

Along the Shores ✦ ✦ ✦ ✦ ✦ ✦ ✦

Confederate flotilla commanded by Flag-Officer William F. Lynch and the much heavier naval division under Commander S. C. Rowan, that resulted in the destruction or capture of all but three of the Confederate vessels.

After the expedition to Hatteras Inlet, the most important movement against the coast was set on foot when Flag-Officer Samuel F. Du Pont hoisted his broad pennant on board the *Wabash,* commanded by Lieutenant C. R. P. Rodgers. This magnificent frigate was to lead the fleet of fighting ships and the transports that were to carry twelve thousand troops, under command of General Thomas W. Sherman, the whole expedition being destined for Port Royal, South Carolina, the entrance to which was guarded by Fort Walker, on Hilton Head, and Fort Beauregard, on Bay Point. Driven in all directions by a violent gale, the fleet reassembled off the bar with the loss of but two vessels, the transports *Governor* and *Peerless.* The crew of the first had been saved through the exertions of the crews of the frigate *Sabine* and the steamer *Isaac Smith,* and only seven men had been lost. This was out of a human cargo of over six hundred and fifty souls. Everyone on the *Peerless* was saved by the crew of the *Mohican.* On the first high tide, all of the vessels were gotten over the bar. At daybreak, on the 7th of November, 1861, the war-ships weighed anchor and started in to attack Fort Walker. The fleet was divided into two columns, the *Wabash* leading.

Lying back of the forts was Flag-Officer Tattnall's little flotilla of Confederate river steamers, but as it would have been madness to have opposed the Federal vessels with such make-shifts, Tattnall withdrew into Skull Creek and took no part in the action. The Confederate forces on shore were commanded by General Thomas F. Drayton. The circling tactics used by Flag-Officer Du Pont and the tremendous and concentrated fire of his heavy guns quickly bore results, and the lighter-draft vessels, which had taken up an enfilading position to the north of Fort Walker, soon had the latter at their mercy. At twenty

MEN OF THE "UNADILLA," AFTER PLAYING THEIR PART IN THE NAVY'S CRUCIAL TEST

Under Lieutenant-Commander N. Collins, the "Unadilla" took part in the expedition that succeeded in capturing Port Royal, November 9, 1861. The "Unadilla" was but one of the fifty vessels that had assembled in Hampton Roads by October 27th to join the largest fleet ever commanded by an officer of the American navy up to that time. In contrast to the number of the vessels was the nondescript character of most of them. The "Unadilla" is described officially as a steam gunboat, but she was typical of the sort of hastily converted vessels that made up the fleet—river steamers, ferryboats, tugs, almost anything that would turn a wheel or propeller. These frail craft, loaded down with heavy guns, set forth in the face of foul weather to engage in battle for the first time with two of the strongest fortifications of the Confederacy. It was a momentous trial of wooden ships against most formidable earthworks. But Flag-Officer Du Pont, who possessed in an eminent degree all the qualities of a great commander, succeeded in demonstrating to Europe that even with a fleet of so uncertain a character the American navy could win by a masterly plan of battle, originated by him.

THE "UNADILLA"

minutes after two in the afternoon, Commander John Rodgers landed with a small force and raised the Federal flag over the deserted batteries. Fort Beauregard, across the harbor entrance, seeing the fate of Fort Walker, was abandoned by Captain Elliott, its commander, late in the afternoon, and now the most important position that either the army or the navy had yet gained was in the possession of the North, and the coveted naval base established.

Early on the morning of January 1, 1863, General Magruder made a vigorous attempt to recapture the city of Galveston, which had been taken by Farragut's squadron the previous October. The side-wheel steamer *Harriet Lane* bore the brunt of the naval attack, and she was captured by two small steamers after her commander and lieutenant-commander had been killed. The ferry-boat *Westfield* was burned. The military force in the town surrendered, and the blockade was broken for a week.

On the 31st of this month, the Confederate iron-clad rams *Chicora* and *Palmetto State,* built and equipped at the navy-yard in Charleston, steamed down past the forts and took the inner line of the blockading fleet by surprise. The *Mercedita* was captured, and the *Keystone State* was badly injured. As it was calm weather, the *Chicora* and the *Palmetto State* proceeded out to sea, and as the outer line of the blockading squadron was far off the coast, they came back and reported that the blockade was raised. In fact, General Beauregard attempted to bring this point before the foreign consuls at Charleston.

It was on the 28th of February that the cruiser *Nashville,* lying up the Ogeechee River above Fort McAllister, Georgia, was destroyed by the monitor *Montauk* while she was waiting for a chance to get to sea. One well-directed shot from the monitor's 15-inch gun struck the *Nashville* fair amidships, and in a few minutes she burst into flame, and blew up.

The Confederate ram *Atlanta,* on the 17th of June, 1863, running down into Wassaw Sound, secure in the protection of

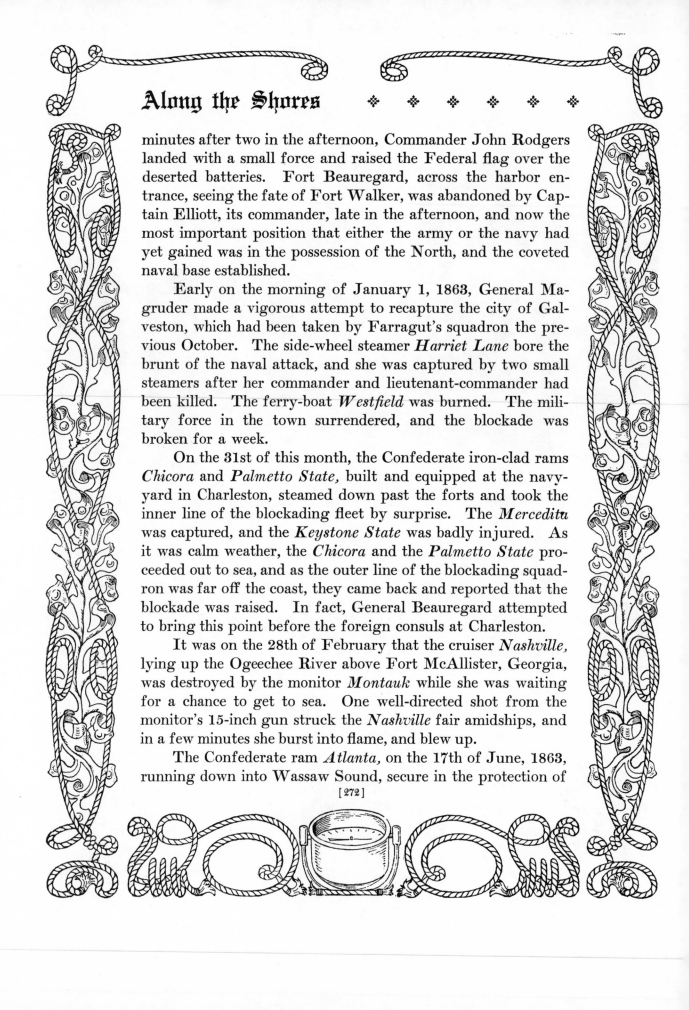

A FEARLESS BLOCKADER—U. S. S. "KANSAS"

This little screw steamer, under Lieutenant-Commander P. G. Watmough, with four other vessels no more formidable than she, stood her ground when the great ironclad ram "Raleigh" came down from Wilmington on May 7, 1864, and attempted to raise the blockade at the mouth of the Cape Fear River. The "Raleigh" trained her ten guns on the little vessels for nine hours. But they replied with vigor, and finally Flag-Officer W. F. Lynch, C. S. N., under whose direction the "Raleigh" had been built, judged it best to retire, since she was hardly in a state of completion to warrant coming to close quarters. To the "Kansas" belongs the honor of capturing the famous blockade-runner "Tristram Shandy," May 15, 1864. The "Tristram Shandy" afterward became despatch vessel to Porter's fleet.

her heavy armor and big guns, was pounded into submission by the monitors *Weehawken* and *Nahant,* and surrendered after a stubborn defense.

The many attempts to gain possession of Charleston Harbor, that were animated as much by sentimental reasons as they were dictated by military necessity, were crowned by at least one success. Part of Morris Island was evacuated by the Confederates on September 7th. The enfilading and breaching batteries in the swamps, together with the combined efforts of the ironclads and other vessels, had not succeeded in the reduction of Fort Sumter. Every kind of invention was tried by the inhabitants of Charleston to raise the blockade. Floating mines were sent out on the receding tides by the score; many were anchored at night in places where the day before the Federal vessels had occupied vantage spots in the bombardment.

On September 6th it was that the *New Ironsides,* directly off Fort Wagner, lay over a huge mine whose two thousand pounds of powder would have been sufficient to have torn her in two. On shore, the engineering officer who had placed the mine and laid the wires, surrounded by a large body of officers, was making every effort to produce the contact that would destroy the hostile ironclad. It was all in vain. By the most miraculous circumstances the wagons that had been driven along the beach to gather sand for the reenforcement of the parapet had rubbed off the insulation of the wires, and they would not work.

It was now that the invention of the torpedo-boat and the submergible came to be enforced on the attention of the public. In all the history of any war there will be found no such record of continuous daring and almost certain death as is to be found in the story of the *H. L. Hunley,* the first submarine boat. This vessel, a cylindrical, cigar-shaped craft only thirty-five feet in length, could actually dive and be propelled under water and rise to the surface. The motive power was furnished by the crew, who, sitting *vis-à-vis* on benches, turned a crank

From the time General Grant established his headquarters at City Point, there was no rest for the gunboats in the James River. There was an active and determined foe to contend with, and alertness was the watchword for every officer and man in the Federal flotilla. Underneath, one of the huge 100-pounder Parrott guns is being brought into position on the gunboat "Mendota" in July, 1864, ready to be trained upon the Confederates whenever they attempted to plant batteries along the shores. The work of the "Mendota's" gunners on July 28th at Four Mile Creek spoke eloquently of their coolness and accuracy of aim. With equal smartness, and scarcely more excitement than is apparent in the picture above, they served their guns under fire of shot and shell.

CONSTANT

PREPAREDNESS

ON THE

"MENDOTA"

1864

LOOKING ALONG

THE

100-LB

PARROTT

GUN

connecting with the propeller-shaft. The torpedo was attached to the end of a spar which could be projected in front of the craft. H. L. Hunley, of Mobile, was the designer, and the vessel was built in his native city.

After several unsuccessful and fatal attempts at Mobile and Charleston, Hunley went to the latter city to take command of his invention in person. Volunteers seemed easy to find, for he picked six men, and starting out in the harbor made several spectacular dives. She was gone overlong on one of these. It was a week before she was brought to the surface. Her inventor and all of his crew were huddled together under one of the manholes. Nothing daunted, Lieutenant George E. Dixon, a friend of the boat's inventor, got together another crew, and on the 17th of February, 1864, silently they moved out to where the fine sloop-of-war *Housatonic* was lying at anchor. The torpedo plunged against her side and exploded, blew her almost out of the water and she sank immediately. But the little *Hunley* never returned. She found a resting-place on the ocean bed beside her gigantic victim.

On the 27th of October, 1864, the indomitable Lieutenant W. B. Cushing, who had been constantly proposing wonderful and almost impossible things, succeeded in getting eight miles up the Roanoke River in North Carolina and sinking, in an open launch, with a torpedo, the Confederate ram *Albemarle*.

The gunboat *Otsego* ran afoul of a torpedo in the Roanoke River on December 9th and went to the bottom, and after the fall of the last fort, Fort Fisher, the *Patapsco* was sunk in Charleston Harbor, January 15, 1865, and officers and crew were lost to the number of sixty. Still later in the war, in April, the monitors *Milwaukee* and *Osage* suffered a like fate. They were in Admiral Thatcher's fleet that was assisting Generals Canby and Steele in the capture of Mobile. After the forts had been taken by the army, the war-ship advanced up the torpedo-filled channel. A tin-clad, a wooden gunboat, and several tugs were also blown up before the ships anchored off the city.

XI

THE SEA LIFE
OF '61

A "POWDER–MONKEY" ON A DEEP–SEA CRAFT

This smart little "monkey" is a sailor, every inch. In the old navy, the powder, before the days of "fixed ammunitions," was brought up in canvas bags or powder buckets, and during an action these brave little fellows were constantly on the run from their divisions to the magazine. Under the break of the poop-deck behind the little lad are to be seen the cutlasses that every sailor wore in the old days and that have now disappeared from the service.

THE MEN OF THE "MENDOTA"

Gathered here on the after-deck are the crew of the gunboat "Mendota," some busy at banjo-playing, checkers, and other diversions more idle. More than one nationality is represented. Although there are many men who probably have followed no other calling than that of the seaman, there are doubtless men from inland towns and farms who, flocking to the seaports, had chosen to enlist in the service. But there is another reason for the foreign-looking faces; the higher pay of the United States navy and the chance for adventure and prize money had caused a good many foreign ships to find it difficult to procure merchant-sailors. Englishmen,

AN IDLE HOUR ON THE AFTER-DECK

Swedes and Norwegians, Danes, Russians, Germans, Frenchmen, Spaniards, and Portugese were to be found on almost every United States ship. To a certain extent sea-language, so far as the terms and orders are concerned, are the same the world over. There was no educational qualification required. Some of the seamen could scarcely speak English. In the foreground is a marine and an able-seaman playing the jack-tar's favorite game of checkers, while a bright-faced little "powder-monkey," leaning picturesquely against the capstan, has looked up to pose for the camera man who has preserved this typical scene of the sailors' idle hour.

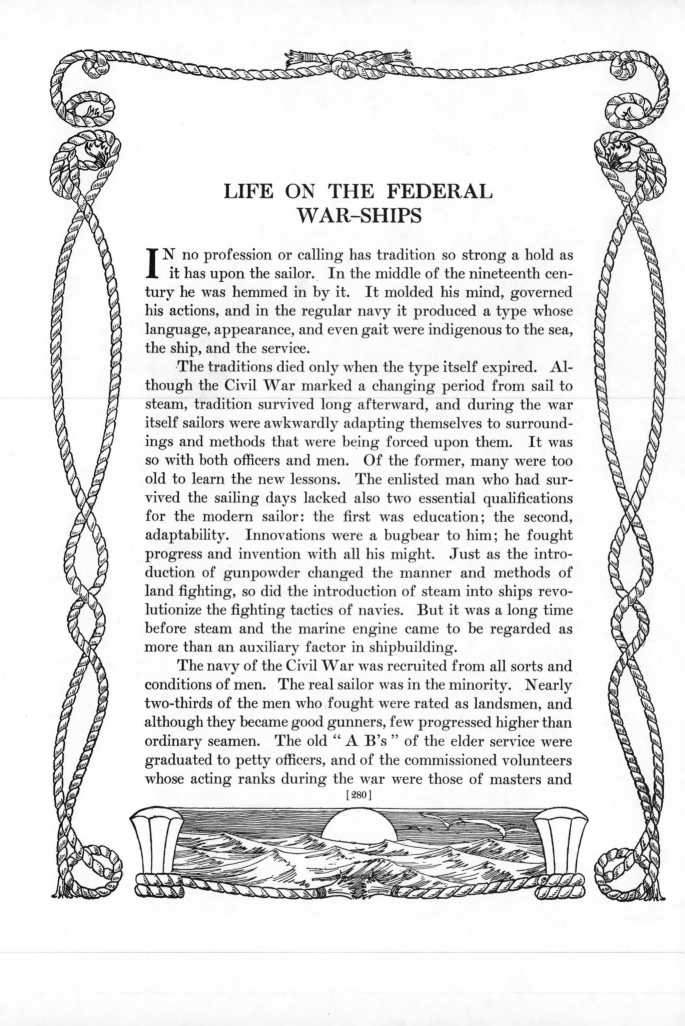

LIFE ON THE FEDERAL WAR-SHIPS

IN no profession or calling has tradition so strong a hold as it has upon the sailor. In the middle of the nineteenth century he was hemmed in by it. It molded his mind, governed his actions, and in the regular navy it produced a type whose language, appearance, and even gait were indigenous to the sea, the ship, and the service.

The traditions died only when the type itself expired. Although the Civil War marked a changing period from sail to steam, tradition survived long afterward, and during the war itself sailors were awkwardly adapting themselves to surroundings and methods that were being forced upon them. It was so with both officers and men. Of the former, many were too old to learn the new lessons. The enlisted man who had survived the sailing days lacked also two essential qualifications for the modern sailor: the first was education; the second, adaptability. Innovations were a bugbear to him; he fought progress and invention with all his might. Just as the introduction of gunpowder changed the manner and methods of land fighting, so did the introduction of steam into ships revolutionize the fighting tactics of navies. But it was a long time before steam and the marine engine came to be regarded as more than an auxiliary factor in shipbuilding.

The navy of the Civil War was recruited from all sorts and conditions of men. The real sailor was in the minority. Nearly two-thirds of the men who fought were rated as landsmen, and although they became good gunners, few progressed higher than ordinary seamen. The old " A B's " of the elder service were graduated to petty officers, and of the commissioned volunteers whose acting ranks during the war were those of masters and

AMUSEMENT DURING THE BLOCKADE

MINSTRELS ON THE FLAGSHIP "WABASH"

A ship's company is a little world by itself. As one of the principal objects of the inhabitants of the earth is to amuse themselves, so it is with the crew of a vessel at sea. The man who can sing, dance, play the banjo or the fiddle is always sure of an appreciative audience in the hours off duty. On many of the larger craft there were formed orchestras, amateur theatrical companies, and minstrel troupes who used to get together to rehearse, and gave entertainments to which very often the officers of all the ships of the fleet were glad to be invited. Time grew heavy and the hours lagged in each other's laps during the tedious blockade. The flagship "Wabash" became renowned throughout the fleet for her minstrels, whose good music and amusing songs helped to pass many a long evening. On more than one occasion regular balls were given that, although not attended by the fair sex, did not lack in gaiety. "A busy ship is a happy one," is an old adage with sea-faring men, but the wise captain was he who remembered also an old saying well known and equally true both afloat and ashore: "All work and no play makes Jack a dull boy."

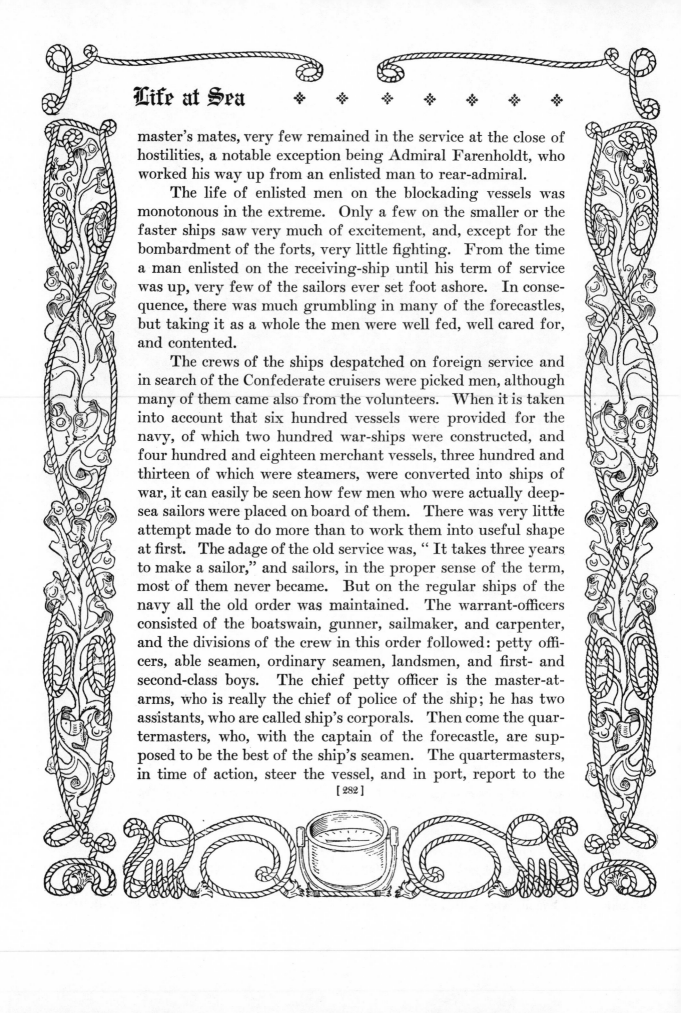

master's mates, very few remained in the service at the close of hostilities, a notable exception being Admiral Farenholdt, who worked his way up from an enlisted man to rear-admiral.

The life of enlisted men on the blockading vessels was monotonous in the extreme. Only a few on the smaller or the faster ships saw very much of excitement, and, except for the bombardment of the forts, very little fighting. From the time a man enlisted on the receiving-ship until his term of service was up, very few of the sailors ever set foot ashore. In consequence, there was much grumbling in many of the forecastles, but taking it as a whole the men were well fed, well cared for, and contented.

The crews of the ships despatched on foreign service and in search of the Confederate cruisers were picked men, although many of them came also from the volunteers. When it is taken into account that six hundred vessels were provided for the navy, of which two hundred war-ships were constructed, and four hundred and eighteen merchant vessels, three hundred and thirteen of which were steamers, were converted into ships of war, it can easily be seen how few men who were actually deep-sea sailors were placed on board of them. There was very little attempt made to do more than to work them into useful shape at first. The adage of the old service was, " It takes three years to make a sailor," and sailors, in the proper sense of the term, most of them never became. But on the regular ships of the navy all the old order was maintained. The warrant-officers consisted of the boatswain, gunner, sailmaker, and carpenter, and the divisions of the crew in this order followed: petty officers, able seamen, ordinary seamen, landsmen, and first- and second-class boys. The chief petty officer is the master-at-arms, who is really the chief of police of the ship; he has two assistants, who are called ship's corporals. Then come the quartermasters, who, with the captain of the forecastle, are supposed to be the best of the ship's seamen. The quartermasters, in time of action, steer the vessel, and in port, report to the

"AL FRESCO" COOKING ON THE FAMOUS "MONITOR"

This is the deck of the original "Monitor," with part of the crew that had participated in the fight in Hampton Roads. The savory smoke is blowing away from the fire, where the ship's cook is preparing the mid-day meal. The crew are awaiting the mess-call, and in the foreground are seated two of the fire-room force. There was one thing that the men on the monitors had a right to complain of: it was the intense heat generated between decks after a day's exposure to the sun. It was difficult to obtain proper ventilation in this class of vessel at the best. The wooden ships, with their high top sides, their hanging "wind sails" or canvas ventilators, and their ranges of open ports, admitted the free passage of the air; but in the iron-decked mon-

itors, whose metal plating often got so hot that it was almost scorching to the feet, the fire-rooms, the galley, and the men's sleeping-quarters became almost unbearable. In still water, while on blockading duty, it became customary for the ship's cook to prepare the men's messes up on deck, and for this purpose stoves were erected that could be easily taken below in time of action, and the men took their meals *al fresco* in the open air. The crew of the "Monitor" were picked men, in a sense, for they were all old sailors who had volunteered for the unknown work that lay before them. Their devotion to the officers who had brought them so successfully through the famous engagement was little short of worship; it is sad to think that most of these men went down with their vessel when she foundered in the storm off Hatteras a few weeks after this picture was taken.

officer of the deck, taking care of signals and other movements in the harbor. Boatswains' mates are assistants to the boatswain, and the medium through which the officers' orders are communicated to the crew. The gunners' mates and quarter-gunners have the guns and all their paraphernalia under their especial charge; to each gun-deck there is a gunner's mate, and a quarter-gunner to each division. The crew proper is divided primarily into two watches, starboard and port watch; and secondarily into subdivisions which in the old days were entitled forecastlemen, foretopmen, maintopmen, mizzentopmen, afterguard, and waisters.

The ship's guns were divided into divisions, each generally under command of a lieutenant, assisted by a midshipman, and to each gun was assigned a crew that, in the muzzle-loading days, was made up of (for the heavier guns) one captain, one second captain, two loaders, two rammers and spongers, four side-tacklemen, five train-tacklemen, and a powder-boy—sixteen in all. Their names indicate distinctly their positions at the gun in action.

On board the faster vessels which acted as scouts on the outer line of the blockading squadrons, things often reached a pitch of great excitement. The appearance of low-lying, black lines of smoke against the horizon late in the afternoon was a sure precursor of the dash of a runner, either to make port or to reach shoal water along the beach—anyhow, to get through if possible. Rich as were the hauls, however, when the vessel was captured, they did not begin to compare in value with those taken from outward-bound blockade-runners loaded with cotton. Some of the blockading vessels had once been in the very business themselves, and there are instances of chases lasting fifty-six hours before the runner either escaped or was brought to, with most of her cargo jettisoned. In 1863, one noted blockade-runner loaded to the gunwales with cotton, brought as prize-money to the captain of the vessel that captured her twenty thousand dollars, and even the cabin-boys

WILLIAM YOUNG
GUNNER'S MATE
OF THE
"ESSEX"

Below appear four picked men from the crew of the "Essex." Seated on the right in the front row is "Bill Young," the medal of honor man whose portrait appears above. W. L. Park, to his left, was a quarter gunner, as were Thomas T. Drew, standing to the right, and Gordon F. Terry beside him. All four are typical faces of the best that service in the inland navy could produce. The firm features of these men tell of a simple heroism that so often rose to great heights in the battles of the gunboats. These men fought under "Bill" (Com. W. D.) Porter, elder brother of the admiral, in a ship named after the famous flagship of their father, Commodore David Porter, in the War of 1812. In that old namesake Farragut had his first training as a fighter and about the newer "Essex" there hung much of the spirit of the navy of former days. Aboard of her too there was abundant opportunity to exemplify that spirit as nobly as was ever done by sailors anywhere. From Fort Henry till

FOUR PICKED MEN
GUNNERS' CREW
OF THE "ESSEX"

the fall of Port Hudson the "Essex" was always in the thick of the fight. One of the "Essex's" most important services came in the action of July 15, 1862. On Aug. 7 the "Arkansas" and two gunboats were lying above Baton Rouge ready to coöperate with the Confederate troops in a combined attack on that place. The troops with the aid of the Federal gunboats were defeated. Then Commander W. D. Porter started up-stream with the "Essex." As he approached the "Arkansas," a few well-directed shots disabled her so that she became unmanageable. Porter, seeing his advantage, loaded with incendiary shells, but at the first discharge the "Arkansas" was seen to be already ablaze. Porter and his men redoubled their efforts. The "Arkansas" managed to get near enough in-shore to make fast but her cable burnt away, and drifting again into the current she blew up. The "Essex" had accomplished the destruction of the last Confederate ram operating on the Mississippi River.

received large sums. If other vessels were in a certain radius of distance or attached to the same station, they also had a share in the money awarded by the prize-courts, and an escaping blockade-runner would remind one of a hare pursued by a heterogeneous pack of hounds—the swiftest to the fore, and then the lumbering, unwieldy boats bringing up the rear.

Of the fifty-one thousand men in the Federal Navy during the Civil War, not a third could have been called by the most elastic stretching of the term, sailors. A great majority rated as landsmen, were so in fact as well as name, and at least twelve or fifteen thousand of the men serving in the fleets along the coast and on the rivers had never set foot on a ship before enlisting.

On the gunboats in the Mississippi and the converted nondescripts that did such good service along the shores, there was very little chance for putting into practice the strict rules that governed life on the regular vessels. The men in some cases had greater comforts, and in others much less. It was a question of give and take and make the best of it between officers and crew.

With the introduction of the monitors there came into sea life an entirely new existence. At sea, if the weather was rough the men were corked up like flies in a bottle. Under a hot sun the sleeping quarters below became almost unbearable, and the iron decks so hot that they almost scorched the feet. This life in the ironclad, modified in a great measure with many comforts, is the life that has developed the seaman of to-day, for the old-time Jack has gone. A man must know more than how to make his mark when he enlists; his knowledge of arithmetic in fact must include the use of decimal fractions. The once-despised duties of the soldier are his also. He must know his manual of arms like a marine, for the ship's crew is an infantry regiment, a light-artillery battalion. The individuality of the sailorman as a class began to disappear when the generation that had fought the Civil War forsook the sea.

XII

THE CONFEDERATE CRUISERS
AND
THE "ALABAMA"

AFTER THE SINKING OF THE "ALABAMA"—
ADMIRAL SEMMES (ABOVE) AND COMMAND-
ER KELL WITH THEIR ENGLISH HOSTESSES

REAR-ADMIRAL RAPHAEL SEMMES

Very few officers in the Civil War had the opportunity of serving in both the army and navy: Admiral Semmes of the Confederate service was one of the small number. This fine likeness represents him at Southampton, England, whither he was taken by the *Deerhound* when the unlucky *Alabama* sank to her watery grave. Upon his return to America he was appointed rear-admiral and put in charge of the James River Squadron. This was February 10, 1865. On April 2d came the order from Secretary Mallory to destroy the ships, for Richmond was to be evacuated. His occupation gone, Semmes did not stand idly by and witness the ruin of his Government, but with a commission of brigadier-general undauntedly led a marine brigade in the last efforts of the expiring Confederacy.

COMMANDER JOHN McINTOSH KELL

THE RIGHT-HAND MAN OF CAPTAIN SEMMES

As first-lieutenant, Kell was Captain Semmes' executive officer on the *Alabama*. The captain gave him "great credit for the fine condition in which the ship went into action" and further stated that he rendered him "great assistance by his coolness and judgment as the fight proceeded." Kell, like his superior, was rescued by the *Deerhound* and taken to Southampton, where this photograph was made. On his return to the Confederate States, he was appointed commander and given the ironclad *Richmond*, in the James River Squadron. The fine features and resolute bearing of these naval officers go far to explain the daring and effective handling of the famous *Alabama*. With such sailors, an extensive Confederate Navy would have added even more dramatic chapters to history.

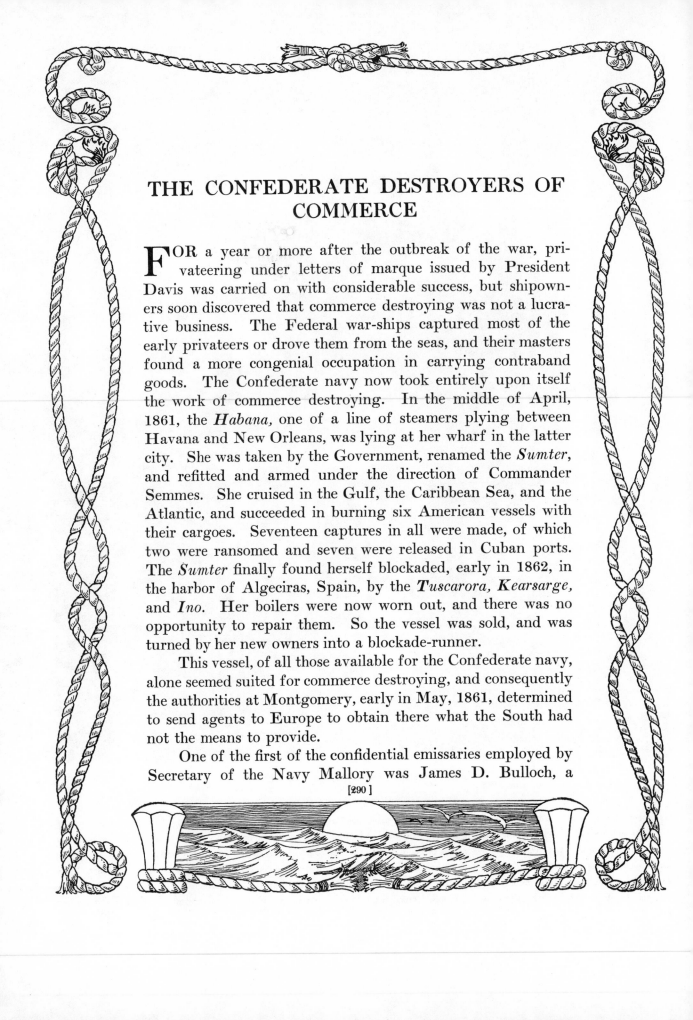

THE CONFEDERATE DESTROYERS OF COMMERCE

FOR a year or more after the outbreak of the war, privateering under letters of marque issued by President Davis was carried on with considerable success, but shipowners soon discovered that commerce destroying was not a lucrative business. The Federal war-ships captured most of the early privateers or drove them from the seas, and their masters found a more congenial occupation in carrying contraband goods. The Confederate navy now took entirely upon itself the work of commerce destroying. In the middle of April, 1861, the *Habana,* one of a line of steamers plying between Havana and New Orleans, was lying at her wharf in the latter city. She was taken by the Government, renamed the *Sumter,* and refitted and armed under the direction of Commander Semmes. She cruised in the Gulf, the Caribbean Sea, and the Atlantic, and succeeded in burning six American vessels with their cargoes. Seventeen captures in all were made, of which two were ransomed and seven were released in Cuban ports. The *Sumter* finally found herself blockaded, early in 1862, in the harbor of Algeciras, Spain, by the *Tuscarora, Kearsarge,* and *Ino.* Her boilers were now worn out, and there was no opportunity to repair them. So the vessel was sold, and was turned by her new owners into a blockade-runner.

This vessel, of all those available for the Confederate navy, alone seemed suited for commerce destroying, and consequently the authorities at Montgomery, early in May, 1861, determined to send agents to Europe to obtain there what the South had not the means to provide.

One of the first of the confidential emissaries employed by Secretary of the Navy Mallory was James D. Bulloch, a

A. P. MASON

JOHN SLIDELL

JOHN BIGELOW

CAPT. JAMES N. MAFFIT,
C. S. N.

The names of Mason and Slidell were linked throughout the war with the diplomatic efforts made in behalf of the Confederacy at the courts of England and France. The most concrete evidence of these efforts were the vessels that were built in English and French shipyards and, eluding the "vigilance" of the two Governments, passed into the hands of the Confederates to strike telling blows at American commerce, then next to the largest on the seas. Actively opposed to Mason and Slidell was John Bigelow, consul at Paris for the Federal Government during the war. His efforts to circumvent the construction of Confederate cruisers were untiring and in great measure successful in keeping in check the foreign tendency to encourage the division of the United States. At the very outset of this diplomatic struggle the Federal Government narrowly escaped becoming involved in war with England when Captain Charles Wilkes, in the "San Jacinto," seized Mason and Slidell aboard the British steamer "Trent," Nov. 8, 1861. Had not the captain of the "Trent" forgotten to throw his vessel on the hands of Captain Wilkes as a prize, hostilities could scarcely have been prevented. While Mason and Slidell were paving the way with diplomacy, a commission of Confederate naval officers, with headquarters in London, were striving energetically to arrange for the purchase

and building of vessels to be used as blockade-runners or privateers. Particularly active among these officers was Captain James Newland Maffit, C. S. N., and he was given command of the first cruiser built with Confederate funds that safely put to sea. In the "Oreto," Captain Maffit proceeded to Nassau; after she had been released by the British authorities there, her armament was again put aboard her and she began her career as the "Florida." She had been out but five days when yellow fever broke out on board. It reduced the working force to one fireman and four deckhands. Maffit, himself stricken, ran into Cardenas, but was soon ordered by the Cuban authorities to bring his ship to Havana. Maffit determined to escape. On Sept. 4, 1862, he took the "Florida" boldly through the blockading squadron into Mobile Bay. The vessel was refitted, and on the night of Jan. 15, 1863, Captain Maffit ran out with her and got safely to sea. He continued to command the cruiser on her adventurous voyages until the latter part of 1864, when his health was so broken that he was relieved. In January, 1865, he took the blockade-runner "Owl" out from Wilmington and over the bar near Fort Caswell, the very night that the forts surrendered to the Federal fleet. Maffit arrived at Bermuda in time to stop the sailing of five blockade-runners.

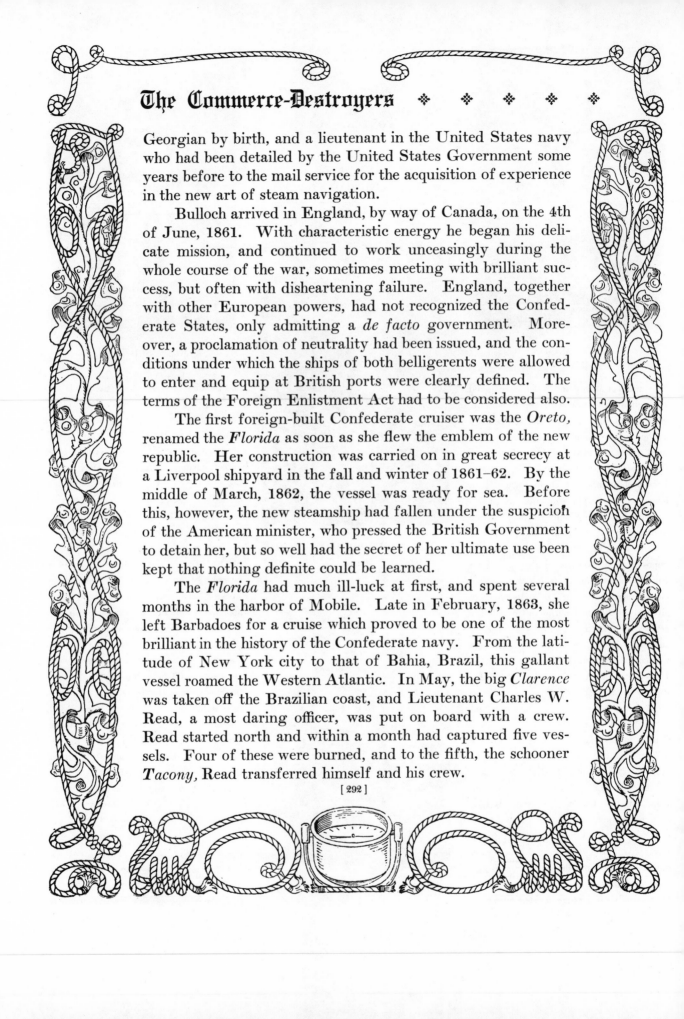

The Commerce-Destroyers ✦ ✦ ✦ ✦ ✦

Georgian by birth, and a lieutenant in the United States navy who had been detailed by the United States Government some years before to the mail service for the acquisition of experience in the new art of steam navigation.

Bulloch arrived in England, by way of Canada, on the 4th of June, 1861. With characteristic energy he began his delicate mission, and continued to work unceasingly during the whole course of the war, sometimes meeting with brilliant success, but often with disheartening failure. England, together with other European powers, had not recognized the Confederate States, only admitting a *de facto* government. Moreover, a proclamation of neutrality had been issued, and the conditions under which the ships of both belligerents were allowed to enter and equip at British ports were clearly defined. The terms of the Foreign Enlistment Act had to be considered also.

The first foreign-built Confederate cruiser was the *Oreto,* renamed the *Florida* as soon as she flew the emblem of the new republic. Her construction was carried on in great secrecy at a Liverpool shipyard in the fall and winter of 1861–62. By the middle of March, 1862, the vessel was ready for sea. Before this, however, the new steamship had fallen under the suspicion of the American minister, who pressed the British Government to detain her, but so well had the secret of her ultimate use been kept that nothing definite could be learned.

The *Florida* had much ill-luck at first, and spent several months in the harbor of Mobile. Late in February, 1863, she left Barbadoes for a cruise which proved to be one of the most brilliant in the history of the Confederate navy. From the latitude of New York city to that of Bahia, Brazil, this gallant vessel roamed the Western Atlantic. In May, the big *Clarence* was taken off the Brazilian coast, and Lieutenant Charles W. Read, a most daring officer, was put on board with a crew. Read started north and within a month had captured five vessels. Four of these were burned, and to the fifth, the schooner *Tacony,* Read transferred himself and his crew.

COPYRIGHT, 1911, REVIEW OF REVIEWS CO.

THE "TUSCARORA" NEAR GIBRALTAR, IN CHASE OF THE CONFEDERATE CRUISERS

The U. S. S. "Tuscarora" with other vessels during the latter half of 1861 was scouring the seas in search of the "Sumter"—the first of the Confederate cruisers to get to sea, eluding the blockading squadron at the mouth of the Mississippi, June 30, 1861. She was a 500-ton passenger steamer with a speed of but ten knots and had been declared unfit for naval service by a board of Confederate officers. Captain Raphael Semmes, upon seeing the report, said: "Give me that ship; I think I can make her answer the purpose." Within a week after she got away, the "Sumter" had made eight prizes. On Nov. 23d Semmes cleverly eluded the "Iroquois," then lying outside the harbor of St. Pierre, Martinique, and cruised to Gibraltar. There the "Sumter" was blockaded by the "Tuscarora," the "Kearsarge" and the "Ino." Semmes, seeing that escape was impossible, sold his vessel and disbanded her crew. Her prizes totalled fifteen, and Semmes was soon making another record for himself in the "Alabama." The "Florida" was the first cruiser built for the Confederacy abroad. She was allowed to clear from Liverpool on March 22, 1862, under the name "Oreto." On August 7th she began her career under Captain John Newland Maffit, with a crew of but twenty-two men. She had an adventurous career till she ran into the harbor of Bahia, Oct. 5, 1864, where she encountered a vessel of Wilke's flying squadron, the "Wachusett." Commander Napoleon Collins, in violation of the neutrality laws, suddenly attacked the "Florida" and received her surrender.

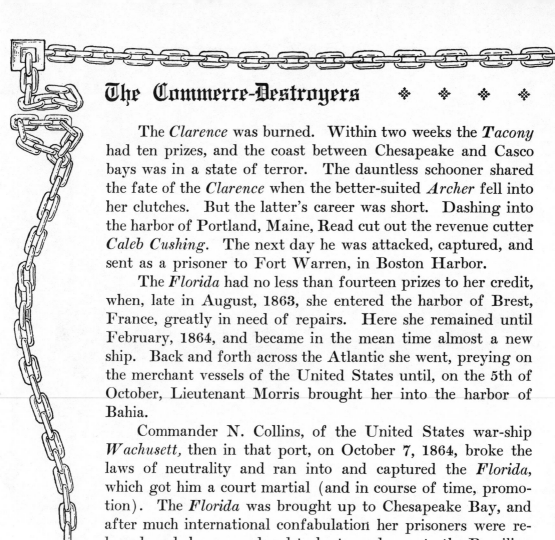

The Commerce-Destroyers ❖ ❖ ❖ ❖

The *Clarence* was burned. Within two weeks the *Tacony* had ten prizes, and the coast between Chesapeake and Casco bays was in a state of terror. The dauntless schooner shared the fate of the *Clarence* when the better-suited *Archer* fell into her clutches. But the latter's career was short. Dashing into the harbor of Portland, Maine, Read cut out the revenue cutter *Caleb Cushing*. The next day he was attacked, captured, and sent as a prisoner to Fort Warren, in Boston Harbor.

The *Florida* had no less than fourteen prizes to her credit, when, late in August, 1863, she entered the harbor of Brest, France, greatly in need of repairs. Here she remained until February, 1864, and became in the mean time almost a new ship. Back and forth across the Atlantic she went, preying on the merchant vessels of the United States until, on the 5th of October, Lieutenant Morris brought her into the harbor of Bahia.

Commander N. Collins, of the United States war-ship *Wachusett,* then in that port, on October 7, 1864, broke the laws of neutrality and ran into and captured the *Florida*, which got him a court martial (and in course of time, promotion). The *Florida* was brought up to Chesapeake Bay, and after much international confabulation her prisoners were released, and she was ordered to be turned over to the Brazilian Government. But a blundering ferryboat ran her down, and Brazil received only an apology, for this time the *Florida* went to the bottom.

While the *Florida* was building, Captain Bulloch visited the shipyard of John Laird, at Birkenhead, and arranged to build a wooden screw despatch-vessel. This ship, when it finally went into commission on the 24th of August, 1862, was the famous *Alabama,* and she was under the charge of Commander Semmes of the dismantled *Florida*. In a month's cruise in the North Atlantic twenty American vessels were destroyed. Then she went south, swept the Gulf, and among her captures was the Federal war vessel *Hatteras*. The

AT ANTWERP—U. S. S. "NIAGARA" AND THE FIGHT THAT WAS NOT FOUGHT

No sooner did it become known that the "Stonewall" was abroad than the Federal vessels in foreign waters began an active search for her. At the very beginning of her cruise she was found to have sprung a leak, however, and put into Ferrol, Spain, for repairs. There, during the first week in February, 1865, the frigate "Niagara" and the sloop-of-war "Sacramento" found her and attempted to blockade her. On March 24th the "Stonewall" steamed out of Ferrol and cleared for action. Commander T. T. Craven, of the "Niagara," had already notified his Government that in a smooth sea the "Stonewall" would be a match for three such ships as the "Niagara." Twice when the sea was rough he had stood out and offered battle to the Confederate ram, but Captain Page refused the offer, choosing his own time on a day when the water was as smooth as glass and no slight advantage could accrue to the Federals. Commander Craven was equally determined not to give his antagonist an inexpensive victory and carefully avoided the encounter. The "Stonewall" after flaunting her flag in his face, sailed jauntily off to Lisbon with the intention of crossing the Atlantic and striking a blow at Port Royal and at the cities of the North, hoping thus to revive the waning cause of the Confederacy. Arriving at Havana early in May, Captain Page learned that the war was over, and surrendered his vessel to the captain-general of Cuba.

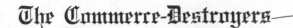

The Commerce-Destroyers

successful cruiser now visited Jamaica, landed her prisoners, and made necessary repairs. Semmes then cruised off the coast of Brazil, making ten prizes, and in company with one of them, taken into the Confederate service and renamed the *Tuscaloosa,* proceeded to the Cape of Good Hope. The vessel next spent six months in Eastern waters, even crossing the China Sea. On this cruise seven vessels were destroyed. In March, 1864, she was back at the Cape, and before the end of the month sailed for Europe. On June 11th, the *Alabama* entered the harbor of Cherbourg, France, in order to coal and to refit. What happened to her now will be told at the end of this chapter.

Among other Confederate cruisers was the *Georgia,* bought in March, 1863, by one of the Confederate agents, Commander Matthew F. Maury, the distinguished hydrographer. The *Georgia* started from England, but her sail power was found to be so small that she was constantly compelled to enter port to take on coal. This circumstance made her useless for long cruises, and she was taken to Liverpool and sold, after a year's activity in the Middle and South Atlantic. The *Victor,* an old despatch-boat of the British navy, was also bought by Commander Maury and, as the *Rappahannock,* was long detained in the harbor of Calais.

With neither of these vessels was it possible to duplicate the *Alabama,* and, as yet, the whaling industry in the Pacific had been quite free from the unwelcome attentions of the Confederate cruisers. The *Sea King* was purchased by the Southern agents in Europe in the summer of 1864. She was refitted and armed, and, as the *Shenandoah,* was sent to the Pacific under command of Lieutenant Waddell. In these far seas he destroyed a large number of whalers, keeping the work up until the end of June, 1865, in ignorance of the termination of the war. Lieutenant Waddell then returned to Liverpool and surrendered the *Shenandoah* to the British Government.

A ship of many names began her adventures as the blockade-runner *Atlanta,* in the summer of 1864. She made two

THE "STONEWALL," A DREAD CONFEDERATE DESTROYER

In this picture, taken after the "Stonewall" was voluntarily delivered by Spain to the United States in July, 1865, is seen the tremendous power for harm possessed by the vessel. Commodore Craven, at his own request, was tried in a court of inquiry for his failure to engage the Confederate ram with the "Niagara" and "Sacramento" and was exonerated of all blame. By taking the less popular course he undoubtedly saved the Federal navy a grave disaster. His were wooden ships, while the "Stonewall" was heavily armored, and her great ram could easily have sunk both her antagonists even if her gunnery should have proved inaccurate. Although the "Niagara" was rated as one of the most powerful vessels of the old navy and perhaps the fastest sailing-ship afloat, under steam she was scarcely a match for the

COMMODORE
THOMAS T. CRAVEN

"Stonewall" in that particular. The condition of her boilers at the time was still further disadvantageous. The "Niagara" could not turn around in less than fifteen minutes, while the "Stonewall" could turn on her center while going either forward or backward in a minute and a half. The battery of the "Niagara" had been condemned as unserviceable by a board of survey. Her target-practice reports showed that the shot from her guns would "tumble." The "Niagara" carried twelve 9-inch smooth-bores and the "Sacramento" ten guns, but unless both ships could bring their broadsides to bear on their antagonist it was bound to be a one-sided battle, for the "Stonewall's" powerful and modern Armstrong rifles were mounted in two turrets and could be brought quickly to bear over a wide range.

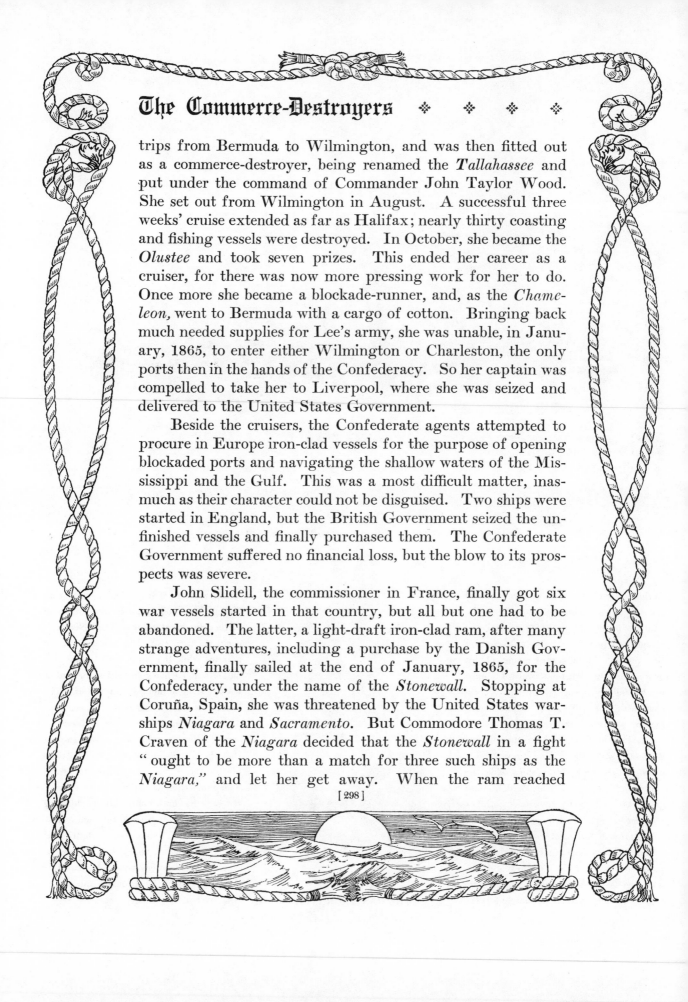

trips from Bermuda to Wilmington, and was then fitted out as a commerce-destroyer, being renamed the *Tallahassee* and put under the command of Commander John Taylor Wood. She set out from Wilmington in August. A successful three weeks' cruise extended as far as Halifax; nearly thirty coasting and fishing vessels were destroyed. In October, she became the *Olustee* and took seven prizes. This ended her career as a cruiser, for there was now more pressing work for her to do. Once more she became a blockade-runner, and, as the *Chameleon,* went to Bermuda with a cargo of cotton. Bringing back much needed supplies for Lee's army, she was unable, in January, 1865, to enter either Wilmington or Charleston, the only ports then in the hands of the Confederacy. So her captain was compelled to take her to Liverpool, where she was seized and delivered to the United States Government.

Beside the cruisers, the Confederate agents attempted to procure in Europe iron-clad vessels for the purpose of opening blockaded ports and navigating the shallow waters of the Mississippi and the Gulf. This was a most difficult matter, inasmuch as their character could not be disguised. Two ships were started in England, but the British Government seized the unfinished vessels and finally purchased them. The Confederate Government suffered no financial loss, but the blow to its prospects was severe.

John Slidell, the commissioner in France, finally got six war vessels started in that country, but all but one had to be abandoned. The latter, a light-draft iron-clad ram, after many strange adventures, including a purchase by the Danish Government, finally sailed at the end of January, 1865, for the Confederacy, under the name of the *Stonewall.* Stopping at Coruña, Spain, she was threatened by the United States warships *Niagara* and *Sacramento.* But Commodore Thomas T. Craven of the *Niagara* decided that the *Stonewall* in a fight "ought to be more than a match for three such ships as the *Niagara,*" and let her get away. When the ram reached

Here are two striking views in the Port Royal dry-dock of the Confederate ram "Stonewall." When this powerful fighting-ship sailed from Copenhagen, Jan. 6, 1865, under command of Capt. T. J. Page, C.S.N., the Federal navy became confronted by its most formidable antagonist during the war. In March, 1863, the Confederacy had negotiated a loan of £3,000,000, and being thus at last

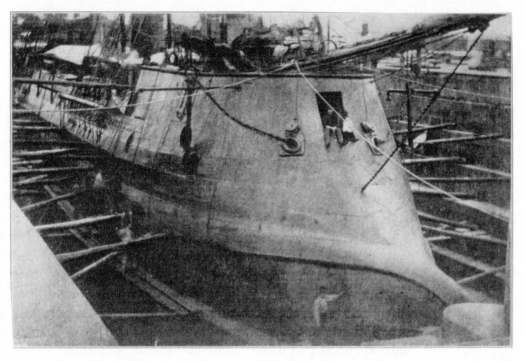

in possession of the necessary funds, Captain Bulloch and Mr. Slidell arranged with M. Arman, who was a member of the *Corps-Legislatif* and proprietor of a large shipyard at Bordeaux, for the construction of ironclad ships of war. Mr. Slidell had already received assurances from persons in the confidence of Napoleon III that the building of the ships in the French yards would not be interfered with, and that getting them to sea would be connived at by the Government. Owing to the indubitable proof laid before the Emperor by the Federal diplomats at Paris, he was compelled to revoke the guarantee that had been given to Slidell and Bulloch. A plan was arranged, however, by which M. Arman should sell the vessels to various European powers; and he disposed of the ironclad ram "Sphinx" to the Danish Government, then at war with Prussia. Delivery of the ship at Copenhagen was not made, however, till after the war had ceased, and no trouble was experienced by the Confederates in arranging for the purchase of the vessel. On January 24, 1865, she rendezvoused off Quiberon, on the French coast; the remainder of her officers, crew, and supplies were put aboard of her;

the Confederate flag was hoisted over her, and she was christened the "Stonewall." Already the vessel was discovered to have sprung a leak, and Captain Page ran into Ferrol, Spain. Here dock-yard facilities were at first granted, but were withdrawn at the protest of the American Minister. While Captain Page was repairing his vessel as best he could, the "Niagara" and the "Sacramento" appeared, and after some weeks the "Stonewall" offered battle in vain.

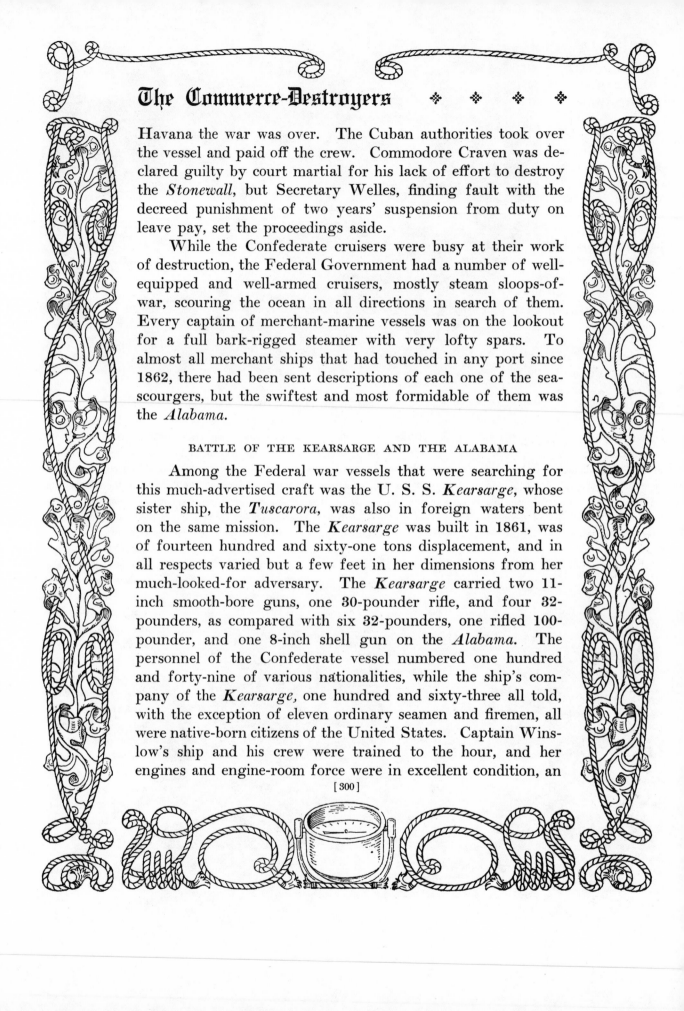

The Commerce-Destroyers ❖ ❖ ❖ ❖

Havana the war was over. The Cuban authorities took over the vessel and paid off the crew. Commodore Craven was declared guilty by court martial for his lack of effort to destroy the *Stonewall*, but Secretary Welles, finding fault with the decreed punishment of two years' suspension from duty on leave pay, set the proceedings aside.

While the Confederate cruisers were busy at their work of destruction, the Federal Government had a number of well-equipped and well-armed cruisers, mostly steam sloops-of-war, scouring the ocean in all directions in search of them. Every captain of merchant-marine vessels was on the lookout for a full bark-rigged steamer with very lofty spars. To almost all merchant ships that had touched in any port since 1862, there had been sent descriptions of each one of the sea-scourgers, but the swiftest and most formidable of them was the *Alabama*.

BATTLE OF THE KEARSARGE AND THE ALABAMA

Among the Federal war vessels that were searching for this much-advertised craft was the U. S. S. *Kearsarge*, whose sister ship, the *Tuscarora*, was also in foreign waters bent on the same mission. The *Kearsarge* was built in 1861, was of fourteen hundred and sixty-one tons displacement, and in all respects varied but a few feet in her dimensions from her much-looked-for adversary. The *Kearsarge* carried two 11-inch smooth-bore guns, one 30-pounder rifle, and four 32-pounders, as compared with six 32-pounders, one rifled 100-pounder, and one 8-inch shell gun on the *Alabama*. The personnel of the Confederate vessel numbered one hundred and forty-nine of various nationalities, while the ship's company of the *Kearsarge*, one hundred and sixty-three all told, with the exception of eleven ordinary seamen and firemen, all were native-born citizens of the United States. Captain Winslow's ship and his crew were trained to the hour, and her engines and engine-room force were in excellent condition, an

OFFICERS OF THE "ALABAMA" IN 1862

From left to right: First Lieut. John M. Kell; Surgeon David H. Llewellyn; Capt. Raphael Semmes; Third Lieut. Joseph D. Wilson; Lieut. P. Schroeder; Master J. P. Bullock; Lieut. Arthur Sinclair; Chief Engineer Miles D. Freeman; Lieut. Richard F. Armstrong; Capt.'s Clerk W. B. Smith; Surgeon Francis L. Galt; Asst. Engineer William P. Brooke; Midshipman Eugene Maffitt; Midshipman E. M. Anderson; Master's Mate George T. Fullman; Lieut. of Marines Becker K. Howell; Carpenter William Robinson; Paymaster Clarence R. Yonge; Fifth Lieut. John Lowe; Asst. Engineer S. W. Cummings. The portraits here grouped were taken in London in 1862 before the departure on August 13th in the steamer "Bahama" to join "Ship No. 290," built at the Lairds' shipyard, which received her guns and crew on the high seas off the Azores.

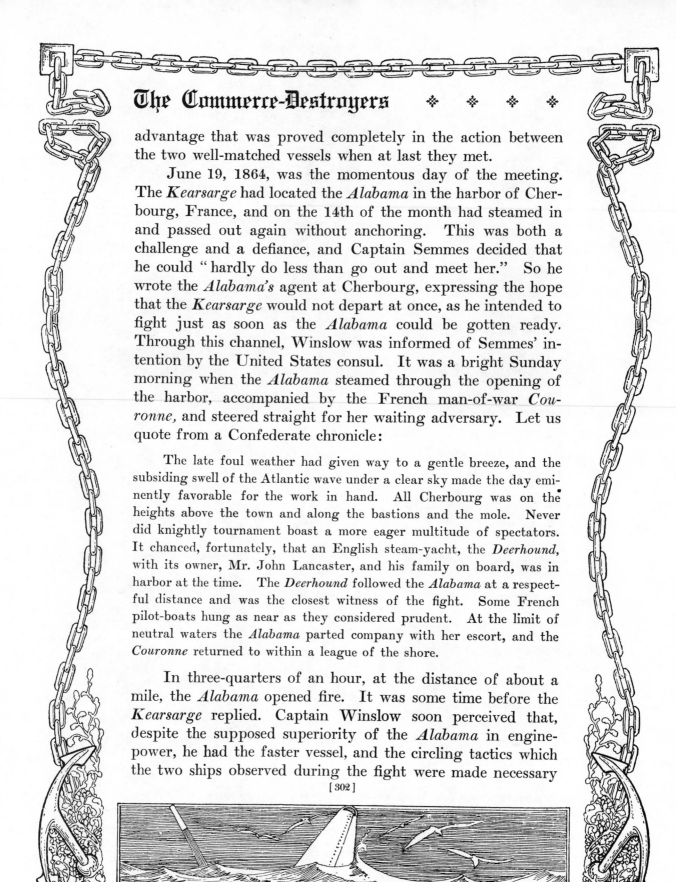

advantage that was proved completely in the action between the two well-matched vessels when at last they met.

June 19, 1864, was the momentous day of the meeting. The *Kearsarge* had located the *Alabama* in the harbor of Cherbourg, France, and on the 14th of the month had steamed in and passed out again without anchoring. This was both a challenge and a defiance, and Captain Semmes decided that he could "hardly do less than go out and meet her." So he wrote the *Alabama's* agent at Cherbourg, expressing the hope that the *Kearsarge* would not depart at once, as he intended to fight just as soon as the *Alabama* could be gotten ready. Through this channel, Winslow was informed of Semmes' intention by the United States consul. It was a bright Sunday morning when the *Alabama* steamed through the opening of the harbor, accompanied by the French man-of-war *Couronne,* and steered straight for her waiting adversary. Let us quote from a Confederate chronicle:

> The late foul weather had given way to a gentle breeze, and the subsiding swell of the Atlantic wave under a clear sky made the day eminently favorable for the work in hand. All Cherbourg was on the heights above the town and along the bastions and the mole. Never did knightly tournament boast a more eager multitude of spectators. It chanced, fortunately, that an English steam-yacht, the *Deerhound*, with its owner, Mr. John Lancaster, and his family on board, was in harbor at the time. The *Deerhound* followed the *Alabama* at a respectful distance and was the closest witness of the fight. Some French pilot-boats hung as near as they considered prudent. At the limit of neutral waters the *Alabama* parted company with her escort, and the *Couronne* returned to within a league of the shore.

In three-quarters of an hour, at the distance of about a mile, the *Alabama* opened fire. It was some time before the *Kearsarge* replied. Captain Winslow soon perceived that, despite the supposed superiority of the *Alabama* in engine-power, he had the faster vessel, and the circling tactics which the two ships observed during the fight were made necessary

THE GUN THAT SUNK THE "ALABAMA"—ON BOARD U. S. S. "KEARSARGE"

On the main deck, showing one of the two 11-inch pivot-guns that were handled with superb skill in the famous fight with the "Alabama." The engagement was in reality a contest in skill between American and British gunners, since the crew of the "Alabama" was composed almost entirely of British sailors. Word was passed to the men in the "Kearsarge" to let every shot tell, and there followed an exhibition of that magnificent American gunnery that had characterized the War of 1812. The "Kearsarge" fired only 173 missiles, almost all of which took effect. The "Alabama" fired 370 missiles, of which but 28 struck her antagonist. An 11-inch shell from the pivot-gun of the "Kearsarge" entered the "Alabama's" 8-inch gun-port, mowing down most of the gun crew. It was quickly followed by another shell from the same gun, and then by another, all three striking in the same place. Although the gunnery aboard the "Alabama" was inferior, one of her 68-pound shells lodged in the sternpost of the "Kearsarge" but failed to explode. Had it done so, in all likelihood it would have been the "Kearsarge" and not the "Alabama" that went to the bottom of the English Channel. Although the "Kearsarge" was wrecked on Roncador Reef in 1894, her sternpost with the shell still imbedded in it was recovered and became a historic relic.

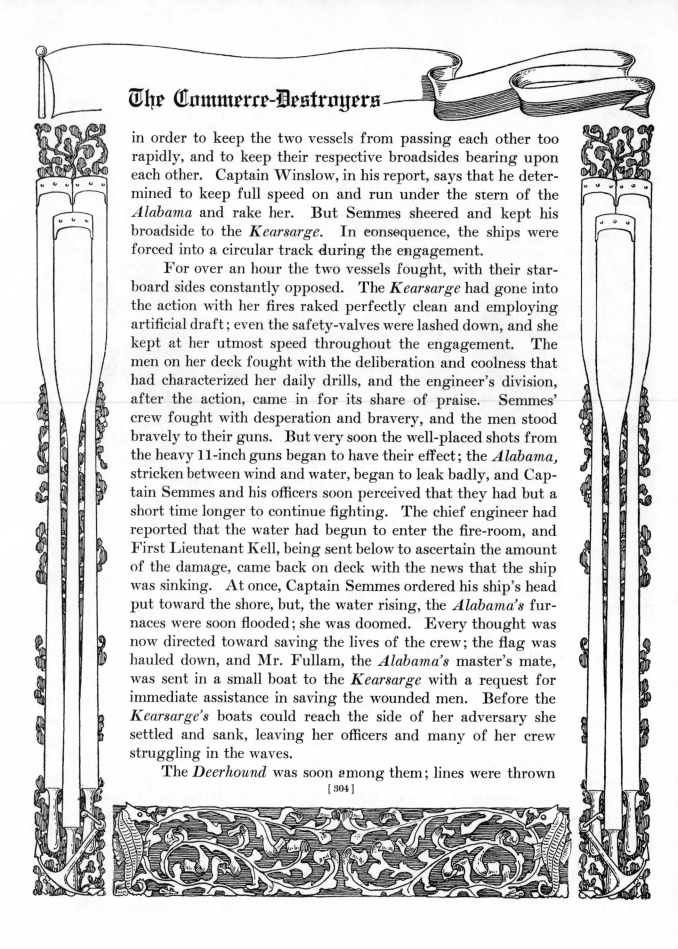

in order to keep the two vessels from passing each other too rapidly, and to keep their respective broadsides bearing upon each other. Captain Winslow, in his report, says that he determined to keep full speed on and run under the stern of the *Alabama* and rake her. But Semmes sheered and kept his broadside to the *Kearsarge*. In consequence, the ships were forced into a circular track during the engagement.

For over an hour the two vessels fought, with their starboard sides constantly opposed. The *Kearsarge* had gone into the action with her fires raked perfectly clean and employing artificial draft; even the safety-valves were lashed down, and she kept at her utmost speed throughout the engagement. The men on her deck fought with the deliberation and coolness that had characterized her daily drills, and the engineer's division, after the action, came in for its share of praise. Semmes' crew fought with desperation and bravery, and the men stood bravely to their guns. But very soon the well-placed shots from the heavy 11-inch guns began to have their effect; the *Alabama,* stricken between wind and water, began to leak badly, and Captain Semmes and his officers soon perceived that they had but a short time longer to continue fighting. The chief engineer had reported that the water had begun to enter the fire-room, and First Lieutenant Kell, being sent below to ascertain the amount of the damage, came back on deck with the news that the ship was sinking. At once, Captain Semmes ordered his ship's head put toward the shore, but, the water rising, the *Alabama's* furnaces were soon flooded; she was doomed. Every thought was now directed toward saving the lives of the crew; the flag was hauled down, and Mr. Fullam, the *Alabama's* master's mate, was sent in a small boat to the *Kearsarge* with a request for immediate assistance in saving the wounded men. Before the *Kearsarge's* boats could reach the side of her adversary she settled and sank, leaving her officers and many of her crew struggling in the waves.

The *Deerhound* was soon among them; lines were thrown

AFTER THE MOST FAMOUS SEA-FIGHT OF THE WAR
CAPTAIN WINSLOW AND HIS OFFICERS ON THE "KEARSARGE"

Here on the deck of the "Kearsarge" stand Captain John A. Winslow (third from left) and his officers after their return from the victorious battle with the "Alabama." On Sunday morning, June 19, 1864, Captain Winslow, who had been lying off the harbor of Cherbourg waiting for the Confederate cruiser to come out, was conducting divine service. Suddenly a cry—"She's coming, and heading straight for us"—rang out on the deck. Laying down his prayer-book and seizing his speaking-trumpet, Winslow ordered his ship cleared for action. He stood out to sea to make sure that the fight would occur beyond the neutrality limit. Meanwhile, people were crowding to every vantage-point along the coast with spy-glasses and camp-chairs, eager to witness the only great fight on the high seas between a Federal and a Confederate cruiser. The two ships were almost precisely matched in tonnage, number of men, and shot-weight of the guns brought into action on each side. The battle was begun by the "Alabama" at a range of 1,200 yards. The "Kearsarge," however, soon closed in to 900 yards, training her guns for more than an hour upon the "Alabama" with telling effect. Precisely an hour and thirteen minutes after the "Alabama" fired her first broadside, her colors were hauled down from her mast-head; the 11-inch shells of the pivot-guns of the "Kearsarge" had pierced her again and again below the water-line; twenty-six of her men were killed and drowned and twenty-one wounded, while aboard the "Kearsarge" only three men were injured. Twenty minutes after the surrender the "Alabama" settled by the stern and sank. Some survivors escaped on the British steam-yacht "Deerhound."

from the yacht, and many exhausted men, including the *Alabama's* commander, were picked up. This done, the yacht steamed away for England.

During the action the *Alabama* fired about three hundred and seventy times, but only twenty-eight of her shots struck the Federal vessel, whose immunity from harm was due, perhaps, in a measure, to the fact that she had slung along her sides her spare chains sheathed with light planking, from which some of the shells and even the solid shot of her foe had bounded harmlessly. The *Kearsarge* fired one hundred and seventy-three projectiles, and the *Alabama* was probably struck about as many times as was the *Kearsarge*. The latter had a narrow escape from destruction, for after the action there was found lodged in her stern-post a 100-pound shell that was unexploded. A close student of such matters and an authority on this special sea-fight, Passed Assistant Engineer Frank M. Bennett, has written about this shell as follows,

" The truth is, however, that this shell struck the counter of the *Kearsarge* at least twenty feet from the stern-post and would have exploded there, where the damage would have been slight, had it possessed any explosive power, for it was a percussion shell. . . ."

When she sank, the famous Confederate cruiser scarcely left a trace behind. A broken whale-boat, a few floating oars and struggling swimmers alone were on the surface. Her loss in killed and wounded was not far from forty, and one officer, Assistant Surgeon Llewellyn, and nineteen men, including the carpenter and one assistant engineer, were drowned. On board the *Kearsarge* there were but three casualties and no deaths, although a brave and gallant sailor, William Gowin, died a few weeks later from his wounds. When the news reached him that the *Alabama's* colors had been lowered, he insisted that the surgeon who was attending him should go on deck and join in the ringing cheers of victory.

[306]

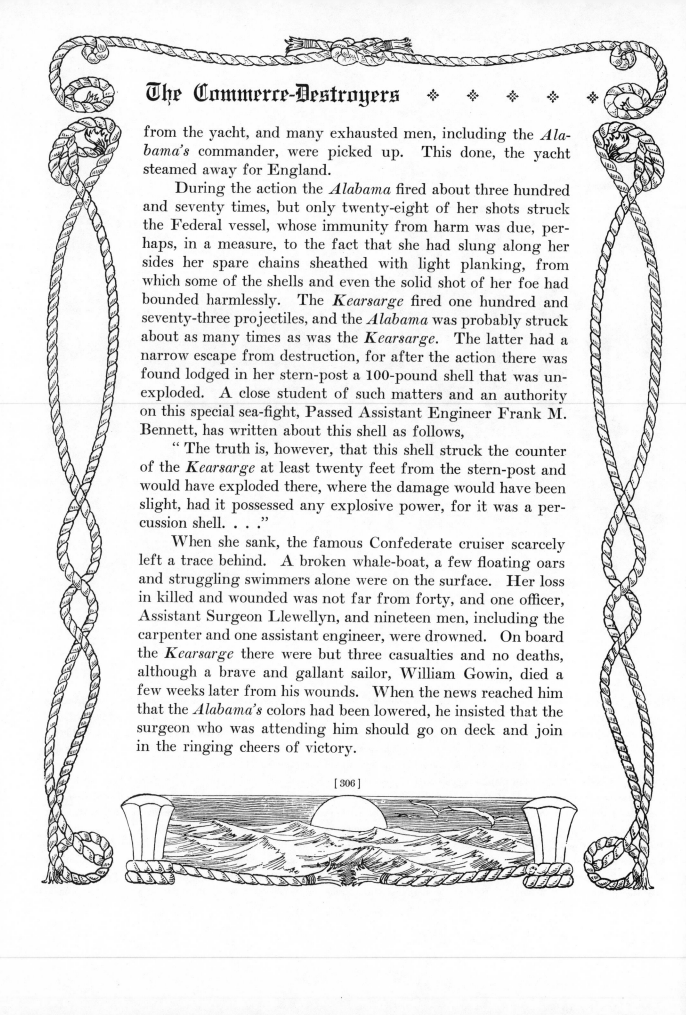

CHAPTER XIII

NAVAL CHRONOLOGY

1861—1865

IMPORTANT NAVAL ENGAGEMENTS
OF THE CIVIL WAR
MARCH, 1861—JUNE, 1865

CHRONOLOGICAL summary of important actions in which the Federal and Confederate navies were engaged, based on official records. Minor engagements are omitted; also joint operations where the army played the principal part.

MARCH, 1861.

20.—Sloop *Isabella,* with provisions, for the Federal Navy-Yard at Pensacola, seized at Mobile by request of Gen. Bragg.

APRIL, 1861.

17.—Seizure of the U. S. transport *Star of the West,* at Indianola, by Texas troops under Col. Van Dorn.

19.—Ports of South Carolina, Georgia, Alabama, Florida, Mississippi, Louisiana, and Texas ordered blockaded by President Lincoln.

20 and 21.—Gosport Navy-Yard, Norfolk, Va., abandoned by Union officers in charge, and seized by Virginia State troops.

27.—Ports of Virginia and North Carolina included in the blockade.

MAY, 1861.

4.—S. S. *Star of the West* made the receiving ship of the Confed. navy, New Orleans, La.

9.—U. S. ships *Quaker City, Harriet Lane, Young America, Cumberland, Monticello,* and *Yankee* enforcing the blockade off Fort Monroe.
—Steamers *Philadelphia, Baltimore, Powhatan,* and *Mount Vernon* armed by U. S. Government, and cruising on the Potomac.

13.—Proclamation of neutrality issued by Queen Victoria, in which the subjects of Great Britain were forbidden to endeavor to break a blockade "lawfully and effectually established."

18 and 19.—Shots exchanged between U. S. S. *Freeborn* and *Monticello* and the Confed. battery at Sewell's Point, Va.
—U. S. S. *Harriet Lane* arrives off Charleston.

26.—U. S. S. *Brooklyn* commenced the blockade of the Mississippi River.
—Blockade of Mobile, Ala., commenced by U. S. S. *Powhatan.*

28.—U. S. S. *Minnesota* begins real blockade of Charleston.
—Blockade of Savannah initiated by U. S. gunboat *Union.*

31.—U. S. S. *Freeborn, Anacostia, Pawnee,* and *Resolute* attacked Confed. batteries at Aquia Creek, Va.

JUNE, 1861.

27.—Engagement between U. S. gunboats *Freeborn* and *Reliance* and Confed. batteries at Mathias Point, Va., Commander Ward of the *Freeborn* killed.

JULY, 1861.

2.—U. S. S. *South Carolina* begins blockade of Galveston.

4 to 7.—U. S. S. *South Carolina* captures or destroys 10 vessels off Galveston.

7.—"Infernal" machines detected floating in the Potomac.

19.—Captain-General of Cuba liberated all the vessels brought into Cuban ports as prizes by Confed. cruiser *Sumter.*

24.—Naval expedition from Fort Monroe to Back River, Va., by Lieut. Crosby and 300 men. Nine sloops and schooners of the Confederates burnt, and one schooner with bacon and corn captured.

COMMODORE VANDERBILT'S PRESENT TO THE GOVERNMENT

This side-wheel steamer was presented to the Government by Commodore Cornelius Vanderbilt in 1861, when the navy was sorely in need of ships, and she was christened after the donor. In Hampton Roads she led one of the two columns of fighting-vessels of all sorts that had been assembled to meet the "Merrimac," in case she made another attack upon the fleet after her encounter with the "Monitor." The "Vanderbilt" mounted fifteen guns and showed great speed. She was employed largely as a cruiser. Her first prize was the British blockade-runner "Peterhoff," captured off St. Thomas, February 25, 1863. On April 16th she caught the "Gertrude" in the Bahamas, and on October 30th the "Saxon," off the coast of Africa. Under command of Captain C. W. Pickering, she participated in both of the joint-expeditions against Fort Fisher.

Important Naval Engagements of the Civil War

28.—Confederate privateer *Petrel*, formerly U. S. revenue cutter *Aiken*, sunk by U. S. frigate *St. Lawrence* near Charleston.

AUGUST, 1861.

22.—The steamer *Samuel Orr* was seized at Paducah, Ky., by Confederates, and taken up the Tennessee River.

26.—Naval and military expedition to North Carolina coast sailed from Hampton Roads, Va., under command of Flag-Officer Stringham and Maj.-Gen. Butler.

28 and 29.—Bombardment and capture of Forts Hatteras and Clark, at Hatteras Inlet, N. C., 30 pieces of cannon, 1000 stand of arms, 3 vessels with valuable cargoes, and 750 prisoners were taken.

30.—Capt. Foote ordered to the command of U. S. naval forces on the Western waters.

SEPTEMBER, 1861.

4.—Engagement on the Mississippi River near Hickman, Ky., between U. S. gunboats *Tyler* and *Lexington* and the Confed. gunboat *Yankee* and shore batteries.

14.—An expedition from the U. S. frigate *Colorado*, under Lieut. J. H. Russell, destroyed the privateer *Judah*, under the Confed. guns at Pensacola.

16.—A naval expedition from Hatteras Inlet, under command of Lieut. J. Y. Maxwell, destroyed Fort Ocracoke, on Beacon Island, N. C.

17.—Ship Island, near the mouth of the Mississippi River, occupied by Federal forces from the steamer *Massachusetts*.

OCTOBER, 1861.

1.—U. S. steamer *Fanny*, with 35 men of the 9th N. Y. Volunteers, captured by the Confederates on the north shore of Hatteras Inlet.

4.—Commander Alden, U. S. S. *South Carolina*, captured two schooners off the S. W. Pass of the Mississippi, with four to five thousand stands of arms.

5.—Two boats from U. S. S. *Louisiana*, Lieut. A. Murray, destroyed a Confed. schooner, being fitted out for a privateer, at Chincoteague Inlet, Va.

12.—Five Confed. gunboats, the ram *Manassas*, and a fleet of fireships attacked the U. S. fleet at the passes of the Mississippi and were repulsed after considerable injury had been done to the U. S. fleet.

26.—Confed. steamer *Nashville*, commanded by Lieut. R. B. Pegram, escaped from Charleston, S. C.

28.—Three Confed. vessels were surprised and burnt at Chincoteague Inlet, Va., by a portion of the crew of U. S. gunboat *Louisiana*, under Lieut. A. Hopkins.

29.—Federal expedition sailed from Fort Monroe, under the command of Flag-Officer Samuel F. Du Pont, comprising 77 vessels of all classes. The land forces, numbering 20,000 men, were commanded by Brig.-Gen. Thos. W. Sherman.

NOVEMBER, 1861.

1.—A violent storm overtook the naval expedition off the N. C. coast. 3 vessels were disabled and returned, 2 were driven ashore, and 2 foundered. 7 lives lost.

7.—Federal fleet under Du Pont captured Forts Walker and Beauregard at Port Royal entrance, and took the town of Beaufort, S. C.

7 and 8.—Two launches and 40 men, commanded by Lieut. Jas. E. Jouett, from the U. S. frigate *Santee*, off Galveston, Texas, surprised and cut out the Confed. privateer *Royal Yacht*.

8.—Capt. Chas. Wilkes, commanding U. S. screw sloop *San Jacinto*, removed by force Confed. Commissioners Jas. M. Mason and John Slidell from British mail steamer *Trent*.

18.—U. S. gunboat *Conestoga* engaged Confed. batteries on the Tennessee River, and silenced them.

19.—The ship *Harvey Birch* was captured and burnt in the English Channel by the Confed. steamer *Nashville*.

—First flotilla of the "Stone Fleet" sailed for the South, from Conn. and Mass.

24.—Tybee Island, in Savannah Harbor, was occupied by U. S. forces under Flag-Officer Du Pont.

[310]

A SIGHT FOR THE OLD-TIME SAILOR—A GUN-CREW ON THE DECK OF THE FLAGSHIP "WABASH"

Here is a sight that will please every old-time sailor—a gun-crew on the old "Wabash" under the eyes of Admiral Du Pont himself, who stands with his hand on the sail. No finer sweep of deck or better-lined broadside guns were ever seen than those of the U. S. S. "Wabash," the finest type of any vessel of her class afloat at the outbreak of the Civil War. Everything about her marked the pride which her officers must take in having everything "ship-shape and Bristol fashion." She was at all times fit for inspection by a visiting monarch. The "Wabash" threw the heaviest broadside of any vessel in the Federal fleet. Her crew were practically picked men, almost all old sailors who had been graduated from the navy of sailing days. The engines of this magnificent frigate were merely auxiliary; she yet depended upon her towering canvas when on a cruise. Her armament was almost identically that of the "Minnesota," although her tonnage was somewhat less. She mounted two 10-inch smooth-bores, twenty-eight 9-inch guns on her gun-deck, fourteen 8-inch on her spar deck, and two 12-pounders. At the time this picture was taken she was flagship of the South Atlantic squadron, flying the broad pennant of Admiral Samuel F. Du Pont.

Important Naval Engagements of the Civil War

DECEMBER, 1861.

4.—Proclamation of Gen. Phelps, attached to Gen. Butler's expedition, on occupation of Ship Island, Mississippi Sound.

17.—Entrance to the harbor at Savannah, Ga., blocked by sinking 7 vessels laden with stone.

20.—The main ship-channel at Charleston Harbor was obstructed by sinking 16 vessels of the " Stone Fleet."

31.—Two boats under Acting-Masters A. Allen and H. L. Sturges, from the U. S. S. *Mount Vernon,* destroyed a lightship off Wilmington, N. C., which the Confederates had fitted up for a gunboat.

—Capture of the town of Biloxi, Miss., by U. S. gunboats *Lewis, Water Witch,* and *New London,* with Federal forces from Ship Island.

JANUARY, 1862.

1.—Confed. Commissioners Mason and Slidell left Boston for England via Provincetown, Mass., where the British war steamer *Rinaldo* received them.

12.—Expedition sailed from Fort Monroe under command of Flag-Officer Goldsborough and Gen. Burnside, for Albemarle Sound, N. C.

13.—Steamship *Constitution* with the Maine 12th regiment, and the Bay State regiment, sailed from Boston for Ship Island, Miss., via Fort Monroe.

26.—Second " Stone Fleet " was sunk in Maffitt's Channel, Charleston Harbor, S. C.

30.—Ironclad *Monitor* was launched at Greenpoint, N. Y.

FEBRUARY, 1862.

6.—Unconditional surrender of Fort Henry to Flag-Officer Foote.

7 to 10.—Lieut. Phelps, of Foote's flotilla, commanding the gunboats *Conestoga, Tyler* and *Lexington,* captured Confed. gunboat *Eastport* and destroyed all the Confed. craft on the Tennessee River between Fort Henry and Florence, Ala.

10.—Destruction of Confed. gunboats in the Pasquotank River, N. C., also of the Confed. battery at Cobb's Point, and the occupation of Elizabeth City by Federal forces from 14 gunboats, commanded by Commander Rowan.

14.—Foote, with 6 gunboats, attacked Fort Donelson, but was repulsed, the flagofficer being severely wounded. Federal loss 60 in killed and wounded.

28.—Confed. steamer *Nashville* ran the blockade of Beaufort, N. C., and reached the town.

MARCH, 1862.

1.—U. S. gunboats *Tyler,* Lieut. Gwin, commanding, and *Lexington,* Lieut. Shirk, on an expedition up the Tennessee River, engaged and silenced a Confed. battery at Pittsburg Landing, Tenn.

6.—U. S. ironclad *Monitor,* Lieut. Worden, sailed from New York for Fort Monroe.

8.—Destruction of the U. S. sloop-of-war *Cumberland* and the frigate *Congress,* in action with the Confed. ironclad *Merrimac,* in Hampton Roads, Va. 120 men were lost on the *Cumberland,* and 121 on the *Congress.*

9.—Combat of the U. S. ironclad *Monitor* and the Confed. ironclad *Merrimac,* in Hampton Roads, Va.

11.—Occupation of St. Augustine, Fla., by Federal naval forces.

12.—Occupation of Jacksonville, Fla., by Federal forces from the U. S. gunboats *Ottawa, Seneca,* and *Pembina,* under command of Lieut. T. H. Stevens.

17.—Federal gunboats and mortars, under Foote, began the investment of and attack on Island No. 10, on the Mississippi.

APRIL, 1862.

1.—During a storm at night, Col. Roberts with 50 picked men of the 42d Illinois, and as many seamen under First Master Johnston, of the gunboat *St. Louis,* surprised the Confederates at the upper battery of Island No. 10, and spiked 6 large guns.

4.—Federal gunboat *Carondelet* ran past the Confed. batteries at Island No. 10, at night, without damage, and arrived at New Madrid.

[312]

HEADQUARTERS OF GENERAL Q. A. GILLMORE AT HILTON HEAD

General Gillmore is not out of place in a volume that deals with the naval side of the Civil War, for almost continually he was directing movements in which the Federal navy was operating or was supposed to lend assistance. Had many of this splendid officer's suggestions been adopted, and had he received better military support from Washington, Savannah and Charleston could not by any possibility have held out, with all the bravery in the world, as long as they did. Had he been given supreme command at the time that he was ranked by General Thomas W. Sherman and had he commanded 50,000 men instead of a small army, the Federal naval victories might have been followed up by army successes. General Gillmore conceived and superintended the construction of the fortifications at Hilton Head, and also planned the operations that resulted in the capture of Fort Pulaski. Transferred to western Virginia and Kentucky, and brevetted for gallantry, he once more returned to the coast as commander of the Department of South Carolina, where he succeeded General Hunter. It was greatly through his efforts that Forts Wagner and Gregg, near Charleston Harbor, were finally silenced. During the latter part of the war he was successively in command of the Tenth and Nineteenth Army Corps.

Important Naval Engagements of the Civil War

11.—Confed. steamers *Merrimac, Jamestown,* and *Yorktown,* came down between Newport News and Sewell's Point, on the Chesapeake, and captured 3 vessels.

14.—Potomac flotilla ascended the Rappahannock River, destroying several batteries. Three vessels were captured.
—Foote's mortar-boats opened fire on Fort Pillow, on the Mississippi.

18 to 24.—Bombardment of Forts Jackson and St. Philip, on the Mississippi.

24.—Federal fleet passed Forts Jackson and St. Philip, destroying 13 Confed. gunboats, the ram *Manassas,* and 3 transports.

25.—New Orleans captured. Confed. batteries on both sides of the river destroyed.

28.—Forts St. Philip and Jackson, La., surrendered; Forts Livingston and Pike abandoned, and the Confed. ironclad *Louisiana* blown up.

MAY, 1862.

2.—U. S. S. *Brooklyn* and several gunboats left New Orleans, ascending the Mississippi, to open the river and connect with the Western Flotilla.

8.—Ironclad steamer *Galena,* assisted by the gunboats *Aroostook* and *Port Royal,* attacked and silenced two Confed. batteries a short distance from the mouth of the James River, Va.

9.—Pensacola, Fla., evacuated by the Confederates after setting fire to forts, navy-yard, barracks, and marine hospital.

10.—Federal gunboats in the Mississippi, under the command of Acting Flag-Officer Davis, were attacked above Fort Pillow by the Confed. River Defense fleet, which after a half-hour's contest, was forced to retire. The Federal gunboats *Cincinnati* and *Mound City* were badly injured, and the Confed. vessels also were considerably cut up.

11.—Confed. ironclad *Merrimac* was abandoned by her crew and blown up off Craney Island, Va.

13.—Confed. armed steamer *Planter* run out of Charleston, S. C., by a negro crew, and surrendered to Comdr. Parrott, of the U. S. S. *Augusta.*
—Natchez, Miss., surrendered to *Iroquois,* Comdr. J. S. Palmer.

15.—Federal ironclad *Monitor,* together with the *Port Royal, Aroostook,* and the mailed gunboats *Galena* and *E. A. Stevens,* attacked Fort Darling, on Drewry's Bluff, 6 miles below Richmond, on the James River. The *Galena* was badly damaged, and lost 17 men killed and about 20 wounded. The large rifled gun of the *E. A. Stevens* burst.

JUNE, 1862.

6.—Engagement between the Federal gunboats and rams and the Confed. rams in front of Memphis, in which all of the latter but one were sunk or captured. 100 Confed. prisoners taken. Memphis occupied by Federals.

15.—U. S. gunboats *Tahoma* and *Somerset,* Lieuts. Howell and English, crossed the bar of St. Mark's River, Fla., and destroyed a Confed. fort and barracks.

17.—Federal expedition up the White River, when near St. Charles, was fired into from masked batteries, and the gunboat *Mound City* received a shot in her boiler which occasioned the destruction of 82 of her crew by scalding, 25 only escaping uninjured. The Confed. works were captured by the land forces under Col. Fitch, who took 30 prisoners.

26.—Three Confed. gunboats burned on the Yazoo River by their officers, to prevent their capture by the Union ram-flotilla, Lieut.-Col. A. W. Ellet, then in pursuit of them.

28.—Flag-Officer Farragut with nine vessels of his fleet ran by the Confed. batteries at Vicksburg, through a severe fire, forming a junction with Western Flotilla on July 1st.

29.—Steamship *Ann,* of London, with a valuable cargo, captured by the U. S. steamer *Kanawha,* in Mobile Bay, under the guns of Fort Morgan.

JULY, 1862.

1.—Porter's mortar flotilla engaged the Confed. batteries at Vicksburg, Miss.

2.—Commencement of bombardment of Vicksburg, Miss., by the combined mortar fleets of Davis and Porter.

4.—Confed. gunboat *Teaser* captured on James River by U. S. steamer *Maratanza.*

ON THE DECK OF THE "AGAWAM"

The easy attitudes of the acting ensign, to the left of the gun, and the volunteer acting-master with him, do not suggest the storm through which the ship on which they stand, the Federal gunboat "Agawam," passed in the spring of 1864. Their vessel was called upon to coöperate in Grant's great military movement that was to bring the war to a close. In February, Acting Rear-Admiral S. P. Lee, commanding the North Atlantic squadron, was ready to assist General Butler with gunboats in the James and York Rivers. The admiral himself remained with his main squadron at Fortress Monroe to convey Butler's expedition to Bermuda Hundred. After that general got himself bottled up and, despite the protests of Admiral Lee, had sunk obstructions in the James to prevent the Confederate gunboats from coming down, the "Virginia" and her consorts came down to reconnoiter the character of the obstructions. The "Agawam," under Commander A. C. Rhind, was lying below Battery Dantzler, with several monitors. They were engaged by the fortification and by the Confederate gunboats concealed behind the Point. The Federal vessels promptly returned the fire and kept up the battle for six hours, inflicting considerable damage on the fort.

Important Naval Engagements of the Civil War

15.—Confed. iron-clad ram *Arkansas* came down the Yazoo River and engaged the Federal gunboats *Carondelet* and *Tyler,* and ram *Queen of the West.* The ram succeeded in escaping to Vicksburg.

22.—Confed. steamer *Reliance* captured by U. S. steamer *Huntsville.*

—Unsuccessful attempt made to sink the Confed. ram *Arkansas,* at Vicksburg, by Lieut-Col. Ellet, with the Union ram *Queen of the West* and ironclad *Essex,* Commander W. D. Porter.

29.—Attack on Fort James, on the Ogeechee River, Ga., by Federal gunboats repulsed.

AUGUST, 1862.

6.—Destruction of Confed. ram *Arkansas* by her commander, Lieut. Stevens, at Baton Rouge, La.

16.—Lieut.-Comdr. Phelps with 3 gunboats and 4 rams, and the 58th and 76th Ohio in transports, left Helena, Ark., sailed down the Mississippi to Milliken's Bend, where they captured the steamer *Fairplay,* with arms, &c., for 6000 men. Further captures made at Haynes' Bluff and at Richmond, La., and property destroyed.

SEPTEMBER, 1862.

5.—Ship *Ocmulgee* burned at sea by Confed. cruiser *Alabama.*

17.—U. S. gunboats *Paul Jones, Cimarron,* and 3 other vessels attacked Confed. batteries on St. John's River, Florida.

25.—Sabine Pass, Texas, captured by U. S. steamer *Kensington* and schooner *Rachel Seaman.*

OCTOBER, 1862.

3.—Confed. fortifications at St. John's Bluff, on St. John's River, Fla., captured by 1500 Federals under Gen. Brannan, assisted by 7 gunboats from Hilton Head, S. C.

—Fight on the Blackwater River, near Franklin, Va., 3 Federal gunboats, *Commodore Perry, Hunchback,* and *Whitehead,* under Lieut.-Comdr. Flusser, engaged a large force of Confederates 6 hours.

4.—Capture of the defenses of Galveston, Texas, after slight resistance by Federal mortar flotilla under Comdr. W. B. Renshaw.

NOVEMBER, 1862.

4.—Bark *Sophia* captured off N. C. coast by U. S. steamers *Daylight* and *Mount Vernon.*

18.—British schooners *Ariel* and *Ann Maria* captured off Little Run, S. C., by U. S. gunboat *Monticello.*

DECEMBER, 1862.

12.—U. S. gunboat *Cairo* sunk in the Yazoo River by a torpedo. The crew saved.

27.—Engagement between the *Benton* and the Confed. battery at Drumgould's Bluff on the Yazoo. Lieut.-Comdr. Gwin mortally wounded.

31.—Ironclad *Monitor,* Commander Bankhead, foundered off Cape Hatteras, N. C.

JANUARY, 1863.

1.—Galveston, Texas, with its garrison of 300 men, recaptured by Confederates under Gen. Magruder, and 2 steamers, *Bayou City* and *Neptune.* 6 Federal gunboats were in the harbor. The *Harriet Lane* was captured after a severe fight, in which Commander Wainwright was killed, and some of his crew. Federal flagship *Westfield* was blown up by Commander Renshaw, to avoid capture, by which he lost his life, with many of the crew.

11.—U. S. S. *Hatteras,* Lieut.-Comdr. H. C. Blake, sunk off Galveston, Tex., by Confed. steamer *Alabama.* 100 of the Federal crew captured.

14.—Four Union gunboats under Lieut.-Comdr. Buchanan, assisted by Gen. Weitzel's troops, engaged the Confed. iron-clad gunboat *J. A. Cotton,* which was aided by Confed. artillery, on the Bayou Teche, La. The *Cotton* was destroyed after several hours' combat. Lieut.-Comdr. Buchanan was killed.

16.—Confed. cruiser *Florida* escaped from Mobile.

27.—First attack on Fort McAllister, Ga.

30.—U. S. gunboat *Isaac Smith* captured in Stono River, S. C.

DISCUSSING THE PLANS—PORTER AND MEADE

On the left sits Rear-Admiral David Dixon Porter, in conference with Major-General George Gordon Meade. There were many such interviews both on shore and aboard the "Malvern" before the details of the expedition against Fort Fisher were finally settled. Porter had been promised the necessary troops to coöperate in an attack on the fort, but it was months before they were finally detached and actually embarked. Grant and Meade had their hands full in the military operations around Petersburg and Richmond and could not give much attention to the expedition. General Butler had more time at his disposal and proposed a plan for exploding close to Fort Fisher a vessel loaded with powder. This was bravely carried out by the navy but proved entirely futile.

Important Naval Engagements of the Civil War

31.—Confed. armed iron-clad rams, *Palmetto State* and *Chicora,* and 3 steamers, under Flag-Officer Ingraham, came down Charleston, S. C., Harbor, and attacked 3 vessels of the blockading squadron, the *Mercedita, Keystone State,* and *Quaker City,* damaging them severely, and capturing and paroling the crew of the *Mercedita.* 30 Federals killed and 50 wounded.

FEBRUARY, 1863.

1.—Second attack on Fort McAllister, Ga. Confed. commander, Maj. Gallie, killed. Federal vessels retire without loss.

2.—Union ram *Queen of the West* ran by the Confed. batteries at Vicksburg, Miss.

14.—Transport *Era No. 5* captured by Federal ram *Queen of the West,* Col. Charles R. Ellet, near Fort Taylor, Red River. The *Queen of the West,* running aground near Gordon's Landing, Red River, fell a prize to the Confederates.

18.—Mortar-boats opened fire on Vicksburg.

21.—Union gunboats *Freeborn* and *Dragon* engaged a Confed. battery on the Rappahannock River, Va. Three Federals wounded.

24.—Gunboat *Indianola* captured near Grand Gulf, Miss., by 4 Confed. steamers.

28.—Destruction of Confed. steamer *Nashville* in Ogeechee River, near Fort McAllister, Ga., by monitor *Montauk,* Commander Worden.

MARCH, 1863.

14.—Adml. Farragut, with 7 of his fleet, attacked the Confed. batteries at Port Hudson. The *Hartford* (flagship) and the *Albatross* passed the batteries and went up the river. The *Mississippi* was destroyed and part of her crew captured.

31.—Adml. Farragut, with the Federal vessels *Hartford, Switzerland,* and *Albatross,* engaged the Confed. batteries at Grand Gulf, Miss., and passed them without serious loss.

APRIL, 1863.

1.—Adml. Farragut's vessels proceeded to the mouth of the Red River.

2.—U. S. gunboat *St. Clair* disabled by Confederates above Fort Donelson on the Cumberland River. She was rescued by the steamer *Luminary.*

7.—Attack on Fort Sumter, Charleston, S. C., by 9 Federal ironclads under Rear-Adml. Du Pont.

14.—Destruction of Confed. ram *Queen of the West,* in Berwick Bay, La., by U. S. gunboat *Estrella* and others. 90 Confederates captured, and 30 lost.

16.—Adml. Porter's fleet of 8 gunboats and several transports ran past the Vicksburg batteries, losing only 1 transport and no men.

22.—Six transports and 12 barges passed the Confed. batteries at Vicksburg.

26.—Confed. shore batteries at Duck River shoals, Tennessee River, silenced by gunboats. 25 Confederates killed and wounded.

29.—Bombardment of Grand Gulf, Miss., by Porter's fleet. Confed. works greatly damaged. Fleet considerably injured.

MAY, 1863.

3.—Confed. batteries at Grand Gulf, Miss., evacuated by the Confederates, and taken possession of by Adml. Porter.

27.—Sinking of the U. S. gunboat *Cincinnati* by Confed. batteries at Vicksburg. 35 of her crew killed and wounded.

JUNE, 1863.

3.—Simsport, La., attacked by Federal gunboats.

10 and 11.—Attack on Morris Island, Charleston Harbor, by Federal gunboats and troops.

17.—Capture of Confed. iron-clad ram *Atlanta,* by monitor *Weehawken,* in Wassaw Sound, Ga. 180 prisoners taken.

22 and 23.—Seven fishing vessels captured off Martha's Vineyard, Mass., by Confed. captured bark *Tacony,* Lieut. C. W. Read.

JULY, 1863.

13.—U. S. gunboat *Baron DeKalb* sunk by Confed. torpedo in Yazoo River, Miss.

THE "KICKAPOO"
WITH TORPEDO–RAKE READY AT THE BOW

THIS NEW WEAPON OF DEFENSE WAS USED EFFECT-
IVELY DURING THE ATTACK ON MOBILE, ON MARCH 28,
1865. THE "KICKAPOO" CAME OUT SAFELY, ALTHOUGH
THE "MILWAUKEE" NEAR-BY FAILED TO DISCOVER
A CONFEDERATE TORPEDO IN TIME AND WAS SUNK

Important Naval Engagements of the Civil War

AUGUST, 1863.

21.—U. S. brig. *Bainbridge* foundered. Only 1 man saved.

23.—U. S. gunboats *Satellite* and *Reliance* captured by Confederates at the mouth of the Rappahannock, Va.

SEPTEMBER, 1863.

2.—Unsuccessful attempt to destroy by Union force, gunboats *Satellite* and *Reliance,* captured by the Confederates.

8 and 9.—An assault made on Fort Sumter by 400 men in 20 boats from the Federal fleet, under Commander T. H. Stevens. The sailors were defeated with the loss of 124.

8.—U. S. gunboats *Clifton* and *Sachem,* attached to an expedition under Gen. Franklin, grounded on the bar at Sabine Pass, Texas, and were captured by the Confederates.

OCTOBER, 1863.

5.—Confederates attempt to destroy the *New Ironsides* with the torpedo-boat *David.*

26 to Nov. 10.—Bombardment of Fort Sumter.

30.—Heavy bombardment of Charleston, S. C.

NOVEMBER, 1863.

2.—Unsuccessful attempt upon Sumter by a boat expedition.

DECEMBER, 1863.

6.—Monitor *Weehawken* founders in Charleston Harbor. Over 30 lives lost.

5.—Fight between the U. S. gunboat *Marblehead* and Confed. batteries on Stono River, S. C. Confederates defeated.

FEBRUARY, 1864.

2.—Capture and destruction of U. S. S. *Underwriter,* Actg. Master Westervelt, by Confed. attack under Comdr. J. T. Wood, in Neuse River, N. C.

18.—Federal sloop-of-war *Housatonic* sunk off Charleston, S. C., by Confed. submarine torpedo-boat *H. L. Hunley.*

16 to 29.—Bombardment of Fort Powell, Ala., by Adml. Farragut.

MARCH, 1864.

6.—U. S. gunboat *Peterhoff* sunk by collision off Wilmington, N. C.

11 to 15.—A naval expedition from Brashear City captures camp, arms, and flag on Atchafalaya River, La.

APRIL, 1864.

1.—U. S. Army stmr. *Maple Leaf* blown up by torpedo in St. John's River, Fla.

5.—Fight betweeen gunboats and guerrillas at Hickman, Ky.

12.—Adml. Porter's Red River fleet attacked at Blair's Plantation by 2000 Confed. infantry on shore, who are beaten off.

14.—Gunboat expedition from Butler's army captures prisoners and stores at Smithfield, Va.

19.—Attack on Federal vessels under Lieut.-Comdr. C. W. Flusser by Confed. ram *Albemarle,* Comdr. J. W. Cooke, at Plymouth, N. C.; sinking of U. S. S. *Southfield* and death of Flusser.

23.—U. S. gunboat *Petrel* captured by Confederates on the Yazoo River.

25.—Confederates in strong force attacked 3 of Adml. Porter's gunboats on the Red River.

MAY, 1864.

6.—U. S. gunboat *Commodore Jones* blown up by Confed. torpedo in James River.

13.—Adml. Porter's fleet above Alexandria Falls released by Col. Bailey's dam.

JUNE, 1864.

3.—Capture of U. S. S. *Water Witch,* Lieut.-Comdr. Austin Pendergrast by boat expedition under Lieut. J. P. Pelot, C. S. N., in Ossabaw Sound, Ga., Lieut. Pelot killed.

19.—The Confed. cruiser *Alabama,* Capt. Semmes, was sunk off the harbor of Cherbourg, France, by U. S. sloop-of-war *Kearsarge,* Capt. Winslow. 70 of the Confed. crew were taken on board the *Kearsarge,* and 115 reached England and France. 3 persons only were wounded on the *Kearsarge.*